Short Stories for Students

National Advisory Board

Short Stories
for Students

Presenting Analysis, Context, and Criticism on Commonly Studied Short Stories

Volume 20

Ira Mark Milne and Timothy Sisler,
Project Editors

THOMSON

GALE

Detroit • New York • San Francisco • San Diego • New Haven, Conn. • Waterville, Maine • London • Munich

THOMSON

™

GALE

Short Stories for Students, Volume 20

Project Editor
Ira Mark Milne

Editorial
Anne Marie Hacht, Michelle Kazensky,
Jennifer Smith

Rights Acquisition and Management
Edna Hedblad, Emma Hull, Sheila Spencer

Manufacturing
Rhonda Williams

Imaging and Multimedia
Lezlie Light, Mike Logusz, Kelly A. Quin

Product Design
Pamela A. E. Galbreath

ISBN 0-7876-4272-X
ISSN 1092-7735

Printed in the United States of America
10 9 8 7 6 5 4 3 2 1

Table of Contents

Why Study Literature At All?

Short Stories for Students is designed to provide readers with information and discussion about a wide range of important contemporary and historical works of short fiction, and it does that job very well. However, I want to use this guest foreword to address a question that it does *not* take up. It is a fundamental question that is often ignored in high school and college English classes as well as research texts, and one that causes frustration among students at all levels, namely—why study literature at all? Isn't it enough to read a story, enjoy it, and go about one's business? My answer (to be expected from a literary professional, I suppose) is no. It is not enough. It is a start; but it is not enough. Here's why.

First, literature is the only part of the educational curriculum that deals directly with the actual world of lived experience. The philosopher Edmund Husserl used the apt German term *die Lebenswelt*, "the living world," to denote this realm. All the other content areas of the modern American educational system avoid the subjective, present reality of everyday life. Science (both the natural and the social varieties) objectifies, the fine arts create and/or perform, history reconstructs. Only literary study persists in posing those questions we all asked before our schooling taught us to give up on them. Only literature gives credibility to personal perceptions, feelings, dreams, and the "stream of consciousness" that is our inner voice. Literature wonders about infinity, wonders why God permits evil, wonders what will happen to us after we die. Literature admits that we get our hearts broken, that people sometimes cheat and get away with it, that the world is a strange and probably incomprehensible place. Literature, in other words, takes on all the big and small issues of what it means to be human. So my first answer is that of the humanist—we should read literature and study it and take it seriously because it enriches us as human beings. We develop our moral imagination, our capacity to sympathize with other people, and our ability to understand our existence through the experience of fiction.

My second answer is more practical. By studying literature we can learn how to explore and analyze texts. Fiction may be about *die Lebenswelt*, but it is a construct of words put together in a certain order by an artist using the medium of language. By examining and studying those constructions, we can learn about language as a medium. We can become more sophisticated about word associations and connotations, about the manipulation of symbols, and about style and atmosphere. We can grasp how ambiguous language is and how important context and texture is to meaning. In our first encounter with a work of literature, of course, we are not supposed to catch all of these things. We are spellbound, just as the writer wanted us to be. It is as serious students of the writer's art that we begin to see how the tricks are done.

Seeing the tricks, which is another way of saying "developing analytical and close reading skills," is important above and beyond its intrinsic literary educational value. These skills transfer to other fields and enhance critical thinking of any kind. Understanding how language is used to construct texts is powerful knowledge. It makes engineers better problem solvers, lawyers better advocates and courtroom practitioners, politicians better rhetoricians, marketing and advertising agents better sellers, and citizens more aware consumers as well as better participants in democracy. This last point is especially important, because rhetorical skill works both ways—when we learn how language is manipulated in the making of texts the result is that we become less susceptible when language is used to manipulate us.

My third reason is related to the second. When we begin to see literature as created artifacts of language, we become more sensitive to good writing in general. We get a stronger sense of the importance of individual words, even the sounds of words and word combinations. We begin to understand Mark Twain's delicious proverb—"The difference between the right word and the almost right word is the difference between lightning and a lightning bug." Getting beyond the "enjoyment only" stage of literature gets us closer to becoming makers of word art ourselves. I am not saying that studying fiction will turn every student into a Faulkner or a Shakespeare. But it will make us more adaptable and effective writers, even if our art form ends up being the office memo or the corporate annual report.

Studying short stories, then, can help students become better readers, better writers, and even better human beings. But I want to close with a warning. If your study and exploration of the craft, history, context, symbolism, or anything else about a story starts to rob it of the magic you felt when you first read it, it is time to stop. Take a break, study another subject, shoot some hoops, or go for a run. Love of reading is too important to be ruined by school. The early twentieth century writer Willa Cather, in her novel *My Antonia*, has her narrator Jack Burden tell a story that he and Antonia heard from two old Russian immigrants when they were teenagers. These immigrants, Pavel and Peter, told about an incident from their youth back in Russia that the narrator could recall in vivid detail thirty years later. It was a harrowing story of a wedding party starting home in sleds and being chased by starving wolves. Hundreds of wolves attacked the group's sleds one by one as they sped across the snow trying to reach their village. In a horrible revelation, the old Russians revealed that the groom eventually threw his own bride to the wolves to save himself. There was even a hint that one of the old immigrants might have been the groom mentioned in the story. Cather has her narrator conclude with his feelings about the story. "We did not tell Pavel's secret to anyone, but guarded it jealously—as if the wolves of the Ukraine had gathered that night long ago, and the wedding party had been sacrificed, just to give us a painful and peculiar pleasure." That feeling, that painful and peculiar pleasure, is the most important thing about literature. Study and research should enhance that feeling and never be allowed to overwhelm it.

Thomas E. Barden
Professor of English and
Director of Graduate English Studies
The University of Toledo

Introduction

Purpose of the Book

The purpose of *Short Stories for Students* (*SSfS*) is to provide readers with a guide to understanding, enjoying, and studying short stories by giving them easy access to information about the work. Part of Gale's "For Students" Literature line, *SSfS* is specifically designed to meet the curricular needs of high school and undergraduate college students and their teachers, as well as the interests of general readers and researchers considering specific short fiction. While each volume contains entries on "classic" stories frequently studied in classrooms, there are also entries containing hard-to-find information on contemporary stories, including works by multicultural, international, and women writers.

The information covered in each entry includes an introduction to the story and the story's author; a plot summary, to help readers unravel and understand the events in the work; descriptions of important characters, including explanation of a given character's role in the narrative as well as discussion about that character's relationship to other characters in the story; analysis of important themes in the story; and an explanation of important literary techniques and movements as they are demonstrated in the work.

In addition to this material, which helps the readers analyze the story itself, students are also provided with important information on the literary and historical background informing each work. This includes a historical context essay, a box comparing the time or place the story was written to modern Western culture, a critical essay, and excerpts from critical essays on the story or author. A unique feature of *SSfS* is a specially commissioned critical essay on each story, targeted toward the student reader.

To further aid the student in studying and enjoying each story, information on media adaptations is provided (if available), as well as reading suggestions for works of fiction and nonfiction on similar themes and topics. Classroom aids include ideas for research papers and lists of critical sources that provide additional material on the work.

Selection Criteria

The titles for each volume of *SSfS* were selected by surveying numerous sources on teaching literature and analyzing course curricula for various school districts. Some of the sources surveyed include: literature anthologies, *Reading Lists for College-Bound Students: The Books Most Recommended by America's Top Colleges*; *Teaching the Short Story: A Guide to Using Stories from around the World*, by the National Council of Teachers of English (NCTE); and "A Study of High School Literature Anthologies," conducted by Arthur Applebee at the Center for the Learning and Teaching of Literature and sponsored by the National Endowment for the Arts and the Office of Educational Research and Improvement.

Input was also solicited from our advisory board, as well as from educators from various areas. From these discussions, it was determined that each volume should have a mix of ''classic'' stories (those works commonly taught in literature classes) and contemporary stories for which information is often hard to find. Because of the interest in expanding the canon of literature, an emphasis was also placed on including works by international, multicultural, and women authors. Our advisory board members—educational professionals—helped pare down the list for each volume. Works not selected for the present volume were noted as possibilities for future volumes. As always, the editor welcomes suggestions for titles to be included in future volumes.

How Each Entry Is Organized

Each entry, or chapter, in *SSfS* focuses on one story. Each entry heading lists the title of the story, the author's name, and the date of the story's publication. The following elements are contained in each entry:

- **Introduction:** a brief overview of the story which provides information about its first appearance, its literary standing, any controversies surrounding the work, and major conflicts or themes within the work.

- **Author Biography:** this section includes basic facts about the author's life, and focuses on events and times in the author's life that may have inspired the story in question.

- **Plot Summary:** a description of the events in the story. Lengthy summaries are broken down with subheads.

- **Characters:** an alphabetical listing of the characters who appear in the story. Each character name is followed by a brief to an extensive description of the character's role in the story, as well as discussion of the character's actions, relationships, and possible motivation.

  Characters are listed alphabetically by last name. If a character is unnamed—for instance, the narrator in ''The Eatonville Anthology''—the character is listed as ''The Narrator'' and alphabetized as ''Narrator.'' If a character's first name is the only one given, the name will appear alphabetically by that name.

- **Themes:** a thorough overview of how the topics, themes, and issues are addressed within the story. Each theme discussed appears in a separate subhead, and is easily accessed through the boldface entries in the Subject/Theme Index.

- **Style:** this section addresses important style elements of the story, such as setting, point of view, and narration; important literary devices used, such as imagery, foreshadowing, symbolism; and, if applicable, genres to which the work might have belonged, such as Gothicism or Romanticism. Literary terms are explained within the entry, but can also be found in the Glossary.

- **Historical Context:** this section outlines the social, political, and cultural climate *in which the author lived and the work was created.* This section may include descriptions of related historical events, pertinent aspects of daily life in the culture, and the artistic and literary sensibilities of the time in which the work was written. If the story is historical in nature, information regarding the time in which the story is set is also included. Long sections are broken down with helpful subheads.

- **Critical Overview:** this section provides background on the critical reputation of the author and the story, including bannings or any other public controversies surrounding the work. For older works, this section may include a history of how the story was first received and how perceptions of it may have changed over the years; for more recent works, direct quotes from early reviews may also be included.

- **Criticism:** an essay commissioned by *SSfS* which specifically deals with the story and is written specifically for the student audience, as well as excerpts from previously published criticism on the work (if available).

- **Sources:** an alphabetical list of critical material used in compiling the entry, with bibliographical information.

- **Further Reading:** an alphabetical list of other critical sources which may prove useful for the student. It includes bibliographical information and a brief annotation.

In addition, each entry contains the following highlighted sections, set apart from the main text as sidebars:

- **Media Adaptations:** if available, a list of film and television adaptations of the story, including source information. The list also includes stage adaptations, audio recordings, musical adaptations, etc.

- **Topics for Further Study:** a list of potential study questions or research topics dealing with the story. This section includes questions related to other disciplines the student may be studying, such as American history, world history, science, math, government, business, geography, economics, psychology, etc.

- **Compare and Contrast:** an "at-a-glance" comparison of the cultural and historical differences between the author's time and culture and late twentieth century or early twenty-first century Western culture. This box includes pertinent parallels between the major scientific, political, and cultural movements of the time or place the story was written, the time or place the story was set (if a historical work), and modern Western culture. Works written after 1990 may not have this box.

- **What Do I Read Next?:** a list of works that might complement the featured story or serve as a contrast to it. This includes works by the same author and others, works of fiction and nonfiction, and works from various genres, cultures, and eras.

Other Features

SSfS includes "Why Study Literature At All?," a foreword by Thomas E. Barden, Professor of English and Director of Graduate English Studies at the University of Toledo. This essay provides a number of very fundamental reasons for studying literature and, therefore, reasons why a book such as *SSfS*, designed to facilitate the study of literture, is useful.

A Cumulative Author/Title Index lists the authors and titles covered in each volume of the *SSfS* series.

A Cumulative Nationality/Ethnicity Index breaks down the authors and titles covered in each volume of the *SSfS* series by nationality and ethnicity.

A Subject/Theme Index, specific to each volume, provides easy reference for users who may be studying a particular subject or theme rather than a single work. Significant subjects from events to broad themes are included, and the entries pointing to the specific theme discussions in each entry are indicated in **boldface**.

Each entry may include illustrations, including photo of the author, stills from film adaptations (if available), maps, and/or photos of key historical events.

Citing Short Stories for Students

When writing papers, students who quote directly from any volume of *SSfS* may use the following general forms to document their source. These examples are based on MLA style; teachers may request that students adhere to a different style, thus, the following examples may be adapted as needed.

When citing text from *SSfS* that is not attributed to a particular author (for example, the Themes, Style, Historical Context sections, etc.), the following format may be used:

"The Celebrated Jumping Frog of Calavaras County." *Short Stories for Students*. Ed. Kathleen Wilson. Vol. 1. Detroit: Gale, 1997. 19–20.

When quoting the specially commissioned essay from *SSfS* (usually the first essay under the Criticism subhead), the following format may be used:

Korb, Rena. Critical Essay on "Children of the Sea." *Short Stories for Students*. Ed. Kathleen Wilson. Vol. 1. Detroit: Gale, 1997. 42.

When quoting a journal or newspaper essay that is reprinted in a volume of *Short Stories for Students*, the following form may be used:

Schmidt, Paul. "The Deadpan on Simon Wheeler." *Southwest Review* Vol. XLI, No. 3 (Summer, 1956), 270–77; excerpted and reprinted in *Short Stories for Students*, Vol. 1, ed. Kathleen Wilson (Detroit: Gale, 1997), pp. 29–31.

When quoting material from a book that is reprinted in a volume of *SSfS,* the following form may be used:

Bell-Villada, Gene H. "The Master of Short Forms," in *Garcia Marquez: The Man and His Work*. University of North Carolina Press, 1990, pp. 119–36; excerpted and reprinted in *Short Stories for Students*, Vol. 1, ed. Kathleen Wilson (Detroit: Gale, 1997), pp. 89–90.

We Welcome Your Suggestions

The editor of *Short Stories for Students* welcomes your comments and ideas. Readers who wish to suggest short stories to appear in future volumes, or who have other suggestions, are cordially invited to contact the editor. You may contact the editor via E-mail at: **ForStudentsEditors@thomson.com.** Or write to the editor at:

Editor, *Short Stories for Students*
The Gale Group
27500 Drake Road
Farmington Hills, MI 48331–3535

Literary Chronology

1864: Miguel de Unamuno (y Jugo) is born on September 29 in the port city of Bilbao, located in the Basque region of Spain.

1885: Isak Dinesen (pseudonym for Karen Blixen, born Karen Christentze Dinesen) is born on April 17 near Copenhagen, Denmark.

1896: Liam O'Flaherty is born on Inishmore, an Aran Island off the coast of Ireland.

1903: Frank Sargeson is born on March 23 in Hamilton, New Zealand.

1908: Richard Wright is born on September 4 on a plantation near Natchez, Mississippi.

1914: Julio Cortázar is born in Belgium but is raised in Buenos Aires, Argentina.

1917: Heinrich Böll is born on December 21 in Cologne, Germany.

1919: Doris Lessing is born (Doris May Tayler) on October 22 in Kermanshah, Persia (later renamed as Iran).

1920: Ray Bradbury is born on August 22 in Waukegan, Illinois.

1922: Grace Paley is born on December 11 in the Bronx, New York.

1923: Liam O'Flaherty's "The Sniper" is published.

1933: Miguel de Unamuno's "Saint Emmanuel the Good, Martyr" is published.

1936: Miguel de Unamuno dies of a heart attack while under house arrest during the Spanish Civil War for criticizing the Nationalist rebellion led by Francisco Franco, who later becomes dictator over Spain.

1940: Frank Sargeson's "A Great Day" is published.

1940: Bobbie Ann Mason is born near Mayfield, Kentucky, and grows up in rural Kentucky on a dairy farm that her father owns.

1947: Ann Beattie is born on September 8 in Washington, D.C.

1950: Isak Dinesen's "Babette's Feast" is published.

1951: Heinrich Böll's "Christmas Not Just Once a Year" is published.

1951: Ray Bradbury's "The Veldt" is published.

1958: Richard Wright's "Big Black Good Man" is published.

1959: Ben Okri is born on Sunday, March 15, in Minna, Nigeria, just sixteen months before the country gains its independence from the United Kingdom.

1959: Julio Cortázar's "The Pursuer" is published.

1960: Richard Wright dies on November 28 in Paris. The official cause of death is a heart attack, though rumors that Wright was murdered persist.

1962: Isak Dinesen dies of malnutrition near Copenhagen on September 7.

1963: Doris Lessing's "To Room Nineteen" is published.

1968: Junot Díaz is born into a *barrio* family and raised in Santo Domingo, the capital of the Dominican Republic.

1972: Heinrich Böll is awarded the Nobel Prize for literature.

1974: Ann Beattie's "Imagined Scenes" is published.

1974: Grace Paley's "The Long-Distance Runner" is published.

1982: Frank Sargeson dies on March 1.

1983: Ben Okri's "In the Shadow of War" is published.

1983: Bobbie Ann Mason's "Private Lies" is published.

1984: Julio Cortázar dies of leukemia and heart disease in Paris on February 12, three years after becoming a French citizen.

1984: Liam O'Flaherty dies in Dublin.

1985: Heinrich Böll dies at his home in Langenbroich from complications of arteriosclerosis.

1998: Junot Díaz's "The Sun, the Moon, the Stars" is published.

Acknowledgments

The editors wish to thank the copyright holders of the excerpted criticism included in this volume and the permissions managers of many book and magazine publishing companies for assisting us in securing reproduction rights. We are also grateful to the staffs of the Detroit Public Library, the Library of Congress, the University of Detroit Mercy Library, Wayne State University Purdy/Kresge Library Complex, and the University of Michigan Libraries for making their resources available to us. Following is a list of the copyright holders who have granted us permission to reproduce material in this volume of *Short Stories for Students (SSfS)*. Every effort has been made to trace copyright, but if omissions have been made, please let us know.

COPYRIGHTED MATERIALS IN *SSfS*, VOLUME 20, WERE REPRODUCED FROM THE FOLLOWING PERIODICALS:

Explicator, v. 47, spring, 1989; v. 50, spring, 1992; v. 56, summer, 1998; v. 57, spring, 1999. Copyright © 1989, 1992, 1998, 1999 by Helen Dwight Reid Educational Foundation. All reproduced with permission of the Helen Dwight Reid Educational Foundation, published by Heldref Publications, 1319 18th Street, NW, Washington, DC 20036–1802.—*Hispanic Review*, v. 54, spring, 1986. Reproduced by permission.—*Journal of Evolutionary Psychology*, v. 1, June, 1979. Reproduced by permission.—*Kenyon Review*, v. 11, summer, 1989 for "The World of Bobbie Ann Mason," by Devon Jersild. Reproduced by permission of the author.—*MELUS*, v. 25, spring, 2000. Copyright, *MELUS: The Society for the Study of Multi-Ethnic Literature of the United States*, 2000. Reproduced by permission.—*Michigan Quarterly Review*, v. 32, summer, 1993. Copyright © The University of Michigan, 1993. All rights reserved. Reproduced by permission.—*Modern Language Review*, v. 76, 1981 for "The Problem of Truth in 'San Manuel Bueno, Martir,'" by C. A. Longhurst. Copyright © 1981 by Modern Humanities Research Association. Reproduced by permission of the author.—*The Nation*, New York, v. 200, January 25, 1965. Copyright © 1965 by *The Nation* magazine/ The Nation Company, Inc. Reproduced by permission.—*Romance Notes*, v. 31, spring, 1991. Reproduced by permission.—*Saturday Review*, August 7, 1976. Copyright © 1976, General Media International, Inc. Reproduced by permission of *The Saturday Review*.—*Third World Quarterly*, v. 11, April, 1989. Copyright © 1989 by *Third World Quarterly*. Reproduced by permission.—*Times Literary Supplement*, August 5–11, 1988. Copyright © 1988 by The Times Supplements Limited. Reproduced from *The Times Literary Supplement* by permission.—*Women and Language*, v. 23, spring, 2000 for "A Matter of Voice: Grace Paley and the Oral Tradition," by LaVerne Harrell Clark. Reproduced by permission of the publisher and the author.—*World Literature Today*, v. 64, spring, 1990. Copyright 1990 by the University of Oklahoma Press. Reproduced by permission of the publisher.

COPYRIGHTED MATERIALS IN *SSfS*, VOLUME 20, WERE REPRODUCED FROM THE FOLLOWING BOOKS:

Conrad, Robert C. From *Understanding Heinrich Böll.* University of South Carolina Press, 1992. Copyright © 1992 by University of South Carolina. Reproduced by permission.—Contemporary Authors Online. "Frank Sargeson," www.gale.com, 2003. Reproduced by permission of The Gale Group.—Hakutani, Yoshinobu. From "Richard Wright," in *Dictionary of Literary Biography*, Vol. 102, *American Short-Story Writers, 1910–1945, Second Series*. Edited by Bobby Ellen Kimbel. Gale Research, 1991. Copyright (c) 1991 by Gale Research. Reproduced by permission of The Gale Group.—Margolies, Edward. From *The Art of Richard Wright.* Southern Illinois University Press, 1969. Reproduced by permission.—Price, Joanna. From *Understanding Bobbie Ann Mason.* University of South Carolina Press, 2000. Copyright © 2000 by University of South Carolina. Reproduced by permission.—Rhodes, H. Winston. From *Frank Sargeson.* Twayne Publishers, Inc., 1969. Copyright © 1969 by Twayne Publishers, Inc. All rights reserved. Reproduced by permission of The Gale Group.—Standish, Peter. From *Understanding Julio Cortazar.* University of South Carolina Press, 2001. Copyright © 2001 by University of South Carolina. Reproduced by permission.

PHOTOGRAPHS AND ILLUSTRATIONS APPEARING IN *SSfS*, VOLUME 20, WERE RECEIVED FROM THE FOLLOWING SOURCES:

Beattie, Ann, photograph. Copyright © Jerry Bauer. Reproduced by permission.—Biafran War soldier, Nigeria, 1968, photograph. © Hulton-Deutsch Collection/Corbis. Reproduced by permission.—Boats in the harbor in Nyhaven, Copenhagen, Denmark, 1980–1990s, photograph by Michael S. Yamashita. Copyright © by Michael S. Yamashita/Corbis. Reproduced by permission.—Böll, Heinrich, right, with Alexander Solzhenitsyn, photograph. Getty Images. Reproduced by permission.—Bradbury, Ray, photograph. The Library of Congress.—Cortázar, Julio, photograph. AP/Wide World Photos. Reproduced by permission.—Díaz, Junot, photograph. Copyright © Jerry Bauer. Reproduced by permission.—Dinesen, Isak, 1957, photograph. Corbis-Bettmann. Reproduced by permission.—Lessing, Doris, photograph. Copyright © Jerry Bauer. Reproduced by permission.—Mason, Bobbie Ann, photograph. Copyright © Jerry Bauer. Reproduced by permission.—Mountains flank Dusky Sound on New Zealand's South Island, photograph by E. O. Hoppe. Copyright © by E. O. Hoppe/Corbis. Reproduced by permission.—O'Flaherty, Liam, photograph by Burs Lond. Copyright © 1939 by Bettmann/Corbis. Reproduced by permission.—Okri, Ben, London, 1991, photograph. AP/Wide World Photos. Reproduced by permission.—Paley, Grace, 1986, photograph. AP/Wide World Photos. Reproduced by permission.—Parker, Charlie, on the bandstand at Billy Bergs Club in Hollywood, California, 1945. AP/Wide World Photos. Reproduced by permission.—Rebellion by Free State Troopers at the Four Courts Building in Dublin, Ireland, on June 12, 1922. Copyright © by Bettmann/Corbis. Reproduced by permission.—Sargeson, Frank, ref# F-527959–1/2. Alexander Turnbull Library, Wellington, New Zealand. Reproduced by permission.—Slums on hillside, Santo Domingo, Dominican Republic, photograph. United Nations. Reproduced by permission.—Soldiers during the Siege of Paris in 1871. Copyright © by Hulton-Deutsch Collection/Corbis. Reproduced by permission.—Street near Burgos Cathedral in Burgos, Spain, ca. 1935, photograph by E. O. Hoppe. Copyright © by E. O. Hoppe/Corbis. Reproduced by permission.—Unamuno y Jugo, Miguel de, photograph. The Library of Congress.—Wright, Richard, photograph. AP/Wide World Photos. Reproduced by permission.

Contributors

Bryan Aubrey: Aubrey holds a Ph.D. in English and has published many articles on twentieth-century literature. Entry on *A Great Day*. Original essay on *A Great Day*.

Liz Brent: Brent holds a Ph.D. in American culture from the University of Michigan. Entry on *Saint Emmanuel the Good, Martyr*. Original essays on *In the Shadow of War*, *The Pursuer*, and *Saint Emmanuel the Good, Martyr*.

Jennifer Bussey: Bussey holds a master's degree in interdisciplinary studies and a bachelor's degree in English literature. She is an independent writer specializing in literature. Entry on *Babette's Feast*. Original essay on *Babette's Feast*.

Laura Carter: Carter is currently employed as a freelance writer. Original essay on *In the Shadow of War*.

Douglas Dupler: Dupler is a writer, teacher, and independent scholar. Original essay on *The Sun, the Moon, the Stars*.

Joyce Hart: Hart, a former writing teacher, is a freelance writer and author of several books. Original essays on *The Sun, the Moon, the Stars* and *The Veldt*.

Diane Andrews Henningfeld: Henningfeld is a professor of literature at Adrian College who writes on literary topics for a variety of publications. Entries on *Imagined Scenes* and *Pri-vate Lies*. Original essays on *Imagined Scenes* and *Private Lies*.

Beth Kattelman: Kattelman holds a Ph.D. in theater. Entry on *The Veldt*. Original essay on *The Veldt*.

Rena Korb: Korb has a master's degree in English literature and creative writing and has written for a wide variety of educational publishers. Entry on *The Sniper*. Original essay on *The Sniper*.

Melodie Monahan: Monahan has a Ph.D. in English. She teaches at Wayne State University and also operates an editing service, The Inkwell Works. Entry on *The Long-Distance Runner*. Original essay on *The Long-Distance Runner*.

Candyce Norvell: Norvell is an independent educational writer who specializes in English and literature. Entry on *Big Black Good Man*. Original essay on *Big Black Good Man*.

Wendy Perkins: Perkins is a professor of American and English literature and film. Entry on *To Room Nineteen*. Original essay on *To Room Nineteen*.

Annette Petruso: Petruso earned a bachelor's degree in history from the University of Michigan and a master's degree in screenwriting from the University of Texas. Original essay on *Babette's Feast*.

David Remy: Remy is a freelance writer in Warrington, Florida. Entry on *The Sun, the Moon, the Stars*. Original essay on *The Sun, the Moon, the Stars*.

Dustie Robeson: Robeson is a freelance writer with a master of arts degree in English. Entry on *In the Shadow of War*. Original essay on *In the Shadow of War*.

Scott Trudell: Trudell is a freelance writer with a bachelor's degree in English literature. Entry on *The Pursuer*. Original essay on *The Pursuer*.

Carey Wallace: Wallace is a writer and poet. Original essay on *The Pursuer*.

Mark White: White is the publisher of the Seattle-based press, Scala House Press. Entry on *Christmas Not Just Once a Year*. Original essay on *Christmas Not Just Once a Year*.

Babette's Feast

Isak Dinesen
1950

Perhaps best known for *Out of Africa* (1937), Isak Dinesen is the pseudonym of Karen Blixen. Having established her reputation as an author in the 1930s and 1940s, she sought to increase her income in the 1950s by having stories published in American magazines. A number of her stories were featured in *Ladies' Home Journal*, including "Babette's Feast," which was first published in 1950. A friend had advised her to write about food because Americans love food, so she crafted a story about the transformative powers of a very special feast. In 1958, "Babette's Feast," along with other stories published in magazines, was compiled into *Anecdotes of Destiny*, which was available as of 2004.

As a child, Dinesen suffered the loss of her father by suicide. In the wake of this tragedy, her grandmother and a nearby aunt helped care for the family. Through this experience, Dinesen came to understand and appreciate the ways women take care of loved ones and of each other. As an adult, Dinesen found herself operating a coffee farm in East Africa, an experience that taught her a great deal about contrasting people and cultures. Dinesen's admirers and scholars often seek parallels between her life and her writing, and in "Babette's Feast" Dinesen seems to draw on her childhood and adult experiences to give the story depth and authenticity.

Author Biography

Karen Blixen (also known as Isak Dinesen) was born Karen Christentze Dinesen on April 17, 1885, near Copenhagen, Denmark. Her father was loosely related to royalty, and her mother was the daughter of a successful shipowner. When Dinesen was ten, her father committed suicide. This was devastating to Dinesen, who had shared a close relationship with her father.

Literature played a prominent role in Dinesen's family; her grandfather had been friends with the fairy tale author Hans Christian Andersen, and her father, brother, a sister, and an aunt were all writers. When Dinesen was twenty-two, several of her short stories were published in literary journals.

On January 14, 1914, Dinesen married her second cousin, Bror von Blixen-Finecke, a baron's son. With the emotional and financial support of their family, the couple bought 700 acres of land in East Africa and began cultivating it for coffee beans. Within the year, however, Dinesen discovered that she had contracted syphilis from her unfaithful husband. Afraid and angry, she returned to Denmark for treatment. She stayed there for most of 1915 and 1916 before reconciling with Bror. With big dreams, they purchased two more coffee farms, but a series of droughts left them profitless.

Dinesen and Bror separated and then divorced in 1925, leaving Dinesen in charge of the failing coffee farms. Her personal life was further complicated by her romance with a longtime friend, an Englishman named Denys Finch Hatton. She had two miscarriages over the course of their relationship, and he had no intention of marrying her. Dinesen's coffee career ended because of a failed loan, fallen coffee and land prices, locusts, and droughts. In 1931, she sold everything to a local developer. A few weeks later, Hatton died when his small airplane crashed.

Prior to leaving Africa and again after returning to Denmark, Dinesen submitted stories to an American publisher (under the name Isak Dinesen). In 1934, her first book of short stories, *Seven Gothic Tales* was published in America. Critical reception was overwhelmingly positive, although the book failed to make waves in Denmark. When *Out of Africa* was published in 1937, American readers and critics alike applauded the author's work. This time, her Danish readership was equally impressed.

In 1959, Dinesen's health was on the decline. Still, she visited America on a four-month tour, where she was toasted by the elite of New York City, including Pearl S. Buck, e. e. cummings, and Marilyn Monroe. After her return to Denmark, her health continued to deteriorate. On September 7, 1962, she died of malnutrition near Copenhagen.

Plot Summary

Part 1: Two Ladies of Berlevaag

In the town of Berlevaag lived an old man and his two daughters, Martine and Philippa. Martine had been named for Martin Luther, and Philippa (one year younger) had been named for Luther's friend Philip Melanchton. The man, called the Dean, was the leader of a small Lutheran religious sect with a faithful following in the small town. He and his daughters led a puritanical life, and the daughters were expected to forego marriage for the sake of leading the sect after the Dean's death.

After the Dean died, the sisters continued his legacy, keeping the church going and ministering to the poor. Now, many years later, the aging churchgoers are bickering and bringing up past wrongs.

Part 2: Martine's Lover

As young women, Martine and Philippa had been strikingly beautiful. At the age of eighteen, Martine caught the eye of a young lieutenant, Lorens Loewenhielm, who then began visiting the Dean in order to see Martine. Despite his frequent visits, he could never manage to tell her of his feelings for her. Being around her made him feel small and worthless, so on his last visit he boldly kissed her hand and declared that he would never see her again. After this he resolved to forget about her and focus on becoming a great military leader so he would never feel small again.

Part 3: Philippa's Lover

A year later, when Philippa was eighteen, a visiting opera singer from France heard her sing at church. The singer, Achille Papin, was renowned in Paris and was convinced that young Philippa could be the toast of Paris with her exquisite soprano voice. The Dean agreed to allow Papin to give the girl lessons, but when Papin rehearsed a romantic duet with her, he kissed her. She returned home and asked her father to write a letter telling Papin she would no longer accept instruction from him. Papin felt a deep loss for the world of music, and he barely remembered the kiss.

Part 4: A Letter from Paris

Fifteen years later, a ragged-looking woman appears on the sisters' doorstep with a letter from Papin. He explains that this woman, Babette Hersant, has fled Paris for her life. He hopes that Martine and Philippa will be kind enough to take her in as a maid, as she has nowhere else to go, having lost her husband and son in an uprising. Babette assures the sisters that she will work as their maid and cook for nothing, and the sisters agree to the arrangement.

Part 5: Still Life

At first, the sisters are wary of their new maid. She speaks only French, looks like a beggar, and is Catholic. As they get accustomed to her, however, they realize that she is strong and kind and has their best interests at heart. Although Papin's letter informed the sisters that Babette could cook, they show her how to prepare the plain dishes to which they are accustomed. Gradually, the sisters' affection for her grows, as does the affection of the members of the church. Martine and Philippa realize, however, that there is much about Babette that they do not know and that she holds painful secrets from her past.

Part 6: Babette's Good Luck

For years, Babette had continued to play the French lottery by mail. As luck would have it, she won the ten-thousand-franc prize just as the sisters were trying to plan a celebration of what would have been their father's hundredth birthday. Babette asked that they allow her to pay for and prepare an authentic French meal for the sisters and their guests. They are nervous about the dishes that will be served, and they are hesitant to accept Babette's generous offer to pay. The sisters reluctantly agree.

Part 7: The Turtle

Babette leaves for ten days to make arrangements for the ingredients for the dinner. Upon her return, Martine and Philippa notice that Babette is particularly bright and enthusiastic in anticipation of the meal. A few weeks later, strange bottles, ingredients (including a large turtle), and other items begin arriving at the house. The sisters become anxious about their guests' response to the foreign dishes, and they appeal to their guests to be as gracious as possible because they are only allow-

Isak Dinesen

ing this meal out of kindness to their servant. The church members, who love Martine and Philippa, gladly agree.

Part 8: The Hymn

The morning of the celebration, Martine and Philippa receive a note that Mrs. Loewenhielm will be bringing her nephew, General Loewenhielm, with her that evening. The General recalls his awkward appearances there as a young lieutenant and looks forward to the chance to show more poise and confidence this time. Martine and Philippa inform Babette that there will be one more for dinner and that it is a man who spent several years in Paris. Babette is delighted.

When the guests arrive, they join hands and begin singing the Dean's favorite hymns. It is a time of sharing and community, and when they sit down to the meal, they are beginning to feel more unified than they have in years.

Part 9: General Loewenhielm

On the drive to the dinner, Loewenhielm had been reflecting on his life and the fact that, despite his military glory, earthly success, and beautiful wife, he is basically unhappy. He had begun to worry about the state of his soul but lacked direction on how to resolve his angst. He remembered the brash young officer he had been years before and how he had dreamed of having everything he now has.

Part 10: Babette's Dinner

A member of the congregation says the blessing over the meal, and Babette's hired assistant begins serving the food and wine. With each course, Loewenhielm is more amazed at how fine the food is and how it reminds him of his days at Paris's finest restaurants. Meanwhile, the conversation at the table revolves around miracles they had all seen during the Dean's years of ministry.

Part 11: General Loewenhielm's Speech

Overcome by the experience of the meal and the feeling of hospitality, Loewenhielm stands up to deliver a speech about righteousness and bliss. He is so eloquent that even though his fellow guests do not understand everything he says, they are moved. Around the table, the men and women of the congregation make amends for their recent bickering and grudges.

As the guests prepare to return home, the sisters walk them to the door. Before leaving, Loewenhielm confesses to Martine that he has never forgotten her and that he never will. They part amicably.

Part 12: The Great Artist

With the meal concluded, Martine and Philippa go to the kitchen to find Babette. She is surrounded by piles of dirty dishes and pots. They thank her for such a fine meal and for all of her work. She admits that she was once the chef at one of Paris's finest restaurants, but when the sisters ask about her return to Paris now that she has money, she answers that she will never go back to Paris. The sisters are relieved but surprised. Babette explains that she prepared the meal that night for herself because she is a great artist and needed to express her artistry. Back in Paris, the life she knew and the people who appreciated her work are all gone. She also tells them that she cannot return to Paris because she has spent her entire lottery winnings on this one meal.

With the understanding of who Babette truly is and how she sees herself, the sisters are moved to compassion. Philippa embraces her and assures her that her art is not lost, because in paradise she will be all God meant her to be.

Characters

Babette Hersant

Babette is welcomed into the home of Martine and Philippa because she is in dire need of a place to stay. She has fled Paris after she and her husband and son participated in an uprising and her two men were killed. Under accusations of arson, she left the country to save her life, taking with her a letter from Achille Papin asking the sisters to take Babette into their home.

Babette is confident, frugal, intelligent, congenial, loyal, and hardworking. She treats the sisters with respect and devotion, despite the many differences between them and herself. Although the sisters do not know it until the end, Babette had been a renowned Parisian chef. This is part of her identity, as she considers herself a great artist who must express her art in order to feel fulfilled. She waits patiently for twelve years before being given the opportunity to prepare a lavish meal for the sisters, an experience that means more to her than it does to them.

Lorens Loewenhielm

When the reader first meets Loewenhielm, he is a young lieutenant in the military, who is smitten with Martine. Never able to bring himself to reveal his feelings for her, he determines to continue his military career and be great so that he will not feel the awkwardness and unworthiness he felt around Martine. Many years later at the dinner, he is a guest. Having become a general with numerous achievements and medals, he feels self-confident entering the house that had intimidated him as a young man. At the same time, he has become introspective in his older age, and he realizes that all the "trappings" of the good life he pursued have failed to make him truly happy.

Martine

Martine is the slightly older sister in the story. As a young woman, her beauty had caught the attention of many men (including Lieutenant Loewenhielm), but she remained loyal to her father's church and his expectation that she and Philippa would oversee it after his death. As a result, she never marries, and she and her sister live together throughout their lives.

Martine is devout, kind, and non-judgmental. She honors her father's memory and loves her sister. Martine and her sister have led sheltered lives, and they both resist change. Martine's anxiety regarding the unknown is evident in the episode in which she sees the large turtle brought in for Babette's meal and is so terrified she has nightmares. Still, she decides that Babette's feelings are more important than her own anxiety. She visits the men and women of the congregation who will be guests at the dinner, asking them to pretend to enjoy the meal, even if the dishes served are very strange. This gesture demonstrates her sensitivity to the feelings of others.

Achille Papin

A great French opera singer, Achille Papin takes a leisure trip to Norway, where he meets eighteen-year-old Philippa. Her voice astounds him, and he arranges to give her private voice lessons. During a duet, however, he kisses her, and she ends the lessons. Though he is disappointed not to see Philippa again, he is more distraught over what the world of art has lost in Philippa's decision not to pursue singing.

Papin is basically a kindhearted man who enjoys his fame and the benefits it brings him. The reader sees how his compassion has grown over the years when he comes to Babette's aid in Paris. With her life at risk, he remembers the two gentle Norwegian sisters and sends Babette to them with a personal letter asking them to care for her.

Philippa

One year younger than Martine, Philippa is the other daughter of the Dean. Together, she and her sister oversee their father's Lutheran sect in their small hometown. Like her sister, she honors her father's desire that they focus on the congregation rather than marry and have their own families. Also like her sister, she seems to bear no resentment for this course in life, and she and Martine live happily together for their entire lives.

Philippa has a beautiful voice, and in her youth it captured the attention of the French opera singer, Achille Papin. She turns from pursuing developing this talent, however, and devotes her life to her father's congregation. Philippa is a kind and religious woman who leads a plain but satisfying life. Her sensitivity is demonstrated in the last scene when, after Babette has revealed her identity as a chef and an artist, Philippa embraces her and encourages her in her art. She assures Babette that her days as an artist are not over because in heaven she will enjoy the fullness of her art as it was meant to be.

Media Adaptations

- In 1987, Danish writer and director Gabriel Axel adapted "Babette's Feast" to film for Orion Pictures. It garnered an impressive following and won the 1988 Academy Award for Best Foreign Film.

Themes

Food

The predominant theme of "Babette's Feast" is how food can transform the hearts of people and the atmosphere of a gathering. Prior to Babette's appearance on their doorstep, Martine and Philippa regarded food as something plain that had the sole purpose of providing their necessary sustenance. Because their lifestyle requires shunning the pleasures of the flesh, they had never considered food a luxurious experience to be enjoyed. Babette, on the other hand, has a very different perspective; she adores preparing exquisite food to delight others, and when she is finally given the chance to do this for the sisters and their congregation, the story takes on new life. The meal she prepares creates an atmosphere that fosters interaction and delight. Dinesen explains: "Usually in Berlevaag people did not speak much while they were eating. But somehow this evening tongues were loosened." She adds:

> Most often the people in Berlevaag during the course of a good meal would come to feel a little heavy. Tonight it was not so. The *convives* grew lighter in weight and lighter of heart the more they ate and drank. They no longer needed to remind themselves of their vow [to pretend to enjoy the meal despite the strange dishes]. It was, they realized, when man has not only altogether forgotten but has firmly renounced all ideas of food and drink that he eats and drinks in the right spirit.

Even before the feast, Dinesen reveals that Babette has unusual powers with food. When she takes over running the house for the sisters, she respects their work feeding the needy. The sisters notice that "the soup-pails and baskets acquired a

Topics for Further Study

- After so many years of living a certain way, Babette reveals much about herself to Martine and Philippa at the feast. Given the ways the characters interacted during the feast, how do you think the women's relationships may be different afterwards? How may they remain the same? Do you think Babette continues to live with the sisters? Write an ''Afterword'' addressing these questions. You may write it in Dinesen's style or approach it as an objective follow-up.

- Imagine that you are in a similar position as Babette after she won the money and offered to prepare an authentic French meal. Consider your own family's background, and prepare a menu for a feast featuring dishes from the native land of part or all of your family. Include at least three recipes with the menu. Be sure to consider every course of the meal and include beverages.

- Research the Evangelical Lutheran Church of Norway. If you have difficulty finding enough information, extend your research to other Scandinavian Lutheran churches. How has it changed since the eighteenth and nineteenth centuries? Were sects like that formed by the Dean common, and what kinds of factors led groups to differentiate themselves slightly from the main church body?

- Babette considers herself a great artist because she is a great chef. Do you agree that cuisine is a form of art? In the story, what does her cooking have in common with other forms of art, and how is it different? Choose one other student in the class whose opinion differs from yours and hold an informal debate with a panel of three students who will decide which of you makes the stronger arguments.

---

new, mysterious power to stimulate and strengthen their poor and sick.'' Whether she is cooking for friends, hostesses, strangers, the needy, or the wealthy, Babette has a special gift with food that fulfills her while satisfying others.

Contrast

Throughout the story, Dinesen sets up a variety of contrasts. Most of the contrast is between Babette and her hostesses, Martine and Philippa. Babette is an entirely different kind of woman than they are, and Dinesen draws these lines very clearly. Whereas Babette is dark, the sisters are fair. Whereas Babette is a French Catholic fleeing danger and unrest, the sisters are Norwegian Lutherans secure in their familiar and predictable environment. Whereas Babette embraces worldly experience and pleasure (though not to excess), the sisters consciously avoid such things. The religious contrast is an important one to the sisters, a lesson they learned from their father, who upon learning that Papin was Roman Catholic "grew a little pale," as he had never actually seen a Roman Catholic in person. Dinesen

writes that the sisters and their congregation "renounced the pleasures of this world, for the earth and all that it held to them was but a kind of illusion." Shedding light on the sisters' upbringing, Dinesen offers a contrast between them and the world beyond the environment created by their father; the sisters are described as having had an "almost supernatural fairness of flowering fruit trees or perpetual snow," and they "did not let themselves be touched by the flames of this world." On the evening of the dinner, Babette's diligent and frantic preparations in the kitchen contrast sharply with the sisters' preparation for the event. Martine and Philippa "put on their old black best frocks and their confirmation gold crosses. They sat down, folded their hands in their laps and committed themselves unto God."

What makes the idea of contrast a theme rather than a stylistic consideration is what Dinesen does with it. Rather than use it as a way to generate interest in the characters, she brings all the contrasts between Babette and the sisters to the moment of the

---

feast, where she demonstrates how their differences ultimately bring them closer together. To everyone's surprise, their differences are not irreconcilable, as General Loewenhielm announces in his toast, "Righteousness and bliss have kissed one another!" By treating each other with kindness and understanding, the women learn that their differences in no way prevent them from achieving emotional intimacy. This closeness is hinted at earlier in the story, when the sisters have taken Babette into their home and are getting to know her better. Dinesen reveals a realization they make: "She had appeared to be a beggar; she turned out to be a conqueror." The contrast between the first impression she made and the person she actually is only important because the sisters keep their hearts open to finding out who Babette really is.

Style

Biblical Allusion

Biblically well-read, Dinesen applies her knowledge of Scripture in "Babette's Feast" to underscore the strong religious overtones of Martine and Philippa's home they share with Babette. Throughout the story, subtle biblical allusions are introduced without reference, giving them the natural context of everyday thought that they have in the hearts of the sisters and the congregation. In describing the sisters' beauty in their youth, Dinesen explains that they caught the eyes of the men in the congregation. She writes that the older men "had been prizing the maidens far above rubies," an allusion to Proverbs 3:15 ("She is more precious than rubies; nothing you desire can compare to her") and Proverbs 31:10 ("A wife of noble character who can find? She is worth far more than rubies").

Babette is also the subject of biblical allusions. At one point, she is likened to Martha and the sisters to Mary, a reference to a story in the book of Luke (Luke 10:38–42) in which Jesus visits the sisters Mary and Martha. While Martha busies herself with hostess duties and preparing food, Mary sits quietly to learn. Babette is also deemed a "good and faithful servant," an allusion to the parable of the talents. In this parable, a master puts some of his servants in charge of money to see what they do with it. The servant who doubles his sum is praised, "Well done, good and faithful servant!" (Matthew 25:21).

The feast itself inspires a reference to the wedding in which Jesus turned water into wine (John 2:1–11). Dinesen writes, "They were sitting down to a meal, well, so had people done at the wedding of Cana. And grace has chosen to manifest itself there, in the very wine, as fully as anywhere." This is a significant reference for the conservative Lutherans at the meal because it gives them biblical permission to enjoy the event and its wine, and it is the first step toward the eventual reconciliation of the pleasures of the world and the fullness of the spirit.

Simile

Perhaps because the Norwegian setting and characters were unfamiliar to her American readers ("Babette's Feast" was, after all, written for an American magazine), Dinesen scatters similes throughout her story to provide her readers with familiar images. This approach begins in the very first paragraph, where Dinesen writes of the small town of Berlevaag that it "looks like a child's toytown of little wooden pieces painted gray, tallow, pink and many other colors." When Babette asks if she may use her lottery winnings to pay for and prepare a lavish French meal, Dinesen writes, "Babette's dark eyes were as eager and pleading as a dog's." General Loewenhielm dresses in his military regalia for the feast, and when he arrives, "in his bright uniform, his breast covered with decorations, [he] strutted and shone like an ornamental bird. A golden pheasant or a peacock, in this sedate party of black crows and jackdaws."

Historical Context

Norway in the 1870s

In the 1870s, Norway was a relatively peaceful, prosperous nation. Although it was under Swedish rule, Norway had been allowed to have its own constitution. This simply meant that rather than being governed by its own monarch, it was under the authority of Sweden. In the Parliament and among the people, however, a growing nationalist movement began to pave the way for Norway's eventual independence. Economically, Norway was healthy. Increased trade and more favorable tariffs brought Norway further into the opportunities offered by the European economy. Modernity was making its way into the country's business and daily life: The first railway had been in operation since 1854, the telegraph was available, and agricultural

Compare & Contrast

- **1870s:** Although Norway has its own constitution and its Parliament is growing stronger, it is under Swedish rule. This and other factors feed a rising nationalism that results in Norway's independence in 1905.

  1950s: Having regained its independence, Norway returns to its government structure of a constitutional monarchy. Norway has deserted its World War I neutrality and joined NATO, making it a more active player in international affairs.

  Today: In the 1990s, Norway maintains its independence from the European Union. The 1994 vote is very close, with a slight majority of 52 percent voting against joining Europe.

- **1870s:** The state church is still the Evangelical Lutheran Church of Norway. Put in place after the Reformation in 1500, the state church is funded by the government. Most Norwegians are members of this church. Having a state church does not, however, prohibit free practice of other faiths and denominations.

  1950s: Little has changed over the years. The Evangelical Lutheran Church of Norway is still the state church, and most Norwegians continue to be members with varying degrees of activity.

  Today: Approximately 90 percent of Norwegians are affiliated with the Evangelical Lutheran Church of Norway. While it is still the state church, a growing number of Norwegians favor separating the church and the government.

- **1870s:** About thirty years after Norway began to establish industrial businesses, such as textile factories, the economy is healthy and strong. During this period, the number of merchant ships in Norway rises substantially, evidence of the growth of Norway's industries.

  1950s: In the post–World War II years, Norway's economy has grown. More attention is given to building welfare programs to provide for the low-income segments of the population.

  Today: As a result of the strong economy and the postwar welfare programs, Norwegian society is less characterized by class distinctions than many Western nations.

- **1870s:** Women are second to men in Norwegian society. Although they won inheritance rights in the 1850s, women are still barred from pursuing higher education, and married women are not allowed to manage money.

  1950s: Progress in women's rights has been made, but inequality still characterizes gender rights and privileges. With the rise of industrialism, more women have entered the workforce, but at lower pay rates than men receive. Women also have the right to vote.

  Today: Women hold visible positions in government and occupy numerous seats in the Parliament. Women comprise at least half of all college graduates each year, and the government has handed down "affirmative action"–type statutes to increase the number of women in the workforce.

---

methods had been modernized. Industry had grown substantially since the 1840s, which, combined with the increased trade, substantially grew the merchant fleet.

With the economic upturns, however, came class conflict and a call for social reforms. This eventually led to the first liberal political block that challenged the predominant conservative thinkers in government. Still, it would not be until 1884 that this block would officially become a political party.

The population in 1870s Norway was quite homogenous. There were very few non-Norwegians, so the language and customs of Norway remained well preserved. Family life was very traditional, with women expected to marry young, have children, and maintain the home, whereas men were expected to work hard to provide for their families.

The 1871 Communard Uprising in Paris

France in the mid-nineteenth century was a place of political turmoil. Between 1852 and 1871, the period called the Second Empire saw the Emperor Napoleon III pursue colonial expansion and foster a strong economy. The Franco-Prussian War, however, lasted from 1870 to 1871 and brought France and its emperor to its knees. A provisional government was put in place as a stopgap until February 1871, when elections were held for a National Assembly. A group of radicals, however, were angry at how quickly France had surrendered to Prussia and how the new government was shaping up to be conservative. In March, these radicals and the National Guard seized Paris and appointed themselves the *Communards* (supporters of *La Commune de Paris*) to take over as the governing body. Government troops were sent on May 21 to destroy the *Communards*, and the week that followed became known as "Bloody Week." After the defeat, punishments were handed down to those who participated. In all, eighteen thousand Parisians lost their lives and seven thousand were deported.

Critical Overview

Critics generally characterize "Babette's Feast" as a triumphant and sensitive story of generosity, grace, and healing. John Simon of *National Review* deems it as "one of the author's finest." The characterization of the women in the story and the relationships between them strike readers as believable and sympathetic. In the *New Republic*, Stanley Kauffmann observed, "Lightly but clearly interwoven in the story are oppositions of cultures—pleasure-loving Catholic France, dour and hell-conscious Protestant Denmark." Despite the differences between Babette and the sisters Martine and Philippa, the women find a way to live contentedly together, caring for each other and finally getting to know each other in meaningful ways. In fact, Bruce Bassoff of *Studies in Short Fiction* notes that "Babette's Feast" features new knowledge and "a desire for transcendence," which are present in other short stories by Dinesen. Her use of these ideas and plot elements in multiple stories suggests that depicting them to her readers was important to Dinesen.

Dinesen's use of food in the story is a frequent topic of critical discussion. Dinesen uses food in the story in two opposing ways: first as an outward reflection of the differences between Babette and her hostesses and then as a means of bringing unity and commonality to a diverse group of people. In *Style*, critic Esther Rashkin comments on the former:

> Food has tended to be viewed allegorically in the story as representing, for example, the schism between the ethical, Norwegian, puritanical sect of Protestantism, nurtured on split cod and ale-and-bread soup, and the aesthetic, sensuous inclinations of French Catholicism, nourished by haute cuisine and epitomized by the master chef Babette.

She adds:

> There is no denying that Babette's sumptuous feast and its aftermath offer a reflection on religion and on the opposition between the spiritual and the carnal, while also raising questions of artistic creation and identity.

More attention, however, is given to the banquet that gives the story its title. With the feast itself, Dinesen not only introduces the sense of sharing that comes with enjoying a meal together, but she adds the elements of generosity, service, mystery, and revelation. Rashkin notes that the feast demonstrates how the differences between Babette and the sisters come together in a unique and transformative way over the course of the evening. Of particular interest to Rashkin is the way the dinner opens up the hearts and mouths of the guests to explore emotional territory previously kept private. She notes that many of the guests, along with the main characters, have suffered loss that remained unspoken until the feast. She explains that the dinner "allows for a communion in loss by enabling loss to be talked about and the process of mourning to begin." Rashkin concludes her commentary by suggesting that writing this story had a similarly cathartic purpose for Dinesen, who endured considerable loss during her years in Africa. Having lost her coffee farms, her husband, her lover, two pregnancies, and almost two decades, she returned to Denmark alone. Rashkin offers this biographical interpretation of "Babette's Feast":

> If Africa was for Dinesen a "child she had buried" and could only talk or write about from a distance, and if "Babette's Feast" is all about the creation of a work of art as the therapeutic medium for "talking" about loss, we may suggest that Dinesen too, like the sisters . . . "used" this narrative for her own therapeutic needs. . . . Created as a symptom of her need to grieve, as a vehicle for facilitating the grieving process, and as a subtle commentary on the intricate relationship between writing and bereavement, "Babette's Feast"

The Siege of Paris in 1871, which drives Babette from her native France to the home of the Norwegian sisters in Dinesen's ''Babette's Feast''

can ultimately be read as a text that humorously and poignantly tells the tale of Dinesen's own recipe for mourning.

Criticism

Jennifer Bussey

Bussey holds a master's degree in interdisciplinary studies and a bachelor's degree in English literature. She is an independent writer specializing in literature. In the following essay, Bussey examines Dinesen's depiction of the unique ways in which women take care of each other in "Babette's Feast," and she relates them to the author's life.

Isak Dinesen's "Babette's Feast" features three main characters, all women, who find themselves as unlikely housemates. Martine and Philippa are sisters who remain unmarried so they can take up the responsibilities of overseeing the congregation of their deceased father's Lutheran sect. The other woman in the story is a French woman named Babette, who fled Paris in great danger and is taken in by the two sisters. Babette and her generous hostesses have little in common, but among the

strongest qualities they all share is the impulse to take care of each other. Despite their differences, they forge a familial bond through the act of mutual support, first out of a sense of duty, but ultimately out of affection.

Initially, the sisters know little of Babette, and her inability and unwillingness to communicate with them makes her difficult to understand at times. Besides the language barrier that exists between Babette and the sisters, Babette carries a great deal of pain and loss at having fled Paris for her life after the deaths of her husband and son. Dinesen writes, "When in the early days the sisters had gently condoled her upon her losses, they had been met with that majesty and stoicism of which Monsieur Papin had written [in the letter introducing her to them]." The lack of communication between the women compels them to take care of each other in practical ways. They want to help and support each other, but as virtual strangers, the only ways they can do so are by attending to each other's obvious needs. The sisters come to Babette's aid by giving her a safe place to stay; by providing food, shelter, and companionship; and by making few demands of her. In turn, Babette looks after the sisters by cooking, cleaning, shopping, and running the house

What Do I Read Next?

- All of the short stories in the collection *Anecdotes of Destiny* (1958), including "Babette's Feast," were written by Dinesen in the 1950s for American magazines and American readers.

- Karen Blixen (as Isak Dinesen) is best known for *Out of Africa* (1937). Largely based on her actual experiences in Africa trying to operate successful coffee farms, this book remains popular because of its descriptions of landscape, animals, and people and its honest portrayal of a difficult lifestyle.

- *Like Water for Chocolate* (1992) is Laura Esquivel's magical yet realistic novel about the emotional and spiritual effects food can have. The novel is set in Mexico and tells the story of a young woman forced to allow her sister to marry her lover. Her ability to cook, however, includes the ability to use her emotions and passions as ingredients.

- Einar Molland's *Church Life in Norway: 1800–1950* (1978) closely examines the role of the state church in Norway and its influence on daily life. Molland also explores challenges to the church's theological views over this time span and how these challenges have affected the church's position in Norwegian society.

---

so they can focus on their congregation and their charity work. Babette shows respect and appreciation for the sisters by working hard without complaining. In all of these ways, the women help lighten each other's loads, and they begin to build a relationship of trust and dependence that will later open up the possibility of emotional bonds.

As their relationships gradually develop over the next twelve years, the sisters and Babette learn to take care of each other in more personal ways. As they get to know each other better, they learn how to be kind, understanding, respectful, patient, and intuitive toward each other in ways that are personally meaningful to each woman. The reader also notices that the three women do not pressure each other, but instead are sensitive enough not to pry into the pain or emotional discomfort of one another. Because Babette is so different from the sisters, they all make special efforts to accommodate each other. Babette wants to cook in her familiar, grand way, but she realizes that the sisters expect to eat exactly as they always have, so she sacrifices her art for their comfort and makes the plain dishes they request. Later, the sisters agree to allow Babette to prepare a large French meal, even though they are very apprehensive about the dishes that will be served. For Babette's sake, however, they determine to pretend to enjoy the food, and Martine asks the guests to do likewise. In this way, the sisters unselfishly accommodate Babette's wishes, as she has done for them for so many years. Gestures such as these reflect emotional growth between the women. By the end of the story, the women have such love for each other that they feel deep sympathy and compassion for each other's pain. Martine and Philippa listen as Babette explains what she lost when she left Paris, and they are moved by her pain. Dinesen explains:

> The strange names and titles of people lost to Babette faintly confused the two ladies, but there was such an infinite perspective of tragedy in her announcement that in their responsive state of mind they felt her losses as their own, and their eyes filled with tears.

The development of the emotional bond is important to Babette because she has been emotionally alone for many years, whereas the sisters have been close all their lives. But the emotional bond with Babette is not meaningless to the sisters. Having led very sheltered lives, they grow in unique ways from knowing her. Their experiences are broadened and their ability to be open emotionally is stretched as a result of this stranger entering their lives.

Dinesen contrasts the sisterly interactions of the women with the ways in which the men in the

> "... the sisters and Babette learn to take care of each other in more personal ways. As they get to know each other better, they learn how to be kind, understanding, respectful, patient, and intuitive toward each other in ways that are personally meaningful to each woman."

story try to take care of women. Martine's and Philippa's father, the Dean, took care of them in practical ways: He provided their food, shelter, clothing, education, and religious upbringing. The women's recollections, however, do not include any warm memories of loving talks, fatherly advice, or emotional connection at all. The reader has the impression that the Dean never asked his daughters what they wanted to do in life but rather communicated to them (and to the congregation) his expectation that they would take over for him after his death. Although Dinesen tells little about what kind of man the Dean was, his parenting style seems consistent with his strict demeanor.

Two mini-chapters tell of each of the sisters' "lovers," which is hardly the correct term for two men who barely knew or interacted with the women. First, Martine is silently admired by Lieutenant Loewenhielm. He is struck by her physical beauty and is so intimidated by her that he cannot speak to her until his final departure. His feelings for her have little to do with wanting to know her, love her, and take care of her. Instead, his feelings are more akin to infatuation, and he is drawn to her by his own longings. He imagines life with her as being "with no creditors, dunning letters or parental lectures, with no secret, unpleasant pangs of conscience and with a gentle, golden-haired angel to guide and reward him."

Philippa's physical beauty, along with her extraordinary soprano voice, catches the attention of a French opera singer named Achille Papin. His de-

sire to be with her is driven by his love for the art of music and the desire to see her rise to fame in Paris. In fact, he gives little indication that he has personal affection for the young woman, even after he boldly kisses her during a duet. He has no interest in knowing her and taking care of her particular needs but rather in seeing her achieve the success *he* values. He tells her that she will

> rise like a star above any diva of the past or present. The Emperor and Empress, the Princes, great ladies and *bels esprits* of Paris would listen to her, and shed tears. The common people too would worship her, and she would bring consolation and strength to the wronged and oppressed.

Later in life, when Babette is in need, Papin seems to understand at some level that women are best in taking care of other women; he sends Babette to Martine and Philippa, confident they will care for Babette. None of these men—the Dean, Loewenhielm, or Papin—displays any interest in attending to the emotional needs of the women in the story. At best, they have practical notions of what the women need, but in no way do they take care of the women the way the women take care of each other. To further emphasize this point, Dinesen tells nothing of the way men take care of each other. Combined, these images of men place the focus squarely on how women take care of each other.

A great deal of literary attention has been given to Dinesen's personal life and its influences on her writing. Her best-known work is easily *Out of Africa*, which relies very heavily on her own experiences in Africa. But her other works also draw from her personal experiences, and "Babette's Feast" is no exception. When Dinesen was a child, her father committed suicide, leaving her mother alone to run the house and rear the children. Luckily, a grandmother and an aunt who both lived nearby took on the responsibility of helping Dinesen's mother and the children manage without a man in the house. Biographers note that the help they lent was material, emotional, and spiritual. This tells the reader of "Babette's Feast" that Dinesen knew a great deal about how and why women take care of each other and that she was deeply affected by this kind of care. It is no wonder, then, that her portrayal of Babette, Martine, and Philippa is so warm and believable.

Source: Jennifer Bussey, Critical Essay on "Babette's Feast," in *Short Stories for Students*, Gale, 2005.

A. Petruso

Petruso earned a bachelor's degree in history from the University of Michigan and a master's degree in screenwriting from the University of Texas. In the following essay, Petruso explores how the idea of art saturates aspects of Dinesen's short story.

According to *The Random House Dictionary*, a definition of art is "the quality, production, expression, according to aesthetic principles, of what is beautiful." This concepts of art and artistry and how they can affect life is a central theme of Isak Dinesen's short story, "Babette's Feast," primarily expressed through characters and their actions. Though Babette Hersant is most obviously an artist with food as the title implies—the story's title claims that she creates a "feast" not a "nice meal"— several primary characters have an artistic element that helps answer questions such as "what is art?" and "how does it affect every day life?" Some believe that life itself is art, and this story explores that concept to the fullest.

The title character, Babette, has the most obvious and the most complicated relationship to art of any character in "Babette's Feast." Dinesen clearly labels Babette an artist. At the end of the story, the author entitles the last section "The Great Artist," and Babette herself declares to the sisters that "I am a great artist, Mesdames." In that section, Babette reveals to the sisters that she was a chef at a famous restaurant in Paris, Café Anglais, before she was forced to leave Paris and came to Norway to become their servant. Babette also tells them that she spent the whole of her winnings in the French lottery on the meal—10,000 francs. Babette sacrifices what could have given her a different, if not better, richer, and fuller life in Paris or elsewhere, to be able to create what she has not been able to do for the past 12 years while she has been in the sisters' employ: an extravagant culinary work of art. Dinesen gives Babette the chance to define what an artist is. She declares, "A great artist, Mesdames, is never poor. We have something, Mesdames, of which other people know nothing." Much of the story is the embodiment of this idea.

It is not until that moment that at least one of the sisters fully appreciates Babette's sacrifice for her art. Philippa is moved by Babette's words in the last pages of "Babette's Feast." Though Babette was against the rich in the French civil war from which she escaped, her style of cooking was meant to be appreciated by such people before the uprising changed life in the city. It is only then that Philippa, and the reader, really understands that while Babette has not been able to be the artist she was meant to be for many years while in the sisters' employ, she has

> "Though it is not local custom to talk during the meal, the guests speak freely of the Dean, his life, and their memories of him. Later, Dinesen writes that the divisions between certain people are overcome and old grudges are forgiven. Babette's culinary art works emotional magic."

made her life a reflection of her artistry. That is, Babette found means of expressing her art in smaller ways—on smaller, odder canvases—than in the one meal she made in honor of the Dean's one hundredth birthday. Achille Papin, the singer/teacher who was connected with Philippa in her youth and who sent Babette to the sisters' door, was able to relate this idea best for Babette. While describing the longing to do one's best as an artist, Babette quotes Papin as saying, "Through all the world there goes one long cry from the heart of the artist: Give me leave to do my utmost!"

Though Babette is grateful to the sisters for providing her a home and a position after she came to their door penniless and alone, the limitations of the sisters' severe and quiet lifestyle affects Babette's ability to express her art the way she had in Paris before the uprising. But for the 12 years in the sister' employ until Babette wins the French lottery, Dinesen describes several ways in which Babette expresses herself culinary artist. When the sisters demonstrate to her what their preferred meal is—split cod and an ale-and-bread soup—Dinesen writes that she masters it like a native of the city. Babette acquiesces in their demand for plain and simple food for themselves, but when told that the food she creates for the poor—"soup-pails and baskets"—is important, she puts much effort into doing the best she could. Her food for unfortunates "acquired a new, mysterious power to stimulate and strengthen the poor and the sick." Babette also is able to be cost efficient. The costs of running the household go down and she is described as winning many battles while haggling over the price of food with local tradesman. Though these small works are not as extravagant as the meals she cooked in Paris, they allow Babette a limited outlet for her artistry. They give her leave to do her utmost and be an artist every day of her life.

Another way that the idea of art works in "Babette's Feast" is in how Babette's art is appreciated and used by those who partake in it. The main place where this occurs is during the meal, primarily described in "Babette's Dinner" and "General Lowenhielm's Speech." Only General Loewenhielm directly verbalizes the extraordinary nature of the dinner that Babette has cooked. He has eaten her culinary art before. In the text, he recounts an original dish he ate in Paris and that a woman, implied to be Babette, was considered "the greatest culinary genius of the age." Loewenhielm is constantly amazed by the courses that she cooks for them, and knows the name of each dish and every beverage. He is a connoisseur of Babette's art.

Though the other attendees at the dinner are not as sophisticated about such culinary matters as the general, Babette's art moves them as well. To compare this appreciation to how an audience views a painting in a museum, the general is an educated viewer who understands the background of the painter and can explain why the piece is beautiful, while the other attendees of the dinner are more casual viewers of the work. Such patrons walk by, perhaps consciously appreciating the color scheme and the subject of the painting, but something about the work jars a memory, creates an emotion, and perhaps starts an unexpected conversation. It affects them deeply. Babette's feast has such an effect on the other guests. Because the sisters, primarily Martine, were concerned that the meal might be bad somehow, all the attendees, members of the Dean's congregation, decide not to comment at all on the food that Babette serves them at the dinner for the sake of the sisters. The attendees—save the general, an outsider added to the guest list at the last minute—stick to this pledge, but the meal greatly affects them. Though it is not local custom to talk during the meal, the guests speak freely of the Dean, his life, and their memories of him. Later, Dinesen writes that the divisions between certain people are overcome and old grudges are forgiven. Babette's culinary art works emotional magic.

Dinesen's definition of the artist also applies to the sisters, whose story makes up the majority of the text, but each in a slightly different way. Like Babette, both sisters choose to live to the utmost, using self-discipline, sacrifice, and faith as their colors. After the meal, however, it is Philippa, the younger sister, who understands better than her elder sister Martine that Babette is an artist. Philippa makes an emotional connection to Babette at the end of "Babette's Feast." Martine compliments Babette as well, saying "They all thought it was a nice dinner," but has a different relationship to art in her life than Philippa. Philippa is more obviously connected because of her singing, but it is Dinesen's description of their lives that makes them artists in their own way.

In her youth, Philippa was recognized for having a lovely singing voice and potential for greatness in that art form. She is discovered by a well-known Paris-based opera singer, Papin, who immediately offers to give her singing lessons. Philippa so inspires him that he makes great plans for her operatic singing career, which she seems to share because Dinesen says that she keeps them a secret from her sister and father. However, after Papin goes too far one day and kisses her while they are working on a scene from Mozart's *Don Giovanni* together, she immediately ends her singing education. Dinesen implies it is because of what the kiss stirs inside of her. Thus Philippa had the chance and the skills to be an artist in song, but she took her gift elsewhere.

Though Philippa turns her back on her singing career, she and her sister live the austere life of artists of their faith. Their father was the leader of a church and had many followers. Though Dinesen does not directly address the issue of whether or not marriage was permitted for the women of this faith, his daughters did not marry, but made their lives a living work of art defined in the image of morality, ethics, and frugality set forth by their father. In the second paragraph of the story, Dinesen describes how they have the figures for fashionable clothes, but they choose to dress only in black or gray. While both sisters have a moment in which they connect with a man and a brief kiss of some sort, their lives are focused on what the Dean preached as important. Dinesen writes of the Dean's church, "Its members renounced the pleasures of this world. . . ." The author also says that the sisters never use foul language, as the Dean taught, and devote all their time and money to charitable works. Everything the pair does in their entire lives was to live to this ideal, a devotion mirrored by Babette's dedication to her culinary artistry in whatever form that was able to take in her circumstances. The sisters' lives are works of art in that they appreciated what was set for them and followed it to the letter. Their lives are beautiful in their purity, their piety, and single-minded focus.

In Bruce Bassoff's essay, "Babette Can Cook: Life and Art in Three Stories by Isak Dinesen," he argues that Martine and Philippa are "shallow" while Babette is "deep." In this argument, Bassoff oversimplifies Dinesen's conclusion in "Babette's Feast." It is Babette's artistic abilities, and the way she has incorporated them in her everyday life for the past 12 years, that has helped refine the artistry of the life of the sisters. When they learn that Babette was once a cook to an elderly priest, Dinesen writes, "the sisters resolved to surpass the French priest in asceticism." Outsiders like Babette are challenged by the sisters' life artistry and forced to find new outlets for their talents. In the end, though it takes Babette's obvious culinary artistry to make the sisters, and their readers, more fully appreciate their lives, Martine and Philippa have already lived the full life of spiritual artists.

Source: A. Petruso, Critical Essay on "Babette's Feast," in *Short Stories for Students*, Gale, 2005.

Ervin Beck

In the following essay, Beck explores associations between the character of Babette and Saint Barbara in "Babette's Feast."

The meaning latent in the name of Babette Hersant, the main character in Isak Dinesen's short story "Babette's Feast," associates Babette with Saint Barbara, thereby enriching the theological implications of the story.

The family name Hersant can be translated, "herself a saint." The syllable *sant* is a reasonable cognate for both the French and English saint, and *san* literally suggests the Spanish *san*, as in San Francisco. According to the OED, *sant* historically has been a rather common Indo-European spelling for saint, as in Old Frisian, Medieval Dutch, and Medieval High German.

Babette can be regarded both as the diminutive form of Elizabeth in French-speaking culture and as the diminutive of Barbara (cf. Babs) in English-speaking culture. Although Babette Hersant was French, other contextual elements suggest the English meaning instead of the French for the nickname in this story. For instance, Babette became famous as a chef at the Cafe Anglais (English Cafe) in Paris.

More important, Dinesen wrote the story in English and first published it for an English-speaking audience in the popular American magazine *Good Housekeeping*. Dinesen clearly allows the English etymology to dominate the story since Babette has very clear and essential connections with St. Barbara, "one of the most popular saints in the Middle Ages."

Like other saints, Babette is a sacrificial victim whose life and death are associated with salvation and the miraculous. Although we assume that Babette does not literally die at the end of the story, sly Dinesen opens the door for that possibility when Philippa, in her final gesture, puts her arms around Babette and feels "the cook's body like a marble monument against her own." Metaphorically, Babette has already become a marble saint's statue. Her figurative "death" has been prepared for by the fact that, following the guests' departure, Martine and Philippa go to the kitchen and find Babette sitting "on the chopping" block, "white and . . . deadly exhausted." Babette on the chopping block alludes to St. Barbara's death by having her head cut off.

Another important correspondence between Babette and St. Barbara is that the latter's feast day in the Catholic church year is 4 December, early in Advent, which is also the time of year when Babette prepares her feast. The food arrives in Berlevaag (through Christiania!) "one December day" and Babette prepares the dinner for 15 December, the anniversary of the pastor's birthday.

But the most significant association of Babette and St. Barbara concerns both women's relationship to the mass as a Catholic sacrament. In many iconic representations of St. Barbara she "carries the sacramental cup and wafer, and is the only female saint who bears this attribute." This image of cup and wafer visualizes St. Barbara's dying wish. Despite her personal anguish, St. Barbara prayed not for herself but for others who die without benefit of the sacraments but remember both Christ's name and her own suffering. Her request for grace for the unshriven has made her "an especial protectress of those in danger of dying without the sacraments"—as are Babette's Lutheran sectarian friends in their quarreling, fallen state.

Dinesen's equivalent for St. Barbara's wafer and cup are Babette's exotic food and drink. The understatement "Babette can cook" flowers not only into the sensory marvels of her culinary art but also into the spiritually saving grace that partaking of her food brings to her guests. Perhaps Babette began mastering this art even prior to her work at the

Cafe Anglais—when as a girl she was cook "to an old priest who was a saint." In any event, the Berlevaag food becomes the actual body (wafer) and blood (wine) of Christ, according to the Catholic doctrine of transubstantiation. One odd detail that emphasizes this "actual presence" is Martine's gruesome recollection, following the feast, of the story of a missionary who discovered that he had eaten "a small fat grandchild of the chief's cooked in honor of the great Christian medicine man." Babette's feast is another such instance of holy cannibalism.

Babette's feast produces the miracle that is required for a holy person, like St. Barbara, to be canonized. Even at the Cafe Anglais her cooking rather miraculously turned a dinner into "a kind of love affair . . . in which one no longer distinguishes between bodily and spiritual appetite or satiety." But her Berlevaag feast absolutely transforms the hearts of the people who partake of it. Babette unwittingly creates a sacramental experience, worthy of St. Barbara, that brings atonement (at-one-ment) to its participants, just as the Catholic mass does.

Many details contribute to seeing Babette's feast as a commemoration of the Last Supper: The meal is served to twelve people; the meal commemorates the death of the founder of a religious sect; it is set on a Sunday in the Advent season; and Dinesen several times quotes Psalm 85:10, which is a traditional reading during Advent, since it prophesies the way the Incarnation will reconcile the rival claims of justice and mercy and of the old and new dispensations:

> Mercy and truth have met together. Righteousness and bliss have kissed each other.

In his 1987 film version of the story, director Gabriel Axel shrewdly emphasizes the eucharistic moment by having General Lowenhielm tap his glass when he stands to repeat Psalm 85:10 and elaborate on the meaning of the meal. His "ping" is the archetypal equivalent of the bell that rings during the Catholic mass to indicate the precise moment when the bread and wine have become the Body and the Blood.

Isak Dinesen wrote "Babette's Feast" in late 1952, at a time when she was hosting dinner parties at which she, a Luthern pastor, a Catholic priest, and other friends discussed theology. Dinesen, who claimed to be a kind of Unitarian-Mohammedan, was more interested in Christian conduct than in Christian doctrine and claimed that, of Christianity,

"any real understanding in a connected sense I have never achieved."

The salvific work of Babette, properly seen as a modern equivalent of St. Barbara, proves the disingenuousness of Dinesen's statement. It also suggests that, in her theological dinner discussions, Dinesen sympathized more with the sacramentalist Roman Catholic priest than with the transcendentalist Lutheran pastor.

Source: Ervin Beck, "Dinesen's 'Babette's Feast,'" in *Explicator*, Vol. 56, No. 4, Summer 1998, pp. 210–13.

Sources

Bassoff, Bruce, "Babette Can Cook: Life and Art in Three Stories by Isak Dinesen," in *Studies in Short Fiction*, Vol. 27, No. 3, Summer 1990, pp. 385–89.

Dinesen, Isak, "Babette's Feast," in *Anecdotes of Destiny and Ehrengard*, 1958, reprint, Vintage Books, 1985, pp. 21–68.

Donelson, Linda G., "Karen Blixen," in *Dictionary of Literary Biography*, Vol. 214, *Twentieth-Century Danish Writers*, edited by Marianne Stecher-Hansen, Gale, 1999, pp. 41–59.

Ewbank, Inga-stina, "Isak Dinesen," in *European Writers*, Vol. 10, Charles Scribner's Sons, 1990, pp. 1281–1305.

Kauffmann, Stanley, "Changes of Voice and Place," Review of films *Babette's Feast* and *Distant Harmony*, in *New Republic*, Vol. 198, No. 12, March 21, 1988, pp. 26–27.

"Norway," in *Worldmark Encyclopedia of the Nations*, Gale, 2001.

Norway.org Web site; URL: http://www.norway.org/culture.

The Random House Dictionary, 1967, s.v. "art."

Rashkin, Esther, "A Recipe for Mourning: Isak Dinesen's 'Babette's Feast,'" in *Style*, Vol. 29, No. 3, Fall 1995, pp. 356–74.

Simon, John, "Food for Thought," Review of film *Babette's Feast*, in *National Review*, Vol. 40, No. 8, April 29, 1988, pp. 50–51.

Further Reading

Danielsen, Rolf, Stale Dyrvik, Tore Gronlie, Knut Helie, and Edgar Hovland, *Norway: A History from the Vikings to Our Own Times*, Scandinavian University Press, 1995.

> Beginning with the mysterious Vikings, Danielsen et al. take the reader through Norway's intriguing history of thought and culture. These five historians account for Norway's economic, social, and political changes over the years. This volume originally appeared in Norwegian.

Hope, Nicholas, *German and Scandinavian Protestantism: 1700–1918*, Oxford University Press, 1995.

> Hope offers a history of the Lutheran church in Germany and Scandinavia, explaining its roots in the Reformation, its place in society, and its handling of the crisis of World War I.

Pelensky, Olga Anastasia, ed., *Isak Dinesen: Critical Views*, Ohio University Press, 1993.

> With twenty-six articles, this collection of literary criticism provides an overview of the works of Dinesen.

Thurman, Judith, *Isak Dinesen: The Life of a Storyteller*, St. Martin's Press, 1982.

> Regarded by many as one of the best biographies of Dinesen, this book takes the reader from Dinesen's birth and childhood, through her tumultuous years in Africa, to her death in Denmark.

Big Black Good Man

Richard Wright

1958

"Big Black Good Man" was published in French in 1958, three years before Richard Wright's death. It appears in the story collection *Eight Men*, one of the author's last works. Its themes of suspense, fear, and alienation mark it as typical of Wright's fiction. The story, although not one of the author's better-known works, is included in *The Art of the Tale: An International Anthology of Short Stories*, edited by Daniel Halpern and published in 1987.

Author Biography

Richard Wright was born September 4, 1908, on a plantation near Natchez, Mississippi. His father, Nathaniel, was a sharecropper who left the family when Richard was a young boy. His mother, Ella Wilson, was an educated woman who worked as a schoolteacher and a cook. Throughout his childhood, Richard moved often, living at various times with his mother, his maternal grandmother, and other relatives in Mississippi, Tennessee, and Arkansas. He attended school sporadically but was an avid reader.

Wright's first short story was published in 1924 in an African American newspaper, the *Southern Register*. For a few years, Wright worked at odd jobs and continued to write. In 1927, Wright moved to Chicago. There he wrote articles for Communist

1 8

Party newspapers as well as short stories, and when Wright moved to New York in 1937, he became editor of the Communist *Daily Worker*.

Four of Wright's short stories were published in 1938 as a collection entitled *Uncle Tom's Children*. The following year Wright married Dhimah Rose Meadman. With financial support from a Guggenheim Fellowship, Wright wrote his first novel, *Native Son*, which was published in 1940. Wright's first marriage was brief, and in 1941 he married Ellen Poplar, with whom he had two daughters. His autobiography, *Black Boy*, was published in 1945 and became, along with *Native Son*, his best-known work.

Wright moved his family to Paris, France, in 1946. He became a French citizen and befriended existentialist authors Jean-Paul Sartre and Albert Camus, whose work influenced his own, especially the novel *The Outsiders* (1953). In the ensuing years, Wright traveled widely and continued to write fiction, nonfiction, and poetry. As the years went by, he suffered increasingly from ill health and financial problems. The story collection *Eight Men*, in which "Big Black Good Man" first appeared, was among Wright's last works and was published in 1961, after his death.

Wright died in Paris on November 28, 1960. The official cause of death was a heart attack, though rumors that Wright was murdered have persisted through the years.

Richard Wright

that, although he is not a bigot, "this particular black man . . . Well, he didn't seem human. [. . .] There was something about the man's intense blackness and ungamely bigness that frightened and insulted Olaf."

Jenson wants to refuse the man lodging but is afraid to do so. As soon as he agrees to give the man a room, the sailor hands Jenson a roll of fifty- and one-hundred-dollar bills to keep in the safe. Wracking his brain for a way to get the man out of the hotel, Jenson plans to tell him that the hotel does not let rooms for one night only. The man, however, says that he is staying five or six nights.

The man refuses to let the elderly porter carry his suitcase, but Jenson shows him to his room. The man asks Jenson to get him whiskey and a woman, which are common requests in this hotel. Still revolted by the man, Jenson returns to the office and reluctantly calls Lena, a prostitute who regularly visits men at the hotel. He warns Lena about the man's size, but she is unconcerned and soon arrives. Jenson worries about her while she is with the man, but she later leaves, first giving Jenson his percentage of her fee.

The next night, the man comes in late and asks for Lena by name. This pattern continues for six

Plot Summary

"Big Black Good Man" opens on an August night in Copenhagen, Denmark. The year is not specified, but the setting seems to be contemporary with the time of the story's writing, the late 1950s. Olaf Jenson sits in the office in a cheap hotel that caters to sailors and students. Jenson, the night porter, will be sixty years old the next day. He finishes a beer, smokes a cigar, and reflects on his comfortable, unremarkable life.

It is late, and Jenson is about to take a nap when a very large black man opens the office door and asks for a room. Jenson is so taken aback by the man's size that he does not answer until the man repeats his request. Jenson asks if the man is an American (yes) and a sailor (yes). The porter thinks nights. Then the man comes to the office to pay his bill and get his money from the safe. The man gives Jenson a tip. Then, instead of leaving, he simply stares at Jenson, who becomes increasingly terrified. Finally, the man commands Jenson to stand up. He then approaches and places his hands around Jenson's neck, grinning. Convinced that he is about to be strangled, Jenson urinates on himself. The man moves his fingers on Jenson's neck gently and then withdraws them. Jenson pleads with the man not to hurt him, and the man replies, "I wouldn't hurt you, boy. So long."

When the man is gone, Jenson weeps out of humiliation, fear, and anger. He wishes that he had killed the man with the gun he keeps in the desk drawer. He calls the hotel owner to say that he is ill, and she comes to take over so that Jenson can go home and change out of his soiled clothes. He lies to his wife also, again saying that he is sick.

For the next year, Jenson fears the man's return and harbors detailed fantasies of revenge. He imagines that the man's ship sinks in a storm and that the man drowns "gasping and choking like a trapped rat." His rotting corpse is eaten by a white shark.

Then, on an August night one year after his first appearance, the man returns. Jenson tells him that there are no rooms available. The man says that he does not want a room. When Jenson asks what he wants, the man grins, opens his suitcase, and takes something out of it. Then he approaches Jenson and again puts his hands around Jenson's neck. Jenson tries to reach the drawer where the gun is, but the man pushes him away from the desk. The man then proclaims, "A perfect fit!" and takes from his suitcase six new white shirts—gifts for Jenson, one for each night that Jenson sent Lena to him.

Jenson becomes hysterical, laughing and crying. The man asks him what is wrong and then tells him to try on a shirt, which Jenson does. Jenson asks the man if it is Lena he wants, adding that she has not returned to the hotel since the man left a year ago. The man answers that he and Lena have been writing and that he is going to her house.

Jenson admits that he thought the man was going to kill him. Incredulous, the man laughs and tells Jenson that he would not hurt him because he, Jenson, is a good man. Jenson tells the man that he is a good man, too, adding, "a big black good man." The man replies, "Daddy-O, you're crazy." As he leaves, Jenson thanks him. The man turns back, grins, and says, "Daddy-O, drop dead."

Characters

Karen Jenson

Karen is Olaf's wife. She appears in the story only in Olaf's thoughts, as conveyed by the narrator. Olaf never talks to her about what happens at the seedy hotel, implying that she is a proper woman.

Olaf Jenson

Olaf is the night porter in the hotel where Jim arrives asking for a room. The story begins on the night before his sixtieth birthday. He is an ordinary man, who is married, owns a home, and likes to garden. As he sits at his desk in the hotel office, he reflects that it would have been nice if he and his wife had had children and if he had saved more money. But, all in all, he is content.

From the moment when Jim first arrives at the hotel, Olaf is overwhelmed by revulsion and terror. It seems to be neither Jim's race nor his size alone that so profoundly affects Olaf but the combination of the two. His reaction to Jim shows his inability to rightly judge people, as he continues to be convinced that Jim is a cruel, threatening man capable of unprovoked violence even though Jim's behavior contradicts this.

Jim

Jim is a black American sailor (on a passenger ship) who arrives at a cheap hotel on the Copenhagen waterfront on the night when the story begins. His clothes and a large roll of cash mark him as well off, but the most remarkable thing about him is his size. He is about six and one-half feet tall and huge in every aspect. The story refers to his "gorillalike arms" and "mammoth hands." As well, Jim's skin is not brown but so black that it has a bluish cast.

Upon his arrival, Jim entrusts Olaf, the night porter, with twenty-six hundred dollars in cash. He also refuses to let the older, much smaller porter carry his suitcase to his room. When he returns a year later, Jim brings Olaf six custom-tailored white shirts—one for each night that Olaf sent the prostitute Lena to him the year before. In contrast to his generous actions, Jim's verbal communication is somewhat ambiguous, giving little clue to his feelings and intentions.

Lena

Lena is a prostitute who regularly visits the sailors who stay at the hotel. It is Lena whom Olaf calls when Jim asks for a woman on the night of his arrival. Lena is a big, strong, blonde, and Olaf thinks that if any woman can handle Jim, it is Lena. He also appreciates that she gives him a larger share of her earnings than the other women do.

Lena has four young children to support and is quite willing to visit Jim. In fact, she visits him on all six nights of his stay, and when Jim returns a year later, he stays at her home. The narrator reveals that Lena never went to the hotel again after the end of Jim's stay there, implying that Jim began supporting her.

Themes

Ambiguity

"Big Black Good Man" is shot through with ambiguity. Wright gives clues to the attitudes and intentions of Olaf and Jim, but some of these clues are contradictory so that, all in all, they lead to question marks in readers' minds. The narrator reports that Olaf is not racially prejudiced and provides some evidence to support this statement: Olaf regularly provides rooms at the hotel for men of all races. Yet Olaf's negative reaction to Jim is extreme and unrelenting, and the terms that the narrator, speaking from Olaf's point of view, uses to describe Jim are clearly racist. Throughout the story Jim is referred to as a "black beast" with animal qualities—"gorillalike arms" and "mammoth hands." Further, Olaf feels that if Jim's skin were brown rather than black, Jim would not convey the same horror.

Jim is equally ambiguous. Most of his actions toward Olaf speak of a trusting and courteous man. He gives Olaf a large sum of money for safekeeping and does not ask for a receipt. He refuses to let the elderly porter carry his suitcase. Yet, as he checks out of the hotel, he places his hands around Olaf's neck without asking permission or explaining his purpose. Most people would feel threatened by such an action, especially given Jim's size, regardless of his race.

The result of this layered ambiguity is that readers' own attitudes and experiences come into play as they attempt to interpret the two characters. At the end of the story, when both characters are finally revealed more clearly, readers also see clearly how their own interpretations colored the men— accurately or not. The term "interactive" probably

had not been coined at the time this story was written, but the author's carefully crafted ambiguity makes it an authentically interactive story.

Racially Based Fear and Alienation

This story shares with much of Wright's fiction the theme of fear and alienation growing out of racial differences. The alienation is one-sided; Jim seems completely comfortable with Olaf. Olaf, on the other hand, has a horror of Jim that seems to stem mostly from his blackness. The old porter may well have been intimidated by any man as large as Jim, but it is hard to imagine that his revulsion and fear could have been as lasting and as extreme if Jim had not been black. Again, this impression is supported by the words the narrator uses to describe Jim as Olaf sees him. These words convey that Olaf sees Jim as something less than human and as someone who therefore cannot be counted on to have human thought processes and responses. To Olaf, Jim is a beast who may kill him in a fit of unprovoked rage.

Olaf's baseless, relentless fear of Jim is echoed in late twentieth century and early twenty-first century studies that find that many white people are afraid of, or at least suspicious of, black men in situations where they are not afraid of white men. It is a long-known fact of human nature that human beings generally react negatively to people who are different from themselves. Further, race has been shown to be a difference that many people find particularly threatening. These facts are the central realities of Wright's story.

Style

Point of View

"Big Black Good Man" has a third-person narrator who tells the story from Olaf Jenson's point of view. The narrator is privy to Olaf's thoughts but not to Jim's. Through this device, Jim's thoughts and intentions remain as much a mystery to readers as they are to Olaf. This means that readers see Jim through Olaf's eyes and at the same time through the lens of their own experiences and attitudes. The result is a heightening of tension and suspense. On one level, the reader gets caught up in Olaf's blind fear of Jim. At the same time, the reader stands outside the story and so has a different, more detached perspective. Depending upon his or her own race, age, and attitudes, the reader may have responses that closely match Olaf's or that conflict

Topics for Further Study

- Jim, who is a sailor on a passenger ship, is well dressed and carries a large amount of cash. Do some research to find out what passenger ships were like in the days before air travel. Is Jim's affluence realistic? What might have been his job on the ship?

- Jim's final words at the end of the story—"Daddy-O, drop dead"—are ambiguous, especially since he "flashed a grin" as he said them. What do you think Jim was thinking and feeling at that moment?

- Discuss the three women who appear or are mentioned in the story. What character types do they represent? What do they have in common with one another, and how are they different?

- What possible reasons might Wright have had for setting the story in Copenhagen? What role does the setting play in the story's mood and effectiveness? Do you think another location would have been more effective?

- Wright implies more about Jim and Lena's relationship than he explains. What can you infer about their relationship, and what clues allow you to make these inferences? What do you think will happen between them in the future?

---

with them. Readers, therefore, struggle to resolve not only the tension between Olaf and Jim but also the tension between Olaf's attitudes and their own. The question of who is right about Jim—Olaf, or the reader, or both, or neither—looms larger and larger as the story progresses, and Jim remains (until the very end) a towering uncertainty.

If the narrator revealed Jim's thoughts throughout the story, the suspense would be greatly reduced. Readers would never be required to confront their own responses to Jim or to wrestle with the question of whether or not Olaf's responses were warranted.

Figurative Language

The story is rich in figurative language, particularly in similes and metaphors that emphasize Olaf's view of Jim as something inhuman. When Jim first appears, the narrator describes him as Olaf sees him: "His chest bulged like a barrel; his rocklike and humped shoulders hinted of mountain ridges; the stomach ballooned like a threatening stone; and the legs were like telephone poles." In these phrases, Jim is a force of nature or an inanimate object. In many other descriptions, he is an animal, with a "buffalolike head," a neck "like a bull's," "gorillalike arms," "mammoth hands," and so on. Jim is repeat-edly described as anything and everything except a human being.

One especially interesting use of figurative language occurs when Lena's first visit to Jim's room is described as an "errand of mercy." The phrase stands out, since the narrator does not generally use euphemistic language to describe the tawdry goings-on at the hotel. Lena is called a whore, not a call girl, and the woman who owns the hotel is a "hard-bitten [b——]." The lone euphemism "errand of mercy" is unexpected and humorous in such gritty company.

Historical Context

Harlem Renaissance

Scholars are divided as to whether Wright should be considered part of the Harlem Renaissance, but all agree that his work was powerfully influenced by the cultural movement that was ending just as Wright's career was beginning. After World War I, the Harlem neighborhood of New York City was home to more African Americans than any other urban area in the United States. It

Compare & Contrast

- **1950s:** A man like Olaf, who is sixty years old, is considered quite elderly, since the life expectancy for men who were born at or before the beginning of the twentieth century is less than fifty years.

  Today: In developed nations, the average life expectancy for men is about seventy-five, and a man of sixty has not yet reached retirement age.

- **1950s:** Europe is still recovering from the economic effects of World War II, while the United States is experiencing unprecedented prosperity. Americans are rich compared to Europeans, as evidenced by Jim's clothing, his roll of cash, and his generous gift to Olaf.

  Today: Americans continue to be among the wealthiest people on earth and to have a higher standard of living than Europeans. Although the economic slowdown in the first years of the new millennium has been a global event, the American economy has proved more resilient than those of European nations. Low interest rates and high productivity have minimized the impact of the slowdown on Americans' standard of living.

- **1950s:** Jazz musicians are the source of popular slang terms such as ''Daddy-O,'' which is what Jim calls Olaf.

  Today: Hip-hop musicians are the source of popular slang terms. An African American man might use the slang term ''Money'' to refer to a man whose name he does not know.

---

soon became a cultural epicenter where musicians, artists, and writers thrived. The impact of what became known as the Harlem Renaissance was magnified by the fact that white audiences embraced its artists and their works. For the first time, large numbers of white Americans supported African American artists by listening to their music in nightclubs and by reading their literary works. It was a time when a broad spectrum of Americans learned about and came to appreciate African American culture.

Wright moved to Harlem from Chicago in 1937 and was part of the area's literary community by virtue of his position as the editor of the Communist newspaper, the *Daily Worker*. He met and was influenced by some of the leading writers of the Harlem Renaissance, such as Langston Hughes, Countee Cullen, Claude McKay, Nella Larsen, and Zora Neale Hurston.

American Artists in Europe

Another phenomenon that began after World War I and continued through much of the twentieth century was the popularity of Europe—particularly France—among American artists and writers. Artists of all races were attracted to France by its rich cultural history and by its high regard for artists and the arts. In addition, African Americans found that they faced much less racial prejudice in France and other parts of Europe than they did at home. Many jazz musicians and singers, artists, and writers, Wright among them, became expatriates, remaining in France for the rest of their lives. Some returned to the United States, temporarily or permanently, when Europe was ravaged by World War II. Harlem Renaissance painter William H. Johnson, for example, spent about fifteen years living in France and traveling throughout Europe before returning to New York in 1939.

Critical Overview

Eight Men, the collection in which "Big Black Good Man" first appeared, was published after Wright's death and contains some of his last writing. The volume is not considered to be among Wright's most important work, and within the volume, "Big

Black Good Man" is not considered to be among the strongest stories.

Most critics were disappointed with *Eight Men* when it first appeared, judging the stories inferior to Wright's earlier fiction. One exception was Irving Howe, according to an article by Yoshinobu Hakutani in *Dictionary of Literary Biography*, Vol. 102, *American Short-Story Writers, 1910–1945*. Hakutani quotes Howe as writing that "Big Black Good Man" shows "a strong feeling for the compactness of the story as a form. . . . When the language is scraggly or leaden there is a sharply articulated pattern or event."

Considering the story collection in *Dictionary of Literary Biography*, Vol. 76, *Afro-American Writers, 1940–1955*, Edward D. Clark writes, "The works in *Eight Men* display the variety and development in Wright's literary and thematic skills. Clark calls "Big Black Good Man" "one of Wright's few humorous stories" and notes that it "develops the theme of black pride through the adventures of a black sailor."

Clark concludes his overview of Wright's work by declaring that Wright is "undeniably one of the most important American writers of the twentieth century," noting that Wright's writing has been translated and read around the world. According to Clark, "no black writer between Frederick Douglass and James Baldwin has offered so moving a testimony and delivered so scathing an indictment of America's racial dilemmas to so large an audience as has Richard Wright."

Criticism

Candyce Norvell

Norvell is an independent educational writer who specializes in English and literature. In this essay, Norvell discusses three types of conflict in Richard Wright's story "Big Black Good Man."

Much of Richard Wright's fiction can correctly be said to be about race. His early stories and novels deal with the experiences of African Americans both in the North and in the South, within their own communities as well as in their relationships with white individuals and white institutions. It is easy, then, to categorize "Big Black Good Man" as a story about race, particularly since it is the story of a relationship between a black man and a white man.

It is not wrong to say that "Big Black Good Man" is about race, but it is not the whole story either. In a mere ten pages, Wright has managed to tell a story about race, a story about maleness, and a story about the nature of goodness.

Clearly, race is a central concern of the story. It is perhaps not coincidental that "Big Black Good Man" is set in the far northern reaches of Europe, in a land of blue-eyed blonds that in every way is about as far from Africa as it is possible to get. The narrator of "Big Black Good Man" comments repeatedly that Jim is the blackest of black men. That he is blue-black, and not brown, is one thing about Jim that disturbs Olaf. The narrator never mentions, however, that Olaf is surely the whitest of the white, just as Jim is the blackest of the black. The two men are not just members of different races, they are the extremes of different races.

Although Olaf repeatedly protests that he is not a racist, it is clear that he is. One place where this becomes evident is in Olaf's gory fantasy of Jim's being drowned and eaten by a shark. The only guilt Olaf feels about the fantasy comes when he thinks about the fact that "many innocent people, women and children, all white and blonde" would die along with Jim when his ship went down. Not only does Olaf value the lives of white people above those of black people, he views Jim as something less than human because of his extreme blackness. The narrator, describing Jim through Olaf's eyes, never refers to Jim by name. Readers only know Jim's name because he tells Olaf to write "Jim" on the roll of cash that he asks Olaf to keep for him. Although Olaf knows Jim's name from that point on, he never uses it. Instead, he consistently likens Jim to an animal or an inanimate object. Jim is a "black beast." Various parts of Jim's body are described as being like rocks, mountain ridges, telephone poles; like parts of bulls, gorillas, mammoths, and more.

Olaf's horror of Jim—his complete misreading of Jim—stems largely from his racist assumption that since Jim is absolutely black, he cannot possibly be human. He must be a brute beast who does not know or care that it would be wrong to murder a defenseless old man. Olaf believes that Jim does not need a reason to kill; violence for the sheer thrill of it must be his nature.

The white man, therefore, is superstitious about race, equating black skin with all that is primitive and dangerous. The black man, on the other hand, is portrayed as being color blind. Olaf's whiteness seems to have no significance to Jim. What the black man notices about Olaf is his age (he refuses to let the old porter carry his suitcase), not his race. One clear message of the story is that the white man is a racist but the black man is not.

But race is only one point of conflict between the two men. Their maleness, and the competitiveness that is a part of maleness, is another. Olaf sees Jim as an adversary and a threat not only because he is black but also because he is bigger, stronger, and more successful. As the story opens, Olaf, on the eve of his sixtieth birthday, is reviewing and evaluating his life. Readers learn that he was a sailor, that he has a wife but no children, and that he owns a home but has little money to see him through the last years of his life. The reason for Olaf's childlessness is not explained. He may or may not be impotent in the sexual sense, but he is portrayed, generally, as a man who, while not a failure, has not amounted to much.

As soon as readers have been given this information about Olaf, Jim appears. While Olaf is a physically small man who is well past his physical prime, Jim is much younger, much larger, and also obviously quite strong. As Olaf once was, Jim is a sailor. Unlike Olaf, though, Jim has done well financially. Olaf is confronted with Jim's affluence, first in the form of his expensive clothing and shoes and next in the form of a large roll of cash. The roll contains twenty-six hundred dollars in fifty- and one-hundred-dollar bills. This amount was worth much more in the 1950s, when the story was written, than it would be in the early 2000s, of course. It is quite possible that Olaf had never before seen that much money at one time. It is even possible that Jim's roll of ready cash represented more money than Olaf had saved after a lifetime of work.

Wright therefore reveals much about the two main characters and leaves it up to readers to reflect on how the facts influence the men's attitudes toward each other. Jim does not know all that readers know about Olaf, but much is easily inferred. The old man is working as a night porter in a cheap hotel instead of being comfortably retired. Jim shows Olaf a modicum of courtesy and trust, but not respect. In deference to Olaf's age and size, Jim carries his own suitcase when Olaf leads him to his room. He trusts Olaf to label and keep a large amount of money. But Jim calls Olaf "boy" and, later, "Daddy-O." The narrator more than once describes Olaf's chafing at Jim's confident manner. Jim has every expectation that Olaf will do as Jim tells him to. To put it another way, Jim is secure in

Copenhagen, Denmark, provides the opening scene where Olaf Jenson first encounters the black American soldier in Wright's "Big Black Good Man"

the knowledge that he is the more successful and powerful man, and this security shows in his classist actions toward Olaf. Conversely, Olaf is aware of his own relative smallness and powerlessness—an awareness that greatly inflames Olaf's hatred of Jim. On this level, the conflict in the story is a conflict between two males and one that would exist regardless of the men's races. Even if Jim were white, his far greater strength and success would have been an affront to Olaf. It is understandable for a man to compare himself to other men, especially in terms of physical prowess and financial success. And it makes sense that the man who grasps his own inferiority would despise the man who is his better.

As was true of the racial conflict, this conflict between males is one-sided. Because of Olaf's age and low social position, Jim does not have any interest in Olaf beyond acknowledging that he deserves, as a human being and as an elderly person, to be treated with decency. Olaf, on the other hand, is obsessed with Jim and feels slighted by his every word and gesture.

The third level of conflict in "Big Black Good Man" is the most basic and universal: the conflict

> **But the story asks readers to consider whether traditional gauges of morality, such as sexual behavior, are really accurate measures of a man's goodness."**

between good and evil. On this level, too, Wright provides readers with certain facts about each man. Olaf lives a quiet, settled life with his wife. Out of respect for her, he never tells her about the unsavory events that routinely occur at the hotel. Even in his old age, he works to support himself and his wife. He limits his drinking, deciding on the first night of the story to take a nap rather than have another beer. He worries about Lena's safety on the night of her first visit to Jim. All of these are hallmarks of a "good" man.

Jim, by contrast, does not seem to be married or to live a settled life. He spends every night with a prostitute, and every night he drinks an entire bottle of whiskey. Many people, even those who are completely free of racial prejudice, would be inclined to judge Olaf as a "good" man and Jim as a "bad" one. But the story asks readers to consider whether traditional gauges of morality, such as sexual behavior, are really accurate measures of a man's goodness. It demonstrates that a man may live a conventionally moral life and still walk around seething with hate toward another man who has done him no harm.

At the end of the story, Jim tells Olaf that Olaf is a good man because he has helped Jim by sending him Lena. Jim says this, even though at the time he has at least some understanding of the dark thoughts Olaf has harbored about him. This makes Jim seem generous in his definition of a "good" man. He is willing to overlook the bad in Olaf and appreciate the good, even though the good that Olaf did for Jim was done under duress.

Similarly, Olaf finally calls Jim a good man. He finally sees Jim more accurately—finally recognizes that he is a human being—and tells him that he is a "big black good man." It is telling that Olaf still puts "big" and "black" in front of "good" and "man"

in his description of Jim. The things that Olaf finds threatening about Jim still loom larger in his mind than Jim's goodness and his humanity.

The story ends with all conflicts between the characters resolved in a mutual declaration of goodness. Whether each man is correct in his evaluation of the other is an issue that Wright leaves up to readers.

Source: Candyce Norvell, Critical Essay on "Big Black Good Man," in *Short Stories for Students*, Gale, 2005.

Yoshinobu Hakutani

In the following essay, Hakutani discusses Wright's short-story collection Eight Men *(which contains "Big Black Good Man") as well as the collection* Uncle Tom's Children *and events from Wright's biography.*

Richard Wright was a preeminent African-American writer whose influence on the course of American literature has been widely recognized. As Irving Howe has said, "The day *Native Son* appeared, American culture was changed forever." The importance of Wright's works, beginning with *Uncle Tom's Children* (1938; enlarged, 1940), comes not so much from his technique and style but from the particular impact his ideas and attitudes have made on American life. His early critics' consideration was that of race. They were unanimous in the view that if Wright had not been black his work would not have been so significant. As his vision of the world extended beyond the United States, his quest for solutions expanded from problems of race to those of politics and economics in the emerging Third World. Finally, his long exile in France gave his national and international concerns a universal dimension. Wright's development was marked by an ability to respond to the currents of the social and intellectual history of his time.

Wright was born on 4 September 1908 near Natchez, Mississippi, to an illiterate sharecropper, Nathaniel Wright, and a well-educated black woman, Ella Wilson Wright. When Wright was six, his family moved to Memphis in search of employment, but his father left the family for another woman. After several more moves to various places, in 1918 his mother fell ill, and the family moved to Jackson, Mississippi, to live with Ella's mother, a fanatic Seventh Day Adventist. The harsh religious code Wright's grandmother imposed on him is well portrayed in the first volume of his autobiography, *Black Boy: A Record of Childhood and Youth* (1945).

What Do I Read Next?

- Wright's first and best-known novel, *Native Son* (1940), is the story of Bigger Thomas, an African American teenager who accidentally kills someone and is sentenced to death.

- *White Man, Listen!* (1957) is a collection of Wright's better-known essays.

- James Baldwin's novel *Go Tell It on the Mountain* (1953) is the story of an African American family in Harlem during the depression. Baldwin, like Wright, was an expatriate living in France, and in fact the two knew each other and had a stormy friendship.

- *Invisible Man* (1952), by Ralph Ellison, became an immediate classic for its portrait of racial intolerance in the United States in the 1950s—an ugly picture painted by the narrator, a young, unnamed black man.

At twelve Wright was enrolled in a Seventh Day Adventist school near Jackson, and later he attended public schools in the city for a few years. In Spring 1924 the *Southern Register*, a local black newspaper, printed a short story, "The Voodoo of Hell's Half-Acre," his first attempt at writing. No complete version is known to exist.

From 1925 to 1927 Wright worked at a few menial jobs in Jackson and Memphis. In Memphis he began reading literature, especially the works of H. L. Mencken, Theodore Dreiser, and Sinclair Lewis. In *Black Boy* Wright tells how he was inspired by Dreiser's *Sister Carrie* (1900) and *Jennie Gerhardt* (1911): "It would have been impossible for me to have told anyone what I derived from these novels, for it was nothing less than a sense of life itself. All my life had shaped me for the realism, the naturalism of the modern novels, and I could not read enough of them."

In 1927 Wright traveled to Chicago and obtained a position as a post-office clerk. As the Depression hit, he lost the position, but the relief office gave him several temporary jobs, including work with the Federal Negro Theatre and later the Illinois Writers' Project. In April 1931 his first major short story, "Superstition," was published by *Abbott's Monthly*. The following year he attended meetings sponsored by the John Reed Club in Chicago, a leftist literary group, and became a member of the Communist party. Before moving to New York in 1937, he had written poems, short stories, and essays, many of which appeared in leftist periodicals.

In New York, Wright became the Harlem editor of the *Daily Worker*, a Communist newspaper, and helped edit *New Challenge*, a short-lived literary magazine. In 1938 four of his stories were collected and published as *Uncle Tom's Children* and won a literary prize from *Story* magazine. The following year he was awarded a Guggenheim Fellowship to complete his first novel, *Native Son* (1940). In August 1939 he married his first wife, Dhimah Rose Meadman, a white dancer. The couple soon separated, however. The year 1940 brought him fame and financial success: the Book-of-the-Month Club chose *Native Son* as its March selection, and an enlarged edition of *Uncle Tom's Children* was published.

On 12 March 1941, after divorcing Rose, Wright married his second wife, Ellen Poplar, a white member of the Communist party, from Brooklyn. In the same year, he published *Twelve Million Black Voices*, the first of a series of nonfiction books on racial issues. His first child, Julia, was born in 1942. By the end of 1944 he had broken with the Communist party, as indicated in his *Atlantic Monthly* (August-September 1944) article "I Tried to Be a Communist" (incorporated into *American Hunger*, the second volume of his autobiography, published in 1977). His novella "The Man Who Lived Underground" was included in *Cross-Section* (1944), an

> There is a distinct change of tone in Eight Men in comparison with Uncle Tom's Children. The earlier racial hatred is replaced by racial understanding in a story such as 'Big Black Good Man.'"

anthology edited by Edwin Seaver (and later collected in Wright's *Eight Men*, 1960). *Black Boy*, published in 1945, captured wide publicity and was a Book-of-the-Month Club selection.

From after World War II until his death in 1960, although he traveled often, Wright became a permanent voluntary exile in Paris. He and his family became French citizens in 1947 and eventually bought a farm in Ailly, which they maintained along with a Paris apartment. Before the publication of his second novel, *The Outsider* (1953), no new books of his had come out since 1945, but he cherished his Parisian life, associating with French and African writers and intellectuals. His second daughter, Rachel, was born in 1949. In 1954 he published a minor novel, *Savage Holiday*. He also continued to travel in Africa, Europe, and Asia, which led him to write several nonfiction books: *Black Power: A Record of Reactions in a Land of Pathos* (1954); *Pagan Spain* (1956); *The Color Curtain: A Report on the Bandung Conference* (1956; first published in French, 1955); and *White Man, Listen!* (1957). Wright's last years were plagued by illness (amoebic dysentery) and financial hardship. He tried his hand at writing English haiku, four thousand of them, most of which were not published. He also tried to write a novel," Island of Hallucination," which was never fully published (part of it—"Five Episodes"—was anthologized by Herbert Hill in *Soon, One Morning*, 1963). Wright did publish another novel, *The Long Dream* (1958), but it was doomed by adverse criticism. Nevertheless, he was successful in preparing another collection of short stories, *Eight Men*, published posthumously. Wright died in Paris at age fifty-two. A few years later *Lawd Today* (1963) was published; he had begun this short novel in 1936.

Wright was a remarkably resilient thinker and writer. His successes are beyond dispute, his failures understandable. He has fascinated not only literary critics, but also philosophers, psychologists, sociologists, and historians. Though many of his works failed to satisfy the rigid standards of New Criticism, his evolution as a writer has excited readers the world over. Biographer Michel Fabre speculates that toward the end of his life Wright "was once again going through a period of ideological change which, had its course been completed, might have caused him to start writing in a new vein. It is highly probable that the civil rights and Black Power movements would have given him a second wind, had he lived another five years."

The enlarged (1940) version of *Uncle Tom's Children*, Wright's first book, consists of five stories about the lives of black people in the deep South. These stories prefigure the theme, structure, and ideology of his later fiction. Wright seems to imply here, as he does in his other fiction, that American social conditions are directly responsible for the degradation of black people. Recent criticism, however, has modified this interpretation, suggesting that Wright went beyond naturalism. The pessimistic determinism often associated with naturalism taught the young Wright the meaning of racial oppression. A victim of oppression himself, Wright directed his energy toward rebellion. While he escaped the pessimistic outlook of naturalism, his respect for that philosophy helped him develop his own individualism and endow his characters with self-awareness. Only vaguely are the black characters in *Uncle Tom's Children* conscious of their racially oppressive environment, but they willfully seek freedom and self-determination.

"Big Boy Leaves Home" (anthologized in *The New Caravan*, 1936), the first story in Wright's collection, features a young boy's escape from his violent southern community. Four innocent, happy-go-lucky black boys are discovered naked by a white woman while they are swimming in a pond on a white man's premises. When she screams, her male companion without warning begins shooting and kills two of the boys. Big Boy manages to overcome the white man and accidentally kills him. Now the two surviving boys must take flight; Bobo is captured, but Big Boy reaches home and is told by church leaders to hide in a kiln until dawn, when a truck will come by to take him to Chicago. While hiding, he poignantly watches Bobo lynched and burned. Witnessing such an event gives Big Boy not only a feeling of terror and hatred but a sense of self-awareness and maturity. Although the events take place in less than twenty-four hours, the story is divided into five parts that correspond to the crucial stages in Big Boy's development from innocence, through violence, suffering, and terror, to freedom.

"Down by the Riverside" (previously unpublished), the next story in *Uncle Tom's Children*, dramatizes the tragic death of Brother Mann, who steals a boat during a Mississippi flood to take his pregnant wife to a hospital for the child's delivery. On Mann's way to the hospital he is discovered by the owner of the boat who tries to shoot him, but Mann, in self-defense, kills the owner. When Mann reaches the hospital, he finds his wife is dead. Later he is asked by the town authorities to join their rescue work for stranded citizens. The first house to which he is sent, with a black companion, both of them on another boat, happens to be that of the owner of the stolen boat, whose family recognizes Mann. Although he considers killing them, he changes his mind and rescues them. Once the boat safely reaches the hills, they tell the white authorities that Mann is a murderer. As Mann flees down the riverside, he is shot to death. The story is filled with coincidental events that foreshadow Mann's doom. In contrast with "Big Boy Leaves Home," this story suggests the futility of a man struggling against the elements of chance and fate that undermine his perseverance and will to survive.

The plot of "Long Black Song" (also previously unpublished) is less complicated than the other stories. A white phonograph salesman seduces a black farmer's wife, Sarah, while her husband, Silas, is away during the day. When Silas returns home, he discovers her infidelity and fumes over it. The next day the salesman comes back, with another white man waiting in the car. Sarah leaves the house with her child to warn the salesman of Silas's presence. Silas then exchanges gunfire with the men, killing one of them. Later white lynchers arrive and set fire to the house with Silas inside. The story is told from Sarah's point of view. On the one hand, Sarah, unconcerned with the materialistic strivings of men, is trying to recapture the memories of a past love; on the other, Silas is trying to realize his dream of owning a farm. Both dreams, however, come to naught in the face of a caste system that allows for the exploitation of others. The success of the story lies in the noble victory of Silas, who realizes at his death that his wife's disloyalty to him has been permitted by the white bourgeois code to which he had so easily acquiesced. When white men

sexually exploited black women other than his own wife, Silas did not think about it seriously.

The last two stories in *Uncle Tom's Children* deal with the Communist ideology as it affects the black communities of the South. "Fire and Cloud" (*Story*, March 1936) takes place during the Depression and presents a black minister trusted by both blacks and whites. His dilemma is whether to dissuade his congregation from demonstrating for the food they need, or to support the march at the risk of violence. While many of the elders in his church cannot break with their traditional faith in passive resistance, the Reverend Mr. Taylor can change and does opt for solidarity and militancy. Similarly, "Bright and Morning Star" (*New Masses*, 10 May 1938)—the story added to the collection in 1940—deals with the change of attitude a black woman takes toward Christianity. Aunt Sue, the mother of two revolutionary black youths, is accustomed to the attitude of forbearance preached by black church leaders, but now that she is awakened by the "bright and morning star" of Communism, she becomes a martyr instead of a victim of white power. When she is summoned by the white authorities to claim the body of her murdered son, she shoots the official dead before she is killed.

The initial critical reception of *Uncle Tom's Children* in 1938 was generally favorable. James T. Farrell, appreciative of Wright's direct and realistic style, remarked in the *Partisan Review* (May 1938) that the book serves as an exemplary refutation for those who wished to write "such fancy nonsense about fables and allegories." In response to those critics who wanted Wright to pace more steadily in his narrative and delve more deeply into his material, Farrell argued that Wright effectively employs simple dialogue "as a means of carrying on his narrative, as a medium for poetic and lyrical effects, and as an instrument of characterization." Most reviewers, both black and white, praised Wright's first work without reservation; all respected him for breaking away from stereotypes. Malcolm Cowley found the stories "heartening, as evidence of a vigorous new talent, and terrifying as the expression of a racial hatred that has never ceased to grow and gets no chance to die" (*New Republic*, 6 April 1938). Cowley considered legitimate the Communist aim to unite black and white and regarded racial violence in the South as inevitable. Many critics were also impressed by Wright's language and art, especially his use of black dialect. Robert Van Gelder compared him to Ernest Hemingway (*New York Times Book Review*, 13 April 1938); Allen

Maxwell likened his style to John Steinbeck's (*Southwest Review*, April 1938).

Some readers were antagonistic to Wright's racial views. As if in return for Wright's unfavorable review of her novel *Their Eyes Were Watching God* (*New Masses*, 5 October 1937), Zora Neale Hurston categorized *Uncle Tom's Children* as a chronicle of hatred with no act of understanding and sympathy (*Saturday Review*, 2 April 1938). She opposed Wright's politics, too, arguing that his stories fail to touch the fundamental truths of black life.

The earliest extended critical analysis of Wright's short fiction was by Edwin Berry Burgum (in the *Quarterly Review of Literature*, Spring 1944), who confirms Wright's skill in structuring the stories in the form of modern tragedy: the hero's individualism collides with the external forces of society. For example, Wright skillfully illustrates a black man's rebellion against society in the heroism of Silas, the protagonist in "Long Black Song." Burgum also finds Wright's style extremely congenial to his material, claiming that his style in the short stories was influenced by Hemingway: both writers use short sentences to describe surface activities; but whereas Hemingway disguises the confusions beneath the surface, Wright clarifies them.

Later estimates of the book concur with Burgum's. Edward Margolies, in *The Art of Richard Wright* (1969), observes that one of the successes of *Uncle Tom's Children* is Wright's use of Marxism for didactic purposes. Portraying conflicts that are true to the facts of life in the South, his stories usually succeed by their integration of plot, imagery, character, and theme. Wright also renders his stories sometimes in biblical terms. The Reverend Mr. Taylor and Aunt Sue, for example, arrive at their moments of truth through Communistic or Christian ideals, but also as a result of "their peculiar Negro folk mysticism." The sweep and magnitude of Wright's stories are, Margolies observes, "suffused with the author's impassioned convictions about the dignity of man." Dignity, as Blyden Jackson, an eminent black critic, suggests, is a central issue in "Big Boy Leaves Home," as it is in Wright's fiction in general. He explains in *Southern Literary Journal* (Spring 1971) that "Big Boy Leaves Home," instead of showing the quality of a black man's will to survive oppression, presents the lynching of Bobo as "the ultimate indignity that can be inflicted upon an individual."

Eight Men, the other volume of Wright's short fiction, comprises seven short stories and one novella, published in various periods of his career. "The Man Who Saw the Flood" (*New Masses*, 24 August 1937—as "Silt") and "The Man Who Was Almost a Man" (*Harper's Bazaar*, January 1940—as "Almos' a Man"), both written in the 1930s, reflect the hard times black farmers faced in the South. The first story portrays a family of three stranded by a flood and then threatened by a white store owner because of their overdue debt; the second deals with the initiation of a black boy whose family all work for Hawkins, a prosperous southern farmer. Dave, the sixteen-year-old black boy, learns the meaning of white oppression the hard way: when he realizes his dream of owning a gun, a symbol of self-respect and power for him, but accidentally kills Hawkins's mule, he is forced to pay for it by working two full years. Rather than accepting this unjust punishment, he jumps on a train that will carry him North.

The stories Wright wrote in the 1940s, in contrast with those of the 1930s, have an urban setting in common. "The Man Who Went to Chicago" (anthologized as "Early Days in Chicago" in *Cross Section*, 1945) is based on Wright's own experience: he was employed first in a Jewish delicatessen—where he saw a woman cook spit in the food she prepared—and later in a hospital, where he observed a scientifically unreliable experiment being conducted in the name of science. "The Man Who Killed a Shadow" (originally published in French in *Les Lettres Françaises*, 4 October 1946) treats the psychology of fear in a black man. Saul Saunders, encountering in a library a white seductress who falsely "cries rape," kills her for fear of being discovered.

"The Man Who Lived Underground" (a short version of which appeared in *Accent*, Spring 1942) is an allegory of any man, black or white, who feels an innate, inescapable sense of guilt. Fred Daniels, a black man falsely accused of murdering a white woman, hides in a sewer and witnesses various aboveground activities: a church service, a business transaction, and a suicide resulting from the false accusation of a crime. In the course of his underground life, Daniels comes to realize, as "the man who went to Chicago" does, that much of life is chaotic and meaningless. When he finally emerges from underground to relate this revelation to the police, he learns that they have caught a white man who was the woman's murderer and that he is exonerated. But Daniels declares that he himself is guilty for the sake of all humanity. He then takes the police down the sewer to show where he had lived. One of them, tired of hearing his strange testimony, kills him, saying, "You've got to shoot his kind. They'd wreck things."

Wright's short stories from the 1950s focus attention on white men rather than black men in dealing with racial issues. "Man of All Work" (written in 1957 but previously unpublished) describes an unhappily married white man, who is shocked after he makes amatory advances to a maid who turns out to be a black man in disguise. "Man, God Ain't like That" (also previously unpublished) portrays a white American painter, John, who adopts a native African boy, Babu, as his servant. Babu privately conducts a secret ritual of making sacrifices to his Ashanti ancestors but publically sings Christian hymns. Impressed by white civilization, he reasons that white men must have killed Christ to create such a civilization and that he must kill John, his master, whom he regards as a Christ figure. "Big Black Good Man" (published in French in *La Parisienne*, January-February 1958) treats humorously the inferiority complex of a Danish hotel clerk confronted by a huge black sailor who asks for a room, a bottle of whiskey, and a woman companion.

Eight Men received a decidedly less positive response from critics than *Uncle Tom's Children*. Saunders Redding, a distinguished black critic, dismissed *Eight Men* as the work of a declining author (*New York Herald Tribune Book Review*, 22 January 1961). Though all the stories in the collection indicated distress with Wright's rootlessness, Redding theorized that his long exile, somehow lightened "his anguish," which was "the living substance of his best books." For Redding, even the most impressive story, "The Man Who Lived Underground," seemed only "a first-class Gothic tale." In a similar vein, Richard Gilman (in *Commonweal*, April 1961) found the collection of stories inept, "dismayingly stale and dated." Wright's attempts at humor, tragedy, and pathos "all fail." *Eight Men*, however, pleased Irving Howe, Wright's consistent champion, for its signs of the author's continuous experimentation despite uneven results. Howe found in "Big Black Good Man" "a strong feeling for the compactness of the story as a form. . . . When the language is scraggly or leaden there is a sharply articulated pattern or event." In "The Man Who Lived Underground" Howe found not a congenial expression of existentialism, as other critics did, but an effective narrative rhythm, "a gift for shaping the links between sentences so as to create a chain of expectation" (*New Republic*, 13 February 1961).

Later critical estimates of *Eight Men* are more favorable. Even James Baldwin, who was critical of *Native Son*, considered the collection a reflection of Wright's authentic rage: "Wright's unrelentingly bleak landscape was not merely that of the Deep South, or of Chicago, but that of the world, of the human heart" (*Encounter*, April 1961). Recent criticism of *Eight Men* has concentrated on "The Man Who Lived Underground." David Bakish regards this novella as Wright's finest accomplishment because it is an intellectualized story based upon an authentic experience. Michel Fabre (in *The Unfinished Quest of Richard Wright*, 1973) testifies to the authenticity of the story, showing that it derives not from Fyodor Dostoyevski, but from an account in *True Detective* (August 1941) of Herbert C. Wright, a Los Angeles white man who lived underground and robbed businesses in 1931 and 1932. Fabre reads "The Man Who Lived Underground" as an "existential parable" that presents a humanist message: while an individual can impose masks upon himself, he "acquires his identity from other men."

There is a distinct change of tone in *Eight Men* in comparison with *Uncle Tom's Children*. The earlier racial hatred is replaced by racial understanding in a story such as "Big Black Good Man." Moreover, Daniels's adventures in "The Man Who Lived Underground" may suggest Wright's own feelings after ten years in the Communist underground. In any event, Wright thrived on naturalism, for when he moved from his naturalistic style in *Uncle Tom's Children* to a more subtle technique in *Eight Men*, he was not as impressive a writer as he was in *Native Son* and *Black Boy*.

Wright's reputation as a major American author was firmly established by his early works: *Uncle Tom's Children*, *Native Son*, and *Black Boy*. His emergence as a black writer was a phenomenon, as *Black Boy* clearly demonstrates, for not only did he endure oppression and lack of freedom in the South and the North but he triumphed over them. His successful transformation of that experience into enduring art has been recognized by readers of different races. Before Wright, the African-American writer primarily addressed himself to the black audience. Had he written for a white audience, he would have been expected to present stereotyped pictures of black people. Exceptions such as W. E. B. Du Bois and Charles W. Chesnutt went largely unheeded, because blacks, as Wright said, "possessed deep-seated resistance against the Negro problem being presented, even verbally, in all its hideous dullness, in all the totality of its meaning." Therefore, it was somewhat miraculous that both black and white readers believed what they read in Wright's early works, in which he destroys the white myth of the patient, humorous, subservient black man.

Source: Yoshinobu Hakutani, "Richard Wright," in *Dictionary of Literary Biography*, Vol. 102, *American Short-Story Writers, 1910–1945, Second Series*, edited by Bobby Ellen Kimbel, Gale Research, 1991, pp. 378–86.

Edward Margolies

In the following excerpt from his The Art of Richard Wright, *Margolies discusses Wright's development as a writer, focusing on the thematic progression of Wright's fiction.*

Wright at his best was master of a taut psychological suspense narrative. Even more important, however, are the ways Wright wove his themes of human fear, alienation, guilt, and dread into the overall texture of his work. Some critics may still today stubbornly cling to the notion that Wright was nothing more than a proletarian writer, but it was to these themes that a postwar generation of French writers responded, and not to Wright's Communism—and it is to these themes that future critics must turn primarily if they wish to reevaluate Wright's work. . . .

Wright not only wrote well but also he paved the way for a new and vigorous generation of Negro authors to deal with subjects that had hitherto been regarded as taboo. [His] portraits of oppressed Negroes have made a deep impression on readers the world over. . . .

Wright's existentialism, as it was to be called by a later generation of French authors, was not an intellectually "learned" process (although he had been reading Dostoevsky and Kierkegaard in the thirties) but rather the lived experiences of his growing years. The alienation, the dread, the fear, and the view that one must construct oneself out of the chaos of existence—all elements of his fiction— were for him means of survival. There were, of course, externals he grasped for as well. . . .

In general, Wright's nonfiction takes one of two directions. The first concerns itself with the devastating emotional impact of centuries of exploitation on its individual victims. The second is the overall cultural characteristics of oppressed peoples. The first is largely psychological; the second socio-anthropological. Obviously no such absolute division obtains since it is impossible to discuss one without making reference to the other, but for purposes of analysis it may be said that Wright lays greater or lesser stress on one or the other of these issues in each of his works of nonfiction. *Black Boy* (1945), Wright's autobiography of his Southern years, serves perhaps as the best point of reference from which to make an examination of his ideas, since, as we have seen, Wright generalizes from his own experiences certain conclusions about the problems of minorities everywhere. . . .

Possibly the problems presented by *Black Boy* are insoluble since the environment in which *Black Boy* operates is so alien to the average reader that it is almost essential for Wright to hammer home in little digressive essays the mores of the caste system so that *Black Boy*'s psychology and behavior may be better understood. As a result, its authority as autobiography is reduced—Wright frequently appears to stand aside and analyze himself rather than allow the reader to make inferences about his character and emotions from his actions—and its strength as sociology seems somewhat adulterated by the incursions of the narrative. Yet, despite these failures—or possibly because of them—the impact of the book is considerable and this perhaps is Wright's artistic triumph. . . .

Wright's theme is freedom and he skillfully arranges and selects his scenes in such a way that he is constantly made to appear the innocent victim of the tyranny of his family or the outrages of the white community. Nowhere in the book are Wright's actions and thoughts reprehensible. The characteristics he attributes to himself are in marked contrast to those of other characters in the book. He is "realistic," "creative," "passionate," "courageous," and maladjusted because he refuses to conform. Insofar as the reader identifies Wright's cause with the cause of Negro freedom, it is because Wright is a Negro—but a careful reading of the book indicates that Wright expressly divorces himself from other Negroes. Indeed rarely in the book does Wright reveal concern for Negroes as a group. Hence Wright traps the reader in a stereotyped response— the same stereotyped response that Wright is fighting throughout the book: that is, that all Negroes are alike and react alike. . . .

[It] is in [*Uncle Tom's Children*] that the reader may find the theme, the structure, the plot, and the ideational content of all his later fictional work.

Although Wright, when he wrote these stories, was a convinced Communist, it is revealing how related they are to the later phases of intellectual and political development. Here, for example, one finds Wright's incipient Negro nationalism as each of his protagonists rises to strike out violently at white oppressors who would deny him his humanity. More significantly his Negro characters imagine whites as "blurs," "bogs," "mountains," "fire," "ice," and "marble." In none of these stories do his heroes act out of a sense of consciously arrived at ideology (most of them, as a matter of fact, are ignorant of Marxism), but rather out of an innate, repressed longing for freedom—or sometimes merely as an instinctive means of self-survival. Often the act of violence carries along with it a sudden revelatory sense of self-awareness—an immediate knowledge that the world in which the protagonist dwells is chaotic, meaningless, purposeless, and that he, as a Negro, is "outside" this world and must therefore discover his own life by his lonely individual thoughts and acts. We find thus in these first short stories a kind of black nationalism wedded to what has been called Wright's existentialism—the principal characteristics of Wright's last phase of political and philosophical thinking.

Paradoxically, Wright's Marxism seldom intrudes in an explicit didactic sense. . . . To be sure, Communists are viewed in a kindly light in the last two of Wright's stories, but they are only remotely instrumental in effecting his heroes' discovery of themselves and their world. Oddly enough, in three of the stories ("Down by the Riverside," "Fire and Cloud," and "Bright and Morning Star"), Wright's simple Negro peasants arrive at their sense of self-realization by applying basic Christian principles to the situations in which they find themselves. In only one ("Bright and Morning Star"), does a character convert to Communism—and then only when she discovers Communism is the modern translation of the primitive Christian values she has always lived. There is a constant identification in these stories with the fleeing Hebrew children of the Old Testament and the persecuted Christ—and mood, atmosphere, and settings abound in biblical nuances. Wright's characters die like martyrs, stoic and unyielding, in their new-found truth about themselves and their vision of a freer, fuller world for their posterity. . . . The spare, stark accounts of actions and their resolution are reminiscent in their simplicity and their cadences of Biblical narrations. The floods, the songs, the sermons, the hymns reinforce the Biblical analogies and serve, ironically, to highlight the uselessness and inadequacy of Christianity as a means of coping with the depression-ridden, racist South. Even the reverse imagery of white-evil, black-good is suggestive in its simple organization of the forces which divide the world in Old Testament accounts of the Hebrews' struggle for survival. . . .

There is a thematic progression in these stories, each of which deals with the Negro's struggle for survival and freedom. In the first story ["Big Boy Leaves Home"] flight is described—and here Wright is at his artistic best, fashioning his taut, spare prose to the movements and thoughts of the fugitive. . . .

Although "Big Boy" is a relatively long story, the rhythm of events is swift, and the time consumed from beginning to end is less than twenty-four hours. The prose is correspondingly fashioned to meet the pace of the plot. The story is divided into five parts, each of which constitutes a critical episode in Big Boy's progress from idyll, through violence, to misery, terror, and escape. As the tension mounts, Wright employs more and more of a terse and taut declaratory prose, fraught with overtones and meanings unspoken—reminiscent vaguely of the early [Ernest] Hemingway. . . .

"Down by the Riverside," the next story in the collection, is not nearly so successful. If flight (as represented by "Big Boy Leaves Home") is one aspect of the Negro's struggle for survival in the South, Christian humility, forbearance, courage, and stoic endurance are the themes of Wright's second piece. But here the plot becomes too contrived; coincidence is piled upon coincidence, and the inevitability of his protagonist's doom does not ring quite as true. . . .

> "Wright at his best was master of a taut psychological suspense narrative. Even more important, however, are the ways Wright wove his themes of human fear, alienation, guilt, and dread into the overall texture of his work."

Yet, there is a certain epic quality to the piece—man steadily pursuing his course against a malevolent nature, only to be cut down later by the ingratitude of his fellow men—that is suggestive of [Mark] Twain or [William] Faulkner. And Mann's long-suffering perseverance and stubborn will to survive endow him with a rare mythic Biblical quality. Wright even structures his story like a Biblical chronicle, in five brief episodes, each displaying in its way Mann's humble courage against his fate. But if Mann's simple Christian virtues failed to save him, it was in part because the ground had not yet been laid on which these virtues might flourish. The recognition that the bourgeois ethic is incapable of providing men with the possibility of fulfilling themselves is an element of Wright's next story ["Long Black Song"]. . . .

The success of the story, perhaps Wright's best, lies in the successful integration of plot, imagery, and character which echo the tragic theme of Silas's doomed awareness of himself and the inadequacy of the bourgeois values by which he has been attempting to live. Silas's recognition is his death knell, but he achieves a dignity in death that he had never known in life. . . .

It is Sarah, though, who is the most memorable portrayal in the story. The narrative unfolds from her point of view—and she becomes, at the end, a kind of deep mother earth character, registering her primal instincts and reactions to the violence and senselessness she sees all about her. But for all that, she remains beautifully human—her speech patterns and thoughts responding to an inner rhythm, somehow out of touch with the foolish strivings of men, yet caught up in her own melancholy memories and desires. . . . Wright conveys her mood and memories and vagaries of character in sensuous color imagery—while certain cadences suggest perhaps Gertrude Stein whom Wright regarded as one of his chief influences. . . .

Sarah is Wright's most lyrical achievement, and Silas, her husband, Wright's most convincing figure of redemption. . . .

Wright's militant Negroes, despite their protestations to the contrary, often sound more like black nationalists than Communist internationalists. It was perhaps this facet of Wright's work, in addition to the obvious, extreme, and frequent isolated individualism of his heroes that [began] to disturb Communist Party officials. Yet regardless of whether Wright had been at heart a Communist, an outsider, or a nationalist when he wrote these pieces, there can be little doubt that they draw a good deal of their dramatic strength from the black and white world Wright saw. There is little the reader can do but sympathize with Wright's Negroes and loathe and despise the whites. There are no shadings, ambiguities, few psychological complexities. But there are of course the weaknesses of the stories as well.

How then account for their overall success? First of all, they *are* stories. Wright is a story teller and his plots are replete with conflict, incident, and suspense. Secondly, Wright is a stylist. He has an unerring "feel" for dialogue, his narrations are controlled in terse, tense rhythms, and he manages to communicate mood, atmosphere, and character in finely worked passages of lyric intensity. But above all they are stories whose sweep and magnitude are suffused with their authors impassioned convictions about the dignity of man, and a profound pity for the degraded, the poor and oppressed who, in the face of casual brutality, cling obstinately to their humanity. . . .

Unlike the pieces in *Uncle Tom's Children*, [the stories in the posthumously published *Eight Men*] are not arranged along any progressively thematic lines; instead the order in which they are assembled indicates that Wright was more concerned with showing a variety of styles, settings and points of view. To be sure, they all deal in one way or another with Negro oppression, but they do not point, as Wright's previous collection of stories did, to any specific social conclusion. . . .

The only significant work of fiction Wright produced in the decade of the forties was his long story, "The Man Who Lived Underground."

Here Wright is at his storytelling best, dealing with subject matter he handles best—the terrified fugitive in flight from his pursuers. Like Wright's other fugitives, Fred Daniels exercises a kind of instinct for survival that he perhaps never knew he possessed. But what makes him different from the others is that he is not merely a victim of a racist society, but that he has become by the very nature of his experiences a symbol of all men in that society—the pursuers and the pursued. For what the underground man has learned in his sewer is that all men carry about in their hearts an underground man who determines their behavior and attitudes in the above-ground world. The underground man is the essential nature of all men—and is composed of dread, terror, and guilt. Here then lies the essential difference between Wright's Communist and post-Communist period. Heretofore dread, terror, and guilt had been the lot of the Negro in a world that had thrust upon him the role of a despised inferior. Now they are the attributes of all mankind. . . .

Fred Daniels is then Everyman, and his story is very nearly a perfect modern allegory. The Negro who lives in the underground of the city amidst its sewage and slime is not unlike the creature who dwells amidst the sewage of the human heart. And Fred Daniels knows that all of the ways men attempt to persuade themselves that their lives are meaningful and rational are delusions. . . . But paradoxically despite Fred's new found knowledge of the savagery of the human heart and the meaninglessness of the aboveground world, he recognizes its instinctive appeal as well, and he must absurdly rise to the surface once more. . . .

The dread, the terror, the guilt, the nausea had always been basic thematic elements in Wright's fiction—and now in "The Man Who Lived Underground," they are made the explicit components of the human personality. Like Wright's heroes, the characters of existentialist authors move about in a world devoid of principles, God, and purpose—and suffer horror at their awesome godlike powers as they create their own personalities and values out of the chaos of existence. But in some respects Wright's heroes are different. They are alienated often enough not from any intellectually reasoned position (at this stage in Wright's career), but by chance happenings in their lives or an accident of birth—race, for example. (In Fred Daniels' case, for instance, he is a Negro who quite by chance happened to be near the scene of a crime.) They arrive then accidentally at their insights, and as a result of having discovered themselves outside the rules of conventional social behavior recognize that they are free to shape (and are therefore responsible for) their own lives. But this is not primarily why they suffer guilt. Wright seems to prefer a Freudian explanation; guilt is instinctively connected with the trauma of birth. Hence, for Wright, a man's freedom is circumscribed by his very humanity. In ways he cannot possibly control, his nature or "essence" precedes his existence. But however different the routes French existentialist authors and Wright may have taken, they meet on common ground in regard to their thrilled horror at man's rootlessness—at the heroism of his absurd striving.

"The Man Who Lived Underground" undoubtedly owes something in the way of plot and theme to [Victor Hugo's] *Les Miserables,* and to what Camus called the "Dostoevskian experience of the con-

demned man"—but, above all, Fred Daniels' adventures suggest something of Wright's own emotions after ten years in the Communist underground. The air of bitterness, the almost strident militancy are gone—momentarily at least—and in their place a compassion and despair—compassion for man trapped in his underground nature and despair that he will ever be able to set himself free. . . .

The fifties saw Wright experimenting with new subject matter and new forms. Problems of race remain the central issue, but are now dealt with from changing perspectives. For the first time there are two stories with non-American settings, and race neurosis is treated more as the white man's dilemma than as the black man's burden. This shift in emphasis from black to white is accompanied by corresponding shifts in social viewpoint. Racial antagonisms do not appear to be immediately—or for that matter remotely—traceable to compelling class interests. It is clear that Wright was trying to broaden the range and scope of his fiction—that he was trying to move away somewhat from the psyche of the oppressed Negro peasant or proletariat toward characters of varying social and ethnic backgrounds. The three novels Wright produced in this ten year period bear out this conclusion. In the first, *The Outsider* (1953), he wrote of his hero that though a Negro "he could have been of any race." *Savage Holiday,* written the following year, contains no Negro characters and deals with the misfortunes of a white, "respectable" middle-aged retired insurance executive. *The Long Dream* (1957) is written from the point of view of an adolescent, middle-class Negro boy. Wright was apparently reaching for a universality he felt he had not yet achieved—but his craft was not quite equal to the tasks he had set for himself. Too often, as before, his whites appear as stereotypes, and his Negroes are a bit too noble or innocent. In the 1930's Wright's social vision lent his stories an air of conviction, a momentum all their own; in the 1950's Wright's quieter catholicity, his wider intellectuality, perhaps removed his stories from this kind of cumulative dread tension, the sense of urgency, that made his earlier works so immediately gripping.

Nonetheless it cannot be said that Wright's new stories do not possess their own narrative qualities. . . . What these stories sorely lack are the charged, vibrant rhythms and vivid lyric imagery that so rounded out character and theme in his earlier works. Perhaps Wright wanted to pare his prose down to what he regarded as bare essentials—just as he may have fancied his idol, Gertrude Stein, had done. Whatever the reasons, the results are only occasionally successful. . . .

Source: Edward Margolies, Excerpt, in *The Art of Richard Wright*, Southen Illinois University Press, 1969.

Sources

Clark, Edward D., "Richard Wright," in *Dictionary of Literary Biography*, Vol. 76, *Afro-American Writers, 1940–1955*, edited by Trudier Harris, Gale Research, 1988, pp. 199–221.

Hakutani, Yoshinobu, "Richard Wright," in *Dictionary of Literary Biography*, Vol. 102, *American Short-Story Writers, 1910–1945*, edited by Bobby Ellen Kimbel, Gale Research, 1991, pp. 378–86.

Wright, Richard, "Big Black Good Man," in *The Art of the Tale: An International Anthology of Short Stories*, edited by Daniel Halpern, Penguin Books, 1987, pp. 786–95.

Further Reading

Coles, Robert, *Black Writers Abroad: A Study of Black American Writers in Europe and Africa*, Garland Publishing, 1999.

Coles catalogues the African American writers who left the United States over the course of two centuries, examining their reasons for moving abroad and the impact of the decision on their work.

Crossman, R. H. S., ed., *The God That Failed*, Columbia University Press, 2001.

Wright is one of six contributors to this collection of essays by respected writers, all of whom had first embraced and later renounced communism. The authors relate their personal experiences with communism and their reasons for rejecting it. André Gide of France and Arthur Koestler of Germany are among the other contributors to what is widely considered an important record of cold war issues.

Lewis, David L., ed., *The Portable Harlem Renaissance Reader*, Penguin USA, 1995.

This volume of short fiction, essays, memoirs, drama, and poetry provides a snapshot of the literature produced during the Harlem Renaissance. More than forty writers are represented.

Wright, Richard, *American Hunger*, HarperCollins, 1982.

This volume, first published seventeen years after Wright's death, is a continuation of the autobiography begun in *Black Boy*.

———, *Black Boy: A Record of Childhood and Youth*, 1945, reprint, Everbind Anthologies, 2003.

Black Boy is the first part of Wright's autobiography, covering his early life in Mississippi and Tennessee.

Christmas Not Just Once a Year

Heinrich Böll

1951

"Christmas Not Just Once a Year" ("*Nicht nur zur Wiehnachtszeit*") was written in 1951 and was first "published" in a German radio broadcast that year. Considered to be one of Heinrich Böll's finest satires, the story was included in German in his 1952 book, *Nicht nur zur Weihnachtszeit*, a collection that was expanded in 1966 and renamed *Nicht nur zur Wiehnachtszeit: Satiren*. In the United States, the story appeared most recently in Böll's collected stories, *The Stories of Heinrich Böll*, published by Knopf in 1986. In addition, "Christmas Not Just Once a Year" is one of Böll's most widely anthologized stories. By 1975, according to Robert C. Conard, writing in *Understanding Heinrich Böll*, the story had appeared in at least twenty-three German and foreign anthologies.

"Christmas Not Just Once a Year" tells the simple story of Aunt Milla's hysterical reaction to the taking down of the family Christmas tree in 1946 and her family's subsequent reaction to her hysteria. Told through the eyes of one of the family's first cousins, the story describes the complete moral and psychological disintegration of a family that refuses to acknowledge Milla's profound psychological problems. Instead of addressing the issue of Milla's breakdown clinically or directly, the family decides to continue with the ruse that every day is Christmas. For two years they go to great lengths and expense to host a nightly ritual of Christmas tree decorations and carol singing in order to keep Aunt Milla from screaming hysterically.

Böll's narrative becomes increasingly absurd as the story develops. Written while Germany was in the early stages of its postwar reconstruction, and during a time when it had yet to fully acknowledge its role in World War II or in the Holocaust (according to J. H. Reid, writing in *Heinrich Böll: A German for His Time*, in a 1954 essay Böll laments the fact that in one particular class of forty German students, not one had heard of the Holocaust), "Christmas Not Just Once a Year" addresses the theme of historical amnesia. Just as the family refuses to accept the fact that things are no longer "like the good old days" of prewar Germany and that Aunt Milla could not become healthy until the family acknowledges this basic fact, Böll believed that Germany would remain stunted if it did not directly address its Nazi past and come to terms with its role in the war.

However, to say that the story is simply about Germany would be to underestimate its strength; critics have pointed out that the characters and symbols Böll uses in the story are universal enough that "Christmas Not Just Once a Year" can be applied to any country, including the United States, with a historical past that it would rather ignore.

Author Biography

Heinrich Böll was born December 21, 1917, in Cologne, Germany. The sixth child of Maria and Viktor Böll, Böll's clearest memories were of Germany's defeated troops returning from the war and the economic instability that Germany experienced following the war. His father, a self-employed furniture maker, lost his business in 1923 when Germany's astronomical rates of inflation rendered its currency virtually worthless, and following the stock market crash of 1929, he was unable to keep up with his loan repayments and lost the family house. Böll would cite these events, along with the rise of Adolph Hitler's Nazi movement during this same time period, as having a profound impact on his writing throughout his career.

Böll was never more than an average student in school. However, his decision to resist joining Hitler's youth movement gave him ample time to read on his own outside of classes. Following high school, he took on a brief stint as a bookseller's apprentice in 1938, and shortly thereafter he was inducted into the army. In 1942, while on furlough, he married Annemarie Cech, a woman he had

known through the Catholic youth group meetings his mother hosted at their house, and over the next three years he wrote his wife nearly one thousand letters, many of them openly critical of the war and of Hitler. Böll was wounded several times in the course of the war, and for a brief spell late in the war, he went underground as a deserter. In 1945, after returning to the front, he was captured by American troops and remained a prisoner of war until the war's end.

Böll and his wife returned to Cologne after the war, and by 1950 his wife had given birth to three children. Böll wrote full time upon his return from the army while his wife worked, and in 1951 he received his first award for his writing—1,000 marks for his short story "Black Sheep." His first novel, *Adam, Where Art Thou*, was published in 1951, and his second novel, *And Never Said a Word*, which appeared in 1953, sold well enough to allow Böll to continue as a full-time writer. The short story "Christmas Not Just Once a Year," considered to be one of Böll's best satires, was written in 1951 and was translated into several languages and anthologized widely.

In addition to his prose fiction, Böll became well known for political work and views, which he expressed widely in his essays and speeches. His work on behalf of imprisoned and politically repressed writers around the world led to his election as president of the German PEN Club in 1970 and his election the following year as president of the International PEN. He was instrumental in bringing Soviet dissident Alexandr Solzhenitsyn's book *The Gulag Archipelago* to the West, and he was the first Westerner to offer the Russian writer refuge after his expulsion from the Soviet Union in 1974. In 1972, he was awarded the Nobel Prize for literature. In the 1980s, shortly before his death, a poll was conducted in Germany, and Böll was considered to be the second most popular figure in Germany, second only to the country's chancellor Helmut Schmidt. Heinrich Böll died at his home in Langenbroich in 1985, from complications of arteriosclerosis.

Plot Summary

Section 1

"Christmas Not Just Once a Year" tells the story of how a German family, shortly following

World War II, is affected by an aunt who suffers a severe psychological breakdown and reacts hysterically to the taking down of the family Christmas tree. Told through the eyes of an unnamed narrator, the nephew of Aunt Milla, the story is a satire, and the events the narrator describes over the course of two years grow increasingly more absurd as his narrative develops.

In section 1 the narrator introduces the members of the family who play important roles in the story and among whom "symptoms of disintegration" are beginning to show: Uncle Franz, "the kindest of men," who is said to have recently become "tired of life"; his sons Franz, a famous boxer who now rejects all praise with utter indifference, and Johannes, whom the narrator fears has become a communist; Lucie, the sister who had always been a "normal woman" but who now frequents "disreputable places"; and Aunt Milla, the "originator" of the family's ills but who "is as well and cheerful as she has almost always been."

Although section 1 offers no details, the narrator makes it clear that it is because of Aunt Milla the family has suffered tremendously and that cousin Franz has warned the family much earlier of the "terrible consequences" of what was, at the time, deemed a "harmless event." Now, as a result of not listening to Franz, things have gotten "so out of hand" that the family is at a "total loss" of what to do.

Section 2

Section 2 provides the background and first details of the source of the family's ills. The setting of the story is an unnamed German city, shortly following the end of World War II. Aunt Milla has always had a "particular fondness" for decorating the Christmas tree and singing Christmas carols, activities that her son Franz always resisted with "vehement indignation." During the war, however, aerial bombardments and the general war-torn state of the country prevented the aunt from having a tree. In fact, her desire for the ritual was so great that she saw the war mainly as a "force" that "jeopardize[d] her Christmas tree."

The family itself was left virtually unscathed by the war. Uncle Franz, a successful importer of fruits and vegetables, had built a strong bunker that protected them from the raids, and his business and political connections kept the family relatively well endowed during most of the war. However, as the

Heinrich Böll

war continued, it became difficult even for Franz to find supplies, so it was not until Christmas 1946, more than a year after the war ended, that Aunt Milla could once again bring her family around the decorated Christmas tree.

There was nothing peculiar about Christmas that year; however, three months later, in March of 1947, as the narrator was nearing his uncle and aunt's house, he could hear the singing of Christmas carols. Later, Uncle Franz explained the situation to him: On the eve of Candlemas, or the "Festival of Lights" that occurs at the beginning of February, Johannes began to strip the tree of its decorations, as was the custom of the region. However, as he was detaching the dwarves that decorated the tree, the tree crashed to the floor, and Aunt Milla began to scream hysterically. For almost a week she continued to scream despite the best efforts of neurologists and psychologists. She refused to eat or sleep, and it was not until Uncle Franz suggested getting a new tree that the aunt finally stopped.

Sections 3–6

The reality of Uncle Franz's "solution" to Aunt Milla's hysteria begins to settle in as the family discovers how difficult it actually is to procure a

Christmas tree outside the Christmas season. But somehow arrangements are made, a new tree is erected, complete with its decorations, and the family continues to meet on a nightly basis, as if each night were Christmas Eve, to sing carols around the tree and eat holiday sweets.

Spring approaches and with it the region's carnival season. As an indication of how deeply disturbed Aunt Milla has become, she complains about the thousands of carnival-goers for not respecting the sanctity of Christmas. Nevertheless, the family and the family priest continue to celebrate Christmas each night. By June, the doctor the family has hired to cure Aunt Milla gives up his efforts, and one night the family priest does not show up, citing other obligations in his parish. A fellow curate is sent to replace him, but in the course of the singing, he laughs hysterically at the absurdity of the situation and refuses to return. Uncle Franz files a complaint with the church, ultimately to no avail, and the family must replace him with a retired priest in the area who agrees to participate in the nightly ritual.

By now, the family has become quite efficient in organizing the ceremonies: The family arrives at the uncle's home and assembles around the tree, the candles are lit, the angels on the tree begin singing "Peace, peace," a few carols are sung, and all end the evening with a "Merry Christmas!" and retire to their regular lives. One item the narrator notes is that the financial cost of keeping up this facade is beginning to add up.

Sections 7–11

Although the actual Christmas of 1947 goes off without a hitch, in January Lucie suddenly begins to scream when she sees fallen Christmas trees littering the streets. Soon thereafter Karl, Lucie's husband, secretly begins to research emigration possibilities to countries where carol singing is not allowed and where Christmas trees do not grow and are not imported; Johannes suddenly resigns from the choral society; and Uncle Franz is rumored to be in an adulterous relationship. Most significantly, Uncle Franz has hired a stage actor to replace him in the nightly ceremonies, a precedent-setting act that ultimately leads to the hiring of a complete ensemble to replace each of the adult members.

Eighteen months following Aunt Milla's initial scream, rumors circulate that Uncle Franz has en-

tered into business practices "that virtually no longer permit the description 'Christian businessman.'" Lucie has come to wear gaudy clothes and has otherwise thrown "all restraint to the wind"—acts she considers to be "existential." Johannes has, indeed, become a communist and has severed all relations with his family. Karl has discovered a country along the equator where he and Lucie will move, and Franz has retired from boxing.

Nearly two years following the start of these extraordinary events, the narrator, on one of his evening strolls, stops by the uncle's house to observe the ceremony. The room is filled with actors who are treating themselves to good food, cigars, and wine. The narrator points out the possible negative effects this constant partying will have on the family children, who continue to participate, and he convinces the uncle to replace the children with wax dummies.

Section 12

The final section mirrors section 1 in that all of the characters and their respective situations are mentioned. Lucie and Karl have emigrated; Johannes has moved out of the city; Uncle Franz has become "tired of life" and complains that the servants are no longer dusting the wax dummies; the aunt and the retired prelate continue to "chat about the good old days" at the nightly ceremonies; and cousin Franz has traded the boxing ring for the monastery, where, according to the narrator, he looks more like a "convict" than a monk. "Our life is our punishment," Franz says to the narrator before quickly departing for his chapel prayers.

Characters

The Actors

After nearly eighteen months of having to participate in the nightly family rituals, Uncle Franz hires an ensemble of local actors to take the places of the adults. As artists who can barely make ends meet, they are quick to take on this assignment, and over time they come to take advantage of the situation by eating expensive asparagus every night, drinking the family's good wine, and smoking its good cigars. Eventually, the children are replaced by wax figures, so in the end the only "true" participants in the ritual are Aunt Milla and the retired priest.

Dr. Bless

Dr. Bless is mentioned briefly as one of the psychologists who is hired, at no insignificant cost, by Uncle Franz to cure Aunt Milla of her condition. However, neither Dr. Bless nor any of the other specialists hired by Uncle Franz is successful in curing Aunt Milla.

Uncle Franz

The narrator describes Uncle Franz on more than one occasion as "the kindest of men." Franz, the patriarch of the family, made his fortune by importing and selling tropical fruits. During the war he expanded his business to include other fruits and vegetables. It is Franz's decision not to commit his wife for her hysteria, choosing instead to organize and finance the daily ritual of decorating the Christmas tree and singing the carols. The narrator suspects early on that Uncle Franz is having an extramarital affair, a suspicion he eventually confirms. A further indication of Franz's moral decay is that rumors begin to circulate that he has begun business practices that can in no way be described as "Christian." Franz eventually gets the idea of hiring an actor to replace him during the evening rituals, a practice that is quickly adopted by all of the family's adult members. Eventually, he is convinced by the narrator to replace the children with wax figures, and at the story's conclusion he is said to be "tired of life" and complains that the servants at the house do not dust the wax children regularly and are taking advantage of him. It can be said that Uncle Franz represents Germany's rush into economic activity as a way to avoid dealing with its past. Instead of addressing the root causes of his wife's hysteria, Franz decides it is best to keep his wife believing that these are still the "good old days," even if he must dive headlong into his business activities and become "un-Christian" as a result.

Cousin Johannes

Uncle Franz's favorite son, Johannes is a highly successful lawyer as the story opens. However, as Aunt Milla's condition worsens, rumors begin to circulate that Johannes has become a communist—a rumor that the narrator confirms by the story's conclusion. Johannes uses his extensive connec-

tions and finds a company that can deliver Christmas trees throughout the year. An indication of the effect his mother's hysteria has had on Johannes comes when he resigns from the choral society and declares in writing that he can no longer "devote himself to the cultivation of German songs"—a sure sign that the family's nightly carol singing had deeply affected him.

Karl

Karl is Lucie's "helpless spouse" who frequents "disreputable" places with Lucie. As Aunt Milla's condition worsens, Karl begins to research countries where no Christmas trees are allowed and where the singing of carols is prohibited. By the story's conclusion, he has found such a country located near the equator, and he and Lucie leave Germany for good.

Cousin Lucie

Up until the moment her mother's hysteria begins, Lucie is generally thought of by the narrator as a "normal woman." Unmarried during the war, she volunteered in a local factory that embroidered swastikas. Following the onset of Aunt Milla's condition, Lucie, along with Karl, her "helpless spouse," is said to frequent "disreputable" places in the evening. Her own condition worsens to such a degree that following Christmas 1947, a year after her mother first became hysterical, Lucie begins to scream uncontrollably herself at the sight of discarded Christmas trees. Karl and she eventually move to an equatorial country that does not have Christmas trees and has a prohibition on the singing of carols. Prior to her departure, the narrator notes that she had essentially taken on an "existential" life; she had started wearing her hair in "bangs," instead of the more acceptable fashion of the day, and sandals instead of shoes, and she had begun dressing herself in corduroys and "gaudy sweaters."

Aunt Milla

Aunt Milla, the narrator's aunt, is the source of the family's "disintegration." She is described by the narrator in several places with warm regard. Generally speaking, she is described as a kindly woman; however, her one peculiarity is "her particular fondness for decorating the Christmas tree"—an attribute the narrator describes as a "harmless if particular weakness that is fairly widespread in our Fatherland." In fact, though, her fondness for the ritual is so strong that she views World War II "merely as a force that . . . jeopardize[d] her Christmas tree." For a six-year period starting in 1940, Aunt Milla's tree falls victim to the war and the country's subsequent shortages of goods and supplies. She is finally able to decorate a tree at Christmas 1946, but when the tree is taken down on the eve of Candlemas, she begins to scream hysterically. The only "cure" for her screaming is for the family to continue the ritual of singing around the tree every evening thereafter, as if every day were Christmas. Symbolically, Aunt Milla, along with her family, comes to represent Germany's unwillingness to recognize its Nazi past and its responsibility in the war.

The Narrator

The narrator is an unnamed nephew of Uncle Franz and Aunt Milla. He does not participate directly in the rituals, though it is as a result of his insistence that Uncle Franz replaces the children with wax figures. The success of the satire depends on the narrator being a member of the family but not one of the members who directly participates in the rituals. As a family member, the narrator is able to view the events with an empathy that would otherwise not be possible, and as a family member who is removed from the daily rituals, he is also able to be objective enough not to become too drawn in or detrimentally affected by Aunt Milla's hysteria. It is Böll's choice of this narrator that gives "Christmas Not Just Once a Year" the conviction it needs to succeed as a satire.

The Priest

The family priest who originally participates in the family's Christmas celebration decides by late spring that enough is enough, and he refuses to participate any longer. He is replaced by a curate who, during the course of the carol singing, laughs uncontrollably and also refuses to return. Eventually, the family finds a retired priest to participate. The priest represents, on one level, the close relationship and favored status Uncle Franz has, by virtue of his wealth and standing, with the church.

Themes

Catholicism

Böll's family was devoutly Catholic, and until 1969 when they were forced to leave the church because of their refusal to pay church taxes, he and his wife remained practicing Catholics. In "Christmas Not Just Once a Year," Uncle Franz uses his connections and his economic standing to build a favored relationship with his parish. When the family priest finally decides, after several months, no longer to participate in the family's evening rituals, a prelate is quickly sent to take his place. However, the replacement laughs throughout the family's ritual and does not return, and Franz files a formal complaint with the church. The complaint is eventually dismissed, but Böll seems to be commenting on the favored relationship that Franz has with the church by virtue of his economic status.

Family

During the 1920s and 1930s, when Böll's father lost his business and the family house because of the economy, and while Hitler was rising to power, Böll's family remained close and provided Böll with a shelter from all the social and economic unrest of the time. Much of his work portrays the family structure in a positive light. In "Christmas Not Just Once a Year" the family structure once again plays a positive role, to a large degree, in the characters' lives. Uncle Franz's bomb shelter keeps the family from harm during the war, and his connections keep the family fed during difficult times. However, while Aunt Milla is devoted at all costs to keeping her family together through the tradition of tree decorating, her inability to accept the changed reality of her circumstances leads to the family's ultimate disintegration. The family structure, in this case, comes to symbolize the greater "family" of Germany. Just as Aunt Milla's family is unable to understand how destructive their refusal to face reality is, Germany's refusal to acknowledge its own reality vis-à-vis the war and the Holocaust was just as destructive.

German Reconstruction

Germany's economic, industrial, and social infrastructures were decimated by the war. Whole sections of cities were left abandoned, and families wanting to start a new life could often move into a house and call it their own by agreeing to its renovations. Cologne itself lost more than seven hundred thousand of its inhabitants in the war. There are some hints of this situation in "Christmas Not Just Once a Year." On his way to visit his uncle and aunt, the narrator must walk by "overgrown piles of rubble and neglected parks." One of Böll's

Topics for Further Study

- One of the main themes of "Christmas Not Just Once a Year" is "historical amnesia." What is meant by the term "historical amnesia?" In particular, how does it relate to Germany immediately following the war? Explain the steps Germany has taken since the 1950s, if any, to address this issue.

- Research the Nuremberg Trials of 1945–1949. What was the purpose of the trials? What effect did they have on German society? Did the trials ultimately achieve their goals?

- Some of the most popular shows ever broadcast on German television have been about the Holocaust. In 1984, for instance, a rebroadcast of the American television serial *Holocaust* was viewed by over 10 million Germans, or one-sixth of the population. What accounts for the huge popularity of that series nearly two decades after the historical events had transpired? Is this phenomenon related to the concept of "historical amnesia"? If so, how?

- For much of his career, Heinrich Böll devoted himself to the "writers of conscience"—writers who, for political reasons, were either imprisoned by their governments or whose writing suffered from severe governmental censorship. Many of the writers whom Böll worked for lived in the eastern bloc or other communist countries. Now that most of the former communist countries have become democratic, is there a primary region of the world where most "writers of conscience" in the early 2000s live? Using Amnesty International and the International PEN Club as the basis of your research, find the names of several writers who would fall in this category and describe their situations. Are there political issues that these writers share?

---

arguments is that in the aftermath of World War II, Germany's headlong rush into rebuilding its economy prevented it from adequately addressing its role in the war. Uncle Franz, a highly successful business man, symbolizes this aspect of German reconstruction for Böll.

Historical Amnesia and the Holocaust

In the early 1950s, when Böll wrote "Christmas Not Just Once a Year," a minority of Germans believed that they were responsible for the war, and very few claimed knowledge about the Holocaust. The Jewish population in Germany had been annihilated, and there were no national moves to discuss reparations or acknowledge the great loss of human lives due to Nazi policies. Böll believed that if Germany was unwilling to address its past and directly confront its own role in the Holocaust, it would "disintegrate" much like Aunt Milla's family disintegrates around her while she lives as if every day were Christmas. Böll's satire is a direct response to the historical amnesia he perceived his country was experiencing.

Tradition

The tradition of Christmas and its rituals is obviously a vital part of Aunt Milla's life. In "Christmas Not Just Once a Year," Christmas comes to symbolize the tradition of Christian Germany's way of life as it existed before the war: Each year families decorate tress, sing carols, and on the eve of Candlemas, they take down their trees to signify the end of the season. World War II interrupted that tradition, and it is Aunt Milla's steadfast and absurd desire to keep the tradition alive year round, as if she can make up for the lost time caused by the war. Böll seems to be saying that while traditions are important, Germany is hiding behind its own traditions as a means of escaping reality. Like Aunt Milla, Germany is not able to set aside its obsession with returning to the "good old days" long enough to recognize the horrors it inflicted during the war.

Another, more subtle comment Böll's use of the Christmas tradition seems to reveal is that although Aunt Milla's experience clearly shows the steep price the family must pay to keep their tradition alive day in and day out, at least they are able to continue with that tradition. Because of German war policies, the entire German Jewish population was annihilated, and with it the many traditions Jews practiced on a daily and yearly basis.

War

World War II was a pivotal event in Germany's history. Prior to the war the country had built the strongest military in Europe, but its defeat at the hands of the Allied forces virtually destroyed every aspect of its society. The role of its citizens in the Holocaust would eventually become an important topic of discussion and debate throughout Germany, but for many years the country refused to acknowledge that as an issue. In "Christmas Not Just Once a Year," the narrator essentially apologizes to the reader for bringing up the war. Although none of the family members was killed during the war, it nevertheless had a profound effect on them, as evidenced by Aunt Milla's hysteria.

Style

Narrative Point of View

It is significant that the narrator of "Christmas Not Just Once a Year" is a cousin of the family that is directly affected by the aunt's hysteria. This point of view allows him just enough distance to view events somewhat objectively, although he admits that throughout much of the time in which the story takes place even he did not notice the extent to which the events had gotten out of control. A daughter or son of the aunt could not remove her or himself enough from the story to narrate it dispassionately, and an outsider to the family would not have the compassion that the narrator portrays for the family's situation. To succeed as a satire about Germany, the story must be told by a family member; thus, although the narrator is literally describing his family, he could also be seen as talking about Germany, his greater family.

Satire

A satire is a literary work, made with irony or wit, which doubles as a kind of a protest or criticism of society or of humanity in general. Satirical works usually use absurd situations or elements to make their points. Famous examples of satire in the twentieth century include Aldous Huxley's *Brave New World* and George Orwell's *1984* and *Animal Farm*. "Christmas Not Just Once a Year" is one of Böll's most famous satirical stories. Although its literal subject is what appears to be a fairly normal, well-to-do family that is suddenly faced with an extreme situation concerning one of its members, its real subject is Germany in general and the way the country refused to acknowledge its Nazi past and the role it played in World War II. By injecting a few absurd, but plausible, elements into the beginning of the narrative, Böll is able to draw the reader into the story—so much so that it makes perfect "sense," for instance, that the children are replaced by wax dummies at the end. Successful satires use comedic elements to address what the writer perceives to be a tragic situation or set of circumstances.

Setting

The setting for "Christmas Not Just Once a Year" is postwar Germany. World War II was started largely because of German aggression, and as a result of the war, Germany itself, as well as the whole of Europe, was now digging itself out of the literal and figurative rubble caused by the war. The war was devastating to both Germany and its enemies. The country's population, due to war casualties, was decimated, and nearly every facet of Germany's infrastructure was in ruins. On a psychological level, the country's citizens had yet to deal with their individual or collective responsibility for the horrors inflicted by their country during war. Germany, through the Nazi policies of Adolph Hitler, was responsible for the annihilation of millions of Jews and other ethnic groups in the Holocaust, and for years thereafter historians, politicians, and psychologists argued publicly about how to best deal with the country's guilt. In 1951, at the time of the story's publication, there was a significant desire among the German population and its leaders to forget about the country's past and to think only of the future. Many writers and other intellectuals, like Böll, insisted that Germany would not be fully healed on a psychic level until it stopped ignoring reality and addressed the role it played in the war. "Christmas Not Just Once a Year" is written to show what can happen when a family's, or a country's, reality or difficult past is ignored and people try to live as if every day was like one of the "good old days."

Compare & Contrast

- **1950s:** There are very few public exhibits or museums devoted to Germany's role in World War II or its role in the Holocaust.

  Today: Several significant museums in Germany are devoted to World War II and the Holocaust, and throughout Germany there are public displays related to various aspects of the war and its victims.

- **1950s:** With the German population decimated by the war and facing severe shortages of trained personnel, laws have been passed to encourage couples to have children. Germany is in the early stages of its economic and social reconstruction. With the assistance of the Marshall Plan, it is attempting to rebuild its once mighty industrial and economic infrastructure.

  Today: The German population has long since recovered, and Germany is one of the economic powerhouses of the European Union and is a major producer of many of the world's most popular brands of cars and electronic devices.

- **1950s:** Many German Nazi leaders have fled the country, relocating free from prosecution in South American countries and other countries around the world.

  Today: So-called "Nazi Hunters" have successfully tracked down most of the high-ranking Nazis and brought them back to trial for their war crimes.

- **1950s:** There is not a central economic or political entity in Europe. The continent consists of many individual nation states, each with its own currency, laws, and political structures.

  Today: Following the fall of the eastern bloc, many European countries have voted to join the European Union. Union members share a currency and agree to abide by many laws and policies that govern various aspects of governmental, economic, and social policies.

Historical Context

Heinrich Böll was first and foremost known as a political writer. In speeches and essays, Böll continually described the purpose of his writing as political, asserting that he did not believe there was a separation between his literary life and his political one. In 1951, he was invited to join "Group 47," writers who were committed to democratic ideals; eighteen years later, in 1969, he was elected president of the West German PEN, an organization devoted to the politics of literature, and in 1971 he was elected as president of the international PEN.

"Christmas Not Just Once a Year" takes place in the years immediately following World War II. Böll himself had participated in the war as a Nazi soldier. In the course of the war, he wrote hundreds of letters home to his wife, many of which explicitly criticized Germany's role in the war, and Böll also spent some time as a deserter before being captured by the Americans, which he celebrated as an act of liberation.

Germany, once considered to be the economic and military powerhouse of Europe, had been reduced to rubble by the war. In Böll's hometown of Cologne, for instance, the population was reduced from over eight hundred thousand before the war to less than thirty thousand. Entire city blocks throughout the country were abandoned, and families trying to rebuild their lives were given opportunities to move into abandoned houses and start anew. The narrator alludes to some of this devastation when he describes walking "past overgrown piles of rubble and neglected parks" as he makes his way to his uncle's house.

More important for the story, however, is the emotional and psychological rubble the war left behind. Germany was the clear aggressor of World

War II. Without Hitler's aggressive military actions prior to the war and without his policy of eliminating European Jewry along with other "undesirables," there probably would not have been a European war. And in the years immediately following its defeat, as the full horrors of those policies were made known to the world, German citizens were forced to deal with their role in those horrors.

Most major politicians, and most of the population, chose not to address the war directly. Instead, they argued, it was best for Germany to look "forward," and not "backward," and the country should let the past be the past. For Böll, however, it was necessary to understand the past in order to move into the future. "Christmas Not Just Once a Year" can be read as his statement to that effect: that by pretending that life is like it was before the war, that by pretending that every day can be like "Christmas," Germany was in danger, like Aunt Milla and her family, of complete "disintegration" and "collapse."

Indeed, one of the strengths of "Christmas Not Just Once a Year" is its timelessness. The issue of Germany's "collective guilt" would continue to be played out in public spheres for the next two decades; it was not until the 1980s and 1990s that German society as a whole—at least West German society—began to discuss the Holocaust publicly in any depth. And by the time the Berlin Wall was finally torn down in 1989 and East and West Germany were once again united, a whole new issue of German guilt, which "Christmas Not Just Once a Year" could also work to address, suddenly arose— namely, the East German's collective guilt over its communist past.

Critical Overview

Several critics, including Erhard Friedrichsmeyer, believe that Böll's greatest work is to be found in his short stories and, more particularly, in his satires. Friedrichsmeyer, writing in his *University of Dayton Review* article, "Böll's Satires," considers his satirical stories his best work, and he calls "Christmas Not Just Once a Year" one of his "masterpieces." Robert C. Conard, writing in *Understanding Heinrich Böll*, concurs: "Böll's work in the

satiric mode has no equal in postwar German literature." He adds, "In *"Nicht nur zur Weihnachtszeit"* Böll created not only a national classic but a satire for all ages." Conard also quotes Friedrichsmeyer as saying that the story is a "satiric gem." Rienhard K. Zachau, in his book *Heinrich Böll: Forty Years of Criticism* discusses the views of German critic Marcel Reich-Ranicki, who had a strong influence on the reception of Böll's work in Germany in the early 1960s. Reich-Ranicki, according to Zachau, believed Böll's short story style was his trademark and that Böll had not written anything perfect "except for a few short stories."

In general, Böll was highly regarded around the world for his writing and his commitment to literature. Because his subjects were most often political and, more specifically, dealt with the less advantaged members of German society, Böll often suffered from the political vicissitudes of reviewers and critics. This was especially true of his reception by critics in former communist countries. Zachau, for instance, points out that Böll was warmly received early in his career in the former Soviet Union and became one of that country's major Western writers, "second only to . . . Ernest Hemingway." Critics pointed to his commitment to working class ideals and his antimilitarist and antifascist stances. However, starting with the publication of his novel *The Clowns* in 1965, Böll began falling out of favor with communist orthodoxy, and following the 1974 publication of *The Lost Honor of Katharina Blum*, Böll was officially banned by Soviet censors, although his books could continue to be sold in the country in foreign languages.

In the United States, Zachau writes that the reception of Böll's works reflected that of German literature in general. Until 1954, with the translation of *And Never Said a Word*, no German author, according to Zachau, had become widely known in academic or critical circles in the United States. For several years, then, at least until the publication of Günter Grass's breakthrough novel *The Tin Drum* in 1959, Böll was considered "the" German writer in the eyes of American critics and academics. However, Böll would continue throughout his career to receive praise in America for his work. Reviewing the posthumously published *The Stories of Heinrich Böll* in the *Chicago Tribune* on March 23, 1986, critic Miriam Berkley concludes her review by writing, "Readers of this volume should have no doubt that Heinrich Boll well deserved his

Nobel Prize." Michael Heskit, reviewing the collection on January 12, 1986, for the *Houston Chronicle*, writes that the "collection provides a powerful entrance to Böll's tragic view of the world, tempered always by wit and compassion: the sordidness and inhumanity of war, the hollowness of Germany's postwar economic recovery, and the moral rot pervading the new Germany." While most of the reviews of Böll's stories were positive, there were some notable exceptions. In the *Los Angeles Times*, for instance, Michael Scammell concludes that "Böll's talent was largely unsuited to the genre of the short story, and that he needed more space to succeed." And although it fell short of being negative, the *New York Times* published a less than enthusiastic review, calling the collection "a memorial to the far more subtle-minded author" that Böll was.

In Germany, Böll became an enormously popular cultural icon. Known for his political work as well as his writing, Böll was, according to a poll conducted shortly before his death in 1985, considered by Germans to be the second most popular figure behind the country's chancellor at the time, Helmut Schmidt. Zachau points out that in 1977 alone, more than fifteen books, twenty dissertations, and twelve hundred newspaper and magazine articles were written about Böll, and by 1993, more than sixty books had been written about him.

Criticism

Mark White

White is the publisher of the Seattle-based press, Scala House Press. In this essay, White argues that Böll's choice of narrator is a crucial element in the tremendous success of the story as a satire on the German postwar situation.

Heinrich Böll's "Christmas Not Just Once a Year" is a satire on Germany's refusal to address the moral implications of its Nazi past. Written in 1951 as Germany was working feverishly to recover from the devastating effects of the war, the story was one of Böll's many warnings that Germany faced an uncertain future of "disintegration" and possible "collapse" if it did not adequately treat the root causes of its historical and moral amnesia.

To convey this warning, Böll chose as the narrative voice a calm and slightly detached nephew of Aunt Milla—the main character whose hysteria is the immediate cause of her family's ills. This choice of narrator was crucial to the resounding success of "Christmas Not Just Once a Year" as a satire. By virtue of his close relationship to his aunt's immediate family, the narrator is privy to enough family history and gossip to offer a comprehensive account of their troubles. However, as a once-removed relation, he is sufficiently protected from the immediate effects of Aunt Milla's hysteria and is therefore able to comprehend the depths to which the family is sinking. And yet—and this is a crucial element to Böll's underlying message—despite his knowledge, the narrator—just like his fellow countrymen who remained silent to the effects of Germany's amnesia—is still unable or unwilling to intervene on behalf of the family's welfare.

There is little disagreement among critics that "Christmas Not Just Once a Year" is not only one of Böll's most successful satires but perhaps one of the Nobel laureate's finest works. Erhad Friedrichsmeyer, writing in his *University of Dayton Review* article, "Böll's Satires," calls "Christmas Not Just Once a Year" one of Böll's masterpieces. Böll scholar Robert C. Conard writes in *Understanding Heinrich Böll* that "Böll's work in the satiric mode has no equal in postwar German literature," and he adds that "Christmas Not Just Once a Year" is "not only a national classic but a satire for all ages."

Set in the years immediately following World War II, "Christmas Not Just Once a Year" tells the story of Aunt Milla and the devastating effects her obsession with the family Christmas tree has upon her family. From 1940 to 1945, the war made it impossible for Aunt Milla and her family to have a Christmas tree. In 1946, the situation in Germany had improved enough to allow the family to renew the celebration, much to Aunt Milla's delight, but when the tree is finally taken down, Aunt Milla begins to scream hysterically, and nothing can stop her. It is only when the family sets up another, fully decorated tree and repeats the celebration that her screaming stops. The narrator of "Christmas Not Just Once a Year," an unnamed nephew of Aunt Milla, describes how the family, rather than ad-

What Do I Read Next?

- W. G. Sebald's *Austerlitz*, widely acclaimed at its publication in 2001, tells the story of Jacques Austerlitz who, as a small child, was sent to England on a kindertransport in 1939, and who, as an adult fifty years after the war is over, is haunted by images and fleeting memories of his past. He follows a dim trail that ultimately leads to the truth of his parents' death in the Holocaust.

- *The Tin Drum* (1959) is Günter Grass's first and most famous novel. A huge commercial success, *The Tin Drum* tells the story of thirty-year-old Oskar Matzerath, who, in protest of the Nazi regime, stopped growing at the age of three. The novel is a moving and hilarious view of German history and immediately cast Grass as German's most popular writer.

- *Missing Persons* (1997), a collection of essays by Heinrich Böll, includes selections from Böll's non-fiction prose work, including his political essays, book reviews, and literary work, and provides a good overview of Böll's political convictions and social views.

- Heinrich Böll's first novel, *Silent Angel*, remained unpublished until 1995, a decade after his death. Like "Christmas Not Just Once a Year," its themes are postwar German decay and reconstruction.

- *The Stories of Heinrich Böll* was first published in the United States in 1986 to widespread and strong reviews. The collection includes most of Böll's previously published stories, as well as stories previously uncollected in English editions, including "Christmas Not Just Once a Year."

- *What's to Become of the Boy? or Something to Do with Books* (1985) is Heinrich Böll's memoir of his teenage years in Germany. Böll describes Hitler's rise to power, the importance of books in his life, and his strong family ties that helped him to eventually become a writer.

---

dressing the source of Aunt Milla's psychosis, celebrates "Christmas" in the family living room every night thereafter. This profound denial of reality gradually takes its toll on the family members, and by the story's conclusion, a full two years has passed since Aunt Milla's screaming had begun, and the narrator has detailed what can only be described as the complete "disintegration," if not utter "collapse," of Aunt Milla's family.

One of the effects Böll's story had was to highlight his country's refusal to acknowledge its Nazi past and the devastation it was responsible for in the war. In 1951, Germany was in the early stages of its headlong rush into postwar reconstruction. Although the rest of the world considered Germany to be the prime instigator of the war and although the horrible truths of the Holocaust were becoming public, the country itself seemed either to be in great denial or in great ignorance of these basic truths.

The vast majority of German citizens at the time did not believe their country was responsible for the war, and four decades later German society would still be debating its role in the Holocaust.

Whereas some critics, such as John Klapper, writing in his essay "The Art of Aggression and Its Limitations: The Early Satires," point to the idea of "traditions" in general being the main theme of "Christmas Not Just Once a Year," the satire works best when it is read as an indictment of Germany's refusal to confront its history. Aunt Milla, in this context, represents Germany's desire to return to its past. However, her "perseverance with which she insisted that everything was to be 'like in the old days'" does not reflect her, or Germany's, desire to return to the country's *pre-Nazi* past; rather it is her desire to return to the days just prior to the war when Adolph Hitler's Nazi movement had peaked and Germany was viewed by the world as a mighty nation. The Christmas tree, in this context, represents the bridge between the prewar Germany of 1939—the last year before the war that the family was last able to celebrate their annual rituals—and the postwar society in which the story is set.

Böll also seems to be using Aunt Milla to comment on Germany's narcissistic view of the war. In Aunt Milla's eyes, the war is "merely . . . a force that began as early as Christmas 1939 to jeopardize her Christmas tree." The war was not a "force" that annihilated millions of Jews and tens of millions of Russians; rather, it was an inconvenience—admittedly a serious one—that disrupted the German way of life.

Böll uses the rituals around the Christmas tree to remind his readers that Germany's problems started long before the war and that simply returning to the ways things were in 1939 would be disastrous. Just as Aunt Milla will never be healed of her psychosis by celebrating Christmas every day as if it were still 1939, Germany itself would not be able to cure its own psychosis without first acknowledging that it was responsible for the war, the Holocaust, and for Hitler's ascendancy in the first place. Returning to 1939 Germany would not be enough, and hiding behind long-standing traditions was little more than a ruse. Both Aunt Milla and Germany must face the fact that their respective situations have undergone irreversible changes that necessitate radical measures. While literally and figuratively decorating the Christmas tree every night might alleviate the screaming, over the long run the psychosis will only deepen.

That Aunt Milla's family represents the greater German "family" is made evident by the narrator's choice of words as the story opens: *"Among our relatives,* symptoms of disintegration are beginning to show" (emphasis added). He adds that a "mildew of decay" has begun to take hold that could bring on "the end of the integrity of the entire clan."

For the story to succeed on this level, it is necessary that the narrator embody several characteristics. First, and most obviously, he must be a respectable member of the family he is describing. Criticism of any organization by one of the organization's accepted "insiders" is more likely to find a sympathetic audience than would the same criticism from an outsider. It is essential for Böll's narrator to be a family member with no bias or agenda that could render his account unreliable.

> The war was not a 'force' that annihilated millions of Jews and tens of millions of Russians; rather, it was an inconvenience . . . that disrupted the German way of life."

Franz, for instance, is a family insider who has been warning the family about his mother's obsession with the Christmas tree for years, but because "he lacked prestige in the family," his words have gone unheeded. In a cultured, upper-middle-class family with strong business and political connections, Franz, a boxer, is a black sheep due to his profession and his proclivity to fistfight "regularly with shady characters in remote parks and dense undergrowth on the outskirts of town."

The narrator, on the other hand, seems to have the ear of Uncle Franz, Aunt Milla's husband, who fills him in with accounts of the early events as they unfold. And nearly two years into the family's ordeal, when stage actors have long since replaced the adults in the nightly rituals, the narrator worries of the "possible effects" of the "unusual daily stimulation on childish minds" and recommends to Uncle Franz that he consider replacing the children with wax dummies, a recommendation the uncle accepts despite the steep costs.

It is also important to Böll's satire that the narrator be removed enough from the problems he describes so as not to be immersed in them. As a nephew, the narrator of "Christmas Not Just Once a Year" has not suffered the way Aunt Milla's husband or children have suffered, and he can therefore offer a more reasonable and detached view of the situation than could one of those immediate family members. Aunt Milla's daughter, Lucie, for instance, becomes so affected by her mother's psychosis that she eventually begins her own bouts of hysterical screaming at the sight of downed Christmas trees, and any account that she could possibly offer would be severely limited by that psychosis. Similarly, the other children and their spouses become deeply affected, if not disturbed: Johannes becomes a communist, moves out of the city, and ends all communication with the family; Franz falls into a deep melancholy, retires from the ring, and joins a monastery, where he looks more like a "convict" than a monk; and Lucie's husband, Karl, has been driven to emigrate with Lucie to an equatorial country where Christmas trees and Christmas carols are not allowed. Even Uncle Franz, considered at the start of these events to be the "kindest of men," has taken a mistress at the age of seventy and has resorted to business practices that can in no way be described as "Christian."

What the narrator has described is the complete "moral disintegration" of the family, and he seems to have successfully kept himself at a safe distance from its disturbing effects. Or has he?

For the sake of the narration—that is, for the sake of the narrator's perceived objectivity in his retelling of the family tragedy—it is true that he has steered clear of the most obvious psychotic elements that plague the immediate family members. By his account, the reader is given no reason to distrust his story. However, he nevertheless suffers from an "ailment" that strikes at the heart of Böll's satire. The narrator, despite his respectable position in the family and despite his ongoing awareness of the family's disintegration, does nothing, aside from recommending that wax dummies replace the children, to intervene in the situation. In effect, his inaction helps contribute to the family's collapse.

In 1996, Harvard professor Daniel J. Goldhagen wrote a controversial book entitled *Hitler's Willing Executioners: Ordinary Germans and the Holocaust* in which he argues that the extent to which everyday Germans, and not simply members of the Nazi party, knew about the genocide of Jews was much greater than had previously been acknowledged. Although the book was eventually criticized widely in academic circles for lax scholarship, it became a bestseller in Germany and provoked intense reaction and debates throughout the country. More than fifty years after the last trains had transported Jews to concentration camps, Germans were still debating their individual and collective roles in the Holocaust.

Böll's "Christmas Not Just Once a Year" addressed this same issue less than five years after the war had ended. Is Böll suggesting that the narrator, by virtue of his knowledge and apathy, is "guilty" of the family's demise? Is he accusing his fellow countrymen of being responsible for the Holocaust? One of the great strengths of "Christmas Not Just

Once a Year" is that it allows for these possible interpretations without bludgeoning the readers with direct accusations. Although Böll did not hesitate to "bludgeon" or "accuse" in his political writings and activism, as an artist he understood life's complexities, and by creating a morally ambiguous and seemingly unaffected and objective narrator, he was able to portray those complexities in a brilliant satire of the German situation.

Source: Mark White, Critical Essay on "Christmas Not Just Once a Year," in *Short Stories for Students*, Gale, 2005.

Robert C. Conrad

In the following essay excerpt, Conrad argues that "the work attacks, first and foremost, West Germany's desire after the war to avoid coming to terms with the Hitler years."

In his conversations with Eckermann, Goethe claimed, "In general the personal character of the writer influences the public more than his artistic talent" (*Conversations with Eckermann* 30 March 1824). Goethe illustrated his point with Corneille, whom, Goethe said, Napoleon did not read, but nonetheless wished to raise to a prince, and with Racine, whom, Goethe said, Napoleon did read, but of whom he made no such statement. Goethe's observation would actually have found more support in the case of Böll. His integrity as a man of conscience was never in doubt, not even by his opponents. His importance as a man of principle and as a critic of society was well recognized. But nowhere did his character and talent blend so well to form a unity than in his satires. Böll's work in the satiric mode has no equal in postwar German literature. As a satirist Böll has won his highest critical acclaim.

The satire "Nicht nur zur Weihnachtszeit," 1951 ("Christmas Not Just Once a Year"), written at the time of Böll's growing displeasure with political, psychological, and social developments in the Federal Republic, was his breakthrough in this genre.

"Christmas Not Just Once a Year" ("Nicht nur zur Weihnachtszeit")

In writing "Christmas Not Just Once a Year," Böll began to distance himself from the general approval of Germany that he felt immediately after the war in the nation's return to what he thought were fundamental values. This change in attitude found praise among critics. James Henderson Reid in his 1973 book on Böll claimed, "'Nicht nur zur Weihnachtszeit' [is] possibly Böll's most telling satire . . . and must be ranked among Böll's most unreservedly successful works" (16, 62). And Erhard Friedrichsmeyer wrote in his study of Böll's satires: "This text ['Christmas Not Just Once a Year'] is a satiric gem. The work's comic richness as well as its virtuosity . . . are indisputable" (83).

The work soon became widely anthologized both in Germany and abroad and in 1970 was made into a film for television. Its acceptance abroad paralleled its success in Germany, where it was frequently used as a school text. Although the work's reputation continues to grow, there is still no consensus about the meaning of the story, even when most critics agree the satire deals with the relationship of Germany's present to its past. Despite disagreement about the target of the satire, the critics are unanimous in their praise of its quality.

In January 1979, West German television broadcast the American television serial "Holocaust." Millions of Germans saw all or part of this dramatized treatment of the Final Solution of the "Jewish problem." The response of the nation to the series again made clear that thirty-four years after the war, many Germans who had lived through those years had not yet dealt honestly with the past. Some still claimed not to have known of the crimes of the Hitler period, and a few even denied that they took place. The phenomenon of German repression of the events of the war years was once again a subject for the world press. The German claim of limited knowledge of the extent of Nazi war crimes was justified at the end of the war, but during the postwar years of the "economic miracle" many Germans slipped into willful ignorance and denial. While many German writers have treated this theme, Böll's bizarre and humorous tale "Nicht nur zur Weihnachtszeit" was one of the earliest works in German literature to deal with this refusal to face reality, and that theme is arguably the real meaning of the story. But the story in its carefully chosen symbolic form transcends the limits of a national satire and contains a message for other nations as well.

The satire is easily summarized. It relates the tale of tyrannical Aunt Milla, who desires to celebrate Christmas every day, and of her tantrums, which force the members of her family to yield to her strange and destructive demand. To recount the tale, Böll chose a first-person narrator, but one not immediately involved in the events. As nephew to Aunt Milla, he is close enough to events to be

> "Hence, the Christmas season functions as institutionalized escapism as it is employed in the work, a permanent flight from reality extending from December to December, a point reinforced in the satire by the twelve narrative divisions Böll gives the story."

informed but not close enough to lose his objectivity. He witnesses some of the action and hears about the rest from members of the family. Despite his effort to be detached, he is more sympathetic to his aunt's attempt to have Christmas every day (to hide reality) than he admits. Because of his sympathy with the older generation, because of his desire to put his relatives in a good light, he becomes a German Everyman, who shares the responsibility of that generation for the repression of history. Most exemplary of his cooperation in the repression of the past is his failure, in an entire story about the Hitler period, to hint at, much less refer to, concentration camps or the Final Solution; he mentions only Germany's own suffering in the war years. What results is a narrative fraught with understatement of bizarre antics. The discrepancy between the understatement and the extraordinary events of the story contributes to the irony of the tale.

In "Christmas Not Just Once a Year" the object of Böll's satire is not primarily false Christian piety or hypocrisy, the commercialization of Christmas, the sentimentality of Germans, or the state of religion in West Germany—all suggested interpretations. Certainly the satire can be read as a critique of these social realities. But the work attacks, first and foremost, West Germany's desire after the war to avoid coming to terms with the Hitler years and that nation's reluctance to learn from recent historical experience. Since this aspect of West Germany's national character is characteristic of all nations' psychological behavior, the satire acquires intercultural importance.

Remarkable about "Christmas" is the way it presents its message with objectivity and cool detachment in a genre not noted for either of these virtues. Böll's satire is in this regard in the manner of the satirist Jonathan Swift, who creates tension in "A Modest Proposal" by confronting outrageous events with calmness. (In fact, Böll uses Swift as a model in another story, "The Thrower-away," discussed later in this chapter.) While the very idea of Christmas every day is a form of hyperbole, the work retains a matter-of-factness and directness that results in a thorough analysis of Germany's postwar social sickness.

The opening sentences of the story suggest Böll's intention:

> Among our relatives, symptoms of disintegration are beginning to show up that for a while we tried silently to ignore but the threat of which we are now determined to face squarely. I do not yet dare use the word "collapse," but the alarming facts are accumulating to the point where they represent a threat and compel me to speak of things that may sound strange to the ears of my contemporaries but whose reality no one can dispute. The mildew of decay has obtained a foothold under the thick, hard veneer of respectability, colonies of deadly parasites heralding the end of the integrity of an entire clan. (*WRE [Werke: Romane und Erzählungen]* 2: 11, Vennewitz translation from *The Stories of Heinrich Böll* 419).

The narrator's story is to be understood as a tale of his countrymen. He achieves this breadth of context with the words, "among our relatives," which indicate the story is one of more than the immediate family and refers to all relations and kin, with the phrase "entire clan," which indicates a tribe, a family group in the largest sense, and with the expression "contemporaries," which informs the reader that the unusual story he is about to hear is a parable ("whose reality no one can dispute") for and about the entire German nation. Lothar Huber in his essay on Böll's satiric method also identifies the family with the German nation, for he sees in "distinguished old" Aunt Milla the figure of "Germania" (52).

Early in the story the narrator humbly apologizes for having to mention the war, admitting he preferred not to run the risk of making himself "unpopular" (*WRE* 2: 13) but was forced to raise the unpleasant topic simply because it had an "influence on the story" (*WRE* 2: 13); however, after once having put the "boring" (*WRE* 2: 13) detail aside, he promises not to bring it up again. With this use of understatement, Böll both sets the tone and provides the background necessary to understand the message of his tale.

The choice of Christmas as a symbol of Germany's forgetfulness (a people's desire not to conquer the past) is actually quite natural. Christmas, in fact, abrogates the concerns of the day. For a brief period people forget their troubles or at least disguise them behind a festive spirit. Traditions by their nature stress the past and in that manner distort the present and neglect the future, but Christmas more than other celebrations emphasizes an idealized and romanticized past. Hence, the Christmas season functions as institutionalized escapism as it is employed in the work, a permanent flight from reality extending from December to December, a point reinforced in the satire by the twelve narrative divisions Böll gives the story.

The past that Aunt Milla wishes to forget is implicit in the tale, "The war was registered by my Aunt Milla only as a power which began in 1939 to endanger her Christmas tree" (*WRE* 2: 13). Two conclusions are necessary from the narrator's observation. First, some Germans only reacted to the war to the extent that it touched adversely upon their personal lives, and second, Germans could hate the inconvenience of war without relating it to the Hitler dictatorship. Both conclusions reveal that the war might be condemned as something not directly resulting from National Socialism and fascism. The leitmotifs of the story—"the good old days" and "Everything should be as before"—refer specifically to the period prior to 1939, not to 1933. "The good old days" refer then to the prewar period when Hitler was in power, Nazism was triumphant, and all was going well for the nation. Böll is saying in this satire of 1951 that the German failure to conquer the past is more than merely a desire to forget the war and a refusal to assume responsibility for it, but it is also a failure to condemn fascism.

The time references in the story are specific. It was "the middle of March" 1947 (*WRE* 2: 16) when the narrator discovered the first signs of permanent Christmas among his relatives. But the family gave in to Aunt Milla's hysterical demand for Christmas every day by treating it as a "harmless weakness" (*WRE* 2: 13). and thus, with the "participation of all" (*WRE* 2: 14), they took up the "costly" (*WRE* 2: 14) burden of continuing the celebration.

The costs are, indeed, more than financial. Aunt Milla's husband, Uncle Franz, described prior to the permanent Christmas as a "goodhearted man" and a "model of a Christian businessman" (*WRE* 2:

12) soon manifests signs of moral decay hinted at in the opening paragraph. He becomes estranged from his wife, takes a mistress, and becomes a greedy, manipulating merchant—the last change a necessary development to maintain the costly permanent Christmas. As the narrator sums it up, "in his case the decay was complete" (*WRE* 2: 29).

Aunt Milla's children, Cousin Johannes, Cousin Lucie, and Cousin Franz, are equally ill affected by the tacit decision not to conquer the past. Johannes, a successful lawyer, becomes a Communist; Lucie has a nervous breakdown. Her husband Karl plans to emigrate to a country "not far from the equator" (*WRE* 2: 31) in order to save his wife and to restore their children's deteriorating health. Thus, the children of Aunt Milla turn to political activism, emigration, or succumb to poor health because of conditions in the German family. These desertions from normal German life are positive alternatives in the story if one considers that their other choice is to accept permanent social deceit.

In order to make his criticism more analytical and historically accurate, Böll departs momentarily from the tradition of satire that conventionally makes no claim to fairness. In fact, satire is normally the least objective of all literary genres because its intention is to present a revealing insight into the condition of society; therefore, it makes no pretense of equity nor claim of realism, relying instead on disproportion either as overstatement or understatement. Such methods are justified in satire because its purpose is not to offer solutions to social problems, but only to point out what the problems of society are.

In "Christmas Not Just Once a Year," Böll departs from the normal exaggeration of satire to tender a fuller view of reality. Although he never accepted the idea of collective guilt in relation to the Hitler period, he did accept the term in relationship to Germany in the postwar period after the currency reform of 1948, when most Germans rushed into the economic miracle at the expense of the past. In the essay "Hierzulande," 1960 (In This Country), he claimed, "If there is anything like collective guilt in this land, then it starts with the moment of currency reform when the sellout of suffering, sadness, and memory began" (*WESR [Werke: Essayistische Schriften und Reden]* 1: 374). And in the same essay he declared with outrage, "Whoever has memory that goes back ten years is considered sick and deserves to be put in a deep sleep so that he can wake up strengthened for the present" (*WESR* 1:

333). Nonetheless, Böll still knew that not all Germans were guilty of even the postwar coverup. Thus, he provides Aunt Milla's family with a symbolic redeeming member in Cousin Franz, whose function in the satire is to act as a foil to his tyrannical aunt. He is a typical Böllian black sheep, a boxer with an inclination to piety. He warns the family from the beginning of the "terrible consequences" (*WRE* 2: 11) of permanent Christmas and is fully aware that what appears to be "'in itself' a harmless event" (*WRE* 2: 11) is in reality a dangerous undertaking.

At no time does Cousin Franz personally take part in the celebrations. He even enhances his unpopularity in the family by suggesting that his screaming mother be subjected to an exorcism or committed to an institution. In this detail Böll points out his view that the refusal to confront the past is, indeed, a devilish obsession or, as a case of willful amnesia, a form of mental illness. Because Cousin Franz as a young man was a mediocre student, became a boxer, and associated with questionable companions, he "possessed . . . too little reputation for the relatives to listen to him" (*WRE* 2: 12). The family considers him of unreliable character and treats him as an outsider. Cousin Franz exemplifies a type common in Böll's stories, the ethical asocial individual. His life is a model of humanity. During the war he treated Polish and Russian POW's with kindness, and after the war he reluctantly assumes the role of a prophet, of one crying out in the wilderness, warning his relatives of the dangers of catering to escapism; later he even intervenes to save Lucie's and Karl's children. However, at the conclusion of the story, he retreats to a monastery to continue his battle to save his German family by other means. He dons a monk's habit and turns to prayer, accepting the fateful conclusion, "We are punished by life" (*WRE* 2: 34).

It is typical of Böll in these early years that he puts religion and the church in a favorable light. Besides Cousin Franz, two clerics, a pastor, and a chaplain refuse to take part in the daily Christmas celebrations. But in the prelate who cooperates with the family, one sees the earliest example of Böll's criticism of the church. Also, the manner in which the wealth of the family determines the institutional church's treatment of the pastor and chaplain reveals Böll's belief that the wealthy bourgeois class influences the church as it does the state. Also implied is Böll's belief that it is the wealthy who benefit most from a society with a façade that conceals the relationship of the present to the fascist past. Erhard Friedrichsmeyer's analysis of the satire also supports this interpretation. He concludes, "Reactionary tendencies establish themselves so that parallels begin to develop between the fascism of the past and growth-obsessed capitalism (*Leistungskapitalismus*)" of the present (60).

Uncle Franz, because of his wealth, has connections in the hierarchy of the church; he sees that charges are brought against the pastor and the chaplain for their "neglect of pastoral duties" (*WRE* 2: 23). Although the two clerics are exonerated in the canonical court, the incident reveals a working relationship between the financially powerful and the church hierarchy. Through this relationship, Böll's story shows that the church shares in the guilt of the postwar repression of the past by its failure to provide moral leadership, or, in the words of the story, begins to share in the responsibility for the "mildew of decay" (*WRE* 2: 11) developing in the heart of West German society.

By being balanced in his presentation, Böll departs from the tradition of satire, but he also deviates from satirical practice in yet another way. He uses satire not only to criticize but also to analyze social reality. Each character has a parabolic role in relationship to the permanent Christmas, and the players fall into more than two camps: those for and those against the celebrations, those who cooperate and those who do not. Within the family only Aunt Milla is totally dedicated to the restoration of "the good old days." She feels no remorse nor does she demonstrate any recognition of the consequences of her actions. Therefore, her physical health is not endangered by the repression of the recent past, "Only my Aunt Milla enjoyed the best of health, smiled, is well and happy as she almost always was" (*WRE* 2: 12). Aunt Milla, therefore, represents the people who see nothing wrong with the years 1933–1945, except that the war years after 1939 began to endanger their Christmases.

For other persons not in this category of the willfully deceived, the repression of the past produces psychological disturbances, family divisions, and generational animosity with undesirable social effects. If such are the negative results of the permanent Christmas, the reader must ask why one would begin—much less continue—such a practice. The answer is indicated in the story. At first the extension of Christmas seemed "'in itself' harmless" (*WRE* 2: 16). "The terrible consequences" (*WRE* 2: 11) were not foreseeable (except by Cousin Franz, to whom no one listened). It was easier to cooperate

with the celebrations than to oppose them because the "costs" were not immediately obvious. It was also an easy way to achieve normality, for, as the narrator states, "Everything seemed to be in order" (*WRE* 2: 20).

The story speaks to the German social situation in the 1990s as effectively as it did in 1951. The current desire of Germans for normality in relationship to the Hitler period and, since unification, in relationship to the crimes of the Stalinists in the former German Democratic Republic is again a major issue of contention with philosophers, historians, politicians, journalists, and intellectuals. Their debate centers on the uniqueness or commonplaceness of Germany's aberrations. In this climate, Böll's formulation of the problem in "Christmas Not Just Once a Year" gives the story a continuing actuality.

Furthermore, the satire suggests a close connection between the repression of the past and the headlong rush into the economic boom. It implies that the more one wants to do away with the unpleasantnesses of recent history, the more one must lose oneself in frantic economic activity. Uncle Franz, representative of the entrepreneur class, is forced to earn more, increase his profits, participate in the *Leistungsgesellschaft* (performance society) in direct proportion to his cooperation with the needs of permanent Christmas.

Böll's satire is effective for at least two reasons. The first derives from the technique of exaggeration used to execute the author's idea and the second from the choice of permanent Christmas as a symbol to represent the theme. While the election of the dual perspective of Aunt Milla's nephew with its advantage of intimacy and objectivity, involvement and detachment, has already been mentioned, this point of view also performs another aesthetic service. The teller of the story is not consciously committed to any of the factions within the family. He tries to be neutral in his presentation, friendly with all, sympathetic to everyone. He sees with the aunt's, uncle's, and the cousins' eyes. He even ends his story with a visit to Cousin Franz in the monastery. This middle position of the narrator (although in reality he is somewhat more sympathetic to Aunt Milla's generation than to her children's) reduces the unpleasant didacticism and overbearing seriousness satire can often have. The narrator's stance aestheticizes and socializes the aggression inherent in the satire by the principle of indirection.

The technique of exaggeration deserves further mention in relation to Böll's development as a satirist because it was his first use of a method that later proved so successful and simple for him to apply that he gave it up as no longer challenging. That is the principle of *executio ad absurdum,* the carrying out of the details of a story to their ultimate self-parodying conclusion. Böll explained this method in a conversation with Karin Struck: "In essence writing a satire is nothing but the development of a very simple mathematical formula, let's say, a plus b in parentheses, squared. A basic idea consistently exaggerated until it can't be exaggerated any more, then you have a satire. To to do that you need imagination, not information" (*WI [Werke: Interviews]* 1: 67).

In "Christmas Not Just Once a Year," this technique is seen in the details of the daily celebration, in the effort to prolong the life of the tree, the itemization of the daily cost of providing the feast, the replacing of the children with wax figures and the hiring of the actors to replace the adults, the sending of the children to cut trees in the state park, the bribing of officials to get out-of-season items, the melting of the candies on the tree in the summer heat, and the angels' constant whispering of "peace, peace." Klaus Jeziorkowski refers to this process in Böll's satires as "a mass of details, nonsense, scurrility, and fantasy" stabilized by a "precise calculated static framework of inner form" (13). The success of Böll's method as employed in "Christmas Not Just Once a Year" and in most of the other satires of the fifties—first-person narrator with a tendency to confessional revelation and the accumulation of details leading to an absurd conclusion—is no doubt the formula that Böll had in mind when he explained in an interview with Marcel Reich-Ranicki in 1967 why he wrote so few short stores in the sixties: "Probably it is a weariness with my own ability. I would like to make the short story the middle point of my work again. But when I try it, I fall again and again into the same pattern. I'm making every effort to change this. Perhaps I will be successful. The short story is still the most beautiful of all prose forms" (*WI [Werke: Interviews]* 1: 67).

In fact Böll published few short stories after the fifties, together no more than about twenty-one are spread throughout various books; about half of these could be called satires, the best of which are "Anekdote zur Senkung der Arbeitsmoral," 1963 ("Anecdote Concerning the Lowering of Productivity"), "Veränderungen in Staech," 1969 ("The Staech Affair"), "Epilog zu Stifters 'Nachsommer'" 1970 (Epilogue to Stifter's *Indian Summer*), "Berichte zur Gesinnunglsage der Nation," 1975 (Report on the Attitudinal State of the Nation), and "Erwünschte Reportage," 1975 (A Desired Report).

The second reason for the effectiveness of "Christmas" is that the symbol of Christmas is timeless. Most satire has a short life because of its usual relationship to rapidly changing current affairs. Böll's story, on the contrary, remains alive because in it he chose to criticize conditions which, though specifically German, still retain a general validity. In the choice of Christmas and the critique of "the good old days," Böll created a certain universality, which transcends the single interpretation of Germany's desire to forget its Nazi past. The story can, in fact, be read with equal application in any country where for political, economic, or psychological reasons a shameful national past has not been adequately dealt with. In such a country where national policy is changed out of opportunism or expediency, where the perpetrators of injustice assume the role of victims. "Christmas Not Just Once a Year" will be rewarding reading. Erwin Theodor Rosentahl makes this point about Böll's popularity in Brazil, "Böll's works are received in Brazil as contemporary critical observations which do not apply exclusively to Germany, but to the entire Western world (and perhaps not only there!)" (150). In "Nicht nut zur Weihnachtszeit" Böll created not only a national classic but a satire for all ages.

Source: Robert C. Conrad, "The Satires," in *Understanding Heinrich Böll,* University of South Carolina Press, 1992, pp. 34–51.

James D. Wehs

in the following essay, Wehs argues that "Böll describes the process of reification [dehumanization] that has crept into . . . the family."

Introduction

Heinrich Böll's short story "Not only at Christmastime" depicts the inherent dangers of the expanding phenomenon or depersonalization in modern society. In this particular narrative, Böll describes the process of reification that has crept into, what has traditionally been considered, the most sacrosanct of all human institutions: the family. Reification is, in essence, a process of dehumanization which is not entirely new in the annals of human kind. While its ramifications were a by-product of the human condition at all stages of man's evolution, its manifestation within the technological era has asserted itself in a position of dominance. Kafka, one of the leading spokesmen of alienation in modern times depicts the process of dehumanization in *Metamorphosis* where the hero, Gregor Samsa, who is deprived of human dignity and respect, turns into a disposable object. This process which goes hand in hand with loss of identity is also the dominant theme in Böll's writings in general and in the work under discussion here in particular.

Aunt Milla: Prototype of the Collective Denial of Reality

In "Not only at Christmastime" Böll protests against the unconscionable attempts of the Germans to blot out the memories of the past seven years after the end of World War II. The religious feast of Christmas which is meant to lead to reflection and introspection is exposed in its current form as superficial hypocrisy. The narrator in this particular story remains unnamed and *sub rosa*. This is psychologically relevant because the narrator entrenches himself at the safe distance of a 'splendid isolation.' This vantage ground enables him to depict this quasi Kafkaesque absurdity with some sort of psychic equanimity. The anonymity of the narrator in turn reflects upon the post-war mentality of the collective German psyche. To this day, the average German denies active participation in and knowledge of the atrocities perpetrated by the leaders of the Third Reich.

Immediately after the war (1946), Aunt Milla, the central figure of the narrator's family, is captivated by the obsessive compulsion that Christmas be celebrated not only in its old form, exactly as it was before 1939, but every single day of the year. "The destruction of the city is completely forgotten by this preoccupation with the destroyed cult of Christmas. Aunt Milla, the 'heroine' of the satire, has completely lost the basic religious significance of Christmas." What, at first glance, seems to be an odd fixation or better, the whimsical caprice of an aging lady, reveals itself as the psychotic behavior pattern of an entire society in the throes of mental imbalance. Aunt Milla is a caricature of the conventional Catholic who is oblivious of the essential content of Christianity and concentrates instead on rituals and traditions to which the average person can no longer meaningfully relate, but which are nevertheless kept alive and supported by the clergy for an appropriate remuneration. Böll's struggle against institutionalized religion is extended to cover the fundamental conceptions of man's freedom and spontaneity as well. In his works *The Clown* and *My Sad Face* the members of the institution face a similar dilemma, namely, that the essence of their cause is in danger of being lost and eventually replaced by ritual and decorous veneer. In "Not only at Christmastime" Böll goes one step further by attacking the nucleus of society itself: the family, whose members are no longer guided by spontaneous love but rather by ceremonious and compulsive 'get-togethers.'

This theme of familial alienation, which eventually leads to reification, has been explored at length by various German authors. Gerhart Hauptmann's drama *Das Friedensfest* (the Peace Party) depicts a family which feels itself called together by duty rather than love. However, the compulsive attitude of the individual family members is the only unifying factor at this ominous reunion which eventually produces a tragedy as it becomes clear that even the formal ritual of Christmas cannot suppress the hateful ambivalences that fill the air at the time when the "Prince of Peace" is to be ushered in. Compulsion within an etiology of affective deprivation generally leads not only to a loss of individual freedom for all participants in human institutional and organizational activity, but to a simultaneous spiritual and emotional retreat as well.

In "Not only at Christmastime," Christianity is portrayed in the negative light of routine and deception. In no uncertain terms, Böll takes issue with the superficial existence of family life. If man cannot truly identify with those who are closest to him, he is equally unable to find roots in the broader spectrum of his existence. "The deep alienation between man and his world becomes most clear in the nonsensical variety of unimportant and unrelated details of which a major portion of visible reality is comprised."

The narrator in this work retains a tichoscopic distance as does the narrator in Böll's *My Sad Face*. In spite of this, he manages to give us an insider's intimate view of a family's slowly progressing demise. This is a technical device, borrowed from the classical Greek drama, by means of which the narrator assumes an intrinsic role within the setup he describes, his otherwise passive stance notwithstanding. However, in this particular case, the narrator is not only the passive bystander but he is also a victim of circumstances in spite of his sarcastic wit and subtle tongue-in-cheek propensity. "The technique of presenting a contemporary scenario with satirical sidelights is something of which Heinrich

Böll is an absolute master. He effectively employs the perspective of the narrator who, in "Not only at Christmastime," apparently declares himself one with the family in order to heighten the assurance that it will be made laughable." Thus it is through the eyes of an 'insider' that we gain access to the manipulations of Aunt Milla as well as the bizarre reactions of the family members she is trying to dominate.

Cousin Lucie is the first family member who falls victim to Aunt Milla's machinations. Compelled to participate in the Christmas festivities which, on Aunt Milla's insistence, take place every evening of the year (!) Lucie suffers a nervous breakdown. Böll's opinion that states as well as institutions have the historical tendency to misuse, abuse, and alienate people is here extended in an alarming manner to the family as the nucleus of organized life per se. Cousin Lucie's mental breakdown and her recovery in an asylum are depicted against the backdrop of psychic bewilderment, retrogression, and chaos. After her release from the asylum and return to the family, she undergoes a drastic change. The narrator informs us Lucie now hangs out exclusively in bars. She wears smart slacks, colorful sweaters, runs around in sandals and has cut off her stunning hair in favor of a pony tail. Although he has not observed any public immorality in her case, only a certain exaltation, which one could perhaps designate as Existentialism, in spite of this he is not happy about this development.

On the other hand, cousin Franz is portrayed as the 'black sheep' of the family. Franz is the only one capable of genuine human emotions and understanding. Early in life he had distanced himself from the family because their hypocrisy was more than he could tolerate. "He met with questionable companions in remote parks and vegetated areas of a suburban nature. There they practiced the stringent rules of boxing without being worried that their humanistic inheritance was being neglected." However, it is the pugilist Franz who, in the end, rejects the world of the flesh and enters a monestary. He "excluded himself from certain festivities . . . called it all rubbish and nonsense, . . . declined to participate in activities which would contribute to the preservation of the same. But . . . he carried too little weight in the family to have any influence."

In Böll's first post-war narratives and novels, he always depicts the 'little man,' his helplessness and isolation amidst the tragic fate thrust upon him by the war and its consequences. In "Not only at

> "Böll's opinion that states as well as institutions have the historical tendency to misuse, abuse, and alienate people is here extended in an alarming manner to the family as the nucleus of organized life per se."

Christmastime" he portrays, for the first time, an entire family in the throes of alienation and its devastating effects. Religion, which is under normal circumstances considered to be a contributory factor to family life and family solidarity, is no longer capable of serving this traditional purpose as it has lost its inherent mythopoesis and is now kept alive by the artificial stimulation of commercial incentives. This decline of truly religious values is manifest in the displacement of the fundamental pastoral message for the sake of veneer and public consumption. In Böll's own words: "The main attraction on Aunt Milla's Christmas tree were glass dwarfs which held cork-shaped hammers in their upraised arms and had bell-shaped anvils at their feet."

After several months of daily Christmas festivities, everything develops into a properly organized business enterprise, and it gradually becomes apparent that all family members—excepting of course Aunt Milla—are feeling more and more alienated by their preposterous activities. Thus, one by one, they concoct devious ways to remove themselves from the scene of religious mockery. In the end, the entire scene is transmogrified into a showcase of deception and illusion. The religious content of Christmas now moves into the background as the brute manipulations of material gain and greed occupy a front seat in the limelight of a ritual depleted of its genuine content. The Priest finds a substitute, a pensioned Chaplain, to replace him for adequate remuneration. Even the importer of Aunt Milla's Christmas trees, which have to be regularly replaced, especially in the summer months, smuggles his product into Germany. This psychotic state of affairs is turned into a flourishing enterprise. In this complete reorganization of a once solid family structure, the sign 'business as usual' dominates the scene.

Böll's portrayal of a declining family is a reflection of the West German society immediately after the war. The readiness of the nation to blot out the atrocities of the Third Reich from the collective anamnesia and to carry on 'business as usual' is here subject to Böll's vituperative attack against the deceptive machinations of the German collective psyche.

The husband of Aunt Milla, Uncle Franz, who plays the role of head of the house, is described as a "genuinely good person." But he too gradually falls prey to the entire scenario. Always the representative of respectability, Uncle Franz initially rejects his son Franz, the 'black sheep' of the family, who exposes the show of religious hypocrisy. After several months, however, even Uncle Franz refuses to attend the endless Christmas celebrations and takes on a young mistress for the satisfaction of his biological needs. On this stage of deterioration of a formerly solid German family, he is no longer affected by the whispers, rumors, and accusations of adultery. "He insists on his right to live in relationships and conditions which can only be seen as exceptions to the prevailing moral code."

It is also Uncle Franz who hits upon the idea to let himself be represented by an actor. This is so spectacularly successful that other family members make the decision to follow suit. "A precise plan has been devised, which is called the 'game-plan' in the family. The actors are more than pleased to play their roles as various family members, because they can earn some extra money and it has also been discovered that there is no lack of unemployment among actors." Everybody is now so estranged from the empty daily Christmas ritual that actors are engaged to substitute for all participants of the family. The ironic side effect of this exaggerated ritualistic cult which now represents the once venerated but now alienated message of love and peace, leads to the unmasking of the spiritual, religious downfall of formerly highly treasured cultural values. Böll's inexorable search for a meaningful renewal of the spirit of Christmas is not only aimed at the adult population. The children too are affected by the so-called 'blessings' of an affluent society. This merciless, if not to say, mercenary retrogression along the entire front of the collective psyche lends the entire setting a clownlike appearance as the children are now represented by wax replicas at the daily Christmas party. The business rationale that everything has a price tag, that everything can be systematically organized and manipulated regardless of the human component is the bone of contention in Böll's "Not only at Christmastime." The vaning human involvement in an age dominated by the computerized Golem is an additional point in question in this process of reification. If the process leads to a negation of man's uniqueness, then only loss of humanity and alienation remain the ineluctable consequences. Böll's contemporary Hermann Kosack sounds a similar alarm in his short story "Der mechanische Doppelgänger" (The Mechanical Double). Kosack's robot can be so minutely programmed that the borderline between man and machine is in danger of being wiped out. Man's dilemma is then not only of becoming a machine but of the machine becoming assuming human shape.

Conclusion

In "Not only at Christmastime," Heinrich Böll warns us of the perils of dehumanization. If we can recognize and identify them, their possible effect can be considerably reduced. The ultimate denigration of the human species is symbolically represented by the wax replicas of the children. This process of dehumanization and reification constitutes the *Leitmotif* in this work in particular and in Böll's writings in general. Böll reminds us that spiritual alienation and dehumanization are but the stepping stones leading to the general decline of man the individual in particular and of human kind in general.

Source: James D. Wehs, "Symbolic Reification in Heinrich Böll's 'Not Only at Christmastime,'" in *Journal of Evolutionary Psychology*, Vol. 1, No. 1, June 1979, pp. 40–45.

Sources

Berkley, Miriam, "Böll's Stories Mark German Culture Reborn," Review of *The Stories of Heinrich Böll*, in *Chicago Tribune*, March 23, 1986, sec. 14 (Books), p. 37.

Conard, Robert C., *Understanding Heinrich Böll*, University of South Carolina Press, 1992.

Friedrichsmeyer, Erhard, "Böll's Satires," in *University of Dayton Review*, Vol. 10, No. 2, Fall 1973, pp. 5–10.

Goldhagen, Daniel J., *Hitler's Willing Executioners: Ordinary Germans and the Holocaust*, Knopf, 1996.

Heskett, Michael, Review of *The Stories of Heinrich Böll*, in *Houston Chronicle*, January 12, 1986, p. 24.

Huber, Lothar, "Introduction," in *University of Dayton Review*, Vol. 24, No. 3, Summer 1997, pp. 3–5.

Klapper, John, "The Art of Aggression and Its Limitations: The Early Satires," in *The Narrative Fiction of Heinrich Böll*, edited by Michael Butler, Cambridge University Press, 1994, pp. 70–88.

Reid, J. H., *Heinrich Böll: A German for His Time*, Oswald Wolff Books, 1988.

Scammell, Michael, Review of *The Stories of Heinrich Böll*, in *Los Angeles Times*, March 30, 1986, p. 3 (in The Book Review).

Stewart, Keith, "The American Reviews of Heinrich Böll: A Note on the Problems of the Compassionate Novelist," in *University of Dayton Review*. Vol. 11, No. 2, Winter 1974, pp. 5–10.

Zachau, Reinhard K., *Heinrich Böll: Forty Years of Criticism*, Camden House, 1994.

Further Reading

Burleigh, Michael, *The Third Reich: A New History*, Hill & Wang, 2001.
    Burleigh focuses on the systematic breakdown of German society that ultimately led to Hitler's rise to power. The book paints a picture of a people so desperate for prosperity and identity that they gradually and consistently ignored their conscience while their country pursued those goals at a great human cost.

Conard, Robert C., *Understanding Heinrich Böll*, University of South Carolina Press, 1992.
    Conard is considered one of the foremost experts on Böll's writing, and he provides a comprehensive overview of Böll war stories, satires, and major novels.

Goldhagen, Daniel J., *Hitler's Willing Executioners: Ordinary Germans and the Holocaust*, Knopf, 1996.
    Goldhagen caused a huge stir in the United States and in Germany with the publication of this book. He argues that the extent to which ordinary Germans knew of the genocidal acts of the Nazi government was far greater than had previously been acknowledged and that hundreds of thousands of Germans were directly aware of the death camps and other aspects of the Holocaust.

Reid, J. H., *Heinrich Böll: A German for His Time*, Oswald Wolff Books, 1988.
    Reid was one of Böll's earliest biographers. This biography, published a few years after Böll's death, is perhaps the most comprehensive study of Böll's life yet published in English. Of particular note is the chapter "Years of Hope (1949–1955)," which covers the years of Böll's early literary life when "Christmas Not Just Once a Year" was written and first published.

Sebald, W. G., *On the Natural History of Destruction*, Random House, 2003.
    The four essays in this collection address the themes of memory and survival in the context of the violent era of postwar Germany. The essay "Air War and Literature," in which Sebald criticizes the silence of German writers on the starvation, mutilations, and killings caused by Allied bombings, provoked great controversy in Germany when it was first published in 1999, an indication that the country had not yet fully healed itself of the war's aftereffects.

Zachau, Reinhard K., *Heinrich Böll: Forty Years of Criticism*, Camden House, 1994.
    Böll's fame as a writer extended beyond Germany to England and the former eastern bloc countries, as well as to the United States. Zachau provides an overview of how Böll's work was received by critics in those countries. The book also includes an extensive bibliography of critical articles on Böll's work.

A Great Day

Frank Sargeson

1940

"A Great Day," a short story by New Zealand writer Frank Sargeson, was first published in Sargeson's collection of stories *A Man and His Wife* (Christchurch, New Zealand, 1940). It was reprinted in Sargeson's *Collected Stories* in 1964 (reprinted, 1965).

Sargeson is one of New Zealand's best-known writers. Beginning in the 1930s, he was instrumental in creating a genuine New Zealand literature that was not derived from British or American models. He deliberately avoided using literary English, and most of his stories, which are often told in the first person, sound like an ordinary person speaking naturally.

"A Great Day" is one of Sargeson's most admired stories. This short tale of an early morning fishing trip undertaken by two friends culminates in a shocking, and surprising, act of violence and betrayal. The story illustrates the spare, compressed nature of Sargeson's art (almost all his stories are very short), as well as his use of informal, colloquial language and working-class characters. In "A Great Day," Sargeson avoids any overt moralizing and leaves the story to speak for itself, inserting many subtle clues within the text to enable the reader to make sense of the final incident.

Author Biography

Frank Sargeson was born on March 23, 1903, in Hamilton, New Zealand. His father was a store-keeper and later the town clerk, and Frank was the second of his four children. After leaving school, Sargeson worked in a Hamilton law office and studied for his law degree. In 1925, he left home for Auckland, where he lived in a small house owned by his father in Takapuna, and the following year he was admitted as a solicitor. After returning from a long visit to England, he found routine work as a clerk for the New Zealand Public Trust in Wellington, from 1928 to 1929. During his spare time, he wrote several short stories.

Depressed by his job, which did not suit him, Sargeson decided to pursue a career as a writer. In 1929, he went to live with his uncle on a farm in Okahakura, where he wrote a novel but failed to get it published. In 1931, he returned to Takapuna and registered as unemployed. During the depression, Sargeson worked at various manual jobs and continued to write short stories and articles. His first published story appeared in the journal *Tomorrow* in 1935, and in 1936 his first collection of stories, *Conversation with My Uncle and Other Sketches*, was published in Auckland.

Ill health prevented Sargeson from serving in World War II, and he received a government invalidity benefit, which enabled him to continue his writing. His second collection of short stories, which included "A Great Day," was *A Man and His Wife*, published in 1940. One of the stories, "The Making of a New Zealander," won the Centennial Literary Competition Prize, and Sargeson's reputation as a fresh voice in New Zealand literature began to grow.

Sargeson's first novel, *When the Wind Blows*, appeared in 1945 and was followed by another short story collection, *That Summer and Other Stories* (1946), and the novel *I Saw in My Dream* (1949). During the 1950s, despite his comparatively small output, Sargeson was regarded as one of New Zealand's finest and most original writers. The publication of his *Collected Stories* in 1964 cemented his reputation, and the remainder of that decade saw the publication of three more Sargeson novels: *Memoirs of a Peon* (1965), *The Hangover* (1967), and *Joy of the Worm* (1969).

Sargeson also wrote several plays, two of which were published in *Wrestling with the Angel* (1964): *A Time for Sowing*, first produced in Auckland in

Frank Sargeson

1961, and *The Cradle and the Egg*, first produced in Auckland in 1962.

Continuing to write well into his seventies, Sargeson published *Man of England Now* in 1972, which contained the novellas *I for One* and *A Game of Hide and Seek*. He also wrote the novel *Sunset Village* (1976) and two memoirs, *Once Is Enough: A Memoir* (1972) and *More Than Enough: A Memoir* (1975). His last work was *En Route*, which was published in 1979 in the book *Tandem* (which also included *The Chain* by Edith Campion).

Sargeson died on March 1, 1982. His *Conversation in a Train and Other Critical Writing* was published posthumously by Oxford University Press in 1983.

Plot Summary

"A Great Day" begins with two friends, Ken and Fred, getting up just before dawn and preparing for a fishing trip. Ken leaves his "bach" (a small, cabin-style house) and carries their dinghy down to the beach. Fred follows with the rest of the gear. The tide is halfway out and the beach is deserted. As they get in the dinghy and begin rowing, the sun comes up, and it looks as if it is going to be a great day. There is not a cloud in the sky.

They head for an island where they have been before. Ken finds the rowing easy, since he is the bigger and stronger of the two men. During the trip, Fred discusses the hardships of being out of work. Ken is also out of work, but life is easier for him because he has some savings and lives rent-free with his aunt. He also has an education, which makes it easier for him to find work. Fred, on the other hand, is a member of the working class. It is he who does most of the talking, and some of his remarks sound strange. He talks, for example, about how men grow old and die and a man might as well die now as at any other time.

About halfway to the island, less than two miles from the shore, Fred says they have gone far enough. They drop anchor and begin to fish. Fred remarks on the fact that Ken has never learned to swim. But Ken replies that this does not bother him, especially on such a calm, still day. They both get bites on their fishing lines, which are crossed. Ken's catch is a very small fish, and Fred throws it back. They put fresh bait on their hooks and try again, but with no success. Fred persuades Ken that they should head for a submerged reef at the end of the island. On the reef they will be able to stand in water up to their knees and pull up the mussels, which could then be used for much more effective bait.

They start out for the end of the island. A wind comes up and the sea starts to get a little choppy. Fred mentions a girl called Mary, whom he has known for years. It appears that they were great friends, but her family fell on hard times, and she had to take up a position as a domestic help. She now lives with Ken's aunt.

Fred looks back at the shore, which is deserted. There is no one else coming out fishing. He puts cotton wool into his ears, saying that he will suffer from earache if he gets spray in his ears.

They reach the end of the island, which is uninhabited. Fred maneuvers the dinghy, and they find the reef. It is several hundred yards out, with deep water all around it. Fred gets out of the dinghy and stands on the reef. The water comes up to his knees and sometimes higher because of the choppy sea. While Ken holds the dinghy steady, Fred pulls up mussels and throws them into the dinghy. After a while, Ken takes over while Fred holds the dinghy. But then Fred shoves the dinghy off and hops into it. He pulls away from the reef, his eyes shut. With the

cotton wool in his ears, it is difficult for him to hear. Halfway back to the shore, he stops for a rest. Then he gathers his strength and capsizes the dinghy. After that he starts on the long swim back to the shore.

Characters

Fred

Fred is Ken's friend and accompanies him on their fishing trip. He is a small, slightly built man, with short legs. He seems to lack self-esteem and refers to himself disparagingly as a "joker." He probably feels that he is a failure in life, and he envies those he perceives to be more successful and attractive than he is. He dresses shabbily, and his old clothes, which he has purchased secondhand, do not fit him properly. Fred is neither strong nor physically fit. When he first rows out from the shore, progress is very slow, and he does not keep the dinghy on course. On the reef, a few minutes' work pulling up mussels leaves him badly out of breath.

A working-class man, Fred lost his job and has been unemployed for some time. He survives on "sustenance," which means a tiny government benefit, which he supplements by selling the fish he catches. But this does little to alleviate his financial anxieties. He lives in a small cabin for which he must pay rent. Fred is uneducated, unlike Ken, with whom he has little in common. Fred is full of envy of the easier, more successful life that he thinks Ken enjoys. He envies Ken's muscular body and his greater success with women. Fred's envy seems to center on a woman named Mary. They used to be the closest of friends, but now Mary is in domestic service at the home of Ken's aunt, where Ken himself lives. Perhaps it is this loss of Mary that provides the final impetus for Fred to plan his spiteful, unprovoked murder. He reveals himself to be a petty, cold, calculating man, who lacks any positive feeling for a man who is supposed to be his friend.

Ken

Ken is Fred's companion on the fishing trip. He is the opposite of Fred in almost every way. About the only thing they have in common is that they both smoke cigarettes. Ken is better educated than Fred. He is also physically superior, being over six feet tall and strongly built. He rows far better than Fred could ever hope to do. Ken also, according to Fred, does well with the ladies. Although Ken, like Fred, is also out of work, his financial situation is not as difficult as Fred's. He regards his time out of work as a holiday. Living with his aunt, he does not have to pay rent, and he also has savings. His one apparent weakness, which Fred ruthlessly exploits, is that he never learned to swim. He says that he has had no need to do so, since he has lived mostly in country towns. Ken regards his companion as somewhat odd, because of some of the remarks Fred makes, but he never for a moment suspects the cold malice with which Fred regards him.

Themes

Envy

Fred is envious of Ken, and it is this that fuels his undeclared hatred of his companion. Fred envies everything Ken has that he does not. This includes physical attributes. Ken, who wears only shorts and a shirt in the boat, is bigger and stronger than the scrawny Fred, who keeps his body covered. "I wish I had your body," Fred says as they are rowing. He refers to Ken's physique more than once, as in "a big hefty bloke like you" and "that big frame of yours." It is as if he is obsessed with Ken's physical superiority.

In his conversation with Ken as they row out to the island, Fred manages to disguise his envy, and Ken appears not to be aware of it. When Fred points out that Ken is better off financially than he—Fred—is and that he has savings and does not have to pay rent, he speaks in an easy, conversational style that does not reveal what must be his true thoughts about the matter. But he cannot get over the fact that Ken has so many advantages in life: "[I]f a man's been to one of those High Schools it makes him different," he says. Although he does not acknowledge to Ken that an educated man is better than one without education, he must secretly feel that this is so. It is clear that the working-class Fred suffers from class envy, since Ken appears to be from the educated middle class.

Vengeance

In addition to the envy that Fred feels, he may also have a specific grievance against Ken. This concerns the woman Mary. Mary appears to have been Fred's best friend, and he feels he has lost her

since she went into domestic service with Ken's aunt. Presumably, Fred's access to her is now limited, whereas Ken, since he is living in the same house, may have supplanted Fred in her affections. Little is said explicitly, but Fred repeatedly hints that Ken has more success with women than he does—another source of envy—so possibly, in Fred's mind, Ken may have stolen his woman. Ken indicates that he is fully aware that Fred and Mary were close: "So I've gathered," he says, which may indicate that Fred has pointed it out to him many times before but more likely indicates that Mary herself explained it to him, which does suggest that he and Mary are on at least familiar, if not intimate, terms. This suggestion of sexual jealousy would provide Fred with a direct motivation for his crime, a motivation far more potent than simply a general feeling of envy. Fred's sexual jealousy of Ken would also make sense of Fred's apparent obsession with Ken's superior physique. He feels invalidated by Ken's masculinity and implied sexual vigor, and the sight of his body is a continual goad to the undersized Fred, with his pervasive feelings of inferiority.

Style

Irony and Foreshadowing

Fred's conversation with Ken appears innocuous until he commits his shocking act of betrayal. The reader then realizes that there is a dark significance lying behind almost everything Fred says. His words are ironic in the sense that they have a hidden meaning that Fred is aware of but that is not apparent to Ken. The discussion about the fact that Ken cannot swim, for example, does not sound out of the ordinary. The malice behind Fred's words is not apparent until it becomes clear what he has been planning all along. When Fred raises the subject of death and dying, it seems to develop quite innocently out of the conversation, and his comment "It might as well be now as anytime, mightn't it?" sounds like nothing more than a harmless philosophical observation, but in fact it reeks with malice. Another apparently innocent remark comes when Fred throws the tiny fish back. "But don't you wish you could swim like that?" he says to Ken. His remark, "Wouldn't you like to stay out here for good?" has a similar biting significance, known only to him. This doubling of meaning can also be

Topics for Further Study

- Most of Sargeson's stories are told from the first-person point of view, but "A Great Day" has a third-person narrator. Why did Sargeson choose this method? Could the story have been told in the first person? How would that have changed the story?

- Compare the way Sargeson uses language in "A Great Day" with a typical story by Ernest Hemingway, such as "The Happy Life of Francis Macomber," "The Killers," or "Hills Like White Elephants." What qualities do these two writers appear to share?

- Research the effect on men of long-term unemployment. To what extent do men acquire meaning in their lives, and a sense of identity, from their work? Could Fred's long-term unemployment have contributed to the twisted nature of his mind?

- Sargeson's stories are often preoccupied with violence, isolation, squalor, and death. He said that this merely reflected the spiritual impoverishment of New Zealand society. Bearing this in mind, should literature reflect what is in society, or should it try to improve society? Does a violent story like "A Great Day" have a good or bad effect on the person who reads it?

---

seen in the title of the story: It is a "great day" for fishing, but also a great day for murder.

The veiled irony in Fred's words suggests an aspect of his character. He appears to be a man who represses his real feelings. He pretends to be a "mate" of Ken's, and he appears on the surface to be amiable and friendly. But underneath that false exterior, Fred seethes with envy, resentment, and hatred. These repressed emotions build up relentlessly until they create the desire to commit murder.

Setting

The setting is described in a way that creates a sense of eeriness, as if the reader were being taken beyond the normal world of people and human relationships into something timeless and strange. In the very early morning, the sea is absolutely calm, and nothing moves except some seagulls. The passage that follows creates the necessary atmosphere in which a violent act that breaks the natural bond between two people can take place: "It was so still it wasn't natural. Except for the seagulls you'd have thought the world had died in the night." Later in the morning, a wind comes up and the sea becomes choppy. The movement from almost surreal calm to rough seas is an appropriate buildup to the violent climax.

Colloquial Language

Sargeson is known for using colloquial language, including slang, in his stories, which was part of what marked his work as a new development in New Zealand literature at the time. Slang expressions include "bloke" (the rough equivalent of "guy" in modern American usage, and a common, usually working-class term in New Zealand today); "bob," which is slang for a shilling, a unit of currency; "tucker," which means food; and "cobbers," which means pals, as in "Mary and I used to be great cobbers." "Bust your boiler" means roughly "strain yourself without too much effort," and a "spell" means a rest.

Historical Context

The Great Depression

New Zealand was badly affected by the Great Depression. In the early to mid-1930s, unemployment reached 12 percent (including Ken and Fred in "A Great Day"); the national income fell 40 percent from 150 million NZD (New Zealand dollars) to 90 million NZD, and the value of exports also fell by 40 percent. The government was forced to cut pen-

Compare & Contrast

- **1930s:** New Zealand literature in English enters a fruitful period. A distinct New Zealand voice begins to emerge, and poetry, the novel, and the short story forms flourish. Much literary output is stimulated by issues raised by the depression.

  Today: New Zealand has a number of world-renowned authors, including novelist and short story writer Janet Frame (1924–2004), the most acclaimed New Zealand author of the twentieth century; and Ngaio Marsh (1899–1982), who is renowned for her crime fiction. There is also an upsurge in the prestige and popularity of Maori literature. Maori novelist Keri Hulme (1947–) wins the prestigious Booker Prize in 1995 for her novel *The Bone People*, and *Whale Rider* (1987) by Witi Ihimaera (1944–) is adapted into the Oscar-nominated film in 2002.

- **1930s:** In 1932, there are riots in Auckland, Wellington, and Dunedin in response to the Great Depression. In the wake of the depression, New Zealand becomes the first country in the world to establish an all-encompassing social welfare system. The system provides aid for the sick, the unemployed, and for families. A wide range of medical care is available free of charge.

  Today: Welfare benefits are targeted at those in need. A range of benefits are available to people on low incomes or those unable to support themselves because of unemployment, sickness, widowhood, single parenthood, or disability. Senior citizens over the age of sixty-five receive a retirement income equivalent to 65 percent of the average annual wage.

- **1930s:** The New Zealand economy depends heavily on a long-standing reciprocal trade arrangement with the United Kingdom, selling meat, butter, and wool and importing large quantities of British goods.

  Today: New Zealand no longer relies on traditional trading partners. It has diversified its products and is attuned to the demands of the global economy. Its export industries compete vigorously in world markets.

---

sions, education, health, and public works. Unemployed men were sent to rural camps to work on low-capital, labor-intensive tasks that paid a pittance.

Sargeson's early stories provide vivid insight into what life was like in New Zealand for many during the depression. In "Cow-Pats," for example, a young boy and his siblings work on a farm, but their old boots leak so much that their mother tells them they would be better off if they did not wear them at all. In "An Attempt at an Explanation," a young mother tries to pawn the family Bible in order to get money to feed her son and herself. Unsuccessful, she and her son are reduced to picking at crusts of bread they find in trash containers. In "A Man and His Wife," the narrator describes what some people were reduced to:

> During the slump people had to live where they could, and a lot of them lived in sheds and wash-houses in other people's backyards. I lived in an old shed that had once been a stable, and it was all right except for the rats.

In 1935, a new Labour government came to power in New Zealand and created a comprehensive welfare state to mitigate the effects of the depression and to ensure against future economic fluctuations.

New Zealand Literature in the 1930s

Settled by Europeans several generations later than Australia, New Zealand is a comparatively young country. The literature of New Zealand has therefore had less time to develop a distinctive character of its own. Before the 1930s, New Zealand literature in English—that is, not including the literature of the Maori, the indigenous inhabitants—reflected the European origins of white

New Zealanders. It was in effect a literature of exile
and was not deeply rooted in the writers' experience
of New Zealand itself. This was typified in the work
of New Zealand's most gifted writer of the early
twentieth century, short story writer Katherine
Mansfield (1888–1923), who left New Zealand at
an early age and wrote of it from her new home in
England. It was not until 1930 that the first anthology of short stories written entirely by New
Zealanders appeared. However, the book consisted
mostly of romances (by the female authors) and
adventure stories, old-fashioned yarns, and comic
sketches by the male writers.

But in the 1930s, New Zealanders began to
create literature that stemmed more directly from
their experience of their own land. Some impetus for this new direction came from the experience of the depression. Many of Sargeson's realistic, depression-era stories originally appeared in
the left-wing weekly *Tomorrow*, published in
Christchurch, which advocated a Marxist solution
to the country's economic and social difficulties.
These Sargeson stories represented a major leap in
the direction of the creation of a national literature.
Another work inspired by the depression was *Children of the Poor* (1934), a novel by John A. Lee,
which exposed the plight of children during these
catastrophic times.

The poetry of the 1930s was also concerned
with issues arising from the depression. Many poets
chose to reexamine the foundations on which New
Zealand society was based; others explored more
deeply than before the implications of what it meant
to be a New Zealander.

These works by novelists, short story writers,
and poets became the basis for a national literature,
the demand for which was neatly expressed in 1936
by a reviewer in New Zealand's *Evening Post*, who
called for "stories of New Zealand people by New
Zealand people for New Zealand people" (quoted in
The Oxford History of New Zealand Literature).

By 1938, writer O. N. Gillespie, pointing to
the work of novelists Lee, Robin Hyde, Gloria
Rawlinson, and Ngaio Marsh, declared that "we are
on the eve of a Golden Age in New Zealand
literature" (quoted in *The Oxford History of New
Zealand Literature*). Critic J. C. Reid was also
optimistic. He wrote that in the fiction of the 1930s
could be seen "a faithful reproduction of certain
aspects of the New Zealand character" (quoted in
The Oxford History of New Zealand Literature).

In 1953, a group of sixteen New Zealand writers paid tribute to Sargeson's achievement in the
1930s and beyond. In an open letter to Sargeson,
published in the New Zealand journal *Landfall* in
1953, the writers declared that his work had "a
liberating influence on the literature of this country." They went on to say that Sargeson had "turned
over new ground with great care and revealed that
our manners and behavior formed just as good a
basis for enduring literature as those of any other
country."

Critical Overview

"A Great Day" has usually been admired by literary
critics, who point out that a number of Sargeson
stories, including "Sale Day" and "Old Man's Story,"
have similarly violent climaxes. David Norton, in
"Two Views of Frank Sargeson's Short Stories,"
has categorized the story as "an elaborated fable
without the moral supplied: it can be taken as
demonstrating the weakness of strength and the
dangers of underestimating the weak." According
to Helen Shaw, also in "Two Views of Frank
Sargeson's Short Stories," "A Great Day" shows
"deep insight into repression. If something deeply
desired is repressed and for too long trapped in the
hideout of the Unconscious, it may escape." Shaw
sees this theme of the repression of desires, with
unfortunate or evil consequences, operating in a
number of Sargeson's short stories.

Not all critics or reviewers have evaluated "A
Great Day" favorably, however. Norman Levine, in
an otherwise appreciative review of Sargeson's
Collected Stories in *Spectator*, declared that when
Sargeson tried to write a conventional story such as
"A Great Day," which Levine described as "the
story with the sting in its tail," he was "not very
effective." Critic J. C. Reid had a more wide-
ranging complaint against Sargeson's stories, arguing that there was an emphasis "on violence, on
mental aberrations, on the sordid, the cruel, the
bitter . . . a total effect of cynicism from which
health is absent" (quoted in C. K. Stead's *Kin of
Place: Essays on 20 New Zealand Writers*).

In an unusual reading of "A Great Day," Joost
Daalder, in "Violence in the Stories of Frank
Sargeson," argues that Sargeson intended the reader
to sympathize with Fred rather than censure him for
his murder of Ken: "[T]he whole strategy of the
story is aimed at justifying a man who gets his own

back on a rival by drowning him." Daalder's point is that Ken destroyed the ideal relationship between Fred and Mary and is therefore to blame for what happens to him.

Criticism

Bryan Aubrey

Aubrey holds a Ph.D. in English and has published many articles on twentieth-century literature. In this essay, Aubrey examines "A Great Day" in light of Sargeson's use of violence in his short stories and his ideal of male friendship.

"A Great Day" is an unusual story. Even its appearance on the page is unusual. Although it has plenty of dialogue, it has no quotation marks. This is a feature of all Sargeson's stories, one that started a trend that many serious writers in New Zealand followed in the 1940s. Perhaps the reason Sargeson adopted this technique was to give his stories a nonliterary, artless quality, a feeling of greater naturalness. He wanted to give the reader the feeling that he or she is eavesdropping on a real conversation, not one filtered through the work of an intermediary, the writer. (This is, of course, an illusion, since the means by which this feeling of naturalness is being attempted is also a literary technique.)

"A Great Day" is also unusual and distinctive for the flatness and evenness of the narrator's tone throughout. This unemotional, detached tone continues even as the story builds to its climax. Fred's actions of leaving Ken behind on the reef, capsizing the dinghy, and swimming to shore—leaving his friend to certain death—are conveyed without any heightening of language or change of pace. Sargeson uses this method of narration to ensure that the violent ending comes across, paradoxically, with shocking, unexpected force. The detached method also well conveys the exceptionally cold, calculating nature of Fred's actions.

It is this violent end that sticks in the mind, just as Sargeson wanted it to. Violent climaxes occur frequently in Sargeson's early stories, and each time, told in that flat, detached manner of his, the climax comes with surprising suddenness and force. In "Sale Day," for example, a young man, irritated by the presence of a tom cat in the kitchen, seizes the cat and dumps it into the fire that is burning under the frying pan, incinerating it. In "How I Lost My

This New Zealand sound in early 1900 sets a scene similar to the one experienced by Ken and Fred in Sargeson's "A Great Day"

Pal," Tom and the narcissistic, sharp-tempered George, both of whom are employed as sheep shearers, fall out with each other. A little while later, Tom is nowhere to be seen. At the end of the story, Tom's friend, the narrator, watches as George strangles a dog that has irritated him with its barking, and in that instant he knows what has happened to Tom. In "A Good Boy," a young man reveals that he has murdered his girlfriend and has no remorse about it; and "Old Man's Story" ends with a suicide. This is what critic C. K. Stead has described as the "dark side" to Sargeson's writing. And Kai Jensen, in *Whole Men: The Masculine Tradition in New Zealand Literature*, has noted that death and violence were a preoccupation of many male writers in New Zealand in the 1930s. It was part of the "masculine emphasis" taken by the literature of the period, which was strongly associated with Sargeson.

In this emerging male literature, there was an emphasis on the working-class man as the ideal embodiment of masculinity. There was also an emphasis on male community and male friendship, what Jensen calls "mateship." This theme can be found in many of Sargeson's stories. "A Pair of

What Do I Read Next?

- *Frank Sargeson: A Life* (1995), by Michael King, is the only full-length biography of Sargeson. It provides invaluable insight into Sargeson's personality and his environment, as well as his creative output.

- The fifteen stories in *The Garden Party and Other Stories* (1998 edition), by Katherine Mansfield, are representative of the work of the renowned New Zealand author whose career as a short story writer preceded that of Sargeson. Mansfield died in 1923, a decade before Sargeson began publishing.

- *The Oxford Book of New Zealand Short Stories* (1994), edited by Vincent O'Sullivan, includes stories from the nineteenth and twentieth centu-

ries. Authors represented include Katherine Mansfield, Sargeson, Dan Davin, Maurice Gee, Janet Frame, and Maurice Duggan. Also included are stories by leading Maori writers, such as Patricia Grace and Witi Ihimaera, and the new generation of writers, including Peter Wells and Keri Hulme.

- *A History of New Zealand* (1988), by Keith Sinclair, was first published in 1959 and quickly became a classic, hailed by general readers as well as scholars. It has continuously been in print since first publication and has gone through several revisions. Sinclair emphasizes the growth of national identity in New Zealand through activities such as politics, war, patterns of speech, and writing.

Socks," for example, is about the narrator and Fred, his "cobber" (New Zealand slang for close friend). They have been friends since childhood, but they fall out because the narrator chooses to buy his employer a gift of a pair of socks. This alienates his friend, presumably because he was not consulted or included in the gift. ("Presumably" is the correct term, because Sargeson is rarely explicit about motivation or causation. He likes to encourage the reader to use his imagination and work some things out for himself.)

"Mateship" appears in Sargeson's stories to be the ideal relationship, superior to that between a man and a woman. In "A Man and His Wife," the narrator is cobbers with Ted, who has had difficulties with his wife and spends more time with his male friend, who lives in an old shed. (The story is set in the depression.) Often in these stories, mateship does not last. As in "How I Lost My Pal," something happens to destroy it. Similarly, in "A Man and His Wife," Ted loses his pet canary, and this so upsets him he drifts back to his wife, and the special friendship he had with the narrator is lost. "The Hole that Jack Dug" is another male friendship story

in which the bond between the narrator and his friend Jack is much stronger than that between Jack and his wife.

When studied in the light of this concern with "mateship," "A Great Day" occupies a somewhat anomalous position. After all, Fred's deepest bond is not with Ken, his fishing buddy, but with Mary. He even describes their relationship with the word usually used to describe a male friend: "Mary and I used to be great cobbers." And a close reading suggests that Ken is not the stuff of which the male cobber should be made: The story is like an ironic reversal of the ideal of mateship. The key here comes early in the story. As Fred busies himself preparing the dinghy for pushing off, Ken takes it easy and rolls himself a cigarette. He does not offer one to Fred, which would have been an act of mateship. And when Fred rows out, Ken neglects to watch out for the direction in which they are going. The reason? He is rolling his own cigarettes again, thinking only of himself. It is only after they change places, with Ken doing the rowing, that Fred points out Ken's omission, asking him for a smoke. Ken apologizes for not offering. The incident is telling, since in a Sargeson short story, no detail is superfluous. A few paragraphs later, the narrator comments that the only thing these two men have in common is that they both have cigarettes dangling from their mouths. But the way the disposition of the cigarettes has been made suggests that even this small commonality hides a large difference.

It appears that Ken is not an ideal "cobber" in other senses either. The Sargeson ideal was that of the workingman, and in the male literature of this period, as Jensen points out, education was presented as something to be distrusted. In "A Great Day," Ken is more educated than Fred, and the latter, although he does not openly admit it—he is of course going to great lengths to disguise his feelings about everything—despises him for it. Education makes a man "different," he explains. In Fred's mind, education opens up a gulf between one man and another. The pitiful smallness of Fred's mind is seen in the fact that, for him, the advantages of education have nothing to do with knowledge, culture, or even earning potential but lie in his belief that an educated man does better with the girls.

If Fred defines himself as a workingman, it is not apparent what occupation Ken follows, or if he even has one. He appears to have money, and he feels no urgency about finding a new job. He is one of life's fortunates. (Fred, of course, is the opposite.) Ken does possess some aspects of the masculine ideal, however: He has a fine muscular body (like Jack in "The Hole that Jack Dug"), and he also possesses the taciturn, inexpressive quality associated with the New Zealand male in literature of the 1930s and 1940s. Although he is the more educated of the two men, he allows Fred to do almost all the talking.

If Ken fails to meet the test of being a true cobber, Fred obviously fails the test, too. Ken's failings hardly mitigate the gravity of Fred's crime, although they may explain something of why Fred has such feelings of animosity toward his friend. The premeditated nature of Fred's act, the quality of cold calculation he brings to it, and what must be his sadistic anticipation of it (as shown by the double-edged remarks he makes to Ken, secretly gloating over his unsuspecting victim) suggest him to be a psychopath. A psychopath is someone who is incapable of empathizing with the feelings of another person.

But this diagnosis of Fred does not quite fit all the facts. It is noticeable that, as he prepares for his crime, he puts cotton wool in his ears, and then, as

> " The premeditated nature of Fred's act, the quality of cold calculation he brings to it, and what must be his sadistic anticipation of it (as shown by the double-edged remarks he makes to Ken, secretly gloating over his unsuspecting victim) suggest him to be a psychopath."

he rows away from the reef, he shuts his eyes. He cannot bear to allow any evidence of what he has done to reach his senses. He must not hear any cries or protests that Ken might make; nor must he see the reaction of the stranded, doomed man. Perhaps, after all, he has a conscience and a knowledge of right and wrong. He knows perfectly well what he is doing, and at some level of his mind, his actions shock and appall him. Perhaps, as the psychologically repressed little man, he is secretly frightened of the big man, Ken, and he dreads—like a child scared of a parent's wrath—Ken's anger and rage being directed toward him, even from a distance. Who knows what murky things lurk in the mind of a man who could do what Fred does?

This picture of a man who shuts his ears and eyes to his own evil suggests that, from the moment Fred arrives back at the beach, his twisted psyche will be even more divided and repressed than before. A man who is well practiced at repressing his true feelings has ensured, in one terrifying act of demented vengeance, that there will always be a corner of his psyche into which he dare not go. Demons will lurk there that would consume him if he were to let them out.

Source: Bryan Aubrey, Critical Essay on "A Great Day," in *Short Stories for Students*, Gale, 2005.

Contemporary Authors Online

In the following essay, the author discusses the nature of Sargeson's writing and Sargeson's place in New Zealand literature.

At the time of his death in 1982, Frank Sargeson was "the unquestioned doyen of New Zealand letters," a London *Times* writer commented. The characters of Sargeson's numerous short stories and seven novels are alienated and isolated from their society, often because of their sexual orientation, and strive for freedom from a Puritanical society. Many of his characters are also from the lower classes, inarticulate, and violent. As H. Winston Rhodes noted in *Landfall Country: Work from "Landfall," 1947–61*, "The world of Sargeson's stories is one inhabited by casual workers and rouseabouts, by station hands and street loungers, by the misfits, the dispirited and the lonely." Rhodes continued, "Because of their mental attitudes and habits they are isolated from the smug conventionalities of the garden suburb. They are separated from social groups and organized communities by their anarchic behaviour, by their inability to accept the recognized prescriptions for achieving respectability and a comfortable bank balance." "Sargeson's attitude is one of pity for people who destroy their own capacity for life," Murray S. Martin explained in the *Journal of General Education*.

One of Sargeson's typical characters was described by E. H. McCormick in *New Zealand Literature: A Survey* as "the 'good,' well brought up boy who breaks away from his respectable parents." This character type is found in such novels as *I Saw in My Dream* and *The Hangover*. *I Saw in My Dream* follows a middle-class young man, Henry, a.k.a. Dave, as he grows to maturity in the New Zealand of the early part of this century. Rhodes, in his introduction to the novel, compared the story to *Pilgrim's Progress*: "Sargeson's 'dream' of a twentieth century, New Zealand pilgrim's progress is no allegory and is less a visionary search for a heavenly goal than a curiously patterned but dramatic portrayal of adolescent deprivation culminating in the pursuit of wholeness and the quest for fulfillment." In Part I of this novel, Henry finds himself in a world where his middle-class values are challenged by others outside his world. This outside world is the landscape beyond the New Zealand suburbs, where immigrants, the unemployed, and the aboriginal Maoris live and wander. In bringing together these two worlds in *I Saw in My Dream*, "Puritanism, conventionality, enclosure and middle-class comfort are contrasted to sexual desire, individuality, freedom, the working class and economic insecurity," Bruce King noted in *The New English Literatures: Cultural Nationalism in a Changing World*. In Part II, Henry takes the name Dave and also takes on new experiences in the New Zealand countryside. "Dave puts up with discomfort, has friends, is more relaxed and in touch with nature, and is open to experience," observed King. This new landscape offers Henry/Dave "a chance to begin again," King pointed out, "a chance to discover [his] authentic self." King concluded that the novel's "blend of symbolist experimental techniques with a kind of realism common to regional literature" makes *I Saw in My Dream* "a remarkable book."

In *Memoirs of a Peon*, Sargeson wrote a satirical account of New Zealand middle class respectability. As in his previous books, the focus is on an innocent young character coming of age. There is a "strange sense of survival . . . in reading this carefully structured narrative of a young innocent who sets out on intellectual and sexual adventures, covering a fair amount of his society in the process," observed Malcolm Bradbury in *Punch*. In Bradbury's opinion, the novel amounts to an "adaptation of the eighteenth-century picaresque manner . . . to present-day New Zealand," and it "is done with the greatest literary assurance, as if this were the ideal form for an essentially provincial and raw society."

In *The Hangover*, the young character Alan enters the drug world of the hippies and "loses both his innocence and his sense of belonging," as Martin explained. Speaking of *The Hangover*, Kay Dick once commented that it was "full of fascination and interest, with its straightforward account of a young man gaining maturity through his association with several offbeat characters. Mr. Sargeson is also much concerned to describe the inherent bisexuality of most relationships. He is an expert at tone and mood, and able to switch from conventional illustration . . . to loose philosophical notation." Similarly, Ian Reid of *Australian Book Review* found that, "as in much of his work, Frank Sargeson [in *The Hangover*] directs his unblinking but not uncompassionate eye towards an adolescent struggling to reconcile the disturbing facts of his widening experience with the assumptions derived from a narrow religious upbringing."

Joy of the Worm offers the story of the Reverend James Bohun and his son, Jeremy, two men who while away the First World War writing letters to each other, letters steeped in so much style that "they entirely blot out the scrawny realities of the external world," Jonathan Raban observed in the *New Statesman*. These letters juxtapose with the more mundane letters of their wives, and Sargeson captures the voice of each writer. For Ian Reid, contributor to *Australian Book Review*, "Sargeson's mimic gift is amusingly displayed in the numerous letters, from various hands, that carry much of the story." In the end, Raban conceded, "a counterfeit style and surface supplant the dismal details of an arid civic and domestic life. *Joy of the Worm* is an idiosyncratic masterpiece; elegant, formal, deliciously ironic."

Speaking of Sargeson's contribution to New Zealand literature, Bruce King wrote: "in a colonial situation where English middle-class social values are inappropriate, the first really believable characters in fiction are usually the eccentrics and outcasts. It was Frank Sargeson who made such types representative of an authentic New Zealand." Sargeson also captured their voices. "His recording of the New Zealand working class vernacular has not been surpassed and has seldom been matched by later writers," commented William Broughton in *Reference Guide to Short Fiction*. "The idiomatic speech, with its flattened cadences, its laconic and sometimes wry ironies, and its cautious and limited vocabulary, became intimately associated with his distinctive sketches and stories."

Sargeson once told *CA*: "Personal data of no interest to anyone except self and half a dozen friends. But my publishers think my longest book, *Memoirs of a Peon*, is one of the funniest books written anywhere this century. They may be right."

Source: Contemporary Authors Online, "Frank Sargeson," in *Contemporary Authors Online*, Gale, 2003.

H. Winston Rhodes

In the following essay excerpt, Rhodes discusses how Sargeson evokes the physical environment and offers "glimpses that are caught of a twisted mind" in "A Great Day."

Sargeson's comparatively slender output is indicative of a refusal to write stories merely for the sake of dramatic narrative and of a desire to explore the varied responses of human beings to the experience of living. "A Great Day," one of the longest of the earlier sketches, is more elaborately developed and sustained; and, partly because it is written in the third person, the attempt to evoke the atmosphere of the harbour and the Rangitoto channel has been successfully achieved. However, there are no slabs of description; and gulls, sun, wind, water, and tide, the mussels on the submerged reef, the rocking and direction of the dinghy with its ill-assorted pair as it moves into what seems a timeless world, all enter imperceptibly into the consciousness of the reader until his senses are tingling and identified with the seascape. It is a story the full impact of which comes only with the second reading, for it is only then on the long pull out to the reef that the conversation, guided by Fred, who lives on sustenance and from the fish he can catch in the harbour, turns into something like an ironic interior monologue of self-justification for the crime he is preparing to commit. This violent but evocative tale with its unpleasant ending is redeemed by the glimpses that are caught of a twisted mind in a weedy body, by a realization that if the blood of one so conscious of failure and physical inferiority has turned to gall, there still remains sufficient sensibility to make his life a misery as he starts on his solitary long pull back to the shore.

Source: H. Winston Rhodes, "The World of Frank Sargeson," in *Frank Sargeson*, Twayne Publishers, 1969, p. 70.

Sources

Ballantyne, David, et al., "A Letter to Frank Sargeson," in *LandFall*, Vol. 7, No. 1, March 1953, p. 5.

Daalder, Joost, "Violence in the Stories of Frank Sargeson," in *Journal of New Zealand Literature*, Vol. 4, 1986, pp. 56–77.

Jensen, Kai, *Whole Men: The Masculine Tradition in New Zealand Literature*, Auckland University Press, 1996, pp. 19–82.

Levine, Norman, Review of *Collected Stories*, in *Spectator*, April 23, 1965, p. 538.

Sargeson, Frank, *Collected Stories*, Macgibbon & Kee, 1965.

Shaw, Helen, and David Norton, "Two Views of Frank Sargeson's Short Stories," in *Critical Essays on the New Zealand Short Story*, edited by Cherry Hankin, Heinemann, 1982, pp. 30–61.

Stead, C. K., *Kin of Place: Essays on 20 New Zealand Writers*, Auckland University Press, pp. 47–64.

Sturm, Terry, ed., *The Oxford History of New Zealand Literature in English*, Oxford University Press, 1991, pp. 222–29.

Further Reading

Allen, Walter, *The Short Story in English*, Oxford University Press, 1981, pp. 331–35.
    Through his analysis of Sargeson's story "A Man of Good Will," Allen describes the qualities that made Sargeson a liberator for later New Zealand writers.

Copland, R. A., "The Goodly Roof: Some Comments on the Fiction of Frank Sargeson," in *Essays on New Zealand Literature*, edited by Wystan Curnow, Heinemann Educational Books, 1973, pp. 43–53.

> Copland discusses point of view in Sargeson, covering Sargeson's extensive use of first-person narrators, but also touching on "A Great Day" as a departure from the norm demanded by the nature of the plot. Copland shows how Sargeson conveys his philosophical and moral vision through the narrow range of sensibilities of his mostly inarticulate working-class characters.

Horsmann, E. A., "The Art of Frank Sargeson," in *LandFall*, Vol. 19, No. 2, June 1965, pp. 129–34.

> This is a reassessment of Sargeson's early work in the light of the later. Horsmann argues that the essence of Sargeson's art is the enacting of a process of discovery and that the early stories are more complex than has generally been supposed.

Jones, Joseph, and Johanna Jones, *New Zealand Fiction*, Twayne's World Author Series, No. 643, Twayne Publishers, 1983, pp. 42–43, 81–82.

> This is a chronological survey of the main tendencies and writers to be encountered in New Zealand fiction. It includes an annotated bibliography.

McCormick, E. H., *New Zealand Literature: A Survey*, Oxford University Press, 1959, pp. 108–135.

> This contains an excellent review of New Zealand poetry and fiction during the 1930s.

Rhodes, H. Winston, *Frank Sargeson*, Twayne, 1969.

> Rhodes traces the path Sargeson followed as a writer, the obstacles he had to overcome, and his unique contribution to the development of an authentic New Zealand literature.

Stevens, Joan, *New Zealand Short Stories: A Survey with Notes for Discussion*, Price Milburn, 1968.

> Stevens discusses many New Zealand short stories and introduces students to matters of literary technique. She includes a discussion of Sargeson and an analysis of his short story "An Affair of the Heart."

Imagined Scenes

Ann Beattie
1974

"Imagined Scenes" by Ann Beattie first appeared in the *Texas Quarterly* in the summer of 1974 and was later published in Beattie's 1976 collection, *Distortions*. Although the original Doubleday edition was out of print as of 2004, the collection was reissued in 1991 by Vintage.

"Imagined Scenes" is the story of an unnamed young wife who cares for an elderly man at night while her husband studies for his Ph.D. oral examinations. While she is out of the house, her husband appears to be entertaining guests or going out himself without revealing his whereabouts to his wife.

In "Imagined Scenes," Beattie explores the fragmentation of contemporary life. Her narrator's sleep-deprived imaginings, as well as the elderly man's stories, compete with the "reality" of their lives. The story has the style, images, and ambiguous ending that are hallmarks of Beattie's writing. Beattie's flat prose and attention to minutia create a world comprised of detail and of gaps, leaving the reader to puzzle out which of the scenes are the imagined ones.

Author Biography

Ann Beattie was born in Washington, D.C., on September 8, 1947, and grew up in the Washington suburbs. She attended American University in the 1960s where she majored in English, studying writ-

Ann Beattie

ers such as F. Scott Fitzgerald, Ernest Hemingway, and John Updike. These writers clearly influenced Beattie's writing. She completed a master's degree at the University of Connecticut, and although she began work on a Ph.D., she did not complete the degree once she began having success publishing her stories.

It was while she worked with writer J. D. O'Hara during the early years of the 1970s that Beattie began placing her stories in such prestigious publications as the *Atlantic* and the *Virginia Quarterly*. After rejecting twenty of her stories, the *New Yorker* published "A Platonic Relationship" in 1974, leading Beattie to a long association with the magazine. "Imagined Scenes" was first published in the *Texas Quarterly* in the summer of 1974.

In 1976, Beattie published her first novel, *Chilly Scenes of Winter*, and her first collection of short stories, *Distortions*, which included many of her *New Yorker* stories as well as "Imagined Scenes." Both books received mixed reviews; however, it was clear from the beginning that Beattie's would be a voice to be reckoned with in contemporary fiction.

Since her first books, Beattie has published fifteen books, including *Perfect Recall: New Stories*

in 2000 and *The Doctor's House* in 2002. In addition, she was awarded a Guggenhiem Fellowship in 1978; an award in literature by the American Academy of Arts and Letters in 1980; and a PEN/Malamud Award for Excellence in Short Fiction in 2000. She has often been referred to as the voice of the generation coming of age in the 1960s, and she continues to chronicle the lives of this group of people. Beattie's work generates heated critical commentary. Increasingly, readers and reviewers alike classify her as one of the major writers of the late twentieth and early twenty-first centuries.

Plot Summary

In the opening scene of "Imagined Scenes," the wife describes a dream to her husband, David: She is in Greece; the weather is warm, and she is on a beach. She then remembers how they awaken together and arrive home from the store at the same time. In addition, she recalls the many ways he has adjusted his life to hers. Nevertheless, in the first scene, she also mentions that David is not going to work in the fall because he is returning to school to finish his Ph.D.

Next, the wife describes a plant that is having a growth spurt in the middle of winter. David takes care of the plant while she is out. She mentions that she has to work that night, so David continues to read while she goes to bed.

The wife has been hired to stay with an old man. His daughter normally takes care of him but she has gone to Florida on vacation with her husband. The old man's sister stays with him during the day, but the young wife, who is a nurse, takes the night shift. The old man tells her about the winter he spent in Berlin and shows her his postcards and photo album.

When the young wife returns home, she finds evidence that people have been in the house while she has been gone, and her husband's books are strewn around the room. He comes in with the dog and encourages her to get some sleep. He tells her that he's met the couple who live down the hill.

Again at the elderly man's house, the woman realizes she does not have her watch. She calls home, but no one answers the phone. Meanwhile, the snow that began earlier in the story continues to fall.

When she returns home, David is not there again, and the plant is gone. David returns and tells her he gave the plant to the couple he met. The next night, she calls home again at 4:00 A.M. No one answers the phone. In the morning, the old man wants to go for a walk in the snow. She helps him get dressed, and they go outside. Some children are in a fight, and when she goes to break it up, one of the boys runs into the old man, and he falls. David is there and helps right the man. He has come to pick her up because there is so much snow. He says he didn't answer the phone because he was asleep.

On the way home, the woman imagines David with the dog. At home, she goes upstairs to sleep, and she hears David cleaning up dishes again. When the phone rings, it is the old man's sister, saying that his daughter cannot get home from Florida because of the snow. She wants the woman to come back to take care of the old man. The story ends with the old woman's whisper on the phone: "You're so lucky. . . . You can come and go. You don't know what it's like to be caught."

Media Adaptations

- "Imagined Scenes" is included in a tape recording of *Distortions*, produced by Books on Tape, Inc., in December of 1979.

Characters

David

David is the husband in the story. He decides rather abruptly in the opening of the story that he is not going to go to work but will instead go back to school to finish his Ph.D. Over the course of the story, David changes from an attentive husband who falls asleep and awakens with his wife to a man who spends a great deal of time out of the house, walking the dog or visiting with his neighbors. Because the story is told from the young wife's point of view, there are large gaps in the reader's understanding of the husband. For example, when the wife calls home to check on her watch, no one answers, so the reader and the narrator are unable to determine what the husband is doing. Indeed, David is even less defined than the narrator in this story; the reader is an even further distance from this character than from the narrator.

Elderly Man

The young wife cares for the elderly man at night, after his sister has left. The elderly man has a book of photographs, and he tells stories to the young woman. He says, "People get old and they can't improve things . . . so they lie." He tries to make a distinction between the "lies," or romantic stories he might make up, and his real stories; however, it is difficult for both the narrator and the reader to distinguish between the two.

The Sister

The old man has a sister who comes to stay with him during the days while his daughter and her husband are on vacation in Florida. The sister is fifteen years younger than the old man but is still elderly herself. Although she seems to care for her brother, she also visits him daily out of duty. The sister herself seems to feel powerless, both in the snow and in her old age. "You don't know what it's like to be caught," she tells the young wife when she calls, asking the young wife to return for another night.

Young Wife

The unnamed, third-person narrator of "Imagined Scenes" is a young wife, married to David. The story is told entirely from the young wife's point of view. The couple has no children. The woman is a nurse who works taking care of an old man overnight. In the beginning of the story, the woman and husband seem in tune with each other. However, as the story continues, the young woman seems to be losing track of her life with her husband. It is difficult to tell if this is because her husband is deceiving her or if her lack of sleep is causing her to become increasingly fragmented and unable to think clearly. It seems clear, however, that she suspects her husband of something, perhaps an affair, because she tries to call him in the middle of the night and seems upset when he does not answer the phone. By the end of the story, the young woman seems groggy with lack of sleep and almost unable to gather her thoughts. It is difficult to know much about this character, other than her profession and the actions she takes in the story, because Beattie deliberately does not develop characters in this story. Rather, she lets the reader discern the young wife's inner life and concerns from the external details the wife chooses to notice.

Themes

Dream and Reality

In "Imagined Scenes," it can sometimes be difficult to discern when the narrator is awake or dreaming. The story opens with a description of a dream. The warm Greek beach clearly contrasts with the cold snow falling outside in the "real" world. Likewise, her initial description of her life with her husband has a dreamlike quality to it: They awaken together, he learns to like Roquefort dressing for her, they arrive home from shopping at the same time. The reality of her marriage is much different, however, from this initial glimpse. When the narrator goes to work caring for the old man, David begins absenting himself from their home, and, it begins to seem, from their marriage.

Yet even David's absence is not unproblematic. When the narrator returns home and finds dishes on the table and evidence that someone has been there, it is almost as if she has stepped into a dream. She finds herself trying to interpret the sensory data before her, yet she is unable to come up with a coherent narration of what is going on in her life.

Back at the old man's house, she falls asleep sitting in a chair watching the old man. Again she dreams of the beach in Greece. Increasingly, the narrative takes on a dreamlike quality. At home again, she can't find the plant, and in the steamy bathroom she is unable to see her face in the mirror. These absences, as well as David's absences and the traces of the people who have been visiting in her house, seem to become stranger and stranger. Meanwhile, snow continues to blanket the landscape, changing the physical reality of the setting.

By the end of the story, the narrator seems unable to separate her reality from her dreams. The old man's daughter is grounded in Florida, the snow making it impossible for planes to land. The narrator imagines planes not only from Florida but from Greece as well. The content of her two earlier dreams subsumes the request from the sister that she

return to the old man's house, and she imagines that everyone is up in the air on a plane above the snow.

This moment forces readers to return to the story. How much of what has just been narrated is a dream, and how much is reality? How many of the scenes are "real," and how many are imagined scenes? Indeed, the strange intermingling of imaginings and dreams reminds the reader that what he or she has just read is a fiction itself and that any "reality" the story presents is just as illusory as the embedded imagined scenes.

Youth and Age

The narrator and her husband, David, are clearly young. They have no children; David is a graduate student; and the narrator seems to be working temporary jobs. There is also a sense that they have not been married long and that they are still in the process of learning to live together. Further, David's romping with the dog, as well as his return to school and his failure to clean up the house in the narrator's absence, also suggests that David is attempting to return to a younger age himself. Although he is married and responsible for at least half of the maintenance and upkeep of their house and at least half of the financial support of the couple, he turns away from this responsibility. In fact, he never discusses his decision to return to school with his wife; he merely informs her without any discussion of how the two will make ends meet while he does not work. Likewise, his new companionship with the couple down the hill and the subtle implication that he may be having an affair with another woman suggest that David is turning away not only from his marriage but also from the responsibilities of adulthood. While the narrator must leave the home to care for another person in order to earn money to support David and herself, David entertains guests in their home or stays out all night. This immaturity stands in stark contrast both to the narrator and to the other characters in the story.

At the other end of the chronological spectrum stand the old man and his sister. The old man is unable to care for himself and needs help from his daughter and from his sister. When the daughter takes a much-needed vacation, the narrator steps in as a paid employee to provide care. In the old man, the reader is able to see the future: This is David, grown old, needing care from all of the females in his life. His life is circumscribed by the boundaries of his bed, his stories, and his photographs. Indeed, he is even afraid to have his pictures leave the room. He tells the narrator that "people get old and they

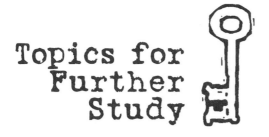

Topics for Further Study

- Sigmund Freud wrote extensively on the subject of dreams and of their usefulness in analyzing both individuals and literature. Read selections from Freud's *The Interpretation of Dreams* and consider the narrator's dreams in "Imagined Scenes" from a Freudian perspective. What do her dreams reveal about her? How do her "imagined scenes" serve like dreams in this story?

- Many studies have been conducted showing the effect of sleep deprivation and shift work on human beings. What happens when a person's sleep schedule is disrupted? What happens when a person loses REM sleep? How do these studies affect the way a reader approaches "Imagined Scenes?"

- Minimalism is a movement that influenced not only literature but also art and architecture. Find a discussion of minimalism in art and/or archi-

tecture, and find photographs of minimalist art and/architecture. In what ways does this study further your reading of Beattie's short fiction?

- Critics often mention Beattie's study of Ernest Hemingway as influential on her development as a writer of short fiction. Read Hemingway's early collection of short stories *Men without Women*, and consider similarities and differences with Beattie's fiction in *Distortions*.

- Beattie is often cited as the spokesperson for the "baby boom" generation, those people born in the years between the end of World War II, in 1945, and about 1965. Research this generation. Why are they of interest demographically? What characterizes this generation, and what has happened to them in the years since the publication of "Imagined Scenes"?

---

can't improve things ... so they lie all the time." Like David, the old man finds that he must improvise the stories of his life to account for his actions—or for his inability to act. A sign of the old man's immaturity is his insistence on going outside in the snow. Because of his age and frailty, this action endangers his life. Even worse, it places him in a highly vulnerable position: A fall would mean enforced bed rest and perhaps even a nursing home. And, at its worst, the old man's insistence on going outside also creates the potential for him to be an even heavier burden on the women in his life.

Although the old man's sister is twelve years younger than the old man, she is, like the narrator, the more mature of the two. She visits the old man daily. She has boots and an umbrella, she tells the narrator, and she tries to do good things for the old man, but not just out of duty. Her altruistic care giving is not without cost, however; she feels caught in the situation she is in, without help, and without a future herself. Like the narrator, she is the responsible one, the one who will not leave the old man

alone without help in his daughter's absence. Thus, while the apparent contrast in this story is between the two young people and the two old people, a more subtle, yet disturbing contrast is between the immature men and the mature women.

Style

Point of View

Point of view is the narrative perspective from which a story is told. Most common points of view include first person and third person. In a first-person story, the narrator is commonly referred to as "I," and she reveals the story from her own perspective and mind. In a third-person narration, the narrative unfolds either from the perspective of an omniscient narrator who can tell the reader everything that is going on with every one of the characters, or from an impersonal voice that merely report events from all perspectives. Beattie, however, in "Imagined

Scenes," creates yet another point of view. Although her unnamed narrator is not an "I," the story is limited to her perspective entirely. Indeed, it is this choice that gives the story its distinctive quality. The reader is limited to seeing, hearing, touching, thinking, and feeling what the narrator does. The reader is not able, for example, to see what David does while the narrator is at work. Like the narrator, the reader must observe the sensory data, such as the dirty dishes, and draw conclusions about the evidence for him or herself.

Beattie also makes an additional adjustment to the traditional third-person-limited point of view. She eliminates much of the expected interior monologue through which information is generally given to a reader in this kind of point of view. Thus, while the reader is privy to the narrator's thoughts and observations, the narrator reveals very little about what she is actually thinking. Instead, the reader only has the bare observations on which to base his or her conclusions. Such manipulation of the point of view suggests one of several things: Either the narrator is not a reflective person, someone who does not internalize external data; or the narrator is deliberately not reading the data in order to hide problems with her marriage from herself, or the narrator is so sleep deprived that she goes about her day in a kind of fog. These choices are not the only ones either. Beattie's deliberate narrowing of the narrative perspective provides the reader with ample room to draw his or her own conclusions. For the reader who wants definitive answers, however, the technique can be frustrating and perhaps disturbing.

Symbols

An author will frequently place an object in the story that both suggests or stands for something else without losing its original identity. Beattie often uses an array of physical objects to impart meaning in her stories without specifically naming what that meaning is. "Imagined Scenes" is no exception. Like many of Beattie's other stories, "Imagined Scenes" contains photographs and postcards and a plant. The photographs and postcards belong to the old man. The old man shows the narrator a postcard with the caption "Joseph Jefferson as Rip Van Winkle." The narrator, naturally, believes that someone the old man knows has sent him the card. However, he tells her that it is one that he found in a store. In other words, the old man has bought someone else's story. Further, the old man says that he can make up a "romantic story" to tell the narrator about the postcard. He distinguishes this

from the "real" stories of his photographs. As symbols, the postcards and photographs function not only as themselves in the story, but they also suggest the power of pictures to both preserve and create stories. The postcards suggest to the old man the potential for the creative act, the act of composing a "romantic story." And although the narrator expects the old man to tell the story, he does not. Likewise, the photographs preserve a trace of the "real" stories of the man's life and, again, suggest the potential for another kind of creative act, that of composing a memoir. However, again, although the man says to the narrator that he will tell her some stories, he does not. Thus, both the photographs and the postcards represent both the creation and repression of stories. As such, they serve a similar purpose in the narrator's real and imagined scenes.

The plant, too, functions both as an image in the story, providing texture and sensory detail, and as a symbol, imparting a deeper meaning to the story of the couple's lives together and apart. The plant has suddenly "begun to grow, sending up a narrow shoot." Such imagery suggests Beattie may be using the plant as a phallic symbol. Indeed, writers often use plants and plant imagery as phallic or yonic symbols, representing male or female characteristics through their choices. In this case, the plant may be symbolic of David's sexual growth and, perhaps, his sexual infidelity. When the couple purchased the plant a year earlier, it was "not very pretty then. It was in a small cracked pot, wrapped in plastic. They replanted it. In fact, David must have replanted it again." Whereas a tall, thin object such as the narrow shoot of the plant can generally be considered a phallic symbol, representative of the male, a short, wide, round object may also be considered a yonic symbol, representative of the female. The cracked pot and the covering of the plant in plastic may suggest that David feels trapped by his marriage. Although the couple replanted the plant together once, the narrator now notices that David has replanted it again himself. Such "replanting" is at least suggestive of David's sexual proclivities. Perhaps he has "replanted" himself with another woman.

Tense

Although traditionally stories are told in the past tense, in the decades of the twentieth century, short story writers, in particular, began using the present tense frequently. Beattie chose to use the present tense in "Imagined Scenes" for important narrative effect. In the first place, by choosing to tell the story in the present tense, she lends immediacy to the story itself. It is as if the story is unfolding before the reader's eyes in real time. Unlike stories told in the past tense, where the story, by implication, has already occurred, a present-tense story postpones the conclusion. That is, when a reader begins a present-tense story, he or she has no idea where the story might lead, since the action of the story has not yet been completed in the chronology of the story itself. Thus, by choosing to use present tense, Beattie delays meaning in her story.

Beattie also chose to use present tense as a means of limiting information to the reader, something she also does through her choice of point of view. Because the story is always in the present moment, there are very few instances when Beattie provides any backstory; nor does Beattie provide a look ahead to the future. Like the very limited point of view, the limited tense creates an almost claustrophobic sense, akin to walking a narrow path in the dark. The reader never knows what might pop up around the bend.

Historical Context

The Nixon Years and Watergate

In 1974, the year Beattie wrote "Imagined Scenes," the United States experienced one of the most disturbing political events of its two-hundred-year history. Two years earlier, in 1972, five men broke into the Democratic National Headquarters, housed at the Watergate Hotel in Washington, D.C. The burglars were caught, tried, and sentenced. No one, however, could have predicted the Pandora's box the break-in would open. By 1973, the scandal had grown to include Richard Nixon, then president of the United States, and most of his staff. In April of 1973, he told the nation in a televised speech that he did not have any foreknowledge of the break-in, nor had he tried in any way to cover up the break-in. He also told the American public that he was worth the sacred trust of the presidency.

There ensued a long investigation that continued to uncover evidence that the president had indeed been involved in both the planning and the cover-up of the Watergate break-in. However, as late as April 1974, Nixon continued to maintain, on television to the public, that the evidence provided from tape recordings made in his office would prove him innocent. He was wrong. By August 1974, it was clear that Nixon would be impeached by the

legislature, and it was also clear that there were not enough votes in the Senate to prevent this from happening. On August 8, 1974, Nixon announced to the American public that he would resign his office on August 9 at noon.

The Watergate scandal, as it came to be called, reverberated throughout the entire United States culture. Its web of deception, lies, constructions, fictions, and illusion informed much of the writing of the period. Indeed, the scandal itself caused a deep distrust not only of the government and politicians but also of truth claims themselves. "Imagined Scenes," with its swirling imagined and real scenes and its clear interest in fiction and reality, is a product of this time and this milieu.

Minimalism: Art and Literature

In the late 1950s, a group of artists led by Frank Stella developed a form of abstraction called minimalism. By the mid-1960s, minimalism had become the most prevalent form of abstraction in the New York art world. According to Marilyn Stokstad in her book *Art History* (2002), the minimalists attempted to rid their art of everything unnecessary to the art itself. Stokstad writes, "They banished subjective gestures and personal feelings; negated representation, narrative, and metaphor; and focused exclusively on the art work as a physical fact." As the movement evolved, the artists continued to create nonrepresentational works, but some began to allow some suggestion of narrative or metaphor back into their work. Minimalists often used space as a medium in their work in an attempt to divorce the art from the intent of the artist. The impact of artistic minimalism on the culture was profound, perhaps nowhere more so than on short fiction.

In literature, the use of space translates to silence. That is, what is not said in a story is at least as important as what is said. For the minimalists, such silences call attention to the story itself through contrast. In the late 1960s, the 1970s, and the 1980s, the impact of artistic minimalism surfaced in the fiction of writers such as Ann Beattie, Raymond Carver, and Mary Robison, among others. There has been considerable critical debate over the quality of minimalist fiction. While many critics find the clean, hard edges of narration and silence to be the stuff of satisfying reading, others rail against what they see as the barrenness and triviality of the prose. Much of this debate has its root in a very old and much deeper philosophical divide: What is it that fiction ought to do? Minimalists seem to suggest

Compare & Contrast

- **1970s:** Richard Nixon becomes involved in the Watergate scandal, a burglary and cover-up that eventually leads to his resignation.

  Today: Although Bill Clinton is censured in the 1990s for misconduct, no president since Nixon has been forced to resign from office.

- **1970s:** Worldwide inflation causes dramatic increases in the price of oil, fuel, food, and materials. In the United States, the Dow Jones index drops to 663 in 1974, after a partial recovery from the 1970 recession.

  Today: The Dow Jones index reaches the ten-thousand mark for the first time since September 2001, and the United States slowly recovers from recession, in spite of significant loss of manufacturing jobs nationwide.

- **1970s:** Members of the so-called "baby boom" are finishing college, getting married, and starting families. They flood the job market, and in many families both partners work full time.

  Today: Baby boomers are starting to retire. The sheer size of their generation and the demands that it will place on health care, pension plans, and social security are issues that confront the government, businesses, and society in general.

---

that fiction functions as art, not reality, and as such calls attention to its own artificiality through the juxtaposition of surface detail with an absence of interior monologue.

Further, Myles Weber links the rise of minimalist fiction with larger social issues. In his 1999 *Northwest Review* article, "Revisiting Minimalism," he writes that minimalist fiction "was a symptom of the larger social crises out of which the authors worked." He continues, "They faced the problems of the past century now in an inflated and accelerated form (murkier rivers and beaches, more brutally mechanized street crime, more lethal sexually transmitted disease)." For the minimalists, the only response to such a world was disengagement and apathy.

Critical Overview

By the time *Distortions* was published in 1976, Beattie had already established herself as a serious writer of short fiction, regularly placing stories in the influential and prestigious *New Yorker*. The simultaneous publication of both *Distortions* and her first novel, *Chilly Scenes of Winter*, therefore, attracted considerable critical attention.

Beattie's former professor and mentor, the writer J. D. O'Hara, wrote a glowing review of her work in the August 15, 1976, edition of the *New York Times*, calling Beattie "the best new writer to come down that particular pike since Donald Barthelme." Likewise, David Thorburn, writing for the *Yale Review* in 1977, commented that Beattie's prose is "not unlike good Hemingway." Susan Horowitz, on the other hand, was less charitable in a review from the August 7, 1976, *Saturday Review*: "The characters . . . are fleshed out (or, rather, painted by number) in a collection of disjointed details, so that, although they are sometimes intriguingly eccentric, they lack an emotional core. Childhood histories, kinship patterns, recipes, and tastes in pop music do not necessarily add up to anyone we care about or remember."

Although few critics mention "Imagined Scenes" directly, one reviewer who does mention the story is John Romano. Unlike some other critics, he finds "Beattie's writing not tedious; there is instead, something graceful and painstaking about her fidelity to the ordinary." He continues with a discussion of the narrator of "Imagined Scenes," noting that she has "no imagination." However, Romano takes this as a "mark of Beattie's respect for this creation." That is, Beattie loves her character like "some impossible ideal of a loving parent who succeeds in not interfering in her children's lives. To love one's characters . . . is to allow them to be who they are."

More recent criticism of Beattie's work focuses on her place as a writer of experimental short fiction. James C. Robison, for example, writes that Beattie's stories "generally combine the realistic surface of traditional fiction and the bitter outlook typical of experimental work." Furthermore, Joseph Epstein, in his 1983 *Commentary* article, "Ann Beattie and the Hippoisie," writes that "[w]hat her fiction strives to achieve is not development of character, accounts of motivation, or moral resolution—no, what she strives to achieve are states of feeling. What is less clear is why the states of feeling her stories reveal are always those connected with sadness and loss." Likewise, Carolyn Porter, in her chapter "Ann Beattie: The Art of the Missing" from *Contemporary American Writers* (1985), edited by Catherine Rainwater and William J. Scheick, writes that "Beattie's most marked talent is for eliminating discrete chunks of exposition, that laying out of background information which the short story must find a way of minimizing." Clearly, for Porter, Beattie's minimalist approach to literature works well.

It is likely that critical attention to Beattie's work will continue in the twenty-first century with the publication of new work and with some historical distance from the height of the minimalist movement. Her style has modified over the years; yet she still retains the sharp edge in her prose, rendering her a continued force in fiction.

Criticism

Diane Andrews Henningfeld

Henningfeld is a professor of literature at Adrian College who writes on literary topics for a variety of publications. In this essay, Henningfeld considers the roles of sleep and snow in Ann Beattie's "Imagined Scenes."

Ann Beattie's 1974 short story, "Imagined Scenes," contains many of the elements of a typical Beattie story: photographs, postcards, and plants. In addition, as in most Beattie stories, the narrator is a woman, the situation is a marriage, and the tense is present. It is likely that these characteristics have caused critics and reviewers alike largely to overlook this story.

Yet even among those critics who choose to treat the story, there seems to be some level of discomfort with just what is going on in the text. Christina Murphy, for example, while applauding the general ambiguity and inconclusivity of Beattie's fiction, nevertheless seems to want to fix the details and meaning of the story. In particular, she zeroes in on the relationship between the narrator and her husband, David. She initially writes that "the adultery in 'Imagined Scenes' is only hinted at." However, rather than allowing the story to remain nebulous, and the supposed adultery a hint, Murphy quickly leaps from the hints to statements about "David's adultery." That she should do so is puzzling, especially given the nature of the body of Beattie's work, work that is noted for its nonlinearity, its fragmentation, and its lack of clear-cut conclusion. In her attempt to make sense of the story, Murphy, as most readers, trusts the perceptions of the narrator to be accurate portrayals of the scenes before her. What Murphy forgets is just what Cynthia Whitney Hallett reminds readers about minimalist fiction in general: "The stories appear as open-ended as life itself, and, as with life, nothing about them should be taken for granted."

Taking the narrator's perceptions for granted creates several problems with the persuasiveness of Murphy's interpretation, however, and there are many hints that the story might be read otherwise. In the first place, the story appears in a collection called *Distortions*, suggesting at least that events within the story may be other than what they appear. Furthermore, the title of the story is "Imagined Scenes," again cluing the reader to the possibility that the narration provided by the young wife might be located within her imagination rather than in the "real" world of the story. Finally, and most tellingly, are the ongoing references throughout the story to dreams, snow, and sleep. Indeed, sleep seems to be Beattie's overriding concern throughout the story.

The story opens directly with the narrator's words as she describes a dream to her husband, David, and it closes with the narrator speaking to the old man's sister in a kind of waking dream. Thus the entire story is framed between these two instances of interrupted sleep. Furthermore, throughout the story itself there are at least nineteen direct references to sleep, or lack of sleep, or need for sleep, or quality of sleep. There are several ways to read these references. A straightforward examination of sleep and the effects of sleep deprivation may provide a deeper understanding of Beattie's thematic purpose in the story itself.

What Do I Read Next?

- Beattie is often compared with Raymond Carver as a writer of minimalist short stories. Carver's *Where I'm Calling From* (1988) is a collection that illustrates the range of Carver's talent.

- Bobbie Ann Mason's *Love Life* (1989) offers a look at short fiction written by one of Beattie's contemporaries. Mason's work also features a close attention to the minutia of the everyday.

- Beattie's *Park City: New and Collected Stories* (1998) allows the reader a retrospective look at Beattie's best stories, with representative stories from the 1970s, 1980s, and 1990s.

- *Contemporary American Women Writers* (1985), edited by Catherine Rainwater and William J. Scheik and published by the University of Kentucky Press, is a collection of essays and photographs treating ten important women writers, including Beattie, Grace Paley, Annie Dillard, and Toni Morrison, among others. Each chapter also includes a very useful bibliography of writings by each of the writers.

- *Chilly Scenes of Winter* (1976) is Beattie's novel published at the same time as "Imagined Scenes." The novel utilizes many of the same devices and themes found in her short stories.

All human beings need sleep. No one is able to function for any length of time without adequate sleep, and sleep studies have demonstrated repeatedly the consequences of both sleep deprivation and interrupted REM (rapid eye movement) sleep. In the twentieth century, electric lights, improved transportation, and the demand for manufactured goods led, for the first time in human history, to the creation of "shift work." In shift work, people work around the clock and often have no control over what shift they will be assigned. This, as well as other fundamental realities of life in the twentieth and twenty-first centuries, has led to widespread sleep deprivation among citizens of industrial nations.

Lack of sleep, according to many sleep studies, causes a variety of physiological and psychological effects in the sleep-deprived. Someone not getting enough sleep will suffer from confusion and memory lapses. Moreover, studies and surveys document that inadequate sleep leads not only to depression but that, in its extreme form, it leads to paranoia and disorientation as well. In addition, without adequate REM sleep, humans are also deprived of their dreams. Because the brain seems to need dreams for memory and for health, humans who do not get enough REM sleep will often suffer from hallucinations or waking dreams. People in the business of prisoner interrogation and brainwashing have long known that depriving a prisoner of sleep is a form of torture.

In the case of the narrator of "Imagined Scenes," the reader discovers that the young woman is working nights, caring for an old man. The assumption is that she has taken on this job to support herself and her husband while he is in graduate school. Because he does not go to work during the day, his schedule is likewise not regular. In addition, the narrator is not sleeping very much during the day. After doing the grocery shopping, for example, early in the story she mentions that she has to work that night. Because of this, "[s]he goes upstairs to take a nap and sets the alarm. She rests, but can't fall asleep." At the old man's house that night, she "drinks tea with him, tired because she didn't nap." Likewise, the old man tells her that he does not sleep well.

The next day in the early afternoon, the narrator notices that there is food on the countertop that she does not remember buying. Certainly, this food could be read as a clue that David is carrying on behind the narrator's back. It could just as easily be read as a memory lapse caused by sleep deprivation. The narrator starts for her bedroom to sleep but is interrupted by David's return to the house. "You should be asleep," he tells her. "You can't work at night if you're not going to sleep in the day." A few lines later he says, "You look like you need sleep." And just a few lines after this, he tells the narrator, "Get some rest." Again, it is possible to read this as David's attempt to get the narrator out of the way for whatever it is he is doing with his time. Certainly, if the reader trusts the narrator's perceptions, the reader will begin to experience a slight paranoia: Just what is it that David is up to? However, is it not just as easy to trust *David's* perception? If the narrator has been working all night and not sleeping during the day, then of course she will look like she needs sleep.

Later, the narrator discovers that she cannot find her watch when she goes to work. In the middle of making tea, she goes to search for it, forgetting about the tea she is preparing for the old man. This is clear because she has to reheat the tea when she returns from searching her car. And not only does the narrator suffer memory lapses concerning the tea, she finds her watch at home in the bathroom where she left it, having forgotten to put it on before work.

Additionally, when the narrator sits with the old man, she is unable to keep herself awake, falling immediately into a dream about Greece, even though she is sitting in a chair by the old man's bed. REM sleep deprivation studies confirm that when a person does not get enough REM sleep, dreams will occur earlier and earlier in the sleep cycle.

In the car on the way home from the old man's house, the narrator nearly falls asleep. At home, "she closes her eyes again. . . . She's very tired." However, even here, her sleep is interrupted: David awakens her to take a call from the old man's sister who wants her to come back. The scene is very strange; the narrator is unable to make sense of what the woman is saying to her, and her conversation becomes mingled with the narrator's dream of Greece. Because all perception is filtered through the narrator, the scene is also strange for the reader, who cannot at this point determine if the narrator is awake or asleep. The story ends in this fugue state of half-waking or half-sleeping, without resolution.

The many references to sleep, of course, could just be part of the background fabric of the story. However, very early in the story Beattie inserts an obvious clue that sleep is not the background of the story but is rather the foreground, something that needs to be accounted for by any reader. When the old man shows the narrator his collection of post-cards, there is one that the narrator "looks longer at

> **In need of relationship as much as in need of sleep, the characters stumble through their days and nights, caught, it seems, by their inability to touch each other."**

than the rest: A man in boots and green jacket carrying a rifle is pictured walking down a path through the woods in the moonlight." The caption of the postcard identifies the figure: "Joseph Jefferson as Rip Van Winkle." Rip Van Winkle, of course, is the protagonist of another story in which sleep itself is the subject: Washington Irving's famous story of the man who sleeps for twenty years while the rest of the world goes on without him.

This allusion suggests that Beattie wants the reader to consider all aspects of sleep, both literal and metaphorical. As noted above, sleep deprivation leads to the kinds of distortions of reality experienced by the narrator. One need not posit an actual affair on the part of the husband to understand why the sleep-deprived narrator might read her environment to support such an interpretation. At the metaphoric level, however, sleep plays yet another function: The narrator is not the only character in the story who sleeps or does not sleep; the old man says he has trouble sleeping. David claims that he is sleeping when the narrator calls him on the phone. Like the omnipresent snow (the mention of which nearly always follows mention of sleep), the sleeping state becomes a metaphor for contemporary, fragmented existence. In a world blanketed by snow, the landscape changes and is muffled. Snow and sleep isolate the inhabitants of this story from each other. In need of relationship as much as in need of sleep, the characters stumble through their days and nights, caught, it seems, by their inability to touch each other.

Further, the sleeping state and the snow serve as metaphors for death. James Joyce's "The Dead," from *Dubliners*, closes as the main character, Gabriel, looks out his window, his wife asleep in the bed bedside him, at snow blanketing the living and the dead. While Beattie's references to sleep and snow may not be a direct allusion to Joyce's famous story, she nonetheless seems to be striving toward a similar association among snow, sleep, and death. The human condition, such that it is, requires not only sleep but also waking; not only work but human companionship. The narrator, David, the old man, his sister, and even the old man's daughter—trapped in an airplane in Florida—all move as if in a dream, not fully awake nor aware of their surroundings nor understanding the need to reach out their arms to each other. Like Rip Van Winkle, they have chosen to sleep their way through their days and their lives.

Source: Diane Andrews Henningfeld, Critical Essay on "Imagined Scenes," in *Short Stories for Students*, Gale, 2005.

Ann Beattie with James Plath

In the following interview, Beattie discusses how she structures her stories, her narrative technique, and characterization.

Book tours have a way of turning writers into gypsies. After Ann Beattie finished reading from *What Was Mine* at a Chicago-area book store, I drove her to her hotel, where, upon finding cold champagne and a fruit tray, compliments of her publisher, she expressed the same measure of surprised delight as a tourist might. Her appearance was equally down-to-earth. Beattie wore a loose tunic, patterned stretch pants, and bold socks. Nothing matched, she explained, because she purchased them on the road because her others were dirty. "My Reeboks," she said, lifting one foot above the coffee table, "I recently bought in Key West. On sale."

Born in Washington, D.C., in 1947, Ann Beattie enjoyed the early support of *The New Yorker*, where a great many of her stories of failed and failing relationships appeared. Her first novel, *Chilly Scenes of Winter* (1976), and *Distortions*, a collection of short stories published that same year, established her as a spokesperson for the hippie-turned-yuppie generation. Other books quickly followed: *Secrets and Surprises* (1978), *Falling in Place* (1980), *The Burning House* (1982), *Spectacles* (1985), *Love Always* (1986), *Where You'll Find Me* (1987), *Picturing Will* (1989), and her latest collection, *What Was Mine* (1991).

During the reading, Beattie sat in a chair on a small platform, rarely looking up from her book to make eye contact with the crowd of sixty or so. Once finished, however, she received the line of autograph-seekers and well-wishers with reception-line enthusiasm, asking each person a question or two, and personalizing every book. By the time she finished, it was well after 10 p.m. Yet, in the hotel room, relaxing somewhat with shoes off and a glass of champagne in hand, she was still gracious, still full of energy, full of interest—and seemingly eager to talk about her work.

[JP:] Like Raymond Carver, you tend to write what I would call "fictions of aftermath," where most of the conflict or turning points have already occurred, leaving the characters to cope with or work through resultant problems. What is it about recovery that seems more interesting to you than the cause and effect process leading up to it all, a process you seem to deemphasize?

[AB:] I don't think you can omit any mention of the cause and effect process in the story, but I'm not sure that it needs to be the beginning. If the stories seem to resemble "ordinary life," then very few things happen with a beginning, middle and end. You often can understand things in retrospect, or something will happen that will precipitate a change. But I don't think that most of us lead orderly lives, and it wouldn't be possible for me to write a story that went along with some status quo that I don't even see in operation.

As your characters try to order their lives, they look to the past so often that it almost seems like returning to the "scene of the crime."

It's true. I think I've very rarely written anything that doesn't invoke the past at some point. At what point that occurs, though, varies a bit. The story that I read tonight, "Home to Marie," certainly could have been told in reverse order. It could have had a different so-called "punch line." It's really just an emotional decision, in a way, if all your material is there, to try to figure out how you want to present it. I'm not saying that *anything* is okay. I don't think you can set a reader up for one set of expectations, and then just reverse course in the story. But I do think that the same information can be given a lot of different ways.

I've juggled a lot. I very rarely make endings beginnings, but I quite often lop off beginnings, because I write many pages before I feel my way into the material. And those things often have more to do with the character's past, how they habitually talk, the physical description. Finally, if you've got it right in your head and you are clear on who they are and you can animate them, you don't need an introduction. I mean, what's more interesting: two hours into the party, or when you're walking through the front door?

A passage from your story "In the White Night" reads, "There were two images when you looked in the finder and you had to make the adjustment yourself so that one superimposed itself upon the other and the figure suddenly leaped into clarity"— which, it seems, could almost serve as directions or a warning label on the side of your fiction for how readers should get through a Beattie story.

Hopefully, that's how the details will work. For me as a writer, the way to make something seem more real is to go at it several times, rather than declaring that it is some particular thing. There are a lot of people who are extremely good at that. Carver, he'll give you some benign landmark—a lamp on a table—and by the time he comes back to the table for the third time, you know the lamp is there and it's gold, whether or not he says that it is. That's just a working method, in a lot of ways, but it also has to do with a personal view of things.

I'm not very interested in looking at the surfaces of things except as starting points. I'm willing to go with the visual detail that strikes me, but it has to be appropriate to the material. It's fairly random if something is going to capture my attention, but when it does, I think you have to hound the reader a little bit about what that means.

I'm thinking not so much about motifs—although they're certainly present in your fiction—but about the way your characters tend to reexamine their childhoods, or estranged couples will meet at houses that hold pleasant memories. They engage in a nostalgic return of some sort in order to find meaning or healing. Has life become so complicated that, like a poem, it has to be "read" more than once?

A lot of the time, people don't see a thing succinctly in the moment, but whether or not they even want to see that thing, other things accrue— and those things are often things from the past that allow the person to more fully see what's happening in the moment. In other words, I'm not talking about people who are out on a quest, or people who are simply sitting and trying to articulate a problem to themselves. I'm talking more about those unexpected moments when people find that they are thinking about the present, and that it's been influenced by the past.

You experiment more in the latest collection with strikingly different narrative voices. I'm thinking of "Installation #6" or "Television." How did

> **"I almost think that readers take my tone as a matter of course, whereas a lot of critics are very alarmed by it, and I'm not quite sure why. It doesn't seem to me to be that shocking a thing."**

the new voices arise? They're quite unlike the "New Yorkerish" voice which has typified your characters' speech.

They *are* distinct voices. *What was Mine* is filled with monologues. Who knows why that becomes interesting to a writer at one point, versus another? When I sat down to write "The Working Girl," for instance, I wrote the first paragraph which began, "This is a story about Jeanette, who is a working girl." And sitting there, I thought, "Oh, Ann, you *can't* execute another story in which you make the presumption that you're the omniscient narrator. I mean, really!" So I undercut it by interjecting a real question. In effect, the question was "Really?" and it ended up being a kind of deconstruction of a short story, and therefore an admission of what the process is, too. But I was funning with myself there; it's not that I wasn't in earnest about what I wrote, but for whatever reason I didn't mind letting people see the skeletal system. Why not?

In some of the newer stories, you deal with people who actually use contractions, who begin sentences with conjunctions. And in Picturing Will, *the style is even more complex, more fluid, less stylized than the short stories with their subject-verb-object patterns.*

That was deliberate, and partly it was because I realized I was going to be taking years out of my life. You want to set yourself some tasks if you're going to do such a thing. However silly they might sound, I just decided that I was going to write compound-complex sentences for a change. Who knows why? But I had to find a reason for it. It wasn't even my notion when I started writing that book that the italicized portions—the journal entries—would be attributed to any particular character. And when I did decide to do that, then it looked like it was overly conceived, in a way. That it was calling attention to its own form by having the author's voice come in. At first I thought about giving them to Jody, but then I realized no, no, no, no, no.

You've referred, in the past, to things like point/ counterpoint, and counter melodies. It seems as if you have relied on these devices, these breaks, in order to give the narrative some sort of texture, some sort of relief or "counterpoint," as you say. I don't want to lead you here, but you seem to be growing more and more fascinated with the whole process of authorial intrusion.

I'm more ill-at-ease with the notion that anyone might think that I was defining something in the story, but I think for my own sake, at least, to be able to look at the story and to point to the fact that there *are* ambiguities, complexities, contradictions, etc., is a pleasing notion—because I'm just the sort of person that if you tell me one story, I won't pay much attention to the story that I'm hearing, or I'll put it in the context of something that I choose.

I'm not really very interested in information. Information is random, so it would be very hard for me to write something that was on some level informative—you know, four-hundred pages of a novel—and to put out something that might be mistaken for being "definitive," that would not be at all pleasing to me. If I could do such a thing, I guess I would stand on the street corner or something and shout it at the sky, or passers-by, or whatever. I don't think that's what the writing is about at all. It just puts me at my ease, personally, to indicate those counternarrative things, if for no one else but myself. And it is to create texture. You're totally right about that.

How do you relate to your characters?

I just plain try to put enough information there so they're believable. I mean, I try to examine them closely—that's how I relate to them. But it certainly wouldn't be of any interest to me to be directly analytical, because I don't even think people would believe it—not the readers that I was interested in having as readers, anyway. You know, that just doesn't seem to me to be the purpose of fiction.

But believe it or not, I'm certainly trying to do a lot of things by delivering the detail or information between the lines. I hope you will realize that I might have given you the same set of facts, but in a different order. I'm trying to elicit particular emotional reactions with the stories, and I'm quite aware that the way I structure something and the way I omit things, as well as the way I include things, can create or fail to create a real world in the story.

In the past you've talked about private lives and secret yearnings. Are these yearnings, in part, responsible for creating the impossible distance that separates your characters?

I'm hard-pressed to think of a writer who doesn't have characters with secret longings. I mean, Raymond Carver is about nothing but longing in a lot of ways. I could think of any number of people: Tobias Wolff, Richard Ford. . . . Those unstated things that happen off the page are so often what contemporary fiction is about. They're not empty spaces—they're referential spaces.

Your characters don't travel as much as they used to.

That's because I traveled *too* much.

But they're still as alone as ever, still not connecting with each other, for the most part. What keeps them distant from others? Personal space? Or are yearnings the culprit?

I don't know that it's just secret yearnings. I don't necessarily assume that my characters have any more social skills than me or anybody I meet. It's a problem to communicate—it's as simple as that. It's extremely difficult. I don't think that, in a lot of ways, this is a culture that really asks people to communicate. It's a culture that asks people to listen. That's why people are so hostile.

In some of your early stories, the connections between characters were so tenuous that they would do anything to relate to one another. In the case of "A Vintage Thunderbird," it was the car that served as the main connection, and in another story, it was the Weimaraners. Now though, it seems as if objects are less the bond between characters than an associative method of leading them somewhere else.

I think that's true. Even *Chilly Scenes of Winter* was a novel about an obsession. Charles would find things that would remind him of Laura all the time. He took all these things to be signposts and guides. He was projecting like mad.

The whole idea of anti-materialism was much in the air when I was going to college. So if we're talking about stories that I wrote in the early or mid- '70s, I was often surrounded by a lot of people who professed not to want material possessions, and who were happy not to own furniture. It was certainly to your credit to have only what could fit in the trunk of your car, including your cat.

I saw a lot of acting-out on the part of a lot of disenfranchised people who were militant about not being ensconced in the world, who were not going to live the status-quo, who were going to have a freewheeling existence. What they tended to do, on however sad or humorous a level, was often to fixate on their pen, or something like that. They didn't have any furniture, no fixed address, no telephone number, no way to get in touch with them, but they absolutely would have had an anxiety attack if they had lost their favorite pen! I never failed to see that, on some level—whether or not they admitted it— there was something that they held onto, and very often in an extremely exaggerated way.

Fixations point to something meaningful, don't they? For an author, as well as a character?

When I was doing *The Burning House,* the copy-editor at Random House wrote me a letter saying, "You and I know these are distinct stories, but if you keep naming the characters Andrew or Andy, the clever reader is going to go through trying to zig-zag and make a pattern between these stories, so don't you want to rethink it and call Andy 'Paul' sometimes?" And that was entirely true.

She also pointed out things like—we're talking about maybe fifteen or sixteen stories—six or seven times somebody has a headache, which seems perfectly believable, in terms of what people suffer in the real world, and I was always sending them off to take an Excedrin. That is, in fact, what I take. I don't think of it as the generic: aspirin. I think of it as Excedrin. She said, "They're going to think you're getting a kickback from the company. You've got to change this. Nobody would believe that every character everywhere is taking Excedrin." Point granted. I was so fixated myself that I didn't *know* I was fixated.

I know you're not talking about those small betrayals of myself—you're talking about elements of plot, that people tend to be fixated on external things that bespeak private desires.

Right. In "Longest Day of the Year," when the Welcome Wagon lady comes, just the sheer irony of her arriving when the marriage is in dissolution is awfully funny. But as she begins to prattle nervously, she starts talking about kids in the neighborhood. That gets her to thinking about rabbits and turtles that also used to be in the neighborhood, which gets her to thinking about the squirrel acrobatics. That leads her to recalling a traveling carnival, which leads her to recalling the animals her husband used to win for her at the carnival, and at that point the narrator/observer concludes: "I was coming to understand that she was suffering too."

It's interesting, I'll tell you that. To tell you the truth, I put that line in and took that line out half a dozen times. I probably made the wrong decision. I should have taken the line out. But I didn't want the woman who was being visited by the Welcome Wagon lady to seem like anyone's fool, either. I didn't want to condescend to her in any way. She just happened to be a victim, and she happened to encounter someone who more overtly thought of herself as a victim. It was playing off of those two vulnerable positions and having them understand each other for what they were, but still not really being able to do anything for one another, or even to get past that without a lot of awkwardness. I wanted the story to be as awkward as those real life encounters can be when somebody just starts spinning out of control and you realize that they're saying more than they want to say, than they know they're saying. That was really a consideration again of trying to figure out how to make the woman in that story not seem to be dense. That's why I wrote such an overt line. Of course, as a writer, what I was trying to do was bring in everything from the natural world—the rabbits that used to run around before the place was so sophisticated—the way the world looks when there's a carnival.

I realize as much as the next person that there are things that people expect to hear. I'm used to people making a lot of small talk with me. Everybody is. You sort of expect that. You're always lulled by that. To make the story seem real, you do have to have that level of small talk, in some way, so that you can make readers comfortable enough to stay with you. Then you can begin to surprise them. If you just launch these characters in some wild way, it is as much an assault literarily as it would be conversationally.

I thought that perhaps some of your characters were just using language as a mask.

Oh, that happens too. I certainly admit that. Even the story that you were talking about, "In the White Night," begins: "Don't think about a cow, don't think about a river, don't think about a car, don't think about snow." Absolutely. That's a mask for not having any real communication during the evening, and as the story goes on you find out why these people would have everything invested in *not* wishing to communicate. What painful conclusion would they arrive at if they did? Probably no conclusion, just more pain, you know? A lot of my stories are about masks, a lot of them are about the smokescreens, the facades, and so forth. Nevertheless, considering the characters, they have to vary. It did seem to me that the Welcome Wagon lady might kind of veer out of control because of who she was, in that setting. To tell you the truth, I encountered such a Welcome Wagon lady.

I figured you might have.

I did. I very rarely write things that are true. And it was only true to the extent that there was a lunatic Welcome Wagon lady who did come to visit near the end of my first marriage—not my third marriage, as I made it in the story. She uttered a great line that I could never use; when she unrolled the map—and I never remember dialogue verbatim, but I've remembered this for twelve years—she said, "I believe they have neglected to imprint the map." It would either look far out, or it would look like the author was just writing outrageous and bad dialogue, to have someone say that. She must have known she was speaking bad dialogue, but it was a mask. She was anxious, and it was a blank piece of paper. She was completely unnerved. So in a lot of the stories I think it's true I want to lead into things, which I do by letting the characters be unnerved.

I thought it was also great use of a symbol to have her sit in the chair that the woman's husband had neglected to properly glue—as she herself is coming unglued.

You may call it a symbol, but as Flannery O'Connor said about her character's wooden leg in "Good Country People," first and foremost, it is a wooden leg. You may want to say that it's loaded, that it's a symbol, but first and foremost, those were the lousy chairs I lived with for years. By the way, it didn't crack, and she didn't go down. But years later, I realized my anxiety was so great that I had not considered that the chair *wouldn't* break. So I wrote the story and let it happen. A retake.

Your stories seem driven by underlying emotion. I get the feeling that at the heart of a lot of your stories is a Welcome Lady who, given the right door, may just spill everything.

That's certainly my sense of the world. I don't know if it's the case that I had a particular personality and therefore I became a writer, or if it's because

now that I'm a writer, people come up and say things to me because they think they intuit a particular sensibility. I mean, it's very hard at some point to ever sort that stuff out. Whether or not I became a writer, I think I would still be sitting here saying to you, "It's amazing what people will say overtly." Forget about covertly.

If you think about the day you spend in New York City, or something like that, the cab driver has a rehearsed routine that he's going to recite. Can you think of the last time anyone in public transportation has been interested in your opinion? I just flew in today from San Francisco. No one on the plane made eye contact. Not only did they not want verbal communication, they didn't even want to acknowledge that you were sitting in the same space they were sitting in.

I think that everybody's a volcano. Today I was reading an excerpt from some book that's coming out about Raymond Carver. Somebody said that Ray always said, when the phone rang, "The phone's ringing. The world will change." That's all it takes. I feel that same way. Otherwise, I would not have an unlisted phone number and screen calls. I do believe that the phone rings and the world changes.

What about Irony and Pity, the name of your corporation? Is that a nutshell expression of how you feel toward your characters, or about the world?

It's a nutshell of what I feel about being told to incorporate. Years ago I had a scandalously inept accountant who told me to do this. It's been nothing but grief ever since, but I did do that for business reasons. I had to pick a title for my so-called corporation, and you know the line, right? Jake Barnes is sitting there talking to one of his friends in *The Sun Also Rises,* and the friend says, "irony and pity, give them irony and pity"—which, when I read it, I just burst out laughing. I was probably sixteen when I read the book. Actually, my ex-husband came up with the best name. It was "Wasted Inc." That's pretty good—but the one that I came up with was Irony and Pity.

Speaking of "Wasted Inc.," I was going to get a group of over-the-hill basketball players in the university intramurals, and we were going to call ourselves "Abilities Ltd." We also had a diet contest on campus, and the English department chose, for our team name, "As I Weigh Dying."

That's very good. I have no ability with puns. It's strange. And often they have to be explained to me. Those don't, but often they do.

And do you have, irony and pity flowing through your work?

I hope so. I don't know that the irony is so strong. It's often remarked upon to me, but I'm not sure. I almost think that readers take my tone as a matter of course, whereas a lot of critics are very alarmed by it, and I'm not quite sure why. It doesn't seem to me to be that shocking a thing. In other words, I think people get the little ironies very quickly when I read aloud, or even just people who have read my work privately, who talk to me. They understand the dual levels. It doesn't seem to stop them dead. It often seems to stop the critics dead.

When you say, "stop them dead," what do you mean?

To make them analyze the work only in terms of where and when it becomes ironic, to overlook any other impetus of a piece, to speak only about where it's ironic and to form opinions and assumptions—even if they've only become personal opinions and assumptions about me based on that.

Look, here's an example: *Twin Peaks* on television. Were you shocked and amazed by *Twin Peaks?* You couldn't be; you've read literature. That was only shocking in the context of its going out to a television audience. Television, as far as I'm concerned, has always essentially condescended to the public. I think there are any number of writers who are communicating clearly to their readers—not condescending—and being understood. But it's only when people come in to do a so-called critical study of this book that they stop dead at point A, as though it's remarkable.

I wanted to wait until a relaxed moment to hit you with the "M-word," so to speak, since you seem to have bristled when minimalism was mentioned in previous interviews. Yet, you admit to having felt Hemingway's influence, and if Carver has been called the godfather of minimalism, Hemingway is certainly a precursor. A passage from your story, "Snow," even reads like a minimalist dictum, or a rewording of Hemingway's "Iceberg Theory" of omission.

Yeah, that one's been turned around as a baseball bat a lot of times: "Any life will seem dramatic if you omit mention of most of it."

That's come back to haunt you?

Sure. I mean, you can always point to the sentence in a book that some critics are inevitably going to turn against you. And then you just think, am I really going to take it out?

Why do you take it as a baseball bat, though?

Because it is always invoked in a negative way, it's always taken as a dismissal. That line has never been used positively. It's only used negatively. It's only been used as a substantiation of someone's own faulty notion of what so-called minimalism is. I don't mind the comparisons. I don't mind a serious discussion about Raymond Carver, Ernest Hemingway, and me. I'm in great company. It's just that I rarely get serious discussions. And as you realize, many interviewers simply mean to be provocative: the "Oh, you're so cute when you're mad" approach[.]

I think most people who know me well think that I do have a pretty wild sense of humor. But I'm really serious about writing, and maybe I was falsely protected, in that being in the academy for so many years, and graduate school, and teaching, and so forth, I didn't know that people tossed things off the way a lot of interviewers do when they talk to me. So I don't necessarily take people at their word if they say that what they most want to talk about is minimalism.

When many young writers engage in what they consider minimalism, they usually combine it with their idea of Chekhovian slice-of-life, and they end up with a piece of nothing.

Look, if I had to generalize, I'd say what I dislike about a lot of so-called minimalist writing is that it has no clear trajectory. I can't stay with anything if it seems there is no necessity to keep reading. I'm interested in how things are put together to form a whole. I'm really not very interested in the kind of egocentricity that I see in a lot of so-called minimalist writing. And certainly I'm not going to sit here and trash people.

According to theory, the final stage of any genre is self-parody. And I'm wondering if minimalism has reached the point where it has become parodic, except in the hands of people who really know what they're doing.

I think even "parody" puts too nice a word on it. I don't think its parodic, I just think a lot of it is bad. When something is complex, there are ways to read between the lines. You might not agree with my interpretation, but if we sat with a Carver story, I could at least tell you where I think something is being said that isn't verbalized, and how I think he's led into that, and so on.

It's not the first mode to be misunderstood. You have to remember that when modernism came in, people were kicking and screaming. Now we speak about "postmodernism" as though modernism is taken for granted, and now there's this often self-referential, humorous, even parodic thing called "postmodernism." Did modernism become legitimized because there's now so-called *post modernism?*

"Postmodernism" and "minimalism" are only buzz-words?

Yeah, which is why I'm very ill-at-ease in having questions asked about that. If I am to take something seriously, what am I being asked?

Alright. The simple sentences style, the preponderance of articles, the absence of contractions—the "I am" instead of "I'm"—what do you feel it accomplishes in a story?

It has a kind of staccato effect, and it has a kind of deliberate artificiality about it that should make you suspect that the article or noncontraction is being invoked for a purpose.

So it's an acknowledgement of the writer/story relationship?

Yes, it is, in a way. It's a kind of tacit admission on the part of the so-called authority figure—the writer—that this is a put-up. It's literature, after all.

Would you go so far as to compare this style to the impressionists—of drawing attention to the process of creation, of diminishing the illusion?

I would almost compare it to the superrealists. I would be more inclined to think about [Richard] Estes, or somebody. Yes, it is the natural world, but it is so *hyper.* Is there ever a moment when you stop and think about the world that way?

I could easily think of a lot of photographers who try to do the same thing. But there are rarely moments in which time is frozen that are quite that pertinent and complex. You may indeed pass by a store window when you least expect it and see that the light is even in a way that allows you to see everything perfectly reflected. Then you go right on. In other words, it's a refinement and an exaggeration presented as being normative. And that's true of a lot of the prose style you were discussing. It's both things, but it's a deliberate masquerade. It's an intensification for a purpose.

How much forethought goes into crafting a story? Does much of the "planting" occur in rewrites?

No. At this stage of my career, more than fifty percent of what I attempt to write ends up in the trash. If the stories don't start to take on a larger life, I just can't follow through. I have to be surprised in the story in the same way I'm surprised constantly in daily life. Of course, I have to realize that there are obviously a lot of things gestating that I don't realize are gestating until I sit down to write—that I'm making comparisons between things in my mind that are not factually related, and so forth. I might have an overheard conversation in a fictional setting, and that fictional setting might be slightly like my best friend's kitchen. But I tend to write about things that are so-called "real" only to the extent that they begin to transform. And if they never transform, then I feel like I'm a reporter. I feel like I'm just on the scene, and that is so deadening in a fictional context that I can't continue.

You say "if they don't transform." Is it a first line that will grab you, a character, a sketch, a situation?

Never a situation, because that would too closely resemble plot, and I never know the plot. It's an emotion that starts me, and then the visual image comes. The visual image may eventually be discarded. I can write several pages to orient myself to the world that I'm talking about, and then there could be a line of dialogue, and I could realize then or later that the line of dialogue is the true beginning of the story. I mean, the first forty-nine and a half pages of *Chilly Scenes of Winter* were thrown out, so that the novel now begins with a line of dialogue—in French no less, because it took that many pages to wade into the material—explaining how Charles and Sam came to know each other, what the house looked like that they lived in, blah, blah, blah. Very nice, once I know it—then I can fly.

Did that happen with Picturing Will *too?*

Oh, everything imaginable happened with *Picturing Will.* It was very hard for me to catch on to what I was doing. I had to write a lot to see what shouldn't be written. Even when I did figure out what my notions were, and which characters were major and minor, and, to a large extent, how the book would be organized, even then it was a real problem to figure out how it could be done as directly as possible, while still keeping the reader's interest.

In other words, that seemed like a book that could turn very discursive, and that would be a terrible disadvantage. It's an entire book about storytelling. Everybody tells a story. They actually sit down physically and *say* things in that book.

This is probably the first time in a novel I so clearly let myself be the manipulator. To have dropped twenty years out of the text was quite calculated. What could I do, though, to make that seem not a cheap shock, or not shocking beyond the obvious, when the reader realizes that here we are in the 21st century, in section three? That was really the question, really the hardest thing to do.

A lot of friends gave me feedback on that manuscript. They understood what I had meant to write. They were very good in being able to say where I had not been clear. Case in point: I thought I had created a pretty cold Jody. I thought I'd presented that dimension to her character rather early on. Her opinions on Atget are not my personal opinions on Atget. I created a character who would have, as far as I'm concerned, a rather odd and insufficient response to Atget, because I meant to indicate something about her character. Point granted in retrospect. I don't think everybody's going to say, "Aha," and spring up out of his or her chair. I finally went back and wrote that scene where her friend hits the deer, and you see Jody jumping out of the car and saying, in effect, I'm going to now photograph the scene for my art, and "Thank you, God . . . for the invention of the autowinder." I put that sentence in point-blank; I knew perfectly well that, at least there, I was announcing something about her character. Therefore, at the end, when you find that she is more than a little removed and more than a little egocentric, if you look back you may not think of her as simply a person under duress and trying to do a difficult job as a single mother. Hopefully, in retrospect, the book will come clear. The last image gets superimposed on the first image, if you will.

Something else in Picturing Will *that struck me is that you included some graphic sexual scenes. That's also new territory for you, isn't it?*

I was absolutely shocked when the motel door closed and I realized what was going to happen. I didn't realize until that door closed what I had intuited but not verbalized to that point. We all know these people who seem to be completely out of control, in an almost charming way. Very egocentric and narcissistic, they are very interesting to watch from afar. Close the door on those people and, like everybody else, they will either be less

crazy or more crazy. So Haveabud's transformation was interesting. But that was not fun to write. I have written things on many occasions that haven't been fun to write.

You were pulled along then.

Yeah, feeling that I had led myself into my own trap, and that I had not articulated the full situation to myself.

Does that happen in a short story as much as it does in a novel?

I wrote a story years ago with a garden hose in it. I had never seen a white garden hose until I visited a friend's house on Long Island where there was this wonderful green lawn and millions of things to observe. I was so stunned, because I had always seen green garden hoses all my life, and there was that glowing white hose in the green grass.

Several years later, when I was writing about that backyard in a completely fictional context— having nothing to do with that man or with me—I remembered the white hose, but only then. I had forgotten it for all those years, and as I was typing the rough draft of the story, I had the character think that it was the East Hampton equivalent of the snake in the grass. And I suddenly realized, at that point in the rough draft, that I had been writing something that referred to the Garden of Eden and to the fall of man.

Your world—at least the characters that you write about—has been somewhat restricted, and I hope that you don't take that in the wrong way, but . . .

I try to make my personal life as restricted as possible!

So you don't exactly do field work like Mike Royko of the Chicago Tribune, *who frequently goes to Billy Goat Tavern to sit and talk with the common folk?*

I don't ever do direct research. I mean, I don't do things and think that I'll file the experience away and use it. I have to admit that many things have come back to me in writing. Not conspicuous things, but the overheard conversation or the ordinary detail that becomes the telling detail in the fictional context does come back, so I have to say that my tentacles are out, whether I mean them to be or not. I'm always knowing things that I don't *know* I know until I sit down to write them. I myself am amazed at how those things both recur and are changed by being put in a fictional context.

How do you remain open to surprise and discovery as you're writing?

To some extent I have to struggle more now than when I began writing, to keep other concerns out of my mind. I never sat there thinking of pitching this to such and such magazine, or what will critic X think about this. I still don't, but so much of my life is encroached upon now with the business of writing that it becomes harder and harder to just plain drop out for a week. Either I have not learned to manage my time very well, or I now realize it cannot be managed well. It's not any longer very interesting to shut out the world. If I go and take the mail from the mailman's hand—and I'm not saying this facetiously, either; I've done that instead of having it dropped through the slot—I've been absolutely amazed at what gets revealed before the mailman leaves the front door.

It's like hopping stones across a river or something, you know? The idea seems logical until you get out there and you realize that the river is wider than you realized, and you've only got three stones. And I think people tell their stories that way a lot. If the mailman stops to say something to me, he may mean it to be quick and brusque, but something either triggers something in his mind, or I look taken aback, and he goes on. And as he elaborates, like the Welcome Wagon lady he finds that he's in deeper, and it can all happen so quickly.

I think people are always vulnerable. You try to pretend that you're not and to keep that out of your conscious mind, but in point-of-fact you are. And as a writer, you really do have to—at least for the physical act of writing—sequester yourself as much as possible. It's enough that these things have been percolating in the subconscious, and hopefully will come to you when you're writing.

So human connection isn't important to you?

I try to forget it when I'm writing. It wouldn't be possible to write if I remembered it. Also, I must say that, with a few notable exceptions, including *Picturing Will,* I mostly write short stories that don't work out in the course of a day. I have three to five pages of rough draft very quickly. They either get abandoned right away, or they do work out. And in most cases, some very primitive sort of a rough draft exists in a matter of hours, whether it be three hours or six hours. We're talking about a fifteen-page story, not "Windy Day at the Reservoir." I can drop out for that long.

How many rewrites does each story undergo now?

Well, "The Longest Day of the Year" probably had six words changed. It was written in three hours. "What Was Mine," the title story of the new collection, had six or seven rewrites before it went off to the magazine.

"In the White Night"?

Right off the typewriter, and that's a rare exception, too. That hardly ever happens, anymore, and when it does, it's something very brief, like "Installation #6" in the new collection. I was sitting on a plane, as a matter of fact. I had very little paper, so the analogies I came up with—like the way people glare at you when your reading light goes on in the airplane, or the way the horizon line looked outside—were because I was on an airplane. I was flying from New York to Houston. I was killing time. I just had a couple of pieces of paper, so I wrote.

Would it be possible to have you do a walk-through on a story?

Well, the genesis of "In The White Night" . . . which, I was told after the fact, is apparently a term for a hangover. I had no idea. You have to understand, this is the same person who wrote *The Burning House* having no idea that it was the Buddhist name for the body [laughter]. Didn't know it. Got to *The Burning House* by way of "ladybug, ladybug, fly away home, your house is on fire. . . . " But I can't tell you what made me sit down to write, Don't think about a cow.

That was the first line that came?

Yeah. I wrote a story years ago called "Dwarf House," a story in the first collection. And the first line is "'Are you happy?' blank said, 'Because if you're happy, I'll leave you alone.'" It seems a good beginning, in retrospect, but where did that come from? Then I wrote, "'Are you happy?' McDonald said," because I had eaten at McDonald's that night. And now there is an article out there titled "Ann Beattie: The Imagery of Old McDonald's Farm." Just amazing! Sometimes a line will pop into my mind, "Don't think about . . ." Remember that game?

Anyway, it really did begin with "Don't think about a cow." So here was somebody saying some perplexing thing, and I had no frame of reference for it. Then you've got the next paragraph. Suddenly, I have to root him visually. I have to put him in the temporal world in some way, so I start them naming things. But I remember when I moved them out from under the protection of the Brinkleys' porch—"the cold froze the smiles on their faces"—I suddenly realized that what seemed to be the case, was not really the case at all. That's a tacit admission to the false level on which they're discussing things, if you know what I mean. The choice of the words, "the cold froze the smiles on their faces," that did something for me. Then I knew it wasn't the cold.

And then, "Don't think about an apple," I was actually thinking of [René] Magritte's painting. I had written "Don't think about a cow" just randomly, as far as I know, but then when I wrote "Don't think about an apple," suddenly I was seeing that painting and wondering, why am I seeing that painting in this context? What's that doing there? Why am I putting that there? So I let it stand in the rough draft, and later we get to it. Later the light, which is red, yellow, and green—the green becomes the apple again. So there you are with the layering. Again, I'm just talking about the physical creation of the story.

Your characters do exactly what you do. They free associate, going from one object to the next, one element to another, in a modified stream of consciousness.

What may start as "free association," that has to stay there. But the prose has to intensify within the free association. It has to build. I mean, there are a few thrown-in lines, but not generally speaking. Then, I had set the scene up—what was going on. And then I had to create my story. I knew my characters. I knew what they were doing now, why they were doing it, and who these people were who thought in terms of images.

I did spend time in the hospital when I was a kid. It is nothing that I usually have reason to think about, but once I had started writing this story, which had nothing to do with the way it really was in my life, I could remember my father so distinctly sitting on the hospital bed. He's a very tall man, and even as a little girl I knew that he looked extremely foolish. And he was out of his element with the plush animals and me horribly ill in the hospital bed and my mother backed up against the door. And I just thought—well, what I never thought at the time, what I only know now, really, being an adult—is that there were unspeakable consequences to what was going on. It became worse in the story than it did in my personal life, but "there were two images when you looked through the finder," and there certainly were, "and you had to make the adjustment yourself so that one superimposed itself on the

other, and the figure suddenly leaped into clarity." So it becomes more her story, in a way, only at that point.

In retrospect, I can see that I could have anticipated. But had the man in the story not gone to sleep, it could have become his story. I could have dramatized. I could have gone from the battlefield and to the animals in the hospital bed. It could have become his story, but, in a way, because she's deferring to him all along, and everybody's out of control—the drunks are out of control, that's why they're hollering this nonsense game; the snow is out of control, because who can control snow? Her memory is out of control, because suddenly something that she knows in one context becomes almost surreal in another. When she stopped at the stoplight, the real world they occupied was out of control—so what are you going to do about illness?

The battlefield is not a random analogy. You can compare a bunch of animals thrown on the floor to a lot of things. The stakes are high, if it's a battlefield. Those things became emotionally loaded enough to cue me as to where I was going. And with the ending, I had a friend who was extremely tall, and who always slept this exact way. It had nothing to do with the world of the story, but when I started imagining what it would be like to have my character's life, I suddenly thought of my friend who was disproportionately tall, draping over everything because nothing was large enough to hold him. When the woman goes back to the fetal position at the end of the story, you know that she is regressing, then you make the analogy between her and the daughter, the young child, the younger person who died.

To some extent it started with the external world, and it got very claustrophobic. So back to the outside world. But by then, hopefully, the wooden leg is loaded—the snow has taken on certain connotations. It's not a neutral snow anymore. And I have to admit that I was thinking of the ending of James Joyce's "The Dead," when Gabriel Conroy goes to the window and sees the snow that's no longer the same snow at all. He's thinking of it as blanketing and uniting everything; I was thinking, that's interesting. Let's see what the snow means in this story.

So in effect, I just said what the snow meant: "the sadness set in, always unexpectedly, but so real that it was met with the instant acceptance that one gave to a snowfall." Well, that sort of brings back the normal everyday world. Who's going to get freaked out by seeing snow on the ground? But if you really think about the consequences of that, it means that the world is different, stranger, a little bit out of control. And by then, hopefully, there's been a story in that. I wanted it to be a controlled story about people who were out of control. And it could best be reinforced by having the natural world be out of control.

I once taught a course on "Middle-Aged Crazy: Updike, Carver and Beattie." Students, light years from their own midlife crises, read the books as if they were fantasy. But they were fascinated by Updike's ten-year reexaminations of Rabbit Angstrom. Have you ever thought about how your characters, though you don't revisit them, have changed over the course of the years that you have written?

Without realizing it, when I started writing, although I was not writing autobiography, I was writing about things that I was curious about, and I was writing about people who weren't exactly like me, but that I certainly thought on some level I understood. I was interested in an almost speculative thinking about those people. I think I've backed off that. I think now you can be speculative all you want, and that won't begin to approach the complexity of what you're dealing with. I just plain didn't know that then. I thought there was some virtue, some personal satisfaction to be taken in that kind of speculation—in going out on a limb, in imagining spacemen coming to earth to take pornographic pictures, or something like that.

When I was writing *Falling In Place,* Skylab was falling and nothing could have been a more perfect metaphor if I had invented it, and I didn't even have to invent it. But now I'm quite skeptical. I don't want to go for the easy thing, even if it is the perfect thing. I'd rather go for situations and metaphors more off-kilter, hoping that they might reveal something in a slightly more complex way. I don't mean to totally dismiss the earlier stories, saying that they were expedient, but I now see that I was kind of bedazzled myself.

The same is true of your readers, presumably.

I do feel a little bit more like I realize my position as the author. I realize when I'm creating a keyhole and having people look through it. The scene in *Picturing Will* in the motel with Haveabud was, in effect, that. Where do readers stand physically in terms of these people that I'm thinking about? I don't ever think about the readers in rough draft. But as I'm trying to make the story seem very actual, then I *am* thinking about the audience. I am

thinking about what should be there and where should it be and when should I go private, when should I not? I think I'm less prone to go private than I was earlier. When I was writing a story like "Downhill," I was presuming to go into the mind of an extremely disturbed woman, I would make those leaps. Fine, that's that. But now what I think I'm interested in is texture or the variance of things—counternarrative. I can't help but realize it as a calculated effect. And knowing that I'm onto myself, I don't want to overuse that device either. I'm on guard.

Generally speaking, I think that the focus is narrower now. I don't mean narrower in terms of honing in on something, but that there is a particular kind of thrust to the story that doesn't have to encompass some of the things the earlier stories had to encompass. There's a difference. Part of it is that I simply understand method better than I used to.

Source: Ann Beattie with James Plath, "Counternarrative: An Interview with Ann Beattie," in *Michigan Quarterly Review*, Vol. 32, No. 3, Summer 1993, pp. 359–79.

Susan Horowitz

In the following review, Horowitz praises Beattie for her craft but calls for Beattie to do more "mining of her own offbeat sensibility."

If the non sequitur were an art form, then Ann Beattie, author of this novel and collection of short stories, would be its matron saint. "Matron" seems apt, whatever Beattie's age, and no matter that both books are firsts, since her style effectively girdles any youthful awkwardness, bulging hyperboles, and the passion that might redeem both.

Her taste for the non sequitur, with its lack of logical causation, lends itself to the creation of characters whose behavior is not conventionally or even recognizably motivated. Charles, the hero of *Chilly Scenes of Winter,* has a mother who strips naked as a jay at the drop of anyone's attention, leaves heating pads dangling about the house, and impulsively gulps fistfuls of laxatives. Charles seems as disconnected from his mother as she does from conventional reality. He also seems emotionally removed from, though certainly obsessed by, Laura, his ex-mistress, and Beattie seems equally alienated from them all.

The characters in both the novel and stories are fleshed out (or, rather, painted by number) in a collection of disjointed details, so that, although they are sometimes intriguingly eccentric, they lack an emotional core. Childhood histories, kinship patterns, recipes, and tastes in pop music do not necessarily add up to anyone we care about or remember.

Chapters and stories seem equally fragmented. We get glimpses of odd, painful, or potentially humorous patterns. But instead of mining her own offbeat sensibility, the author scurries off to a safer ground of more facts.

Beattie's most successful stories are those that deal with the directly bizarre: "Dwarf House," which is about the marriage of two dwarfs, and "The Lifeguard," in which a disturbed child sets fire to a boat and drowns himself and three other children. Both these stories have an emotional resonance and a sense of direction and completion that the other, more episodic stories lack.

Beattie has an instinct for the grotesque that verges on the edge of real wit and pain. She is obviously a first-rate craftswoman with an eye for idiosyncratic detail. I only hope that in her future work she will not keep her instincts and characters so much under glass.

Source: Susan Horowitz, Review of *Chilly Scenes of Winter* and *Distortions*, in *Saturday Review*, August 7, 1976, p. 37.

Sources

Beattie, Ann, "Imagined Scenes," in *Distortions*, Doubleday, 1976, pp. 54–63.

Epstein, Joseph, "Ann Beattie and the Hippoisie," in *Commentary*, Vol. 35, No. 3, March 1983, pp. 54–58.

Hallett, Cynthia Whitney, *Minimalism and the Short Story: Raymond Carver, Amy Hempel, and Mary Robison*, Edwin Mellen Press, 1999, pp. 10–15.

Horowitz, Susan, Review of *Distortions* and *Chilly Scenes of Winter*, in *Saturday Review*, August 7, 1976, p. 37.

Murphy, Christina, *Ann Beattie*, Twayne United States Authors Series, No. 510, Twayne, 1986.

O'Hara, J. D., Review of *Distortions* and *Chilly Scenes of Winter*, in *New York Times Book Review*, August 15, 1976, pp. 14, 18.

Porter, Carolyn, "The Art of the Missing," in *Contemporary American Women Writers*, University Press of Kentucky, 1985, pp. 9–30.

Robison, James C., "1969–1980: Experiment and Tradition," in *The American Short Story*, edited by Gordon Weaver, G. K. Hall, pp. 82–83.

Romano, John, "Ann Beattie & the 60's," in *Commentary*, February 1977, pp. 62–64.

Stokstad, Marilyn, *Art History*, 2d ed., Prentice Hall, 2002, pp. 1146–47.

Thorburn, David, Review of *Chilly Scenes of Winter*, in *Yale Review*, Vol. 66, No. 4, Summer 1977, p. 586.

Weber, Myles, "Minimalism Revisited," in *Northwest Review*, Vol. 37, No. 3, 1999, pp. 117–25.

Further Reading

Aldridge, John W., *Talents and Technicians: Literary Chic and the New Assembly-Line Fiction*, Scribner's, 1992.
    Aldridge's book is a disparaging critical view of the minimalist fiction of Ann Beattie and Bobbie Ann Mason, among others.

Montresor, Jaye Berman, *The Critical Response to Ann Beattie*, Greenwood Press, 1993, pp. 1–18.
    Montresor's book is an essential compilation of criticism on Ann Beattie from 1976 to 1993. She includes not only excerpted criticism but also a complete and well-documented bibliography.

Parini, Jay, "A Writer Comes of Age," in *Horizon*, December 1982, pp. 22–24.
    In addition to offering good background information, this article also discusses the stories in *Distortions*.

In the Shadow of War

Ben Okri

1983

Ben Okri published an early version of "In the Shadow of War" in the London publication *West Africa*, in 1983. Subsequently, he included a rewritten version of the story in his 1988 collection, *Stars of the New Curfew*. Both the English and United States editions of *Stars of the New Curfew* were out of print as of 2004; however, the story was also anthologized in 1999 by Daniel Halpern in *The Art of the Story: An International Anthology of Contemporary Short Stories*.

Like much of Okri's writing, "In the Shadow of War" focuses on a young main character, who in this case is a Urhobo boy, age seven or eight, named Omovo. Omovo appears as the main character in two of Okri's other works, *The Landscapes Within* and *Dangerous Love*. Here, Omovo is forced to explore issues of morality against the landscape of the Nigerian Civil War. In question is his morality as well as that of his father and the soldiers who kill a woman whom they presume to be a spy. In fact, she may simply be aiding other women and children who are impoverished and displaced by the war.

"In the Shadow of War" marks a significant turning point in Okri's career. Most important, this story, as well as those that appear with it and those in Okri's earlier short fiction collection, *Incidents at the Shrine*, mark a shift away from realist writing to writing that skillfully incorporates the realm of the imagination and the fantastic. By incorporating fantastical elements into the work, Okri opens the story to a myriad of interpretations, all of which

conspire to fortify his theme that, in the face of war, the distinctions between right and wrong become unclear.

Author Biography

Ben Okri was born on Sunday, March 15, 1959, in Minna, Nigeria, just sixteen months before the country gained its independence from the United Kingdom. Okri was born to Silver Oghenegueke Loloje Okri, an Urhobo man from Warri on the Niger delta, and to his Ibo wife, Grace. Okri spent his early life in Peckham, England, in the borough of Southwark and was one of four siblings, three boys and one girl. At the age of six, Okri returned to Nigeria, a country marked by military coups d'etat and ultimately a three-year civil war. Okri remained in Nigeria until 1978, when his failure to gain entry into the universities' science programs prompted him to return to London with the manuscript of his first novel in hand. In England, Okri attended the University of Essex while successfully publishing his first and second novels, *Flowers and Shadows* (1979) and *The Landscapes Within* (1981).

In 1983, Okri became the poetry editor for the weekly magazine *West Africa*, in which "In the Shadow of War" was first published during that same year. By the mid-eighties, Okri's talent began to be recognized, and he continued to publish. His subsequent publications included *Incidents at the Shrine* (1986), his first collection of short stories; *Stars of the New Curfew* (1988), in which a revised version of "In the Shadow of War" appeared; *The Famished Road* (1991), a novel; *An African Elegy* (1992), a poetry collection; *Songs of Enchantment* (1993), the second volume of *The Famished Road*; *Birds of Heaven* (1995), a brief nonfiction collection of his essays and speeches; *Astonishing the Gods* (1995); *Dangerous Love* (1996), which is a revision of his second novel, *The Landscapes Within*; *A Way of Being Free* (1997), a more extensive collection of his essays, reviews, and speeches; *Infinite Riches* (1998), the third volume in *The Famished Road* series; *Mental Fight* (1999), a poetry volume; and *In Arcadia* (2002).

In addition to winning the prestigious Booker McConnell Prize for Fiction in 1991 for *The Famished Road*, Okri has been distinguished by the following awards and recognition: an Arts Council of Great Britain scholarship (1984); the Commonwealth Prize for Fiction and the Paris Review Aga

Ben Okri

Khan Prize for Fiction (1987) for *Incidents at the Shrine*; a two-year Fellow Commonworship in Creative Arts at Trinity College, Cambridge (1991); the Chianti Rufino-Antico Fattore International Literary Prize (1993); the Premio Grinzane Cavour Prize (1994); and the Crystal Award from the World Economic Forum (1995). Additionally, Okri was awarded a Doctor of Letters *honoris causa* by the University of Westminster and elected as a vice president of the English Centre of the writers' association, International PEN, in 1997. In 1998, he was elected as a fellow of the Royal Society of Literature, and in 2000 he served as the chairman of the judges for the Caine Prize for African Fiction.

Plot Summary

"In the Shadow of War" begins in an unknown Nigerian village. Three soldiers arrive in the afternoon, disturbing the animals that roam the streets, as they proceed to the local bar to drink palm-wine "amidst the flies."

Next, the narration turns to a young boy and his father. The father and son are at their home, which from the window offers the son, Omovo, a view of the soldiers. As the father and son listen to their old

Grundig radio, which they purchased inexpensively from a family who was escaping the war, they hear news of "bombings and air raids in the interior of the country." As the father grooms and then dresses himself in a coat that is "shabby" and too small for him, Omovo continues to peer out the window. He is "irritated" with his father and is focused on looking for a woman who has been passing his house every day for the past week. The woman wears a black veil over her face and is headed for the forest by way of the village paths and the Express road. While Omovo continues to watch for the woman, the war news finishes and the radio broadcaster announces that there will be an eclipse of the moon that night. Omovo's father chides bitterly, "As if an eclipse will stop this war." An exchange ensues in which the father tells Omovo that an eclipse is "when the world goes dark and strange things happen." He warns Omovo not to stay out late because "Heclipses hate children" and that "they eat them." Omovo does not believe his father, who smiles and gives him his allowance of ten kobo. Before leaving, Omovo's father instructs him to turn off the radio because "it's bad for a child to listen to news of war." After taking a drink and praying to his ancestors, Omovo's father picks up his briefcase and departs.

Omovo watches his father leave and board the bus before he turns the radio back on. With the radio on, Omovo continues to sit in the windowsill waiting for the woman, whom he remembers to have worn a yellow smock the last time she went by. He also remembers that the last time she went by the children stopped what they were doing and threw things at her. The children said that the woman had no shadow and that her feet never touched the ground. Unaffected by the children's efforts, the woman continued on her way without flinching, looking back, or walking any faster.

As the story continues, Okri describes the oppressive heat and the way in which the villagers continue with their daily activities "as if they were sleep-walking." The soldiers continue to drink palm-wine and play draughts. Still watching them from his upstairs window, Omovo notices that each time children pass the bar, the soldiers call them over and, after speaking with them briefly, give them some money. Omovo goes downstairs and passes the soldiers, but they do not call to him. On his return, they do call to him, however, by asking him his name. Omovo replies that his name is "Heclipse." As the soldier laughs at his reply, he sprays spit on Omovo's face. The other soldiers appear not to be interested in Omovo as they continue to play their game and swat flies. Standing so close to the soldiers, Omovo sees their guns and the numbers that appear on them. One of the soldiers asks Omovo about the name Heclipse, wondering if his father gave him that name because he had big lips. The other soldiers laugh at this inquiry and Omovo nods. The soldier then asks Omovo if he has seen the woman who wears the black veil. When Omovo replies that he has not, they tell him that she is an enemy-helping spy. Giving Omovo ten kobo, the soldier tells Omovo to tell them if he sees her. Refusing the money, Omovo returns home to sit in the windowsill. The soldiers periodically look up at Omovo. In the oppressive heat, Omovo falls asleep sitting up. He awakes to the sound of cocks crowing and the hourly radio news. The soldiers sleep in the bar as Omovo listens "without comprehension to the day's casualties." Also affected by the heat, the radio announcer yawns, apologizes, and continues to catalog the day's fighting.

When Omovo looks up again, the woman has already passed, and the soldiers are following her. Omovo runs to catch up with the men, one of whom has removed his shirt. The other soldier, Omovo notices, has such large buttocks that he has split his pants. Omovo follows the men across the Express road and into the forest. Once in the forest, the soldiers take a different route than the woman, but Omovo continues to follow her through "dense vegetation." The woman wears "faded wrappers and a grey shawl" with her black veil and a red basket on top of her head. While in pursuit of the woman, Omovo fails to notice if her feet are touching the ground. As he continues through the forest, Omovo passes "unfinished estates" with "ostentatious signboards" and "collapsing fences," a cement factory in disrepair, and a tree with a large animal skeleton under it. A snake descends from a tree, and up ahead he hears "loud music and people singing war slogans." Finally, they come upon an encampment, where the woman stops to give "children with kwashiorkor stomachs and women wearing rags" her basket and its contents. The people thank her, and she leaves, heading back to a muddy river. At the river, Omovo sees what he thinks are "capsized canoes and trailing waterlogged clothes" and floating sacrificial items such as bread, gourds filled with food, and Coca-Cola cans. Looking more closely, he sees that the canoes look to have changed into "swollen dead animals" and that there is outdated money along the riverbank. He then hears the voice of one of the soldiers and hides in the shadow of a tree. After the soldiers pass, Omovo hears a scream as they come upon the woman. They demand that she tell them where "the others" are, and when she remains silent, they call her a witch and ask her if she wants to die. She still does not answer. One of the soldiers removes her veil and tosses it to the ground. As she bends to pick it up, her bald and disfigured head is exposed. She also has a "livid gash" across her face. The bare-chested soldier pushes her down and falling onto her face, she remains still.

The lighting in the forest changes, and Omovo sees that the things floating in the river are actually corpses of men. After another scream, the woman gets up, spits in the fat soldier's face, and with the veil waving in her hand, she begins to "howl dementedly." Two of the soldiers step back, but the fat soldier pulls out his gun. Just before the gunshot, Omovo hears "the beating of wings" above him. He runs through the forest screaming, the soldiers following him. He sees an owl, trips over a tree root, and blacks out as his head hits the ground. When Omovo awakes, he fears he is blind because he cannot see his hand move in front of his face. He runs into a door and then begins to hear voices and a radio broadcast about the war. He finds himself on his balcony and sees his father drinking palm-wine with the three soldiers in the bar. He rushes down to tell his father what happened in the forest, but his father first tells him that he should thank the soldiers for bringing him back from the forest. Omovo again tries to tell his father what happened, but "smiling apologetically," his father picks him up and takes him back to bed.

Characters

Heclipse

See Omovo

Omovo

Omovo is the main character of "In the Shadow of War." He is a young Urhobo boy who is about seven or eight years old. In the story, he acts primarily as an observer. He watches as his father gets ready and leaves for work, as well as for a woman in a veil who has been passing his house every day for the past week. He also watches as three soldiers, who have newly arrived in town, talk to the village children and give them money. Intrigued, Omovo invites an exchange with the

Media Adaptations

- The BBC maintains a Web page about Okri (http://www.bbc.co.uk/arts/books/ author/okri/index.shtml) that contains a brief overview of his work and life. The site also includes a link to an article about one of Okri's poems, as well as information about other postcolonial authors, including Chinua Achebe.

soldiers by walking past them. After telling them that his name is Heclipse, he turns down the ten kobo that they offer him in exchange for information about the woman in the veil. He lies to the soldiers, telling them that he has not seen her. Omovo then returns to his home to watch for the woman in the veil again. After the woman passes, Omovo dashes off to the forest, where he watches the woman give a basket of goods to some women and children. When the woman then sets off again, Omovo continues to follow her. Ultimately, the soldiers also catch up with the woman and murder her. While this happens, Omovo hides in the shadow of a tree. Horrified by what has transpired, Omovo attempts to run out of the forest, but he falls and blacks out. He awakes to find himself at home, where just below his window, he sees his father drinking palm-wine with the soldiers. Omovo tries to tell his father what happened in the forest, but his father simply asks him to thank the soldiers for bringing him home and takes Omovo off to bed.

Although the narrator at one point mentions that Omovo does not understand the news of war that he hears on the radio, Omovo seems to have an instinctive humanitarian side that prompts him not to disclose information about the woman in the veil. When he tries to tell his father what the soldiers have done, Omovo reveals an allegiance to the woman in the veil rather than to the soldiers, who claim that she is a spy who is helping their enemies. As a young boy, Omovo may not understand the political implications of his loyalty; however, for readers, such fidelity points out how war makes human beings do terrible things to each other. It is inconsequential to Omovo whether the woman in the veil is a spy—or a witch, for that matter. For him, her murder is wrong because it is a crime against another human being. Having seen the woman give her basket of goods to starving children and obviously needy women, Omovo likely feels even more strongly that the soldiers' actions are wrong. Omovo's youthful perspective confirms Okri's belief that, in war, morality and ethical behavior are not the norm.

Omovo's Father

Omovo's father appears only in the beginning and the end of the story. In the beginning, he is getting ready for work and teases his son about the coming lunar eclipse. He works in a professional capacity of some sort, yet he is not a man of substantial means, as indicated by the "shabby coat" he wears that no longer fits him. He believes that there is something inherently bad about war, and he does not want his son listening to news of it on the radio. In the end, Omovo finds his father drinking palm-wine with the soldiers, and when he tries to tell his father about the day's events, his father smiles "apologetically" and takes Omovo off to bed. If one reads this story as a dream that Omovo has, the father's presence can be read as a reflection of the boy's earlier irritation with him. If, however, one reads the story as an actual series of events, the father's presence with the soldiers demonstrates either his allegiance to the national war effort or his way of protecting his son, should the boy's sympathy toward the veiled woman be revealed.

Radio Announcer

The radio announcer provides details about the war and broadcasts the news that an eclipse of the moon is expected. While reporting the news about the day's fighting, the announcer yawns, indicating that, to a certain extent, he has become desensitized to the horrors of war.

Three Soldiers

The three soldiers are responsible for the death of the veiled woman. In the story, they remain nameless and are only recognizable by their physical traits and actions. One soldier speaks to Omovo from the bar and tries to bribe him with ten kobo to tell them if he sees the woman in the veil. Another soldier removes his shirt, and the third soldier is described as fat with large buttocks that split his pants. The soldiers believe that the woman is a spy who is helping the Biafrans. When the soldiers find the veiled woman in the forest, the bare-chested soldier pushes her down, and the fat soldier shoots her after she spits in his face. The soldiers are not portrayed as admirable, hardworking men. They spend their day in the village bar, drinking and playing draughts while they bribe the children to help them find the veiled woman. After napping at the bar, they pursue the veiled woman, who they see has sustained injuries to her face and head, and kill her.

The Veiled Woman

The veiled woman is a mysterious character who is figured as a spy, as a witch, and as a humanitarian. The soldiers believe that she is a spy for the Biafrans, and they ultimately kill her. The children in the village believe that she is a witch. They say that she has no shadow and that her feet never touch the ground. Readers may believe that the woman is simply a humanitarian who values human life regardless of political designations. The woman passes through Omovo's village every day for a week on her way to a Biafran encampment where, on the day that she is killed, she gives a basket of goods to malnourished children and impoverished women. By aiding the non-national side of the war, the woman exposes herself to the danger of being caught by the Nigerian soldiers who are monitoring her efforts. The woman, whose face and head are disfigured, demonstrates a clear dislike for the soldiers who confront her in the forest; however, it remains uncertain whether she is a spy, or a benevolent soul, or a witch.

Themes

Truth

One of the overriding themes in "In the Shadow of War" is truth and the absence of it. On more than one occasion, Omovo is dishonest. First, he does not tell the soldiers his real name. Second, he lies when he tells them that he has not seen the woman in the veil. The fact that Omovo has the propensity to lie and that his initial perceptions are sometimes proved wrong, as with the corpses that he at first believes are capsized canoes, makes it possible to read his account of the events in the forest as somehow less than true. Another way to read Omovo's dishonesty, however, is that he is acting morally by protecting the woman in the veil. The narrator in the story

Topics for Further Study

- Locate a copy of the first version of "In the Shadow of War" that appeared in the magazine *West Africa* in 1983. Compare and contrast this version with the one that appeared in the 1989 collection, *Stars of the New Curfew*. What are the most noticeable changes? Why do you think that Okri made these changes? Do you think Okri was trying to communicate the same things in both versions? If not, what is different about the two versions, and how do those differences make you arrive at different readings?

- Have a debate about whether Omovo behaved admirably in this story. Consider whether he should have taken the ten kobo from the soldiers, whether he should have told them the truth about seeing the woman in the veil, whether he should have alerted the woman to danger, and whether he should have protested more as his father took him back to bed.

- Civil war is a reoccurring event in world history. Aside from researching the Nigerian Civil War, choose another country that has been involved in a civil war in the last one hundred years, and prepare an overview of the conflict for your classmates. How did the causes of the Nigerian Civil War and those of the country you chose differ? In what ways were they similar? How does each of these events compare and contrast to the American Civil War?

- Do you think that the soldiers or Omovo believed that the woman with the veil was a witch? Research the Salem witch trials, which occurred during the late 1600s in the Massachusetts Bay Colony. Do you think that everyone believed that the women who were killed in Salem were really witches? What other motivating factors might have contributed to the deaths of the Salem women and the woman in this story?

---

makes the claim that Omovo is listening to things on the radio about the war that he does not necessarily understand; however, Omovo's dishonesty suggests that there are some aspects of war that are not lost on him. He seems to understand that telling the soldiers about the woman would place her in danger. By showing how telling a lie can be seen as a moral act, Okri points out one of the ways in which war creates ambiguities in issues of right and wrong.

The theme of honesty is first introduced in the story when Omovo's father tells him that "Heclipses hate children. They eat them." The father's smile suggests that he does not intend for Omovo to believe this statement, which Omovo indeed does not. While this is a small, harmless untruth that can be read as a playful joke between a father and his precocious son, the exchange also functions as an introduction to the notion that not everything that is said or stated as fact can be believed as true. At the same time, Omovo's father's statement that an eclipse is "when the world goes dark" shows readers

that some information can actually be true. In addition to suggesting that honesty and dishonesty often go hand in hand, this opening scene prompts readers to be mindful that some factual elements of the story may be true, whereas others may not. For example, in the end, readers are left to wonder if the veiled woman is a spy or a witch. Perhaps more important, readers must also determine if they believe that all of the events in the forest really take place or if they are a dream or the product of Omovo's fanciful imagination.

War and Morality

"In the Shadow of War" is set during the Nigerian Civil War. Using this backdrop, Okri explores morality and the ways in which war breaks down the usually clear distinctions between what constitutes moral behavior and what does not. As mentioned in the earlier section on the theme of truth, Omovo's dishonesty is one way that Okri points out how a normally immoral act can be moral in wartime. Omovo's lie about not having seen the veiled woman prevents him from having to tell the soldiers that he has seen her going into the forest via the village paths and the Express road and thus shields her route from the soldiers, at least in the short term. Earlier, Omovo disobeys his father by turning the radio back on after his father leaves for work. Under normal circumstances, such behavior would demonstrate willful disobedience; however, to the extent that what Omovo learns on the radio informs his decision to lie to the soldiers and reject their bribe, his disobedience can be seen as a path to rightful living and informed decisions when it comes to protecting the veiled woman. While Okri explores ambiguities around moral behavior, he also clearly points out the injustices of war, the most obvious of which is perhaps that the veiled woman is killed by the soldiers for coming to the aid of malnourished children and women. In the end, readers do not know if the veiled woman is indeed a spy or if she is simply helping some unfortunate casualties of the war; however, the lack of resolution on this point only reinforces Okri's perspective that murdering anyone is wrong.

Loyalty

One of the most prominent themes in "In the Shadow of War" is that of loyalty. The theme manifests itself in many ways: loyalty to country, loyalty to humanity, and loyalty to family. The soldiers' pursuit of the veiled woman demonstrates their loyalty to the national cause. They are fighting to unite Nigeria once again and to prevent Biafra from becoming an independent republic. In contrast, the veiled woman does not demonstrate loyalty to the national cause. Instead, she shows clear disdain for the soldiers when she spits in the face of one of them. By bringing the basket of goods to the impoverished and displaced Biafran women and children, the veiled woman demonstrates loyalty, perhaps to the Biafran cause but most definitely to her fellow human beings. Whether the woman is a spy is not clearly resolved before her death; however, her commitment to helping people who are suffering despite their political affiliations is readily apparent. Omovo also demonstrates loyalty to humanity when he lies to the soldiers about whether he has seen the veiled woman. The theme of loyalty as it pertains to family is brought out in the end of the story when Omovo's father tells him to thank the soldiers and then takes Omovo back to bed after "smiling apologetically" to the soldiers. Read in one way, this scene suggests that the father's loyalty lies with the soldiers and that he somewhat hushes his son's excited tale of the day's events. Read in

another way, however, Omovo's father can be seen as protecting his son from the harm the soldiers might do to him if Omovo appears to defend the veiled woman's actions in any way. Ironically, by taking his son home, Omovo's father is showing the greatest loyalty because he is protecting his son from a political and violent world that he may be too young to understand.

Style

African Literature

Okri's work belongs to the ever-growing canon of African literature, which in the United States and Europe refers to literature written in English or French by writers from Africa. Africa has a long history of oral literature and literature written in indigenous languages; however, as African nations began to achieve independence in the 1950s and 1960s, a collection of writing began to emerge that was written in the languages of nations who had colonized the continent. West Africans, especially Nigerian writers, have been particularly prolific. First-generation-African writers, like Chinua Achebe, wrote in response to the stereotypes that colonial nations had long created about Africans. While these efforts were effective in redefining Africa and its people and cultures, early African writing, which was largely written by men, has been criticized for failing to accurately represent women. Hence, in the 1960s and beyond, female African writers, including Flora Nwapa, Buchi Emecheta, and Ama Ata Aidoo, began to write literature that exposed not only colonial repression and oppression but oppression of African women by African men. Okri belongs to the second generation of African writers. As a group, these writers have focused not only on the social, cultural, and political ramifications of colonization but also on post-independence challenges, failures, and opportunities for change throughout the continent.

Magic Realism

As its name suggests, magic realism is a genre of literature that includes both realistic and magical elements. Unlike fantasy writing, literature written in this genre is not wholly fantastical. Instead, the world in which stories unfold is both fantasy and reality. German art critic Franz Roh originally coined the term "magic realism" in 1925; however, the term is largely associated with literature written in the 1980s and afterward. Magic realism is most often associated with Latin American writers because authors such as Gabriel Garcia Marquez and Isabel Allende popularized this form. Despite this association, magic realism appears in fiction outside of Latin America. "In the Shadow of War" is one example. In this story, Okri incorporates elements that seem to be other-worldly like the veiled woman who the children say walks without touching the ground.

Setting

When authors sit down to write literature, whether it be a novel, a short story, or a play, they must decide where their story should take place. The place in which a story takes place is called its setting. In some cases, authors intentionally make the setting of their work unknown or vague. In other cases, however, the setting of the work plays an integral role in the development of the author's themes. The latter is true with "In the Shadow of War." This story takes place during Nigeria's civil war, which continued from 1967 to 1970. Using this as his setting, Okri was able to explore the impact that war has on people and the moral predicaments that they find themselves in during civil strife.

Historical Context

Okri and Nigeria

Okri was born in Nigeria and spent much of his childhood as well as his adult life living in England. Despite his predominantly western residency, Okri's writing has been deeply informed by the years he spent in Nigeria during the country's three-year civil war and the subsequent, highly turbulent postwar years. Writing for the *South African Literary Review* in September 1992, Carolyn Newton writes that Okri's novel *The Famished Road* "could not have been born of England's green and pleasant land; his is a heady cocktail of African legend and western classicism." The same can be said of his short stories, which served as the testing ground for the writing style that he popularized with *The Famished Road*.

From 1967 to 1970, Nigeria was embroiled in a bloody civil war, also known as the Nigerian-Biafran War or the Biafran War, during which an estimated 1 million people were killed. Okri lived in Nigeria during the violent war and postwar years up until 1978. After this time, he remained deeply connected with his country's ongoing political and social struggles.

Okri has been and continues to be deeply affected and engaged in the issues, challenges, and injustices faced by his countrymen. In 1985, following a visit home, he published several essays about Nigerian political concerns and the state of the nation. Ten years later, Okri remained active in Nigerian events, including those surrounding Nigerian author Ken Saro-Wiwa's imprisonment and subsequent trial for treason. Despite pleas from around the world, including those from Okri and South African president Nelson Mandela, Saro-Wiwa was ultimately hanged along with several others who were detained with him.

The Civil War Years and Beyond

The Nigerian Civil War began in 1967; however, seeds of discontent and destabilization date back to 1963 when Chief Obafemi Awolowo, the first premier of the newly created Mid-Western Region of Nigeria, was accused of and imprisoned for working against the national leadership. During 1966, Nigeria lost civilian administration of the country during two successful military coups d'etat in January and July. The latter coup d'etat left Lieutenant-General (later General) Yakubu Gowon at the helm of the country. He quickly divided the country into twelve states, which prompted Lieutenant-Colonel (later General) Odumegwu Ojukwu to announce the secession of the three easternmost states. The three states were to become the autonomous Republic of Biafra, and thus began the war. Literary figures, like Christopher Okigbo, one of Nigeria's best poets and someone Okri admired, joined the fight for Biafra. Others like Wole Soyinka, who is a well-known and respected novelist and playwright, opposed the war. By 1970, the Biafran resistance had diminished considerably, and on January 15, 1970, a delegation from Biafra surrendered and ended the war.

Despite the end of the war, Nigeria's political landscape continued to be marked by leadership assassinations, multiple military coups d'etat, and the ongoing division of the country into numerous states. In 1979, a reprieve seemed possible when civilian ruler Sheu Shagari was elected president of the Second Republic. In 1983, however, Major-General Mohammed Butari deposed Shagari in yet another military coup and gained control of the country. Butari created the Supreme Military Council that was aimed at curbing all democratic rights. In 1985, General Ibrahim Babangida overthrew

Compare & Contrast

- **Late 1960s:** There are fewer than ten Nigerian novels published per year.

  1980s: There are approximately fifty Nigerian novels published per year.

  Today: There are approximately twenty Nigerian novels published per year.

- **Late 1960s:** Civilian administration in Nigeria ends following two successive military coups d'etat.

  1980s: General Ibrahim Babangida overthrows Major General Mohammed Butari, stating his intention to return Nigeria to civilian rule in the 1990s.

  Today: The Nigerian president Olusegun Obasanjo issues a press statement about his unwillingness to accept any actions aimed at destabilizing his democratically elected presidential administration.

- **Late 1960s:** Famous Nigerian poet Christopher Okigbo resigns from the Cambridge University Press and enlists as a major in the Biafran army.

  1980s: Because of governmental changes in Nigeria, Okri's Nigerian-sponsored scholarship at the University of Essex ends. Okri leaves for London, where he is homeless before finding a flat in Seven Sisters.

  Today: Author Ken Saro-Wiwa is taken into custody by the government, charged with treason, and hanged despite protests and appeals by Okri and South African president Nelson Mandela.

Butari and pledged to return the country to civilian rule within the next decade. On the economic front, the eighties were challenging years for Nigeria. The country's real gross national product (GNP) declined so significantly that Nigeria was reclassified by the World Bank as a low-income country for the first time since 1978. In the face of a collapsing economy, the internal ethnic tensions continued to build, and despite successfully forming a transitional government in 1993 comprised of a military National Defense and Security Council and a council of civilian ministers, Babangida was unable to fulfill his pledge. He eventually stepped down, but not until 1999 did Nigeria experience its first peaceful transition to civilian leadership.

Critical Overview

Stars of the New Curfew received less attention than Okri's more well-known work, *The Famished Road*; however, the work did not go unnoticed in 1988, when it was released in England, or the following year, when it was published in the United States. In "Beneath the Waves," which Sylvester Ike Onwordi wrote for the *Times Literary Supplement* in August 1988, Onwordi commends *Stars of the New Curfew* as some of Okri's "finest writing to date." He notes that Okri "appears now to have come into his own stylistically and creatively." In addition to saying that Okri writes without "self-indulgence," Onwordi praised Okri's writing as "concise without being arid." Writing for the *New York Times Book Review* in August 1989, Neil Bissoondath seems to agree. Taking special note of the first paragraph of "In the Shadow of War," Bissoondath writes that Okri's "language is simple" and that his details are "striking."

Okri has been praised for the ways in which his fiction accurately reflects Nigerian culture. Onwordi notes of *Stars of the New Curfew*, "this is a book on Nigerian life which perfectly captures the emotional temperature of that turbulent country." At the same time, Okri has also been recognized by critics for the universality of his themes, particularly as they apply to Africa's greater continental experience of colonization and subsequent independence. In his review of *Stars of the New Curfew* in *World Literature Today* in the spring of 1990, Michael Thorpe notes that:

> Okri's fabular and allegorical journeys, three of which are excursions into the forest, are more patently linked with the life Africans endure and struggle through in the here and now. Everywhere images of sudden violence and random, cruel power erupt.

Bissoondath concurs and calls Okri a "natural storyteller" who writes "tales that resonate well beyond their immediate settings, striking chords of recognition in anyone with more than a nodding acquaintance with underdeveloped countries."

Critics have also remarked that *Stars of the New Curfew* as well as Okri's preceding short fiction collection, *Incidents at the Shrine*, signal a transition in his writing. *Postcolonial African Writers: A Bio-Bibliographical Sourcebook*, which is edited by Pushpa Naidu Parekh and Siga Fatima Jagne, takes note that the stories found in these collections

> mark a turning point in [his] aesthetic development because they increasingly use African narrative techniques as an essential aspect of their narrative strategy. *Stars of the New Curfew* particularly develops the rich imagination, complex mythical imagery, and episodic adventures that are found [in the writings of Okri's predecessors].

Okri's predecessors include Amos Tutuola, Gabriel Okara, and D. O. Fangunwa. This same source also states that "critics have praised Okri for his ability to creatively experiment with new literary forms." One such critic is Robert Fraser. Writing in the April 1989 issue of the *Third World Quarterly*, Fraser calls attention to Okri's particular strength in drawing on the traditions of oral storytelling without "compromising anything of his fractious modernity." Stylistically, *Stars of the New Curfew* is also known by critics as some of Okri's earliest use of magic realism. In his early review of *Stars of the New Curfew*, Onwordi reflects that Okri's "work will probably be described as magic realism because, dealing with fable and the collision of dream and reality, he takes liberties with perceived notions of time and place."

Criticism

Dustie Robeson

Robeson is a freelance writer with a master of arts degree in English. In this essay, Robeson ex-

Scene from the Nigerian Civil War in 1968, which provides the setting for Okri's "In the Shadow of War"

plores the issue of morality as figured in Okri's "In the Shadow of War."

In the Spring 1990 issue of *World Literature Today*, Michael Thorpe notes that in *Stars of the New Curfew*, Okri "probe[s] unsparingly the self-inflicted wounds of 'freedom.'" In this statement, Thorpe refers to the irony that in the wake of colonial independence, Nigeria found itself embroiled in a violent civil war. Instead of fulfilling the promise of freedom in a united state of empowerment, Nigerians turned on themselves and were bitterly divided in a bloody, three-year conflict.

Thorpe continues by noting that in the wartime worlds depicted in *Stars of the New Curfew*, "No virtues have scope to thrive, whether love, loyalty, or integrity." Indeed, love, loyalty, and integrity are often compromised by war, and Okri skillfully exposes this fact throughout his works of short fiction. In *The Encyclopedia of Post-Colonial Literatures in English*, Bruce King states that the "underlying theme [of Okri's work] is the failure to find love and caring relationships in a society that has become brutalized through the harshness needed to survive." King concludes with the observation

What Do I Read Next?

- *The Famished Road*, which was first published in 1991, is one of Okri's best-known works. He earned the Booker McConnell Prize for Fiction for this novel, and in 1993 and 1998 respectively he published sequels to the work titled *Songs of Enchantment* and *Infinite Riches*.

- Chinua Achebe's *Things Fall Apart* is known as one of the founding novels of African fiction in English. In this novel, Achebe considers the social realities faced by his people in the wake of colonialism. Published in 1959, *Things Fall Apart* is a must read for anyone interested in becoming more familiar with African fiction, specifically that which is written by Nigerian authors.

- *War Stories: A Memoir of Nigeria and Biafra* (2002), by John Sherman, is a first-person account of the author's time in Nigeria as a Peace Corp volunteer in 1966 and later, during the country's civil war, as a member of the Interna-

tional Committee of the Red Cross. Sherman's story provides a graphic account of the impact of the Nigerian Civil War on children.

- Flora Nwapa is the first Nigerian woman to be published in Nigeria and the first black African woman to be published in England. *Efuru* (1966) is about a woman who, despite failure in marriage and child rearing, is an example of female independence and spiritual transcendence.

- Tsitsi Dangarembga, who is from Zimbabwe (formerly part of Rhodesia), is another African writer who writes about a young main character. In *Nervous Conditions* (1988), Dangarembga explores the coming of age of a young woman in colonial Rhodesia during the 1960s. In the novel, Tambu faces issues surrounding gender, cultural identity, colonialism, wealth, education, and eating disorders.

---

that Okri also expresses what he perceives to be a "lack of communal morality" in Nigeria "through images of excrement, disease, and poverty, spiritual disorder finding its physical counterpart in filth, stink, clogged sewage, electricity failures, and rotting bodies." Social and familial relationships, communal morality, as well as the need to survive, are all explored in "In the Shadow of War." More specifically, Okri uses this story to examine the ways in which families and society grapple with the issues of morality, humanity, selflessness, and self-preservation against the backdrop of war.

In the beginning of the story, Omovo's father tells him that during eclipses "strange things happen." Okri suggests that the same can be said of war, by naming the story "In the Shadow of War," thus creating a parallel between an eclipse, during which "the world goes dark," and shadows. Omovo's father warns him that "the dead start to walk about and sing," two events not normally associated with the dead. Likewise, during wartime, people do not

always act as they normally might. It is likely not a coincidence then that Omovo faces his most challenging moment while hidden "in the shadow of a tree." From this shaded vantage point, Omovo must decide if he should attempt to help the veiled woman and expose himself as a friend of the "enemy" or if he should remain hidden. In the shadow, Omovo is symbolically encased in the shadow of war, or the place where his behavior may be inconsistent with what it would be during non-wartime situations. In this one scene, Okri reveals how, in the shadow of war, individuals may sometimes place their own safety above their moral convictions about violence.

Okri explores Omovo's individual dilemma around the issues of survival and morality in a broader social context through the character development of Omovo's father, the soldiers, and the veiled woman. He does so by setting up oppositional relationships within the story that mirror the social divisions that occurred during the civil war between

Biafra sympathizers and those who supported the national Nigerian position. Symbolically, the soldiers and Omovo's father represent the Nigerian national side of the war, whereas Omovo and the veiled woman represent the Biafran side.

The associations between Omovo's father, the soldiers, and the Nigerian national cause are quite clear. As soldiers, the three village newcomers obviously are representative of and are fighting for the reunification of Nigeria. Their primary occupation is to prevent the successful separation of the nation's three easternmost states. Though Omovo's father never clearly states his political position, Okri draws subtle likenesses between him and the soldiers that create a link between these patriarchal authority figures. For example, Omovo's father drinks "a libation" before going to work, just as the soldiers, who are presumably always on duty, order "a calabash of palm-wine" at the "palm-frond bar." Physically, Omovo's father wears a "shabby coat that he had long outgrown," while one of the soldiers has "buttocks so big they had begun to split his pants." In addition, like Omovo's father, the soldiers try to give Omovo ten kobo. Omovo seems equally displeased with his father and the soldiers throughout the story. In the beginning, Okri writes that Omovo is "irritated with his father," and he seems to display equal annoyance with the soldiers when he lies to them and rejects their bribe. Further, with both the soldiers and his father, Omovo demonstrates disobedience. He turns the radio back on when his father leaves for work, even though his father had told him to turn it off because "it's bad for a child to listen to news of war." And later, despite the soldier's instruction, Omovo fails to alert the threesome about seeing the veiled woman.

Although these linkages exist, they can be read as tenuous. Okri makes these parallels apparent and yet understated in an effort to make more than one reading of the story possible. On the one hand, the story can be read in such a way that the father supports the soldiers' activities. This reading is supported by the fact that he asks Omovo to thank the soldiers for bringing him back from the forest and that he smiles "apologetically" at them for his son's behavior. Another interpretation of this same scene, however, is that Omovo's father is actually protecting his son by carrying him back to bed. If one favors the second reading, then Omovo's father's actions, though they seem on the surface to be disloyal to his family, are actually quite loyal. He protects his son from the danger of appearing to be loyal to the Biafran side of the war. Ironically, Okri

> Okri uses this story to examine the ways in which families and society grapple with the issues of morality, humanity, selflessness, and self-preservation against the backdrop of war."

uses the relationship between the soldiers and Omovo's father to suggest that to befriend people who murder humanitarians can in some ways be seen as justifiable and thus moral during war.

Okri continues to explore the issues of self-preservation and morality through the connections he creates among the veiled woman, Omovo, and Biafra. At the outset, the veiled woman's allegiance to the Biafran people is evident. In addition to being thought of as a spy by the soldiers, she is seen giving her basket of goods to "children with kwashiorkor stomachs." The word *kwashiorkor* describes the distension of the stomach that results from severe malnutrition. During the civil war, this was a life-threatening yet common experience for Biafran children. By the end of the story, readers do not know whether the woman is indeed a spy or simply a humanitarian. What is apparent, however, is her faithfulness to the Biafrans who are suffering as a result of the war, as well as her contentious anger toward the soldiers and, by extension, the Nigerian national cause for its part in the marginalization of the Biafran people. The veiled woman's anger is clearest during the scene just prior to her death when, having had her veil torn off, she picks it up and then stops "in the attitude of kneeling, her head still bowed." Her feigned deference lasts only shortly and is soon followed by a demonstration of pride and power. Okri writes, "she drew herself to her fullest height, and spat" in the soldier's face. Okri complicates the character of the veiled woman by creating questions around whether she is a witch; however, although her identity is less than clear, readers never have any doubts about where she focuses her compassion and loyalty.

As someone who may be too young to have strong political affiliations, Omovo cannot necessarily be said to be a Biafran supporter. Nevertheless, Okri writes Omovo as sympathetic to and seemingly aligned with the veiled woman. The linkages between the two are both overt and symbolic. On the overt side, Omovo's loyalty to the veiled woman is clearest when he lies to the soldiers about never having seen her, despite the fact that he had been watching her pass by his house at the same time for a week. Okri makes another one of the more obvious connections between the two when Omovo follows the veiled woman and the soldiers into the forest. He writes:

> When they got into the forest the men stopped following the woman, and took a different route. They seemed to know what they were doing. Omovo hurried to keep the woman in view. He followed her through dense vegetation.

Despite the perception that the soldiers know what they are doing, Omovo elects to follow the veiled woman's path into the forest. This suggests an allegiance to her rather than to the soldiers. One of the perhaps less obvious parallels between Omovo and the veiled woman surrounds their identities. Because she wears a black veil, the woman has an obscured identity. She cannot be easily recognized. In a different but somewhat similar vein, Omovo also has an obscured identity. Instead of telling the soldiers his real name when they ask him, Omovo tells them that his name is "Heclipse."

The connections between the black veil and the name Heclipse as well as the characters that these images represent continue. Both a veil and an eclipse create a shadow or darkness. In the Nigerian flag, which consists of a central, vertical white band flanked on the left and right by two vertical green bands, the color white symbolizes national unity. In that a veil and an eclipse are associated with darkness, or the opposite of white, both Omovo and the veiled woman can be symbolically linked to the concept of disunity, which in this case refers to the formation of a new Republic of Biafra. At the same time, if light can be read as a symbol of truth, then Omovo and the veiled woman's actions can be associated with the obstruction of truth. Just as Omovo is not always honest, the veiled woman appears to withhold information from the soldiers when they confront her in the forest. She refuses to tell them where "the others" are. Whether "the others" are the Biafra soldiers or the women and children with whom she left her basket, readers do not know. Regardless, the woman remains silent. Ironically, Omovo and the veiled woman's shared dishonesty can be seen as admirable. Both Omovo and the veiled woman make decisions that compromise their own safety in an effort to ensure the safety of others. If one reads this story altruistically, this loyalty can be seen as loyalty to fellow human beings who are suffering because of the politics and injustices of war.

Through the development of these main characters, Okri aptly points out that war has an impact not only upon the soldiers who occupy the front lines but on society at large, including children. When Okri writes that Omovo calls himself Heclipse, he figuratively suggests that Omovo himself is an eclipse, or that which darkens the world in shadow. Taken a step further, this symbolism suggests that as the one who creates the shadow of war, Omovo is complicit in creating the moral dilemma in which he finds himself. This is perhaps what Thorpe means by the "self inflicted wounds of freedom." In the newly independent and war torn Nigeria, the cost of freedom for Biafrans, as well as for those caught in the crossfire of the conflict, was their own morality. Yet, in an ironic twist, Okri suggests that perhaps such lack of morality is in fact the very basis of that freedom. In the context of war, siding with murderers and being dishonest proves to have moral currency. Ironically, in the case of war, it is sometimes true that acting in less than moral ways is the most moral thing one can do. It is in such moral ambiguity that people free themselves from the destructive nature of violence and war. As symbolized by his upstairs perch in the window, Omovo, like the veiled woman and perhaps like his father, observe the world from a moral high ground. In the end, Okri thus asserts that both the selfishness and selflessness of these characters express moral positions that demonstrate an admirable concern for family and humanity at large.

Source: Dustie Robeson, Critical Essay on "In the Shadow of War," in *Short Stories for Students*, Gale, 2005.

Liz Brent

Brent holds a Ph.D. in American culture from the University of Michigan. In this essay, Brent discusses the motif of vision in Okri's "In the Shadow of War."

Ben Okri utilizes vision as a recurring motif in "In the Shadow of War," contrasting images of light, vision, and visibility with images of darkness (or shadow), blindness, and invisibility. Light, vision, and visibility function as metaphors for truth, knowledge, and understanding, while darkness, invisibility, and blindness function as metaphors for lack of knowledge, comprehension, or a clear perception of the truth.

Okri in "In the Shadow of War" represents the experience of war from the limited and uncomprehending perspective of a young child. The narrative is thus restricted to the sights, sounds, and smells that the boy perceives. In representing the boy's limited understanding of what he sees in the war-torn world around him, Okri refrains from explaining to the reader the broader meaning or context of Omovo's observations and perceptions. As a child, Omovo lives "in the shadow of war." His lack of understanding of the war is indicated by the narrator's statement that he "listened without comprehension to the day's casualties" announced on the radio. Omovo's understanding of the war is limited to his perceptions as a child.

"In the Shadow of War" opens with Omovo's perspective as he gazes from the window balcony of his home, looking down onto the street. This thematically places Omovo in the position of an observer, who watches the world around him, as figures "appear" and "disappear" from his sight. For example, as the story opens, Omovo is waiting for the woman in the black veil to "appear" on his street, recalling that every day she has walked past his window then "disappeared" into the forest.

The title "In the Shadow of War" clues the reader into the story's recurring motif of shadows, light, and darkness. This motif is emphasized when the radio announcer states that an eclipse of the moon will occur that night. An eclipse of the moon, or lunar eclipse, occurs when the Earth passes between the sun and the moon, and the shadow of the Earth blocks the sunlight from reaching the moon. This phenomenon causes the moon to go dark, from the perspective of a person looking up at the night sky from Earth. Hearing the announcement of the eclipse, Omovo's father comments, "As if an eclipse will stop this war." When Omovo asks his father what an eclipse is, his father responds enigmatically, "That's when the world goes dark and strange things happen." This statement could also describe the effect war has on a society. Metaphorically, one might say that war eclipses human understanding and human experience by casting a shadow over an entire society.

The motif of the shadow occurs again in reference to the black veil worn by the mysterious woman. The narrator explains the children's superstitious belief that the woman in the black veil has no shadow. While to the children this suggests something supernatural and perhaps evil, it symbolically functions in the story to resonate with the motif of shadows and light. Omovo's concern with watching and vision is again indicated when he follows the woman in the black veil into the woods, hurrying after her in order to "keep the woman in view." The black veil worn by the woman connects the story's motifs of darkness and shadow, as it conceals her face for most of the story, in effect keeping her face in shadow.

The actions of the woman with the veil are further described in terms of shadows, darkness, and invisibility. Omovo sees the woman enter a cave in the woods where "shadowy figures moved about in the half-light." After the woman leaves the cave, where she has apparently brought food to the starving people living there, Omovo follows her to a dark, muddy river. The dark, muddy water of the river suggests the obscured and muddied perceptions of Omovo's level of understanding of the war at this point. Omovo's visual perceptions are further described by the impression that the woman "moved as if an invisible force were trying to blow her away." From Omovo's perspective, "invisible forces" seem to be determining the course of events, because he lacks a full understanding of the circumstances of war that affect the woman's actions.

When he realizes that the soldiers are following the woman too, Omovo hides in the shadow of a tree. The soldiers stop the woman and one of them removes the dark veil from her head and throws it to the ground, revealing that her head and face have been mutilated. At this point, after the woman's veil is removed, Omovo's perception of the bodies floating in the river suddenly changes. Whereas he thought he had seen the carcasses of dead animals in the river, he now realizes that they are the corpses of men. The removal of the veil, and the revelation that the woman has been mutilated, probably in the course of the war, occurs along with the removal of the veil or shadow of incomprehension that shrouds Omovo's perceptions of the war. Thus, at the moment when the veil is removed from the woman's head, Omovo sees the contents of the river clearly for the first time. He further notices that the eyes of the corpses are bloated. This detail describing the misshapen eyes of the corpses conveys the notion that war destroys the human capacity for clarity of vision and distorts human perceptions of the world around them.

After Omovo experiences this brief moment of clarity, when the veil is lifted from his perception, he runs out of his hiding place in the shadow of a tree and runs into the woods "through a mist which seemed to have risen from the rocks." As he runs, he notices an owl staring at him, and then he trips and blacks out after his head hits the ground. Mist obscures the ability to see clearly, and so suggests that Omovo's moment of clarity and understanding will be once again obscured. The owl staring at him represents his moment of clarity about war, for the owl is able to see at night—that is, symbolically, to see clearly the truth of war that is normally hidden in the shadow and darkness of ignorance. The owl thus symbolizes the true perception of war that has been revealed to Omovo by the removal of the veil from the woman's face. Just as the veil has been removed, revealing the ravages of war on the woman's face, so metaphorically the veil, or shadow, of ignorance has been removed from Omovo's eyes, and the true horror of war is revealed to him.

When Omovo regains consciousness after falling and blacking out in the forest, he is in his home and it is dark. He at first thinks that he has gone blind. When he goes to the balcony and is able to look out he is "full of wonder that his sight had returned." Omovo's adventure, as related in "In the Shadow of War," takes him through an allegorical journey from a level of ignorance and incomprehension of the realities of war to a moment of revelation in which he perceives the true nature of war with a new level of clarity. Omovo thus passes through a symbolic experience of blindness and restored vision that parallels his original blindness to the horrors of war and sudden vision of the true nature of war and the human devastation it causes.

Source: Liz Brent, Critical Essay on "In the Shadow of War," in *Short Stories for Students*, Gale, 2005.

Laura Carter

Carter is currently employed as a freelance writer. In this essay, Carter considers the transformative powers of light and shadow in Okri's work.

The title of Ben Okri's childhood recollection of a war-torn Nigeria, "In the Shadow of War," is reflective of the climate he describes, a nation whose collective conscience is overshadowed by the carnage and violence of conflict. Okri uses the events of an eclipse to flesh out his work. Through shifting shape and changing shadow, Okri reveals first hand the power of war to gravely impact the conscience of an entire nation.

At the outset of the story, Omovo asks his father what an eclipse is. He tells him that it is "When the world goes dark and strange things happen." Omovo wishes to know what to expect; in response his father claims, "The dead start to walk around and sing." The eclipse in Okri's work is a powerful metaphor that resonates throughout the story. The contrast between light and shadow that permeates Okri's work plays tricks on Omovo's perception of reality, giving the eclipse transformative powers. With this play of light and shadow is a discernable shifting. Omovo's visual reality is not static; it is ever-changing, mirroring his father's own words.

A cloaked figure passing by at a certain hour for the past seven days, in grey with a black veil covering her face, piques Omovo's interest. In a short time this figure has reached mythic proportions, called an enemy by soldiers, viewed as supernatural by others. The neighborhood children claim "that she had no shadow ... that her feet never touched the ground." And although the children persist in throwing things at her, as she passes by, Omovo observes that "she didn't quicken her pace, and didn't look back." Omovo is to discover the magic of the eclipse, which, through shifting light and shadows has transformative powers. For instance, the light reveals that the "spy that helps our enemies" is merely an old woman, a balding and beaten woman.

Similarly, enemies initially Omovo perceives to be "shadowy figures" moving about "in the half-light of the cave, appear in the light to be children with kwashiorkor stomachs and women wearing rags. In the changing light of the riverbed, Omovo also witnesses canoes changing to swollen dead animals, and eventually, to discarded bodies: "The lights change over the forest and for the first time Omovo saw that the dead animals on the river were the corpses of grown men." He is not a witness to supernatural events, rather, his attempts to focus in on or adjust to the changing light reveal the carnage at the riverbank. The woman is not an enemy, she is one of many victims.

Perception, the ability to see, is a precious commodity. At the story's climax, Omovo is alarmed by the loss of his vision. He is literally terrified by the darkness of his own home. In the story, "He found his way to the balcony, full of wonder that his sight had returned." When he approaches his father, Omovo is overcome with delirium and "frantically" attempts to tell his father what the soldiers had heard. Omovo challenges, he questions, he tries to make sense of the unspeakable horrors he has witnessed. His father simply carries him away. At this point it could be argued that the reader really "sees" the implications of wartime for Omovo and his father. The kind of censorship that leads to his father's ultimate conformity is not only implied, it is profoundly understood. The climax is not dictated by the events in the forest. The terror is not so much what is revealed by the light, visions of eerie grotesques floating in the river, or the leveling of a pistol at the stomach of a badly beaten woman, but what lurks in the shadows of the collective conscience.

In her work on Okri, Felicia Alu Moh discusses the short story's economy of form in relation to Okri's work. Because the short story is used to relay Okri's childhood experiences, the economy of the genre leaves no room for bias. The events are witnessed without judgment, magnifying the horror. Characters are undeveloped, their actions impulsive rather than explained. Moh builds on her assessment of Okri's chosen literary medium, asserting that by the very nature of its form, the short story reveals a sense of urgency on the part of the writer to record an event, feeling, phenomenon, or slice of life. Consequently, says Moh, the subject matters of the West African short stories are most often "urbanity, war (especially the Nigerian Civil war), conflict and cultural assertion, coupe d'etat and the world of children." Okri relies heavily on the issues of urbanity and the Nigerian Civil War to flesh out his work.

The short story, the medium Okri chooses for recalling his childhood experiences in a war torn Nigeria, exposes the cultural malaise of which he so adamantly speaks. In a lecture entitled "The True Issue of this Century Is Not Terrorism, or Religion. It Is Freedom. We Need to De-Censor Our Minds," Okri speaks of the censorship of self. Specifically, "In the Shadow of War," examined in relation to Okri's own writings, draws some rather striking parallels, illuminating the ramifications of absorbing, without thought, the terrors of war. Self-censorship, says Okri, renders humankind easily manipulated and bullied. Failing to question the atrocities surrounding our circumstances, then, means that "we collude in the great outrages and follies and injustices of our age" when we do not actively refute our tendencies to censor "our own minds, our fears, our doubts, our anxieties."

Silent consent has consequences, says Okri, who asserts "our children are horrified to learn that

> " By following the shadowy figure of the woman rather than share the information of her whereabouts with the soldiers, he chooses to question the chaos around him rather than comply with it and witnesses the murder not of a spy but of a humanitarian among his own people."

we were present and adult and alive when unacceptable outrages against humanity are perpetrated under our very noses, and we did nothing. And so we implicate whole generations; and, in extreme cases, a whole nation." Consequently, the stifling of thoughts, of the impulse to translate our sense of outrage into action, become part of a matrix of self-censorship:

> When we do not let ourselves think the thought which our flesh recoils from, when we do not let conscience speak that which the heart screams as unacceptable, when we give ourselves many excellent reasons for refusing to participate in some way in this grand drama of our interconnected lives, then we are victims of censorship within.

The end result of self-censorship for Okri is a bland existence. Potential lies dormant; emptiness prevails. Self-censorship results in a nation devoid of creativity, dreams, or genius. Consider the backdrop of Okri's story—it is characterized by an oppressive heat, flies, and zombie-like villagers. Life drones on: "The heat was stupefying. Noises dimmed and lost their edges. The villagers stumbled about their various tasks as if they were sleepwalking." The reader observes evidence of another Nigeria, as Omovo follows the mysterious woman past a crumbling cement factory, unfinished estates "with their flaking ostentatious signboards and their collapsing fences," and a skeleton of a large animal under a tree. The war has stymied the growth of Omovo's country, an eclipse overshadowing a sleeping nation. Omovo's father also discounts the fact that there are soldiers and, as the reader comes to discover, extreme violence in their midst. "Turn off the radio. It's bad for a child to listen to news of war." The rationale for this command stands in stark contrast to what horrors await Omovo at the river. It is nonsensical.

So too is his father's response to Omovo's hysteria over the events at the river. Omovo dares to rise above the din of his everyday existence. By following the shadowy figure of the woman rather than share the information of her whereabouts with the soldiers, he chooses to question the chaos around him rather than comply with it and witnesses the murder not of a spy but of a humanitarian among his own people. Consequently, the horror of finding his father drinking with men who, moments ago, have murdered an innocent woman overwhelms him. To compound matters, his father responds to Omovo's terror by asserting only that his son has been "saved" by the soldiers, then by whisking Omovo away to bed before he can mention the bloody episode.

Omovo is discounted, treated as if the entire episode was a dream, and is returned to a world of shifting shadows. His father is pressed to discount the horrors witnessed by his son, engaging in censorship without guile, in order to protect Omovo, but, in doing so, he succumbs to the weight of oppressive forces which serve to psychically destroy him. The scene is anticlimactic, the real criminals vindicated of what is probably one of many horrific war crimes. "In the Shadow of War," matters of conscience, or consciousness, ultimately determine the legacy one leaves behind.

Source: Laura Carter, Critical Essay on "In the Shadow of War," in *Short Stories for Students*, Gale, 2005.

Michael Thorpe

In the following review, Thorpe describes the violence and torment captured in Okri's collection Stars of the New Curfew.

Where there is no order, "reality" is anarchy and constant fear of life. Ben Okri's six stories are all quest narratives, one a quest through horrors "to find where you can be happy," but its end is death. Another captures a compulsive aimlessness of these antiquests: a bodiless voice warns the seeker, naïvely "fired by memories of ancient heroes," "Your thoughts are merely the footsteps of you tramping round the disaster area of your own mind."

Okri's settings are Nigerian—Lagos, a provincial capital, the village-dotted bush—but could belong to many another tormented country of tropical Africa; the mode of apprehension is hallucination, dream, and nightmare. In this, though not in language, one is reminded of Tutuola, yet Okri's fabular and allegorical journeys, three of which are excursions into the forest, are more patently linked with the life Africans endure and struggle through in the here and now. Everywhere images of sudden violence and random, cruel power erupt: the whip-flailing, gun-cradling soldier; the bloated, bodyguarded big men "who create our reality." It is against these that the narrator of the long title story, himself "a salesman of nightmares," finally turns after a quest for self-judgment and responsibility.

Through "Stars of the New Curfew" sounds the ironic refrain of the outlandish, derided Rastafarian (himself an impostor in a wig): "Africa, we counting on yuh!" No virtues have scope to thrive, whether love, loyalty, or integrity; suffering "hardens you," does not ennoble. A talking dead man's verdict is the ultimate aphoristic judgment: "First they [sh——t] on us. Now we [sh——t] on ourselves." So Okri continues, as in *Incidents at the Shrine* (1987), to probe unsparingly the self-inflicted wounds of "freedom." (It must be added that, in the standard English narrative, alert editing should have removed some occasional lapses of usage or grammar, such as "Her eyes glowed like that of a cat.")

Source: Michael Thorpe, Review of *Stars of the New Curfew*, in *World Literature Today*, Vol. 64, No. 2, Spring 1990, p. 349.

Robert Fraser

In the following review, Fraser praises Okri for his ability to evoke the beauty and ecstasy hidden in the despair of the African ghetto.

In the penultimate story in this collection there is a perfunctory act of love between a would-be pop star and his reluctant girlfriend. He is trying to break down the girl's inner resistance: "'It's good to be alive,' he said with a sentimental quaver in his voice. 'Who disputed it?' 'No one.'"

Casual readers of this second volume of stories in three years might be excused for thinking that if anyone disputed the general joyousness of existence, it was Ben Okri. When his last volume. *Incidents at the Shrine,* appeared in 1986 some of its less perceptive reviewers observed that Okri seemed to possess a nose for squalor as sharp as a retriever's nose for game. If this was true of *Incidents,* it is even truer of this collection. Okri's locale is the ghetto: that neutral, desolate terrain betwixt town and country in which the detritus of the new African societies so often winds up. His people are that detritus: the aspirant entrepreneurs, inspired con-men, drunkards and ne'er-do-wells of a paradise run to seed. His theme is their despair.

That is one way of describing Okri's achievement, though not necessarily the correct one: the evocation of dereliction. But where such a reading falls down, and where all readers will fail to follow Okri if they happen to be deaf to his particular medley of tone, is in a failure to recognise that his perception of these people and of this terrain possesses in itself nothing of the despairing. These stories are about despair, and for those unacquainted with such absolute destitution the encounter can be gruelling. In mood, however, they are closer to a series of concerto movements in which the bleak, upper tonalities are continually undermined and reproached by an impertinent ground bass, full of a sort of sombre jocularity. The squalor and hopelessness of the ghetto is here, but so is its capacity for improvisation, its mordant, facetious cunning. The title story has for its protagonist a vendor of power-drugs, the havoc of which is strangely released into his own life and those of his townsmen. The transformations thus wrought in their circumstances approximate to a variety of nightmares, but they are also oddly, quirkily beautiful, like the incandescent colours of decay in the festering townscape in Okri's earlier 'Hidden History'. We are watching the mind turning inside out, but the revealed innards have something of the gaudy brilliance of a butterfly devoured by ants:

> I saw the secrets of the town dancing in the street: young men with diseases that melted their faces, beautiful young girls with snakes coming out of their ears. I saw skeletons dancing with fat women. I passed the town's graveyard and saw the dead rising and screaming for children.

The character is of course hallucinating, but the hallucination has in it nothing of the self-indulgence which might mark such an episode in a work by one of Okri's European contemporaries. Such nightmares are the strange fruit of the ghetto itself, and part of its incantatory beauty. Okri is especially powerful at such moments. He is also particularly good at that syncretic progeny of African and European religion: the cultic efflorescence of the desperately believing mind. Nobody is quite as adept as he at capturing the spirit of the Nigerian urban occult: even Wole Soyinka, despite his interest, always seems to be looking down on it. Okri on the other hand seems to get right inside such ecstatic move-

ments, and to come out on the other side having lost very little of his artistic composure.

What is the source of this particular strength? One is reminded of Okri's antecedents. It is perhaps possible to speak of two schools of Nigerian fiction, one of which has for long been in the ascendent. The first, and most frequented, is the School of Achebe, the social realism which for thirty years has cauterised the social conditions of that unfortunate country while apparently doing very little to set it to rights. The second, unduly neglected, is the School of Tutuola, and it is to this that Okri belongs. This might seem an odd statement, for Okri is a quintessentially metropolitan—nay cosmopolitan—artist, while Amos Tutuola in the eyes of his more patronising readership is no more than a country bumpkin. But this is to take the surface as all. The excellence of Tutuola lies not in the hit-and-miss quality of his language—that rather is his downfall—but in his tapping of deep wells of mythic imagination which lie beneath the surface of modern life only to erupt at times of particular difficulty or stress, or at moments akin to the ecstatic.

It is with just such difficulty and stress, and with just such states of near-ecstasy that Okri presents us in his stories, where in consequence the wells of the mythic imagination are for ever breaking surface. Tutuola's own roots lay in that master of Yoruba folklore, D O Fagunwa, and beyond him in centuries of inspired oral story telling. It is Okri's strength that he is able to draw on such traditions without compromising anything of his fractious modernity. The effect can at times be chilling, but it can also be intoxicating.

It ought to be unnecessary to add that this is the equipment, and these are the talents of a major novelist. It is several years since Okri gave us a novel. Until he does so, he is a tiger crouching, much of his considerably quixotic power held in check. When eventually he elects to pounce, his leap will be magnificent. His audience awaits.

Source: Robert Fraser, "Incantatory Beauty," in *Third World Quarterly*, Vol. 11, No. 2, April 1989, pp. 181–83.

Sylvester Ike Onwordi
In the following review, Onwordi praises Okri for coming "into his own stylistically and creatively."

Ben Okri, another Nigerian, has also written about his homeland. *Stars of the New Curfew,* his latest collection of short stories, contains some of his finest writing to date. The biblical cadences of his earlier work suggested that he was aspiring to some quality just beyond his grasp. He appears now to have come into his own stylistically and creatively. There is a simplicity and clarity that give his his modern-day fables the resonance of myth. Greek myth or African myth, it hardly seems to matter.

Okri is a story-teller who, unlike Saro-Wiwa, can express the intricacies of emotional conflict and the drama of life without Nigerian Bigmanism—the compulsion to wear his learning on his sleeve. His work will probably be described as magic realism because, dealing with fable and the collision of dream and reality, he takes liberties with perceived notions of time and place. But he writes without self-indulgence and is concise without being arid. Each of his stories deals with an aspect of life in present-day Nigeria. Some are nostalgic in tone—distorted memories of the civil war, for example; others deal with power and the obsessions, prejudices, hopes and fears of simple, exploited folk. His heroes are market women, prostitutes, down-at-heel drunks like Marjomi, who has a rare blood type and survives by selling it with perilous frequency and using the money to pay for alcohol. Or like the salesman who peddles dangerous potions in the market place and is hounded from town to town by the clamouring voices of his victims. They are love stories because, despite the confusion and poverty of life they reveal, some rich power pervades them all. Soldiers, insane and cruel politicians, policemen, murderers and thieves exist in an elaborate spider's web of fact and fantasy. This is a book on Nigerian life which perfectly captures the emotional temperature of that turbulent country, of a world in fact turned in upon itself and thriving against all the laws of reason. Ben Okri has created a style to match his subject and does it effortlessly well.

Source: Sylvester Ike Onwordi, "Beneath the Waves," in *Times Literary Supplement*, August 5–11, 1988, p. 857.

Sources

Bissoondath, Neil, "Rage and Sadness in Nigeria," in *New York Times Book Review*, August 13, 1989, p. 12.

Fraser, Robert, "Incantatory Beauty," in *Third World Quarterly*, Vol. 11, No. 2, April 1989, pp. 181–83.

King, Bruce, "Okri, Ben," in *Encyclopedia of Post-Colonial Literatures in English*, Vol. 2, edited by Eugene Benson and L. W. Conolly, Routledge, 1994, p. 1178.

Moh, Felicia, *Ben Okri: An Introduction to His Early Fiction*, Fourth Dimension Publishers, 2002.

Newton, Carolyn, "An Interview with Ben Okri," in *South African Literary Review*, Vol. 2, No. 3, September 1992, pp. 5–6.

Okri, Ben, "In the Shadow of War," in *The Art of the Story: An International Anthology of Contemporary Short Stories*, edited by Daniel Halpern, Penguin Books, 1999, pp. 477–80.

———, "The True Issue of This Century Is Not Terrorism, or Religion. It Is Freedom. We Need to De-censor Our Minds," in the *Herald* (Glasgow, UK), August 11, 2003, p. 9.

Onwordi, Sylvester Ike, "Beneath the Waves," in *Times Literary Supplement*, August 5–11, 1988, p. 857.

Parekh, Pushpa Naidu, and Siga Fatima Jagne, eds., in *Postcolonial African Writers: A Bio-Bibliographical Source-book*, Greenwood Press, 1998, pp. 367–70.

Thorpe, Michael, "Nigeria," in *World Literature Today*, Vol. 64, No. 2, Spring 1990, p. 349.

Further Reading

Boehmer, Elleke, ed., *Colonial and Postcolonial Literature: Migrant Metaphors*, Oxford Press, 1995.
    In this collection, Boehmer explores colonial and postcolonial writing in English from 1770 to the present, tracing its development and comparing it to western writing.

Martin, Phyllis M., and Patrick O'Meara, eds., *Africa*, Indiana University Press, 1995.
    This collection includes a host of articles about the continent's history, art, music, social customs, economics, and politics. Of particular interest are the following articles: "African Literature" by Eileen Julien; "The Colonial Era" by Sheldon Gellar; and "Decolonization, Independence, and the Failure of Politics" by Edmond J. Keller.

Oliver, Roland, and J. D. Fage, *A Short History of Africa*, Penguin Books, 1990.
    Oliver and Fage's book provides a concise overview of the continent's history, including chapters on the colonial period and the early years of independence.

Parekh, Pushpa Naidu, and Siga Fatima Jagne, eds., *Postcolonial African Writers: A Bio-Bibliographical Source-book*, Greenwood Press, 1998.
    This source provides readers with an overview of Okri's life, his works and major themes, and the critical reception that his work has received over the years.

Soyinka, Wole, *The Open Sore of a Continent: A Personal Narrative of the Nigerian Crisis*, Oxford University Press, 1996.
    In this collection of his previous speeches, Nobel Prize laureate and well-known Nigerian playwright and novelist Wole Soyinka offers a critical overview of Nigeria's political history and the country's future.

The Long-Distance Runner

"The Long-Distance Runner" by Grace Paley is the last story in the collection *Enormous Changes at the Last Minute*, which appeared in 1974. The story is also available in *The Collected Stories* (1994). The story features Paley's lead protagonist, Faith Darwin Asbury, who at forty-two has taken up long-distance running. This semi-autobiographical character shares Paley's concern for social justice and her awareness of the cultural and economic divisions between the races, recurrent themes in Paley's fiction. The short story foregrounds Paley's skillful use of dialogue as a way of dramatizing differences between individuals in a given neighborhood. In this story, Faith travels back to her childhood neighborhood in Brooklyn and witnesses from the inside the deterioration of the now all African American tenement where her family once lived.

Grace Paley

1974

Author Biography

Grace Paley was born on December 11, 1922, in the Bronx, New York. Her parents, Manya Ridnyik Goodside and Dr. Isaac Goodside, were Russian Jews who immigrated to the United States in 1906. Paley's parents were socialists who had engaged in political resistance efforts against the Russian czar and had been exiled (her father to Siberia; her

Grace Paley

mother to Germany) as a result. They settled originally in lower Manhattan where they were joined by his mother and two sisters, who, along with his wife, supported Isaac Goodside while he studied medicine.

By the time Paley was born, the family was living a middle-class existence in the Bronx. Theirs was a multilingual world: Russian was spoken in the home; Yiddish was used in the neighborhood; her father's first employment-based language was Italian; and English was spoken at school and in the city beyond. A childhood colored by such distinct sounds and colloquial expressions early sensitized Paley to how speech patterns convey character. Moreover, her family's concern for the under classes and for social justice, along with their family stories of oppression, predisposed Paley to see the political component as fundamental to individual circumstance. Indeed, when she came, in the 1950s, to write fiction, she focused on urban neighborhoods full of individuals whose ways of speaking both revealed their backgrounds and connected them to different ethnic communities.

Having survived political oppression, Isaac and Manya Goodside recognized how vulnerable people are to social upheaval and economic change. They urged Paley to learn secretarial skills so she would always be able to support herself. After attending Hunter College her freshman year, Paley went to Merchants and Bankers Business and Secretarial School, and thereafter she worked as a secretary for a reinsurance company, for some social agencies, and for Columbia University. Later she attended New York University. At home, she typed her poetry and later her stories. She married Jess Paley in 1941 and had two children (Nora in 1949 and Danny in 1951). The couple separated in 1967 and divorced in 1971, and in 1972 Grace Paley married Robert Nichols.

During the 1950s and 1960s, while becoming increasingly active in Leftist protest activities, Grace Paley continued writing and caring for her children at home. In 1959, Doubleday published her first collection of stories, *The Little Disturbances of Man*. Among her political activities, she was involved in the 1961 establishment of the Greenwich Village Peace Center, and her 1966 participation in an antimilitary protest at an Armed Forces Day parade led to her serving a brief sentence in jail. She protested for the legalization of abortion and supported the Civil Rights movement. Professionally, in 1966 she began her twenty-two-year connection with Sarah Lawrence College where she taught writing. During these years she continued to publish. *Enormous Changes at the Last Minute* was published in 1974 ("Long-Distance Runner" is the last story in this collection), and in 1985 *Later the Same Day* appeared. Also in 1985, she published her first book of poetry, *Leaning Forward*, followed by *Long Walks and Intimate Talks* in 1991 and *New and Collected Poems* in 1992.

Grace Paley's work gradually garnered widespread critical attention, and Paley began to win awards for her writing. For example, she received the 1970 National Institute of Arts and Letters award for short fiction. She won the PEN/Faulkner Prize for fiction in 1986 and the Senior Fellowship of the Literature Program of the National Endowment for the Arts in 1987. In 1987, Grace Paley became the first New York State Author, and she also won the fiction writers' Edith Wharton Citation for Merit. She won the Lannan Literary Award in 1997. In 2001, Grace Paley and Robert Nichols began a small literary press, Glad Day Books, which they operated from their Thetford, Vermont, home. Their intention, according to a *Publishers Weekly* article, was to publish works, both political and literary, which other presses could not or would not publish.

Plot Summary

When "The Long-Distance Runner" begins, Faith Asbury is preparing to leave home for a long-distance run. She leaves her two sons and a neighbor friend, Mrs. Raftery, watching television. Faith takes the train to Brighton Beach, changes her clothes in a locker, and runs along the boardwalk for a mile or more. Then she cuts away from the beach and heads into her old neighborhood in Brooklyn.

Almost immediately, Faith is surrounded by a crowd of African Americans who comment on her presence and appearance. She is undaunted by them, engaging them in conversation and commenting back in their language. She points out to the crowd her old apartment, and the Girl Scout Cynthia suggests that Faith go inside the building and meet the current tenants in Faith's childhood apartment.

On the first floor of the apartment building, Faith resists Cynthia's suggestion to visit Mrs. Luddy, the resident in Faith's old apartment. Faith excuses herself with the lie that her mother is dead, and she does not want to see the place. This comment arouses Cynthia's fears about losing her own mother, to which Faith replies that if Cynthia's mother were to die, Cynthia could come to live with Faith and her sons. Suddenly, Cynthia is afraid of Faith and lets out a yell. Afraid, in turn, of the fear she has aroused in Cynthia, Faith runs to Mrs. Luddy's door and begs to be admitted. Mrs. Luddy lets Faith in and bolts the door.

Faith remains with Mrs. Luddy for the next three weeks, sharing the work of tending to three little girls and offering to engage the second-grader, Donald, in reading lessons. As women and as mothers raising children alone, Mrs. Luddy and Faith are able to talk about mutually interesting subjects. But they are separated by racial, economic, and education differences. From Mrs. Luddy's window, they can see across the street into burned-out buildings and garbage-laden empty lots and down into the street below to people on the steps and sidewalk. They discuss men and sex and children; they express their separate conclusions on these subjects. Faith's naive and idealistic assumptions about cleaning up the neighborhood and bringing Donald's reading up to level contrast with Mrs. Luddy's matter-of-fact resignation to her bleak surroundings.

Then one morning Mrs. Luddy wakes up Faith with the announcement that it is time for Faith to leave. Mrs. Luddy says, "This ain't Free Vacation Farm. Time we was by ourself a little." Faith fails to return Mrs. Luddy's strict look. She says, "I tried to look strictly back, but I failed because I loved the sight of her." With a kiss on Donald's head, Faith leaves.

Faith runs back to her home and finds her lover, Jack, and her one son, Richard, beginning to clean up. It is Saturday, and her other son, Anthony, is just leaving to visit his friends in institutions such as Bellevue and Rockland State. That evening Faith tries to explain where she has been, but Jack, Richard, and Anthony do not understand. The story concludes with a kind of summing up: "A woman inside the steamy energy of middle age runs and runs. She finds the houses and streets where her childhood happened. She lives in them. She learns as though she was a child what in the world is coming next."

Characters

Anthony Asbury

Anthony, also called Tonto, is Faith Asbury's second son. He is a social activist like his mother and visits friends in institutions on the weekends.

Faith Darwin Asbury

Faith Asbury is Grace Paley's lead protagonist, a woman with an absent husband, Ricardo; two sons, Richard and Anthony; and a sometimes live-in lover, Jack. Politically, Faith is a radical liberal, and as a mother raising children mostly alone, she is sensitive to women's rights and issues. She lives in New York. Her parents live in a seniors facility called Children of Judea.

Richard Asbury

Richard Asbury is Faith's older son. He and his brother Anthony are watching television when Faith leaves for her long-distance run.

Cynthia

Cynthia is a Girl Scout in Brooklyn who meets Faith in the street and ushers her into the apartment where Faith lived as a child. While Cynthia encourages Faith to meet Mrs. Luddy, the tenant of the apartment where Faith lived years before, Cynthia is frightened by the idea that Faith could serve her as an adoptive parent if Cynthia's mother were to die.

Jack

Jack is Faith's lover. When Faith returns from her three-week absence, Jack is cleaning house with Richard.

Donald Luddy

Donald Luddy is a second grader and the oldest of Mrs. Luddy's four children. He is bright and cordial. Mrs. Luddy keeps him in the apartment most of the time because there are dangerous people in the streets who could hurt him. While Faith stays in the Luddy apartment, Donald composes a poem.

Eloise Luddy

Eloise is the two-year-old sister of Donald Luddy. There are also twin baby girls in the Luddy family.

Mrs. Raftery

Mrs. Raftery is a neighbor and friend of Faith Asbury. Mrs. Raftery looks in on Faith's sons and sometimes makes them a meal. When Faith leaves for her run, Mrs. Raftery is watching television with Richard and Anthony.

Tonto

See Anthony Asbury

Themes

White Flight

"The Long-Distance Runner" suggests the effects of "white flight," a term coined in 1967 to describe the movement of white people to the suburbs as urban neighborhoods and schools became increasing African American. As cities lost population and tax base, urban neighborhoods decayed. Poor people were left to cope with deterioration and increasing crime, and urban neighborhoods were called ghettos. In this story, Grace Paley imagines a situation in which a middle-class white woman and an African American woman in the ghetto are able to bridge the gap created by white flight. Faith runs through her Brooklyn childhood neighborhood and is able to meet and live with people there. She witnesses the changes that have transpired since her family moved away. She is able to talk with Mrs. Luddy about the problems that confront poor people and middle-class people alike. Faith's idealistic responses to the tenement culture and problems are

countered by Mrs. Luddy's discouraged resignation. Mrs. Luddy has adapted to her environment, learned to exist in it; Faith visits with the simplistic hope of extending herself to these people, but in the process she becomes more aware of the unanswered questions that permeate the problems of racial prejudice, poverty, and urban decay.

Racial Segregation

"The Long-Distance Runner" dramatizes how people in an all-black, poverty-stricken neighborhood react when a white woman runs through its streets. Time and shifting populations have separated Faith Asbury from her childhood neighborhood, and when, as a forty-two-year-old, she returns, she is hooted at and challenged by the people on the street. Now a stranger, an interloper, Faith is at risk in the streets where she played safely as a child. The people in the street shout out their comments about her while she tries to make connection with them by talking about the names of flowers. By being in their midst, she learns from them, and they see her as an individual despite her race. Moreover, the fiction allows for Faith to stay with Mrs. Luddy for three weeks. This temporary integration gives Faith understanding about what it is like to live in the urban ghetto and what it is like to be an African American woman who must raise her children in a threatening environment. It also implies the limitations of white drive-by platitudes, such as "Someone ought to clean that up."

Cross-Racial Female Relationships

By enacting a story in which women separated by race, economics, and education spend three weeks living together, Paley indirectly addresses the historical separation of the races in the white middle-class pursuit of women's rights. The feminist movement was mainly a middle-class white woman's movement, which suggested no female alliance across color lines. "The Long-Distance Runner" enacts an implausible fiction in which two women meet despite those lines, and the white woman's education is achieved through this exposure.

Significantly, the meeting occurs on the African American woman's turf. Mrs. Luddy is immediately in charge: "You in my house. . . . You do as I say. For two cents, I throw you out." Reversing the racial power structure puts Faith in the position to see more and learn more. That arrangement is important because it is Faith who comes with the "answers"; in other words, Faith comes to Mrs. Luddy with conclusions that Mrs. Luddy then chal-

Topics for Further Study

- Research urban decay in the early 1960s, and make a chart that correlates social unrest of various forms with the rate at which urban poverty increased and white populations decreased.

- Read about Grace Paley's social activism, and then write a report on ''The Long-Distance Runner'' that analyzes how her socialist views and stand for equal rights are suggested in the fiction.

- Return to a former neighborhood, noting the changes that have taken place during your absence. Write a short story in which the main character not only returns but takes up residence among the more recently established neighborhood dwellers. Let the story expose the differences between the character who returns and the

current residents, and hint at ways in which these differences can or cannot be bridged.

- Research the correlations between poverty and three factors: race, gender, and single head of household with dependent children. Draw a chart to show how these factors correlate in three decades: 1950s, 1970s, and 1990s.

- Study a map of a metropolitan area with which you are familiar, and research population according to race across the area. Then reproduce the map so that you can color it in for racial distribution. Reach conclusions about the frequency of segregation and integration based on your research.

---

lenges. For example, regarding the vacant lot across the street, Faith says, "Someone ought to clean that up." Mrs. Luddy matter-of-factly retorts, "Who you got in mind? Mrs. Kennedy?" Readers get the chance here to see just how this new "meeting of minds" transpires. In effect, Paley creates a world in which the traditional lines that divide African American women from white women are crossed, and it is that crossing that reveals the complicated questions that refuse easy, one-liner answers.

Style

Setting

"The Long-Distance Runner" takes place mostly in Brooklyn, New York, in the childhood neighborhood of Faith Asbury. The story takes place some twenty or more years after her departure from the neighborhood. She now lives in a middle-class white neighborhood. However, Faith takes the train to Brighton Beach and runs along the boardwalk

and then into the neighborhood where she spent her childhood. The place has deteriorated, and the residents are now all African Americans. To the crowd who gathers around this forty-two-year-old white jogger, Faith explains: "I used to live here." Crowd members answer back: "Oh yes . . . in the white old days." Since the "white old days," many abandoned houses have been knocked down, vacant lots are littered with discarded furniture and trash, and crime dictates people's behavior on and off the streets. A white woman running through this neighborhood is an anomaly, a person who stands out in every sense from the setting and who residents assume is at risk.

From Mrs. Luddy's apartment window, Faith can look down on empty lots and burned-out houses. She sees what has happened in this neighborhood in the past couple decades. She concludes: "The tenement . . . had been destroyed, first by fire, then by demolition (which is a swinging ball of steel that cracks bedrooms and kitchens). Because of this work we could see several blocks wide and a block and a half long." Whites have moved away, people's homes have been knocked down, and African Americans have remained. Now vacant lots hold overturned sofas, and animals prowl in the trash at night. Setting heightens differences between characters and helps explain why connection cannot be sustained across racial lines.

Characterization

Dialogue is the main tool for characterizing individuals in "The Long-Distance Runner." Otherwise unidentified individuals on the street comment on Faith: "Who you? Who that? Look at her! When you see a fatter ass?" A man from Africa states haughtily, "I will learn the fine old art of sailing in case the engines of the new society of my old inland country should fail." Cynthia, a Girl Scout, asks Faith, "Whyn't you go up to Mrs. Luddy living in your house, you lady, huh?" These disparate voices encircle the intruder, Faith, distinguishing their speakers from one another and from Faith. Grace Paley does not use quotation marks in this story; thus, the voices rather than the punctuation identify separate voices. The way characters use language reveals their background and identifies them as members of certain groups.

Plot

The implausible plot of this story is that a white woman can run through her old neighborhood, which has changed from immigrant Jewish and Irish to poor African American, and decide to drop in at the apartment her family occupied when she was a child. She gets into the apartment suddenly and unexpectedly and then ends up staying there three weeks, living with the current residents and participating in their daily activities. This imagined storyline reveals some basic truths about what separates racial and economic groups and how that separation leads people on both sides to certain prejudicial conclusions.

Historical Context

Gender and Racial Prejudice

In the nineteenth century and through much of the twentieth century, when white middle-class women worked for gender equality, many of them refused to make alliances with women of color or with poor women. While all women experienced unequal treatment, African American and Native American women faced the additional oppression that white women exerted over them. This pattern of exclusion by white women was measurable in the so-called social agencies designed to improve women's lives. For example, the Women's Christian Temperance Union denied membership to black women in the South, and the Young Women's Christian Association (YWCA) did not allow African American women to serve on its board. Even in the late twentieth century, this pattern could still be traced in the absence of African American women from some conferences on feminism, from professional associations, and from positions of power in universities and corporations. Toward the end of the twentieth century, cross-racial collaboration increased, and awareness deepened concerning the multi-layered prejudices at work that affected race relations between women.

In 1974, when "The Long-Distance Runner" appeared in *Enormous Changes at the Last Minute*, the United States continued to be in social and racial upheaval. The 1960s disruption caused by race riots, antiwar protests, the Civil Rights movement, and abortion debate left its aftershocks. Moreover, in 1973, the Supreme Court in *Roe v. Wade* legalized elective abortion in the first trimester. This decision came too late for women like Mrs. Luddy in Paley's story. Mrs. Luddy is a single parent who is responsible for a second-grader, a two-year-old, and twin baby girls. Her poverty and her self-defensive imprisonment in a ghetto apartment surrounded by dangerous streets and crime are made all the more difficult because she has four little children to rear. Mrs. Luddy is oppressed by her class, her sex, and her race. Faith Asbury gets an education by being able to live with Mrs. Luddy for three weeks, an exposure that reveals how complicated Mrs. Luddy's problems are and how resistant they are to easy, liberal solutions.

Critical Overview

Critics have noted the small size of Grace Paley's oeuvre, but her literary reputation is significant, nonetheless. When *The Collected Stories* appeared in 1994, it was nominated for a National Book Award, and the volume drew widespread affirmation of Paley's fiction. Pointing to its central issue, Cynthia Tompkins in her *World Literature Today*

Compare & Contrast

- **1970s:** After decades of resistance to the distribution of contraceptive information or devices, contraception devices are now available. *Roe v. Wade* legalizes abortion in 1973, and women gain the right to choose to end unwanted pregnancies within the first trimester. However, in 1976, Congress outlaws the use of Medicaid funding for abortions, a decision that mostly affects poor women.

  Today: While thousands of elective abortions are performed across the United States, pro-life advocates continue to fight against legalized abortion.

- **1970s:** The 1970s are shaped by the possibility of an Equal Rights Amendment to the Constitution that would state that men and women are equal before the law. In 1972, Phyllis Schlafly organizes Stop ERA, but in 1973 the proposal for an Equal Rights Amendment passes in Congress. State ratification gets bogged down, however, and by 1979 the ratification period has ended, and ERA fails.

  Today: Equality between the sexes is sought in the workplace via the 1964 Civil Rights Amendment, particularly Title VII, which makes discrimination based on "race, color, religion, sex or national origin" illegal.

- **1970s:** The ratio of poverty among African Americans compared to that of white Americans is three to one.

  Today: While the percentage of poor African Americans has declined (for example, from 55.2 percent in 1959 to 31.9 percent in 1990), the ratio of poverty among African Americans to white Americans remains three to one. Among all African American households, the highest rate of poverty occurs in those with a single female head of household and dependent children. The occurrence of poverty for this group exceeds 50 percent.

- **1970s:** The Civil Rights Act of 1968 becomes fully operational in January 1970. It makes discrimination in housing and apartment rental on the basis of "race, color, religion, sex or national origin" illegal, and it applies across the U.S. housing market with small exceptions, such as privately owned, single-family homes sold without the assistance of a realtor.

  Today: The Civil Rights Act of 1968 has little effect on housing discrimination because of its limitations in enforcement.

---

review stated that the collection "encapsulates the moral dilemmas" raised by the question: "How are we to live our lives?" Like other critics, Tompkins also pointed out Paley's "'ear' for idioms and speech patterns," which enhances her handling of characterization and depiction of social interaction between members of different groups. Moreover, in the fiction since the 1970s, Tompkins pointed out that "Paley's texts illustrate the feminist dictum: the personal is the political." These various elements in the work—thematic issues, characterization, and social interaction—are all dramatized in "The Long-Distance Runner," the story of a white woman's return to her childhood neighborhood, now an African American ghetto.

This story focuses on the gulf African American and white women have to bridge in order to make connection. The whole question of spanning a chasm is connected to Paley's political activism. Adam Meyer stated that the stories Paley writes "create a forum wherein she can question her own real-life activism" and where the well-meaning but naive white activist can confront realities that check idealistic platitudes. In fact, regarding Paley's lead protagonist, Faith Darwin Asbury, Meyer stated that the reader comes to "question the inconsistencies in Faith's reasoning." Paley's fiction puts liberal beliefs to the test, and stories such as "The Long-Distance Runner" create scenarios that challenge solutions people may actually espouse but do not necessarily run the risk of putting into action. In her article on marginality, Victoria Aarons stated that Paley's stories create characters "*in relation to others*, to a community."

In an interview with three *Paris Review* writers, Paley's stories were described as "rigorously pruned [so] that they frequently resemble poetry as much as fiction." In sum, one might say that Paley's work allows readers to see through new eyes and to witness possible intersections that may not yet be lived in real life. In these ways, the fiction envisions a new reality. That the prose has the intensity of poetry is another plus.

Criticism

Melodie Monahan

Monahan has a Ph.D. in English. She teaches at Wayne State University and also operates an editing service, The Inkwell Works. In the following essay, Monahan explores the cross-cultural, cross-racial homecoming that is enacted in "The Long-Distance Runner."

Grace Paley's "The Long-Distance Runner" begins with a common enough experience, a long-absent adult's return to the childhood neighborhood. People occasionally drive through their old neighborhoods to look at the homes and buildings in which they spent earlier years. If a new ethnic or racial group occupies the neighborhood, the returning visitors may remark on the culture they remember and contrast it with the culture they now observe. Indeed, as they register local changes, they may wonder about the people who now live in what used to be their homes; they may slow down or park near the old house and imagine themselves reentering it. This commonplace fantasy is literalized with matter-of-fact detail in Grace Paley's story about a woman who not only returns for a look-see but takes up temporary residence in her childhood apartment.

Grace Paley's implausible story is a fictional attempt to span the geographical, social, economic, and racial chasms that separate Faith Darwin Asbury's white middle-class life from the urban ghetto she once called home. Purportedly out for some exercise, Faith takes a train to Brighton Beach, runs along the boardwalk for a mile or so, and then veers off into a once-familiar Brooklyn, New York, neighborhood. Returning after the 1960s' White

Flight and rampant urban decay have gouged this landscape, Faith is both struck by the setting's deterioration and made to feel all the more the outsider by her conversation with people on the street. Nonetheless, the street talk, particularly with Cynthia, a Girl Scout who encourages Faith to enter her old apartment house, propels Faith to knock on the door that once marked entry to her family's home. In this imagined encounter, the current residents take her arrival in stride and accept the way in which the white woman immediately begins to share their everyday lives. When Faith returns to her current home three weeks later, her own family greets her with little surprise and less inquiry. In the interim, she has gone all the way back to her childhood, geographically and in some ways psychologically, and she has remained there long enough to connect with the present tenement and a few of its residents. The truism that Thomas Wolfe used as a title, *You Can't Go Home Again*, is thus tested in Grace Paley's "The Long-Distance Runner."

Grace Paley's use of dialogue to capture diversity and her radical activist stand for civil rights and gender and racial equality intersect in "The Long-Distance Runner" to dramatize specifically a white middle-class woman's encounter with an African American mother, Mrs. Luddy, who is raising four children alone and mostly behind a bolted tenement door. Suddenly afraid of the people outside the apartment building, Faith runs toward her old apartment door and knocks and begs for entry. This point in the story is curiously and tellingly handled. Quotation marks are not used in the text, and a reader might miss the shift that occurs at this point. When Faith knocks, Donald Luddy, a second-grader, refuses to open the door: "Mama not home, I ain't allowed to open up for nobody." Faith responds, "It's me," and then, as if suddenly a child herself running to her own mother, she says, "Mama! Mama! let me in!" Suddenly she is a little child, fearful of strangers outside, begging her mother to open the door. In letting Faith in, Mrs. Luddy takes charge as if Faith were indeed a child. Mrs. Luddy insists, "You in my house. . . . You do as I say."

Thus the intersection is created, and once on site Faith sees (perhaps more like a child might see) how her naive solutions and well-intended aspirations bump up against local realities. Looking down on the vacant lots strewn with discarded furniture and trash, Faith remarks, "Someone ought to clean that up," to which Mrs. Luddy counters, "Who you got in mind? Mrs. Kennedy?" When Donald expresses his mother's criticism of the porch slackers,

What Do I Read Next?

- Grace Paley's essays are collected in *Just as I Thought* (1998). This compilation includes her views on topics ranging from abortion to women's action for peace to reflections on Paley's father and her life in Vermont.

- In *The Collected Stories* (1994) readers can find selections of stories from *The Little Disturbances of Man* (1959), *Enormous Changes at the Last Minute* (1974), and *Later the Same Day* (1985).

- Gloria Naylor's novel *The Women of Brewster Place* follows the lives of seven women living in Brewster Place, a ghetto housing project in a northern U.S. city. The poignancy of these women's lives and their hopes and challenges clearly depict the difficulty poor African American women face living in poverty and coping with racial and sexual prejudice.

"They ain't got self-respect," Faith intellectualizes, "he ought to learn to be more sympathetic." She tells him, "There are reasons that people are that way." Then Mrs. Luddy checks her, "Don't trouble your head about it if you don't mind." When Faith thinks about leaving the apartment, she admits feeling trapped by fear: "I'd get to the door and then I'd hear voices. I'm ashamed to say I'd become fearful. Despite my wide geographical love of mankind, I would be attacked by local fears." Just being on Mrs. Luddy's turf, inside her reality, informs Faith about the daunting complications inherent in social problem solving.

Regarding improving Donald, Faith suggests bringing him "up to reading level at once." She tells him he is "plain brilliant" when he composes a poem full of his mother's words. But Mrs. Luddy corrects her: "You fool with him too much." Then Mrs. Luddy tells the story her grandmother told her mother, about standing in the slave cabin door when a field boy came running through announcing, "Sister! It's freedom." Ironically, Mrs. Luddy, who daily copes with a necessarily locked-in existence, is the teller of this tale about sudden freedom. Paley's handling seems to suggest that story is one way of learning what was and is. As she tells her grandmother's story, Mrs. Luddy's circumscribed existence is juxtaposed with the cabin-door slave girl's life. The fiction gives us a sense of history, but not a sense of progress. Faith's hopes for making a difference here are diminished by the long shadow

slavery casts, a darkening that reaches into the 1960s and 1970s to engulf its descendents. Then, as abruptly as Faith arrives and takes up residence, she is forced to leave. Mrs. Luddy tells her, "This ain't Free Vacation Farm."

Returning home via the park where she played with her own children, Faith sees young mothers and thinks, They will "be like me, wrong in everything." What she has learned at Mrs. Luddy's makes her doubt her initial certainties. At home, her family greets her with mild surprise. When she explains where she has been, Richard tells her to "Cut the baby talk." It is as if she has come home younger, more childlike, more aware, as children are freshly aware when they have made unexpected connections. The grown-up Asbury family members cannot understand what she has learned because only she has had the chance, Paley states at the end, "to [learn] as though she was still a child what in the world is coming next."

In her essay, "The Value of Not Understanding Everything," Grace Paley suggests an alternative to the writer's first rule, to write what one knows. Paley argues it is better by far to write about what one does not know. She admits that she has written a number of stories with Jewish themes because she was an outsider to Judaism. "There were families of experience I was cut off from. You know, it seemed to me that an entire world was whispering in the other room. In order to get to the core of it all . . . I made fiction." Now in this 1960s essay, she believes

---

> The truism that Thomas Wolfe used as a title, <u>You Can't Go Home Again</u>, is thus tested in Grace Paley's 'The Long-Distance Runner.'"

she "knows" her Jewish past and can no longer write those stories. Now she needs to enter new questions life presents. Paley states, "The writer is not some kind of phony historian who runs around answering everyone's questions with made-up characters tying up loose ends. She is nothing but a questioner." In "The Long-Distance Runner," Paley imagines a plot that literalizes an encounter, that dramatizes a most unusual kind of connection. This story maps out the what-ifs that generate from the fictional premise of a white woman's taking the time to see and learn about the life of an African American mother living in the ghetto. Marginalizing the easy solutions such a white woman might have, the story privileges the hard questions such an encounter causes. Facing those questions constitutes the homecoming education Faith Asbury achieves.

Source: Melodie Monahan, Critical Essay on "The Long-Distance Runner," in *Short Stories for Students*, Gale, 2005.

Ethan Goffman

In the following essay, Goffman examines how "The Long-Distance Runner" and "Zagrowsky Tells," another of Paley's short stories, "begin the process of decentering and rewriting identities both Jewish and American by reflecting them through African American perspectives."

Grace Paley is steeped in traditions of community, social activism, and the struggle for transformation. A descendant of the East European Jewish socialist tradition, who developed as a writer in the tumult of the 1960s, Paley remains a political activist. Like her politics, the often-noted power and charm of her literary voice is not merely a personal idiosyncrasy but derives from extensive roots. Her Yiddish heritage blends with urban dialect and African American inflections to create a quirky expressiveness, a cross-section of the everchanging American language. These influences coalesce in the proto-typical ethnic mix of New York City, the scene of a plethora of linguistic styles, an exotic territory familiarized through Paley's community of voices. The urban milieu is crucial in portraying a Jewish American community branching out and cross-pollinating with other peoples, creating a (post)modern multicultural persona. Simultaneously, Paley tests and refines Jewish American identity against the African American experience. The Black presence forces an engagement with past Jewish marginalization, calling into question a comfortable incorporation into mainstream America. American minority communities must define themselves not just against a presumed American center but against each other. Americanization as simple assimilation into a preordained culture is revealed as untenable. "The spatial topography of center and margin," Henry Louis Gates suggests, "has started to exhaust its usefulness in describing our own modernity" (189). There is no stable framework into which one fits one's cultural patterns, but an everchanging aggregation in which various communities interrogate each other in an incessant reshaping.

Paley's New York is the ideal setting for a (post)modern literature: polyglot, multilingual, interethnic. As early as 1924 Mikhail Bakhtin defined modern literature as surmounting the limitations of earlier forms to create a dialogic blending. Monologism is pierced by a multiplicity of voices, an expanding variety of classes and backgrounds, so that "the world becomes polyglot, once and for all and irreversibly. The period of national languages, coexisting but closed and deaf to each other, comes to an end. Languages throw light on each other" (Bakhtin 12). This view of literature as an instrument of change proves somewhat idealistic in practice. Bakhtin overlooks the elite nature of the institutions through which literature is transmitted; the spectrum of voices is inevitably filtered through an educated class. From a position not only of difference but of power, privileged authors may choose to write across class and racial boundaries; their authority and authenticity, however, is problematic.

The posture of speaking for the Other has long marked Jewish speakers and writers regarding African Americans; in Andrew Lakritz's terms such representations "make risky incursions on the uncommon grounds of groups that have not been accorded the authority to speak for themselves" (4). Speaking for another often leads to representing one's own concerns, distorting or even erasing that other identity. So Michael Rogin argues that by adopting blackface guise, such Jewish figures as Al

Jolson created themselves as Americans through contrast with the excluded Other. The minstrel guise "passed immigrants into Americans by differentiating them from the black Americans through whom they spoke, who were not permitted to speak for themselves" (Rogin 56). However most situations in which Jews attempt to represent or speak for African Americans are ambiguous, characterized by mixed motives and mixed results.

In representing the African American presence within a larger cultural imagination, Paley, despite her obvious sympathy with Black communities, ratifies and interrogates her own Jewish American identity. As she herself explains, "if you speak for others—if you really perform that great social task . . . you'll really begin to be able to tell your own story better" ("Conversation" 35). Paley tells her stories from a more comfortable standpoint than earlier Jewish cultural figures, and with a keen awareness of African American needs. She seeks not just to define herself relative to the excluded Other, but to recuperate and legitimize the lost history of Otherness, both Black and Jewish. Her reexamination of American Jewish identity redefines America as a society of overlapping margins, or rather of overlapping communities, superseding the old margins-versus-center dichotomy.

Two stories, "The Long Distance Runner" and "Zagrowsky Tells," begin the process of decentering and rewriting identities both Jewish and American by reflecting them through African American perspectives. In these stories easy assimilation becomes untenable; America is (re)presented as a collection of unfinished, interlocking histories. Yet even in the midst of stylistic and cultural blendings ethnic communities often remain segregated. This is particularly true for African America which becomes, willingly or not, a test case against which other groups define themselves. For Jewish Americans the Black presence is a jarring reminder of a past history of ghettoization and marginalization. A comfortable version of assimilation in which ethnic groups participate fully in American life while maintaining at least a portion of their traditions is called into question. A more extensive American vision is needed, one epitomized by multi-ethnic New York. Yet this new vision is fraught with danger, with unfamiliar contacts and potential misunderstandings.

Issues of interpenetration remain controversial, making for a vexed literary treatment. "The Long Distance Runner" and "Zagrowsky Tells" employ

> ❝'The Long Distance Runner' and 'Zagrowsky Tells' employ two vigorous yet highly divergent Jewish narrative viewpoints, which powerfully compress and individuate larger interactions."

two vigorous yet highly divergent Jewish narrative viewpoints, which powerfully compress and individuate larger interactions. Triangulated among tradition, exclusion, and assimilation, Jewish Americans perceive Blacks through a complex, often conflicting, matrix of subject positions: as a people alien to Judaism, as a similarly oppressed minority group, as a nonassimilated version of the Other. Like many progressive Jews, especially during the social movements of the 1960s, Paley seems at once determined not to forget her people's past and resolved to help similarly oppressed groups join— and thus revise—a larger social collectivity, and, in so doing, end the history of terror inflicted on subnational groups which has so devastated world Jewry.

Paley's recurring protagonist, the free-spirited activist Faith Darwin Asbury, is the narrator of "The Long Distance Runner" and a central character in "Zagrowsky Tells." Having survived a difficult divorce and raised two children singlehandedly, Faith is an ideal subject for dramatic treatment of feminist themes. Her migration from a domesticated status generates a perspective sympathetic to the similarly, though not equivalently, marginalized African American community. Faith's ambiguous position may serve as a bridge to reconstructing other marginalized perspectives as it is made familiar to the reader via Faith's consciousness. A eurocentric perspective is ruptured by historical alienations both Jewish and female.

Despite her newfound independence, Faith's self-doubt lingers; she begins "The Long Distance Runner" ill-equipped for the kind of freedom romanticized in the masculine adventure novel. As a middle-aged woman she starts to run, explaining that "though I was stout and in many ways inadequate to this desire, I wanted to go far and fast."

Adventures epitomized in the masculine adventure novel—vast sea journeys and cross-country excursions—are untenable for a middle-aged women with children to tend; in restlessly exploring her identity, Faith embarks upon the nearest available substitute. Yet her journey out is also a journey in, or rather back. Her running takes her to her original home in Brooklyn, now psychologically and socially distant in ways that parallel the faraway lands of countless adventure novels. Like the prototypical male adventurer, Faith finds the alien, the dark Other, in large numbers: "Suddenly I was surrounded by about three hundred blacks." As in Joseph Conrad's novels, in confronting these others she is confronting herself, yet her heart is not of darkness but of benevolent curiosity. The terror associated with the Other is negligible. True to her heritage of striving for sisterhood and brotherhood, Faith attempts to familiarize the strange, to bring it into harmony with her notions of identity and culture, of an America remade in the image of the many.

The Blacks Faith sees are people like herself, living lives as best they can in a neighborhood alienated from mainstream norms, as she did when a child. In confronting the history of her neighborhood, she reacts not only with fear but, even more, with a delighted curiosity. Conscious of her own implication in a racist history, Faith is anxious to make connections, to humanize. She exemplifies the well meaning, progressive White, telling the gazing Black crowd that "I like your speech. . . . Metaphor and all." In praising the richness of the Black vernacular she does more to explain her own sympathies than to engage the crowd. In addition, she makes a historical connection: "Yes my people also had a way of speech. And don't forget the Irish. The gift of gab," a statement prefiguring current notions of American multiculturalism, of a stream of languages, customs, and approaches to life that are flowing together. The ideology of assimilation into a prefigured European-based culture is called into question; the philosophy of many peoples continually inventing and reinventing a culture is ascendant.

It is impossible to tell how much of "The Long Distance Runner" is represented as literally happening and how much occurs in Faith's imagination since increasing leaps in plausibility render much of the story fictive, even from the viewpoint of the fictional Faith. The story is about an imaginative, internal awakening. From her position as sympathetic political activist, vastly separate from the realities of Black life yet committed to bridging the

gap, Grace Paley plays a delicate balancing game. Blacks for her can never entirely escape their role as a projection of White (in her case Jewish liberal) needs. Her dialogue seems self-conscious in struggling to give her African American characters agency, a life of their own. Faith's viewpoint, though sympathetic, shades into a liberal version of the discerning White gaze, a judgmental stance which the story itself satirizes. Adam Meyer suggests that Paley is "asking herself why she, a white woman, should have the right to speak about African Americans in the first place" (80). Yet the alternative, silence, is worse: whatever the pitfalls, "both collective action and coalition would seem to require the possibility of speaking for others" (Alcoff 102). Given her political motivation and the close relation of African American issues to both Jewish and 1960s progressivism, she cannot but speak. Of course her stories are not meant to be definitive, but are merely one stage in a continuing dialogue.

Paley endows her Black characters with dialect as authentic as she can manage, as when one member of the crowd exhorts respectful treatment of Faith: "Poor thing. She ain't right. Leave her you boys, you bad boys." A moral sense, a sympathetic reaching out, is evident. Rather than being a monolithic whole the Black crowd begins to acquire individuation through dissension, dialogue, and brief, telling description: "You blubrous devil! said a dark young man. He wore horn-rimmed glasses and had that intelligent look that City College boys used to have when I was eighteen and first looked at them." This description purposefully defies preconceptions of the "non-intellectual" Black while linking its subject to intimate remembrances of adolescent anxiety and hope, bridging barriers of color, dramatizing the common human experience.

Yet the dialogue in which Faith engages with the Black crowd is limited; to them she always retains a strong element of White Other, a representative of an alien society powerfully mythologized in the collective Black consciousness. A barrier remains, an inability to understand: "She ain't right." White is interpreted as displaced, as Other, a mysterious ghost from a separate world. The crowd remembers those they have displaced from "the white old days. That time too bad to last." Paley renders Black dialect to subvert dominant norms; from the perspective of the ghetto residents the good old days were, and are, a nightmare of exclusion. The White Other appears as an omnipresent force surrounding the Black ghetto both physically and psychologically. Whiteness in African American perspectives mirrors the inescapability of Blackness as naturalized in White racial ideology. This inverted gaze reclaims at least some of the authority lost due to Paley's elite position.

Despite intimations of a larger African American cultural perspective, "The Long-Distance Runner" maintains the experience of its Jewish protagonist. In returning to her home, Faith revisits her past, updates and revises a crucial part of her psyche. She stops at the apartment of the fat and tragic Mrs. Goreditsky, a Jewish resident from the old times left behind in the ghetto, whose death was discovered due only to the smell: "They couldn't get [her] through the front door. It scraped off a piece of her." Just as history, as the old neighborhood, remains with the Jews who have left, so a piece of them remains, part of the overlapping cultures, the palimpsest of American society. The old and impoverished are left literally behind to die while symbolically the history of ghettoization remains in the Jewish people.

If Mrs. Goreditsky exemplifies one fate for America's Jews, Faith bears witness to the extreme opposite: abandonment of one's improversihed childhood, along with any sense of responsibility for the continuing existence of poverty and marginalization. She remembers one deserter from the neighborhood who is now

> the president of a big corporation, JoMar Plastics. This corporation owns a steel company, a radio station, a new Xerox-type machine that lets you do twenty-five different pages at once. This corporation has a foundation, The JoMar Fund for Research in Conservation. Capitalism is like that, I added, in order to be politically useful.

Capitalism with its plastic facade (like plastic, both everchanging and superficial) is endlessly accumulating, multiply tentacled, and ideologically self-replicating through its incessant funding of think tanks. Implicit in this passage is Faith's critique derived from her socialist mother, her need to preach, "to be politically useful," to empower people to understand their social situation with an implicit long-term goal of change. Between the extremes of impoverished ghetto resident and capitalist entrepreneurship, Faith struggles to reclaim her people's history, to retain their historical conscience while developing a modern identity. Her return to her (transformed) neighborhood (re)opens a connection between her (transformed) neighborhood (re)opens a connection between her own history and the plight of the marginalized, which assimilating Jews are tempted to jettison.

When Faith finally enters the apartment of her childhood, "my old own door," the story thoroughly enters the realm of the metaphorical, of Faith's imaginative exploration of her homeplace as interrogated by the Black presence. The return dramatizes the Jewish psychological reaction to a Black America which has taken over both its neighborhoods and its estranged status. Despite being "attacked by local fears," by a separation from this ghetto with its new strangeness, Faith's impulse to dialogue continues. Engaging Mrs. Luddy in somewhat one-sided conversation, Faith is conscious that she "is constantly intruding into the lives of these black people, offering advice as if she knows, and can teach them, what is right." She discusses, analyzes, criticizes, and seeks to improve. The temptation to overstatement, to the grandiose, is hard to resist; Faith's good-natured liberalism often borders on the self-righteous, as when she suggests that "someone ought to clean up" the outside terrors of the slum, and Mrs. Luddy rebukes her with "Who you got in mind? Mrs. Kennedy?" The authority of Faith (and by implication Paley) to analyze and speak for another community is questioned, with a partial answer implied in the existence of dialogue. A dialectic between the liberal idealist, spewing her opinions in long streams, and the realist, blunt and brief, tempered by a harsh reality, articulates something of this neighborhood's dilemma. Faith's and Mrs. Luddy's differing attitudes derive at least partly from their contrasting histories: the African American experience of promises repeatedly denied, of the slow-paced life of a recently rural people; the Jewish American experience of purposeful immigration, of escaping the New York ghetto in a generation.

Her three weeks in the slum, with its fatalistic psychology, may not have altered the neighborhood, yet Faith returns home with her questing spirit intact: "A woman inside the steamy energy of middle age runs and runs. She finds the houses and streets where her childhood happened. She lives in them. She learns as though she was still a child what in the world is coming next." Her position as middle-aged explorer, driven to run but thriving on the forces that drive her, is interrogated but not greatly changed by her glimpse of an ethnic Otherness. She has seen what her preconceptions encourage her to see. As an exemplar of the enlightened subject—but one interpolated by other positions: Jewish, feminist, socialist—she remains convinced, through her encounter with the Other, of the value of learning and exploration. She glimpses a future multiculturalism in which the barrier of Otherness dissolves. In her childhood this dream is already planted; from her past, her situation as an ethnic poised on the edge of society, she imaginatively (re)constructs the Black situation and glimpses an American future.

In "The Long Distance Runner" Blacks and Jews ultimately remain in separate communities, as happened after, or despite, 1960s upheavals. Any kinship postulated between Blacks and Jews seems to have fractured, leaving a relationship far from familial, or perhaps that of a bitter, estranged family. Yet Black-Jewish relations of the closest kind did arise out of the 1960s, leading to mixed-race children, if only in limited numbers. If in "The Long Distance Runner" a Jewish character crosses into terrain ostensibly reserved for African Americans, in "Zagrowsky Tells" a Jewish milieu is infiltrated by a Black, the child Emanual. If dialogical processes question essential racial identities, biological processes, together with the right historical circumstances, can expunge them. Surprisingly, it is not the sympathetic Faith, but Izzy Zagrowsky, a character tinged with racism, who appears with a (half) Black child. The confrontation between Faith, an examplar of Jewish progressivism, and the more conservative Zagrowsky allows Paley to explore a range of Jewish attitudes regarding African Americans. These responses are further problematized through the use of Zagrowsky as narrative consciousness. His slippery inclinations exemplify the ambivalent, multiple nature of Jewish responses to Blacks, while his ability to hold conflicting views yet remain unaware of the contradictions is psychologically convincing. At times Zagrowsky identifies with dominant society, at times he views himself as Jewish, an outsider, almost a Black.

Emanual is the object of these contradictory identifications, the motivating force provoking Zagrowsky's internal dissonance, his evolving consciousness. "Emanual" means "messiah" in Hebrew, and the child indeed heralds a new vision. Judith Arcana explains that he serves "to heal the grief and misery in his family, embodying a bond that holds the generations together" (163). The healing occurs not just to Zagrowsky's immediate family, not just to the split between conservative and progressive Jews, but to society's larger racial wound. The child is the catalyst for confronting the pain of old enmities. Yet ultimately such racially mixed children are active agents in redefining the meaning of ethnicity in America through subverting

rigid racial boundaries and facilitating cultural blending, roles only implied in "Zagrowsky Tells."

Racial discord persists in the aftermath of 1960s protest, a period of trauma that, in its search for a new beginning, dredged up ancient divisions. The mistreatment of Blacks and other marginalized groups, a wound in the facade of the American republic since before its inception, was confronted but not healed. In "Zagrowsky Tells" this division is an omnipresent backdrop of contention. Years before Faith had participated in a boycott of Zagrowsky's pharmacy, accusing him of refusing to serve minorities. Having previously delivered medicine to Faith's deathly ill child, Zagrowsky feels betrayed, enacting a microcosm of difficulties between progressive and more conservative Jews. To Zagrowsky, Faith is patronizing and self-satisfied as she suggests ways he should raise his grandchild. The edge of satiric self-criticism which permeated "The Long-Distance Runner" is made explicit here in Zagrowsky's characterization of Faith as the "Queen of Right." In lecturing him about how to raise his son, she again enacts a version of self-satisfied liberalism. Yet when Faith tells Zagrowsky that "we were right" to protest segregation, it is hard for him to disagree given his subsequent acceptance of a mixed race child. A distinction between right and wrong is suggested here, whether defined by evolving social attitudes or by a larger moral code.

Yet Zagrowsky cannot admit that he was wrong in his treatment of non-White customers; instead he serves up a litany of guilt-relieving excuses: "naturally, you have to serve the old customers first . . . and to tell the truth I didn't like the idea my pharmacy should get the reputation of being a cut-rate place for them. They move into a neighborhood . . . I did what everyone did." That Zagrowsky's people have been similarly marginalized escapes him at this moment. Running through his head is a catalog, zigzagging and contradictory, of Jewish responses to African Americans. He remembers his wife's comment that "We kept them down," and his reply: "We? We? My two sisters and my father were being fried up for Hitler's supper in 1944 and you say we?" If the Holocaust may be an important bridge from Jews to Blacks in their role as the oppressed, it is here used to deny responsibility for other forms of racism. My people, my immediate family, have been the victims, not the perpetrators, of racism, Zagrowsky angrily contends. Mentally his role shifts from a member of the dominant culture to a marginalized outsider, depending on his immediate psychological needs. Later in the story he shifts again, pondering about his blond-haired daughter: "Out of my Cissy, who looked like a piece of gold, would come a black child." Zagrowsky understands blond and black miscegenation as dangerous, an understanding formulated by dominant culture in its attempt to keep the races separate. The irony he misses is that Cissy's blond hair might come from some long-ago rape by a Polish peasant, that she herself is a product of miscegenation from a violent society practicing its own racial politics, that her people were once the "dark Other."

Zagrowsky's awareness of racial ideology, then, is acute yet inconsistent. Elsewhere he shows himself aware of the connection between Blacks and Jews, that both have been victims of racism. Worried how outsiders will take the sight of him with a black child, he rationalizes, "They think the Jews are a little bit colored anyways, so they don't look at him too long." If here it is pragmatic for him to identify with Emanual, the overall effect of Emanual's existence goes far beyond pragmatism, forcing a realignment of Zagrowsky's social and psychological landscape. As Zagrowsky puts it: "A person looks at my Emanuel and says, Hey! he's not altogether from the white race, what's going on? I'll tell you what: life is going on." Racial mixtures such as Emanual are one means of undermining hatred, forcing a coming-to-terms with difference. Neil Isaacs explains that Zagrowky's "experienced love" speaks "louder than his learned hate." Furthermore, Zagrowsky's Jewish heritage provides material for a counter-ideology consistent with his new experience. He begins to unearth long-term kinships: "They tell me long ago we were mostly dark." An immediate family link awakens historical connections. Zagrowsky, like Faith in "The Long Distance Runner," has confronted a past and, in doing so, redefined a present. If an exploration of the African American presence motivates Faith to reexamine her Jewish identity, Zagrowsky's ties of blood are even stronger.

Within the story Emanual is a focal point for others' reflections, stimulating change through his very existence. He is a product of historical trauma, of a time fraught with questions and changes. If the sixties produced crises—fissures between generations, genders and ethnicities—they were a time also of struggle for togetherness, of hope for an eventual end to the racial division that has tainted American history. Emanual is a product of sixties upheaval, and "Zagrowsky Tells" is a parable of healing. If Emanual is the object of others' perceptions and struggles, an emblem of familial and societal restoration, outside the story's time-frame such multiracial, multicultural individuals will actively confront their ambiguous status. Emanual will be an outsider to Black America through his Jewishness, an outsider to Jewish America through his Blackness, an outsider to mainstream America through both. Paradoxically this alienated, indeterminate status will make him prototypically American, a progenitor of new identity. Outside the pages of "Zagrowsky Tells," narratives such as that of Emanual will help to define an American in transition, a world in flux where the meanings of color and transracial identity are perpetually reinvented. Paley's stories should not be considered in isolation from this process. Her narratives are entangled in multiple cultural networks through which they speak and to which they contribute, part of a clamorous dialogue, an evolving if convoluted inquiry into what we believe and who we are.

Source: Ethan Goffman, "Grace Paley's Faith: The Journey Homeward, the Journey Forward," in *MELUS*, Vol. 25, No. 1, Spring 2000, pp. 197–208.

LaVerne Harrell Clark

In the following essay, Clark examines narrative technique, including that of folk oral traditions, in Paley's short stories.

> My sister says to him, Marv. You look like a pig half the time. You look like a punk, you don't look like an auctioneer. What do you look like? Name it. Schlep, he says. Laughs. Right-o. Schlep. Listen, Marv, give me this warehouse for 70,000. I'll slip you back 7 and an Olds. Beautiful car, like a horse, she says. I know your wife's a creep, she don't put out. I'll fix you up nice. You don't deserve to look such a bum. Right away he's grateful. Hahahah, breathes hard. He thinks he's getting laid. What? My sister? Anna Marie. Not her. No. She wouldn't do that. Never. Still, that's what he thinks. (*Enormous Changes at the Last Minute* 69)

This voice belongs to Jerry Cook, the boyfriend of Kitty—a chum of Grace Paley's most autobiographical character, Faith Darwin Ashbury. Kitty recalls Jerry's garment-district-sounding talk in a monologue set at a time when she and Faith are young mothers living on the same block. Her story in Paley's second collection exudes the kind of earthy, New York City neighborhood speech that, with its distinctiveness, persists as a hallmark of Paley's prose. In such capacity, it characterizes a kind by which Paley has developed and maintained her fiction to secure for it a literary voice that has endured for almost five decades. Like her biographers—Judith Arcana and Neil Issacs—I yearned

> Sometimes when the narrator is particularly Paley-like, she employs the device of addressing the reader in folksy terms, as in 'The Long-Distance Runner.'"

to put a finger on how Paley achieves this voice, especially its oral dimensions. Arcana feels that Paley

> opens up the act of storytelling, revealing her manipulation of language, but like . . . master magicians . . . "reveal[ing]" the mechanics of their tricks while stupefying audiences by performing those very tricks, she has integrated that manipulation so that her narratives are both story and voice. No intrusive external consciousness or voice "interrupts" her narration, for the voice is always present" (187).

To further pinpoint its "idiosyncraticity," Isaacs assesses that Paley's voice is "more than a matter of distinctive style" and maintains that because of the "unique sound" she has perfected, her stories have a "kind of handsome aural presence" to them. Reminding us of how "the concept of voice in literature subsumes such properties as cadence, tone, intonation, register, lilt, rhythm, pacing, timbre, resonance, volume, dialect and diction," he suggests that the presence of all of these in Paley's "voice" is the literary attribute by which we can "mark her achievement." He specifies that the "aural presence" to her prose may be distinguished by such singular properties as having a kind of "airborne tone" to it, with a "wit" and an "harmonic sense" to the lines that "reject" the presence of "cliches." He goes on to note a point that, for the most part, has been previously neglected: while "often admired" and "occasionally described," Paley's voice has nevertheless been "rarely analyzed." Particularly is this true, he says, with regard to its use of language" to achieve its "genuinely original" sound (5).

In full agreement with the truth of these words, I decided, as a fiction writer and folklorist with a history myself of being attracted to the oral dimensions of Paley's literary voice, I would single out the devices from oral traditions that she borrows and blends into her narratives, which in turn equip them with this vocal power. To understand her process, I re-read her fiction with a close look at how she uses speech and other orally-inspired techniques to enrich it, and at the same time investigated how her procedures in writing especially assist her in conveying her singular prose message.

In reviewing her four collections, *The Little Disturbances of Man* (1959), *Enormous Changes at the Last Minute* (1974), *Later the Same Day* (1985) and *Long Walks and Intimate Talks* (1991), I saw that first of all, her oral techniques can be characterized by her concerted use of folk speech to blow breath into her lines. Admirably, besides the talk of her more erudite and intellectual characters with similar ethnic roots, her collections offer a sampling of almost every major dialect of working-class New Yorkers: Jewish, Irish, African American, and Puerto Rican. She renders each character's speech with an accuracy and a naturalness that arises from not attempting too much. Just enough of a speaker's language is captured to lead to a simple and honest story well told.

So important is Paley's process of transporting the everyday speech she hears around her onto the page that in an interview with Leonard Michaels, she affirms that the sound of talk itself can sometimes suggest a story to her:

> I begin, often . . . with a person speaking, because I have an awful lot of speaking in my ear, an awful lot of words, ideas, of persons having spoken to me, or persons whom I would like to speak through me, and other voices, and so I will often begin with a sentence, (or) a couple of sentences of people speaking. (4)

In recalling the early part of her career to Michaels, Paley went on to observe: "I used to start simply from language, especially in the first book. I would write a couple of sentences and let that lay there. Not on purpose, but just because I couldn't figure out what was going to come next." She maintained that she could not begin to construct a story until she became a "listener," hearing the voice of the person inside her head telling the story (4). In another interview—this one with Peter Marchant and Mary Elsie Robertson—she expanded on how this "listener" technique operates: "It's as though in a way that's how I began to be able to write stories. I heard enough voices so I could make my own out of them" (607). The practice itself grew out of a method that W.H. Auden suggested to Paley when she took his course in poetry-writing at the New School for Social Research:

> Auden talked to her about the language she used in her poems, about her ear, and about the voices she heard and spoke in her poetry. He asked if she really "talked

like that" or heard other people talk the way she was writing. "I was using words like 'trousers,' which of course I'd never actually say in conversation." Essentially, he urged her to write in her own language—to write what she actually heard and spoke. (Arcana 43)

Along with her device of "listening" to her narrator tell the story, Paley defines the impetus as the need to say to the listener, "I want to tell you something." She points out, "Almost all stories come from that" (Shapiro 44).

Paley was an avid reader as a child. She acknowledges especially the influence of Russian authors such as Dostoyevsky and Chekhov (Ross 199). Yet she insists that her absorption of language and subject matter comes purely from her own upbringing, from her neighborhood and streets and family, sources never sufficiently credited in connection with her writings (Marchant and Robertson 614).

Daughter of Russian-Jewish immigrants Isaac and Manya Ridnyik Gutseit (Goodside in America), who came to New York at the turn of the century, Grace Paley was born and raised in the Bronx. She has continued always to live basically in New York City. Through his perseverance, her father achieved in America his dream of becoming a doctor. Still, in politics, he retained his belief in a kind of old-world socialism, the subject which he and his talkative brothers perpetually discussed. Accordingly, as Paley recalls, she was "brought up with a lot of their kind of idealism," and through her intent "listening," she "just kind of inhaled their early lives" (Olendorf 397). Which, of course, means that hers was a family who told stories. In fact, Paley often expresses her gratitude for the material she gleaned from listening constantly to stories she heard around her in childhood. Further, she attempts to record the vigorous influence of her father on her creative evolution, even if some of his input was that of opposition. In one of the narratives Paley has admitted is autobiographical (Arcana 185), a father and daughter agree on a preference for simple stories. But his ideal is for an unadorned tale in the style of Chekhov, governed "by plot, the absolute line between two points which," as the narrator-daughter explains, "I always despised" (*EC* 161–162). Paley has long maintained that a story can unfold by a "simpler dialectic" than the one involving "conflict," a term she emphasizes she also dislikes (Issacs 128).

The stories told during her childhood especially captivated Paley. So powerful was their effect that her renditions of folk speech often have a Jewish, or more specifically, a Yiddish cadence. As she explains, "That's what's in my ear, so it got through my Eustachian tubes or whatever into my throat and made [me] . . . write with an accent. . . . The three languages spoken around me when I was a kid [were] English, Russian and Yiddish" (Lidoff 5).

Readers hear a host of memorable Jewish voices in *Little Disturbances*: those of immigrants like Faith's parents, the Darwins, and their friend Mrs. Hegel-Sthein, all residents of the Children of Judea Nursing Home, Coney Island Branch. Constant banter, often containing local references, has prominence in this society. For example, one character, Shirley Abramowitz's talkative Brooklyn-oriented father says, "From Coney Island to the cemetery; it's the same subway; it's the same fare" (*LD* 55). And Paley characterizes Shirley herself as possessing such oral attributes as a singing voice that is so vibrant she is chosen in a competition over several Christian classmates to narrate the school's Christmas pageant. In another tale, a young man accidentally kills his monkey "brother," and sentences himself to the worst punishment he can think of, to abstain permanently from the joking and wordplay of his neighborhood (*LD* 149–71).

For me, however, Paley's most effective uses of Yiddish cadences are voiced by three characters: Iz Zagrowsky; Faith's friend Kitty (especially that of the passage offered at the beginning of this piece, which contains the talk of her lover Jerry Cook); and Rosie Lieber. Here is the voice of Iz Zagrowsky: "So this old woman comes up to me, a woman minus a smile. I said to my grandson, 'Uh oh, Emanuel. Here comes a lady, she was once a beautiful customer of mine in the pharmacy I showed you'" (*LD* 152).

The chatter that Kitty recalls in the quoted passage exists in "Come On, Ye Sons of Art" (EC 69). The inflections of Kitty's voice carry the nuances of the tale as she reports on some of the brags Jerry has passed on to her about his sister Anne Marie's knack for business. A failed businessman himself, Jerry, particularly admires his sister's ability to manage a shark like her associate Mary. He praises Anne Marie's know-how while he lolls in bed with Kitty, who is pregnant with his child, and later, too, as he prepares their breakfast.

Topping both this garrulous offering and Zagrowsky's is the voice of Aunt Rosie Lieber from the first volume. Addressing Lillie, the daughter of her disapproving sister, Aunt Rosie defends her love affair with Volody Vlashkin, chief actor of the

Yiddish Theater and the Valentino of Second Avenue. Rosie wagers that if her niece's mother only understood her, "she would know my heart is a regular college of feelings, and there is such information between my corset and me that her whole married life is a kindergarten" (*LD* 9).

The range of Paley's narrative voice includes black speech, as in the interior monologue titled "Lavinia, An Old Story," included in *Later The Same Day*. Lavinia's mother, Mrs. Grimble, fancies that she is speaking about her daughter to the girl's suitor Robert, and that at the same time, she is letting him know what she thinks in general about men:

> What men got to do on earth don't take more time than sneezing. . . . A man restless all the time owing it to nature to scramble for opportunity. His time took up with nonsense, you know his conversation got to suffer. A man can't talk. That little minute in his mind most the time. Once a while busywork, machinery, cars, guns (*LTSD* 63).

Both the speech in this monologue and the next coming from Charlie, the male narrator of "The Little Girl," in *Enormous Changes,* verify Paley's convincing use of black speech:

> Why Carter seen it many times hisself. She could of stayed the summer. We just like the UN. Every state in the union stop by. She could have got her higher education right on the fifth floor front. September, her mama and dad would come for her and they whip her bottom, we know that. We been in this world long enough. We seen lots of the little girls (*EC* 157).

The monologue, the form framing both of these stories, is a better vehicle for directly rendering the force conveyed by spoken language than is the third person narration provided in the ensuing talk from "The Long Distance Runner." Here the emphasis is more on the reaction of a narrator much like Paley herself as she listens to the talk of Mrs. Luddy, who speaks the black speech now used in the formerly Jewish neighborhood where Paley grew up:

> "Girl, you don't know nothing," she [Luddy] said. Then for a little while she talked gently as one does to a person who is innocent and insane and incorruptible because of stupidity. She had had two such special pleasures for hard times, she said. The first men, but they turned rotten, white women had ruined the best, give them the idea their dicks made of solid gold. The second pleasure she had tried was wine. She said, I do like wine. You has to have something just for yourself. Then she said, But you can't raise a decent boy when you liquor-dazed every night (*EC* 192).

Dolly Raftery, whose Irish brogue is one of Paley's triumphs, appears in the same story that

Mrs. Luddy does. Dolly, who made her debut in *Little Disturbances,* returns in still another selection from *Enormous Changes*—"Distances." There, with her accustomed check, she recalls that when it came to drinking beer or wine during her days in her dad's "home," he, though only "a mick in cotton socks," offered people "a choice" (24). In a later scene, Dolly, guilty of over-indulging in spirits since the time when her husband deserted her for "a skinny crosstown lady" who wears "a giant Ukrainian cross," describes how she now waits daily on the steps of her apartment building to intercept her son John (23). He commutes in from Jersey to visit his mistress who lives downstairs from Dolly. While she waits to catch sight of him, Dolly confesses that she is prone to join "all the dirty kids and the big nifty boys with their hunting-around eyes" at the ice cream truck and then to add "a touch of burgundy," besides, to her "strawberry ice cream cone as my father said we could on Sunday." In reference next to how her self-righteous and nosey neighbors react to her practice with her cone, she declares: "it drives these sozzle-headed ladies up the brown brick wall, so help me Mary" (26).

Other characters with distinct varieties of speech appear in "Gloomy Tune." It has the street speech of the brothers Dode, Neddy, Yoyo and Put Put, and effectively distinguishes between their Lower East Side-sounding, grubby Anglo-based usage and those of their Puerto Rican rival-playmates, the Gomez boys—Chuchi, Ramon and Edie. Though the narrator is never named, it seems female and gives the impression that Paley herself might be telling the story. In any case, upon mentioning the boys' use of the expressions of neighborhood toughs like "Go suck your father's dick," the narrator becomes overt enough to voice this aside: "I don't think they really understood what they were saying" (*EC* 55). Overall, the oral dimension provided by the piece indicates that the words come from a voice steeped in New York City street talk. This next quotation of an exchange between Chuchi and Yoyo shows how the dialogue distinguishes between their dialects and the way it is spelled out according to each:

> You dumb bastard, you push me. I feel over here on my shoulder, you push me. Aah go on, I didn push you, said Yoyo. I seen you push me. I feeled you push me. Who you think you go around pushin. Bastard. Who you callin bastard, you big mouth. You call me a bastard? (*EC* 55).

Besides furnishing such dialogue, another device with an oral-edge to it is one Paley utilizes from time to time in connection with direct address.

Sometimes when the narrator is particularly Paley-like, she employs the device of addressing the reader in folksy terms, as in "The Long-Distance Runner." After Faith snaps at Dolly: "Cut the folk shit with me, Raftery," the narrator steps in to note: "[Dolly's] eyes filled with tears because that's who she is: folkshit from bunion to topknot. That's how she got liked by me, loved, invented and endured" (*EC* 80). As Mickelson notes, Paley's use of folk speech "enlarges the confines of [her] characterization in the way Joyce's language transforms his characters. . . . It has punch and is so well-suited to the people . . . that the reader cannot help chuckling over the absolutely right image" (223).

Similarly Sorkin suggests, the energy of Paley's stories derives from "the bright tonality and often wildly funny, colloquial twists" rather than from any kind of plot to evolve finally as a "terse, comic" oral narrative (1982, 225). While the outpourings of speech that constitute a Paley story might in other hands border on excessive chatter or long-windedness, an essential brevity and a rare kind of compression control her presentations of New York City talk, as the various examples above illustrate.

As the dimensions of her oral style grew, Paley developed her own method of creating humor, providing it largely through asides and wisecracks. Often these interpolate in a manner reminiscent of nineteenth century fiction, only briefer. It is as if Paley is keeping up a running communication with a listener, which means of course a great reliance on audience or implied reader. The high degree of flexibility in these asides expands into a seriocomic effect that Christopher Lehman Haupt sees as the distinguishing characteristic of her art (3).

For Paley a comic sense goes beyond the mere invention of a humorous story to provide a laugh:

> If you're not blind, or cockeyed, you need jokes in order to be able to look out at the cold street, but then if the jokes don't come off, you're left with your thin skin. If they come off too well, you've hidden the stress away altogether. And the nagging question keeps returning: What in the world after all could be looked at without the filter of fun (Paley quoted in Wood 21–22).

Paley is serious about her humor. In a panel discussion on fiction, she listened while William Gass said: "I suppose I'm one of the few writers left still trying not to write funny. I'm interested in tragedy." Paley's prompt comeback was, "Well, all humorists are" (Barthelme et al. 31). In agreement with Mark Twain that "everything human is pathetic," she sees the source of humor to be as often

sorrow as it is joy (Mickelson 233). Blanche Gelfant, it seems to me, best describes the profundity of Paley's joking:

> [It] seems a way of searching within life's inevitabilities for a loop-hole—some surprise opening in the concatenation of events that seem to serious and acquiescent observers inexorably linked. Refusing to follow the absolute straight line of causality, which she sees as the tyranny of plot, Paley traces loops and twists and unexpected turnings that circumvent doom. These curlicues seem comic jokes that Paley plays on life (281).

In considering "A Conversation with My Father" as autobiographical—and as earlier mentioned, Paley herself "acknowledges it is" (Arcanen 185), the piece can be seen as recording a key moment in her recognition of the essential link between comedy and tragedy. As in the story, Paley's own father was the parent with a sense of humor—a trait her mother admitted to not having. In the narrative, when the father disparaged his daughter's perennial joking in her stories, he told her, "As a writer, that's your main trouble. You don't want to recognize it. [You need] tragedy. Plain tragedy!" The daughter protested that pity and humor intertwined do fulfill her responsibility toward "not only art but also life." She illustrated her point by saying about one of her fictional characters, "She's my knowledge and my invention. I'm sorry for her. I'm not going to leave her there in that house crying" (*EC* 166–67). It would seem, therefore, that it was at this point in her career that Paley, like her narrator, decided on humor as the best armor against despair.

Several critics have written perceptively about the nuances that make Paley's tragedy through humor successful. Nancy Blake stresses the skillful manipulation of the irony underlying Paley's "quiet laughter" (55–56). In Mariannne DeKoven's opinion, the humor is never "the hollow laughter, the mocking, alienated distance that is characteristic of serious modern fiction." Instead in the resolution of a Paley story, "transformation undercuts tragedy—functional structure becomes tragedy's antidote," and, at the same time, in Paley's capable hands "transformation undercuts the sentimentality that so easily trivializes pathos" (221). Mrs. Hegel-Shtein's confrontation with gloom illustrates:

> Sickness comes from trouble . . . Cysts, I got all over inside me since the Depression . . . Gall bladder I have since Archie [her son] married a fool . . . Varicose veins, with hemorrhoids and a crooked neck, I got when Mr. Shtein got social security and retired. For him that time nervousness from the future came to an end. For me it first began. You know what is a

responsibility? To keep a sick old man alive. Everything is like the last supper before they put the man in the electric chair (*LTSD* 23).

If a certain case of composition is implied by Paley's oral and free-floating form, such is by no means the case. Jonathan Baumbach points out that "it is as if she begins each time to learn what it is to make a story," so that the "improvisatory casualness" actually disguises "a high degree of sophistication" (301). Her most difficult decision, according to Paley, is choosing a frame for the narrative (Lidoff 17–18).

Bits of conversation dropped in passage can be the origin of a story, or they can help Paley find its proper frame. Yet she admits that working this way with talk she hears sometimes leaves her in the dark about how she should move the story forward. She might have nothing to go on but a fragmentary statement from a character still in embryo. Therefore, she adopted the habit of keeping a file of possible stories her sources have prompted her to tell. Or she puts scattered snatches of conversation that might serve as segments of a story in a desk drawer and refers to them from time to time until they indicate a direction in which to go (Michaels 4).

She reported to Lidoff (17) having taken twenty-five or thirty years to find the proper shape for "The Immigrant Story," which appears (169–75) in *Enormous Changes*. At last, unearthing a couple of pages of notes on beginning a story, she knew at once the way to tell this troublesome tale: It was simply to begin with "two people speaking to each other" (Lidoff 17). "The Long-Distance Runner" in the same collection (*EC* 179–198) caused a struggle she remembered in this way: "I wrote the first page and a half, and then I didn't know what the devil to do for about a year. I didn't know which way it was going, and then about a year later, I wrote the next three or four pages, and . . . a few months after that I finished it" (Barthelme et al. 31).

On the other hand, a story's frame can reveal itself to her in a form readily associated with oral tradition, as with "Debts" in *Enormous Changes*. The form is that of a narrative associated with oral history. When using such a form, the narrator usually proceeds to tell the history of the tale before telling the tale itself. Folklorists make use of this device for tales collected orally from an informant—from someone passing along a story heard from someone else. "Debts" reveals the strategy at once with the narrator alluding to the process involved in this way:

Because it was her idea, the . . . story is Lucia's. I tell it so that some people will remember Lucia's grandmother, also her mother, who in the story is eight or nine. The grandmother's name was Maria. The mother's name was Anna. They lived on Mott Street in Manhattan in the early 1900s. Maria was married to a man named Michael. He had worked hard, but bad luck and awful memories had driven him to the Hospital for the Insane on Welfare Island (*EC* 10).

Another folk technique, which Paley resorted to in "The Long-Distance Runner" (*EC* 194), is the form of a tale within a tale. Here, the tale is told to Faith by her black friend, Mrs. Luddy, about how her grandmother first heard about emancipation (*EC*, 194).

From time to time, Paley also observes a practice familiar to oral historians—indicating within the narrative its ownership. Sometimes she does so by simply including this information in the title, as in these two from *Later the Same Day:* "A Man Told Me the Story of His Life" (129–130) and "This Is a Story about My Friend George, the Toy Inventor" (147–148). Using these techniques, however, does not mean that Paley is specifically interested in recording folklore or oral history for its own sake. She once refused to assist a woman she did not know in writing about the woman's grandfather, a famous man in the Yiddish theater, though the woman offered a share of any profits. The project would have meant research with a stranger to whom Paley felt she owed nothing, not a friend like the Lucia in the example from "Debts."

As might be expected, Paley's experiments with narrative patterns from oral transmission do not always succeed. For example, in "This Is A Story About my Friend George, the Toy Inventor" (*LTSD* 147–148), the tag "we said" is inserted now and again to point up the tie-in with oral history. Later too, when George takes center stage and addresses his listeners as "you," the purpose seems to be to involve the reader more directly in the story. I find this "you" technique, along with the "we said" tags, too concocted to convey the kind of naturalness that other Paley oral borrowings achieve so effectively.

Paley insists that a prime purpose of stories should be to contribute to the vanishing sense of community (Sorkin, 1982, p. 148). "People ought to live in mutual aid and concern, listening to one another's stories," she once observed (Barthelme et al. 31). As a reviewer of *Later the Same Day* put it, she believes that "the process of telling stories is in itself a redemptive and necessary act" (Kakutani 19).

Stories told by the women of her family particularly engrossed Paley as a youngster, and she took to heart the way they spoke of how a company of women can sustain each other. Her women relatives' stories powerfully affected her writing: the majority of her protagonists and other characters are women—individuals often telling about recoveries from failed relationships, or of efforts to hold their families together. Sometimes they appear as young girls relating the experiences of their first love affairs. Stressing her focus, Paley has one character assert to her granddaughter: "Women . . . have been the pleasure and consolation of my entire life" (*LD* 28). Moreover, all the talk of her female characters, as Gelfant observes, is "inseparable from place, from the neighborhood streets, playgrounds, parks where urban congestion fosters intimacy and interest" (284).

The two stories in which Paley says she first discovered her voice concern the romances of Jewish women. "The Contest" (*LD* 67–68) reflects an interior monologue about Dotty Wasserman's retreat from her scheme to capture Frederick P. Sims for a husband. "Goodbye and Good Luck," already discussed, centers on the dramatic monologue containing Rosie Lieber's observations. In her fourth collection, *Long Walks and Intimate Talks* (1991), which also includes poems, the narratives contain the most women-centered talk of all. Since many of the selections Paley has presented as stories can just as easily be considered autobiographical, it is no simple matter to decide which are actually short stories and which might be better designated as memoirs. But certainly the best known of the selections, "Midrash on Happiness," though much like a meditation, was judged to be representative enough of the short story form as to be chosen for the 1986 O. Henry Prize Stories anthology. To me, this rendering in prose of Faith's idea of happiness, as conveyed to her friend Ruthy through the third-person of the particularly Paley-sounding narrator, rolls off the page with a chant-like ring to it—the kind that Biblical texts, which in themselves have been worked upon by oral transmission, often carry. Paley has acknowledged to Michaels (6) and Lidoff (5), as well as to others, that the Bible, and her frequent readings aloud from it, are among her major influences. In this case, the chant-like effect seems to me achieved mainly through the incremental repetition of the piece's wording.

Arcana defines a midrash as "a narrative/commentary often on the Torah, which deals with ideas and ethics, historically Jewish" (p.224, n. 3). Addi-

tional beneficial light on "Midrash on Happiness" is furnished by Jacqueline Taylor in her fine 1990 study, *Grace Paley: Illuminating the Dark Lives*. Taylor uses a feminist's perspective to reveal the methods with which Paley's language, especially her language in performance, addresses women's issues. Citing this narrative as "a particularly interesting example of how Paley continues to develop the short story," Taylor explains that "in rabbinic literature, midrash is 'Sa genre of biblical exegesis' that 'engages in ever-new revelations' of an originary text." According to her:

> The originary text in this case might well be understood as the dominant culture, which would never define happiness according to Paley's woman-centered terms. [Thus the] project of definition is a complex one, for each definition is made of dominant terms which must be redefined from Faith's muted perspective (105).

Taylor further illustrates her point by calling attention to the way Paley opens the story:

> "What she meant by happiness, she said, was the following: she meant having (or having had) (or continuing to have) everything. By everything she meant, first, the children, then a dear person to live with, preferably a man, but not necessarily, (by live with, she meant for a long time but not necessarily)" (*LW* 6).

Paley frequently discusses the social bonding that occurs as women exchange stories in terms of "women's gossip." Used in a context of this kind, the gossip can be considered still another form of oral history. First, Paley distinguishes between the sexes by declaring that when men talk in this fashion they are "telling stories . . . except that men don't tell stories anymore," they "talk shop." She concludes that women are the last practitioners of oral tradition, "handing down stories from grandmother to granddaughter" (Barthelme et al. 31). In turn, this gossip-related form often combines with what Paley labels the "argument" form. She first introduced such a combination in *Enormous Changes,* where it renders a chatty sort of intimacy like that induced over a cup of coffee with a friend. The selections—"Wants" (3–6), "Politics" (139–142), and "The Northeast Playground" (145–148)—all evolve in this manner.

Taylor has examined the last three stories and some others named above in a chapter of her study. Though the focus of Taylor's work, unlike that undertaken here, concentrates entirely on the "links between Paley's work and women's oral tradition," particularly as such links are "manifested in personal narratives" (9), hers is nevertheless the first and only other investigation that to my knowledge finally takes up this all-important matter of the orality in Paley's works. Taylor defines personal narratives as "oral stories told by women about our experiences" (92–93). She places "Northeast Playground" in this category, and believes it is also a story that "can be seen as redefining what constitutes narrative event" (98). She makes the additional point that since some past reviewers originally dismissed this story as weak, along with various of the others that fall under the personal narrative classification, "they must now be re-evaluated." Understanding that Paley draws strongly on a woman's oral tradition makes possible a reassessment" of them, Taylor emphasizes (9). She supports her point that language is central to the originality of Paley's work throughout her study. This means, of course, that Taylor also considers language use to be a mainstay of Paley's for achieving her unique voice.

Despite experimentation with various techniques over the years—some of them complicated—Paley, in general, has practiced a simple linear form of storytelling—one that she endorses for use by future writers (Barthelme et al. 31). The parallels from traditional oral forms that Paley has indicated as her ideals in fiction are narratives whose shapes and sounds readily show kinship to those of legend and myth. An excellent example of the way Paley worked with such a form, and shaped her prose into sounding the way a legend does, occurs in the ending of "A Man Who Told Me the Story of His Life":

> The next morning I called the doctor. I said: She must be operated on immediately. I have looked in the book. I see where her pain is. I understand what the pressure is, where it comes from. I see clearly the organ that is making trouble.
>
> The doctor made a test. He said: She must be operated on at once. He said to me: Vicente, how did you know? (*LTSD* 130)

According to Moffett and McElhenny, tales of this type, with their concentrated narrative, present a distilled subject in such a way as to make it accessible to the cultural experience of the listeners, yet in spite of the economy, the tone is generalized enough to make the story universal (252). As the foregoing example demonstrates, Paley achieves this effect in her stories, not by narrating action, but by a few choice words of dialogue. Once she explained to Michaels how using a method involving the use of spoken words can be employed advantageously to convey even "large events," and

"really clarify what everybody [is] talk[ing] about," or to "give the substance" of it (5).

But inevitably, the more a story is carried by dialogue, the less it will contain chronological reports of action that build the plot of the traditional short story. Consequently some commentators complain that nothing happens in Paley's stories, that there are no plots, plainly reflecting an assumption that every good story must have one, as well as endorsing such an idea at a time when this kind of requirement was, and is, no longer of major concern. Paley protests criticism of this sort, and accuses those offering it of paying insufficient attention to what she does achieve: "A great deal happens in almost any one of [my] stories . . . sometimes . . . enough to make a novel . . . Plot is only movement in time. If you move in time, you have a plot; if you don't move in time, you don't have a plot" (Lidoff 18).

Instead of concentrating on plot, Paley's prose depends on a steady cooperation between writer and reader, an interchange that is among the principal concerns of her fiction. She contends that her form of story is one of the most accessible, given the right sort of participation from an audience. It requires readers who exercise imagination to share with her as author the re-creation of the story (Barthelme, et al. 7–8). Never, she insists, should a writer underestimate the readers or assume they are "total dummies." Rather, she says, they can bring "more knowledge" or "truth" to the work "than the writer ever knew, had planned, or ever wished" (Barthelme et al. 18). And gradually but increasingly since the early 70's, Paley's readership has grown to include this, the kind of listening audience she has always aimed for. During the same time, a sizable number of critics have come to applaud the techniques with which she has steadily been experimenting in her fiction.

The varied techniques from oral tradition that we have now considered are those, then, that Paley has blended into her prose. All contribute to her voice, and in considering each, the salient features of her process of creation emerge. What amazes is that her use of these techniques, though skillful, succeeds so well today, when fiction has been submitted to radical re-examination and subjected to a wide range of experimentation. But, as illustrated, Grace Paley has always had the courage to experiment, though to be sure, offering her efforts with a touch that assures just the right blending of speech and conversational ingredients.

Moreover, with Paley, it is chiefly a matter of voice—a voice enduring through its awesome power. And that primary power lies in her ability to capture the sounds of her native New York City speech and render that speech within the frames of two of the oldest types of story-telling still alive: the straightforward narrative and the complex, though seemingly simple, word-of-mouth creation of a tale.

Source: LaVerne Harrell Clark, "A Matter of Voice: Grace Paley and the Oral Tradition," in *Women and Language*, Vol. 23, No. 1, Spring 2000, pp. 18–25.

Sources

Aarons, Victoria, "A Perfect Marginality: Public and Private Telling in the Stories of Grace Paley," in *Studies in Short Fiction*, Vol. 27, No. 1, Winter 1990, pp. 35–43.

Meyer, Adam, "Faith and the 'Black Thing': Political Action and Self Questioning in Grace Paley's Short Fiction," in *Studies in Short Fiction*, Vol. 31, No. 1, Winter 1994, pp. 79–89.

Paley, Grace, "The Long-Distance Runner," in *The Collected Stories*, Farrar Straus Giroux, 1994, pp. 242–58.

———, "The Value of Not Understanding Everything," in *Just as I Thought*, Farrar Straus Giroux, 1998, p. 188.

Paley, Grace, Jonathon Dee, Barbara Jones, and Larissa MacFarquhar, "Grace Paley: The Art of Fiction CXXXI," in *Paris Review*, Vol. 124, Fall 1992, pp. 181–209.

Tompkins, Cynthia, Review of *The Collected Stories*, in *World Literature Today*, Vol. 69, No. 1, Winter 1995, p. 42.

Further Reading

Feagin, Joe R., comp., *The Urban Scene: Myths and Realities*, Random House, 1973.
  This book is a compilation of excerpts from other books on the subject. Topics covered range from grieving for a lost home to the American dream to perspectives on poverty and the political economy of the African American ghetto.

Jargowsky, Paul A., *Poverty and Place: Ghettos, Barrios, and the American City*, Russell Sage Foundation, 1997.
  In this book, Jargowsky examines the inner city and the urban poor. He also addresses the importance of community development and race relations.

Private Lies

Bobbie Ann Mason

1983

"Private Lies," first published in the March 1983 issue of *The Atlantic* and a classic Bobbie Ann Mason story, is set in the western Kentucky of her youth—a landscape dotted with a growing number of fast food restaurants and big box stores. As Laura Fine notes, "The people of Mason's stories are predominately lower-middle class white heterosexuals who could live in any subdivision or farm in the country," and the characters of "Private Lies" are just those kind of people. Like Mason's other characters, Mickey, Tina, and Donna are in transition.

Appearing in Mason's collection of short stories, *Love Life* (1989), "Private Lies" introduces themes of loss, grief, and mourning by characters who seem divorced from their own inner feelings, as well as from each other. Furthermore, in "Private Lies," Mason explores the shaky ground of gender in contemporary culture.

"Private Lies" has not received the kind of critical attention lavished on Mason's other stories such as "Shiloh," "Big Bertha Stories," and "Love Life." Nevertheless, with its laconic, spare style, and in its attention to painful moments of the heart, "Private Lies" is a story worth studying, one that reveals the importance of past relationships to present lives.

Author Biography

Bobbie Ann Mason was born near Mayfield, Kentucky, in 1940 and grew up on a dairy farm her father owned in rural Kentucky. Her early experiences in the country provided many of the settings for her later fiction. Mason attended the University of Kentucky, graduating in 1962. She left Kentucky immediately and moved to New York, where she earned a living writing for a variety of fan magazines. After several years of this work, she completed a master's degree program at the State University of New York at Binghamton in 1966. She then earned a Ph.D. from the University of Connecticut in 1972, writing her dissertation on Vladimir Nabokov. Her early work was primarily academic and critical; however, she soon began writing and publishing short stories.

After submitting some twenty stories to *The New Yorker* magazine, Mason's short story "Offerings" was accepted in 1980. Mason published many short stories in prestigious magazines and journals over the next several years, and by 1982, her short story collection *Shiloh and Other Stories* was published, and her reputation as a master of the short story was established. Mason followed this book with several novels: *In Country* (1985); *Spence + Lila* (1988) and *Feather Crowns* (1993). In 1989, *In Country*, probably Mason's most famous book, was made into a major motion picture, directed by Norman Jewison, and starring Bruce Willis.

Mason published a collection of her earlier short stories, *Midnight Magic*, in 1998, as well as *Clear Springs: A Memoir* in 1999. She returned to short fiction in her 2001 collection, *Zigzagging Down a Wild Trail*. In 2003 she wrote a biography of Elvis Presley, published by Penguin as part of the publisher's short biography series. Over the years, Mason has won a wide variety of awards for her work including an Ernest Hemingway Foundation Award, Southern Book Award, and the National Book Critics Circle Award, as well as many nominations for other awards.

Mason generally sets her fiction in the western Kentucky of her youth. Her characters are most often working-class people, caught in various kinds of personal and cultural transitions, their lives dangling between where they have been and where they are going. "Private Lies" shares these characteristics. The story appeared in *The Atlantic* magazine in March, 1983. The story also was part of the collection *Love Life*, published in 1989.

Bobbie Ann Mason

Mason's continued productivity as a writer, as well as the ongoing critical attention her work receives, has earned her a position as a major American writer.

Plot Summary

"Private Lies" is the story of Mickey Hargrove, his wife Tina, his ex-wife Donna, and the baby Mickey and Donna gave up for adoption eighteen years before the story opens. The story begins with Tina and Mickey talking about the baby; Mickey wants to find her, but Tina wants nothing to do with it.

Mickey is drinking scotch laced with cream, because he is developing an ulcer and believes that the cream will counteract the damaging effects of the alcohol. Tina, a nurse, thinks this is silly. Mickey is a real estate salesman, but he has been unable to sell a house for six weeks. Although the couple and their two children seem to be financially stable, there are a few hints that money is tight.

Mickey's desire to find his daughter puts pressure on the marriage, as does Tina's move to working the night shift at the hospital. Tina, in the past, has taken care of everything and made sure that their lives maintained "regularity." Now that she is no longer home in the evening, Mickey is responsible for keeping "the schedule rolling." This includes helping his son Ricky with his homework and supervising both children while they watch television. Tina's absences, however, also make it easier later in the story for Mickey to talk to Donna on the phone.

Mickey considers issues of privacy. He is uncomfortable with his job of selling houses because of the way people poke and prod into other people's houses. He compares this to Tina's poking and prodding into other people's bodies as a nurse. The one place where privacy is being maintained in the story is in the adoption records.

Mickey then reflects on his relationship with Donna, his high school sweetheart. When she got pregnant, her family sent her to Florida to stay with her aunt. She gave birth there and gave the baby up for adoption. Mickey and Donna married after she graduated from high school, but the marriage was unworkable and only lasted three years. Donna later married again, but her husband died about three years before "Private Lies" begins.

In the next scene, Mickey is at Donna's apartment. He has not seen her since her husband died, but he has called her on the phone to arrange the meeting. He wants to talk to her about going to find their daughter, whose birthday is the next day. When he watches Donna move around her apartment, he realizes that this is a much different woman than the girl he married and divorced. She is somehow "prettier and more assured," taller, and with a husky voice and sexy smile.

Later, back at home, Tina tells Mickey to sign a paper so that their son Ricky can have speech therapy for a lisp Mickey does not believe Ricky has. As Mickey signs the paper, he recalls that, eighteen years ago, "he had signed a kid away completely."

Time passes. Mickey shows a house to a young couple, and while there, decides to visit Donna again. Donna tells him about her life since her husband has died, and her plans. They end up in each other's arms and begin an affair.

Mickey regularly visits Donna at her apartment on afternoons when he can get away from his office. When he finally sells a house, he decides he will take Donna to Florida. He tells Tina that he's going to Florida to find his daughter. Although Tina supposedly has no inkling about his affair, as Mickey

prepares to leave, she bursts into tears. She seems to know that he is leaving her.

Donna and Mickey fly to Florida and stay in a beachfront hotel. The scene is very different from when they visited Florida on their honeymoon and nothing worked out right. This time, it is all perfect. When Mickey brings up the search for their daughter, however, Donna breaks down. She cries and tells Mickey about why she made the decision to give up the baby rather than have an abortion. She finally tells Mickey that she does not want to "dig up the past." Their daughter, she tells him, has "got her own life."

Mickey responds that perhaps their daughter wants to find them. The two walk on the beach, looking at the ocean. The story ends with Mickey imagining them years in the future, still on this beach, "crunching the fragments of skeletons."

Characters

Mickey Hargrove

Mickey Hargrove is the third person narrator of "Private Lies." He is probably about forty years old, a self-described "grouchy, preulcerous, balding bore." A real estate salesman in bad economic times, Mickey is married to Tina, a nurse, with whom he has two children. As a teenager, Mickey got his girlfriend Donna pregnant. She gave up the baby for adoption. Although they later married, their marriage only lasted three years, as it was tainted by the memory of the lost baby. Now, eighteen years later, Mickey is obsessed with finding his daughter.

Mickey lacks confidence in his career; he is uncomfortable appraising houses and looking into private spaces. He also is uncertain about his life and wonders how his lost daughter would view him. "If she could appraise his life, as he would a house," Mason writes, "she might find its dimensions too narrow, its ceilings too high, its basement cluttered and dank with memories and secrets."

Further, Mickey seems disconnected from his family. He says that being married to Tina is "like riding a bus. She was the driver and he was a passenger." Since Tina makes all the decisions, Mickey seems superfluous. Yet he is grateful to Tina; he believes if he had not met her, he might be a lonely bachelor living out of a rented room. In addition, Mickey seems to have little relationship to his children; they seem more Tina's children than his. This is particularly ironic, given Mickey's current need to find the child Donna gave up.

Eventually, his search for his daughter leads him back to Donna, with whom he has an affair. Mickey discovers that Donna is like a new woman to him, and, like the Coke and lemon icebox cake Donna gives him, she is a "forbidden" substance. This, however, makes her more desirable to him.

When Mickey takes Donna to Florida to search for their child, even Mickey himself does not seem to know what he is doing. Is he leaving Tina? Starting a new life with his first wife? Since not even Mickey seems to know, it is almost impossible for the reader to determine Mickey's future.

Tina Hargrove

Tina Hargrove is Mickey's current wife. She works as a nurse, and as the story opens, she has been put on night shift, so her schedule is out of kilter. Tina is a self-possessed, confident woman who makes all of the decisions in the house. Mickey believes that Tina has rescued him. Tina's favorite television show is *M.A.S.H*, and she likes to watch and criticize the surgical techniques of the doctors. Above all, Tina is orderly, organized, and regular. She deals with life by putting it on a schedule. As Mickey reveals to Donna, "Tina was the sort of person who had separate garbage bags for everything, even tiny ones for scraps from each meal."

In addition, Tina seems to have a hard time connecting with her feelings, compartmentalizing the parts of her life as surely as she does the garbage. Although she suspects that Mickey is leaving her as he prepares for his trip to Florida, she talks about her niece and about a surgery for breast cancer. She finally cries, "You can't just up and leave all you've worked so hard for." The statement is telling: Mickey is not the one who has worked hard for all this, Tina has. She fails to recognize Mickey's growing alienation from her and from their children as he obsesses over the child he does not have. Her refusal to talk to Mickey about the lost child, and her unwillingness to be a part of the search may, in the final analysis, have cost Tina her marriage.

Donna Jackson

Donna is Mickey Hargrove's first wife. While they are in high school, she becomes pregnant with

Media Adaptations

- In 1989, Mason's novel *In Country* was made into a major motion picture, directed by Norman Jewison and starring Bruce Willis.

their child, whom she gives up for adoption. Her parents have some wealth and force her to go to Florida for her pregnancy and the adoption. Although Donna marries Mickey after the adoption, they are not happy together and eventually divorce. She subsequently marries Bill Jackson, who dies about three years before the story opens.

As a young woman, Donna was a whiner, according to Mickey, and she had problems with their poverty. As an older woman, however, Donna seems to have matured; she works, she travels, she has a life of her own. She has had bridgework, which makes her smile seem sexy to Mickey. Most of all, Donna has put into her past the child she gave away.

Not surprisingly, Donna works as a cosmetologist. Her job is to make women look more beautiful than they are, to cover up the imperfections in their appearances. Donna, likewise, tries to cover up her own grief and mourning for the lost child, and for her failed marriage to Mickey. Her clothing and her bravado all suggest that something more is going on with this character. When they finally reach Florida, Donna breaks down and shares with Mickey her feelings about giving up the baby.

Themes

Gender Roles

In many of her short stories, Mason examines the way that men and women relate to each other in

Topics for Further Study

- Read about the economy of the United States between the years 1975 and 1985. What happened during this period? How does this economic picture affect the characters of "Private Lies" as well as the characters of Mason's other short stories?

- Research teen pregnancy and adoption policies in the twentieth century. How have policies changed since the setting of "Private Lies?" How might the story be different if Mickey and Donna were in high school during the 1990s rather than in the 1960s?

- Read several of Mason's short stories from the collections *Shiloh and Other Stories* and *Love Life*. Make a list of popular culture references in the stories such as brand names, movies, television shows, or pop music, etc. Are there any patterns in the references Mason chooses to make? How do these pop culture references contribute to or detract from the stories?

- Read *In Country*, Mason's novel set in the post-Vietnam War era. Compare and contrast this novel with the story "Private Lies." Imagine the life of Mickey and Donna's baby, using Sam Hughes as your model. Write a short story in the style of Bobbie Ann Mason using Mickey and Donna's daughter as the main character.

---

a time when gender roles are undergoing transition. As Kenneth Millard writes, "Since the successes of feminism in the 1970s, women have begun to exercise more control over their lives and move towards greater autonomy and independence as they strive for forms of personal fulfilment less dictated to them by old social pressures." In "Shiloh" for example, the story opens with the wife, Norma Jean, lifting weights to build her biceps, while her husband Leroy, an injured trucker, is learning needlepoint and crafts. "Private Lies" also explores the changing landscape of gender roles and the need for women to express themselves in new ways.

Donna, Mickey's first wife, is a good example of the change occurring for women during the time since her pregnancy with Mickey's child. As a high school student, she had no choice but to leave school as her parents required. Indeed, her parents sent her to Florida so that they could avoid the social stigma of Donna's pregnancy. Now, as a recent widow, Donna chooses to travel, and she considers starting her own business. There is no man in her life who is telling her what to do. This new strength and energy makes her particularly attractive to Mickey.

Likewise, Mickey's wife, Tina, is a nurse, working outside the home to support the family while Mickey's real estate sales are down. She makes all the decisions in the house, something that Mickey seems to have valued at one time, but now feels constrained by.

In Mickey, Mason has created a sympathetic male character, albeit one who seems afloat in the changing world. Millard confirms this, noting that "Mason . . . offer[s] a generous analysis of the predicament of men, one which shows how they might learn to free themselves from outmoded roles to their decisive benefit and to the benefit of women too." Mickey's belated sense of responsibility for his first child, while too little too late, at least suggests the possibility of his maturing into a loving father and husband. Nevertheless, his choice to desert Tina and his children speaks also of escapist fantasies. What he will choose ultimately is not clear; Mason, however, allows him room to grow.

Marriage and Divorce

Many of Mason's stories have characters that are in shaky marriages, or are already divorced. "Private Lies" uses marriage and divorce as one of its primary themes in that it demonstrates how even marriage does not necessarily imply relationship. For example, Mickey and Donna marry just out of high school after their earlier pregnancy and the subsequent adoption of their baby. Donna's parents sent her away for the birth and the adoption, and Mickey only briefly saw her and the baby at the time of the birth. Although this was an intimate detail of their lives together, it was not something they shared. When Mickey goes to see Donna at her apartment years later after the death of her second husband, Mickey realizes that the woman in front of him is nearly a stranger. He somehow thinks that she has changed dramatically over the years. However, he fails to understand that he never knew Donna in the first place.

Likewise, although Mickey credits his current wife Tina with having rescued him from self-destructive bachelorhood after his divorce, Mickey's descriptions of Tina are all superficial. She is like a "bus driver," she likes to watch "M.A.S.H.," she makes sure their bills are paid. In the story, there are very few hints that any of the characters feels anything like love for another, although the hints that are there are poignant. This is particularly true because the characters seem unable to do anything about their love for each other. Their inability to really know or understand each other impedes their ability to have happy marriages or relationships. These are characters who seem to walk through life alone, always wanting relationship, but not knowing how to manage it.

As a side note, Mason's title contains an oblique reference to another literary work that has marriage and divorce as its subject. In 1930, English writer Sir Noel Coward wrote a play called *Private Lives*. In the play a divorced couple arrive, with their new spouses, at the same vacation spot. The previously married couple begin an affair in spite of their current spouses' presence. Both the closeness of the titles and the similarity of subject suggest that Mason had her tongue in cheek when she named her short story: the characters of Coward's play (as in all his plays) are witty, urbane, sophisticated, and rich. Their escapades with marriage and divorce are the source of comedy. Mason's characters, on the other hand, are clumsy, rural, unsophisticated, and barely holding on financially. Their troubles, however, are not comedic in any way. Rather, they are the bittersweet problems of life in contemporary America.

Style

Realism

According to William Harmon and C. Hugh Holman in *A Handbook to Literature*, realism is "fidelity to actuality in its representation." By this they mean that realistic literature calls for the writer to accurately and truthfully depict real life in their writing. Harmon and Holman continue, "Generally, too, realists are believers in democracy, and the materials they elect to describe are the common, the average, the everyday." Realists are interested in everyday details as opposed to large issues; further, they understand that any fiction truthfully reflecting life will be without linearity or even, at times, without plot.

Any student wishing to understand Mason's work needs this basic understanding of realism. Mason has been famously labeled as a "K-mart" or "dirty" realist, and these terms crop up in most critical discussions of the writer. Certainly, "Private Lies" offers evidence in its construction for why Mason has been so described.

In the first place, Tina, Mickey, and Donna are middle class people. Of them, Tina has the most education, since she works as a nurse; however, her values are solidly middle class. Mason describes the smallest details of their everyday lives, from Mickey's penchant for scotch and milk and Donna's work as a cosmetologist.

Mason chooses to include details in the story from popular culture as well. Tina's favorite television show is *M.A.S.H.* Mason not only tells the reader this, she also includes details from the show itself. "'B.J. shouldn't ask for a retractor at that point,'" Tina tells Mickey. The characters of "Private Lies" drink Coke and eat lemon ice box cake, their children go to Enrichment classes, and they relax in La-Z-Boy chairs. Their houses have Formica countertops, they eat out at McDonalds, and a luxurious apartment might look like a Holiday Inn.

Details such as these firmly place "Private Lies" in a specific time and place. Nevertheless, it is details such as these that cause some critics to denigrate Mason's fiction, suggesting that it is all surface detail without depth. Most critics, however, see Mason's surface detail as a way of suggesting the inner lives of her characters without judging them, without delving into the "private lies" each character (and each real person) carries with him or her.

Compare & Contrast

- **1980s:** Unemployment reaches 10.8 percent in 1982, and high inflation rates seriously depress the house market. New home sales and sales of existing homes are down dramatically.

  Today: The post–September 11, 2001 economic downturn results in rising unemployment rates, although not to the level of the 1980s. Low inflation, however, keeps mortgage rates historically low, resulting in a strong housing market.

- **1980s:** Pregnant young women are permitted to remain in public school by the 1980s, a marked change from the 1960s and early 1970s when girls were often sent away during the time of their pregnancies.

  Today: Public school districts permit pregnant young women in classes and also often provide special classes or schools, sometimes with daycare, to assist these young women with their education.

- **1980s:** With the 1973 *Roe v. Wade* Supreme Court decision permitting legal abortion, abortion rates rise through the 1980s.

  Today: Abortion rates drop through the late 1990s and early 2000s. Reasons for this are contested but may include increased access to birth control, abstinence, decreased access to abortion, use of a morning-after pill, and increased use of ultrasounds.

- **1980s:** Although pregnancies in teenagers have dropped slowly since the 1950s, there is a steep upward climb in the 1980s.

  Today: Teenage pregnancies reach a United States record low in 2000, although the rate is still higher in the United States than in other developed countries.

- **1980s:** The United States divorce rate reaches 5.3 divorces for every 1000 people, a historic high.

  Today: The divorce rate is slightly lower than in the 1980s, largely due to the dropping marriage rate.

Historical Context

The Reagan Years

Ronald Reagan was elected president of the United States in 1980, defeating incumbent Jimmy Carter, just three years before the story "Private Lies" appeared in *The Atlantic*. Carter's presidency was marred by the taking of hostages in Iran, an event that led to an oil embargo and caused shortages in gasoline as well as skyrocketing gas prices.

During the early years of the Reagan administration, the country suffered from inflation, that is, rapidly rising prices, and stagnation in the growth of new jobs. Journalists quickly dubbed this situation "stagflation." It was a new phenomenon in American history, and the combination of little work and rising prices was particularly difficult for the lower middle classes who came to be called the "working poor." Like Tina and Mickey Hargrove, these people struggled to make ends meet, often while one of the couple is out of work.

Reagan's response to the economic woes was to cut taxes and government spending. This is often called "supply-side" economics, or "trickle down" economics. By giving corporations and wealthy people tax cuts, the reasoning goes, there will be more money available to stimulate economic growth.

Reagan's policies, especially during the first years of his administration, did not seem to materially affect the lower middle classes. Even with tax cuts, prices continued to soar, and jobs evaporated. Simultaneously, interest rates on home mortgages reached historic highs; it was not unusual to see mortgage rates of 14 percent in this time. These rates effectively put the cost of home ownership out of reach of many Americans. In addition, the high rates also depressed the construction industry as new home sales plummeted. Again, because many members of the lower middle class were employed as construction workers, the drop in new home sales put many out of work.

Although Reagan promised to cut government spending, by 1984, the federal deficit had exploded to $200 billion dollars due to decreasing revenues and increased spending. Tax cuts continued to be popular among voters, however, and Reagan was returned to office on his pledge not to raise taxes. By the time Reagan left office, the national debt, at $834 billion when he took office, had risen to $2.3 trillion, and the deficit was still a hefty $160 billion.

Also during Reagan's tenure as president, his administration deregulated the banking industry, particularly in the areas of savings and loans. This deregulation helped both bankers and investors by allowing risky ventures; however, when housing values went down, there were many defaults on loans. Because the loans had been sheltered by government insurance, the defaults put even more pressure on the federal budget. When a savings and loan went bankrupt, the federal government bailed it out. These losses had to be covered through tax revenues. This policy, then, had the lower middle classes paying through their tax dollars for the failed investments of the higher income members of the country.

Overall, the early 1980s were materially difficult in many ways for the members of the working classes. In addition, the changing fabric of American culture put stress on families and couples across the nation.

Critical Overview

"Private Lies" first appeared in *The Atlantic* in 1983 and was collected in *Love Life* in 1989. The publication of the collection generated a good deal of critical commentary, garnering strong reviews from both Lorrie Moore in *The New York Times Book Review* on March 12, 1989, and from Michiko Kakutani in *The New York Times* on March 3, 1989. Moore comments that Mason's real strength as a writer is demonstrated in her short story collections, while Kakutani notes that Mason's stories are "finely

crafted tales." Nevertheless, few reviewers mention "Private Lies" specifically.

Likewise, although Mason's work in general is the subject of ongoing critical attention, "Private Lies" seems overshadowed by some of Mason's other work, such as "Shiloh," "Residents and Transients," and *In Country*.

Nevertheless, there is much critical commentary useful in a reading of "Private Lies." Robert Brinkmeyer, for example, writes that

> Mason's stories are filled with broken relationships—between people and their friends, husbands and wives, parents and children, people and their extended families—that together embody the collapse of family and community.... Rather than standing apart from the cultural chaos ... Mason's families are as much a part of the cultural confusion as the strips of franchise restaurants and K-Marts where they eat and shop.

Certainly, in "Private Lies," readers are witness to a breakdown of two marriages.

Other critics have chosen to concentrate on Mason's inclusion in a group of writers known as "minimalists." Kathryn B. McKee, for example, writes in *The Southern Literary Journal*, "Known for spare prose and 'Kmart realism,' Bobbie Ann Mason's fiction typically offers minimalist portraits of life in a twentieth-century South, increasingly carpeted by fast food restaurants and discount chains." Although Mason herself often questions the label of "minimalist," most critics agree that her spare, lean prose and her attention to the prosaic details of the modern landscape are characteristic of her writing.

Mason herself comments on the differences she sees in the stories from her earlier collection, *Shiloh and Other Stories* and *Love Life* in an interview with Bonnie Lyons and Bill Oliver. "I think the characters' worlds changed a good bit between the two. I think life was changing so fast that they got more sophisticated, they've gotten more mobile, and I'd like to think that the stories have gotten more complex. I think my characters' lives were a lot simpler in the first collection."

In the same interview, Mason comments on her use of present as opposed to past tense. Unlike many of her earlier stories "Private Lies" is told in past tense. Mason says the stories,

> in the back of *Love Life* are more recent, and they're in past tense. This signaled a change for me.... I think mainly it has to do with the author's authority.... If the author starts in the past tense, if he says, "Once upon a time," then you assume he has sorted events

out, he has a perspective on them, has judged them in some sense."

This reflection demonstrates a deliberate choice on Mason's part, a way of melding past, present, and future in "Private Lies."

Given the continued critical interest in Mason's work, it is likely that in the future there will be additional articles and commentary on both *Love Life* and "Private Lies." The collection, and the story, offer a showcase of what may be seen as a transitional period between her earlier, leaner stories, and her later, fuller ones.

Criticism

Diane Andrews Henningfeld

Henningfeld is a professor of literature at Adrian College who writes on literary topics for a variety of publications. In this essay, Henningfeld considers how the unresolved grief and mourning over events in the past impinge on the characters' present conditions and render their futures ambiguous.

For the characters in Bobbie Ann Mason's short stories and novels, the past is a troubled landscape, one that they strive to keep hidden from their present lives in every way possible. Yet the past always manages to bubble up in some way, and the grief and mourning they refuse to acknowledge in the past have very real consequences in the present.

In her book *Understanding Bobbie Ann Mason*, critic Joanna Price alludes to this: "In several of the stories, Mason explores the effect of the past on the present, as her characters attempt to reconcile them through the process of mourning, whereby a grieving for cultural losses is incorporated into personal mourning." Certainly for Samantha Hughes, the main character of Mason's 1985 novel *In Country*, private grief for the father she has never known ultimately manifests itself in a trip to the Vietnam Veterans Memorial, a place of public mourning and reconciliation. Her mourning for her father moves the reader toward the closure of the "cultural losses" of the Vietnam War.

Price points out, however, that Mason's short "stories express little movement toward closure of the process of mourning, although there are occasional glimpses of the possibility of personal or cultural 'healing.'" Mason defers closure for her short story characters with several artistic moves. In

the first place, she generally uses present tense, particularly in her early stories. The present tense emphasizes the characters' denial of their pasts, and offers no glimpse into the future.

In addition, Mason deliberately refuses to give her short stories any kind of narrative closure. Price writes that the "lack of closure is emphasized by Mason's use of the short story form: the open endings reveal little sense of how to move from the present into the future."

"Shiloh," perhaps Mason's most famous and most anthologized short story, demonstrates both of these techniques, as well as attention to grief and mourning. The story of Leroy and Norma Jean Moffitt is told exclusively in the present tense, and Leroy only dares mention the baby they lost in oblique comments, or in his reports of conversations he overhears between Norma Jean and her mother. The ending of the story is nothing if not inconclusive: Norma Jean stands on a river bluff some distance away from Leroy, flapping her arms. Neither Leroy nor the reader knows what this gesture signifies. Because this scene takes place on the Shiloh battlefield, the site of one of the bloodiest battles of the Civil War, the reader also knows, however, that whatever the gesture means, there is great loss behind it.

In "Private Lies" Mason returns to the themes of past and present, grief and mourning that she opens in *In Country* and "Shiloh." In *In Country*, readers find a nearly eighteen-year-old woman searching for her dead father, a Vietnam War veteran who died before she was born. In "Private Lies," the seeker is the father, looking for a daughter he gave up for adoption nearly eighteen years earlier. Like Mickey, Samantha Hughes has kept her grief hidden away; yet once she begins to unravel her father's life, she reveals herself to be a very good researcher. She reads history texts, uncovers her father's journal, interviews other Vietnam veterans, and finally takes a camping trip alone to try and recreate her father's experience in Vietnam. By the end of the story, she has discovered her father's story, and has also located him on the Vietnam Veterans Memorial Wall.

Mickey, however, has had less success transitioning his past into his present. Until shortly before the story opens, he has kept his past grief in the past very deliberately, largely through projection and passivity. He and Donna divorce, just three years after their marriage, as a result of their inability to work through the mourning process. Now,

What Do I Read Next?

- *A Spring-Fed Pond: My Friendships with Five Kentucky Writers over the Years* (2001), by James Baker Hall, is a collection of photographs of Mason and four other Kentucky writers.

- Bobbie Ann Mason's *Elvis Presley* (2003) is a short biography of the famous singer and is a good example of Mason's nonfiction.

- *Minimalism and the Short Story—Raymond Carver, Amy Hempel, and Mary Robison* (1999), by

Cynthia Whitney Hallett, offers an overview of literary minimalism, looking at some of the stories of the movement's most characteristic writers.

- *In Country* (1985) is Mason's novel of a young Kentucky woman looking for information about her father, who died in the Vietnam War before she was born. This is an excellent coming of age story from a female perspective.

---

some fifteen years later, he reflects on why the marriage did not work: "Mickey often got drunk and left Donna alone at night. He blamed her for giving up the baby. After a while, he blamed her parents. In a later period, he blamed society. And more recently, he blamed himself." This movement from external to internal blame, however, differentiates Mickey from other male protagonists in Mason's short stories. No longer projecting the blame for his loss on others, Mickey has begun, however haltingly, to take responsibility for his own shortcomings. In addition, Mason's choice to use the past tense in this story allows Mickey to indulge in some self-reflection, something not available to Leroy Moffitt in "Shiloh." While this creative choice does not solve Mickey's problems for him, there is at least a sense that he might work his way through some of his issues. As Mason tells the reader, "If Mickey hadn't had a daughter born out of wedlock eighteen years ago next Tuesday, he'd have nothing on his mind now worse than the recession."

Mickey also strives to hide his grief and mourning through his passivity. He describes his current marriage to Tina as "like riding a bus. She was the driver and he was a passenger. . . . Tina rescued him. With her, life had a regularity that was almost dogmatic." The rigid attention to schedule and responsibility imposed by Tina offers Mickey an escape from his own shortcomings as a father. Nevertheless, his dissociation from his children, Ricky and Kelly, suggests that the early loss of his

first child impedes his ability to participate in any way other than materially to the wellbeing of his children from his second marriage. Ironically, the daughter he does not have stands in the way of the children he has now.

Mickey also demonstrates his discomfort with the way the secrets of the past reveal themselves in his discomfort with his career: "Mickey was uncomfortable whenever he appraised houses. The owners hovered over him while he measured the rooms and ran through his checklist of FHA-approved specifications." Such musings turn inward as he thinks of his lost daughter and what she might think of him: "If she could appraise his life, as he would a house, she might find its dimensions too narrow, its ceilings too high, its basement cluttered and dank with memories and secrets. A dangerous basement." For Mickey, returning to the past to find his daughter means going down the basement stairs.

Mickey's grief and loss also bubble into the present in a very physical form: in bubbles of pre-ulcerous stomach acid that give him almost constant pain. Although he hides his pain from his conscious mind, Mason seems to suggest, he feels in his gut the pain and sorrow of his youthful decision some eighteen years earlier.

And, although Mickey seems to be rousing himself to some level of action through his contact with Donna, he is unable to figure out how to

> "By initiating an affair with Donna, and by taking her back to Florida--both the site of the adoption and of their disastrous honeymoon--it is almost as if Mickey believes that he can start over again with the woman he once loved, by finding the child they first made and then gave away."

translate that need for action into efficacious results. He is certainly not as skilled a researcher as Samantha Hughes. He does not make inquiries of the adoption agency, nor does he advertise in any papers. Unlike Samantha, who goes to her father's family for answers, he does not contact Donna's family. Without Tina's help in organizing himself, he seems utterly unable to think of what he might do to find his daughter. Instead, he continues to drink alcohol, laced with half-and-half as a grudging concession to his ulcer. In many ways, this ridiculous nod to the pain in his gut mirrors the ridiculousness of his own strategy for finding his daughter: go to Florida with Donna, and maybe he will run into her there.

Clearly, this is not a wise nor sensible strategy, no more so than drinking scotch and milk. What he seems to want is not to reconcile the past, but to recreate it. By initiating an affair with Donna, and by taking her back to Florida—both the site of the adoption and of their disastrous honeymoon—it is almost as if Mickey believes that he can start over again with the woman he once loved, by finding the child they first made and then gave away. He tries to creatively recreate the life he wishes he had had. For Mickey, there is "a sense of relief" in looking out over the ocean. For a moment, he is able to see into the future: "Mickey saw himself and Donna years from now, holding hands, still walking on this beach. They stepped back, then forward, like dancers." In this beautiful image, Mickey somehow seems able to account for past, present and future.

And yet, Mason does not close the story unambiguously. Mickey and Donna are walking on a coral beach, the sand comprised of the thousands of houses of tiny, ancient, dead marine animals. In the last line she writes, "They were moving like this along the beach, crunching the fragments of skeletons." This sentence serves to remind readers at what cost Mickey and Donna have come to terms with their grief. While they may have opened and cauterized the wound left by their early loss, they have, at the same time, created more loss. In leaving Tina and his children, Mickey creates a troubled future for himself: in this desertion he leaves not one child, but two, as well as a wife who loves him. Thus, any future happiness with Donna depends on further "private lies." At the same time, the image of the coral beach also suggests that ultimately, private lies or no, all ends in death and loss. Since this is the case, Mason seems to suggest, and since there is no changing the past, nor the future, present love offers the only hope in the face of despair.

Source: Diane Andrews Henningfeld, Critical Essay on "Private Lies," in *Short Stories for Students*, Gale, 2005.

Joanna Price

In the following essay excerpt, Price explores character relationships and themes in Mason's Love Life *collection.*

In *Spence + Lila* Mason's depiction of the encroachments of contemporary culture upon traditional ways of life is etched lightly upon the vitality of remembered lives, but in her next work, *Love Life* (1989), Mason focuses on the difficulty of loving and "loving life" in a contemporary culture whose subjects feel alienated from the self and society. This collection of short stories, set mainly in western Kentucky, is unified by themes familiar from Mason's earlier fiction, such as the "culture shock" and sense of exile experienced by her characters as the traditions of rural life are eroded by consumer culture and the effect on her characters' sense of identity of such "democratizing" discourses as education, feminism, and the interpretations of life offered by television. Within individual stories, these "themes" are frequently only glimpsed through allusive images, narrative suggestion, and partial characterization. Lorrie Moore has observed in her review of the stories that "many of the stories in *Love Life* splay out unexpectedly, skate off, or in, at odd angles, displaying a directional looseness. . . . Certainly the beginnings and endings do illuminate each other, but only indirectly, diffusely. Along the way elements are seldom developed in a linear fashion, and are often, once introduced, abandoned altogether." Moore comments that the overall effect of the stories, however, is one of "cumulative beauty," the achievement of "accumulation, a supply," as each story offers a meditation on the possibility, or failure, of different types of love in small-town Kentucky. Through the form of "the story *collection*," Moore remarks, "Mason depicts most richly a community of contemporary lives, which is her great skill." Such "community" is largely unrecognized by its members but is constructed between the author and her readers as the repetition of stylistic, structural, and thematic elements, often with unexpected variations, enables the reader to perceive common concerns among the characters. Whereas Moore discerns a cumulative "depth" and "profundity" in *Love Life,* Devon Jersild remarks that a "cool surface" is produced by Mason's tendency "to refrain from comment, extrapolations, conclusions." In *Love Life,* Jersild argues, this "authorial restraint mirrors her characters' distance from emotion and produces a certain numbing effect."

Many of the characters in *Love Life,* as in *Shiloh,* are locked in the present moment. As Lorrie Moore has put it, Mason's "use of the present tense in the majority of her stories serves as the expression of [their] trapped condition, but also as a kind of existential imperfect: the freeze in time suggests the flow; the moment stilled and isolated from the past and future is yet emblematic of them both, of the gray ongoingness of things." In several of the stories, Mason explores the effect of the past on the present, as her characters attempt to reconcile them through the process of mourning, whereby a grieving for cultural losses is incorporated into personal mourning. In contrast to *In Country,* the stories express little movement toward closure of the process of mourning, although there are occasional glimpses of the possibility of personal or cultural "healing." This lack of closure is emphasized by Mason's use of the short story form: the open endings reveal little sense of how to move from the present into the future.

In the title story, which opens the collection, Mason focuses on the sympathetic cross-generational relationship between Opal and her niece, Jenny. Opal, a retired schoolteacher, has adjusted to her increased leisure time by enjoying the escapist fantasies stimulated by watching MTV and listening to rock and roll. Never having "cared for stories," Opal is mesmerized by the way in which "the

> " Mason focuses on the difficulty of loving and 'loving life' in a contemporary culture whose subjects feel alienated from the self and society."

colors and the costumes change and flow with the music, erratically, the way her mind does these days." These rapidly changing images allow her to remain in a fluid present, where she does not need to rely for sustenance on the impoverished memories of a past constrained by provincial censoriousness about the behavior appropriate to a single woman. It quickly becomes clear, however, that Jenny feels more adrift. Having availed herself of the social changes for women that have occurred between Opal's generation and hers, Jenny has been waitressing in Denver. But, in another variation on the theme of staying at home, leaving, or returning, Jenny "was growing restless again, and the idea of going home seized her. Her old rebellion against small-town conventions gave way to curiosity." Back in Kentucky, Jenny pursues her fantasy of recovering her roots as she dates a local man, Randy Newcomb, and buys a plot of land because she wants "a remote place where she can have a dog and grow some tomatoes." Jenny's sense of exile from the "home" to which she has returned creates a feeling of culture shock through which the South is rendered strange: "In the South, the shimmer of the heat seems to distort everything, like old glass with impurities in it." Her estrangement from the South makes its seem grotesque as, in her first two days there, her attention is drawn to "two people with artificial legs, a blind man, a man with hooks for hands, and a man without an arm." Sensitive to her own difference, she imagines herself becoming a grotesque spectacle, fantasizing about being attacked by a pit bull "in an arena, with a crowd watching." Although Randy Newcomb tells her "we're not as countrified down here now as people think," Jenny perceives the local people as types, noticing that there were "two kind of women" in a bar she visits, which makes her feel "odd" as "she was neither type."

It becomes apparent that Jenny's estrangement from her surroundings is part of a process of mourning for personal and cultural losses. This association of mourning with a defamiliarizing perception and a sense of the grotesque recurs throughout the collection. In "Love Life" Jenny's attempt to recover her "roots" and connect herself with the past becomes increasingly focused on her aunt's collection of crazy quilts, and the family burial quilt in particular. This "dark and somber" quilt is comprised of blocks, on each of which "is an appliqued off-white tombstone—a comical shape, like Casper the ghost. Each tombstone has a name and date on it." Opal, who tells Jenny "I try to be modern," refuses to romanticize the women's history, community, and labor represented by the quilt. She is happy to pass the "burden" of the quilt on to her niece, as it signifies to her "miserable, cranky women, straining their eyes, stitching on those dark scraps of material." The communal rite of mourning represented by the quilt prompts Jenny to tell her aunt that she has just received news of the death of a former lover with whom she had lost touch. The isolation of the contemporary subject through geographic mobility, historical dislocation, and transient social relationships, unrecognized by ritual or tradition, is articulated in Jenny's explanation that "If I still knew him, I would know how to mourn, but now I don't know how. And it was over a year ago. So now I don't know what to feel." The story ends ambiguously as Opal consoles herself with the alternating fantasies of violence and sexual freedom on her television: an image of "smoke emerg[ing] from an eyeball," which may belong to "a woman . . . lying on her stomach on a car hood in a desert full of gas pumps," segues into a classroom scene of pupils "gyrating and snapping their fingers to wild music." Opal, whose image of her own "freedom" is signified by a memory of a liaison with a man in a motel room "devoid of history and association," in Nashville, fantasizes that "the teacher is thinking about how, when the bell rings, she will hit the road to Nashville."

Mason returns to her exploration of mourning in a culture of transient relationships in "The Secret of the Pyramids." Barbara's married former lover has just been killed in a car crash. Her friend tells her that "you have to work out your grief somehow," but Barbara responds: "Grief? . . . Is that what it is? Yesterday I hated him, and today I feel—I don't know what." Isolated from a community of mourners that would publicly recognize her bereavement, Barbara is unable to interpret the past in a way that would make sense of the present. She fondly recalls visiting Cairo, Illinois, with her lover and his story about how "young boys come to Cairo . . . to learn the secret of the pyramids," but this fragment of historical lore remains extraneous to her understanding of her own culture. Her sense of being stranded in the present is heightened by her perception of the alienating nature of the shopping mall where she works and where her lover owned a store: "It is the only quality mall for more than a hundred miles, and people from the country and the small towns congregate here on the weekend. . . . Everyone looks dazed." Dissociated from her own grief, Barbara witnesses how the process of mourning has become a public spectacle. As she reads in the newspaper about the death of her lover, she observes that "in print, he was a distant figure, like a celebrity," and visiting the funeral home, she approaches his body "lying in the casket like a store display." At the end of the story, Barbara "locates his traces" in the only private tokens of the relationship that she possesses: the memorabilia she has collected on her travels with him. The concluding image reveals how, fittingly, all that she keeps from these is an icon of the commodification of another figure by consumer culture: a "pink Elvis Presley clock shaped like a guitar."

Mason returns to explore the dislocation of the subject that grief produces in "Bumblebees." Ruth, whose husband and daughter have been killed in a car crash, and Barbara, who is divorced, are trying to "rebuild their lives" in a house in the country. Barbara attempts to restore herself by working in the garden, and Ruth is "working on quilt pieces." Barbara's daughter, Allison, has returned, changed, from college and is "trying to get centered." Each day Allison "brings in some treasure: the cracked shell of a freckled sparrow egg, a butterfly wing," and Barbara believes that "her daughter, deprived of so much of the natural world during her childhood in town, is going through a delayed phase of discovery now." Despite their attempts to replenish themselves through their contact with nature, each of the women continues to feel dissociated from herself. Ruth has thrown away the photographs of her dead husband and child because, as she explains, "one day I realized that I knew the faces in the pictures better than I knew my memories of their faces." Barbara also experiences moments of detachment from herself, as for example, when she "sees the three of them, on the porch on that hillside, as though they were in a painting. . . . Barbara sees herself in her garden, standing against her hoe handle like a scarecrow at the mercy of the breezes that barrel over the ridge."

Throughout the story the women's relation to the house and garden that they are attempting to restore serves as a symbol for their continuing grief and alienation. The floor of an upper room of the house is covered with dead bumblebees, and live bees torment the women. The garden supplies Barbara with a metaphor with which to interpret her situation: "She had the feeling that she was tending too many gardens; everything around her was growing in some sick or stunted way, and it made her feel cramped." Her sense of dislocation also defamiliarizes the landscape around the house. In a moment reminiscent of Raymond Carver's stories, Barbara's perception of her ordinary, everyday environment is profoundly unsettled: "But sometimes it suddenly all seems strange, like something she has never seen before. . . . in this light, with this particular dog, with his frayed bandage, and that particular stick and the wet grass that needs mowing—it is something Barbara has never seen before in her life." Mason does, however, imply some movement toward healing through her focalizing character's perception of images associated with the house and garden. As Barbara continues to walk through the woods, she notices "a fantastic array of mushrooms": "The mushrooms are so unexpected, it is as though they had grown up in a magical but clumsy compensation for the ruined garden." The story concludes with Allison teasing the distressed Ruth that the bundle of rags she has found in the attic contains a dead baby. Barbara, who realizes the rags are just "old stockings with runs," watches her daughter burn them: "The smell of burning dust is very precise. It is like the essence of the old house. It is concentrated filth, and Allison is burning it up for them."

In "Big Bertha Stories" Mason again explores the suffering of a Vietnam veteran and his relatives. The story is told from the point of view of Jeanette, who is married to a veteran, Donald. Donald spends most of his time away from home, working at a strip mine in Muhlenberg County, occasionally returning "like an absentee landlord checking on his property." In this story, as in *In Country,* Mason evokes some of the symptoms of trauma presented by the veterans: Donald suffers from depression, nightmares, and a sense of meaninglessness. He tells his son, Rodney, "strange stories" about "Big Bertha," the name he has given to the strip-mining machine, informing Rodney that "Big Bertha is just like a wonderful woman, a big fat woman who can sing

the blues." Rodney "loves the stories," but the phantasmagoric images of Big Bertha return in his dreams and the troubled pictures he draws. Jeanette regularly visits a therapist whom she calls "The Rapist," and she feels "her family disintegrating like a spider shattering."

When he first went to work at the strip mine, Donald tried to explain to Jeanette how the American despoliation of Vietnam was like strip mining: "America was just stripping off the top, the best. We ruined it," but such accounts have been replaced by the Big Bertha stories. However, in this story, as in *In Country,* the veteran's expression of silenced memories leads to his desire to find resolution of a grief that has remained open since the war. Donald tells of meeting a Vietnamese woman, Phan, who "was beautiful, like the country," and of how he did not know what happened to her because although the "jungle was the most beautiful place in the world. . . . we blew it sky-high." "Big Bertha" has become a hallucinatory configuration that fuses the destructive power of American technology, the luxuriance and devastation of the Vietnamese landscape, and the bodies of the Vietnamese women whom the American soldiers desired and killed. Donald's articulation of his sense of guilt enables him to agree to undergo treatment in the Veterans Hospital. While he is there, Jeanette gets a job and recognizes what her own expectations of Donald have been: "she has thought of Donald primarily as a husband, a provider, someone whose name she shared, the father of her child." Despite the increased self-reflection of both characters, the story ends ambiguously. Jeanette buys a trampoline for Rodney and imagines herself on it when Donald returns "and sees her flying," an image of apparent freedom. But Donald's troubled memories seem to haunt her own dreams as "that night, she has a nightmare about the trampoline. In her dream she is jumping on soft moss, and then it turns into a springy pile of dead bodies."

An adolescent's first encounter with bereavement is one of the themes of "State Champions." The frame of the story is one of cultural loss, emphasizing the disjuncture between past and present. The story opens with the narrator recounting how "in 1952, when I was in the seventh grade, the Cuba Cubs were the state champions in high-school basketball." The narrator recalls how, twenty years later, she met a Kentuckian in upstate New York who pointed out that the Cuba Cubs were "just a handful of country boys who could barely afford basketball shoes." To the child, Peggy, these boys were "the essence of glamour," and in part her story recounts the awakening of desire through her infatuation with one of the players. But the Kentuckian's comment has prompted her to reinterpret her history, and the story changes direction, as, interpolated into her memories, is the recollection of hearing the news of the death of her best friend's sister. She recalls her self-consciousness in the presence of her bereaved friend, who seems to have "some secret knowledge that lifted her above us." Desire is superseded by awe of death and bereavement as she approaches her celebrating hero: "I wanted to tell him what it was like to be at home when such a terrible thing happened, but I couldn't." The story is tinged with nostalgia for a rural childhood, but it evokes the loss of innocence through an awakening self-consciousness accompanied by increased social sophistication.

A sense of loss informs the remainder of the stories in the collection, where Mason explores the difficulty of sustaining relationships in an alienating culture. Here, as in *Shiloh*, Mason examines the effect of changing gender roles on working-class men. This is the focus of one of the more disturbing stories in the collection, "Midnight Magic," which begins with the protagonist, Steve, reflecting on how, "prowling in his car ['Midnight Magic'] at night, he could be Dracula." In the introduction to *Midnight Magic: Selected Stories of Bobbie Ann Mason*, Mason has elaborated on both the significance of the title story and her conception of the writing process. She comments on her empathy with the protagonist of the "Midnight Magic," explaining that "The mystery of writing is much like driving into the darkness in the middle of the night. It's both dangerous and fraught with possibility. After all, the nighttime is double-edged. It may be the dark night of the soul, but it's also night life: the time for seduction and transformation—the creation of magic." Further, Mason comments: "When I wrote these stories, I was venturing along roads that looked familiar, but which I found myself seeing in a new way. I discovered that a backlog of imagery is stored in the dark recesses of the mind, as if waiting to emerge at night—like Dracula. That's what the creative act is for me—a challenge to inhibition, a delving into the hidden and forgotten."

Mason's identification with her protagonist's fascination with the darkness, and her association of the creative process with the retrieval of what lies hidden in "the dark recesses of the mind," offer some insight into the ambiguous tone she sustains throughout "Midnight Magic." She has also commented on the development of her characterization of Steve, explaining that the story "was inspired by a guy I saw sitting in a car eating chocolate-covered doughnuts and drinking chocolate milk. . . . While I was writing it I couldn't make the person I had seen follow through in my imagination. The real person looked like he could be a rapist and really mean. But I couldn't write him that way. I made him a whole lot nicer that I thought he would be. . . . " The imaginative tensions with which Mason wrestled in writing the story remain imprinted on it. The unsettling ambiguity of "Midnight Magic" is produced by the discrepancy that Mason reveals between Steve's point of view, through which it is the world that seems strange, and other characters' perceptions of Steve's actions, whereby it is his behavior that seems at best misguided and at worst menacing. This discrepancy is mirrored by Steve's sense of dissociation from himself, as is indicated, for example, by his observation that "He has on running shoes, but he was sure he had put on boots. He touches his face. He hasn't shaved." These sentences immediately establish the disjuncture between what Steve thinks he has done and what he has actually done, or failed to do.

Through Steve's eyes the solace that popular culture offers its alienated subjects seems increasingly bizarre. His girlfriend, Karen, seeks spiritual guidance at meetings held by "Sardo," who is "a thousand-year-old American Indian inhabiting the body of a teenage girl in Paducah," while his jailed father has been converted by TV evangelism. The story acquires a Carveresque inflection as Steve's sense of the oddness of his culture becomes tinged with an undertone of violence. While Steve's girlfriend, Karen, lives in fear of a rapist who is striking in her neighborhood, Steve alarms a woman in the laundromat as he scrutinizes her laundry, and he frightens Karen by pretending he is the rapist. What Steve considers to be an affectionate embrace Karen perceives as what "cats do . . . when they want to rip out a rabbit's guts." As Steve fantasizes about how, if he were the rapist, he would lay in wait for Karen, the reader is led to wonder whether this is the disorientation produced by a seemingly random and at times violent culture upon an impressionable man or whether Steve has become so alienated that he cannot discern the bounds of acceptable behavior. Albert Wilhelm notes that "the rapist . . . lingers as an ominous echo—the penumbral image of an identity that Steve has barely avoided."

Steve's sense of being "empty inside, doomed," resonates with Karen's observation about an albino deer: "'It was like something all bleached out. It wasn't all *there*.'" The end of the story emphasizes Steve's immobilizing detachment from his surroundings and his inability to feel the appropriate emotional response to people or situations. Driving along the interstate, he sees what he thinks is a dead man at the side of the road. He drives past, unable to respond, but eventually does report the sighting. The final image is ambiguous, however. Suspended in midconversation in the telephone booth, he observes the car, which symbolizes the latent power he feels he lacks: "His muffler has been growing throatier, making an impressive drag-race ramble. It's the power of Midnight Magic, the sound of his heart."

Mason evokes this sense of dissociation again in "Private Lies," the story of Mickey, who is married to Tina but begins an affair with his ex-wife, Donna. Mickey's betrayal of his wife is informed by his mourning for the daughter whom he and Donna gave up for adoption before they married. While Tina becomes "uncharacteristically helpless," Mickey persuades Donna to accompany him to Florida to search for their daughter. The concluding images evoke how his optimism about the future depends upon his freeing himself from what he regards as the deathly burden of his personal history. As he looks out at the ocean, "he felt, with a sense of relief, that nothing private was left here." He imagines walking along the beach with Donna in the future: "They stepped back, then forward, like dancers. They were moving like this along the beach, crunching the fragments of skeletons."

A sense of the dissociation of the self in an alienating culture also pervades "Piano Fingers" and "Coyotes," but Mason also hints here at the transformative potential of love. In "Piano Fingers" the twenty-six-year-old, unemployed Dean "feels suspended somewhere between childhood and old age, not knowing which direction he is facing." Dean is a dreamer who fantasizes about opening an ice-cream parlor or attending a seminar in real-estate investment, but he realizes that he is adrift. While Dean dreams, his wife, Nancy, who "expects more of him than he has been able to give," "zooms through" "Bodice Busters" and yearns for her "dream-house" in the new subdivision. Nancy informs him that "it makes her feel powerless not to be in charge of certain things." Dean's sense of dislocation is mirrored in his pessimistic vision of his culture. As he sits in his car in a subdivision, he reflects that "on this street in the last couple of years one man, a school-board member, was arrested for molesting a child at the playground; a young woman tried to commit suicide; a child died of leukemia." However, Mason attributes to Dean both a heightened reflectiveness and a redeeming love for his children. He observes that "the sound of wet leaves against the car on a late-autumn day makes him feel nostalgia for something, he can't remember what. He realizes that there are such moments, such sensations, that are maybe not memory but just things happening now, things that come into focus suddenly and can be either happy or sad." Like many of Mason's characters, Dean believes that "there are too many choices." However, Dean makes a choice, although one he can ill afford. His daughter's piano teacher tells her that she has "piano fingers," which Dean regards as "a God-given talent." He buys her an electronic keyboard, and as he sits watching her with a sense of wonder, "she seems like someone he has suddenly dreamed into reality. He can hardly believe his eyes."

Cobb, the protagonist of "Coyotes," feels that he has been changed by meeting his girlfriend, Lynnette Johnson. He recalls how, in his childhood, "his mother didn't read much. She was always too tired. She worked at a clothing store, and his dad drove a bread truck. There were four children. Nobody ever did anything especially outrageous or strange." Lynnette, however, has "made him feel there were different ways to look at the world," and together they find "the unusual in the everyday." Cobb's increased sensitivity to ordinary life defamiliarizes "the everyday," revealing, for example, the disturbing flatness of situations where one might expect to find emotional investment. He is haunted by a "strange scene in a Wal-Mart," where he witnessed two teenagers telling the clerk that they had married. Cobb is "confused," wondering "why weren't these three young people excited and happy?" As in "Midnight Magic," Mason hints at a connection between a pervasive cultural lack of affect and contemporary violence. Lynette, who works in a "film developing place," breaches social etiquette at dinner with Cobb's parents by telling them about how photographs of the victims of violent death are "all mixed in with vacations and children." She comments that "the thing is, they're not unusual at all. They're everywhere, all the time. It's life." Cobb gains some insight into this "morbid" trait of Lynnette's character when she tells him how she fears becoming like her mother, whose psychological illness led to her suicide attempt. The conclusion of this story suggests the redemptive possibility of love, however, as it focuses on Cobb's transfiguring perception. As they watch a feather floating in the creek, Cobb "tried to comprehend all that might happen to that feather as it wore away to bits—a strange thought. In a dozen years, he thought, he might look back on this moment and know that it was precisely when he should have stopped and made a rational decision to go no further, but he couldn't know that now." But, as he watches Lynnette, he realizes that "she couldn't see the way the light came through her hair like the light in spring through a leaving tree."

Other stories in the collection also explore various types of loss associated with recent social changes. In "Marita," for instance, a mother tries to persuade her daughter to terminate her pregnancy so that she will "have choices." The daughter reluctantly agrees, but the story depicts her sense of grief after the termination as she retreats into a protective world of childlike fantasy, which she inhabits with her mother's cats: "We're like the Borrowers. . . . We're tiny and quiet, living in the cabbage roses." The narrative withholds judgment about Marita's decision but ends on a positive note as she recalls how she smashed the "flour baby" that she and her fellow schoolgirls were required to make "to teach us the responsibility of having a baby": "I ran away from the gym, tracking flour down the sidewalk, out into the soccer field where I ran free—like a young dog after a flying Frisbee, like someone in love."

Another story that ponders recent changes, especially the effect of feminism on relations between men and women, is "Hunktown." Here, Mason depicts the strain placed on Joann's and Cody's marriage when the unemployed Cody decides to pursue his dream of playing in a band in Nashville. As a waitress in the bar where Cody is playing explains to Joann that she had her "tubes tied" because "I hate it when people *assume* . . . that I'm the one to make supper because I've got reproductive organs," Joann concludes that the waitress "should have sung a song about it, instead of getting herself butchered." Angry as Joann is that she must look on "like an innocent bystander" while the middle-aged Cody irresponsibly pursues his dreams, she can distinguish between "his wild side [and] the part she loved." The concluding image suggests her recognition that she must not neglect this love: "On the porch, the impatiens in a hanging basket had died in the recent freeze. She had forgotten to bring the plant inside. Now she watched it sway and twist in a little whirl of wind." "Airwaves" also traces the disintegration of a relationship after the male partner has become unemployed. When the protagonist,

Jane, is also made unemployed, she refuses to let her partner return to support her. Her espousal of "freedom" is troubled, however. She buys a "travel kit" but "wasn't sure where she was going." The conclusion of the story evokes her loneliness as, returning to her apartment for some laundry, she realizes that "she has left the radio on, and for a moment on the landing she thinks that someone must be home."

In "Sorghum" Liz, who believes she has "something like a commuter marriage," searches for "roots" in traditional culture by going to see an old man making sorghum molasses. His son, Ed, informs her, however, that his father "could do everything the old way. But he doesn't have to anymore." Liz begins an affair with Ed, but her sense of having lost her roots becomes more acute as she attends a dinner party held by Ed's monied friends. Her feeling of displacement, which is compounded by being out of her class, is expressed through her memory of a picture "of a vase of flowers, impossible combinations. . . . The arrangement was beautiful, but it was something you could never see in real life." Her belief that her alienation from her roots, her class, and her husband and children is decadent, and corrupting is conveyed by her decision to climb into the Jacuzzi: "It seemed too hot to bear, but she decided she would bear it—like a punishment, or an acquired taste that would turn delicious when she was used to it."

Again in "Memphis," Mason traces a woman's desire for "freedom." Beverley reflects how, during the last months she lived with her former husband, "she had begun to feel that her mind was crammed with useless information, like a landfill, and there wasn't space deep down in her to move around in, to explore what was there. . . . She felt she had strong ideas and meaningful thoughts, but often when she tried to reach for one she couldn't find it. It was terrifying." Her divorce does not seem to have brought her the increased autonomy she desired: she feels only "disembodied" and immobilized, as though she and her former husband are "stalled at a crossroads." The story does, however, end with an increased sense of possibility as Beverley reflects: "Who knew what might happen or what anybody would decide to do on any given weekend or at any stage of life?"

The final story, "Wish," takes a different perspective on change. It is told from the point-of-view of the eighty-three-year-old Sam, who is musing with his sister, Damson, on the past. Damson, who has never married, regrets her father's intervention in an early relationship and the subsequent death of her suitor, complaining that "'Pap mined my life.'" Sam, however, is more acceptant of the events in his life. His wife, he believes, died "without needing him at all. And now he didn't need her." His life now reduced mainly to his memories and "the small room where he had chosen to sleep," Sam realizes "he was happy."

Source: Joanna Price, "*Spence + Lila* and *Love Life*," in *Understanding Bobbie Ann Mason*, University of South Carolina Press, 2000, pp. 86–116.

Devon Jersild

In the following essay, Jersild provides an overview of Mason's earlier works, focusing on Mason's character portraits.

It was seven years ago, in 1982, that Bobbie Ann Mason published *Shiloh and Other Stories*, her first collection of short fiction. Except for some nitpicking reviews which complained that Mason was female, wrote in the present tense, and published in the *New Yorker* (qualifications apparently comprising a genre), the critical reception of that volume was noisy and positive; critics saw in Mason a newcomer who showed not only promise but also maturity of vision and technique. Since then, she has published two short novels, *In Country* (1985) and *Spence and Lila* (1988), and now, a collection of stories called *Love Life*.

In *Shiloh*, Mason introduces us to the people who remain her focus: the country folk of western Kentucky, people just past the old ways and into the new, just off the farms and into the factories, caught between the garden and the "Burger Boy." She writes about truck drivers and supermarket clerks and carpenters, real estate agents and teachers. The details of their lives are perfect, as they should be—this is where Bobbie Ann Mason grew up. Indeed, in some of the stories I felt I could see the shadow of a little girl playing in the corner; one imagines, anyway, that such rightness of dialogue and precision of imagery could have come only from an insider.

Yet Mason maintains a rather distanced authorial stance; she, with the reader, looks into her characters' living rooms and watches them as they reveal themselves. It's a pretty funny show, most of the time, as Mason zeros in on the foibles and eccentricities of ordinary folks. She knows about how widows arrive at card parties "in separate cars, not trusting each other's driving," and she knows that at least one widow would refuse to sit at a table set on a bulldozer sprocket, "for fear she will catch her foot

> "Certainly Mason often writes about the confused and uneducated, but I do not believe that she implies a causal relation between emotional clumsiness and social class."

in one of the holes at the base." Humor and pleasure inhere in the simple feeling that the language is just right, that one of these widows *would* say, "Stephanie comes from a kind of disturbed family. Her mother's had a bunch of nervous breakdowns and her daddy's a vegetarian."

To me, one of the more poignant features of these stories is how amiably the characters go along with the changing times which leave them so bewildered. They rarely argue with or protest against change, and they waste precious little time on nostalgia. Rather, they seem eager to demonstrate that they are keeping up. They, too, have microwaves and know about newfangled diseases. It is a truth self-evident that the new and the young are better than the used and the old, the storebought better than the homegrown. A carpenter who makes a table for his wife to commemorate their twenty-first anniversary—and fashions the top out of twenty-one odd shapes of wood—feels obliged to apologize: "It's not something you would buy in a store." The old people sometimes feel distressed by shifting norms, but they rarely object, partly because they feel helpless, but also because they admire "this day and time, [when] people just do what they please." The young people get divorced, the even younger get abortions, and lots of them smoke dope.

Still, the puzzlement of young and old is always evident, and the fear of meaninglessness—always pervasive in cultures unsettled by change—rustles through these stories like wind in a grassy field. In "The Rookers," a daughter home from college provides her parents with a metaphor for their anxiety from quantum mechanics:

> "There's some things called photons that disappear if you look for them. Nobody can find them."

"How do they know they're there, then?" asks Mack skeptically.

"Where do they go?" Mary Lou asks.

. . . "If you try to separate them, they disappear. They don't even *exist* except in a group. Bob says this is one of the most *important* discoveries in the history of the world. He says it just *explodes* all the old ideas about physics."

Later, the mother thinks about how her family has scattered, and she muses, "If you break up a group, the individuals could disappear out of existence."

In the face of this anxiety, Mason's characters rely on physical facts—the sound of a drill, the pictures on a table—to prove to themselves that they are still *alive*. The load of sensory detail by which the author locates us in time and place also suggests the means by which her characters attempt to define themselves, to anchor themselves to their lives. Here, I think, is where Hemingway most strongly makes himself felt in contemporary fiction. In his story "Big Two-Hearted River," for instance, a shell-shocked soldier goes on a camping trip and tries to steady himself by taking in one detail at a time, registering it with his senses, and using each successful transaction with reality to pull himself along a little further. In Bobbie Ann Mason's stories, characters also feel reassured by the physical world, only now they rely not on grasshoppers under stones but on factory-waxed congoleum floors to measure how *real* they are—that is to say, how closely their lives approximate the image of modern life they carry around in their heads. When Mason's characters watch TV—and they do a lot of that—they watch shows like "Real People," and the irony is not to be missed. Advertising and television become a major frame of reference; their own lives become important to the extent that they identify with movie stars and sit-com characters.

Mason's men can be especially detached from their emotional centers. In the title story of *Shiloh*, Leroy, a thirty-four-year-old truck driver home after an accident, suspects that his wife is falling away from him. After avoiding the topic of their baby's death for sixteen years, he recalls the incident. He and Norma Jean had gone to a drive-in movie, and the infant died while sleeping in the back seat:

"It just happens sometimes," said the doctor, in what Leroy always recalls as a nonchalant tone. Leroy can hardly remember the child anymore, but he still sees vividly a scene from *Dr. Strangelove* in which the President of the United States was talking in a folksy voice on the hot line to the Soviet premier about the bomber accidentally headed toward Russia. He was in the War Room, and the world map was lit up. Leroy remembers Norma Jean standing catatonically beside him in the hospital and himself thinking: Who is this strange girl? He had forgotten who she was. Now scientists are saying that crib death is caused by a virus. Nobody knows anything, Leroy thinks. The answers are always changing.

Leroy makes a connection between the doctor's "nonchalant tone" and the "folksy voice" of the president in the movie as he informs the Russians that they are about to be blown up—an association the more touching because it is unconscious. The movie provokes a bizarre sense of unreality. (What does a "War Room" have to do with a war? Or a lit-up "world map" with exploding cities? What does *any* of it have to do with political actualities?) Indeed, its very incongruousness expresses Leroy's sense of disconnection: he remembers the movie but not the child. In the hospital, he forgets his relation to his wife. His reflex is to move quickly from the painful recollection of this moment to a generalization which might help him make sense of the experience: "Now scientists are saying that crib death is caused by a virus," but "Nobody knows anything." Hidden in this passage is Leroy's anger at these strange, removed authorities: these careless doctors, folksy presidents, and fickle scientists who seem to have power over Leroy. Yet Leroy is as much removed from his anger as from his sense of loss. Life is out of his control. He is helpless. So it's best to go along as best he can.

Some critics have charged that Mason condescends to her characters, that she portrays them as confused, uneducated, lower-middle-class types who are trapped in their pain because they don't have the tools to understand their dilemmas, while she and the reader look on with superior understanding. Certainly Mason often writes about the confused and uneducated, but I do not believe that she implies a causal relation between emotional clumsiness and social class. It seems to me that respect for other people—including fictional characters—has something to do with letting go of one's own standards and bias long enough to understand them in their own context, with their particular conflicts and specific ways of seeing the world. Mason tends to refrain from comment, extrapolations, conclusions. She rarely appears to identify with her characters or to invite identification. She simply lets them be.

This cool surface can make it hard to engage with her stories. Still, one of their common features is a movement toward a character's moment of realization, when the self is, however briefly, acknowledged and confirmed in its suffering. These moments, always beautifully accomplished, create a sense of kinship with the characters and render them suddenly more complex. The revelations at the end of each story often throw certain preceding details into a context that reveals the intrinsic shape of the whole.

Published in 1985, *In Country* explores much the same world encountered in *Shiloh,* this time from the point of view of a seventeen-year-old girl named Sam. With its jaunty high spirits, the novel entertains from the beginning. Here is Sam taking her grandmother to the bathroom at a gas station:

> The restroom is locked, and Sam has to go back and ask the boy for the key. The key is on a ring with a clumsy plastic Sunoco sign. The restroom is pink and filthy, with sticky floors. In her stall, Sam reads several phone numbers written in lipstick. A message says, "The mass of the ass plus the angle of the dangle equals the scream of the cream." She wishes she had known that one when she took algebra. She would have written it on an assignment.

> Mamaw lets loose a stream as loud as a cow's. This trip is crazy. It reminds Sam of that Chevy Chase movie about a family on vacation, with an old woman tagging along. She died on the trip and they had to roll her inside a blanket on the roof of the station wagon because the children refused to sit beside a dead body. This trip is just as weird.

Like other Mason characters, Sam's first points of reference are TV and movies. A baby when her father was killed in Vietnam, she feels no sense of bereavement until, years later, she watches an episode of M*A*S*H in which Colonel Blake gets killed. She lives with her Uncle Emmett, who, unlike her father, returned from the war alive. Her mother has moved to Lexington with a new husband and baby; Sam refuses to go because "Somebody had to watch out for Emmett," and she doesn't want to switch schools her senior year. More to the point, Sam feels the burden of being cut off from her past, and tries, through her uncle, to reestablish a sense of connection. Together they listen to sixties music and watch M*A*S*H reruns—media versions of history—and Sam spends much of the novel obsessing over whether the ache on Emmett's face is a sign of exposure to Agent Orange.

What Sam wants is a context in which to define herself. She is caught between her desire to make sense of herself in terms of the past and the impulse to make herself new—to cut loose, drive off somewhere, get a job and find "all new friends." While less compelling than the short stories, *In Country* is more hopeful; in the end, Sam achieves an exhilarating, fresh idea of herself while visiting the Vietnam Memorial in Washington, D.C., a self taking shape in spite of the dissolution—cultural, familial—in evidence everywhere she looks.

Spence and Lila is something altogether different. About a farm couple married for over forty years, the novel is in many ways an idyll, a look at the mythic past from which Mason's contemporary characters have fallen. The landscape is still one of change—marijuana plants grow up amid the cornfields, the children have scattered with problems of their own, and Spence and Lila face their own mortality when they discover that Lila has breast cancer. Yet Spence and Lila as a couple represent that time when life seemed to hold together, when husband and wife moved from love to work and back again with the ease that comes from knowing both are always there, and that they are needed.

The novel celebrates, indirectly, a time when families transcended the animosities that divide many of them today. In the hospital, between operations, Lila remembers being a young wife and mother living with Spence's parents while he was in the navy. When her child caught pneumonia, Lila wanted to take her to the doctor, but her in-laws protested, "Why, he would charge! We can doctor her." Lila wrapped the baby's chest in greased rags and "prayed so hard she was almost screaming." The baby survived, and gradually, the "shared silent worry about Spence" drew Lila and her in-laws together until she loved them "as though they were her own."

Perhaps this is less than convincing. Indeed, authentic as moments in *Spence and Lila* may be, they disappoint if read too literally—that is, as realistic drama. But this would be a mistake. I read the novel as a modern pastoral, a rendition of the bucolic past written by someone who belongs to a newer world—like Virgil dreaming his idyll from the heights of Roman sophistication or Robert Frost, with his college education, inventing a region of the mind that supposedly exists somewhere north of Boston. Mason's idealizations, likewise, say less about the past itself than about the modern longing for a life in harmony with nature, a time and place where one's work provided satisfying metaphors of self in relation to the world.

Lila, for instance, is a gardener; she tends her garden with love and devotion, and it, in turn, nurtures her in body and spirit. The novel ends with Spence and Lila standing amid the vegetables. "I've got a cucumber that needs pickling," Spence teases her. He goes on:

> The way she laughs is the moment he has been waiting for. She rares her head back and laughs steadily, her throat working and her eyes flashing. Her cough catches her finally and slows her down, but her face is dancing like pond water in the rain, all unsettled and stirring with aroused possibility.

Similarly, some of the most beautiful passages in the novel describe Spence on his farm; he is a gentle caretaker, an uneducated but wise old man who understands his place in the world. Here he is as he "follows the creek line down toward the back fields":

> In the center of one of the middle fields is a rise with a large, brooding old oak tree surrounded by a thicket of blackberry briers. From the rise, he looks out over his place. This is it. This is all there is in the world—it contains everything there is to know or possess, yet everywhere people are knocking their brains out trying to find something different, something better. His kids all scattered, looking for it. Everyone always wants a way out of something like this, but what he has here is the main thing there is—just the way things grow and die, the way the sun comes up and goes down every day. These are the facts of life. They are so simple they are almost impossible to grasp.

It's a great risk to write a novel like *Spence and Lila*, to put into words facts "so simple they are almost impossible to grasp." Mason pulls it off by the sheer lyricism of her prose, the earthy humor of her characters, and the uncanny way she has of tracking surprising turns of thought. I was especially moved by Spence's vivid flashbacks to World War II and the way they haunt him throughout the novel. The impossibility of making sense of that time—of figuring out how "his destroyer fit in the larger picture, a whole world at war"—accentuates the beauty of the life he makes for himself with Lila on the farm.

Many of the stories in *Love Life* are familiar as extensions of themes discovered in *Shiloh*. The characters exhibit the same difficulty with the process of translating feeling and thought into purposeful action. Desire becomes a vague and unsettling impulse, but desire for what? More money? More sex? More love? A new dress? Mostly, the characters don't *know* what they want, and so what the businessman says in the story "Sorghum" sounds ruefully true: "Everybody's always dissatisfied."

They have different ways of distancing themselves from the pain of their longing. The old lady of the title story drinks peppermint schnapps and watches TV to forget the risks she never took—like

driving off to Idaho in a shiny Imperial with a man whose beard was too "demanding." In "Midnight Magic," a young man's dislocation from himself approaches schizophrenia. The story begins:

> Steve leaves the supermarket and hits the sunlight. Blinking, he stands there a moment, then glances at his feet. He has on running shoes, but he was sure he had put on boots. He touches his face. He hasn't shaved.

Steve's metaphor of self becomes a car, "deep blue and wicked. . . . The car's rear end is hiked up like a female cat in heat. Prowling in his car at night, he could be Dracula." There's a rapist on the loose in "Midnight Magic," and by the end of the story, through some wonderfully eerie turns, we begin to wonder if Steve is forgetting far more than we had realized.

There are stories of healing here, too. In "Bumblebees," a story with rich and beautiful images, two women, Barbara and Ruth, buy a farmhouse intending to restore it together, one to get over a divorce, the other to recover from the death of her husband and child. Their attempts to mother each other, to nurture their gardens and Barbara's daughter seem doomed from the start. On the other hand, the rot and decay of the old place suggest in themselves the potential for renewal, and Barbara, at least, determines not to shrink from the painful process of making changes. The story ends with her daughter touching a match to a bundle of disintegrating stockings that she finds in the attic:

> In the damp air, the flame burns slowly, and then the rags suddenly catch. The smell of burning dust is very precise. It is like the essence of the old house. It is concentrated filth, and Allison is burning it up for them.

The more I read Mason's stories, the more I am impressed by her natural sense of metaphor, the organic shape of her stories, and the richness of her language. The more, also, I feel the depressive effect of much of her work. Why should this be? Artful stories about grueling circumstances *can*, of course, leave one elated—that's one of the great paradoxes of art. The feeling one is left with depends largely, I think, on authorial stance; the artist's genius (in the sense of the word as *spirit*) determines the final effect. It seems to me that Bobbie Ann Mason's authorial restraint mirrors her characters' distance from emotion and produces a certain numbing effect. A huge burden of feeling stays often at arm's length, as if it would be too difficult to take it on entirely, as if Mason herself prefers to keep it at a distance. Thus the sense of helplessness and defeat that occasionally threatens the reader as well as Mason's characters.

Not all of her characters are quite so cut off from feeling, of course. "Coyotes" is a beautiful story about a young man, Cobb, who has become acutely sensitive to other people's pain—noticing, for instance, "how people always seemed to be explaining themselves. If his stepfather was eating a hamburger, he'd immediately get defensive about cholesterol, even though no one had commented on it." He falls in love with a girl named Lynette "who made him feel there were different ways to look at the world. She brought out something fresh and unexpected in him. She made him see that anything conventional . . . was funny and absurd."

But Lynette has her fears. She is afraid that she will commit suicide because her mother did, the past inexorably gathering her in its tragic web. She asks Cobb, rather daringly, "Do you have any idea how complicated it's going to be?" He reassures her, "Down here, we just call that taking care of business." Both characters recognize the potential for pain ahead of them, and they know that one day they may regret how close they have become. "But he couldn't know that now," Mason writes of Cobb. Here, as in "Bumblebees," she admires the simple braveries of characters who, with a rich sense of ambiguity, still direct themselves toward the future. These stories give *Love Life* some momentum and make the reader care, too, about where Bobbie Ann Mason might go from here.

Source: Devon Jersild, "The World of Bobbie Ann Mason," in *Kenyon Review*, Vol. 11, Summer 1989, pp. 163–69.

Sources

Brinkmeyer, Robert H., Jr., "Finding One's History: Bobbie Ann Mason and Contemporary Southern Literature," in the *Southern Literary Journal*, Vol. 19, No. 2, Spring 1987, pp. 20–33.

Fine, Laura, "Going Nowhere Slow: The Post-South World of Bobbie Ann Mason," in the *Southern Literary Journal*, Vol. 32., No. 1, Fall 1999, pp. 87–97.

Harmon, William, and C. Hugh Holman, *A Handbook to Literature*, Prentice Hall, 2000, pp. 427–28.

Jersild, Devon, "The World of Bobbie Ann Mason," in the *Kenyon Review*, Vol. 11, No. 3, Summer 1989, pp. 163–69.

Kakutani, Michiko, Review of *Love Life*, in the *New York Times*, March 3, 1989, Sec. C, p. 35.

Lyons, Bonnie, and Bill Oliver, Interview with Bobbie Ann Mason, in *Contemporary Literature*, Vol. 32, No 4., Winter 1991, pp. 449–70.

Mason, Bobbie Ann, "Private Lies" in *Love Life*, Perennial Library, 1990, pp. 147–60.

McKee, Kathryn B., "Doubling Back: Finding Bobbie Ann Mason's Present in Her Past," in the *Southern Literary Journal*, Vol. 31, No. 1, Fall 1998, pp. 25–50.

Millard, Kenneth, *Contemporary American Fiction: An Introduction to American Fiction since 1970*, Oxford University Press, 2000, p. 266.

Moore, Lorrie, Review of *Love Life*, in the *New York Times Book Review*, March 12, 1989, p. 7.

Price, Joanna. *Understanding Bobbie Ann Mason*, University of South Carolina Press, 2000, pp. 100, 111.

Further Reading

Gholson, Craig, "Bobbie Ann Mason," in *Bomb*, Vol. 28, Summer 1989, pp. 40–43.

In this interview, Mason covers issues such as class and the importance of television in the lives of her characters.

Peach, Linden, "'K-Marts and Lost Parents': 'Dirty Realism' in Contemporary American and Irish Fiction," in *Critical Survey*, Vol. 9, No. 2, 1997, pp. 61–79.

Peach discusses both the definition of "dirty realism" and its use in the writing of Raymond Carver, Bobbie Ann Mason, and Tobias Wolff, among others.

Ryan, Maureen, "Stopping Places: Bobbie Ann Mason's Short Stories," in *Women Writers of the Contemporary South*, edited by Loren Logdsden and Charles W. Mayer, Western Illinois University Press, 1982, pp. 133–41.

In her examination of Mason's early short stories, Ryan focuses on issues of change as characters attempt to adjust to a changing rural landscape.

Wilhelm, Albert, *Bobbie Ann Mason: A Study of the Short Fiction*, Twayne's Studies in Short Fiction, Twayne Publishers, 1998.

Wilhelm's book examines Mason's short stories, including several interviews, additional criticism, and a bibliography.

The Pursuer

Julio Cortázar

1959

In 1959, the Argentine writer Julio Cortázar published a short story entitled "El Perseguidor" ("The Pursuer") that vividly brought to life the bebop scene of 1950s Paris. Taking the final months in the life of the prodigious jazz musician Johnny Carter as its subject, the story is in many ways an exploration of the career and personal life of the famous alto saxophonist Charlie Parker, the most influential musician of the style of jazz music known as bebop. "The Pursuer" offers a glimpse into Johnny's personal life, from his severe drug addiction and psychological instability to his profound philosophical insights, and it follows the key moments of Johnny's relationship with his biographer and critic Bruno, the narrator of the story.

With its daring narrative structure, which uses shifting verb tenses as a way of reinforcing its challenging conception of time and philosophy, Cortázar's short story is clearly the work of a talented and ambitious writer. By the time he published his early short stories, such as "The Pursuer" in Paris, Cortázar had begun to establish himself among an international community of innovative writers. His depiction of the tensions between the critic and the artist, the theme of pursuit in art and life, and newly emerging philosophies of time and space, have earned "The Pursuer" a place among the classic texts of post-World-War-II literature. The story was originally published in the collection *Las Armas Secretas* (*The Secret Weapons*), but Paul Blackburn's translation from the Spanish became

available in *End of the Game and Other Stories*, published by Random House in 1963.

Author Biography

Julio Cortázar was born in Belgium in 1914 and raised by his mother in a suburb of Buenos Aires, Argentina. Throughout his youth he developed a passion for classic literature, but he was forced because of his family's financial situation to drop out of the University of Buenos Aires after one year and become a teacher. He continued to read foreign literature and published a book of sonnets entitled *Presencia* (*Presence*) in 1938, under the pen name Julio Denis. In 1944 he took a post teaching French literature at the University of Cuyo in Mendoza. After his imprisonment for participating in demonstrations against the Argentine president Juan Perón in 1946, Cortázar resigned his teaching position and began working for a publishing company in Buenos Aires. Meanwhile, Cortázar completed a course in public translation so rapidly that it led to neuroses, which (the author later noted) were reflected in the short stories he wrote during this period.

Cortázar published his first collection of short stories, *Bestiario* (*Bestiary*), and was awarded a scholarship to study in Paris in 1951. He left Argentina for Paris, where he resided for the rest of his life, in part because of political pressure that Perón was placing on the Argentine literary elite. Continuing to travel frequently throughout the world, however, Cortázar frequently gave lectures advocating social change in Latin America, and he remained an active socialist and human rights advocate throughout his life. In 1953, he married another translator, Aurora Bernández, whom he divorced after many years. Later in his life, he married the Canadian writer Carol Dunlap.

An extremely prolific poet, novelist, essayist, and short story writer, Cortázar produced early in his career the short story "Axolotl," a story about a man that is turned into a salamander, as well as "The Pursuer," which is not magical or mythical but challenges the reader's understanding of time. In 1963, the author published his most famous novel, *Rayuela* (*Hopscotch*), which employs a revolutionary narrative structure by way of chapters that are not read in chronological order but can be skipped through in at least two coherent sequences. Cortázar's later writings range widely in theme, from fantasy to political commentary to meditations on reality

Julio Cortázar

and perception. He died of leukemia and heart disease in Paris on February 12, 1984, three years after becoming a French citizen.

Plot Summary

After a dedication to "Ch. P.," which stands for Charlie Parker, a quote from the final book of the New Testament, and a quote from the Welsh poet Dylan Thomas, "The Pursuer" opens with its narrator Bruno entering a trashed Paris hotel room. Inside, in "worse shape than usual," sits his friend about whom he has written a biography, the prodigious jazz musician Johnny Carter, and his current girlfriend Dédée. Johnny is recovering from another bout of heavy drinking and drug use, he has once again lost his sax, and he is in a bad mood. While the three of them drink rum and coffee, Johnny talks about time, one of his "manias," or intense obsessions, using the subway and an elevator as examples of time not working in a rational way.

Bruno tells Johnny that he will get him another sax and gets ready to leave, but while Bruno is saying goodbye to Dédée Johnny throws off the blanket that was covering his naked body. After giving Dédée some money and telling her not to let

Johnny shoot up heroin before his first concert, Bruno leaves feeling grateful that Johnny would no longer make him see what he "didn't want to see."

Two or three days later, Bruno visits Tica, or "the marquesa," a rich friend and sometime lover of Johnny, to find out if she has been giving him heroin, or "junk." She is talking with two musicians, Art Boucaya and Marcel Gavoty, who are excited because of Johnny's excellent recording session with them on the previous day. Although Tica made up with Johnny at the recording session, Bruno discovers that she had gotten into a fight with him two months earlier, so it must have been Dédée that has been giving him heroin. Then Johnny arrives, in "great shape" (with a moderate amount of drugs in his system) and optimistic about the concert that night.

Next comes a brief section of Bruno's thoughts during the intermission of that night's concert, about Johnny and the music he uses "to explore himself, to bite into the reality that escapes every day." Then, four or five days later, Bruno finds out from Art Boucaya that Johnny had refused to play more than two songs at a recording session and started talking obsessively about funeral urns. Bruno delays going to see him until the next day, but he finds out in the police reports the next morning that Johnny set his hotel room on fire and escaped, running naked through the halls. Bruno is not able to get into the hospital where Johnny is under observation until Dédée calls him five days later to say that Johnny wants to see him.

Johnny is emaciated, or extremely thin from illness, but his temperature is normal, and he talks to Bruno about his visions of fields with urns that contain the ashes of dead people, as well as his conviction that the doctors and scientists that are so sure of themselves do not understand the world at all. He uses the example of cutting a loaf of bread, which he cannot understand because it seems that the bread must change into something else when he touches it or cuts it. Then Johnny falls asleep and Bruno observes that Johnny is not a genius "walk[ing] in the clouds," but a man more real than anyone else.

When Bruno goes with Art and Dédée to listen to the two songs Johnny recorded before this breakdown, he finds "terrible beauty" in the song *Amorous*, despite the deficiencies that led Johnny to demand that the engineer destroy the recording. Bruno then receives a call from Tica who says that Johnny's youngest daughter, Bee, has died in Chicago. Bruno goes to Johnny's hotel room and listens

to Johnny explode about his friends keeping the recording of *Amorous*.

Bruno next sees Johnny while sitting at a cafe with Tica and Baby Lennox, another woman that adores Johnny. Tica goes over to deal with Johnny while Bruno flirts with Baby and finds out from two musicians in Johnny's new group that Johnny is "barely able to play anything." Suddenly, Johnny gets up, kneels at Bruno's feet, and cries for his daughter; and everyone in the cafe stares at them until Tica gets him to sit down. After everyone else leaves, Johnny and Bruno walk to the Seine River, and Bruno asks him about his biography, which has just been translated from French into English. Johnny says he liked it but there are things missing.

Considering his decision not to include Johnny's psychological and physical abnormalities and illnesses in the biography, Bruno asks him again about the book and Johnny responds, "what you forgot to put in is me." Before finally going to the hotel, Johnny speaks to Bruno about how the biography misses the point of Johnny and his music, and how once he, Johnny, came close to getting to "the other side of the door," when he was playing and looking at his ex-wife Lan's red dress, and how he doesn't believe in God.

Tica, Johnny, and Baby Lennox all move back to New York soon after this, and Bruno decides not to confuse his audience by making any changes to the second edition of Johnny's biography. Bruno then receives a telegram from Baby Lennox saying that Johnny has died. Bruno finds out that he was at Tica's place and likely died of a severe drug overdose. Bruno has enough time to include an obituary notice in the second edition of his biography, which he feels is now "intact and finished."

Characters

Bee

Johnny's youngest daughter with Lan, Bee dies of pneumonia in Chicago. Her death is quite a blow to Johnny, who later says about his music: "What I'm playing is Bee dead."

Dr. Bernard

Dr. Bernard, whom Johnny calls a "sad-assed idiot," is the physician taking care of Johnny in Paris.

Art Boucaya

Art is a musician, perhaps a bassist, and a friend of Johnny. Bruno calls him a "teahead," or a marijuana smoker, and he sometimes feels sorry for him because Johnny has let him down in Paris. Bruno also recognizes that, like Tica and Dédée, Art takes advantage of Johnny. Like Johnny, Art is from the United States, and he has had "conversations with his agent about going back to New York as soon as possible."

Bruno

Bruno is a prestigious music critic who has recently published a very successful biography of Johnny. The narrator of the story, he is a Parisian intellectual who, although he is close friends with Johnny and the jazz crowd, does not take drugs or mix in much with their social life. Bruno is like Johnny's lovers, friends, and fellow musicians who exploit Johnny for their own devices, since Bruno's book and much of his career is founded on Johnny's genius. Yet Bruno seems to be the only person aware that he is doing this, and Bruno also (as becomes clear while he is listening to *Amorous*) understands Johnny's music, as well as his obsessions and philosophies, better than any of the other characters. Indeed, Bruno seems to understand more about Johnny's real self than anyone else, which is perhaps why Johnny considers him such a great friend.

Bruno's relationship with Johnny is quite complex. Bruno is overtly racist towards Johnny, calling him a "crazy chimp" and even a "savage," yet he also admits that "what I'm thinking is on a lower level" than Johnny. Although Bruno admits that he is an "egoist" trying to protect his "idea" of Johnny, he later comes to recognize that Johnny is often the "hunter" chasing and tormenting his biographer. Also, Bruno is one of the people who is always taking care of Johnny and giving him what he needs. However, by the end of the story, Johnny's combination of intriguing and tormenting Bruno results in Bruno's refusal to include Johnny's complex personal life in the second edition of the biography.

Johnny Carter

A prodigious jazz saxophonist and one of the great talents of his time, Johnny Carter is the main subject of the story. His character is closely based on the famous bebop musician Charlie "Yardbird" Parker, and, like Parker, Johnny is a heroin addict and an alcoholic with severe psychological ill-

Media Adaptations

- Cortázar's "Las babas del Diablo" from the collection *Las armas secretas* was the basis for Michaelangelo Antonioni's 1966 film *Blowup*. The film features David Hemmings and Vanessa Redgrave.

---

nesses. He has abandoned his wife, children, and an unknown number of other lovers, he continually loses or sells his saxophone, he fails to come to performances or refuses to play while there, he has a tendency to be suicidal, and it is sometimes necessary to confine him to a psychiatric hospital because he is a danger to himself or other people. But Johnny is also a unique genius whose understanding of life and psychological problems are inextricably connected to his philosophical and artistic insights.

These insights, expressed in Johnny's monologues to Bruno and his other friends, tend to have much in common with some of the new philosophical theories of the 1950s. The most pronounced of Johnny's obsessions is time, which confounds him because he sees that it is not a linear or collective phenomenon. This relates to the rhythmic innovations of his music and the fact that he is a "pursuer" or "hunter," which Bruno sees as a desperate struggle to find a crack in the "door" and discover a new way of thinking about the world.

Although Johnny often disappoints his friends and family, he is also a person who is almost universally revered and admired. His genius (although Bruno insists that he is not a "genius") is in the combination of his personal life, his music, and his philosophical theories, and Bruno's racist caricature of him as a "chimpanzee who wants to learn to read" also, ironically, suggests that he is struggling to evolve and understand things that his species, the human race, has not understood before. Johnny is ahead of his time, struggling to reach a new level of existence, and normal society, including his biographer Bruno, is ultimately unable to accept or understand him.

Miles Davis

Confusing reality with fiction, Bruno mentions an interview with Miles Davis, the famous jazz trumpeter who played with Charlie Parker during the peak of his career in New York. Davis was, together with Parker, one of the most influential jazz musicians of the bebop era. During his climactic discussion with Bruno near the end of the story, Johnny refers to playing with Davis when "the door open[ed] a little bit," and he found, or nearly found, what he was looking for.

Dédée

Dédée is Johnny's girlfriend who lives with him during most of "The Pursuer," although she stays behind in Paris when he moves to New York. By the time the story begins, she is already quite worn down by Johnny and the lifestyle they lead. Finding the red dress she is wearing during the opening scene repulsive, Bruno notices that she has "gotten older." She later reveals that she is jealous of Tica. Bruno originally hopes that Dédée will refuse to let Johnny abuse heroin, but it appears that she shoots up with him frequently. Nevertheless, Dédée is constantly taking care of Johnny when he is sick and seems quite devoted to him, although she becomes "happily settled" with a trombonist after he goes to New York.

Delaunay

Delaunay is from Paris and seems to be a manager or producer of some kind, since he runs things in the studio but does not play an instrument.

Marcel Gavoty

Marcel is Johnny's friend and fellow musician, likely a trumpet player from the United States. He enjoys joking with Tica, and he takes away Johnny's saxophone after a recording session so Johnny does not sell or destroy it. Bruno feels that Marcel, like Art, fails to understand Johnny as well as he does.

Lan

Lan is Johnny's wife, although they seem to have been separated for a long time. She lives in Chicago with her daughter Bee, who dies of pneumonia. During Johnny's description of the moment when, as he was playing a solo, "time" began to "open out," he remembers Lan's red dress, and he also tells Bruno that Lan's red dress is one of the things Johnny's biography is "missing." Nevertheless, Johnny seems to have abandoned Lan, as he has abandoned many people.

Baby Lennox

The twenty-year-old beauty that goes back to New York with Johnny at the end of the story, Baby is one of Johnny's admirers. Bruno calls her stupid and promiscuous, but she seems to know how to handle Johnny despite Bruno's suspicion that she would readily shoot up heroin and become "lost" with him.

The Marquesa

See Tica

Pepe Ramírez

Pepe is the musician who talks with Art and Delaunay about Lester Young, the alto saxophonist that was Charlie Parker's hero when he was growing up, in the hotel after Johnny learns that his daughter died.

Tica

Although her name is Tica, Bruno often refers to Johnny's friend and sometime lover, the wife (now separated) of a marquis, as "The Marquesa." Tica met Johnny in New York, when he was just beginning to create a sensation in the jazz world, and immediately admired him. Since then she has given him money, sometimes slept with him, shot up heroin with him, and used her unique ability to calm him down and provide comfort when he has needed it. Tica is both an enabler for Johnny's drug addiction, since she is the person who most frequently supplies him with heroin, and a sophisticated and generous friend that often saves him in social situations.

Two months before the opening of "The Pursuer," Johnny had a falling-out with Tica, which is why Bruno is the one to pay for a new saxophone when Johnny loses his on the metro. But Johnny "makes up" with her during a recording session, and they remain close until the end of the story, when they both leave Paris for New York. In many ways, Tica's character is based on the Baroness Pannonica ("Nica") de Koenigswarter, a benefactor and socialite who befriended and financially supported many jazz musicians, including Charlie Parker and

Thelonious Monk. Like Tica, Nica separated from her rich husband because of "dope and other, similar, reasons," and moved to New York and then Paris in pursuit of the bebop scene. She became quite famous, or infamous, after Parker died in her New York luxury apartment from complications due to drug and alcohol abuse.

Themes

Pursuit

As is clear from the title and the frequent speculation about who is "hunting" whom in the short story, Cortázar is very interested in the concept of both ideological and personal pursuit. Bruno's entire career is, in a sense, based on "pursuing" Johnny and Johnny's musical talent. He helps Johnny, in part, in order to make sure that his biography is successful, and he tries to keep Johnny off of drugs, in part, so that Johnny will remain famous for his music and not for his incredibly complex psychology, which Bruno's biography completely omits. As Bruno admits, "we're a bunch of egotists; under the pretext of watching out for Johnny what we're doing is protecting our idea of him." He is trying, as the critic, to confine and limit Johnny in order to pursue what Johnny's music means to him and his readers.

Bruno later suggests, however, that the theme of pursuit is more complex than this. When he states that Johnny "is the critic of us all," and that "Johnny pursues and is not pursued," Bruno is highlighting the fact that Johnny is not simply the prey of a critic like Bruno, a friend like Art, or a lover like Baby or Dédée. Johnny pursues a new definition and realm of possibility in art, and he pursues his friends as well; in his struggle to find what he is looking for with his prodigious music, he hunts and exposes his friends' weaknesses. Bruno admits that he is haunted by what Johnny reveals about his own failures and unhappiness and especially his "prestige," and he feels sorry for Art because Art could not succeed in Paris without Johnny. Although Bruno seems to have less sympathy for the women in Johnny's life, in many ways they seem to be hunted intensely, since Johnny has a tendency to abandon them once he has successfully caught them.

Cortázar uses these relationships and instances of pursuit in order to comment about more general themes. For example, one of his chief interests is in the relationship between the critic and the artist; critics like Bruno must pursue and clarify the truth or the nature of the artist so that the art itself can be comprehended. Critics are very often, like Bruno, successful in identifying key traits of the artwork while finding that some aspects of the artist and his/her work remain impenetrable. Similarly, artists like Johnny are constantly engaged in pursuing some of the basic values and assumptions of a society, trying desperately to open the door to a new understanding of the world. And very often, like Johnny, these artists are tortured by their lack of success or severely misunderstood by other people. Finally, the friendships and sexual relationships in Cortázar's story suggest that there is a common theme of hopelessness and inability to connect between lovers and friends in pursuit of one another.

Time and Metaphysics

Although Bruno has a tendency to dismiss Johnny's discussions of time after he is finished talking with him, these speculations are central to "The Pursuer." The story consistently questions the notion that time is linear or collective, and it often suggests that Johnny may not be crazy at all, but absolutely right about some or all of his convictions. In fact, many of his obsessive rants relate to some of the most pressing philosophical issues of the post–World War II era, particularly in the area of metaphysics, the branch of philosophy that deals with the "nature of reality." For example, Johnny's description of the realization that he is looking at himself in the mirror may relate to the French psychoanalyst and philosopher Jacques Lacan's theory of an infant's self-recognition during the "mirror stage." Also, Johnny's insistence that touching or cutting a loaf of bread "changes" it may be a reference to the influential idea that an observer cannot interact with the natural world without altering its properties—an idea used to support theories that it is impossible to make objective claims about the world.

Since Johnny is principally an artist and not a philosopher, Cortázar seems to be suggesting that art is somehow connected to this new understanding of time and metaphysics. As Bruno admits, Johnny's moments of true artistic genius, as reflected in the recording of *Amorous*, occur not when he is technically accurate but when he is most desperately fighting against convention and searching for an "outlet" in time and existence. Charlie Parker was perhaps most famous for his innovations with rhythm

Topics for Further Study

- Listen to some of Charlie Parker's recordings, such as *Confirmation: The Best of the Verve Years* (Polygram Records, 1995). What stands out to you about ''Bird,'' as Charlie Parker is often called? Listen to other saxophone players such as Lester Young (Parker's hero when he was young) and Cannonball Adderley. How is Bird's style different from Young's and that of other saxophonists popular in the 1930s? How does Bird's sound differ from that of his contemporaries such as Adderley? What does Bird's music have in common with the literary style of ''The Pursuer?'' Explain the similarities and differences.

- Read several short stories by the Argentine writer Jorge Luis Borges, such as ''The Garden of Forking Paths'' (1941). How does Cortázar compare to Borges, who was considered the master of Latin American fiction when Cortázar began writing? Do the compatriots have similar interests and do they explore similar themes? How are they different? What was the relationship of the two writers? Choose a Borges story and compare it to ''The Pursuer'' in theme, style, and subject matter.

- Research some of the French theorists that were influential during the 1950s, such as Jacques Lacan and Claude Lévi-Strauss. How would you describe their theories? What do they say about art, metaphysics and time? How do their theories relate to ''The Pursuer?'' Discuss what Cortázar's story says about psychology, philosophy, language, and time. How are these themes influenced by French critical theory from the 1950s? Which theories and theorists do you think are the most influential over the story?

- Cortázar was writing around the same time as the American ''Beat'' writers such as Allen Ginsberg and Jack Kerouac. Read some Beat poems or prose such as Kerouac's *On the Road*. What do the Beats have in common with Cortázar? How are they different? Consider the authors' philosophies, influences, approaches to music and other forms of culture, as well as styles, and themes in order to construct your answer.

---

and musical time, and bebop music is an appropriate metaphor for Cortázar's theme because it uniquely stretches the boundaries of the commonly accepted understanding of time.

Race

Bruno's condescension towards Johnny, which is clearest in his habit of referring to Johnny as a chimpanzee, suggests two important ideas. First, it emphasizes that Bruno uses racism as a way of dealing with his insecurity around Johnny. Bruno can feel better about himself and his "prestige" by convincing himself that because Johnny is a black man his "mental age does not permit him to understand" the biography's profundity. Second, the racism in the short story allows Cortázar to suggest that art critics make false judgments about racial inferiority, especially in such a black-dominated

medium as bebop music, in order to convince themselves that the art form is simple and straightforward. The author may be suggesting that such racist judgments and simplifications are delusional.

Style

Verb Tenses

The most important stylistic technique of "The Pursuer" is its unique use of past, present, and future verb tenses to narrate the story. Bruno does not follow any commonly accepted standard of dramatic unity or narrative structure and insists on using awkward verb structures. He most frequently uses the present perfect verb tense, a verb form that is usually used to discuss events that happened at an uncertain point between the past and present. "Dédée has called," "I have gone," and "We have recognized," are examples of the present perfect tense translated literally from the opening paragraphs of the story, and they suggest how the persistent use of this verb tense challenges the distinction between past and present.

It is vital to recognize the distinction between the literal Spanish version of the verb usage in "The Pursuer" and the version presented by the translator. The above quotes are not identical to the translation by Paul Blackburn, for example, and Doris Sommer suggests in her article "Pursuing a Perfect Present," that this is because the translator "refuses to respect the redundant awkwardness" of Cortázar's language. Blackburn's translation does shift into different tenses, but it avoids the repetitive use of the present tense of "haber," or "to have," ("he, has, ha, hemos, han") that is so striking in the original Spanish.

Cortázar has at least two reasons for employing this unique mode of storytelling. The first, as Sommer argues, is to imitate the improvisational genius of Charlie Parker's bebop music. Parker, like Johnny, was able to move in and out of normal understandings of time and rhythm in order to create an entirely new understanding of music. Also, the story's use of verb tenses reinforces Cortázar's questions on the nature of time and metaphysics (see above), as well as the relationship of these questions to art, music, and storytelling.

Biographical Fiction

Johnny Carter's character is in many ways meant to refer to the alto saxophonist Charlie Parker. In fact, the details of Johnny's life, including the years of his travels, his drug habits, his musical style, and his relationship with a rich friend and benefactor, suggest that Johnny may actually represent Charlie Parker. But "The Pursuer" uses a fictional medium to approach the famous jazz musician, and Johnny is presented as a fictional character, so in this sense the story is not strictly biographical fiction, but fiction inspired by real persons and events. As Cortázar makes clear by describing Bruno's biography of Johnny, telling the story of a person's life in the format of a biography often fails to actually capture someone's life. But the fictional dramatization of loosely biographical material reveals Cortázar's experimentation with a new and better way of recording the essence of a real person.

Historical Context

Bebop and Charlie Parker

Jazz began in the early years of the twentieth century as a combination of Western classical music and African American folk and blues music. Musicians such as Louis Armstrong soon became extremely popular with both white and black audiences, and by the time the "big band" era peaked in the 1930s, jazz was the mainstream music of the United States. Many black musicians began to be dissatisfied with the strict forms of big band or "swing" music during the 1940s, however, and bands with a new sound known as "bebop" began to earn a reputation because of their radical rhythms and experimental tonality.

Bebop bands were notable for their new style and distinct instrumentation, which they soon found worked better in small ensembles; they also were associated with a number of wider artistic and cultural movements, particularly after the big band era came to an end. Bebop was the musical form of the late 1940s and 1950s American and European counterculture; it occupied a very different political and racial climate, and it tended to be associated with artists, intellectuals, and big cities. Instead of mainstream dance music played in ballrooms and large restaurants, bebop music became associated with smoky nightclubs and musicians that ignored their audiences. Dixieland jazz and swing musicians such as Armstrong were so popular among whites, and made such an effort to please their white critics, that they developed a reputation among some black musicians as "Uncle Toms"—a label from Harriet Beecher Stowe's novel *Uncle Tom's Cabin* that was used to describe servile or accommodating blacks. Black bebop musicians, although they were popular with many whites, were often antagonistic to critics and had little interest in being a part of popular culture.

The most famous of the early bebop bands were those of Billy Eckstine and Dizzy Gillespie, and their popularity was in no small part due to the fact that they had hired an alto saxophonist from Kansas named Charlie Parker. One of the prodigious musi-

Compare & Contrast

- **1950s:** Bebop is the hip style of music in the big city. Listeners cram into nightclubs to hear the stars of the day improvise.

  Today: Live jazz is popular with an older crowd, and disc jockeys, playing everything from hip-hop to drum and bass, have taken over the nightclubs.

- **1950s:** Heroin, a highly addictive opiate, is the most dangerous of the illegal drugs popular with jazz musicians.

  Today: Heroin is still in use, although the potential danger to users is considerably greater because of the risks of contracting HIV (Human Immunodeficiency Virus) from shared intravenous needles and because the (street) purity of the drug is greater. According to the 2002 National Survey on Drug Use and Health, 1.6 percent of the United States population aged over twelve has tried heroin at least once.

- **1950s:** In Paris, a group of foreign artists and intellectuals congregate on the Left Bank of the Seine River to listen to music, sit in cafes, and discuss art and philosophy. They have become known as the second wave of the Lost Generation, a group of expatriates that came to Paris in the years following World War I.

  Today: Although Paris retains its reputation as one of the cultural capitals of the world, it is no longer as popular a destination for expatriate writers and musicians.

- **1950s:** Magical realism is an exciting new technique among prodigious Latin American writers like Cortázar and Gabriel García Márquez.

  Today: Latin American literature still tends to make use of myth and fantasy, but currently much critical interest is focused on previously neglected works by female authors and literature that focuses on women's issues.

---

cians of the twentieth century, Parker is often considered to have almost single-handedly created the style of bebop. Parker, later known as "Bird" or "Yardbird" throughout the jazz world, grew up in an abusive family and developed severe drug habits by the time he dropped out of school at fifteen. Although he never learned music formally, he practiced the alto saxophone constantly, emulated the tenor saxophonist Lester Young, and played in various groups in Kansas City, Chicago, and New York. In 1942 he made his first recordings, in 1944 he joined Billy Eckstine's band, and by 1945 he had changed jazz music forever.

Parker suffered a number of major breakdowns, due to his psychological illnesses and drug addictions, and spent a six-month term in a state hospital in 1946. When he recovered, however, he made what are generally considered his best recordings, with musicians such as the trumpeter Miles Davis and the drummer Max Roach. Parker's 1949 debut in Paris was a tremendous success, and during the

following five years he met with a mix of triumphs and disastrous failures due to his personal problems. In 1955, after traveling back to New York City, Parker had an ulcer attack in the room of his friend and benefactor Baroness "Nica" Ponnonica de Koenigswarter, and died three days later of complications due to heroin and alcohol abuse.

The Hispanic Avant-garde

Like Jorge Luis Borges, the Argentine author famous for his innovations in literature following the modernist movement, Cortázar was a member of a diverse group of writers and intellectuals known as "avant-garde" because of their departure from previous artistic styles and philosophies. Borges was already famous by the time Cortázar began writing, and he was a major influence over his countryman; in fact, Borges was the publisher of Cortázar's first short stories. Cortázar acknowledged this influence, particularly regarding Borges's challenging narratives, which resist traditional, linear understandings of time and space, and his interest in "intertextuality," the process by which texts refer not to the natural world or actual ideas, but solely to other texts.

While Borges was instrumental in the early development of some of these themes, Cortázar was one of the younger Hispanic avant-garde who were beginning their careers during the time when postmodernist ideas were in great vogue. In the years following World War II, French critical theorists such as the psychoanalyst Jacques Lacan were publishing their most influential theories, and the literary and cultural elite were rapidly moving away from the standards of modernism. While modernist writings tend to stress the unity of the work of art and frequently employ allegorical representation, postmodernist texts often call into question the very possibility of representation and highlight metaphysical problems, or problems that relate to the "nature of reality."

Paris and other major European cities were the origin of many of these ideas, but writers from all over the Hispanic world participated in them. One important new style that flowered in the 1940s and 1950s and was particularly Latin American in origin was "magical realism," or a fusion of fantasy and myth with realistic fiction. Like other writers of the Latin American avant-garde, Cortázar had a complex relationship with his home country of Argentina; Buenos Aires was never lost in his fiction and, on the contrary, became more important in much of his later writing. But he became associated with an international elite, and he never actually lived in Argentina after his departure for Paris in 1951.

Postwar Politics in France and Latin America

The 1950s was a decade of great turmoil in the French colonial world, as well as a decade of major political changes in the Hispanic world. By 1954, France had finally lost a costly war in colonial Indochina, and in 1958 a rebellion in Algeria by a combination of colonials and militarists effectively toppled the French government, resulting in Charles de Gaulle being called back to power as president of France. Meanwhile, in 1955, a military-civilian uprising in Argentina had overthrown President Perón (against whom Cortázar had protested) and begun a series of dictatorships. And the Cuban socialist revolution in 1959 was extremely influential over the left-wing Hispanic elite. These political events deeply influenced Cortázar, but their effect on the Parisian social world depicted in "The Pursuer" is unclear.

Critical Overview

Cortázar was not yet very well known when he published "The Pursuer" in 1959, and the story met with mixed reactions in the press. Stanley Kauffman, for example, called the story "outstandingly the worst [in *End of the Game, and Other Stories*]: a juvenile and crude story," in his *New Republic* review of the English translation, although Kauffman praised the other stories in the collection. As Cortázar developed a reputation as a masterful and influential writer, however, the story's reputation benefited, and it came to be considered one of his classic texts.

Some critical analyses of "The Pursuer" have tended to focus on its portrayal of Charlie Parker and bebop music, as well as its theme of the relationship between the artist and the critic. Robert W. Felkel, for example, suggests in his article "The Historical Dimension in Julio Cortázar's 'The Pursuer'" that Charlie Parker's life corresponds in almost every way to that of Johnny Carter. Other critics, such as Doris Sommer in her essay "Pursuing a Perfect Present," discuss the relationship of the critic and the artist as it relates to the story's innovations in narrative structure: "Bruno needs the unfettered genius as the featured subject of an academic career and the catalyst for his own probing performance, while Johnny needs Bruno's sensible attentions in order to survive."

Criticism

Scott Trudell

Trudell is a freelance writer with a bachelor's degree in English literature. In the following essay, Trudell explores the ways in which Cortázar's short story is a breakthrough in literary style and discusses how it reflects some of the new philosophies and artistic theories of the 1950s.

In her essay "Pursuing a Perfect Present," Doris Sommer observes that Cortázar's linguistic style in

Charlie Parker, seen here in 1945 at Billy Bergs Club in Hollywood, California, is the basis for the character Johnny Carter in Cortázar's ''The Pursuer''

"The Pursuer," including his repetitive use of the present perfect verb tense and his tendency to rapidly and often vaguely switch between the past, present, and future tenses, is partly a method of capturing the style of bebop music. Cortázar, himself a great fan of bebop, is clearly interested in applying some of the musical form's most important innovations to a literary context. He recognizes that the "terrible beauty" of a song like *Amorous* is an important artistic development, and his language is an attempt to translate the sense of this style into the form of a short story.

But this unique style is more than simply an emulation of bebop; it is a method of expressing a variety of philosophical and intellectual concepts for which bebop music serves as an excellent metaphor. Cortázar was part of a group of international artists and intellectuals who, in the years following World War II, were experimenting with new forms of expression and attempting to develop unique forms of art. The members of this group did not have a common agenda, and they did not necessarily employ a similar style, but they were often, like Cortázar, living in Paris and exploring new approaches to time, structure, and metaphysics in their writings. Influenced by postmodern theorists such as the psychoanalyst Jacques Lacan, they were largely dissatisfied both with the conventions of the modernist era and the mainstream culture of their time. "The Pursuer" is a prime example of a post-modern story that departs from such conventions and envisions artistic creation as a multi-layered and ultimately futile attempt to access a vague goal such as "reality."

With a growing reputation as a radical thinker and writer, Cortázar was quite self-conscious about the ways in which his fiction departed from previous forms. As the title of the story suggests, he is interested in the idea of a "pursuer," which could refer to any number of characters, seeking a variety of goals. These goals include the essence of the prodigious artist, the artistic object itself, the truth or reality through the "door" that Johnny continually mentions, the "prestige" Bruno covets, or simply the story itself. But one thing that the pursuers all have in common is a difficult and frustrating desire to achieve their goals. For Cortázar, the attempt to find this goal has much in common with one of Johnny's solos or one of his obsessive conundrums about time—which frustrate Johnny so thoroughly that he cries and shakes and goes over the edge.

In order to accentuate this theme, Cortázar has erected a number of barriers and layers in the story that lie between the pursuer and the pursued, and the reader continually confronts obstacles while attempting to discern what is actually happening. Indeed, one of the most important "pursuers" is the reader of the story, hunting through the text in order to discover its meaning. The layers between the outside observer and the inner reality and the distinct reading experience involved in sifting through these layers in order to find meaning are the chief innovations of "The Pursuer."

One of the first barriers the reader encounters, as well as one of the most important, is the divide between the fictional world of the story and the real world of the 1950s Parisian bebop scene, particularly the real life of Charlie Parker. Cortázar dedicates his story to Parker's memory and, as Robert Felkel argues in his article "The Historical Dimension in Julio Cortázar's 'The Pursuer,'" very few details of Johnny's life deviate from Parker's. However, while the reader naturally imagines that the story is an exploration of Parker's personal life, the

What Do I Read Next?

- Cortázar's most famous novel, *Hopscotch* (1963), is the story of an Argentine intellectual caught between the worlds of Buenos Aires and Paris. It is famous for its revolutionary narrative organization, which requires the reader to jump around the chapters, out of order, in order to read the novel. There are at least two sequences in which one can read the story, and this structure challenges linear notions of time and space.

- *Bird Lives!: The High Life and Hard Times of Charlie (Yardbird) Parker* (1996), by Ross Russell, is a compelling biography of Parker that explores his music without passing over his destructive and infamous personal life.

- Jorge Luis Borges, who was a major influence over Cortázar and probably the most influential Argentinian author of the twentieth century, published the short story "The Garden of Forking Paths" in 1941. Now available in Anthony Bonner's 1989 translation of *Ficciones*, "The Garden of Forking Paths" is a detective story as well as an exploration of time and metaphysics.

- *One Hundred Years of Solitude* (1967), by Gabriel García Márquez, is an entrancing novel of "magical realism," the style of Latin American writing sometimes associated with Cortázar. It depicts the history of a small Columbian town using myth and fantasy in combination with striking realistic detail.

---

entirely fictional pose of "The Pursuer" nevertheless prevents the reader from feeling as though he/she is actually pursuing the real bebop master. It is as though Cortázar dangles the actual biographical interest in front of the reader, suggesting that he is capturing Johnny's "me" as Bruno's biography cannot, yet refusing to completely remove the veil of a fiction. One of the most disorienting examples of this practice is the fact that Miles Davis, the famous jazz trumpeter who played with Parker, is a character mentioned in the story.

Cortázar's use of the traditional, analytical critic Bruno as the filter through whom the reader hears about Johnny's life is another example of an obstacle to the source of the reader's intrigue. Bruno's narration, which eventually falls into a clear past tense during the last section, continues to remind the reader that the critical and biographical eye is the sole access to imagining Johnny. Nevertheless, Bruno seems to allow the reader much closer to Johnny's real self and the essence of his musical talent than, presumably, his biography does, because Bruno exposes Johnny's desperate drug abuse problems and philosophical obsessions (Johnny's "me") in addition to his music. This is

another example of Cortázar's effort to vaguely suggest the goal and the meaning for which the reader is searching but deny full access to it.

The layer of critical distance, however, is perhaps less insistent than the stylistic barrier to "reality" formed by Cortázar's language. As Sommer notes her article in "Pursuing a Perfect Present," "The Pursuer" constantly draws attention to its departure from typical past tense narrative by using a "clumsy," "redundant," and "anxious present perfect tense." Not only does this throw the narrative into a confusing ambiguity about past, present, and future events; it acts as a barrier to the action, forcing the reader to think about how he/she is receiving information and question the "reality" of the story. This is clearer in the original Spanish version, since the translator Paul Blackburn has edited out some of the awkwardness in language. But the disorientation and ambiguity of Cortázar's style is perfectly clear, even in the English translation, in the scene of Johnny's breakdown at the cafe, which is introduced by the phrase, "Two empty weeks will pass." Beginning in the future tense, time rapidly becomes so ambiguous in the course of the evening that tenses even begin to change in the

> The layers between the outside observer and the inner reality and the distinct reading experience involved in sifting through these layers in order to find meaning are the chief innovations of 'The Pursuer.'"

middle of a thought: "My reaction is that human, I wanted to get Johnny up."

Sommer goes on to write that Bruno "may be serving as Johnny's instrument to be played on and with," and this is an important point not only for understanding the dynamic of their relationship, but for emphasizing that even the instrument of expression itself, the artistic tool without which the artist cannot express him/herself, is a barrier to the "real." The very object for which Johnny is famous, his saxophone, acts in Cortázar's story as simply another barrier between the reader and the essence of what the story is attempting to capture. Perhaps this is one reason Johnny continually loses his saxophone; he desires to be taken not simply for his music but for himself. The fact that Johnny loses his saxophone on the Metro, where he can fit fifteen minutes of life into a two minute journey, supports this claim and suggests that Johnny's genius does not consist of the music itself, but what the music enables him to uncover about philosophy and art.

The solo of the bebop musician is the central metaphor of "The Pursuer" and, in many ways, the most important way in which Cortázar allows his reader to visualize his new style of fiction. So it is quite important to note that this artistic effort is characterized by such frustration and even futility in its ability to discover its goal and successfully find what it is seeking. Throughout the story, Cortázar portrays bebop with terms like "interminable," "continuous," and "infinite"; he is careful to emphasize that it is multi-layered and endless:

Incapable of satisfying itself, useful as a continual spur, an infinite construction, the pleasure of which is not its highest pinnacle but in the exploratory repeti-

tions, in the use of faculties which leave the suddenly human behind without losing humanity.

This description, particularly the phrase "infinite construction," is an excellent paraphrase of the new aesthetic ideas of the 1950s. Cortázar takes bebop music as his subject, chooses a musician nicknamed because his music is as elusive and free as a "bird," and portrays Johnny as a hunter "with no arms and legs" who is constantly unable to find what he is seeking, because this is the best way to represent the postmodern "infinite construction" that the author saw as literature's new direction. "The Pursuer" is a radical work of art because it erects so many barriers between the pursuer and the pursued that—it becomes clear—these barriers are endless. More than the particulars of Johnny's new and unique vision of the world, this stylistic development is the story's major contribution to the period's changing philosophies of art and narrative.

Source: Scott Trudell, Critical Essay on "The Pursuer," in *Short Stories for Students*, Gale, 2005.

Liz Brent

Brent holds a Ph.D. in American culture from the University of Michigan. In this essay, Brent discusses religious symbolism in Cortazar's "The Pursuer."

Cortázar's short story "The Pursuer" is narrated by jazz critic Bruno V., who recounts his experiences with a brilliant but self-destructive jazz saxophonist by the name of Johnny Carter. Bruno's narrative is an attempt to make up for the element that was "missing" from his published biography of Johnny. As Johnny tells Bruno, "what you forgot to put in is me."

In Bruno's attempt to capture the essence of Johnny that was left out of his biography of the jazz musician, he makes many references to God, angels, devils, and religion. Johnny is repeatedly described by Bruno as a sort of angel or a god. Ultimately, Bruno represents Johnny as a Christlike figure who suffers for the sins of mankind, and his own role as that of a preacher, whose task is to testify to the spiritually transcendent power of Johnny's music.

Bruno struggles to express the essence of what makes Johnny and his music so awe-inspiring. In the process, he explores a number of different explanations of the phenomenon of Johnny. Throughout "The Pursuer," Bruno makes frequent reference to both angels and devils in describing Johnny and his music. He describes Johnny as "this angel who's like my brother, this brother who's like my angel." At another point in the story Bruno states, "I really feel like saying straight off that Johnny is some kind of angel come down among men," and then, in the same sentence, suggests, "maybe what is really happening is that Johnny is a man among angels, one reality among the unrealities that are the rest of us."

However, Johnny is also referred to in terms that associate him with hell and the devil. Bruno describes Johnny's "supreme indifference" to the wellbeing of those around him, stating, "Johnny doesn't give a good [g——d——] if everything goes to hell." Bruno later describes Johnny as a devil, commenting, "Anyone can be like Johnny if he just resigns himself to being a poor devil." And Johnny likewise describes himself as "a poor devil . . . with more plagues than the devil under his skin."

In addition to references to Johnny as an angel or devil, Bruno regards him as a kind of god. In describing the effect of Johnny's music on him, Bruno asserts, "he played like I imagine only a god can play an alto sax, given that they quit using lyres and flutes." Later, Art, another musician, describes Johnny's astounding performance during a recording session in terms of his godlike qualities, asserting, "If God was anywhere yesterday, I think it was in that damned recording studio where it was as hot as ten thousand devils." Art goes on to describe Johnny's greatest moment of musical brilliance as a spiritually transcendent experience, telling Bruno, "all of a sudden he lets go with a blast, could of split the . . . celestial harmonies."

That Bruno regards Johnny's musical abilities as godlike is further expressed when he struggles to describe the awe-inspiring effect of Johnny's live performance at a club one night, observing,

> I think I understand why prayer demands instinctively that one fall on one's knees. The change of position is a symbol of the change in the tone of voice, in what the voice is about to articulate, in the diction itself.

Bruno thus regards his own role as jazz critic as that of a devout worshipper prostrating himself before the awesome power of Johnny's music. Bruno's attitude of religious faith in his deification of Johnny is echoed in the first scene of the story, when Bruno comes to visit Johnny, who describes him as "faithful old buddy Bruno."

While Johnny is described variously as an angel, devil, or god, Bruno also describes Johnny's followers as angels of a sort. In one part of the story,

> **"** Bruno ultimately comes to regard Johnny as a Christ-like figure, whose music offers a form of spiritual transcendence to his listeners, while his self-destructive behaviors represent a Christ-like form of suffering for the sins of others."

Bruno refers to the group of musicians and their friends who congregate around Johnny as "sick angles, irritating in their irresponsibility, but ultimately valuable to the community." Later, Bruno refers to *himself* as an archangel, when he describes a group of friends who gather around him when he enters the room "as if I were the archangel himself." Thus, Bruno paints an allegorical picture of Johnny as a godlike figure, his friends and supporters as angels, and himself as the archangel, a sort of right-hand man to Johnny as god.

Other references to spirituality, religion, and god within the story are less direct. Bruno, for example, describes Johnny and two of his friends who greet each other by "exchanging . . . a complicated onomatopoetic ritual which made everybody feel great." This reference to ritual in relation to Johnny resonates with the narrator's representation of Johnny as a spiritual being who somehow transcends everyday humanity and whose followers engage in ritualistic forms of worship in his presence.

Bruno ultimately comes to regard Johnny as a Christ-like figure, whose music offers a form of spiritual transcendence to his listeners, while his self-destructive behaviors represent a Christ-like form of suffering for the sins of others. Late in the story, Bruno describes Johnny's role among his friends and listeners as that of a religious martyr, who provides a spiritual cleansing of the world by suffering for the sins of mankind. Bruno remarks,

> every time Johnny gets hurt, goes to jail, wants to kill himself, sets a mattress on fire or runs naked down the

corridors of a hotel, he's paying off something for them, he's killing himself for them. Without knowing it, and not like he was making great speeches from the gallows or writing books denouncing the evils of mankind or playing the piano with the air of someone washing away the sins of the world.

Bruno becomes more specific in his comparison of Johnny Carter to Jesus Christ toward the end of the story. One night at a café, Johnny, who is distraught over the recent death of his daughter, goes down on his knees in front of Bruno in a burst of tears. Bruno, embarrassed by this public display, tries to get Johnny to sit down in a chair. He describes the reactions of the other people in the café, noting, "they all look at me as if they were looking at someone climbing up on the altar to tug Christ down from his cross."

Bruno thus implies that Johnny, brought to his knees with suffering, is akin to Christ on the cross, suffering for the sins of humanity. Further, the onlookers seem to derive some comfort or satisfaction from Johnny's display of suffering, and thus resent Bruno's efforts to end this display, just as, the narrator suggests, people derive a kind of comfort from the religious martyrdom of Jesus Christ.

Even Johnny Carter's initials—J. C.—align him with the figure of Jesus Christ. Other ways in which Bruno's narrative equates Johnny Carter with Jesus Christ include such details as Johnny's showing Bruno "what a pretty scar I got between my ribs." As Jesus is often portrayed on crucifixes with a knife wound in his chest, this comment subtly reinforces the narrator's representation of Johnny as a Christ-like figure. Later, Johnny refers to the "holes" in his hands, an image which evokes the stigmata of Christ, whose hands were nailed to the cross.

While Bruno describes Johnny's music in religious terms, Johnny describes his own relationship to organized religion as contentious. In explaining his childhood to Bruno, he equates both his parents' fights over money (specifically, over their home mortgage) with the religion they imposed upon him as aspects of his childhood that he found unbearable. Johnny tells Bruno that, when he plays the saxophone, he is able to find temporary relief from the stresses of "the mortgage and the religion."

Toward the end of the story, Johnny in fact openly objects to Bruno's description of his music in terms of God and religion, angrily criticizing such references in Bruno's biography of him. He tells Bruno, "I don't want your God, he's never been mine." Johnny continues,

> Why've you made me accept [your God] in your book? I don't know if there's a God, I play my music, I make my God, I don't need your inventions.

Johnny further asserts that he resents Bruno's imposing of religious connotations on his music, telling him, "If I play and you see angels, that's not my fault."

While he regards Johnny as a Christ-like figure, Bruno regards himself as a sort of priest or proselytizer, spreading the gospel of Johnny Carter. "I'm beginning to compare myself to a preacher," he says. According to this metaphor, Bruno's biography of Johnny may be regarded as a biblical text, describing the religious message he derives from Johnny's music. After heavily criticizing Bruno's references to religion in his biography, Johnny ironically refers to the biography as "the good book," which is a phrase generally used in reference to the Bible. Johnny thus mocks Bruno's representation of his music as a religious phenomenon.

Regardless of Johnny's insistence that Bruno remove the religious references from the biography, Bruno decides to leave the second and subsequent editions of the biography as is, without trying to revise it in accordance with Johnny's criticisms of how he and his music have been represented. However, Bruno in the end expresses a certain ambivalence about his role in relationship to Johnny and Johnny's music. He questions the validity and value of his own methods of preaching the message delivered by Johnny through his music, when he asks himself, "What kind of preacher am I?"

Source: Liz Brent, Critical Essay on "The Pursuer," in *Short Stories for Students*, Gale, 2005.

Carey Wallace

Wallace is a writer and poet. In this essay, Wallace maps Cortázar's explosion of the categories of writer and character as well as his exploration of the entire project of writing.

An artist of great talent must, at some point, make a choice. One can stay comfortably, and probably successfully, within the borders of one's art as they have already been mapped. Or one can strike out into uncharted waters, unknown lands.

Julio Cortázar was a writer of great talent. Even before the publication of his first book of stories, *Bestiary*, his name was familiar to other Latin

American greats such as Jorge Luis Borges, widely regarded as the father of Latin American realism, and an early publisher of the young Cortázar. In *Bestiary*, Cortázar played with the limits of realistic fiction, introducing elements of the fantastic into his sketches, in the tradition of the French surrealists and of Borges himself. But by the time Cortázar began work on his next collection, which would appear in English as *The End of the Game*, he could no longer be satisfied with writing again as he had already written.

"When I wrote "The Pursuer,'" Jaime Alazraki quotes him as saying in *The Review of Contemporary Fiction*, "I had reached a point where I felt I had to deal with something that was a lot closer to me. I wasn't sure of myself anymore in that story. . . . Fantasy itself had stopped interesting me. By then I was fully aware of the dangerous perfection of the storyteller who reaches a certain level of achievement and stays on that same level forever, without moving on. I was a bit sick and tired of seeing how well my stories turned out. In 'The Pursuer' I wanted to stop inventing and stand on my own ground, to look at myself a bit."

Cortázar turns his own lens on himself through the character of Bruno, a jazz critic living in Paris at the time the action of "The Pursuer" unfolds. Bruno has made his name with a book on Johnny Carter, a brilliant alto saxophonist closely modeled on Charlie "Bird" Parker. Like Cortázar's collection of stories, Bruno's biography has met with critical success—a success that is most deeply threatened by Carter himself, who both exceeds the limits of Bruno's descriptive skills with his brilliance and endangers Bruno's purely aesthetic portrait of him with his raw humanity. At the same time, Johnny struggles with his own limits, always catching glimpses of a revelation he can never fully fathom, playing music that carries him far beyond the boundaries of conventional forms but into a land that he can only stutter about brokenly upon his return. In drawing the complicated friendship between the two men, Cortázar examines the strained relationship between any author and any character, and finally turns his light on the cracks in the base of literature itself. In many ways, "The Pursuer" is a manifesto, not just on the limits of a fictional jazz critic's ability to describe a fictional musician, but on the ability of modern literature to describe the great mystery of this life and what may lay behind or beyond it—a mystery Cortázar himself would spend the rest of his literary life pursuing, with some of the most highly experimental work of the century.

> [The character of Johnny Carter is] every character who ever begged a writer to give him a heart strong enough, lungs real enough, to truly breathe. He's every reader who ever depended on a writer to express for him . . . the only thing he's ever really wanted to say. . . ."

"The Pursuer" opens with a conversation about limits—not Bruno's, but Johnny's. Johnny is fascinated by the glimpse of transcendence he gets through his music, and profoundly frustrated by his inability to put it into words. So he turns to Bruno, whose art is working with words, for help. "Bruno, maybe someday you'll write" he says, before launching into an attempt at describing the way time stops and the known world fades for him when he plays. And Bruno is able to help him communicate, to a point, translating Johnny's almost incomprehensible assertion that "I'm playing that tomorrow" into clear, even lyrical, critical language: "Johnny is always blowing tomorrow, and the rest of them are chasing his tail, in this today he just jumps over, effortlessly, with the first notes of his music." But after this foray into capturing Johnny through criticism, Bruno offers the first hint of his own limitations: "I realize that what I'm thinking is on a lower level than where poor Johnny is trying to move forward with his decapitated sentences, his sighs, his impatient anger and his tears." This is the central tension of the story: Bruno is able, again and again, to translate Johnny's speech, which often borders on nonsense, back into comprehensible language. But he is always left with the sense that he has, perhaps, lost something in the translation, that he has not gone with Johnny over the boundaries, merely brought him back. It is a tension that Johnny uses to torment him, even in this early conversation. "It's easy to explain," he tells Bruno, "But it's easy because it's not the right answer. The right answer simply can't be explained."

Bruno's help may not actually help Johnny much. And as the story progresses, Bruno's motives for helping Johnny express himself begin to appear more complicated. When Johnny descends into another round of addiction and debauchery, his fellow musicians, patrons, and critics gather round, ostensibly to protect him from himself. But in a moment of clarity, Bruno realizes that "under the pretext of watching out for Johnny what we're really doing is protecting our idea of him. . . . All this has nothing to do with the other Johnny . . . Johnny with no horn, Johnny with no money and no clothes, Johnny obsessed by something his intelligence was not equal to comprehending." Bruno, and his friends, have made a character out of Johnny—one they all need, for various reasons. Their problem is that Johnny is still a living man, still capable of defying everything they think, or have written, about him.

It is a problem that every writer who works with true characters, with the crazily unpredictable winds and sparks of real life, should have. And it is an especially tempting problem for a writer of great talent, who can easily hide his small cheats, his capitulations to tradition and cliché, to solve forever by creating an airtight literary world, without surprises or true complications, in which he can move his characters like wonderfully-made dolls. Watching Johnny's descent, Bruno, and perhaps Cortázar, recognizes this tendency in himself, writing, "I prefer the words to the reality that I'm trying to describe."

But unlike a writer of fiction, whose success or failure in portraying a character can be measured finally only in their own hearts, Bruno the critic has the opportunity, or the punishment, of coming face to face with the man he has tried to capture in his now-famous biography. Johnny has not forgotten his early hope, that Bruno's talent for words will somehow help him to speak what for him is unspeakable. When he first brings up his own biography, Johnny refers to a clumsy metaphor he used in the story's initial conversation, in which he described being shocked to see his own reflection in a mirror, and his sense that the man looking back could not possibly be him. It is an almost universal moment: a person's recognition of everything in oneself that a mirror cannot reflect. And Johnny hopes that Bruno, with words at his command, may have some way to express what the mirror cannot. "At first I thought that to read something that'd been written about you would be more like looking at

yourself and not into a mirror," he says. But, he adds, Bruno's book is missing something.

Bruno, terrified by Johnny's criticism, which, voiced to the wrong person, could ruin his career, retorts, "What more do you want? Mirrors give faithful reflections." And then, frightened and infuriated by the effect the living man could have on his static portrait of him, Bruno admits, "Sure, there are moments when I wish he was already dead." But for Bruno, and for any writer, the death of a living man, or the stifling of a living character, will not really solve the problems they are capable of causing. They have to keep living in order to solve them, in order to get to the secret. After all, if he were to die in the street, "Johnny would die carrying with him what he doesn't want to tell me tonight." The dead man, the static character, may be controllable—but he also offers no revelation, no glimpse into the mystery.

Johnny, after a moment, is ready to let the discussion of Bruno's book pass, but Bruno cannot let it go at that. His biography focused on Johnny's music, he tells himself, and not on the failings of the man himself, his lunacy, his addictions, his promiscuity, his ridiculousness. If anything, he was protecting Johnny. What was wrong with the book? What was missing? Bruno asks. What did I forget?

"What you forgot to put in is me," Johnny tells him. "A man can't say anything, right away you translate it into your filthy language. . . . Old Bruno writes down everything in his notebook that you say, except the important things."

His statement is an indictment of Bruno's writing, but it could very well be an indictment of Cortázar himself, and of any writer with the facility to easily trap a caricature on a page, while ignoring the more grueling work of building a language and a literature with the capability of conveying a whole life, or a whole character.

For Cortázar, the character of Johnny Carter in "The Pursuer" is not simply a jazz musician at odds with his critic. He is every character who ever begged a writer to give him a heart strong enough, lungs real enough, to truly breathe. He is every reader who ever depended on a writer to express for him the one thing he has never known how to put into words, the only thing he has ever really wanted to say, the only thing that means anything. And Cortázar's Carter is bigger than all of these: he stands for the mystery of life itself, for everything that is not there when you glance back, for all the glimpses of glory, for all the filth in the streets, for everything that does not make sense the first time, for everything that cannot be captured easily. And Carter insists, again and again, that Bruno's efforts—and by extension, Cortázar's—have not yet, have never, in fact, been enough for him.

Bruno cannot rise to Johnny's challenge. After Johnny's death, he slaps together a quick obituary in time for the second printing of his false biography, further cementing Johnny in the jazz pantheon in which Bruno insists he belongs, and further obscuring the real man and his tortuous, failed search.

But for Cortázar, "The Pursuer" is a point of departure. Cortázar takes up Johnny's search himself and runs it down for the rest of his life. The question of what lies beyond the closed door, what is really glimpsed in those moments of revelation, will haunt the balance of the literature he produces, and Cortázar's quest to find new ways of stalking and revealing the secret will lead him to generate some of the most successful experimental prose of his century—and, some might even argue, in history. Johnny's suspicions and strife may be lost on his fictional critic, but, in the end, his struggle infects the actual writer who created both musician and critic. Cortázar claims Carter's struggle as his own. And unlike Bruno, in his future work he breaks free from the stifling perfection of his early successes, and takes his readers with him into the outer reaches of literature's unmapped borderlands.

Source: Carey Wallace, Critical Essay on "The Pursuer," in *Short Stories for Students*, Gale, 2005.

Peter Standish

In the following essay, Standish examines "The Pursuer" as an important milestone in Cortázar's writing, calling it "the deepest exploration yet of what it is to be authentic."

In Pursuit of Oneself

For quite different reasons, "El perseguidor" (The pursuer) and "Las babas del diablo" (Devil's spittle), two of the stories included in *Las armas secretas* (1959), were to prove to be milestones in Cortázar's development as a writer; thematically, both can be said to mark the path toward his *magnum opus,* the novel *Rayuela* (*Hopscotch*).

On one level "El perseguidor" is a sentimental homage to jazz, specifically to one of its great

> **''** 'El perseguidor' was, he said, the beginning of a new phase of awareness of his fellow man. Ultimately, it would lead him into political involvement."

exponents, Charlie Parker: hence the story's dedication "*In memoriam* CH. P" ("CH" rather than "C" because the former used to have the status of a separate letter in the Spanish alphabet). Cortázar reincarnates Parker in the personage of a self-destructive drug addict called Johnny, a man whose behavior imperils his career and places a great burden on those around him, for he is volatile and frequently abusive. Yet he can also be tender, and when playing his saxophone he comes into his own, so much so that he seems godlike. It is through the free forms of jazz that Johnny, who otherwise appears to be incoherent, disorderly, and unappealing, finds a true way of expressing himself. In daily life, he is attended and protected by his wife and by his biographer, a music critic called Bruno. Bruno narrates the story, and in the course of it reveals how equivocal his attitude to Johnny is, because he serves and protects him, but he is motivated by a mixture of human concern and self-interest; after all, Johnny's life is Bruno's living.

Among the Cortázar stories published prior to this time few had been cast in so realistic a mold. "Los venenos" (The poisons), included in the first edition of *Final del juego* (1956), is something of an exception. That story, a good part of which is autobiographical, delves quite deeply into human sentiments. "El perseguidor" is also remarkable for its concentration on personal, human concerns. In his interview with González Bermejo, Cortázar would later acknowledge that a transformation had come over him when he moved to Paris, a transformation that is reflected in "El perseguidor," for the story revolves around character, rather than vice versa. Although the earlier Cortázar (the Cortázar of *Bestiario* and *Final del juego*) had created believable characters and had felt personally involved with some of them, he had been at least as concerned with aesthetic matters and had sometimes sacrificed character development in favor of narrative effects. "El perseguidor" reflects the fact that Cortázar had, by the time he wrote it, been living in Paris for some years, and his life there had been much more intense, more filled with human experiences than the somewhat bookish and withdrawn one he had led in Buenos Aires. The emotional and intellectual readjustment represented by the move to Paris, his "road to Damascus," had generated a feeling that what was bothering him had to be expressed in writing.

Though faithful in many ways to the biography of Parker, Cortázar projects onto Johnny some of his own preoccupations, such as his suspicion vis-à-vis our concept of time, the feeling that the *métro* is an environment that invites different modes of perception, and the belief that music may allow one to express what language will not. The main interest in the story centers on the dynamics between Johnny and Bruno although the contrast between them is not as clear as one might at first be tempted to assume. Moreover, we should note that the title in Spanish is ambiguous—"The pursuer" or "The persecutor." It is not at all clear that it refers only to the musician. In his music, Johnny is the pursuer of something that cannot be defined, something that Bruno's more intellectual mind can only glimpse, something that has to do with personal authenticity and self-expression. Although Bruno seems genuinely concerned about the way in which Johnny is destroying himself and wasting such talent, he pursues him out of professional interest, rather as *paparazzi* pursue the objects of their attention. Delving into his own motives, Bruno asks himself how far he is really concerned about Johnny's life. Isn't he really worried that Johnny might go his own way and end up undermining Bruno's conclusions in his book? Johnny is difficult, even incoherent, in his dealings with others, and yet, paradoxically, he provokes in Bruno a reaction that is at once patronizing and awestruck.

Bruno is always aware of the task that faces him as biographer and makes a number of references to his difficulties in writing. Except in the closing paragraphs of this long story, he insistently (and unusually, although perhaps one might ascribe it to the influence of French) uses the perfect tense, as if to remind the reader that this is a biography in the making, its subject as protean as are the means to capture it. Ironically, perhaps it is Johnny who expresses that particular dimension most clearly: "No one can say anything without you immediately translating it into your own filthy language." It is as if Johnny were warning that once language takes over and the biography is published the "truth" is fixed, and falsified in the process.

According to comments he made three decades later to Prego, for years prior to writing "El perseguidor" Cortázar had felt "pursued" by the idea of writing a story in which he would confront himself; already familiar with Charlie Parker's music, he settled on him as the focus for the story when, following Parker's death, Cortázar read a brief biography of him in a newspaper. This leads one to wonder what motivated Cortázar to call his protagonist Johnny Carter. A musicological explanation might be that it combines parts of the names of two other well-known saxophone players, Johnny Hodges and Benny Carter. Another explanation follows from the idea that in this story Cortázar is in some sense confronting himself: in other words, CH. P. becomes J. C. in order to allude to Julio Cortázar. This equivalence, however, must not be taken too literally, for it is clear that Cortázar is in Bruno as much as in Johnny. Thirdly, the initials perhaps allude to that most famous of persecuted people, Jesus Christ. Critics have been quick to notice a plethora of religious references in "El perseguidor," ranging from the description of Johnny as a god or an angel or a devil, to Bruno calling himself an evangelist or one of the damned, to the fact that Johnny calls attention to a wound in his side, or the fact that Bruno goes down on his knees before him, or the fact that the epigraph taken from the Apocalypse is associated with John, or the fact that there are some phrases and images in the story that have a biblical ring to them. This is not to imply for a moment that Cortázar sees himself in Christian terms; rather, Christianity provides a cultural framework that is exploited in the construction of the narrative, suggesting that the story's implications extend beyond the author's self-exploration to encompass all of humanity. It is important, however, to realize that one cannot read this story in terms of the simple dialectic opposition of the divine versus the evil.

Johnny and Bruno are complex, overlapping characters, both of whom may be assumed to reflect certain personal characteristics or concerns of the author. One becomes aware of these complexities, of the ethical grayness, so to speak, and, perhaps for that reason, when Johnny dies and Bruno declares the biography complete and final, one has an uncomfortable feeling of escapism, of matters being too tidily resolved. As Bruno puts it at the funeral: "The biography was, so to speak, finished. Perhaps I shouldn't be saying that, but naturally I'm just seeing it from an aesthetic angle."

Many of Cortázar's stories were written in a single sitting, but "El perseguidor" was begun in Paris, halted by writer's block for some three months, and finished during a visit to Switzerland. By Cortázar's standards it is long, even rambling, and lacks the economy and drive that characterizes most of his stories. That said, its importance is not to be underestimated. Above all, this story is important for its themes: in "El perseguidor" we have the deepest exploration yet of what it is to be authentic, of the tension between opposites, of intellect versus instinct, of order versus spontaneity, all of these being matters that will be fully explored later on, especially in *Rayuela*. The author told Evelyn Picón Garfield that some time after the appearance of *Rayuela* he came to realize that its protagonist and Johnny had much in common and that, had he not written the story, he would never have been able to write the novel. "El perseguidor" was, he said, the beginning of a new phase of awareness of his fellow man. Ultimately, it would lead him into political involvement.

Source: Peter Standish, "The Stories," in *Understanding Julio Cortazar*, University of South Carolina Press, 2001, pp. 27–30.

Sources

Alazraki, Jaime, "From *Bestiary* to *Glenda*: Pushing the Short Story to It's Utmost Limits," in the *Review of Contemporary Fiction*, Vol. 3, No 3, Fall 1983.

Cortázar, Julio, "The Pursuer," in *End of the Game and Other Stories*, translated by Paul Blackburn, 1963, reprint, Lowe & Brydone, 1968, pp. 182–247.

Felkel, Robert W., "The Historical Dimension in Julio Cortázar's 'The Pursuer,'" in *Latin American Literary Review*, Vol. 14, Spring-Summer 1979, pp. 20–27.

Kauffman, Stanley, Review of *End of the Game and Other Stories*, in *Modern Latin American Literature*, Frederick Ungar Publishing, 1975, p. 264; originally published in *New Republic*, July 15, 1967, p. 22.

Sommer, Doris, "Pursuing a Perfect Present," in *Julio Cortázar: New Readings*, Cambridge University Press, 1998, pp. 211–36.

Further Reading

Alazraki, Jaime, ed., *Critical Essays on Julio Cortázar*, G. K. Hall, 1999.
  Alazraki is one of the leading scholars on Cortázar and provides a diverse collection of essays about a wide range of the author's work.

Alazraki, Jaime, and Ivar Ivask, eds., *The Final Island: The Fiction of Julio Cortázar*, University of Oklahoma Press, 1978.
  The essays anthologized in this book are by the best and most influential of Cortázar's critics.

Garfield, Evelyn Picon, *Julio Cortázar*, Ungar, 1975.
  Based on interviews with Cortázar, Garfield's book is one of the most important critical commentaries on the author that is written in English.

Hodeir, André, *Jazz, It's Evolution and Essence*, translated by David Noakes, Grove Press, 1956.
  Hodeir, a biographer and critic largely grouped with the 1950s Parisian literati, is in many ways a model for Bruno. His analysis of jazz music, originally published in French in 1954, is most famous for the light it sheds on Charlie Parker.

Saint Emmanuel the Good, Martyr

Miguel de Unamuno

1933

Miguel de Unamuno was one of the most highly celebrated and widely influential Spanish intellectuals of the twentieth century. In "San Manuel Bueno, martir" (1933; "Saint Emmanuel the Good, Martyr"), the story of a priest without faith, Unamuno grapples with his lifelong questioning of received religious and philosophical ideas.

"Saint Emmanuel the Good, Martyr" is narrated as a memoir of Angela Carballino, a woman in her fifties who reflects back upon her family's experiences with Don Emmanuel, the priest of their remote mountain village. At the time of her writing, the Catholic Church has begun the process of proclaiming Don Emmanuel a saint. In her confessional story, Angela reveals Don Emmanuel's true attitudes about religion. Over the years, during which she and her brother Lazarus become close associates of Don Emmanuel, his secret loss of faith in God is revealed to them. Angela's memoir reveals a complex paradox at the heart of the priest's outward devotion and inner loss of faith.

"Saint Emmanuel the Good, Martyr" explores religious and philosophical questioning about the meaning of life and death. Unamuno describes the experience of the man without faith as one of solitude, loneliness, and despair, while he suggests that religious faith is merely an illusion, maintained by the common man as a means of comfort against the desolation of a world without God or Heaven.

Author Biography

Miguel de Unamuno (y Jugo) was born September 29, 1864, in the port city of Bilbao, located in the Basque region of Spain. When he was six years old, his father died. At sixteen, he enrolled in the University of Madrid, completing his Ph.D. in philosophy by the age of twenty. Unamuno obtained a position as professor of Greek at the University of Salamanca in 1891. At this time, he married a young woman from his home town, with whom he had ten children. In 1901, he was appointed to the prestigious position of rector of the University of Salamanca.

While continuing to teach and serve as rector, Unamuno published numerous stories, poems, and essays. He became associated with the Generation of 1898, a set of writers whose works grapple with questions of Spain's national identity in the modern world. Unamuno's first volume of essays, *En torno al casticismo* (*On Authentic Tradition*), was published in 1902. *Vida de Don Quixote y Sancho* (1905; *The Life of Don Quixote and Sancho*), a literary analysis, is one of his greatest works. The essay collection *Del sentimiento tragico de la vida en los hombres y en los pueblos* (1913; *The Tragic Sense of Life*), his best known work, expresses the fundamental ideas of his personal philosophy. Unamuno's greatest novel, *Abel Sanchez* (1917), is a modern retelling of the biblical story of Cain and Abel. His greatest work of poetry, *El Cristo de Velazquez* (1920; *The Christ of Velazquez*), is a book-length blank verse poem based on a painting of the crucifixion of Christ by the seventeenth-century Spanish artist Diego Velazquez.

During World War I, when Spain claimed official neutrality, Unamuno was an outspoken supporter of the Allied forces. Because of his political differences with conservative pro-German elements within the university, he was removed from his post as rector in 1914 but was later reinstated. Unamuno again met with trouble over his political views in 1924, soon after the dictator Primo de Rivera rose to power in Spain. Because of his outspoken opposition to Rivera, Unamuno was forced into exile, without his family, on Fuerteventura, one of the Canary Islands. Friends soon arranged for him to secretly escape to France, where he lived until Rivera was removed from power in 1930. As a writer in political exile, Unamuno became a cause célèbre, and his international reputation as an important contributor to modern thought and letters increased. Upon returning to Salamanca, he soon

Miguel de Unamuno

resumed his post as professor and rector of the university.

During the period of Spain's Second Republic, from 1931 to 1936, Unamuno worked at the university and published his writings without encountering political difficulties. His story "Saint Emmanuel the Good, Martyr" (1933) was published during this period. In 1936, in the early stages of the Spanish Civil War, Unamuno was in favor of the Nationalist rebel forces, led by Francisco Franco. However, when he changed his political views and publicly criticized the Nationalist rebellion, Franco had him put under house arrest. Two months later, on December 31, 1936, the seventy-two-year-old Unamuno died of a heart attack.

Plot Summary

"Saint Emmanuel the Good, Martyr" is narrated by Angela Carballino. In a private memoir, Angela describes her changing perceptions of Don Emmanuel, the parish priest of a small mountain village in Spain, where she grew up and lived throughout most of her life. Angela explains that the bishop of the diocese of Renada is initiating the process of beatification of Don Emmanuel, now that he is dead. Over the course of the story, Angela describes how she came to learn the secret of Don Emmanuel's soul.

Angela explains that Don Emmanuel was her "spiritual father." Her mother, like everyone in the village, worships and loves Don Emmanuel. Angela's brother Lazarus lives and works in America, and sends money to support Angela and her mother. When she is ten years old, Angela is sent to a convent school.

Angela leaves the convent school at the age of sixteen and returns to her village. She notes that the whole life of the village by this time revolves around Don Emmanuel. Don Emmanuel is a very active participant in the daily life of the community, sometimes working in the fields alongside the peasants, sometimes accompanying the doctor on his rounds, sometimes helping to teach at the village school. He counsels troubled families, comforts the sick, aids the poor, cares for the children, and attends to the dying. Blasillo, a man in the village who is mentally retarded, becomes especially attached to Don Emmanuel.

As a young woman, Angela helps Don Emmanuel with his various tasks and duties in the church and the community. When she is almost twenty-four, her brother Lazarus returns from America. Lazarus has been influenced by his experiences away from the village and is disdainful of the religious faith of the peasants and their reliance on Don Emmanuel. Lazarus openly expresses atheistic, anti-religious sentiments. But after he goes to hear one of Don Emmanuel's sermons, and learns of his role in the community, Lazarus comes to respect the priest.

Simona, the mother of Angela and Lazarus, becomes mortally ill. As she is on her deathbed, she asks Lazarus to promise that he will pray for her after she is gone. Lazarus is at first resistant, because he is a non-believer, but Don Emmanuel convinces him to make this promise to his mother. After his mother's death, Lazarus begins spending more and more time with Don Emmanuel, taking walks with him along the lake and discussing questions of religious faith and doubt. Before long, Lazarus starts to attend mass on a regular basis.

Lazarus eventually takes holy communion from Don Emmanuel, which the villagers happily interpret as a sign that his atheism has been converted to faith. After the communion, however, Lazarus confesses in private to Angela the true nature of Don Emmanuel's attitudes about religion. He explains that Don Emmanuel convinced him to pretend to believe in God for the sake of the villagers and to keep his religious doubts to himself. When Lazarus asked Don Emmanuel if he truly believes in God, the priest indicated that he does not. Angela describes this revelation of Don Emmanuel's lack of faith as the "tragic secret" of his soul. She is deeply saddened to learn that Don Emmanuel only pretends to believe in God and prays that he and Lazarus will experience a true conversion to genuine faith.

Lazarus further explains to Angela what Don Emmanuel has told him regarding his true attitudes about religion. Don Emmanuel asserted that, although he himself does not have faith, it is important to maintain the faith of the community because without their faith they would be lost. He regards religion as an illusion held by the villagers that gives them comfort in life. He thus encourages Lazarus to do everything he can to maintain the illusion of faith in the community for the sake of their happiness.

After revealing Don Emmanuel's secret to Angela, Lazarus becomes more and more active in helping the priest with his various tasks and duties, both in the church and in the community. He continues to spend much of his time alone with Don Emmanuel, walking along the lake and pursuing his line of questioning, in order to learn the true nature of the priest's attitudes about religion.

The years go by, and Don Emmanuel becomes ill. Knowing that he will soon die, the priest has himself carried to the church, where he gives his final sermon to the people of the village. After the death of Don Emmanuel, Lazarus begins to write down conversations he had with the priest over questions of faith and doubt. Angela later refers to these recorded conversations in the process of writing her memoir. In the absence of Don Emmanuel, Lazarus seems to lose his will to live. Eventually, he grows ill and dies.

Angela, now in her fifties, explains that the story she relates is her private memoir of her life with Saint Emmanuel the Good. She explains that the bishop who has initiated the process of naming Don Emmanuel a saint is writing a biography of the priest. This bishop has asked Angela for information about Don Emmanuel's life. While she has given him plenty of factual information about the priest, she does not reveal the "tragic secret" of Don Emmanuel's lack of faith.

Characters

Bishop of Renada

After the death of Don Emmanuel, the bishop of Renada begins the process of applying to the Catholic Church to proclaim him a saint. The bishop is also in the process of writing a biography of Don Emmanuel and approaches Angela for information about the life of the priest. Although Angela provides the bishop with plenty of factual information, she does not tell him about Don Emmanuel's secret loss of faith.

Blasillo

Blasillo is described as a "congenital idiot" and later referred to as "the fool." Blasillo becomes emotionally attached to Don Emmanuel, who pays a lot of attention to him and patiently teaches him things no one else thought he was capable of learning. After a particularly moving sermon, Blasillo repeats the words from the Psalms, "'My God, my God, why hast Thou forsaken me?'" Over the years, Blasillo can often be heard repeating this quotation, although it is not clear if he has any idea what it means. During Don Emmanuel's last church sermon, Blasillo holds tightly onto his hand; when Don Emmanuel dies during this sermon, Blasillo's eyes close and he, too, dies at the same moment.

Angela Carballino

Angela Carballino, nicknamed Angelita, is the narrator of "Saint Emmanuel the Good, Martyr." Her name means "angel" in Spanish. The story itself represents Angela's memoirs, written while she is in her fifties, of her experiences with Don Emmanuel. Angela is sent to a convent school when she is ten years old and returns to her village at the age of sixteen. She becomes especially devoted to Don Emmanuel and helps him with various church activities. She describes him as a man who "pervaded the most secret life of my soul, who was my true spiritual father, the father of my spirit, the spirit of myself."

When Angela is twenty-four, her brother Lazarus reveals to her Don Emmanuel's "tragic secret": he does not actually believe in God or an afterlife. Angela is shaken and upset by this revelation. Although her brother explains to her the details of Don Emmanuel's attitudes about religion, Angela herself never seems to lose faith. While she at first regards Don Emmanuel as a father figure, she later develops a maternal attitude toward him, feeling that she must serve as his spiritual caretaker. On one occasion, Angela goes to make her confession to Don Emmanuel, and seek his forgiveness; however, it is Don Emmanuel who indirectly confesses his lack of faith to Angela, begging her forgiveness, which she gives him. After the death of Don Emmanuel and of her brother, Angela records in a memoir her understanding of the complex religious attitudes of this saint.

Lazarus Carballino

Lazarus Carballino is Angela's brother. As a young man, Lazarus leaves his small village in Spain to live and work in America. He regularly sends enough money back to his mother and sister to support them in relative comfort. When he returns from America, Lazarus is full of new ideas that he has acquired while away from the village. He does not believe in God or religion and is disdainful of the villagers, whose lives are centered around the church. However, he soon gains respect for Don Emmanuel, whom he feels is not like other priests.

Lazarus grows closer and closer to Don Emmanuel, helping him with church and community activities. Eventually, he decides to take holy communion, an outward sign that he has been converted from non-belief to faith in the tenets of the church. However, Lazarus explains to Angela that neither he nor Don Emmanuel truly believes in God or an afterlife. Rather, Lazarus comes to believe, based on the teachings of Don Emmanuel, that religion is a vital source of comfort to the people of the village, who would fall into despair if they lost their faith.

The name Lazarus is that of a biblical figure who was raised from the dead by Jesus Christ four days after he had been buried. The name Lazarus has thus come to symbolize one whose life has been renewed. In Unamuno's story, Lazarus, referring to his biblical name, tells Angela, "'I was a true Lazarus whom [Don Emmanuel] raised from the dead.'" He does not mean that the priest literally brought him back from the dead but that he helped to renew Lazarus's faith in "'the charity of life, in life's joy.'" After Don Emmanuel dies, Lazarus seems to lose his desire to live, and he soon grows ill and dies.

Simona Carballino

Simona Carballino is the mother of Angela and Lazarus. Simona's husband died young, and she was left to care for her two children. Simona is deeply devoted to Don Emmanuel, to the point that her memory of her husband has been eclipsed by her emotional attachment to the priest. When Lazarus claims that he wishes to move his mother and sister to the city, Simona refuses to go, insisting that she cannot leave the lake, the mountain, or Don Emmanuel. As she lies dying on her bed, Simona begs her son, Lazarus, to promise that he will pray for her after she is gone. Although Lazarus is known to be a nonbeliever, the priest encourages him to make and keep this promise, which is his mother's dying wish.

Don Emmanuel

Don Emmanuel is a Catholic priest who presides over the church in the small mountain village of Valverde de Lucerna. Don Emmanuel is deeply loved by all of the villagers, and the entire community centers on him. He is extremely active in the life of the community, personally engaging in their work, their family lives, their physical wellbeing, and their religious needs. Angela's memoir of the experiences of her family with Don Emmanuel reveals his "tragic secret": that he was without faith in God or heaven. Don Emmanuel begins to spend much of his time with Lazarus, who is openly atheistic. He convinces Lazarus to maintain the outward appearance of faith, even if he does not believe. When Don Emmanuel dies, the people of the village, who consider him a saint, mourn their loss. After his death, the bishop of the diocese of Renada, in which the village is located, initiates efforts to officially name Don Emmanuel a saint.

Themes

Existential Thought

Unamuno was an important precursor to the branch of philosophy that came to be known as existentialism. While the term existentialism did not gain currency until the World War II era, the philosophical questioning subsequently regarded as existentialism has roots deep in Western culture. Existentialism, broadly speaking, addresses the nature of human existence. Existentialism is in essence concerned with the human condition, insofar as the human condition is defined by the birth and inevitable death of every individual. Existentialism focuses on the unique qualities of each individual and emphasizes the fact that each person is faced with a multitude of choices by which to conduct her or his life.

Existential thinking has influenced such diverse fields of inquiry as philosophy, psychology, theology, atheism, humanism, literature, metaphysics, and phenomenology. Many important modern thinkers have examined existential questions. Among the most important may be included Friedrich Nietzsche, Søren Kierkegaard, Albert Camus, Jean-Paul Sartre, Martin Heidegger, and Karl Jaspers. In Spain, Unamuno and his contemporary José Ortega y Gasset are regarded as important early existential thinkers.

The characters in "Saint Emmanuel the Good, Martyr" explore some of the basic questions posed by existential thought. In this story, Don Emmanuel's preoccupation with death is characteristic of existential thought. Because he does not believe in an afterlife, Don Emmanuel is painfully aware of the limitations placed on the existence of each individual by the fact of death. This awareness leads him to make specific choices as to how he conducts himself as the priest of a small village. Don Emmanuel's primary concern is to help the people around him by easing their suffering and facilitating the experience of joy and happiness. He regards it as his duty to distract the villagers from thinking about the fundamental reality of human existence (as he sees it): that each individual must one day die.

Because of its focus on death as the end of existence for the individual, it may seem that existentialism is by definition an atheistic philosophy. However, existentialism is not necessarily incompatible with religious faith, and existential theology is an important branch of religious thought. Thus, Unamuno has been regarded as a Catholic existentialist, in that he grapples with the apparent contradictions between Christianity and existentialism. Unamuno regards the act of confronting one's faith and doubt as more important than finding absolute answers to age-old questions regarding the human condition.

The New World and the Old World

Through the character of Lazarus, Unamuno creates a set of oppositions that serve as a central thematic focus of his story. Lazarus, upon first returning from America, represents a set of values associated with the New World, the city, and modern society. The villagers, on the other hand, represent a set of values associated with the Old World,

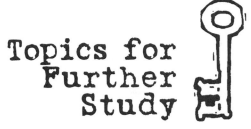

Topics for Further Study

- Unamuno lived through many important events in the history of Spain. Research one of the following major events or eras in Spain's history: the Carlist Wars, the Spanish-American War, the dictatorship of Primo de Rivera, the Second Republic, or the Spanish Civil War. What form of government did Spain have during the period you have chosen? What changes took place in Spanish government over the course of this period? What major social and political issues were of concern to Spanish citizens during this period? What role did the Catholic Church play in social and political conflicts in Spain during this time?

- In "Saint Emmanuel the Good, Martyr," the narrator describes her experiences with a man who exerted a tremendous influence on her life. Think of someone in your own life who has been an important influence on you, such as a teacher, parent, religious leader, older sibling, friend, or perhaps a famous person you have never met. Write an essay describing this person's outstanding characteristics, and how this person has influenced your life. Give specific examples of circumstances in which you made an important decision inspired by the influence of this person.

- Unamuno was one of the writers of Spain's Generation of 1898. Write a report on one other important Spanish writer of the Generation of '98, such as the essayists Azorín and José Ortega y Gasset, the novelists Pío Baroja, Vicente Blasco Ibáñez, and Ramón María del Valle-Inclán, or the poets Juan Ramón Jiménez, Antonio Machado, and Manuel Machado. What significant historical or cultural events in Spain influenced this writer's thinking? What central ideas did this author stress in his writings? In what ways was this author an important influence on Spanish thought and literature?

- Some of the world's greatest artists have lived and worked in Spain. Research an important Spanish artist, such as Bartolomé Murillo, Diego Velázquez, Francisco de Goya, Pablo Picasso, Joan Miró, or Salvador Dali. Where and when did this artist live in Spain? Name some of the major works of this artist, and describe key characteristics of his work. Pick one major work by this artist; in a library book, find a photo reproduction of a drawing, painting, print, or sculpture by this artist. Describe the work of art in specific detail, then discuss your own interpretation of this work.

- Unamuno is regarded as an early existentialist writer, whose ideas were formulated a generation before existentialism emerged as a prominent intellectual movement in philosophy and literature. Learn more about a key figure in existential thought, such as Søren Kierkegaard, Albert Camus, Jean-Paul Sartre, Martin Heidegger, Karl Barth, Paul Tillich, Rudolph Bultman, or Karl Jaspers. What major works of existential thought did this writer publish? Learn about the basic ideas put forth by this existentialist, and explain the ideas to the best of your ability. Then discuss your own response to these ideas. To what extent do you find them convincing? Why are they convincing or why are they not?

- One of the themes of "Saint Emmanuel the Good, Martyr" is the importance of actively participating in one's community as a way of giving meaning to the life of the individual. Make a list of all the different communities which you are a part of, such as your neighborhood, your town, your ethnic group, your church, as well as any extracurricular groups or organizations you are a part of (a sports team, band, or orchestra, etc.). Pick one of these communities that you consider to be especially important to you. Write an essay describing this community. What is your role in this community, and why is it important to you? Give specific examples of how your participation in this community has influenced your life.

the country, and medieval society. Lazarus associates the New World with logic, reason, and atheism, while he associates the Old World with ignorance, cultural backwardness, and outmoded religious beliefs.

When he first returns from America, Lazarus plans to move with his mother and sister to the city, which he considers to be more culturally enlightened than the country. However, the two women refuse to leave their village, because they are so strongly attached to the spiritual life of their rural community, as well as to their priest Don Emmanuel. When Angela goes to visit a school friend in the city of Madrid, she feels stifled by the spiritual emptiness of the urban world and rushes back to the village as soon as possible. With the influence of Don Emmanuel, Lazarus comes to appreciate the values of this devoutly religious Old World community.

Community

Unamuno places a strong emphasis on the life of the remote village community in "Saint Emmanuel the Good, Martyr." The villagers as a group are portrayed as if they were a single composite character. The narrator rarely names or describes individuals within the community but often describes the thoughts and desires of the village as if its people were a homogenous body. After Don Emmanuel and Lazarus die, Angela finds that she is able to go on living through her active engagement in the life of her community. In the end, Angela realizes that Don Emmanuel has taught her the meaning of life, which she interprets as a spiritual merging of her self with the spiritual life of her community.

The Catholic Faith in the Modern World

In "Saint Emmanuel the Good, Martyr," Unamuno explores questions about the role of the Catholic Church in the modern world. The narrative of the story includes many references to Catholic rituals, saints, prayers, and biblical figures. The village in which the story takes place is focused on the activities of their local church, and all of the characters in the story were raised Catholic. This remote village and its rural community in this story come to represent the age-old traditions of the Catholic faith. The challenges Lazarus raises to

Catholicism represent the challenges facing the Catholic church in the modern world of the twentieth century. While Lazarus at first regards the religious devotion of the villagers as a sign of ignorance and backwardness, he eventually comes to appreciate the value of a faith deeply rooted in the age-old traditions of the Catholic Church.

Style

The Nivola

Unamuno coined the term "nivola" to describe his own style of fiction writing. Unamuno considered a nivola to be a work of fiction in which the setting and events of the plot are less important than the ideas expressed by the characters. "Saint Emmanuel the Good, Martyr" is an example of Unamuno's concept of the nivola. In this story, the fictional characters are portrayed primarily in terms of their spiritual struggles, with most other character traits and life events left out of the story. Unamuno thereby foregrounds the story's central theme of religious and philosophical questioning, and the characters in the story are only developed insofar as they express specific ideas about religious faith and doubt.

Narrative Voice and Confessional Fiction

"Saint Emmanuel the Good, Martyr" is written in the first person narrative voice, meaning that the story is told exclusively from the perspective of one character. In the form of a memoir, Angela tells the story of Don Emmanuel from her own perspective. Angela's memoir may also be categorized as "confessional" fiction, meaning a story in which the narrative emerges as an expression or admission of particularly private feelings or experiences. Angela has withheld the "tragic secret" of Don Emmanuel's lack of faith from the bishop who is writing a biography of him. However, she feels the need to record the story of his secret, although she claims that she does not wish her memoir to fall into the hands of the bishop. Thus, Angela confesses to her knowledge that Don Emmanuel, who is regarded as a saint, in fact harbored grave doubts about his faith.

Metaphor and Symbol

Unamuno makes use of recurring metaphors in "Saint Emmanuel the Good, Martyr" through references to the story's setting in a village that is nestled "like a brooch between the lake and the mountain reflected in it." Throughout the story Angela, as narrator, utilizes metaphors comparing Don Emmanuel and the village to the lake and the mountain. The figure of Don Emmanuel is frequently described with reference to this setting, as a man who "carried himself the way our Buitre Peak carries its crest, and his eyes had all the blue depth of our lake." The voices of the villagers reciting from the Bible in unison are described as "a kind of mountain whose peak . . . was Don Emmanuel." Yet Don Emmanuel's voice is sometimes "drowned in the voice of the populace as in a lake." Through this use of metaphor, the mountain and the lake come to symbolize the spiritual life of the community, with Don Emmanuel as its spiritual leader.

A folk myth believed by the villagers states that there is an ancient city submerged in their mountain lake. Lazarus compares the city submerged in the lake to Don Emmanuel's spiritual state, asserting that "at the bottom of Don Emmanuel's soul there is a city, submerged and inundated." This submerged city symbolizes the secret of Don Emmanuel's soul, his complex set of beliefs and non-beliefs about the true nature of religion. The submerged city also symbolizes the age-old spiritual life of the village community. In this sense, the timelessness and immortality of the natural landscape symbolize the everlasting life promised by the Catholic faith.

Epilogue

Unamuno adds an epilogue to the story of "Saint Emmanuel the Good, Martyr." An epilogue is a short section at the end of a story that is meant to stand apart from the content of the central story, while commenting on the story itself. While the fictional Angela is the narrator of the central story, Unamuno narrates the epilogue as himself, Miguel de Unamuno, the author of "Saint Emmanuel the Good, Martyr." In his epilogue, Unamuno asserts that he cannot reveal the secret of how Angela Carballino's memoir fell into his hands. He goes on to question the idea that his fictional characters are not real, suggesting that perhaps the fictional story is more real than the author who created it. Unamuno concludes his epilogue with the assertion that he

hopes the characters in this story will live on forever, although its author will one day die.

Historical Context

Spain in the Nineteenth Century

Spain in the nineteenth century experienced a number of tumultuous changes in its form of government. At the time of Unamuno's birth in 1864, Spain was a constitutional monarchy under Queen Isabella II. However, the revolution of 1868 forced Queen Isabella II into exile. With the end of the revolution in 1870, Amadeo (a son of the king of Italy) was chosen to rule as king of Spain in a constitutional monarchy. In 1873 Amadeo abdicated, under pressure of a revolt, and Spain was declared a republic. This short-lived First Republic lasted until 1875, when Alfonso XII, son of Isabella II, was declared king of Spain. The Constitution of 1876 reinstituted a constitutional monarchy. When King Alfonso XII died in 1885, his young son, Alfonso XIII, was declared the new king of Spain.

The Spanish-American War

Unamuno was in his thirties during the period of the Spanish-American War, which lasted from 1895 to 1898. The Spanish-American War concerned Cuba, which had been a Spanish colony. Cubans wishing to gain national independence from Spain started a rebellion which Spanish forces were unable to put down. After the United States decided in 1895 to support the Cuban rebellion with military force, the Spanish suffered a humiliating defeat. In the peace treaty that followed, Spain lost most of its remaining colonial holdings, which included Puerto Rico as well as Cuba. As part of the treaty, Spanish holdings in the Philippine Islands were sold to the United States. Spain, once the most powerful colonial force in the world, was left with colonial control of only the Canary Islands and Morocco.

Spain in the Twentieth Century

During World War I (1914–18), Spain remained officially neutral, thus avoiding the turbulence that ravaged much of Europe in the early part of the

Compare
&
Contrast

- **1930s:** Spain experiences several major transitions in government. The dictatorship of Primo de Rivera, begun in 1923, is ended in 1930. The Second Republic lasts from 1931 to 1936. The Spanish Civil War begins in 1936. With the end of the Civil War in 1939, Francisco Franco rises to power as dictator of Spain.

  Today: Spain is a constitutional monarchy. King Juan Carlos I serves as head of state. Based on a constitution ratified in 1978, the prime minister oversees a parliament (known as the Cortes Generales), which includes a Congress of Deputies and a Senate. Members of parliament are elected primarily by popular vote via universal suffrage.

- **1930s:** With the outbreak of World War II in 1939, Spain retains a stance of official neutrality. However, Spain secretly supports the Axis forces of Germany, Italy, and Japan during most of the war. Toward the end of World War II, Spain switches unofficial allegiances to the Allied powers.

Today: Spain is an active member of the international community, with membership in the United Nations (since 1955), the North Atlantic Treaty Organization (since 1982), and the European Union (since 1993) after being part of the European Community (joining in 1986).

- **1930s:** During the era of the Second Republic (1931–1936), the Spanish government institutes a separation of church and state. The Spanish education system, once the realm of the Catholic Church, is secularized. With the conclusion of the Spanish Civil War in 1939, Franco quickly restores the powers of the Catholic Church as the state-sponsored national religion of Spain. Franco also reinstates a church-sponsored education system.

  Today: The Spanish government maintains a complete separation of church and state, although the majority of Spaniards are members of the Roman Catholic Church. Public schools in Spain are completely secularized.

---

twentieth century. The Spanish government remained a relatively stable constitutional monarchy from 1885 until 1923, when King Alfonso XIII allowed Miguel Primo de Rivera to take power as dictator of the country. The king, though remaining head of state, deferred to the rule of Rivera. In 1930, however, King Alfonso XIII forced Primo de Rivera to resign. In 1931, amidst growing unpopularity, the king left Spain, in effect abdicating his power. With the king gone, Spain declared the Second Republic and adopted a new constitution. This Second Republic lasted until the outbreak of civil war in 1936.

The Spanish Civil War pitted the right-wing rebel Nationalists, under the leadership of General Francisco Franco, against Loyalists to the left-liberal Republican government. While the Nationalists were aided by military supplies from the fascist states of Hitler's Germany and Mussolini's Italy, the Repub-

licans were aided by supplies from the Soviet Union. In addition, many foreigners, particularly Americans, volunteered to fight in support of the Republican cause. The Nationalists under Franco achieved victory in 1939, thus initiating the Franco dictatorship. With the death of Franco in 1975, King Juan Carlos I was named head of state and oversaw Spain's peaceful transition to a democratic constitutional monarchy.

Spanish Literature

Unamuno was one of the most influential Spanish writers and thinkers of his generation. His place in the history of Spanish letters is associated with a group of writers known as the Generation of 1898. With Spain's humiliating defeat in the Spanish-American War and the resultant demise of the Spanish empire, these writers began to question

Spanish national identity and the role of Spain in the modern world. Writers associated with the Generation of '98 include critics Azorin and José Ortega y Gasset, novelists Pio Baroja, Vicente Blasco Ibanez, and Ramon Maria del Valle-Inclan, and the poets Juan Ramon Jimenez, Antonio Machado, and Manuel Machado, as well as Unamuno.

Unamuno lived to see the emergence of another generation of Spanish writers, known as the Generation of 1927. The writers of the Generation of '27, most of whom were poets, were influenced by movements in early twentieth century European literature, such as Futurism, Surrealism, and Symbolism. The best known writers of the Generation of '27 are Rafael Alberti, Vicente Aleixandre, Damaso Alonso, Luis Cernuda, Gerardo Diego, Angel Ganivet, Jorge Guillen, Federico Garcia Lorca, and Pedro Salinas.

The Roman Catholic Church in Modern Spain

During the twentieth century, the question of what role the church should play in national government was a major source of conflict among Spaniards. Throughout most of the history of modern Spain, the Roman Catholic Church was the official state religion, endorsed by the Spanish monarchy. However, many Spaniards, referred to as anticlericalists, favored a separation of church and state. Popular resentment of the political powers wielded by the Catholic Church led to public outbursts in 1909 and 1931, during which people burned churches and monasteries, killing priests and nuns in the process.

During the era of Spain's Second Republic (1931–36), anticlerical laws were instituted, proclaiming a separation of church and state. However, during the Spanish Civil War (1936–39) the church backed the Nationalist forces under Franco. Thus, Franco's victory in the civil war and his ascendance as dictator of Spain resulted in the reinstitution of the Catholic Church as the state religion. With Franco's death in 1975 and the ratification of a new constitution in 1978, the Spanish government once again declared a separation of church and state.

Critical Overview

Unamuno was one of the most influential Spanish writers of his generation. His stories, poems, and essays garnered an international readership, and were translated into many languages. Although he regarded himself as a poet above all else, Unamuno is remembered primarily as an important writer of essays and stories that grapple with religious and philosophical questioning in the modern world.

Unamuno's fictions are regarded primarily as stories of ideas, with a minimum focus on traditional elements of narrative. In his Introduction to *Abel Sanchez and Other Stories* (1956), in which "Saint Emmanuel the Good, Martyr" is published, Anthony Kerrigan described Unamuno's stories as

> sparse, unstylistic, the bare bones of narratives; but then they are also hot-spirited, intent on righting injustice, and terribly serious about the matter of death. As regards a terrible and troubled honesty, their like is seldom seen.

Unamuno is regarded as an early existentialist thinker, whose works explore themes that were to become the defining concerns of the existentialist movement. In an *Encyclopedia Britannica* article on Unamuno, his fictions are described as "intensely psychological depictions of agonized characters who illustrate and give voice to his own philosophical ideas." These philosophical ideas form the basis of his widely influential contributions to modern thought.

Criticism

Liz Brent

Brent holds a Ph.D. in American culture from the University of Michigan. In this essay, Brent discusses the religious philosophy of the priest in Unamuno's "Saint Emmanuel the Good, Martyr."

Unamuno's central concern in "Saint Emmanuel the Good, Martyr" is with religious faith and religious doubt. As a young woman, Angela expresses complete devotion to the Catholic faith, fully accepting its religious tenets. Her brother Lazarus, on the other hand, returns from America confident in his lack of religious faith. Through their association with Don Emmanuel over a period of years, Angela and Lazarus learn of the priest's secret loss of faith,

This Spanish Cathedral in Spain, circa 1935, sets a scene similar to the village portrayed in "Saint Emmanuel the Good, Martyr"

which he conceals with an outward display of devotion. Through the writing of her memoir, Angela comes to understand and appreciate the complexity of Don Emmanuel's lack of faith, as well as his conviction that people need religion in order to live.

Don Emmanuel tells Lazarus that he does not believe in God or an afterlife; however, he believes it is his duty to maintain the religious faith of the villagers. Lazarus comes to understand the reasoning behind Don Emmanuel's seemingly hypocritical stance of leading the villagers to believe that he is a devout worshipper of God, while secretly harboring a complete lack of faith. Lazarus is thus "converted" to Don Emmanuel's religious philosophy, making it his duty to display outward devotion and encourage devotion among the villagers, while privately maintaining the conviction that God does not exist.

When Angela learns through Lazarus of Don Emmanuel's secret lack of faith, she confronts the priest directly with her own religious doubts and questions. She asks if he believes in the devil, in hell, and in heaven. While Don Emmanuel asserts

that he does, Angela knows that he is lying. Indirectly admitting to her his lack of faith, the priest finally insists that she should keep her religious questioning to herself and never reveal it to others. Angela continues to harbor her own private doubts, while praying that Lazarus and Don Emmanuel will one day be converted to a true faith in God and belief in an afterlife.

Don Emmanuel believes that to live without faith is to live in agony. His own lack of faith causes him to experience lifelong feelings of sadness, loneliness, and despair. As he explains to Lazarus, a man who does not believe in God suffers unbearable torment. He asserts, "The truth, Lazarus, is perhaps something so unbearable, so terrible, something so deadly, that simple people could not live with it!"

Through his characterization of Don Emmanuel, a priest who does not believe in an afterlife, Unamuno explores the significance of death to religious faith. Because he does not believe in heaven, hell, or an afterlife, Don Emmanuel anguishes over thoughts of death. He confesses to Lazarus that his greatest temptation is the urge to commit suicide by drowning himself in the lake. He explains that he has struggled against a lifelong urge to commit suicide, so that his life "is a kind of continual suicide, or a struggle against suicide, which is the same thing."

Because Don Emmanuel himself does not believe in an afterlife and suffers despair over his awareness of his own mortality, he does his best to maintain the belief of the villagers that they will go to heaven when they die. He feels it is his duty to encourage religious faith in the villagers, because he feels that belief in an afterlife is the only thing that keeps people from falling into despair and committing suicide. Angela asserts that Don Emmanuel, who was always called to the bedside of the dying, "helped everyone to die well." That is, he did his best to comfort the dying with the promise of an afterlife, although he himself was tormented by his lack of belief in an afterlife.

From an early age, Angela intuitively perceives Don Emmanuel's despair and thus regards him with "profound pity." Aware of Don Emmanuel's "infinite, eternal sadness," Angela regards herself as the caretaker of his soul, as if he needs her strong sense of faith in order to keep him from descending into utter despair over his own lack of faith. Over the

What Do I Read Next?

- The novel *La Lucha por la vida* (*The Struggle for Life*, 1904), by Pío Baroja, a Basque novelist and one of the Generation of '98, concerns the living conditions of the poor in Madrid.

- *Don Quixote* (Vol. 1, 1605; Vol. 2, 1615), by Miguel de Cervantes, is considered to be the first great modern Spanish novel. Don Quixote is a country gentleman who recruits his faithful servant Sancho Panza to ''sally forth'' into the world and seek adventures requiring knightly chivalry. Don Quixote is in fact a deluded older man who sees a windmill as a giant, a roadside inn as a castle, and a slovenly peasant girl as a beautiful princess.

- One of the strongest novels by Vicente Blasco Ibáñez, one of the Generation of '98, is *Sangre y arena* (*Blood and Sand*, 1908), the story of a bullfighter victimized by the forces of society and tradition.

- Antonio Machado, one of the writers of the Generation of '98, is known for his poetry and essays exploring existential themes. The volume *Poesias Completas* (*Complete Poems*, 1928) is among his best works.

- *Meditaciones del Quijote* (*Mediations on Quixote*, 1914), by José Ortega y Gasset, was inspired by Unamuno's writings on *Don Quixote*. In this collection of essays, Ortega y Gasset reflects upon Cervantes' *Don Quixote* in terms of existential questions about the meaning of human life.

- *The Lone Heretic* (1963), by Margaret Thomas Rudd, is a biography of Unamuno that focuses on his struggles with religious faith and philosophical questioning.

- *Abel Sanchez* (1917), considered to be Unamuno's greatest novel, is a modern retelling of the biblical tale of Cain and Abel. Unamuno's story describes the relationship between two brothers, Joaquin and Able. Joaquin suffers from intense envy of his brother who, as a successful painter, possesses the possibility of becoming immortal through his art.

- *Don Quijote y Sancho* (*Don Quixote and Sancho*, 1905) is a collection of Unamuno's essays on the novel *Don Quixote*. Unamuno argues that the fictional characters of Don Quixote and Sancho Panza transcend the limitations of Cervantes' narrative. Unamuno regards these two characters as representative of distinct strands of thought in Spanish culture.

- *El Cristo de Velazquez* (*The Christ of Velazquez*, 1920), Unamuno's greatest work of poetry, is a book-length blank-verse poem that contemplates a painting of the resurrection of Christ by the seventeenth-century Spanish painter Diego Velazquez.

- Unamuno's *Del sentimiento tragico* (*The Tragic Sense of Life*, 1913) is a collection of his essays expressing his personal philosophy as he grapples with questions of religious faith and existential doubt in the modern world.

---

years, however, this sense of despair takes its toll on Don Emmanuel, and the "deep rooted sadness which consumed him" causes his health to fail.

Don Emmanuel believes that religion is a dream, fantasy, or illusion, by which the common people stave off their fear of death. In private conversation with Lazarus, he refers to God as "our supreme dream." Don Emmanuel feels that his task as the village priest is to do everything he can to maintain the illusion of God and heaven among the villagers. He thus believes it is in the best interests of the people for him to conceal his lack of faith; he advises Angela and Lazarus, also, to conceal their questioning and doubts about religion. Lazarus, repeating Don Emmanuel's lesson, tells Angela, "The people should be allowed to live with their

> Don Emmanuel thus regards it as his duty to promote joy and happiness among the villagers, so that they will be motivated to go on living and will not give in to the despair that comes with realizing that they are 'born only to die.'"

illusion"—that is, the illusion supplied by religious faith.

At one point, Don Emmanuel quotes the socialist theorist Karl Marx, saying, "religion is the opiate of the masses." Marx intended this statement as a criticism of religion, implying that religion distracts people from protesting against unfair economic systems, by lulling them into a false sense of contentment. Don Emmanuel, however, believes that providing people with the fantasy of religion is a positive act, for "We should give them opium, and help them sleep, and dream."

Don Emmanuel particularly feels that it is important to maintain the dream of an afterlife in heaven, to keep the people from falling into despair over the idea that they will one day die. He regards it as his duty to the villagers to "make them dream they are immortal." He goes on to say that all religions serve the same purpose of consoling the people "for having been born only to die."

Don Emmanuel repeatedly asserts that the most important thing is for the people to live, and to go on living. He believes that religious faith gives life meaning, thereby providing people with a reason to go on living. Because he himself has no faith in God, he feels that life is meaningless, and this sense of meaninglessness causes him great despair. Don Emmanuel thus regards it as his duty to promote joy and happiness among the villagers, so that they will be motivated to go on living and will not give in to the despair that comes with realizing that they are "born only to die." Don Emmanuel asserts, "the village must be happy; everyone must be happy to

be alive. To be satisfied with life is of first importance." He tells Lazarus, "let them console themselves for having been born, let them live as happily as possible in the illusion that all this has a purpose." As he is dying, Don Emmanuel advises Angela and Lazarus to continue his mission of maintaining the fantasy of religion in the villagers, to "Let them dream, let them dream."

Toward the end of her memoir, Angela develops a more complex understanding of Don Emmanuel's "tragic secret," which is ultimately a paradox. She begins to wonder if Don Emmanuel secretly *did* have faith in God, and yet merely told Lazarus that he secretly did *not* have faith in God, as a means of indirectly bringing the young man to have faith in the priest's lack of faith. On the other hand, Angela speculates, perhaps Don Emmanuel truly believed that he lacked faith in God, not knowing that, deep down inside, he in fact *did* have faith. Thus, Angela asserts that she believes both Don Emmanuel and her brother "died believing they did not believe, but that, without believing in their belief, they actually believed." She adds, "I believed then, and I believe now, that God—as part of I know not what sacred and inscrutable purpose—caused them to believe they were unbelievers."

Angela ultimately asserts that Don Emmanuel, religious doubt and all, was a saint, and that her brother, too, was a saint. She further suggests that perhaps all of the saints harbored doubts similar to those expressed by Don Emmanuel and that they were no less saintly for their doubt. In fact, Don Emmanuel tells Lazarus that he believes many of the saints, and perhaps even Jesus Christ himself, had also died without truly believing in an afterlife. Angela comes to believe that it is this very doubting of faith, coupled with a commitment to promote religious faith in others, that makes a person saintly. Unamuno thus poses to the reader a philosophical and religious paradox on the nature of faith and doubt, putting forth the notion that, while it is possible to doubt one's faith, it is also possible to have faith in one's doubt.

Source: Liz Brent, Critical Essay on "Saint Emmanuel the Good, Martyr," in *Short Stories for Students*, Gale, 2005.

Gregory Peter Andrachuk

In the following essay, Andrachuk argues that Lázaro, Don Manuel, and Ángela form a trinity for an "alternative religious system," which is the Church of Valverde de Lucerna.

At the thematic and structural centre of Unamuno's *San Manuel Bueno, mártir* (1931), lies a passage whose significance has been completely overlooked. Here, the narrator, Ángela Carballino, describes her brother's reception of the Holy Communion:

> Y llegó el dia de su comunión, ante el pueblo todo, con el pueblo todo. Cuando llegó la vez a mi hermano pude ver que Don Manuel, tan blanco como la nieve de enero en la montaña y temblando como tiembla el lago cuando le hostiga el cierzo, se le acercó con la sagrada forma en la mano, y de tal modo te temblaba ésta al arrimarla a la boca de Lázaro, que se le cayó la forma a tiempo que le daba un vahido, y fue mi hermano mismo quien recogió la hostia y se la llevó a la boca. (Valdés 120)

Until this point Ángela's narrative has concentrated the reader's attention on the actions and thoughts of Don Manuel, but now the focus of the novel broadens to include both Lázaro and Ángela as more active participants. Don Manuel ceases to be the sole source of interest because Lázaro, and to a lesser extent, Ángela, privy now through her brother to the priest's spiritual anguish, adopt the motives and responsibilities once borne by him alone. While the behaviour and beliefs of this trinity appear to be thoroughly Christian to all observers (apparently even to the bishop of Renada), the reader sensitive to indicators Unamuno has placed in the text will see that they form the hierarchy of an alternative religious system. It is one whose goal is not the salvation of the faithful in an eternal after-life, worked out in a contemplative earthly existence. Its aim is, rather, the happiness of the people of Valverde de Lucerna here on earth, achieved through an active involvement in their lives. Although it is essential to the purpose of Don Manuel, Lázaro and Ángela that the faithful believe them to be orthodox Roman Catholics, the reality is that these three are maintaining a fiction. Through this fiction they provide the people with the "opiate" of a religion which is active rather than contemplative, and which allows them and their flock to bear the pain of life. The creation and maintenance of this fiction is motivated by what Mario Valdés has termed their "santa misión de proteger y nutrir la fe" (75). I intend to show that by means of the experiences and interactions of Don Manuel, Lázaro and Ángela, Unamuno has prepared the reader to accept the priest's declaration of the existence of an alternative Church, that of Valverde de Lucerna.

As Manuel prepares for death he calls Ángela and Lázaro to his side, and in words which recall

> **"**The creation of this alternative Church is a natural result of Unamuno's anguish of doubt and at the same time of his recognition of the potential of the Church to mitigate that anguish."

Christ's injunction to Peter that he should feed the sheep (John 21:17), he encourages them to remain steadfast in the faith, and to care for their people. He thus explicitly and succinctly defines their function as pastors within a new construct:

> Oíd: cuidad de estas pobres ovejas, que se consuelen de vivir, que crean lo que yo no he podido creer. Y tú, Lázaro, cuando hayas de morir, muere como yo, como morirá nuestra Ángela, en el seno de la Santa Madre Católica Apostólica Romana, de la Santa Madre Iglesia de Valverde de Lucerna, bien entendido. (137)

For Manuel, Lázaro and Ángela, the theology and liturgy of the Roman Church serve as an appropriate screen, because they are identical in almost all respects to those of the Church of Valverde de Lucerna.

But if this is the only specific mention of the alternative Church, it is not the only indication of its existence. There are, in fact, throughout the novel indicators of ambiguity and alternativity, so that Manuel's statement comes simply as the confirmation of what we should have already discovered. The concept of ambiguity pervades the novel from beginning to end; it is expressed in the description of Manuel as "aquel varón matriarcal" (85), in the existence of another Valverde de Lucerna beneath the waters of the lake, and in Ángela's relationship with the priest. Manuel's confirmation of the alternativity of the Roman Church and the Church of Valverde de Lucerna is the most important example of ambiguity in the novel. The novel itself, in fact can be seen to be alternative construction. Ángela writes in reaction to the bishop's proposed *Vita* of Manuel, and her entire narrative is launched by the phrase: "Ahora que el obispo. . . . " In other words, had the bishop not undertaken the cause of Manuel's beatification, Ángela's story, her "confession," might never have been told. Furthermore, her tale ends with a declaration that although the bishop had solicited from her many details of Manuel's exemplarity as a parish priest for his *Vita*, she has hidden from him the "secreto trágico de Don Manuel y de mi hermano" and she declares her hope that what she now writes will never come into his hands because "les temo a las autoridades de la tierra, a las autoridades temporales aunque scan las de la Iglesia" (48). She is fearful because in writing an alternative *Vita* to that prepared by the bishop she acts as a sort of "advocatus diaboli" or "promotor fidei"; in casting doubt on Manuel's orthodoxy, she does so on her own as well.

Don Manuel's Christ-like behaviour (semiotically suggested in the name Manuel/ Immanuel) is an apparently selfless effort to make his flock secure in their hope of the afterlife, and therefore content as members of the Church militant. But to the orthodox theological concept of the Church militant he adds an intrahistorical interpretation of the Church expectant and triumphant, that is, of the people of Valverde de Lucerna. Together with the living, the dead who inhabit the Valverde de Lucerna submerged in the lake form the "comunión de los santos" (103). Thus Manuel says to Lázaro and Ángela's mother as she lies dying: "usted no se va; usted se queda. Su cuerpo aquí en esta tierra, y su alma aquí también, en esta casa viendo y oyendo a sus hijos, aunque éstos ni le vean ni le oigan" (118).

The fostering of "community" is largely achieved by Don Manuel's personal charisma; it is the focus for the practice of the faith in Valverde in terms of works of mercy as well as the liturgical and extra-liturgical services. One of the latter is the recitation of the Creed by all the townspeople as a separate service. Ángela insists on the unanimous quality of this recitation: "reuniendo en el templo a todo el pueblo, hombres y mujeres, viejos y niños, unas mil personas, recitábamos al unísono, en una sola voz, el Credo" (103). This is the Creed of the Church of Valverde as well, except for the omission of the clause "creo en la resurrección de la carne y la vida perdurable." For this is what Manuel cannot bring himself to believe, despite his desire to do so. Manuel's altruistic work is as much the result of his own anguish, his sense of the futility of life, as it is of his concern for others. His overwhelming desire that his people escape his fate, and that they live this life happily (because to his mind it is the only one which exists) leads him to do things which in another priest of the Roman Church would be considered deficiencies. Thus he does not preach against the humanistic tendencies of the times, he refuses to participate in bringing a criminal to justice lest he be punished for his crime, and he takes an active part in secular pastimes, which as Ángela remarks "en otro hubiera parecido grotesca profanación del sacerdocio, en él tomaba un sagrado carácter y como de rito religioso" (107). In the light of the theology of the Church of Valverde such activities are indeed liturgical in nature because the Church has as its end the salvation and happiness of its people, not in heaven, but here on earth. In Manuel's own words "Lo primero es que el pueblo esté contento, que estén contentos de vivir" (111).

Ángela first becomes aware of the concept of an alternative Church in the course of a conversation with Don Manuel, although she is as yet unaware of her role in it. As he explains to her that he has never felt attracted to the contemplative life of the cloister, where the solitude would be life-threatening for him, he states that his monastery is Valverde de Lucerna; that is, it is a visible community of believers in which he acts as spiritual superior. Ángela immediately accepts this metaphor of Valverde de Lucerna, for in the very next paragraph she states: "volví del colegio de religiosas de Renada a nuestro monasterio de Valverde de Lucerna. Y volví a ponerme a los pies de su abad" (111). In writing her narrative Ángela describes her work during the early years before Lázaro's return as that of a deaconess, and this indeed is what Don Manuel calls her. The traditional duties of a deacon are described in Ángela's own account of her activities: "Yo le ayudaba cuando podía en sus menesteres, visitaba a los enfermos, a las niñas de la escuela, arreglaba el ropero de la iglesia, le hacía, como me llamaba él, de diaconisa" (114). Her ministerial work is not limited to that of a deaconess, but if Ángela never comes to share in the fullness of sacerdotal ministry, she does exercise at least one priestly function, that of confessor.

The theme of confession appears repeatedly in the novel, and is, in fact, the vehicle for the narrative, for in the first paragraph Ángela claims that she writes "a modo de confesión" (85). Her first real knowledge of Don Manuel comes as she confesses to him, and it is here that she first becomes aware of the ambiguity of her position. Rather than confessing to him, she feels that she has heard his confession: "al encontrarme en el confesionario junto al santo varón, sentí como una callada confesión suya en el susurro sumiso de su voz" (112). The confession theme is linked to Ángela's ministerial function most clearly after Lázaro's "conversion." As she continues to act as Don Manuel's deaconess, the ambiguity of her role is now resolved into an "alternativity": "en el tribunal de la penitencia—¿quién era el juez y quién el reo?" (125). Now the emotional turmoil with which Ángela at first confessed to Manuel is shared by him: "no sé ya lo que me digo desde que estoy confesándome contigo" (126). And Manuel recognizes in her a priestly authority as he asks absolution in the name of the Church of Valverde de Lucerna, that is, in the name of the people. Ángela "como penetrada de un misterioso sacerdocio" (127) complies, but grants absolution in the name of the Trinity. In her rejection of the Valverdian formula proposed by Manuel, and her use of the Catholic formula, Ángela demonstrates her attachment to the "faith of the charcoal-burners." For while she has come to share in some of Don Manuel's anguish, she is one of those who does believe in an afterlife. Thus hers is an incomplete priesthood.

But Lázaro's case is different. He returned from the New World imbued with anticlerical, and liberal ideas, and efforts are made to show us that he is an unbeliever. Nevertheless he soon recognizes that Manuel is not as he supposed him to be. Although he does not know any other priests, he is certain that Manuel is different. Even he, Lázaro, is attracted by Manuel's charisma, and feels pulled to hear him preach. From the beginning he intuits that Manuel does not believe what he professes: "es demasiado inteligente para creer todo lo que tiene que enseñar" (118), which is nothing less (as the reader has already learned) than "todo lo que cree y enseña a creer la Santa Madre Iglesia Católica, Apostólica, Romana" (114). It is the death of his mother which acts as a catalyst in Lázaro's conversion. As Manuel asks Lázaro to tell his mother that he will pray for her so that she may die contented, Lázaro comes face to face with the practical application of Manuel's theology, and he sees its effectiveness. From this time forward Lázaro becomes a disciple of Manuel. While Ángela's narrative does not explicitly reveal it, we are led to believe that the reason Manuel concentrates so much effort on Lázaro is that he recognizes in him a potential co-religionist, that is, someone who can wholeheartedly share his ideas. There is no one in the village apart from Lázaro who can fulfill this function, because to convert any of the others to his ideal of service would undermine their belief in the eternal life, and thus cause them to share Don Manuel's anguish. In Lázaro's case, however, the situation is clearly different, because he enters the narrative already in a state of agnosticism. It is a relatively simple matter for Manuel to show him the benefits of feigning belief in order to promote unity and tranquility in the community. With the happy death of his mother, Lázaro has proof positive of the efficacy of this system of action. Lázaro's sympathy with Don Manuel's goals leads to his regular attendance at Mass, and to a promise that he will take Communion.

The importance of the Communion episode has been overlooked, perhaps because critics have not read it in the light of Catholic eucharistic practice. If we take into account the prevailing attitudes towards the sacrament at the time the novel was written, it becomes clear that Unamuno intended this passage to affect the reader's interpretation of the work. Lázaro's announcement that he will take Communion, not privately, but publicly, indicates an apparent solidarity with the people, a joining in communion with them: "se dijo que cumpliría con la parroquia, que comulgaría cuando los demás comulgasen" (120). The public or liturgical aspect of this act is emphasized in the narrative: "Y llegó el día de su comunión, ante el pueblo todo, con el pueblo todo" (120). As he prepares to administer the sacrament, Don Manuel is so moved by Lázaro's reception of the Holy Communion that he drops the Host.

Until the Vatican II Council (1962–65), the eucharistic doctrine of the Roman Church was essentially that developed by St. Thomas Aquinas, codified in the decrees of the Lateran IV Council (1215) and reaffirmed in the decrees of the Council of Trent (1545–63). According to this doctrine of transubstantiation, the bread and wine are changed in substance into the Body and Blood of Christ, leaving only the "accidents" or appearances of the original elements. Thus the bread and wine, after consecration, are in a real sense the sacramental Presence of Christ. Emphasis on this physical change (as opposed to the exclusively spiritual change allowed by the Reformers) led to a fastidious observance of propriety with regard to the handling of the consecrated elements. Thus only a priest could normally touch the Host; the laity were most certainly not permitted any contact with the Host except on the tongue. The use of the houselling cloth and the communion plate or paten held beneath the chin of the communicant was designed specifically to prevent such contact. Lázaro's act of retreiving the Host and administering it to himself can only be seen as an act of sacrilege, which would normally cause scandal in a public ceremony. Yet the syntax used in Ángela's reporting of this act is designed to draw the reader's attention to Lázaro's role here: "Y fue mi hermano mismo quien recogió la hostia y se la llevó a la boca" (120).

It follows that if laymen were not permitted to touch the Host, then Lázaro, in touching it, must in some sense have acquired sacerdotal privileges. In administering the sacrament to himself, Lázaro, in effect, demonstrates that ordination in the Church of Valverde de Lucerna is open to anyone who wholeheartedly embraces its beliefs. The reality of his ordination is made clear to the reader in the "confession" he makes to Ángela immediately afterwards. When Ángela commends him for the joy he has brought to the whole "communion of saints" ("a todos, a todo el pueblo, a todo, a los vivos y a los muertos, y sobre todo a mamá" [120]), he reveals that he has done it for this reason, and not because of his belief in the sacrament. His sharing of priesthood with Manuel is emphasized when Ángela describes him as "mi hermano, tan pálido y tan tembloroso como Don Manuel cuando le dio la comunión" (120). After revealing Don Manuel's theology to Ángela, Lázaro shows his full acceptance of it: "me rendí a sus razones, y he aquí mi conversión" (122), and his entrance into the hierarchy of the Church of Valverde de Lucerna when he says: "y ahora hay otro más para consolar al pueblo . . . para corroborarle en su fe" (123). From this point on, Lázaro takes a full share in the works of Manuel, even liturgically: "le acompañaba en sus visitas a los enfermos, a las escuelas, y ponía su dinero a disposición del santo varón. Y poco faltó para que no aprendiera a ayudarle a misa" (128).

The aspects of community-building and sharing inherent in the liturgical act of Communion are emphasized not only in Lázaro's reception of the sacrament, but in that of Ángela. Her Communion provides the opportunity for Don Manuel to share with her his most daring and heretical thought: that even Jesus Christ is needful of intercession. Ángela, greatly disturbed by this idea, later asks Manuel to identify the people's "sin" and their resultant need for prayers. Manuel's answer is a first attempt to identify an alternative Church, here called the "Iglesia, Católica, Apostólica, Española" whose theology has been defined by its premier theologian, Pedro Calderón de la Barca:

> ¿Cuál?—me respondió.—Ya lo dijo un gran doctor de la Iglesia Católica, Apostólica, Española, ya lo dijo el gran doctor de *La vida es sueño*, y dijo que "el delito mayor del hombre es haber nacido." Ése es, hija, nuestro pecado: el del haber nacido. (136)

The very next passage tells of Manuel's approaching death, and his charge to his fellow ministers that they care for the faithful, consoling them with the theology and sacraments of the Church of Valverde de Lucerna.

The intrahistorical "theology" which underlies the entire novel finds expression in the Church of Valverde de Lucerna. The creation of this alternative Church is a natural result of Unamuno's anguish of doubt and at the same time of his recognition of the potential of the Church to mitigate that anguish. *San Manuel Bueno, mártir* is the narration of the theology of the Church of Valverde de Lucerna at work in the life of one of its saints.

Source: Gregory Peter Andrachuk, "'He That Eateth of This Bread Shall Live Forever' (John 6:58): Lázaro's Communion," in *Romance Notes*, Vol. 31, No. 3, Spring 1991, pp. 205–13.

M. Gordon

In the following essay, Gordon argues that "San Manuel Bueno, Mártir" does not represent a new direction in Unamuno's concept of personality.

Unamuno's fictional writings, widely recognised as among the most original and innovative of their time, are, paradoxically, more often approached from a philosophical, rather than a strictly literary point of view. In view of Unamuno's own insistence on the centrality of existential problems, his oft-repeated scorn for all forms of aestheticism and literariness, and his cultivation of a rather stark prose style which can easily—too easily, perhaps—encourage us to believe that his fictions wear their heart upon their sleeves, this is not too surprising. There are, however, dangers in approaching Unamuno's novels in this way, dangers which are graphically illustrated by *San Manuel Bueno, mártir*. Those who approach this work from a primarily philosophical point of view are apt to assume that its eponymous hero is yet another mouthpiece or fictional alter ego of his creator and to concern themselves with the nature and extent of his belief or unbelief. Since the hero in question is an unbeliever who nonetheless wishes to preserve his flock from the painful implications of the existential uncertainty by which he himself is assailed, such critics are left with the problem of trying to account for what, on the face of it, is a radical volte-face on the part of Unamuno, much of whose life and work was devoted to shaking his readers out of their complacency and forcing them to face the tragic contradictions of the human condition—to confront, in other words, precisely those truths which Don Manuel so assiduously suppresses.

One explanation often adduced to account for this apparent change is the crisis allegedly undergone by Unamuno in his later years and which is often held to be reflected in works like *Cómo se hace una novela* and *San Manuel Bueno, mártir*. A. Sánchez Barbudo is perhaps the best known, as well as the most radical, exponent of this point of view, regarding these works as a kind of repudiation or retraction of all that had gone before—as Unamuno's final disavowal of his earlier *agonista* self. Sánchez Barbudo's view seems to be shared, at least to some extent, by José Luis Abellán, who speaks of 1925 (the year of Unamuno's Paris exile and the first version of *Cómo se hace una novela*) as having produced "una auténtica conversión de la personalidad," the result of a profound crisis in which "se plantea la lucha entre dos Unamunos que eran cada día más irreconciliables: el histórico, el de la leyenda, el de la novela, que de sí mismo había hecho, y el real, el íntimo y profundo, que llevaba sus vicisitudes por el mundo." The outcome is a "giro total" in Unamuno's concept of personality: "aunque sigue considerando que la personalidad es una manifestación histórica, y no trata de absolutizarla, ni de suplantar a Dios por el yo. Unamuno ha centrado su preocupación en torno al sentimiento divino y se despreocupa de la historica, del sueño y de la personalidad, en suma."

While *Cómo se hace una novela* may indeed reflect the agonised search for a self which is "real, íntimo y profundo," it is debatable, to say the least, whether that complex work represents anything like its discovery. Terms like *Dios* and *sentimiento divino* are even more questionable. Yet even C. Blanco Aguinaga, in an article which is far more sensitive than most to the literary complexity of *San Manuel Bueno, mártir*, seems to share the view that this work somehow represents a turning of the page:

> La vida de don Manuel, si en efecto fue como Angela cree recordarla, debió ser, indiscutiblemente, una tragedia agónica; pero lo sorprendente para quien conoce otros agonistas creados por Unamuno es que el relato de esa vida—la novela *San Manuel Bueno, mártir*—no tiene dimensiones trágicas precisamente porque la narradora ha logrado hablar de sí misma, de su personaje central y de su mundo desde "más allá de la fe y la desesperación," desde "fuera de la historia," única fuente y origen constante de la agonía. (p. 586)

Tragedy and *agonía,* in other words, are not so much repudiated as transcended, a kind of final peace being achieved through an essentially intrahistoric view of life.

> "Angela's situation at the end of her narrative, poised between agonised consciousness and the dissolution of that same consciousness in the mists of <u>intrahistoria,</u> was, it could be argued, Unamuno's own for much of his life."

Yet this sense of difference—the feeling that *San Manuel Bueno, mártir* and other later novels represent new directions in Unamuno's attitudes and concerns—does not appear to have been shared by Unamuno himself. In his Prologue to *San Manuel Bueno, mártir y tres historias más*, he writes: "tengo la conciencia de haber puesto en ella todo mi sentimiento trágico de la vida cotidiana." He also explicitly goes out of his way to repudiate the idea that these stories (or at least three of them, since *Una historia de amor*—a much earlier work—is treated somewhat as an afterthought) were written in a new and different frame of mind. What unites them is "el pavoroso problema de la personalidad, si uno es lo que es y seguirá siendo lo que es" (p. 19). He then goes on:

> Claro está que no obedece a un estado de ánimo especial en que me hallara al escribir, en poco más de dos meses, estas tres novelitas, sino que es un estado de ánimo general en que me encuentro, puedo decir que desde que empecé a escribir. Ese problema, esa congoja, mejor, de la conciencia de la propia personalidad—congoja unas veces trágica y otras cómica—es el que me ha inspirado para casi todos mis personajes de ficción. (p. 19)

The same idea—of a continuity, rather than a discontinuity, of outlook and preoccupation—surfaces again in the Prologue to the second edition of *Amor y pedagogía* (written in 1934):

> En esta novela está en germen—y más que en germen— lo más y mejor de lo que he revelado después en mis otras novelas: *Abel Sánchez, La tía Tula, Nada menos que todo un hombre, Niebla,* y, por último, *San Manuel Bueno, martir y tres historias más.* (Magisterio ed. [Madrid, 1970], p. 34)

Unamuno, I suspect, is closer to the truth than the critics aforementioned: *San Manuel Bueno, mártir* is indeed about the problem of personality—the problem which haunts the greater part of Unamuno's fiction—and its implications, so far from transcending the tragedy of the human condition, point insistently towards it. Unamuno's frequent disavowals of literary artifice—his claim to be writing in a direct, unstructured and even haphazard way ("a lo que salga")—should not be taken at face value, for his wayward approach to literary convention often masks a considerable artistry. *San Manuel Bueno, mártir* is no mere ideological transparency, but a complex literary artefact, much of whose meaning does not lie readily accessible on the surface, but is locked into the very structure of the novel and, in particular, in the implications of the first-person narrative mode in which it is cast.

In *San Manuel Bueno, mártir,* form and content are inextricably intertwined. However, if purely philosophical approaches to the novel are poor guides to its meaning, we are nonetheless not likely to get very far by dispensing with philosophy altogether and treating the novel as some kind of self-contained verbal artefact. A recent article by C. A. Longhurst does precisely this. His argument is too complex for summary to do it much justice, but what it boils down to is this: Angela's narrative is largely unreliable, since her own emotions (and in particular her repressed and sublimated love for Don Manuel) colour it at almost every turn; we thus know very little about Don Manuel, only what Angela thinks, or wants us to think, about him; even the evidence of his lack of faith is dubious and stems more from Angela's disturbed consciousness (a mixture, possibly, of subconscious resentment and the desire to project on him her own religious doubts) than from any objectively verifiable source; the novel is thus less about the nature and origins of Don Manuel's supposed unbelief than "an exploration of the nature of perception and belief" (p. 594). As important as Longhurst's analysis of the novel are the critical assumptions about post-Realist fiction which underpin it, and which appear to exclude not only philosophy or ideas as useful instruments for apprehending the meaning of the novel, but the very idea of its having a meaning at all:

> An approach to Unamuno's fiction based on a theological, philosophical or biographical search for the meaning or the message is unlikely to get to the hub of Unamuno's art. Most novelists after all do not write novels to voice meanings; they turn to novels in order to construct artefacts out of language. In Western fiction of the post-realist mode, of which Unamuno is

a prime example, the clear tendency was to allow the narrative to speak with its own voice. The meaning or the message was banished as something extra-literary; but what remained had its own kind of truth, its poem-like structure, its internal justification for existing. (p. 597)

We are clearly a long way here from traditional approaches to the so-called "Generation of 1898" and to Unamuno's fiction. That is in itself by no means necessarily to be deplored: the concept of a Generation of 1898 is in many ways a rather parochial and limiting one and there is much to be said for attempting to set early twentieth-century Spanish fiction in a wider European context. Yet the model of Modernism implied in the above quotation seems to me to be a debilitatingly narrow one. True, post-Realist fiction shows a marked tendency towards aesthetic self-consciousness and formal experimentation and a distinct preoccupation with its own problematical status. However, though questions of form—and the adventurous exploration of its possibilities—lie somewhere close to the centre of much of the fiction which Unamuno produced after 1897, he was no believer in the autonomy of art. Moreover, it is important to remember that if writers around the turn of the century had lost faith in Realism, it was in large measure because they no longer believed in the stable, objective reality with which Realism purported to deal. Increasingly, therefore, objective reality is supplanted by subjective realities and by a concern with individual consciousness, whether as the mode of apprehending these realities or as itself the ultimate, if somewhat problematical, reality. It is this latter aspect of Modernism which is more directly relevant to *San Manuel Bueno, mártir.*

Angela's memoir, apparently so simple, is in fact a deeply ambiguous document, the style of whose narrative is apt to undercut its surface meaning. Even the reasons why she is writing it at all are far from clear, least of all, one suspects, to Angela herself. On the one hand, it is written ("a modo de confesión," she says in the opening paragraph) as a counter to the version of Don Manuel's life being prepared by the local bishop (with beatification in view). On the other hand, we are told at the end of the story of her efforts to conceal Don Manuel's secret from this self-same bishop and her anxiety lest her memoir get into the wrong hands. Similarly, there is an obvious tension between her desire to tell all and her anxiety to shore up the legend of Don Manuel. Angela visibly recoils from the truth which she has to tell, seeking to convince herself that Don Manuel, if only in extremis, believed somehow in spite of himself (a belief, incidentally, which his dying words do little to support). Angela's glowing testament to the public Don Manuel and her awareness of the truth behind the façade thus sit rather uneasily together.

Much of this ambiguity undoubtedly stems from the nature of Angela's relationship with the priest. The precise nature of this relationship is, admittedly, not easy to pinpoint, for Angela, with the possible exception of the closing pages of the novel, is remarkably reticent about her own motives and feelings. We are thus obliged to read between the lines and, to that extent, her account may be said to be less than wholly reliable. However, enough is said, or implied, to make it clear that Don Manuel occupies a very important place in her life and that her relationship with him is inextricably bound up with her emotional and spiritual life. Angela is drawn, almost obsessively, to Don Manuel even when she is at school and the early part of her memoir is strongly coloured by starry-eyed adolescent hero-worship. She returns to Valverde "ansiosa de conocerle, de ponerme bajo su protección, de que él me marcara el sendero de mi vida" (p. 27). Their first direct encounter after her return is, on her part at least, a highly charged occasion:

> Cuando me fui a confesar con él, mi turbación era tanta, que no acertaba a articular palabra. Recé el "yo pecador" balbuciendo, casi sollozando. (p. 35)

A similar emotional intensity is discernible in many of their subsequent encounters.

Longhurst is probably quite right in detecting in all of this symptoms of a form of repressed or sublimated love. Indeed, the following description of a period of her schooldays—which Longhurst interprets, correctly I think, as a form of psychological displacement—suggests as much:

> Desde muy niña alimenté, no sé bien cómo, curiosidades, preocupaciones e inquietudes, debidas, en parte al menos, a aquel revoltijo de libros de mi padre, y todo ello se me medró en el colegio, en el trato, sobre todo, con una compañera que se me aficionó desmedidamente y que unas veces me proponía que entrásemos juntas en un mismo convento, jurándonos, y hasta firmando el juramento con sangre, hermandad perpetua, y otras veces me hablaba, con los ojos semicerrados, de novios y de aventuras matrimoniales. (pp. 26–27)

She then goes on to describe how her schoolfriend is fascinated by the figure of Don Manuel. What is interesting in this passage is how, in a particularly adolescent form, romantic and religious feelings are intertwined, suggesting that Angela's "curiosidades,

preocupaciones e inquietudes" are not merely emotional, but intellectual and religious too. And in fact, while Angela may assert the orthodoxy of her belief in the face of Don Manuel's and Lázaro's lack of it, evidence of a nagging religious doubt surfaces time and time again in her narrative. All of which suggests not merely that she is unconsciously in love with Don Manuel, but that she needs him as some sort of bulwark for her own, evidently rather shaky, belief. It is this aspect of her character that accounts for the mixture of fascination and recoil with which she responds to the evidence of Don Manuel's lack of faith.

Angela's doubts make themselves felt in a more obvious and anguished form at the end of her narrative. Whether all this, however, makes that narrative itself unreliable, leastways in the conventional sense, seems to me to be somewhat debatable. There is little to suggest that the essential facts of the case (Don Manuel's public self and his inner doubts) are untrue. Longhurst's contention that they are seems to me to rest on a misunderstanding both of the principles of unreliable narration and of Angela as a character. It does not follow that because we rely on Angela for most of our information about Don Manuel, the information in question is ipso facto suspect: narrative techniques based on unreliable first-person narrators evolved out of a rather older convention—that of their reliable counterparts—and our natural instinct is to trust a first-person narrator unless we are given rather solid indications that we should not—more solid, I would venture to suggest, than Longhurst's rather adventurous interpretations of Angela's psychology. The significance of Angela's narrative, and its peculiarly complex and paradoxical quality, derives largely from the tension alluded to earlier: between the novel as testament (i.e. a work written in praise and endorsement of Don Manuel's intrahistoric "faith"), and the novel as confession (the revelation of Don Manuel's secret and its unsettling reverberations in Angela's own mind).

Angela's narrative is characterised by a carefully constructed inward progression. In the early stages of her story (the account of her childhood and schooldays), we are left in no doubt about Don Manuel's importance in her life, but as yet the view we get of him, though clearly tinged with hero-worship, is fairly remote. In the second phase of the story—between Angela's return from school and her first confession with Don Manuel—we begin to learn more, but even now the view we are offered is still an essentially external one. What this section does, and with remarkable economy, is to establish in our minds the image of the public Don Manuel. The section consists largely of habitual actions and representative anecdotes, with no definite chronology and a distinct emphasis on the imperfect tense, which not only serves to underline the generic quality of the actions and events described, but also, as Aguinaga has pointed out, to reinforce the impression of continuity which is so marked a feature of the portrayal of Valverde de Lucerna. Thus far there is little hint of the secret which is to come. Of course, the silence of Don Manuel at the crucial moment in the recitation of the creed and the identification of him with the crucified Christ crying out in anguish at being abandoned by His Father contain powerful hints to the reader who is at all familiar with Unamuno, but Angela herself appears to narrate them innocently, betraying no awareness of their significance.

With the episode of the puppeteer and his dying wife, all this begins to change. Hindsight, and with it the first overt hint of a mystery behind the public face of Don Manuel, makes its first significant appearance in Angela's narrative:

> Y más tarde, recordando aquel solemne rato, he comprendido que la alegría imperturbable de don Manuel era la forma temporal y terrena de una infinita y eterna tristeza que con heroica santidad recataba a los ojos y a los oídos de los demás. (p. 34)

This is immediately reinforced by the reference to Don Manuel's fear of solitude and his mysterious walks by the side of the lake, as well as by his own remarks about being unable to bear alone the burden of "la cruz del nacimiento" (p. 34). As the focus of the narrative shifts to the increasingly highly charged encounters between Angela and the priest, to her challenges to him on matters of doctrine and his corresponding discomfort and evasiveness, her—and our—sense that Don Manuel is concealing some kind of inner doubt and suffering grows apace. The still withheld revelation is now clearly casting its shadow before, and Blasillo's aping of Christ's cry on the cross is charged with ominous, if still unspecific, meaning.

Yet the use of hindsight in producing our sense of Don Manuel's hidden inner self remains rather sparing. In other words, Angela's knowledge of the future is seldom projected backwards into her text. Rather, we are encouraged to see Don Manuel through her eyes, to experience directly her changing awareness of him. Hence that inward progression alluded to earlier: from an initially remote and external view of Don Manuel, we are drawn ineluctably towards his inner core. The power with which that inner core seizes our imagination and comes to dominate the narrative derives in part from its inherent mysteriousness and in part from the fact that these encounters between Angela and her confessor have an immediacy and intensity which the earlier portrait of the public Don Manuel largely lacked.

All of which gives rise to some rather interesting paradoxes. To begin with, in a work which purports to be an endorsement of Don Manuel's "faith" and of the charms of the intrahistoric way of life of Valverde de Lucerna, our sense of Don Manuel's inner *agonía* looms inconveniently large. And yet at the same time, and despite the fact that that *agonía* comes to dominate the narrative, its precise nature and origins remain disconcertingly elusive. We are of course given some insight into it through Don Manuel's conversations with Lázaro in the third phase of the narrative, but those are still mere gobbets. Our glimpses of the inner Don Manuel are precisely that—mere glimpses, given a further imprecision by being seen at two removes (i.e. Lázaro's recollections as filtered through Angela's). Again, the reader familiar with Unamuno may feel that he can deduce something of the reasons for Don Manuel's lack of belief, but Angela does not (and, perhaps more importantly, cannot) supply them. The "real" Don Manuel remains beyond our grasp. Thus Angela's narrative leads us inescapably towards Don Manuel's inner self, while at the same time condemning that inner self to recede into unknowability.

In doing so, it illustrates with particular sharpness that problem alluded to by Unamuno himself in his Prologue—"el pavoroso problema de la personalidad, si uno es lo que es y sigue siendo lo que es." Implicit in Angela's narrative is that double question: who and what is Don Manuel and what is he destined to become? The answer to these questions is not a matter of whether or not Angela is lying about him—consciously or otherwise—but whether he, she, and we can find in Don Manuel a solid self to which to cling. The ultimate inscrutability—and, one might add, irrevocable loss—of Don Manuel's *yo íntimo* is an index of its insubstantiality. What we are left with is the self as external projection, the self condemned to time and history. In other words the public Don Manuel, the Don Manuel who is projected upon the world through his acts, whose legend survives to become incorporated into the intrahistoric continuity of Valverde and who, like Lázaro (or so Angela would have us believe), becomes "otra laña más entre las dos Valverdes, la del fondo del lago y la que en su sobrehaz se mira" (p. 56).

To Unamuno's double question, therefore, Angela's narrative appears to return a double answer: that man is inescapably his public (or historic) self, and that he can find ultimate meaning and survival (of a sort) in the collective continuity of *intrahistoria*. This is precisely the kind of survival to which Don Manuel himself clings, for his activities are not merely directed towards sustaining the intrahistoric life of Valverde, but to losing himself within it, to finding refuge in it for his own ravaged soul. As Unamuno puts it in the Prologue, Don Manuel "busca, al ir a morirse, fundir—o sea salvar—su personalidad en la de su pueblo" (p. 19).

And yet Angela's answers—or at least such answers as one might cull from the surface of her narrative—are fatally undercut by that narrative's underlying implications. For if the record of Don Manuel's life—his "obras" and the public self embodied in them—ultimately squeezes out the *yo íntimo*, the latter nonetheless remains a powerful and haunting presence which, from the margins of the novel, calls the usurper false, for the Don Manuel whom the other inhabitants of Valverde see and whose legend lives on in their collective memory (and is shortly to be pressed between the covers of the bishop's book), is not the "real" Don Manuel. And when Lázaro comments on his deathbed that "conmigo se muere otro pedazo del alma de don Manuel" (p. 56), we are reminded that even legends wither and die. In short, Angela's narrative, by virtue of the subjective (and therefore limited) vision to which it is inescapably tied and the confusions and uncertainties in her own mind which inform it, is successful neither as hagiographical testament nor intimate record, for the "real" Don Manuel is destined forever to elude us. Thus we have a novel which is not simply about belief and unbelief, death and immortality, but about the tragic paradox of human personality, torn between a public self which is the prisoner of history and external image, and an intimate self which is condemned to insubstantiality. So, far from transcending the tragedy of the human condition, therefore, Unamuno's novel would seem to enshrine it.

One reason why that tragedy is less conspicuous than it otherwise might be is the gentle mist of *intrahistoria* which shrouds the portrait of Valverde and Don Manuel, and in which Angela seeks to envelop herself at the end. Valverde, with its lake and mountain, is presented by Angela as the living embodiment of that intrahistoric continuity to the contented continuation of which Don Manuel, and subsequently Lázaro and Angela, bend their endeavours. As portrayed by Angela, the village, and its attendant symbols of mountain and lake, is suffused with a sort of poetic glow. The mountain symbolises the life and faith of the living Valverde; the lake, and the mythical village beneath its waters, the accumulated sediment of its "tradición eterna"— "el cementerio de las almas de nuestros abuelos," to use Angela's description (p. 41). Both symbols are identified insistently with Don Manuel and appear more often than not together—"el lago y la montaña que se mira en él"—thus continually reminding us that past, present and future are all aspects of the intrahistoric continuity that Valverde represents and in which Don Manuel seeks to submerge himself as a refuge from his inner *agonía*.

The note of celebration of this intrahistoric continuity—and with it of ringing endorsement of the gospel according to San Manuel—comes through clearly at the end of Angela's narrative:

> ¡Hay que vivir! Y él me enseñó a vivir, él nos enseñó a vivir, a sentir la vida, a sentir el sentido de la vida, a sumergirnos en el alma de la montaña, en el alma del lago, en el alma del pueblo de la aldea, a perdernos en ellas para quedar en ellas. El me enseñó con su vida a perderme en la vida del pueblo de mi aldea, y no sentía yo más pasar las horas y los días y los años, que no sentía pasar el agua del lago. Me parecía como si mi vida hubiese de ser siempre igual. No me sentía envejecer. No vivía yo ya en mí, sino que vivía en mi pueblo y mi pueblo vivía en mí. Yo quería decir lo que ellos, los míos, decían sin querer. (p. 57)

Yet one of the more intriguing features of the novel is the way in which these symbols, so generously used by Angela, are invested with implications of which she seems largely unaware and which, while not basically altering their meaning, serve to undercut the poetic glow with which she surrounds them. A less comforting use of these symbols can be seen in the following comment of Don Manuel, as reported by Lázaro: "¿Has visto, Lázaro, misterio mayor que el de la nieve cayendo en el lago y muriendo en él mientras cubre con su toca a la montaña?" (p. 47). The snowflakes are individuals: clustered together on the mountaintop (an image of the communal life and faith of Valverde), they acquire a kind of substantiality, albeit a collective rather than an individual one. Yet in the lake, for all that it symbolises continuity, they are doomed to perish. The symbol of the lake is two-edged, a symbol of *intrahistoria*, certainly, but also of its inescapable corollary, individual death. We can see, then, a deeper meaning in the reiterated association of Don Manuel's secret with the image of the lake and the narrator's comment that, when Don Manuel falls silent at the crucial part of the creed, "la voz de don Manuel se zambullía como en un lago" (p. 30), and she herself hears the bells of the submerged village ringing out.

As in the passage quoted above, therefore, there is in Angela's apparently resounding endorsement of Don Manuel's "gospel"—the claim that he taught them to "sumergirnos en el alma de la montaña, en el alma del lago"—an implication of which she herself is unaware. Moreover, there is more than a suggestion here of the lady protesting too much: seen in context, its air of confident certainty takes on the appearance of an attempt to still the anguished questions which immediately precede it:

> Y ahora, al haber perdido a mi San Manuel, al padre de mi alma, y a mi Lázaro, mi hermano aún más que carnal, espiritual, ahora es cuando me doy cuenta de que he envejecido y de cómo he envejecido. Pero ¿es que los he perdido? ¿es que he envejecido? ¿es que me acerco a mi muerte? (pp. 56–57)

We return to the "ahora" where the narrative began, but it is a rather different Angela whom we now see. The story which commenced with a confident assertion of her identity, ends on a note of puzzlement and insecurity. Those doubts of hers, which have been so central to the construction of her strange narrative, now overtake it and her completely, for Angela, despite her best efforts to convince herself otherwise, cannot really live the intrahistoric gospel according to San Manuel. The still, small voice of consciousness will not be silenced. Almost inadvertently, she lets slip the difference between her and the intrahistoric souls who inhabit Valverde and whom she has sought to resemble: "Yo quería decir," she says, "lo que ellos, los míos, decían sin querer," and between her "quería decir" and their "decían sin querer" yawns the gulf between genuine *inconsciencia* and one which, being willed, is inevitably incomplete.

The last pages of Angela's narrative show us the last flickerings of a consciousness which senses its own imminent dissolution. Alone before the page on which she writes, Angela feels everything receding into insubstantiality, or, as she puts it, echoing Don Manuel's image earlier on, disappearing beneath the snow:

> Y al escribir esto ahora, aquí, en mi vieja casa materna, a mis más que cincuenta años, cuando empiezan a blanquear con mi cabeza mis recuerdos,

> está nevando, nevando sobre el lago, nevando sobre la montaña, nevando sobre las memorias de mi padre, el forastero; de mi madre, de mi hermano Lázaro, de mi pueblo, de mi San Manuel, y también sobre la memoria del pobre Blasillo, de mi Blasillo, y que él me ampare desde el cielo. Y esta nieve borra esquinas y borra sombras, pues hasta de noche la nieve alumbra. Y yo no sé lo que es verdad y lo que es mentira, ni lo que vi y lo que sólo soñé—o mejor lo que soñé y lo que sólo vi—, ni lo que supe ni lo que creí. (p. 58)

Even the paper on which she writes, and the story which she has written, take on the quality of snow:

> Ni sé si estoy traspasando a este papel, tan blanco como la nieve, mi conciencia, que en él se ha de quedar, quedándome yo sin ella. ¿Para qué tenerla ya . . .? (p. 58)

Angela, in short, is filled with doubts as to the reality of her own story:

> ¿Es que sé algo? ¿Es que creo algo? ¿Es que esto que estoy aquí contando ha pasado y ha pasado tal y como lo cuento? ¿Es que pueden pasar estas cosas? ¿Es que todo esto es más que un sueño soñado dentro de otro sueño? ¿Seré yo, Angela Carballino, hoy cincuentona, la única persona que en esta aldea se ve acometida de estos pensamientos extraños para los demás? ¿Y éstos, los otros, los que me rodean, creen? ¿Qué es eso de creer? Por lo menos, viven. Y ahora creen en San Manuel Bueno, mártir, que sin esperar la inmortalidad los mantuvo en la esperanza de ella. (p. 58)

She still asserts the value of Don Manuel's life-sustaining gospel, but the assertion is more than ever half-hearted, its applicability now limited to "ellos" rather than herself.

This evolution in Angela from the confident assertion of her personality at the start of the novel to the anguished sense of its dissolution at the end, should give pause to those who believe that in *San Manuel Bueno, mártir* Unamuno has somehow risen above the dualities and contradictions of the human condition through the reconciling vision of *intrahistoria*. It is no coincidence, moreover, that Angela's doubts about what she has written should bulk so large in her final agony, for Don Manuel has not merely challenged her beliefs in a conventional sense (i.e. by his own belief), but the ultimate mystery and elusiveness of Don Manuel—the gaping absence at the heart of her tale—challenge them in a more radical way. "Un sueño soñado dentro de otro sueño" is not merely as good a description as any of the tale she has told, it is also a no less accurate description of the precariousness of human personality which that story reflects.

Angela's situation at the end of her narrative, poised between agonised consciousness and the dissolution of that same consciousness in the mists of *intrahistoria*, was, it could be argued, Unamuno's own for much of his life. In that sense, *San Manuel Bueno, mártir* represents no radical new departure, no new conversion or consoling balm conjured from the intrahistoric mist. To understand why it does not, one must be attuned not merely to the intrahistoric vision which sits readily accessible on the surface of the book, but to the tragic implications which are locked into the novel's very structure and the consciousness of its narrator. *San Manuel Bueno, mártir* is no mere ideological skeleton. Nor is that most fashionable of objects—the novel—studiously engaged in the contemplation of its own navel. Hispanism's conventional distinctions between *modernismo* and the so-called "Generation of 1898" may well be somewhat suspect, and there may well be a case for giving Unamuno the place in Modernist fiction that he deserves. We shall, however, have to ensure that our model of Modernism is adequate to accommodate him. Simplifications about a largely mythical novelistic autonomy (however brightly that ideal may have shone in the minds of certain writers of the period), about mediums rather than messages, will not do. As *San Manuel Bueno, mártir* shows, the message is not something extraneous to the medium: the medium and the message are one.

Source: M. Gordon, "The Elusive Self: Narrative Method and Its Implications in 'San Manuel Bueno, Mártir,'" in *Hispanic Review*, Vol. 54, No. 2, Spring 1986, pp. 147–61.

C. A. Longhurst

In the following essay, Longhurst suggests that "the gospel of San Manuel written by Angela" is "her novel: not a record of a life but a personal interpretation of it, the work of Angela's imagination and fantasy. . . . "

We all know that fiction is the opposite of fact. A novel is called fiction, not fact; it is therefore not true. Yet while we are reading it we treat it *as if* it were true. What we are told in a novel, then, is true in a limited sense, that is to say it is true within the confines of the book. But if we happen to hold that truth is not absolute but relative to the observer, not merely something out there but something in the mind, then this can have interesting consequences for the novel, for it raises the possibility that what was regarded before as the truth within a fiction may now no longer be the truth. In modern novels (those of the post-realist era) there is always the chance that there may be different levels of truth or even of untruth. From Conrad's *Lord Jim* onwards, various

novelists (Scott Fitzgerald, Ford, Gide) have taught us to be on our guard against too easy an acceptance of the narrator's view. William Faulkner in particular has exploited the device of contradictory evidence from multiple narrators (for example in *Absalom, Absalom!*), while Franz Kafka's *The Trial* must stand as the prime example of the widespread practice among twentieth-century novelists of attenuating the authority traditionally invested in the narrative voice. Many earlier novelists had of course been aware of the possibilities of unreliable narration. It is a mode of narration frequently adopted in ghost stories and supernatural or implausible tales, the object of which was a simple one: to absolve the author of the tale from the accusation of writing nonsense by raising the possibility or probability that, even on the plane of the characters in the book, the events narrated never actually happened (even Cervantes used this technique in *El coloquio de los perros*). The tremendous resurgence in the use of unreliable narration in the twentieth-century novel has other roots. Here we are not usually dealing with the question of whether an event actually happened or not, but rather with the way in which a real object or occurrence is perceived, construed, represented, or distorted by the human mind. The new view of reality as the creation of human consciousness has led modern novelists to move away from the novel based on events and towards the novel based on the *perception* of events. Events and objects in themselves cease to have any absolute meaning and are important only in so far as they are perceived by or have an effect upon a consciousness. The neo-Kantian philosophical stance so prevalent in the late nineteenth and early twentieth centuries resulted in the wide acceptance of the view that an individual's apprehension of reality is governed by his own conceptions. That human beings are prone to over-interpretation and embellishments of phenomena is another now long-established view. Put the two together and the traditional view of the novel as objectively true on its own plane looks more than a little questionable. Why should it be objectively true? If in real life truth does not come to us in its virgin, undistorted form, why should we assume that it does so in a novel?

This question has implications for both writers and readers. In the case of a novelist it puts before him the choice (or the obligation, if he feels strongly enough about it) of formulating his work in such a way that he offers not the truth of a person or event (since no-one can perceive the world with complete objectivity), but merely the reconstruction of a

> "... is Angela a reliable witness? The answer must be in the negative, not so much because Angela is relating falsehoods, but because her vision is coloured by her own psychological problems, both religious and emotional."

particular consciousness, whether that consciousness belongs to an impersonal or to a personalized narrator. In the case of the reader it confronts him with the need to go beyond the surface of the narration, to make allowances for the distorting filter that is the narrating consciousness and to arrive if he can at his own version of the truth instead of relying passively on the narrator.

Unamuno's *San Manuel Bueno, mártir* has often been called the most perfect, most satisfying of Unamuno's novels, and more than one critic has described it as a prose poem. Yet almost the entire critical debate on this novel has revolved around the mainly theological or philosophical question of whether the protagonist exemplifies religious scepticism or uncertainty or an unusual kind of faith. There are indeed a whole host of questions about the nature of Don Manuel's beliefs which the work poses, questions which have understandably, if inconclusively, aroused a good deal of critical interest. But in pursuing these questions which have to do with finding the meaning *of* the work, other questions more specifically directed to finding meaning *in* the work have largely been ignored. Why did Unamuno employ a personalized narrator? Why did he choose a female narrator? Why should Angela want to write down Don Manuel's story anyway? Questions such as these, important from a literary point of view if not from a religious or philosophical one, have scarcely been formulated and remain largely unanswered.

The following proposition will serve as my basic premiss: there is no way we can get to know the truth about Don Manuel because we do not see Don Manuel directly; all we see is Angela's reconstruction of him. We get absolutely no other view of Don Manuel, not even Lázaro's, because Lázaro's account of him is given through Angela. The only objective knowledge we possess of Don Manuel (objective within the fiction, of course) is that he had a reputation for sanctity and that because of this reputation the bishop of the diocese is promoting the process of beatification. Indeed the reader learns this fact (i.e. the promotion of the beatification process) in the very first sentence of Angela's narrative: it stands out as a significant fact. Obviously for beatification to take place the Church will require not only sanctity but also orthodoxy: it is not going to beatify someone who does not believe in the resurrection of Christ. The bishop and the villagers appear to have no doubts about Don Manuel's orthodoxy. Now suppose that Angela's memoir fell into the hands of the bishop and the ecclesiastical court considering Don Manuel's beatification: how would they react to it? This, after all, is exactly the position the reader of Angela's account is in at the start of the novel. Like the bishop and the ecclesiastical court of inquiry the reader will want to establish the truth about Don Manuel. The bishop and other members of the court of inquiry, then (and by analogy the reader), if they were honest and conscientious, would want to consider two questions in connexion with Angela's account: (1) Is there any external evidence to support Angela's view of Don Manuel? (2) What sort of a person is the writer of this document: is she a completely reliable witness, reliable enough for what she says to be taken literally? The answer to the first question must be no; Angela has not a single supporting witness upon whom to call. Lázaro, who might have shed further light, is by now dead (and the notes which he left behind appear to contain Don Manuel's teachings, not evidence of his disbelief—Angela never actually quotes from these notes). The answer to the second question is of course crucial to the interpretation of the novel. In what follows I address myself first and in detail to this question, that is to say to analysing the character of the narrator, the particular *way* that she writes, and her motives in writing. I shall then briefly switch my attention to the author of the novel and consider the implications for Unamuno's narrative art as it reveals itself in this particular work.

Angela's avowed aim is not of course to write about herself. Yet we can build up a picture of Angela's character and personality from what she feels compelled to say directly about herself and from what she reveals about herself indirectly in the process of writing down her account. There is a caveat to be made here: we must not be content to take everything the narrator tells us at face value; we must look critically at the information and judge the extent to which it is being distorted or manipulated by the narrating mind. It is not so much a matter of questioning the basic facts of the story as of questioning the interpretation of them which is implied in their presentation.

One of the facts of Angela's circumstances which I believe to be important is that she found herself without a father very early on: 'se me murió siendo yo muy niña', as we read on the first page (p. 583; references are to vol. XVI of the *Obras completas*). Her mother came under the spell of Don Manuel and the memory of her husband soon faded, so that Angela lacked not only the physical presence of her father but also the image of him: 'mi buena madre apenas si me contaba hechos o dichos de mi padre' (p. 583). This simple fact about Angela's upbringing, which the casual reader will invariably forget, will come through powerfully in the memoir she composes late in her life, as I hope to demonstrate.

Angela confesses to entertaining, since her tender years, 'curiosidades, preoccupaciones e inquietudes' (p. 585), and although she does not specify what these preoccupations are, she mentions the works of literature she read and in the same breath ascribes certain romantic and religious fantasies to a school friend. The tell-tale phrase 'por cierto que no he vuelto a saber de ella ni de su suerte' (p. 585) suggests the irrelevance or even the unreality of this friend. The whole paragraph in which Angela tells us of her childhood fantasies, clearly unnecessary from the point of view of Don Manuel's story, is rather suggestive from the point of view of Angela's characterization, and it seems reasonable to suppose that Unamuno had this particular function in mind when he included it in the novel. The language used reveals a distinct amorous sensitivity, to the point of mystical rapture: 'me proponía que entrásemos juntas a la vez en un mismo convento, jurándonos, y hasta firmando el juramento con nuestra sangre, hermandad perpetua, y otras veces me hablaba, *con los ojos semicerrados*, de novios y de aventuras matrimoniales. . . . Cuando se hablaba de nuestro Don Manuel . . . ésta exclamaba *como en arrobo*: "¡Qué suerte, chica, la de poder vivir cerca de un santo así, de un santo vivo de carne y hueso, y poder besarle la mano!"' (p. 585; my italics). The attribution of amorous and mystical inclinations to a companion can be seen as displacement—for why else tell us about it? Or why

should this attachment live on in the memory of the narrator? Angela, we should remember, has passed her fiftieth birthday as she writes, yet she vividly relives—remembering or imagining, it makes no difference—the raptures of her friend at the thought of living close to Don Manuel. Romantic and religious fantasizing occur simultaneously and inseparably in Angela's mind. This is accompanied by a noticeable aestheticism which finds its outlet in listening to Don Manuel officiating at High Mass: 'Su maravilla era la voz, una voz divina, que hacía llorar. Cuando al oficiar en misa mayor o solemne entonaba el prefacio, estremecíase la iglesia y todos los que le oían sentíanse conmovidos en sus entrañas. Su canto, saliendo del templo, iba a quedarse dormido sobre el lago y al pie de la montaña' (p. 587). Some of the episodes recalled by Angela reveal her excessive sensibility and lachrymose nature, for example Blasillo's parrot-like repetition of Don Manuel's singing: 'Y al irme hacia mi casa topé con Blasillo el bobo, que . . . repitió—¡y de qué modo!—lo de "¡Dios mío!, ¡Dios mío!, ¡por qué me has abandonado?" Llegué a casa acongojadísima y me encerré en mi cuarto para llorar' (p. 597). Angela's identification with Don Manuel becomes ever more complete; serving as his personal assistant and constant companion, she refers to 'nuestros enfermos' (p. 598), and she cannot bear to be parted from him; when she is absent for a few days 'sentía sobre todo la falta de mi Don Manuel y como si su ausencia me llamara, como si corriese un peligro lejos de mí, como si me necesitara' (p. 598). There is, needless to say, not a shred of evidence that Don Manuel missed or needed Angela. The emotional flow is all in the opposite direction. Angela gives herself away by her choice of words: she says 'su ausencia', whereas logically she should have said 'mi ausencia' since *she* is the one who has gone away from Valverde; but for Angela it is Don Manuel who is absent, absent, that is, from her life. Similarly, she believes or avers that she went to confession with Don Manuel in order to console him. Yet Unamuno has contrived to allow us a glimpse that hints at a different explanation, for if we consider Don Manuel's own words we get the impression that he is getting a trifle impatient with Angela's frequent visits to the confession box: 'Despachemos, que me están esperando unos enfermos de verdad' (p. 597), he tells her, suggesting that her spiritual illness is 'de mentira', that she is indulging in unreal self-accusation and that her frequent visits to the confessional are unnecessary. Angela's mother, too, remarks upon her daughter's excessive devotion to confession: 'Me parece, Angelita, con tantas confesiones, que tú te me vas a ir monja' (p. 597).

In fact Angela firmly rejects the idea of becoming a nun; but, what is more interesting, she equally rejects the idea of marriage. It is Don Manuel who first raises the possibility of Angela's marriage when he makes a harmless remark to the effect that she must now prepare herself 'para darnos otra familia' (p. 595), a remark which, retrospectively, turns out to contain a deep irony, since the cause of Angela's spinsterhood is Don Manuel himself. To her mother, Angela's marriage appears a natural and likely event, as it suggested by her words 'hasta que te cases' (p. 597). This is the second time that the possibility of Angela's marriage is raised, and Angela counters with a curt dismissal of the idea: 'no pienso en ello' (p. 597). The third time that the question is brought up it is Don Manuel who raises it, and Angela's reaction on this occasion is much more complex and interesting. The entire passage deserves careful scrutiny:

—¿Y por qué no te casas, Angelina?

—Ya sabe usted, padre mío, por qué.

—Pero no, no; tienes que casarte. Entre Lázaro y yo te buscaremos un novio. Porque a ti te conviene casarte para que se te curen esas preocupaciones.

—¿Preocupaciones, Don Manuel?

—Yo sé bien lo que me digo. Y no te acongojes demasiado por los demás, que harto tiene cada cual con tener que responder de sí mismo.

—¡Y que sea usted, Don Manuel, el que me diga eso!, ¡que sea usted el que me aconseje que me case para responder de mí y no acuitarme por los demás! ¡que sea usted!

—Tienes razón, Angelina, no sé ya lo que me digo; no sé ya lo que me digo desde que estoy confesándome contigo. Y sí, sí, hay que vivir, hay que vivir.

Y cuando yo iba a levantarme para salir del templo, me dijo:

—Y ahora, Angelina, en nombre del pueblo, ¿me absuelves?

Me sentí como penetrada de un misterioso sacerdocio y le dije:

—En nombre de Dios Padre, Hijo y Espíritu Santo, le absuelvo, padre.

Y salimos de la iglesia, y al salir se me estremecían las entrañas maternales. (p. 608)

This reported exchange between Don Manuel and Angela is ambiguous and may be seen to have implications beyond the surface meaning. Angela's answer to Don Manuel's first question is, for the reader, far from obvious. Don Manuel may know

why Angela cannot marry, but the fact is that Angela has not told us. Nor does Don Manuel voice that knowledge that Angela ascribes to him: he merely rejects the validity of Angela's reason and gives instead his own reason why she should marry. Those preoccupations mentioned by Don Manuel and queried by Angela remain unspecified; but the kind of 'preocupaciones' that are cured by marriage are fundamentally sexual ones: after all the Church itself teaches that one of the objects of marriage is the allaying of concupiscence and the simultaneous fulfilment of the natural drive to procreate. I am not arguing that Angela is motivated by concupiscence; simply that Don Manuel realizes what Angela does not, namely that the nature of her attachment to him is fundamentally sexual but is sublimated into a spiritual or mystical one. The phrase 'responder de sí mismo' is also ambivalent: it means to be in charge of, or responsible for, especially in a moral sense, as in 'Los padres deben responder de sus hijos', but in the way used by Don Manuel it can also mean to be responsible for one's actions. Angela's overreaction, in which she accuses Don Manuel of double standards, suggests her discomfort and confusion. She clearly resents Don Manuel's insistence on the advisability of marriage and implies that he is in no position to look for comfortable solutions to her problem. Don Manuel, in the face of Angela's reaction, backpedals and asks for forgiveness for his hurtful insinuation, which Angela willingly grants. The lovers' reconciliation after the argument, for such it seems as Angela presents it, is clothed in religious language, but Angela betrays the hidden nature of her feelings by the use of words which have other associations. The word 'penetrada' (where 'invadida' or 'imbuida' would have been more appropriate in a purely religious context) tells its own tale, but is in any case reinforced by the explicit 'se me estremecían las entrañas maternales'. Angela does not write 'salí de la iglesia' but 'salimos de la iglesia', which recalls the public emergence of husband and wife together after the marriage ceremony. Thus, in reliving her association with the priest as she writes her memoir she gives away her unconscious fantasies and desires.

There is an image which Angela repeatedly associates with Don Manuel and which tends to confirm that her attachment to him is not purely religious. She repeatedly casts him in the role of father; and I am not referring to the role of spiritual father which it is Don Manuel's priestly duty to fulfil, but to a rather more concrete paternity or fatherliness which Angela emphasizes, a paternity which nurses and fosters in a much more physical sense. The explanation which Angela gives for Don Manuel entering the priesthood is that he wanted to look after the children of a widowed sister, 'servirles de padre' (p. 586). She also relates various anecdotes which show Don Manuel in the role of protective parent. When on a certain occasion he meets a child sent out by his father on a wintry day to look for a cow, he sends the child home and proceeds to do the father's job for him. When an unmarried girl returns to the village with a baby it is to Don Manuel that Angela ascribes a crucial intervention in finding a father for the child. Don Manuel is depicted, too, as extremely interested in pregnancies ('se interesaba sobre todo en los embarazos') and in child-rearing. The paternal role of Don Manuel is accompanied by virile qualities that enable him to fulfil a masculine role in the community. He engages in manual labour, 'con sus brazos', collaborating in such tasks as ploughing and cutting logs for the poorer homes in winter. In all this there is discernible a desire to present Don Manuel as a father, but as a father with the clear attributes of a dominant and protective male figure. The masculinity of Don Manuel acquires its particular significance when we connect it to the narrating consciousness, that of Angela, and even more when we consider that Angela herself comes very close at times to presenting herself in the role of unfulfilled mother. I have already commented upon one occasion in which Angela refers to her 'entrañas maternales'. This, however, is not the only time Angela uses this kind of image. When she relates the effect of her first confession with Don Manuel she uses the same image: 'Era yo entonces una mocita, una niña cast; pero empezaba a ser mujer, sentía en *mis entrañas el jugo de la maternidad'* . . . (p. 596; my italics). It is of course a hankering for maternity that remains unfulfilled as Angela chooses to enter 'nuestro monasterio de Valverde de Lucerna' and place herself 'a los pies de su abad' (p. 595). The sublimation of her love for Don Manuel into a mystical devotion to her village-monastery (a mystical sublimation further suggested by Don Manuel's advice that she stop paying so much attention to St Teresa) cannot hide the ingrained female instinct to regard man as a potential medium of maternal fulfilment. This is variously revealed in Angela's characterization of Don Manuel as a fully masculine figure with a strong paternal role, in her apparently unconscious revelation of her own maternal instincts, and finally in the unexplained feeling of guilt that so disturbs her: '¿pecadores? ¿nosotros pecadores? ¿y cuál es nuestro pecado, cuál? Y

anduve todo el día acongojada por esta pregunta' (p. 614). Indeed there is much in the narrative that is indicative of the unconscious mind at work: Angela's attribution of enamourment of Don Manuel to her mother or of a 'grito maternal' to a figure of the Virgin, both of which could be read as unconscious displacement; or the reference to 'hijos ausentes' of women for whom Don Manuel serves as amanuensis; or the death of a pregnant woman in the arms of Don Manuel; or the reference to a recently-widowed woman who wants to follow her husband but is dissuaded by Don Manuel; all of which could be interpreted as an unconscious revelation of Angela's frustrated motherhood and enforced sterility in the face of her attachment to Don Manuel. The inexplicable feeling of guilt, the frequent tears, the mental confusion, taken in conjunction with the narrator's highly significant references to dreaming can be seen as the embodiment in covert form of the conflict or anxiety which the conscious mind has censored. Thus, while the theme of maternity, fulfilled, vicarious or frustrated, appears in several of Unamuno's works, in this particular one it is given novel treatment, both because of the nature of the potential father (not a brother-in-law as in *La tía Tula* but a saintly priest) and because of the confessional nature of the account.

Perhaps we are now a little closer to answering the question formulated earlier: is Angela a reliable witness? The answer must be in the negative, not so much because Angela is relating falsehoods, but because her vision is coloured by her own psychological problems, both religious and emotional. Far from being objective, neutral and detached, Angela is subjective, idiosyncratic, and emotionally involved with the subject of her memoir. Not only does she not give a balanced view of Don Manuel, but she oscillates alarmingly between the panegyrical and the captious. One thing stands out: Angela is determined to interpret Don Manuel's behaviour as indicating a lack of faith. But the evidence is entirely circumstantial (with the possible exception of Lázaro's witness) and its value depends totally upon a subjective interpretation. From the very first, the narrator regularly inserts phrases which act as a process of persuasion at a subliminal level and which therefore have the effect of pre-empting the issue. Here is a sample of such phrases:

Después, al llegar a conocer el secreto de nuestro santo . . . (p. 589)

Bien comprendí yo . . . que algún pensamiento le perseguía. (p. 590)

Y más tarde … he comprendido que la alegría, imperturbable de Don Manuel era la forma temporal y terrena de una infinita y eterna tristeza que con heroica santidad recataba a los ojos y los oídos de los demás. (p. 593)

Me retiré, pensando no sé por qué, que nuestro Don Manuel, tan afamado curandero de endemoniados, no creía en el demonio. (p. 597)

Leí no sé qué honda tristeza en sus ojos, azules como las aguas del lago. (p. 598)

— . . . Pero lee sobre todo libros de piedad que te den contento de vivir, un contento apacible y silencioso.

¿Le tenía él? (p. 601)

These examples of Angela's subjective interpretation are all taken from the earlier part of the story, before Lázaro has struck up a friendship with Don Manuel and provides Angela with confirmation of her view of the priest. We could of course assume that Angela's recollection of Don Manual and of her association with him up to this point has been retrospectively affected by Lázaro's subsequent revelations; in other words, that Angela, under the influence of Lázaro's reports, interprets Don Manuel's words and actions before the time of Lázaro's involvement as indicative of disbelief. But the fact remains that prior to this development there is no good evidence that Don Manuel is lacking in faith; all that happens is that Angela assumes or imagines that this is so and slants the narration in such a way as to put the idea in the reader's head. Even Lázaro's witness need not be interpreted as proof of Don Manuel's unbelief; there is an obvious alternative interpretation, without having to adopt the extreme position of regarding Angela's explanation as a complete fabrication on her part: that Don Manuel, realizing that Lázaro, a liberal intellectual, was hardly likely to be won over to his cause by theological argument, decided instead to adopt an entirely different approach and win him over by an appeal to his caring conscience, exactly the method he had successfully employed earlier at Lázaro's mother's deathbed. This would put the question not on a theological plane but on a purely pragmatic one—is Christianity of value or not?—in which the question of deception would be irrelevant. But Angela, instead of asking the straightforward question: why did Don Manuel act in this way?, which would have yielded the foregoing answer as an obvious possibility, inverts the terms, asking instead: '¿por qué—me he preguntado muchas veces—no trató Don Manuel de convertir a mi hermano también con su engaño, con una mentira, fingiéndose creyente sin serlo?' (p. 625). Since Angela *assumes* that Don Manuel is feigning in his attitude towards

the people of Valverde, she asks why he ceases to feign in the case of her brother. The question is thus formulated in a thoroughly tendentious manner, a manner which allows her to bring up the idea of *engaño* and *engañar*, words which she employs repeatedly throughout her narration. Indeed Angela is unwilling to accept Don Manuel's own declaration that he believes, and bombards him with a string of questions, some of them rather too emotional to be relevant to a purely religious affair:

—Pero usted, padre, ¿cree usted?

Vaciló un momento y, reponiéndose, me dijo:

—¡Creo!

—Pero ¿en qué, padre, en qué? ¿Cree usted en la otra vida?, ¿ cree que al morir no nos morimos del todo?, ¿cree que volveremos a vernos, a querernos en otro mundo venidero?, ¿cree en la otra vida?

El pobre santo sollozaba.

—¡Mira, hija, dejemos eso!

Y ahora, al escribir esta memoria, me digo: ¿Por qué no me engaño? ¿Por qué no me engañó entonces como engañaba a los demás? ¿Por qué se acongojó? ¿Porque no podía engañarse a sí mismo, o porque no podía engañarme? Y quiero creer que se acongojaba porque no podía engañarse para engañarme. (p. 607)

Once again this passage tells us nothing about the priest—although it purports to—but it does tell us something about Angela. Firstly, Angela contrives to turn the priest's statement of belief into a tacit admission of unbelief by playing on his evasiveness and discomfort and then interpreting this as a sign of lack of faith. But bearing in mind that this occurs during an emotional scene and immediately before Don Manuel's suggestion that Angela should marry, his evasiveness and discomfort may have other roots, apart from which his way of winning over Lázaro has landed him in an awkward position once the latter has given his own version to his sister. Secondly, Angela states that Don Manuel is deceiving everyone, except her; and here we have what amounts to a leitmotif in her account, never explicitly stated in so many words but consistently implied: that unlike the simple village folk, she was too intelligent for Don Manuel and saw through his false front from the very beginning.

Angela does not condemn Don Manuel overtly for what he does; her criticism is subtle and insidious, but no less present for that. Her attitude to him is ambivalent, an ambivalence exemplified in the contradictory phrase she uses to describe his behaviour: 'piadoso fraude.' Having left us in little doubt that Don Manuel's faith is a pretence, she then goes on to label him a martyr and a saint, and to suggest that both he and Lázaro were believers without knowing so. There is certainly something admirable about Don Manuel as he emerges from Angela's portrayal; yet at the same time there are details in this portrayal which strongly suggest that Angela's attitude hides some kind of unexplained resentment. The first kind of detail I have already mentioned: Angela's frequent references to deception, as if she resented Don Manuel's exemplary adherence to his priestly and pastoral—duties, as in the following exchange with her brother:

> —Y ahora—añadió mi hermano—hay otro más para consolar al pueblo.
>
> —¿Para engañarle?—dije. (p. 606)

Angela presents Don Manuel as an actor playing a role, an actor who has a magnetic effect on his audience through his presence and vocal qualities: 'la acción de su presencia, de sus miradas, y . . . sobre todo la dulcísima autoridad de sus palabras y sobre todo de su voz—¡qué milagro de voz!' (p. 587). The high point of Don Manuel's act is his playing of the part of Christ in the Good Friday service, with the enunciation of the words, 'My God, my God, why hast Thou forsaken me?', but several other actions of Don Manuel as presented by Angela strike a theatrical note: his tears in the presence of Angela, his use of catch-phrases such as 'doctores tiene la Santa Madre Iglesia', his last general communion in which as he gives the host he whispers to Lázaro 'no hay más vida eterna que ésta' and to Angela 'reza también por Nuestro Señor Jesucristo', and finally his death in the church in front of his entire congregation. It is not so much a person as an actor that we are presented with, an actor publicly playing the part of a saint. It is this role-playing, this 'fingimiento' or pretence, that must make us question Angela's attitude towards Don Manuel.

The second kind of detail involves irony on the part of the narrator: 'Y el pueblo al ver llorar a Don Manuel, lloró diciéndose: "!Cómo le quiere!" Y entonces, pues era la madrugada, cantó un gallo' (p. 603). This gratuitous comment adds up to an accusation of hypocrisy. It reveals the narrator's covert or unconscious disapproval of Don Manuel's and Lázaro's action: just as Peter betrayed Christ, so they are betraying the beliefs of their people by going through the mechanics of a conversion that is false. Angela's comment is also at variance with what follows:

> Al volver a casa y encerrarme en ella con mi hermano, le eché los brazos al cuello y besándole le dije:
>
> —¡Ay Lázaro, Lázaro, que alegría nos has dado a todos, a todos, a todo el pueblo, a todo, a los vivos y a los muertos y sobre todo a mamá, a nuestra madre! ¿Viste? El pobre Don Manuel lloraba de alegría. ¡Qué alegría nos has dado a todos!. (p. 603)

These words necessarily strike a hollow note coming, as they do, immediately after the symbol of falsehood or betrayal that Angela has inserted in her account, because the symbol pre-empts the explanation that Lázaro is about to provide. The narrator, at the moment of narrating, has seen fit to label Don Manuel's and Lázaro's action as false and hypocritical, even though she already knew their explanation for acting in this way, an explanation which she proceeds to offer to the reader. The contradiction reveals either disingenuousness or confusion in the mind of the narrator. On the occasion of Don Manuel's death we read: 'Y no hubo que cerrarle los ojos, porque se murió con ellos cerrados' (p. 618). In its sheer redundancy, the latter phrase smacks of ironic insinuation—he remained blind to the end. Just how aware is Angela of the implications of her comments? One cannot be sure whether Unamuno intended us to read these gratuitous remarks as the narrator's ironic commentary on the protagonist or as the author's ironic commentary on the narrator, but in any case one can observe a deliberate tension created by the novelist between the facts of the story themselves and the narrator's presentation of them.

The third and final kind of detail I wish to mention in connexion with Angela's ambiguous portrayal of Don Manuel involves the inclusion of references to certain objects which are mentioned but not commented upon by Angela and which would appear to have a built-in ambivalence. The word *lago*, though referring of course to the lake of Valverde de Lucerna, is intimately associated in Angela's mind with Don Manuel: the very first time the lake is mentioned, it is used as an aid to describe the priest's eyes, and priest and lake are repeatedly mentioned in the same breath after this. Critics have usually attached a philosophic or Jungian symbolism to the word *lago*. But another kind of symbolism is possible; at one point Angela writes: 'Don Manuel emprendió la tarea de hacer él de lago, de piscina probática' (p. 587), and later she says: 'me contó una historia [about Don Manuel] que me sumergió en un lago de tristeza' (p. 604). In the first sentence Don Manuel is a lake in whose waters sick people find a cure; if we ascribe the same value to the word 'lake' in the second instance, the sentence acquires distinct Freudian resonances. First used by

Angela to suggest the secret lying undetected in the depths of Don Manuel's personality, the symbol can be restored to its owner and regarded as representing Angela's unconscious desires. The same ambivalence is detectable in the *clavellina desecada* found in Don Manuel's breviary: 'Mi hermano guardó su breviario, entre cuyas hojas encontró, desecada y como en un herbario, una clavellina pegada a un papel, yen éste, una cruz con una fecha' (p. 619). Since Angela is including this curious detail in her account it must have some meaning for her, contain some information which she deems important. If we take the account at this point to be factual, the simplest and the logical explanation would be that this is a record of the gift of the breviary made to the priest, perhaps at his ordination or at the time when he entered the seminary. But this would not explain why Angela felt it necessary to mention it. The meaning that Angela may be wanting to convey without being too explicit is that Don Manuel lost his faith on a particular date a long time ago, the dessicated bloom suggesting loss of illusions. This is a possible reading and the conventional one (though not an entirely logical one: does one lose one's faith on a specific date?). But on another level we can read the symbol differently: *clavellina* is a diminutive of *clavel*, and *clavel* is a flower popularly associated in song and folklore with romance. We have therefore a romantic as well as a religious association in this symbol, entirely as if Angela were fantasizing about her own relationship with Don Manuel: the *clavellina desecada* would symbolize Angela's infertile love, her withered romance. The choice of diminutive is interesting, for there is a phonemic coincidence between *clavellina* and the name that Don Manuel uses to address Angela in the privacy of the confessional: Angelina (her mother and brother never use this form of the diminutive; they use 'Angelita'). Another object with an implied symbolic value that lends itself to conflicting interpretation is the walnut tree out of which Don Manuel carves himself six planks:

> Cuando se secó aquel magnifico nogal—'un nogal matriarcal' le llamaba—a cuya sombra había jugado de niño y con cuyas nueces se había durante tantos años regalado, pidió el tronco, se lo llevó a su casa y, después de labrar en él seis tablas que guardaba al pie de su lecho, hizo del resto leña para calendar a los pobres. (p. 591)

The image recurs later:

> Cuando me entierren [Angela makes Don Manuel say], que sea en una caja hecha con aquellas seis tablas que tallé del viejo nogal, ¡pobrecillo!, a cuya

sombra jugué de niño, cuando empezaba a soñar...¡Y entonces sí que creía en la verdad perdurable ! Es decir, me figuro ahora que creía entonces. Para un niño, creer no es más que soñar. Y para un pueblo. Esas seis tablas que tallé con mis propias manos, las encontraréis al pie de mi cama. (p. 616)

It is important once again to distinguish between the facts of the story and the use to which those facts are put by the narrator. The only accessible or verifiable fact (verifiable, that is, on the level of the fiction, by the bishop and the ecclesiastical court, for example) is that Don Manuel was buried in a coffin made of wood which he himself had cut. Why did he keep part of the tree in the form of planks and why did he want his coffin to be made out of them? The facts, of course, do not speak for themselves, but one could reasonably presume, firstly, that Don Manuel was using those planks to sleep on (to sleep on hard beds is after all a custom traditionally associated with clerical asceticism), and secondly, that the wood represented a bond with his people: he had shared the tree with them and in death he wants to remain symbolically united to them (again, to express a wish about one's burial is a perfectly common human occurrence). But this is not how Angela uses the symbol. She quite specifically connects the tree to Don Manuel's innocent childhood, and the priest's attachment to those wooden planks and his instructions for his burial are seen as a longing on his part to recover the strong and simple faith of infancy ('Except ye be converted and become as little children, ye shall not enter into the kingdom of heaven', Matthew 18. 3). Hence some critics have quite reasonably interpreted the symbol as one of hope in a religious sense. But suppose we consider instead the process by which Angela creates the symbol. The first reference makes it look as if she had known all along about the wooden planks in Don Manuel's bed; but it was really at the time of Don Manuel's death that she learnt about them. (This is not an assumption on my part; it is a logical consequence of the text as it stands.) So far as the narrator is concerned, it is her recollection of Don Manuel's poignant request on his deathbed that triggers off the idea of the tree as a symbol. And in the second passage, the key one, she elaborates upon the facts and presents Don Manuel's request in such a way as to characterize his religious faith as something unfounded and unreal. But the sentiments she puts in the mouth of Don Manuel parallel her own present sentiments. When she makes him say 'me figuro ahora que creía entonces' she is echoing her own question to herself *at the moment of writing*: '¿Y yo creo?' (p. 625). When she makes him equate his childhood faith with dreaming (both in this and in an immediately preceding passage when Don Manuel says 'quiero dormir sin soñar'), she is reflecting her own tendency, *as she writes,* to see the past as a dream: '¿Es que esto que estoy aquí contando ha pasado . . . ? ¿Es que todo esto es más que un sueño soñado dentro de otro sueño?' (p. 626). By elaborating in this way Angela converts the 'hopeful' symbol into a 'hopeless' one. After his death Don Manuel will continue to sleep on those wooden planks which have been his bed for so long, emphasizing the process of the total abandonment of faith: living tree, dead tree, wooden planks, coffin. The walnut tree whose fruit Don Manuel enjoyed eating as a boy becomes a symbol of mother earth, both the source and ultimate destiny of human life, a symbol not of faith in an after-life but of an earth-bound existence. Nor is this all; for the ambiguity of the symbol—simple religious faith or telluric bondage—acquires disquieting undertones when we come across the third and final reference to it: 'Las endemoniadas venían ahora a tocar la cruz de nogal, hecha también por sus manos y sacada del mismo árbol de donde sacó las seis tablas en que fue enterrado' (p. 620). It is impossible not to wonder whether there is an intended, and even cruel, irony contained in this sentence. The wood of the walnut tree has been fashioned into a cross by the hands of a priest of whom the narrator has earlier told us 'no creía en el demonio' (p. 597); and this cross, we are now told, is serving to attract precisely those over whom the Devil himself has taken possession. Angela sees Don Manuel's tomb not as a place of rest but as the Mecca for devilish women. This Satanic vision of Don Manuel (if such it is) would imply a strongly subjective, even disturbed, consciousness at work in the narrative. Indeed Angela had earlier wondered whether she herself was not 'endemoniada', possessed, perverse, or hysterical.

I would submit, then, that Angela's personal re-creation of Don Manuel is an equivocal and contradictory one, governed by her own ambiguous relationship with him. It is a portrayal of Don Manuel in which the overt aim of presenting him in a saintly light is undermined by a covert reprobation which has no very clear cause but which reflects her lonely and unhappy situation at the time of writing. If speculation about a fictitious character's real motives were not such a debatable exercise one might conjecture that she is suffering from a suppressed resentment caused by rebuff or frustration. But in any case what emerges perfectly clearly without any

need to speculate is her mental confusion and disorientation, her bewilderment and even perturbation. This is not merely implicit in her ambivalent portrayal of Don Manuel but is explicitly recognized by her at the end of her story: she confesses that she can no longer tell truth from falsehood, reality from imagination; she wonders whether what she relates actually happened the way she relates it. Curiously she brings in the idea of conscience: 'no sé si estoy traspasando a este papel . . . mi conciencia' (p. 625), suggesting that writing down her memoir has some therapeutic or cathartic value. Angela had forged a relationship with Don Manuel which, on her side, clearly went further than the normal one between confessor and penitent or between priest and acolyte. For Angela, Don Manuel became a father-figure with a latent sexual role. Just as a nun entering a convent and taking her vows becomes 'the bride of Christ', so Angela on entering her own convent of Valverde de Lucerna (as she herself calls it) becomes in her own imagination the bride of Don Manuel. Psychologically this ties in perfectly with what we learn of Angela's childhood. The loss of her own father when very young provokes a search for a surrogate father, and given her mother's devotion to Don Manuel, the child's attention is drawn towards the priest. This initial conditioning is reinforced by Angela coming under the tutelage of the priest at a particularly impressionable age: sixteen. On returning to the village from school she immediately becomes emotionally involved (as is evident from her first encounter with Don Manuel) with the figure of the priest whom her mother has for so long held up to her as a father-figure; the surrogate father becomes a surrogate husband. What is recognized by developmental psychology as being only a passing phase in female adolescence becomes, in Angela's case, a permanent state of affairs; indeed this possibility has already been adumbrated by the early reference in the text to the lure of the convent and the visions of romantic and matrimonial adventures all in the same breath. Angela *qua* narrator and Angela *qua* character are thus beautifully consistent.

This view of Angela not only appears to fit the facts of her life-story, but also goes some way towards explaining why she writes. For her, Don Manuel has been at the centre of her life. When he dies, she still has Lázaro to help maintain alive the image of the priest and to act as a link with her past: 'Él, Lázaro, continuaba la tradición del santo y empezó a redactar lo que le había oído' (p. 620). Lázaro's death signifies a break in Angela's life, and this break, exacerbated by the bishop's insistent questioning and by his decision to write a book about Don Manuel thus threatening to take over from Angela the creative function of keeping alive the image of the priest, precipitates a crisis that leads directly to her memoir. (Angela's references to the present, that is the time of narration, indicate that she writes not long after Lázaro's death and at the time of the ecclesiastical inquiry into Don Manuel's life.) For Angela, now old and lonely ('desolada', 'envejecida'), the memoir is a life-support: it enables her to relive in fantasy her association with Don Manuel, to try and find meaning and consolation in the past as she searches for some sense of purpose in the present. As she consciously consigns her memories to paper she also subconsciously betrays feelings of perplexity and regret at having given her life to Don Manuel's spiritual cause only to find herself in the end sad, lonely, and confused. It is evident that Angela's reconstruction of Don Manuel's life, her revelation of his 'secreto trágico' or of his 'piadoso fraude', represents a reply and a challenge to the orthodox biography that the bishop is preparing. Angela, who has been a doubting Thomas all her life, from the time she started reading her father's books to the moment of writing her memoir, makes an even greater one of Don Manuel. This 'togetherness in doubt' compensates for the simple fact that she never succeeded in being as close to Don Manuel as Lázaro and Blasillo: she did not enjoy the affection of Don Manuel as the village idiot did, nor did she enjoy the confidence of Don Manuel as her brother did. The unconscious recognition that Don Manuel did not fully reciprocate her infatuation leads her to write a double-edged account of the priest's life, encomiastic yet subtly critical. But the memoir allows us to infer much more about Angela herself than about the priest: *she* is the real doubter. The only real truth in the novel is the truth of the narrator herself; the real Don Manuel, hidden behind the impenetrable barrier of Angela's personality, uncertainties, and emotions, is inaccessible. One could in theory go further and put forward the view that the entire memoir was conceived by the novelist as a mere piece of fantasy on the part of the fictional narrator, with no basis in reality (fictional reality, that is). But such an explanation, though perfectly admissible in the case of certain stories by Poe, Borges, and others, seems to me unhelpful in this particular case. The theme and tone of the story suggest that what Unamuno had in mind was not a stark true/false alternative but an exploration of the nature of perception and belief, that is, of an individual's own intimate reasons, motivations, or pressures for accepting or not ac-

cepting something as true and real. At any rate we can be fairly certain that one of the reasons why Unamuno chose a personalized narrator, and a very particular one at that, was in order to eschew the 'truth' or the 'reality' within the fiction, in other words to provide us, the readers, with sufficient grounds on which to question the exactitude of Angela's account. One of the aims of Unamuno in *San Manuel Bueno, mártir*—any rate one of the results of the technique he employs—is to raise the question of narrative authority, in which he was deeply interested, with special reference to the Gospels. Narratives, whether historical or fictitious, speak in hidden and personal ways and cannot simply be taken as mere records of facts. Just as the Gospels of Christ written by Matthew, Mark, Luke, and John were described by Unamuno (both in this work and elsewhere) as novels and not history, so the gospel of San Manuel written by Angela is her novel: not a record of a life but a personal interpretation of it, the work of Angela's imagination and fantasy having only partial links with an external reality, as she herself comes close to recognizing at the end. If we were to examine Angela's memoir from the point of view of its documentary value, several levels of factualness would be clearly distinguished, ranging from the totally factual to the non-factual. These levels could be schematized briefly as follows:

Totally factual

The basic elements of Angela's story: her family circumstances and certain events in her life; the existence of Don Manuel, his reputation for sanctity, the process of beatification; Lázaro's public conversion.

Semi-factual

A good deal of information about Don Manuel: Angela's anecdotes about him (she was not present), her impressions, recollections, reminiscences and reconstruction of distant events and conversations, all of which merge in her memory to give the account its oft-noticed dreamlike and poetic qualities.

Uncertain

The motives behind Lázaro's conversion and his relationship with Don Manuel: did Don Manuel tell Lázaro the complete truth about himself?; did Lázaro tell Angela the complete truth about Don Manuel?; did he tell her the truth about his own motives? A certain amount of critical information about Don Manuel is allegedly obtained through Lázaro; but Lázaro is not a neutral witness: according to Angela he is an atheist who thinks Don Manuel 'demasiado inteligente para creer todo lo que tiene que enseñar' (p. 601). Has Angela been unduly influenced by her brother? Or is Lázaro the excuse for her subtle denunciation of the priest?

Non-factual

Angela's personal interpretation of Don Manuel's religious ideology; her constant insinuations in the direction of unbelief.

Unconscious

Angela's self-portrayal: certain anecdotes about herself and her use of particular words and phrases in the account of Don Manuel which betray the submerged and unconfessed nature of her attachment to the priest and her ambivalent attitude towards him.

In giving his novel a structure based on levels of factualness or truth, Unamuno is moving away from an extra-literary reality and towards the fictive form itself. Indeed it is not even enough to talk conventionally of structure in this particular instance; it is the novel's *infrastructure* that gives it its special quality and ambiguity. But this ambiguity is not that of a capricious writer who merely seeks to mystify his readers or deviously to defend his own personal ideology; it is not the obfuscation and the 'aesthetic ambiguity' denounced by Frances Wyers (p. 120); for while the work is certainly ambiguous, this ambiguity has its own internal justification: it is more than just a cheap attempt at fashionable obscurity; it is an integral part of the story, an essential dimension without which this particular novel would collapse. Another kind of narrator would write quite another kind of work. Angela's history, her personality, her circumstances, create the fiction. On this level the work is perfectly meaningful and intelligible and there is no need to resort to Unamuno's own biography in search of the rosetta stone with which to decipher his novelistic hieroglyphics.

In offering my interpretation of the novel I have of course treated it as the creation and revelation of a fictitious consciousness. In so doing I have quite simply collaborated with the novelist in accepting the fictional form which he has chosen to give his work. Far from offering an apology for my procedure, I hold it to be mandatory. To ignore or to repudiate the fictional form is to throw the artist's craft back in his face. Having brought Angela's memoir to its conclusion with absolute artistic integrity, Unamuno could not resist the urge to speak with his own voice, and so, as was his customary practice (some would say mis-practice, but then what about Henry James's 'Prefaces', or Joseph Conrad's 'Author's Notes'?), he created a little niche for himself by appending a personal interpolation. I should like to conclude this article by briefly considering the relevance of part of Unamuno's authorial interpolation to Angela's account.

Having first acknowledged the creative role of the narrator, that is, the crucial nature of her intervention, Unamuno goes on to insert a short paragraph which is both obscure and at the same time potentially decisive in any attempt to infer the author's attitude towards his fictional narrator The paragraph ends with the phrase 'Y el que quiera entender que entienda', a phrase of biblical origin which functions as an invitation to look beyond the surface for the deeper implication of the speaker's words. In this cryptic paragraph, on the face of it rather superfluous, Unamuno, quoting the epistle of St Jude, verse 9, reminds us of St Michael the Archangel's reproof to the Devil, who was claiming Moses's body: 'El Señor te reprenda.' There are three entities involved in this biblical anecdote: Moses, St Michael and the Devil. Since (1) Don Manuel has earlier been explicitly associated with Moses, since (2) Unamuno is explicitly identifying with St Michael (he reminds us that St Michael is his patron saint), and since (3) the only other person responsible for transmitting the story is Angela (as Unamuno has just reminded us in the immediately preceding paragraph), the clear possibility arises that Angela is being associated with the Devil (the association of angels with devils occurs in St Jude's epistle too), and that the dispute between St Michael and the Devil over who was to have jurisdiction over the body of Moses is meant to represent a divergence of views between Unamuno and his narrator. But why, one might well ask, should Unamuno choose this strange way of giving an authorial nod to the reader? Why should he cast Angela in the role of the Devil? The answer to this is beautifully simple and says a great deal for Unamuno's artistry, for the explanation is contained in the circumstances of composition of the life-story of Don Manuel. What prompts Angela to write her memoir is the beatification process initiated by the bishop of the diocese (this is mentioned twice by Angela, at the beginning and at the end of her memoir). Don Manuel is now the subject of an inquiry by an ecclesiastical court that will have to sit in judgement and decide whether he is a worthy candidate for beatification. In such a court of inquiry the Church always appoints a prosecutor (technically *promotor fidei* but more widely referred too as *advocatus diavoli*) whose function it is to oppose the promoters of the beatification process by questioning the evidence put forward for beatification and by looking for contrary evidence. In the case of Don Manuel it is the bishop (in accordance with canonical procedure) who is promoting the process of beatification and who is writing his life as an example of perfect priestliness. Contrariwise Angela, in her testimony, is presenting Don Manuel as a man lacking in faith, and is consequently hitting at the very heart of the case for beatification. In the context of a canonical beatification process (the starting-point for Angela's story), Angela and the bishop are antagonists. It follows that Angela is cast in the role of *advocatus diavoli*. There is further evidence that this is indeed what Unamuno was getting at, for in the very same paragraph he includes, at first sight gratuitously, a definition of the Devil which fits in exactly with the role of Angela as *advocatus diavoli*: 'diablo quiere decir acusador, fiscal' (p. 627).

Having given us what amounts to a cryptic but intelligible warning not to take Angela's account of Don Manuel at face value, Unamuno ends his interpolation by claiming the superiority of imaginative literature over historiography, of *novela* over *cronicón*, and he goes on to say that his *relato* is not history because in it nothing happens; 'más espero que sea porque en ello todo se queda, como se quedan los lagos y las montañas . . .' (p. 628). If these symbols of permanence are going to attain their full value, it will be only by virtue of the opportunity that imaginative literature gives to the reader to respond to and keep alive the creative consciousness not of the individual, for that is lost forever, but of the artist. An approach to Unamuno's fiction based on a theological, philosophical, or biographical search for the meaning or the message is unlikely to get to the hub of Unamuno's art. Most novelists after all do not write novels to voice meanings; they turn to novels in order to construct artefacts out of language. In Western fiction of the post-realist mode, of which Unamuno is a prime example, the clear tendency was to allow the narrative to speak with its own voice. The meaning or the message was banished as something extra-literary; but what remained had its own kind of truth, its poem-like structure, its internal justification for existing. In *San Manuel Bueno, mártir* Unamuno has given us an artistic 'document', as he calls it, which invites the reader to search for the truth within the story. But the skilful arrangement of the narrative—with its subtle use of personalized narration and of Janus-like symbols and suggestive language—keeps the truth tantalizingly beyond our reach. The fact that ultimately there can be no truth, no reality, except that of the story itself, the fact that we the readers can never hope to be in possession of the truth about Don Manuel, is but a reflection on one level of man's limited access to knowledge of

others and on another of the potential that literature has for creating self-contained worlds that are ever-beckoning but ever-mysterious. Angela will have one view of reality, we may have another one; but the truth itself must always elude us.

Source: C. A. Longhurst, "The Problem of Truth in 'San Manuel Bueno, Mártir,'" in *Modern Language Review*, Vol. 76, 1981, pp. 581–97.

Sources

Kerrigan, Anthony, Introduction, in *Abel Sanchez and Other Stories*, by Miguel de Unamuno, Regnery/Gateway Press, 1956, pp. vii–xvii.

"Miguel de Unamuno," in *Encyclopedia Britannica*, 2004, Encyclopedia Britannica Online, at http://search.eb.com/eb/article?eu=76165 (accessed January 22, 2004).

Unamuno, Miguel de, "Saint Emmanuel the Good, Martyr," in *Abel Sanchez and Other Stories*, translated by Anthony Kerrigan, Regnery/Gateway Press, 1956, pp. 207–67.

Further Reading

Basdekis, Demetrios, *Unamuno and Spanish Literature*, University of California Press, 1967.
    Basdekis provides critical discussion of the ways in which Unamuno's stories, poems, and essays have influenced, and been influenced by, Spanish literature.

Enders, Victoria Loree, and Pamela Beth Radcliff, eds., *Constructing Spanish Womanhood: Female Identity in Modern Spain*, State University of New York Press, 1999.
    Enders and Radcliff offer a collection of essays by various authors on the social conditions of women in Spain during the nineteenth and twentieth centuries. These essays are organized into broad thematic categories, such as socio-cultural roles, work, and political conditions.

Esdaile, Charles J., *Spain in the Liberal Age: From Constitution to Civil War, 1808–1939*, Blackwell Publishers, 2000.
    Esdaile provides a history of Spain from the Spanish War of Independence in 1808 to the end of the Spanish Civil War in 1939.

Shaw, Donald L., *The Generation of 1898 in Spain*, Barnes & Noble, 1975.
    Shaw provides an overview of the major works of literature by writers of Spain's Generation of '98 and discusses the influence of this group of writers on Spanish literature and culture.

Smith, Bradley, *Spain: A History in Art*, Doubleday, 1971.
    Smith provides a history of Spain from its early civilization through the twentieth century, focusing

on pictorial documentation through painting, sculpture, and photography.

Valdes, Mario J., *Death in the Literature of Unamuno*, University of Illinois Press, 1964.

Valdes examines the recurring theme of death in the poems, stories, and essays of Unamuno, focusing on Unamuno's existential questioning of religious faith regarding the afterlife.

Vincent, Mary, *Catholicism in the Second Spanish Republic: Religion and Politics in Salamanca, 1930–1936*, Oxford University Press, 1996.

Vincent examines the intersection of Roman Catholicism and the political climate of Spain's Second Republic, focusing on the cultural and political context of the university town of Salamanca, where Unamuno lived and worked for much of his life.

The Sniper

Liam O'Flaherty

1923

"The Sniper," a story about the Irish civil war, was Liam O'Flaherty's first published piece of fiction. It appeared in 1923 in the London publication *The New Leader*. Over the years, it has been reprinted several times, and as of 2004 it could be found in O'Flaherty's *Collected Stories*. "The Sniper" helped set O'Flaherty firmly on the writer's path. Upon reading it, Edward Garnett, an influential London editor, recommended a publisher bring forth the novel that O'Flaherty had just completed. Thus began a literary career that lasted for three decades.

O'Flaherty was intensely involved in Irish politics as a young man, joining both the Communist party in Ireland and later the Republican army. Nonetheless, throughout his career, O'Flaherty only wrote a handful of overtly political stories. In the fall of 1922, after taking part in the Four Courts incident as a Republican soldier, O'Flaherty fled Ireland. Settling in London, O'Flaherty procured a typewriter and wrote "The Sniper" while the devastating Irish civil war was still going on. O'Flaherty drew upon his experiences to create a piece of fiction that shows that the civil war had repercussions stretching far beyond the field of battle. O'Flaherty places his protagonist, a sniper, in a kill or be killed situation. After the sniper shoots an enemy soldier, he discovers he has just killed his brother. The sniper's emotional detachment throughout the story, coupled with this startling ending, allows O'Flaherty to indirectly address the way in

which the Irish civil war led to the disunity of Irish society.

Author Biography

Liam O'Flaherty was born in 1896 on Inishmore, an Aran Island off the coast of Ireland. O'Flaherty wrote his first piece of fiction when he was about seven years old. He also proved to be an exceptional student, and a visiting cleric thought he showed an aptitude for the priesthood. In 1908 O'Flaherty won a scholarship to attend a Catholic school, Rockwell College, on Ireland's mainland, where he studied until 1912. He continued his education at Blackrock College from 1912 to 1913, also run by priests, where he organized a group of students who supported the Republican cause in Ireland. In 1914 he entered Holy Cross College in Dublin, which was a seminary designed to prepare young men for the priesthood. O'Flaherty, however, did not want to become a priest, and left after one semester. He then went to University College, also in Dublin, where he studied for a year from 1914 to 1915.

World War I disrupted O'Flaherty's studies. He left college in 1915 to join the Irish Guards of the British army. During the war, he served in France and Belgium. Due to shellshock, O'Flaherty was given a medical discharge from the military in 1917.

After a few months in Ireland, O'Flaherty spent the next two years traveling about and doing odd jobs. He went to London, South America, Canada, and the United States. He also crewed on ships sailing the Atlantic Ocean and Mediterranean Sea. During this period, his brother urged him to write about his experiences. O'Flaherty wrote four short stories, but they were rejected by publishers, and O'Flaherty gave up writing.

O'Flaherty returned to Ireland in 1920 and became involved in politics. He supported the Republican cause and also joined the Communist party. In 1922 he and a group of unemployed men seized control of a public building. They raised the Communist flag over it and declared an Irish socialist revolution. In the Irish civil war, he aligned himself with the Republicans, opposing the division of Ireland, and took part in the Four Courts rebellion. A fugitive from the Irish authorities, O'Flaherty fled to London in 1922.

Once again O'Flaherty took up writing. In 1923, he published his first short story, "The Sniper,"

Liam O'Flaherty

in a British weekly paper. After that, he wrote steadily. Later that year, he published his first novel, *Thy Neighbor's Wife*. He spent the next three decades as a professional writer.

Most of O'Flaherty's novels and short stories take place on the Aran Islands of his youth. However, some of his most well-known works have Dublin as their setting, like *The Informer* (1925), which won the 1926 James Tait Black Memorial Prize in England for the best novel of the year, as well as a prize in France. O'Flaherty also wrote nonfiction and stories in his native tongue, Irish Gaelic. In 1932 O'Flaherty and a group of other well-known writers founded the Irish Academy of Letters.

O'Flaherty retired from writing in the mid-1950s, moved to Dublin shortly thereafter, but spent much of his time traveling. He died in 1984 in Dublin.

Plot Summary

Late at night, a lone Republican sniper waits atop a rooftop in Dublin, Ireland. It is June of 1922. Nearby Republican and Free States forces battle over the Four Courts judicial building and throughout the city.

The sniper has been on the rooftop since the morning. Now he eats a sandwich and drinks some whiskey. He risks lighting a cigarette for a quick puff. The light from his cigarette alerts an enemy soldier to his presence. A bullet flies toward the sniper's rooftop. He puts out the cigarette and switches position.

However, the flash of the rifle tells the sniper his enemy's location. The sniper realizes that his enemy also has taken cover—on the roof of the house across the street.

In the street below, an armored car moves. The sniper knows it is an enemy car but it would be useless to shoot at it. As he watches, he sees an old woman approaching the car. She speaks to the soldier manning the turret, pointing at the sniper's rooftop. As the turret opens and the soldier looks out, the sniper raises his rifle and shoots him, killing him. Then the sniper shoots the old woman as she tries to run away.

From the roof opposite, the enemy sniper fires. His bullet hits the sniper in the arm, and he drops his rifle. The sniper examines his wound. He realizes that the bullet is still lodged in his arm and that the arm is fractured. He painfully applies a field dressing and then rests from his effort.

The sniper knows he must devise a plan. He cannot leave the roof because the enemy is blocking any exit from the building, but if he is still on the roof in the morning, Free State soldiers will come for him and kill him. He must kill his enemy before morning so he can escape.

The sniper places his cap on the muzzle of the rifle, which is now useless because he cannot operate it with only one good arm. He pushes the rifle upward so the cap appears over the edge of the roof. In response, the enemy sniper shoots, hitting the cap dead center. The sniper lets his rifle fall forward. He lets the hand holding the rifle dangle over the side of the roof. Then the rifle clatters to the street. Finally, the sniper drags his hand back.

When the sniper peers over the roof, he sees that his plan has fooled the enemy into thinking he is dead. The other sniper now stands uprights and looks across the street that separates the two houses. The sniper lifts his revolver. Taking careful aim, the sniper fires and hits the enemy. The other sniper falls over the edge of the roof down to the pavement below. On the street below, he lies still.

Now that the battle is over, the sniper feels remorse. He curses the civil war and his own role in it. Then he hurls the revolver to the ground. It goes off, sending a bullet past his head. The shock of the near miss returns him to his senses.

The sniper takes a drink of whiskey and decides to descend from the roof and try to rejoin his company. Retrieving his revolver, the sniper crawls down into the house. Once at the street level, the sniper has an urge to see the man he killed. He might know the man from the army before the civil war began. The sniper runs into the street, drawing a spate of machine gun fire from a distance. He throws himself on the ground besides the corpse of the enemy sniper. He turns the body over. He looks into the face of his brother.

Characters

The Enemy Sniper

The Enemy Sniper is the Sniper's main opponent in the story. A member of the Free State army, he still shares similarities with the Sniper. The two men are engaged in the same role. The Enemy Sniper, too, is a good shot, enough so that he wins the respect of the Sniper by the end of the story. His physical presence, on a rooftop across the street, further reinforces the idea that he is a mirror image for the Sniper.

The Enemy Sniper wants to kill the Sniper. He appears to have the advantage after shooting and injuring the Sniper. He makes a fatal error, however, when he falls for the Sniper's ruse. Once he thinks he has killed the other man, the Enemy Sniper stands up on his rooftop, thus making himself a clear mark. The Sniper shoots him, and he falls to the street below, dead. After that, the Sniper—along with the reader—discovers that the two snipers are brothers.

The Old Woman

The Old Woman points out the Sniper's location on the rooftop to the Soldier in the Turret. The Sniper shoots and kills her.

The Sniper

The Sniper is the main character of the story. This young man is a member of the Republican army and his eyes have "the cold gleam of the fanatic." A hardened fighter, the Sniper has become a man "used to looking at death." In his role as a soldier, he functions efficiently and automatically. For instance, when he gets shot, he applies his own field dressing despite the excruciating pain. Only occasionally does he allow himself to make poor decisions, notably when he decides to risk lighting a cigarette, which alerts the enemy soldiers to his location on the roof. He also runs into the street to find out the identity of the Enemy Sniper, drawing machine gun fire upon himself.

The Sniper has been positioned atop a roof in Dublin. His role in the battle is not clear, but the streets of Dublin are awash with fighting, and he likely has been assigned to shoot enemy targets in the streets below. Once the Free State soldiers learn of his presence, the Sniper becomes involved in a standoff with the Enemy Sniper on a rooftop across the street. The Sniper cannot leave his rooftop since the Enemy Sniper has him covered. Nor can he risk staying on the roof until morning, which assuredly would lead to his death at the hands of Free State soldiers. Injured by the Enemy Sniper, the Sniper devises a clever plan to draw fire and make the Enemy Sniper think he is dead. Once his ruse succeeds, the Enemy Sniper lets down his guard and stops keeping his cover, so the Sniper is able to fatally shoot him.

Once the Enemy Sniper is dead, the battle-hardened Sniper undergoes a transformation. The excitement of the battle fades. Looking over the rooftop at the three people he has just killed—the Soldier in the Turret, the Old Woman, and the Enemy Sniper—the Sniper feels remorse. His disgust for the civil war manifests itself physically, as his teeth begin to chatter, and he starts cursing both himself and the war. When the Sniper recovers his senses, his fear dissipates so much that he even risks being shot at to learn the identity of the Free State soldier he has just shot. Only then does he realize that he has killed his own brother.

Throughout the story, the Sniper remains a somewhat mysterious, one-dimensional character. The narrative reveals little of his feelings about what is happening around him, nor does it even share his reaction to the knowledge that he has become his brother's murderer. Instead, the story directs the Sniper's actions and thoughts to the battle. The Sniper's only identity is that of a solider.

The Soldier in the Turret

The Soldier in the Turret is a member of the Free State army. He learns of the Sniper's location on the rooftop from the old woman. Before he and his men can go after the Sniper, the Sniper kills him with a rifle bullet.

Themes

Civil War

The complementary themes of civil war and warfare are the most obvious in "The Sniper." The story takes as its setting Dublin, Ireland, during the Irish civil war. The fighting began in 1922, after the Irish Parliament voted to accept the Anglo-Irish Treaty dividing the island of Ireland into northern and southern parts. Before the treaty, Irish nationalists had united against the British, their common foe, or against Northern Irish Protestants who supported union with England. After the treaty was signed, however, Irish aggression was turned inward. Over the next few years, the Irish people remained bitterly split, and some took up arms against their friends, family members, and countrymen.

O'Flaherty sets the stage of the civil war in his opening paragraph with sensory descriptions such as the "heavy guns [that] roared" at the "beleaguered Four Courts" and the "machines guns and rifles [that] broke the silence of the night, spasmodically, like dogs barking on lone farms." O'Flaherty concludes this first paragraph with the factual statement, "Republicans and Free Staters were waging civil war." This simple statement both serves to place the conflict and to undercut the devastation that this war has caused.

Though the story is quite brief, the reader can infer that the Irish civil war has brought great change to its protagonist. The phrase that the sniper has "the face of a student, thin and ascetic" implies that the sniper may have recently been a student but has taken up the arms of a soldier. Now warfare has transformed him. His "deep and thoughtful" eyes are "used to looking at death," and they even hold "the cold gleam of the fanatic" in his dedication to

Topics for Further Study

- Research the Irish civil war. After you have conducted your research, write a paper analyzing ''The Sniper'' from a historical point of view.

- Imagine that you are directing a movie version of ''The Sniper.'' How would you direct the final scene? What kind of emotions would you ask your actor to convey?

- Write an essay describing how you think the sniper feels at learning he has killed his brother and what he does next. Does this event keep him from further participation in the Irish civil war?

- Investigate another civil war or conflict that has divided families, friends, and communities. Use what you have learned to write your own short story exploring the way that such conflict affects members of society.

- The events surrounding the Irish civil war brought to the forefront many important political leaders. Research one of these leaders, either a Republican or a Free Stater, and find out about his influence on Irish history.

- Find out more about the role that religion has played in Ireland's history from the late 1800s through the present day.

---

the Republican cause. The protagonist is only one of many young men who have joined either one side or the other of this brutal civil war.

The story also makes clear that this civil war has driven enormous rifts into Irish society. After the sniper has killed his enemy, he grows curious about the other man's identity. "He wondered did he know him," and he even speculates, "Perhaps he had been in his own company before the split in the army." With the final sentence, however, the civil war's power to divide takes on even greater significance: "Then the sniper turned over the dead body and looked into his brother's face." This sentence tells the reader that members of the same family could become enemies because of civil war. It also underscores the long-lasting repercussions of warfare that breaks up a society.

Warfare

A few key details in the story emphasize the bizarre landscape of warfare. The sniper undergoes a number of emotional responses to the battle that non-soldiers or those who have not taken part in battle are likely to find unusual. At the beginning of the story, during his stakeout, the sniper "had been too excited to eat." Right before he shoots the enemy sniper, his "hand trembled with eagerness." When he sees that he has hit his enemy, he "uttered a cry of joy." All the words O'Flaherty uses to describe the sniper's reaction to meeting and vanquishing his enemy are positive, anticipatory words. In the world of warfare, killing a fellow human being is a victory; for in war, soldiers, like the sniper, face a situation where they must kill or be killed.

By the end of the story, the protagonist has undergone a wide range of feelings stemming from his own actions. With his enemy dead, the sniper feels regret at what he has done. After the "lust of battle died in him," his body reacts by shuddering and sweating, and his teeth chatter. His mind gets involved in denying his situation as "he began to gibber to himself, cursing the war, cursing himself, cursing everybody." However, even these regrets only last a short time. He throws down his revolver, and it accidentally goes off, returning him to his senses. He also bolsters his courage and brings himself back to the proper state of mind by taking a drink of whiskey. Again able to face the state of warfare, laughing, the sniper descends from the rooftop to rejoin his company and continue his role as a soldier. By the end of the story, the sniper's emotions have moved in a circular pattern, from excitement to nervousness to remorse and back to excitement.

Survival and Isolation

The concept of survival underscores the entire story. Even before the sniper kills any of the Free State soldiers, he knows "there were enemies watching." The sniper's actions are driven by his desire for survival. He must kill anyone who has the capacity to bring about his destruction. So the soldier manning the armored tank must be taken out. Indeed, anyone who takes part in this warfare can become an enemy, even an old woman who becomes an informer with a few simple words and the point of a finger.

The sniper's main combatant and the biggest obstacle to his survival is the Free State sniper on the rooftop across the street. The man has the power to keep the sniper pinned down throughout the night, but he knows that "[M]orning must not find him wounded on the roof." Such an event would mean certain death. The sniper has little choice but to devise a plan, even though it is a long shot, to kill his enemy first.

The fact that the sniper is isolated on his rooftop emphasizes his need to depend upon his own wits, courage, and abilities for survival. Though other men fight side by side with their companies, for instance, at the Four Courts and in the streets of Dublin, the sniper conducts his fight alone. It is up to him to kill the other sniper. No one will come to his aid. Because of his isolation, the sniper finds the resources within himself to overcome fear and pain and continue to fight.

Style

Setting

The setting of "The Sniper" is integral to the narrative, for it draws its action from the Irish civil war. The story takes place in Dublin, Ireland, in June 1922. At this time, the Irish civil war has been going on for several months. The Republicans hold the Four Courts judicial building, but the Free Staters are attacking them with heavy arms.

"The Sniper" also takes place between the hours of dusk and dawn. Beginning as "twilight faded into night," the action of the story instantly becomes more dangerous. The sniper must conduct his battle in the dark. He has only "the dim light of the moon that shone through fleecy clouds" to see by. This lack of clarity has a realistic impact in making his task—difficult even in the light of day—even more challenging. The sniper has to aim at his enemy, about fifty yards away, and get off one fatal shot with a revolver. The lack of light also has symbolic significance: it underscores the murky, ambiguous situation that a civil war poses. The civil war pits friends, neighbors, and even family members against one another. As is borne out by the story's ending, people cannot see very clearly during such a conflict.

Point of View

The narrative takes a limited, third-person point of view. The action is entirely funneled through the protagonist. The reader sees only through his eyes, hears sounds through his ears, and processes events through his thoughts. Despite this limited point of view, readers can clearly follow the action. The sniper observes the old woman on the street below as she talks to the soldier in the turret of the armored car. "She was pointing to the roof where the sniper lay," and the sniper—and the reader—knows that she is pining down his location and that the soldiers may well come after him. When the sniper carries out his plan to trick the enemy sniper into thinking that he is dead, he can tell that he has been successful. For the enemy "seeing the cap and rifle fall . . . was now standing before a row of chimney pots, looking across, with his head clearly silhouetted against the western sky." Though the story never gets deep in the mind of the enemy, the reader, like the sniper, knows that the Free Stater "thought that he had killed his man."

This point of view works well with the emotional detachment of the narrative. Rarely does the protagonist show his reaction to the events around him, other than the excitement of the battle and his momentary repulsion at having killed another human being. Even when he learns that the man now lying in a "shattered mass" is his brother, the sniper does not react. Instead, the story ends, leaving the reader to only speculate about his feelings.

Details and Sound

O'Flaherty employs a number of specific details to make his story realistic. He describes the battle sounds taking place around the sniper, and he refers to actual events and places, such as the Four Courts siege and the nearby O'Connell Bridge. The description of the sniper's first aid efforts is also filled with many concrete details, like the "bitter fluid" of the iodine, the "paroxysm of pain [that] swept through him," and his need to tie the ends of the bandage with his teeth. Such details help ground the reader in the action.

O'Flaherty also uses details to emphasize the darkness. The sniper can see only by the "dim light" from the moon and, later, approaching dawn. Even the flare from lighting a cigarette is easily seen. The sniper decides to risk the cigarette, striking a match, taking a drag on the cigarette, and then putting out the light. Though this process takes only a matter of seconds, if that, "[A]lmost immediately, a bullet flattened itself against the parapet of the roof."

Although the story is rooted in reality, O'Flaherty employs descriptive sound imagery to emphasize the stillness and dark of the night. Throughout Dublin, the machine guns and rifles "broke the silence of the night, spasmodically, like dogs barking on lone farms." When the sniper gets shot and drops his rifle with a clatter, he "thought the noise would wake the dead." Once his personal battle is over, and he has killed all his immediate enemies—the soldier in the turret, the old woman, and the other sniper—"Everywhere around was quiet." This technique emphasizes the danger of the situation, as well as the sniper's complete isolation and his need to vanquish his enemies on his own.

Ending

A. A. Kelly writes in *Liam O'Flaherty: The Storyteller* that "The Sniper" "with its surprise ending based on coincidence is in the older tradition of Maupassant and O'Henry." Such an ending hinges on an unexpected revelation at the end, be it light-hearted or tragic. Few writers have been able to employ the surprise ending effectively. However, O'Flaherty does so successfully because he has already engaged the reader through the fast-paced action and the unique detachment of the protagonist. The shocking ending seems likely to challenge that detachment, but O'Flaherty refuses to reveal the sniper's reaction to the knowledge that he has murdered his brother. Instead, O'Flaherty leaves it up to the reader to draw conclusions and to wonder how, or if, this event will affect the future choices the sniper makes.

Historical Context

The English in Ireland

In the twelfth century, the English monarch, backed by a large army, declared himself overlord of Ireland. For the next several centuries, English rule was generally confined to the area around Dublin. The English monarchy, however, continued efforts to subdue the entire island, resulting in ongoing Irish rebellion. In the early 1600s, the monarchy overthrew the native Irish political system, bringing the entire country under its control. For the next hundred years, the English created colonies in Ireland. As part of this effort, they drove many Irish from their land and gave estates to English landowners. Religious problems arose as well, since most Irish were Roman Catholics while the new English settlers, who mainly lived in the north, followed the Protestant faith. Laws continually favored Protestants over Catholics.

By the late 1700s, Irish rebels were making repeated efforts to gain some kind of independence. Their efforts were to little avail, and in 1801 the Act of Union formally united Great Britain and Ireland. This law abolished the Irish Parliament; instead, Ireland voted for representatives who served in the British Parliament.

Beginning in the 1870s, a Home Rule movement was on the rise among Irish nationalists, most of whom were Catholics. Supporters demanded some form of self government. They were opposed by Irish Protestants, who were called unionists because they wanted to preserve Ireland's status in the United Kingdom. Irish political leader Charles Parnell, who sat in the British Parliament, led a nationalist party and demanded a separate Irish Parliament. Later, in 1902, a new nationalist political party known as Sinn Féin was formed. Its goal was to secure Irish independence.

Because of these nationalist efforts, by the 1910s, the British Parliament enacted a Home Rule bill. While most of Ireland supported this bill, Protestants in Northern Ireland vowed to resist any home rule by force; they feared that the island would become dominated by the Catholics. The onset of World War I, however, delayed the enactment of home rule in Ireland.

The Easter Rising

Irish home rule supporters were frustrated by this delay. In April 1916, a rebellion known as the

Compare & Contrast

- **1920s:** Ireland is part of the United Kingdom. Many Irish have long been unhappy with this situation. In the late 1910s, Irish forces rebel and begin fighting with British forces. They seek independence from British rule.

  Today: Four-fifths of the island of Ireland makes up the independent Republic of Ireland, or Eire in the Irish language. Northern Ireland makes up the rest of the island, and it is part of the United Kingdom.

- **1920s:** Republicans and Free Staters engage in a deadly and destructive civil war. Republicans refuse to accept the Anglo-Irish Treaty, which makes southern Ireland a dominion within the United Kingdom, known as the Irish Free State. The Republicans want all of the island of Ireland to have independence. Free Staters, however, support this treaty. The civil war carries on from 1921 until 1923, when a cease-fire is declared, with the Free Staters victorious.

  Today: After decades of fighting between Protestants in Northern Ireland and the Irish Republican Army—the paramilitary arm of Sinn Féin, the two sides agree to a cease-fire in 1998. Troubles, however, still brew in Ireland over the division of the island. In 2004, Protestant and Catholic political parties struggle over ways to share power, and allegations of kidnapping and violence on the part of the IRA still take place.

- **1920s:** Irish political leaders are all men, such as Michael Collins, Eamon de Valera, and Arthur Griffith.

  Today: Women take a much more active role in politics. In 1990, Mary Robinson becomes the first woman to serve as president of the Republic, and women serve as leaders of political parties.

Easter Rising began in Dublin. About 1,000 Irish forces rose against British rule. Over the next week, street fighting sprang up throughout Dublin, and Republicans seized some government offices. British soldiers, however, forced the Republican leaders to surrender and executed some of the leaders.

In the aftermath of the Easter Rising, when the elections of 1918 took place, Irish voters backed many members of the Sinn Féin political party as their representatives in the British Parliament, over members of the more moderate Irish party. Sinn Féin advocated complete independence for Ireland, and instead of taking their seats, these Irish Republicans set up a revolutionary government and formed an Irish assembly called Dáil Éireann in Dublin.

Until 1921, a brutal war rocked Ireland. The newly created Irish Republican Army (IRA) fought against the British, resisted efforts to renew British rule, and forced Britain to recognize the Irish government. They relied on guerrilla tactics, to which the English government, represented by the police force known as the Black and Tans, responded with brutal reprisals.

During this period, the divisions between north and south grew, with northern unionists threatening to rebel if they were cast free from Britain. In response, the British government passed the Government of Ireland Act in 1920, which called for two separate parliaments for Northern Ireland and Southern Ireland. Finally, in 1922, leaders of the Dáil Éireann signed the Anglo-Irish Treaty with Britain. This treaty made 26 of Ireland's 32 counties into the Irish Free State, a self-governing dominion within the British Commonwealth of Nations, while the six counties of Northern Ireland remained part of the United Kingdom.

Irish Civil War

Within Ireland, not everyone supported the Anglo-Irish Treaty. The British prime minister had even threatened open war on Ireland if the treaty was not accepted. Republicans particularly objected to the oath of allegiance that members of the Dáil Éireann would have to make to the British monarch, as well as the provision that allowed Northern Ireland to remain out of the Irish Free State. Eamon de Valera, head of the Dáil Éireann, would not support the treaty, and he resigned. Elections were held for the new Irish Parliament, which led to the ousting of most of the Republicans. Before the new Parliament could meet, a civil war had broken out between supporters of the treaty, known as Free Staters, and its opponents, called Republicans. In April 1922, Republican forces occupied Dublin's justice buildings, the Four Courts. They came under siege from the Free State forces. For several days in June, the Free Staters bombarded the Four Courts. They retook the buildings and captured the enemy leader. Before their capture, however, the Republicans blew up the Four Courts. Despite this Free State victory, battles continued to take place in Dublin until early July, when Free States forces gained control of the city.

Fighting continued outside of Dublin, and the Irish government (still controlled by Free Staters) initiated official military operations. The government took strong measures to quell the civil war, including executing Republican leaders. Within a few months as well, the Dáil Éireann met to draft and ratify a new constitution for Ireland.

The Irish Free State

The Republican resistance became less organized. By early 1923, Republican forces had ceased fighting. De Valera, the Republican leader, ordered a cease-fire. A few years later, he re-entered the Irish political scene. He formed a new political party and served several times as Ireland's prime minister. In 1937 De Valera drafted a new constitution that made Ireland into a new state, called Éire, which was a republic in all but name. In 1948, Ireland finally gained complete independence. The six counties of Northern Ireland, however, remained part of the United Kingdom.

Critical Overview

"The Sniper" was O'Flaherty's first published short story, and as it would turn out, was different from the main body of his short fiction. O'Flaherty became most known for his stories about nature,

animals, and Irish peasants, not for the stories he wrote about urban Ireland. Of his numerous stories, only four stories deal with the Irish civil war, while another handful are set in Irish cities. However, according to James M. Calahan, author of *Liam O'Flaherty: A Study of the Short Fiction*, O'Flaherty's political stories cannot be separated from the others, for "politics permeate all of his works." In a story like "The Sniper," politics are simply more obvious.

Generally, O'Flaherty's urban stories present a bleak view of humankind. A. A. Kelly, writing in *Liam O'Flaherty: The Storyteller*, noted that such stories "contain much despair and any humour is at man's expense." The protagonist in "The Sniper" might well fall into the role of an urbanized character "imbued with various forms of self-interest based on . . . fear."

The few critics who have directly explored "The Sniper" tend to disagree over a crucial aspect: O'Flaherty's position on the Irish civil war. In his 1929 essay "The Position of Liam O'Flaherty," which was published in *Bookman*, William Troy commended "The Sniper," along with the short story "Civil War," both of which deal with the "real and imagined circumstances" of the Irish civil war. Troy wrote that these stories "constitute the most remarkable record of the period which we are likely to receive: the most complete because derived largely from personal observation and participation; the most reliable because written without any other bias than that of artistic selection." Years later, A. A. Kelly contradicted parts of Troy's statement. Kelly did agree that O'Flaherty drew upon his personal experiences to write "The Sniper." However, she believed that O'Flaherty's "reason for writing is to damn warfare in general as inhuman and debasing." Another critic, James H. O'Brien, would also seem to agree that O'Flaherty condemns warfare. In his discussion of O'Flaherty's short stories, entitled *Liam O'Flaherty*, O'Brien wrote that "the open, matter-of-fact presentation of the shooting and the pain of the wound makes the revelation that brother has shot brother the final atrocity in a barbaric world." The critics, however, do generally emphasize O'Flaherty's careful attention to detail, although Kelly did believe that the "historic aspect and factual accuracy of the work is secondary."

Of all the critics, Kelly has paid the most attention to "The Sniper." She highlighted such elements as its surprise ending and O'Flaherty's "abruptness and economy of style." Similarly,

Calahan noted that, as a writer, O'Flaherty was a "master of the art of omission." Kelly also proposed her belief that the sniper served as a "type figure illustrating all those caught up by warfare and forced to shoot the enemy."

Criticism

Rena Korb

Korb has a master's degree in English literature and creative writing and has written for a wide variety of educational publishers. In this essay, Korb considers how "The Sniper" demonstrates the division the Irish civil war has inflicted on society.

In crafting his first published short story "The Sniper" O'Flaherty took as his setting and dramatic impetus an issue that he knew well: the Irish civil war of the early 1920s. In this story, two snipers on opposing sides of the conflict face off in a duel. The hero of the story prevails. He kills his enemy, thus assuring his survival, at least for the moment. Only after his enemy is dead, however, does the sniper make a startling revelation: the enemy sniper is his own brother.

The story does not address the problems of the civil war from any historical perspective; notably, O'Flaherty makes no mention of the Anglo-Irish Treaty that sparked the civil war or the ongoing problems the native Irish had with the British rulers. O'Flaherty need not do so, for the Irish and British reading audience in the 1920s was well versed in the ongoing troubles that surrounded Ireland and its relationship to the United Kingdom. Modern readers, as well as non-Irish readers, however, likely may need to be reminded that in the spring of 1922, fighting broke out in Ireland over the Anglo-Irish Treaty. This agreement would make southern Ireland an independent state within the British Commonwealth and leave the six counties in northern Ireland part of Great Britain. Free Staters, who supported the treaty, and Republicans, who opposed it, took up arms and fought for control of Ireland's government and national spirit.

O'Flaherty—who fought for the Republicans at the famous Four Courts rebellion—wrote "The Sniper" within months of this incident; "The Sniper" first appeared in a London magazine in January 1923. So, at the time of the story's writing and publication, the civil war was still going on. The

Four Courts Building in Dublin, Ireland, seen here in 1922, is the location of the standoff described in the "The Sniper"

cease-fire between the two Irish armies was not called until spring of that year. This detail of timing may cause readers to more closely examine O'Flaherty's story for a political message about the civil war. It also immediately renders more provocative O'Flaherty's choice to create a narrative with what A. A. Kelly, writing in *Liam O'Flaherty: The Storyteller*, calls a "controlled emotional response." Many readers will be struck by the sniper's emotional detachment from the violence around him and the very deaths that he causes. There are different reasons O'Flaherty may have chosen to treat the subject this way, however. By making the sniper less of an individual and more of a type character, O'Flaherty imbues him with him greater symbolic meaning. The sniper comes to represent all soldiers, both Republican and Free Starters. Indeed, the sniper could be any soldier, caught up in any deadly conflict. O'Flaherty's stylistic device also shows his lack of interest in using his writing as any sort of political propaganda. He does not try to use words and thoughts to win the reader into siding with the sniper, though the man served in the same army as O'Flaherty. Nor does he try to manipulate the reader into feeling that the sniper is a monster. Instead, with his carefully chosen words he presents

What Do I Read Next?

- O'Flaherty's novel *The Informer*, first published in 1925, is set in the aftermath of the Irish civil war. It tells about an outlaw who is the object of a Dublin manhunt. *The Informer* is one of O'Flaherty's most well-known pieces of fiction.

- Like "The Sniper," O'Flaherty's short story "Civil War," included in the 1925 collection of the same name, explores the experience of the war through two Republican soldiers—one an idealist and one a realist—who are trapped on a rooftop, waiting for death.

- *Liam O'Flaherty's Ireland* (2001), by Peter Costello, features biographical information about O'Flaherty, excerpts from his fiction, and photographs from his time period.

- *The Letters of Liam O'Flaherty* (1996), edited by A. A. Kelly, can provide additional information on this writer.

- O'Henry's "The Gift of the Magi" (1905), Guy de Maupassant's "The Necklace" (1884), and Saki's "The Open Window" (1914) all provide variations—both humorous and tragic—on the same type of surprise ending employed by O'Flaherty.

- James Joyce's *Dubliners* (1914), a collection of short stories about the lives of people in Dublin, includes the masterpiece "The Dead."

- Sean O'Casey's play *Juno and the Paycock*, perhaps his most popular, was originally staged in 1924 and set during the Irish civil war. This tragicomedy chronicles the fortunes of one family as they struggle for Irish independence.

- Sean O'Faolain's first collection of short stories, *Midsummer Night Madness and Other Stories*, was first published in 1932.

---

the situation in as straightforward a manner as possible and then retreats, allowing the reader to draw conclusions. He even resists temptation to comment on the sniper's discovery that he has killed his brother. Instead, O'Flaherty ends the story on this devastating, potentially life-altering fact.

Such narrative detachment is in keeping with O'Flaherty's choice not to present an overall picture of the Irish civil war. O'Flaherty does not describe such incidents as the raging battles, the Four Courts seizure and bombing, or the assassinations of major leaders from both sides of the conflict. Instead, O'Flaherty creates only four characters—two of whom appear only briefly—and selects a few specific details that show the effects of the conflict on Irish society. O'Flaherty begins this task in his opening paragraph, describing the noise from the machine guns and rifles that "broke the silence of the night, spasmodically, like dogs barking." O'Flaherty also references the sniper's nearness to the "beleaguered Four Courts [where] the heavy guns roared." However, despite having comrades on the ground who work as a unit in their fight, the Republican sniper faces the conflict alone. He is pinned on a rooftop by the enemy sniper across the street and the armored cars and soldiers down below. Thus in a few sentences, O'Flaherty effectively sets the scene, both for the battle that lies ahead, as well as for the sniper's supreme isolation.

On the one hand, this battle between the two snipers represents the larger battle between the Republicans and the Free Staters. The Republican sniper becomes engaged in fighting both the Free State sniper on the opposing rooftop, as well as Free State forces in the streets below. When the Republican sniper descends from his rooftop at the end of the story, even more Free States forces at the end of the street fire upon him with their machine guns. However, it is the enemy sniper who emerges as his main foe. This is the man whom the Republican sniper most fears and who seems to have the most capability of either killing him or cutting off his escape. The two soldiers thus become engaged in a deadly battle, for the Republican sniper must kill the other if he wants to get off the rooftop alive.

O'Flaherty creates the men as mirror images. Both men have positioned themselves on opposing rooftops, thus reinforcing the idea of similarity. Both men are good shots; the enemy sniper delivers his bullet to the center of the sniper's cap, while the Republican sniper kills his enemy with a single revolver shot from fifty yards away, which is "a hard shot in the dim light." The sniper even notes that he and his enemy may have been in the same company before the disintegration of the Irish army into Republican and Free State companies. O'Flaherty's artistic decision to make the two men so similar reinforces the idea that the civil war has broken strong ties throughout Ireland and shows the extent of the division in Ireland's current political situation. Men in opposing armies only become enemies because they disagree over the governing of their country. If not for this problem, these men could have been colleagues or friends—even brothers. O'Flaherty's subtle demonstration of the snipers' similarity underscores that this disunity is occurring throughout the country and destroying the very fabric of society.

Through O'Flaherty's writing, the Irish civil war also emerges as a battle between individuals. All citizens must take sides. The old woman who alerts the Free State soldier to the sniper's presence on the rooftop becomes an enemy in this act. By pointing out the sniper's location, she directly involves herself in the battle. Because of it, she pays the ultimate price with her life; the sniper kills her with a bullet from his rifle. This detail points to the way that the Irish civil war affects all of Ireland, not merely those directly involved in warfare.

While the civil war holds all the Irish people in its clutches, the fighting has a much greater effect on the combatants, significantly dehumanizing them. The sniper on the rooftop is driven by fear and excitement—at the beginning of the story, O'Flaherty writes that "his eyes had the cold gleam of the fanatic." The sniper also operates superbly, but more like an automaton than a man. When the sniper gets shot, he feels no pain, "just a deadened sensation"; the arm becomes symbolic of the numbness that he must make himself feel to take part in the war at all. Despite the pain, the sniper proceeds to apply his own field dressing to his broken arm and come up with a plan to kill his enemy. Throughout these events, up through the death of his enemy,

> " While the civil war holds all the Irish people in its clutches, the fighting has a much greater effect on the combatants, significantly dehumanizing them."

the sniper carries himself coolly and efficiently. No doubts about his actions or about the war itself distract him, not even when he kills the raggedy old woman who dies like a dog in the gutter. Only after the gunfire is over, however, after "the lust of the battle died in him," does the sniper show any human response to the deaths that he has caused. "[R]evolted by the sight of the shattered mass of his dead enemy," he shudders, sweats, and becomes "bitten by remorse." He even, for a brief moment, "gibber[s] to himself, cursing the war, cursing himself, cursing everybody." This lapse into human feeling is momentary, however. His nerves soon steady, at which point he even laughs—a gesture that may strike the reader as stunningly inappropriate, though, in fact, it may be a reaction to the insanity of war.

The most significant detail that shows how the civil war disunites the people of Ireland does not emerge until the very end of the story, however. Unbeknownst to them, the two snipers—neither of whom can see the other's face—are brothers. Throughout the ordeal, the sniper had remained true to his cause and pursued the sole aim of vanquishing his enemy. While the men battled it out, the enemy sniper had no individuality; he was simply a Free State soldier. Not until the enemy is dead and his selfhood thus eradicated does the sniper feel a spark of curiosity as to the man's identity. Only when the other man ceases to be a threat does the sniper acknowledge his status as another human instead of merely an enemy soldier.

O'Flaherty chooses to end his story with this surprising sentence, "Then the sniper turned over the dead body and looked into his brother's face." The reader is left to wonder about this unexpected development. What kind of relationship did the brothers have? How did two members of the same family come to take opposing sides in the civil war?

How will this incident affect the sniper and his future? While these questions remain unanswered by the narrative, the reader sees in this simple statement the breach that the civil war has caused in Irish society. No longer are neighbors, friends, or even family members united. And this dissent, though perhaps with less extreme results, is playing out in other households across Ireland. Further, this dramatic ending highlights the terrible stakes of the civil war. The sniper will carry for the rest of his life the knowledge that he has killed his brother.

By presenting his stark ending but not exploring it, O'Flaherty also emphasizes the universality of civil war. History abounds with examples of how civil wars have broken up families. In the American Civil War, for instance, one man might have fought for the Confederate states while his brother may have enlisted in the Union Army. O'Flaherty's story could exist, with details and locations changed, and tell the tale of any civil war. This universality allows "The Sniper" to be a universally applicable condemnation of civil war. This additional layer only enhances the literary richness of "The Sniper" and makes it a tale that surpasses borders and time.

Source: Rena Korb, Critical Essay on "The Sniper," in *Short Stories for Students*, Gale, 2005.

William Troy

In the following essay, Troy categorizes O'Flaherty's works by theme and setting, calling "The Sniper" and other works "the most remarkable record" of Dublin's revolutionary period of the early twentieth century.

Liam O'Flaherty, at the age of thirty-two, has written five novels, four volumes of short stories, a biography and a large number of sketches and short stories soon to be gathered together in another collection. His reputation, however, is commensurate neither with this record of sustained creative energy nor with the easily recognizable distinction of his work. Literary popularity is never a matter of significance in speaking about a serious artist; but the reasons behind the critical apathy in the present instance are more interesting than usual. To consider them is to discover something about the mechanism of literary popularity at any time. It is also one excellent means of approaching certain of the essential features of this writer's contribution to the literature of our age. For the two things which are responsible for the neglect of O'Flaherty are at the same time inseparable from the deepest meaning and value of his work: his nationality and his fondness for melodrama.

The disadvantages of being an Irish writer today would be numerous even were it possible for the English reviews to be less loyal to their country and their class. Liam O'Flaherty has had at least as much to overcome in detaching himself from the settled mist of the "Celtic renaissance" as the writers of that movement had in detaching themselves from the earlier schools of Lever and Boucicault. The unfortunate result is that O'Flaherty has perhaps suffered more than he has gained by the association. It would seem pretty definite that the critical portion of the public is as avid of novelty as the common reader; and both certainly have had reason of late to become rather stalely habituated to the periodic emergence of ambitious talent in Ireland. At any rate an unmistakable tone of weariness has become the custom in whatever is written about this writer in the few literary journals which do not altogether ignore him. Actually, O'Flaherty's relation to the double tradition of Anglo-Irish literature is unique and distinct. He is on the side of Synge and Joyce, as against the side of Swift and Shaw; but he does not belong unreservedly with either of those writers. Neither intellectual refinement nor the impedimenta of culture and religion operate to confuse the complete identification with nature which is the predominant feature of his work. He is closer to the unknown writers of the early Gaelic folk literature than to any of his contemporaries. He is less the product of any modern school than of that period when European culture had not yet entirely lost its innocence.

There can be no question that all the novels of O'Flaherty belong to the category of melodrama; there can be equally little doubt that judgment of their value has been affected by the prevailing distrust of this mode. The objections to the mode have never been clearly formulated, although adherence to it has often been enough to discredit much of the work of Conrad and Dostoievski in the eyes of some critics. In the Greek sense, a melodrama meant simply a play with music; but the term was never used to differentiate such entertainment from a tragedy by Æschylus, for instance, which has nevertheless most of the objectionable features of a modern melodrama. Today we signify by the term any composition in which the element of action seems exaggerated or strained beyond certain vaguely determined limits. What we probably mean is the extension of action beyond the boundaries to which we are accustomed in normal social experience.

This restriction may apply with considerable justice to certain works of drama and fiction of inferior merit; but applied to other more pretentious works of the imagination it seems to involve an inconsistency. Perhaps the misconception rests on a failure to determine the nature of the relationship between action and theme, on the failure to recognize that the treatment of certain themes requires the extension of action on a more strenuous and heroic plane than the normal.

Melodrama, so considered, might be accepted as the elaboration of human motives on a grand scale, against immense backgrounds, and to the accompaniment of enormous music. In terms of function, one might discover in this form the most appropriate medium for the working out of certain crises or highly intensified human situations, the proper conditions for which depend on a heightening of the common laws of circumstance. However, any such defense of melodrama as a legitimate mode has nothing to do with its value in comparison with other recognized modes or with any possible system of values of its own. It is possible to write *good* melodramas, like *Macbeth* or *The Duchess of Malfi*; it is also possible to write *bad* melodramas, like any number of plays written in Shakespeare's time or like any number of books written in our own. It is part of O'Flaherty's distinction as a novelist that he has had the courage, throughout all his five novels, to adopt what is at once the most dangerous and the most unpopular of literary modes.

The fact that all of O'Flaherty's novels, from *Thy Neighbour's Wife* to *The Assassin*, adhere to the one mode suggests that it is inevitable for the particular pattern of life that has shaped itself in his imagination. His themes dictate the choice, themes which resolve themselves always into the larger and more violent conflicts of melodrama. Should this explanation prove insufficient, there remains the exceptional nature of the background against which these themes are represented. Modern Ireland is a portion of the earth's surface which it would be necessary to imagine if it did not exist. The Aran Islands, in which O'Flaherty was born, are not unlike those western islands around which Odysseus sailed and adventured; and Dublin, in the civilized modern mind, often takes on the colors of the Elizabethan version of the Italian cities of the Renaissance. It is clear that whatever temperamental predilection O'Flaherty may have had toward the writing of melodrama was strengthened by the inherent conditions of his environment.

> "Of the Dublin group, The Informer, The Assassin, and two earlier stories, 'The Sniper' and 'Civil War,' are based on real or imagined circumstances of the period of insurrection and disorder through which that city has passed in the last twelve years."

For convenience O'Flaherty's work may be divided into those novels and tales which have Dublin, and those which have his native Aran, for their setting. Of the Dublin group, *The Informer*, *The Assassin*, and two earlier stories, "The Sniper" and "Civil War," are based on real or imagined circumstances of the period of insurrection and disorder through which that city has passed in the last twelve years. As a whole they constitute the most remarkable record of the period which we are likely to receive: the most complete because derived largely from personal observation and participation; the most reliable because written without any other bias than that of artistic selection.

The Informer, as the title suggests, is a novel of the revolutionary half-world, the story of Gypo Nolan who betrays his friend to the police for twenty pounds. Less than one page is devoted to the actual capture and death of the betrayed man. All the interest is centered on the subsequent psychological history of the informer; his failure to liberate himself from the consciousness of the crime except through the expiation of death affords the theme. To appreciate his state of soul it is always necessary to remember the peculiar ambient of shame and horror that surrounds his crime in Ireland. Although low enough down on the moral scale of society, Gypo Nolan proves himself at bottom hopelessly loyal to the one code of morality that he can understand. How his guilt makes him give himself away at every turn, at every word, every movement, until he is finally shot down on his own doorstep, is told with a profound command of the Judas psychology. *The*

Informer is a study in conscience; it might even be described as a melodrama of the conscience.

In *The Assassin*, his last published novel, O'Flaherty essays the most ambitious study of the revolutionist psychology yet attempted in fiction. Here the object of the action, its specific political or social aspects are completely ignored. Also, the whole explicit action is subordinated to the conflict of motives, sometimes clear, sometimes strangely obscure, operating in the mind of the chief conspirator. Every step in Michael McDara's procedure from the moment of his return to Dublin—his selection of confederates, his preparations for the deed, his conduct after the deed—is described in a minute and exciting manner. At the beginning he is presented as the perfect and idealized archetype of the tyrannicide. As such he is thoroughly contrasted with each of his colleagues: Ketch, the professional thug, expert in murder as a trade; Tumulty, a mouthy sentimentalist, an inveterate patriot of the old order. Neither is able to rise to the hard purity of McDara's own philosophy of revolution. "Nobody had the *idea*," he explains, referring to the past. "Without an idea behind it, every political act becomes immoral and unnecessary. Such an act as this should be done in cold blood, not for motives of revenge or greed or for the purpose of seizing power or for anything else. Merely to cut off the head that is blocking the foreward movement of the mass. . . . This act must also be directed against the idea of God." In such speeches as this McDara is sustained by his reason and his eloquence; but at other moments he reverts to his peasant origin, remembering his own mother and the creed of his childhood, feeling suddenly terrified at the enormity of the gesture he is making against society. In the finest scene of the book the contrasted mental states of the three conspirators are shown as they sit about in a cheap furnished room on the eve of the murder. Here the closeness of observation is consummate; no movement, no vibration of the tense atmosphere is left unobserved as a possible source of intimate revelation. The style is attuned to the mood of the situation with a precision calculated to make the reader also share in the physical suspense. Ketch lies stretched out on the bed; Tumulty moves about nervously, talking foolishly to conceal his terror; but McDara, at the climax of his dream, ruminates on the sordidness of his surroundings, the cowardice and worthlessness of his companions, the essential waste and futility of his scheme.

If *The Informer* was a melodrama of the soul, with conscience as the principal protagonist, this last novel of O'Flaherty's is a melodrama of the intellect, founded on the immemorial strife between the will and the memory, between what the mind would determine and what life has decreed. At the end McDara is not strong enough to unbind the cords of tradition and sentiment which chain him to his emotional past, to whose aggregate symbol, on bended knees, he finally succumbs: "Mother, forgive me!" He has been clever enough to make his escape after the assassination quite certain; but the train which hastens him away from Ireland, of whose every beauty he is now made suddenly aware, bears an outcast and a failure. Suicide awaits him as soon as he reaches London.

Mr. Gilhooley represents an interesting effort on the part of O'Flaherty to extend his range of interest into a new sphere of Dublin society, the more quiescent, distinctly more bourgeois, society that is now forming out of the old. Gilhooley is a successful, middle-aged engineer who has come back to Ireland to recover his health after twenty years spent in South America. His is a full-length portrait of *l'homme moyen sensuel*. The sure sense of a wasted capacity for strong feeling, the depression of autumnal yearning make him ripe for his affair with the girl whom he picks up one night on the pavements. The differences in age and sensibility make the relationship impossible from the beginning. Tragedy becomes certain when Gilhooley's affection burns gradually into the fierce passion of middle-age. Perhaps the meaning of their last terrible scene in the flat, with its resolution of the theme into the familiar nightmare of jealousy and death, can be felt only by recognition of the man's age and essential normalcy. The girl's betrayal is for him the defeat of his life. But about this book as a whole one feels a lessening of strain, especially of poetic strain, as though O'Flaherty were telling Mr. Gilhooley's story more out of duty than out of any profound desire of the imagination.

The stories in *Spring Sowing* and *The Tent* should make their appeal even to those readers who are unable to respond to the larger patterns of the novels. The trained intensity of style, the economy of detail, the exact sharpness of perception appear here with special appropriateness and combine to place these stories among the most distinguished of our time. Almost every phase of Irish life is touched on, although for the most part they deal with the land. Such stories as "Milking Time," "Three Lambs" and the title-story of "Spring Sowing" are themselves like the rich exhalations of the soil; "Going into Exile" is a record of its tragedy, "The Bladder" and "The Old Hunter" of its robust humors. Perhaps the most perfect in achievement of all these little stories is "Birth" (published in the limited edition entitled *The Fairy Goose*), which is the simple account of a group of peasants gathered together near a meadow at night to attend the birth of a calf. But the most individual are those in which O'Flaherty writes about a lost thrust, or the capture of a fish, or a sea gull's first flight—unsentimental studies of animal life written with a fastidious interest usually reserved for human beings alone. From all of O'Flaherty's stories, however, one takes away a similar impression of the profound solidarity of nature, all of her manifestations being of equal importance to the artist who admits her superiority.

This conviction of the impenetrable identity of all physical nature receives its grandest expression in *The Black Soul*, the second, and the most majestic, of O'Flaherty's novels. "*The Black Soul* overwhelms one like a storm," wrote AE, but closer is the resemblance to a symphony, a vast prose symphony, whose most proper divisions are the four seasons of the year. The setting is Inverara, "the island of death, the island of defeated peoples, come thither through the ages over the sea pursued by their enemies"; its characters are its people, seated "on the cliffs dreaming of the past of their fathers, dreaming of the sea, the wind, the moon, the stars, the scattered remnants of an army, the remains of a feast eaten by dogs, the shattering of a maniac's ambition." Into this world comes the Stranger, bringing with him the sick body and tired soul of one who has lived too long on the mainland. The whole tempestuous drama of the book is in full process in Fergus O'Connor's brain before it is realized in explicit action. There begins at once his long struggle to yield himself to life as life becomes crystallized for him in his love of Little Mary, the wife of the peasant with whom he has taken lodging. Mary is a kind of island Cybele; she has no more character, in the usual sense, than nature herself; she is as hard, as wild and as beautiful. But Fergus is obliged to bore down through every layer of sentiment, culture, illusion which buries the reality of his being. The old conflict between nature and the intellect—the single underlying theme of all O'Flaherty's novels—here is staged against the most opulent background of physical nature, elaborated with all the resources of a rich, poetic prose, and resolved finally in one of the most powerful scenes in modern fiction. During the fierce struggle with Red John in the cleft of rocks on the coast,

Fergus is made to see the meaning of life through the meaning of death. Through action he is at last able to free himself. It would be much closer to a certain tradition of romantic fiction to have Fergus, instead of Red John, meet his end in this scene. But such a solution would cause the deeper implication of the novel to be lost. The victory of Fergus is essential if the positive import of the theme is to be established: the complete reaffirmation of physical experience as the means of bringing man back into harmony with his universe.

The Black Soul is the best of O'Flaherty's novels because of the grandeur and sonority of the theme and because of the abundance of those qualities of language and perception for which his work as a whole is distinguished. These qualities are essentially of a poetic order and, as such, difficult to define or describe by means of any available critical equivalents, although plainly manifest on every page. Moreover, they are qualities which should make a potent appeal to any modern reader. (The theme of *The Black Soul*, for example, is profoundly modern, but it is also *more* than modern.) Nature, not as the dark intoxicant of the earlier romanticists, but as something apprehended in the flesh, may come to be more and more accepted by our writers as the superstructure of our intellectual world crumbles about their feet. In the meantime, when most of our novelists seem to be frantically entrapped among the ruins, the reading of O'Flaherty is like a tonic and a promise.

Source: William Troy, "The Position of Liam O'Flaherty," in *Bookman*, Vol. 69, March 1929, pp. 7–11.

Sources

Calahan, James M., "Politics," in *Liam O'Flaherty, A Study of the Short Fiction*, Twayne Publishers, 1991, pp. 30–40.

Doyle, Paul A., "Liam O'Flaherty," in *Dictionary of Literary Biography*, Vol. 162, *British Short Fiction Writers, 1915–1945*, edited by John H. Rogers, Gale Research, 1996, pp. 282–92.

Kelly, A. A., "Urban and War Themes," in *Liam O'Flaherty: The Storytellers*, Harper & Row Publishers, 1976, pp. 23–36.

O'Brien, James H., "The Short Stories," in *Liam O'Flaherty*, Associated University Presses, 1973, pp. 92–117.

Troy, William, "The Position of Liam O'Flaherty," in *Bookman*, Vol. LXIX, March 29, 1929, pp. 7–11.

Further Reading

Bates, H. E., "The Irish School" in *The Modern Short Story: A Critical Survey*, The Writer, 1972, pp. 148–62.
    Bates, himself a writer of numerous novels and short stories, places O'Flaherty's work within the context of other important twentieth-century Irish writers.

Brewer, Paul, ed., *Ireland: History, Culture, People*, Courage Books, 2002.
    This volume provides an illustrated introduction to Ireland, focusing on its history through the early 2000s, its people, and its culture.

Doyle, Paul A., *Liam O'Flaherty*, Twayne Publishers, 1971.
    Doyle's work provides a good overview of O'Flaherty's entire body of fiction, both short stories and novels, as well as a detailed biographical chapter.

Kiely, Benedict, *Modern Irish Fiction: A Critique*, Golden Eagle Books, 1950.
    Kiely discusses the preeminent Irish writers of the first half of the twentieth century and dubs O'Flaherty a romantic.

Ranelagh, John O'Beirne, *A Short History of Ireland*, Cambridge University Press, 1995.
    This updated edition covers Irish history from ancient times through the end of the twentieth century.

Zneimer, John, *The Literary Vision of Liam O'Flaherty*, Syracuse University Press, 1970.
    Zneimer's detailed work investigates O'Flaherty's personal life, the themes of his work, and specifically analyzes his body of short fiction.

The Sun, the Moon, the Stars

Junot Díaz

1998

The story came about after Díaz spent a summer working as an interpreter for a U.S.-sponsored dentistry mission in Santo Domingo. The job gave Díaz an opportunity to visit his native Dominican Republic and experience it again from the perspective of someone who has lived for years in the United States. According to Díaz in the "Contributors' Notes" in *The Best American Short Stories 1999*, that summer they "pulled . . . five thousand teeth on the trip and . . . rubbed shoulders with many of the country's elite," a contrast Díaz sought to capture in a story. After a year of revising the story, Díaz realized that he should delete all references to dentistry and focus more on the dissolution of the relationship between his two main characters. "Once I got that insight," says Díaz, "I finished the story in a single day, the culmination of sixteen months of work." This achievement represented something else for the author, however. "I still remember that day. The first piece I'd finished since my book [*Drown*] was published. My hands were shaking." The story first appeared in *The New Yorker* and was later included in the anthology *The Best American Short Stories 1999*.

"The Sun, the Moon, the Stars" recounts the ways in which Yunior, a proud Dominican male, manages to sabotage his relationship with Magdalena, a woman who seems very much like every man's ideal. The story progresses from one miscue to another as Yunior attempts to remedy the damage he has caused by having an affair. The couple

travels from metropolitan New York to Santo Domingo to celebrate an anniversary, but the vacation, instead of reviving their love for each other, only brings an end to their relationship. Yunior does not think of himself as a bad guy, yet his actions contradict him at every turn. Charming and engaging, he is, nevertheless, his own worst enemy.

Author Biography

In 1968, Junot Díaz was born into a *barrio* family and raised in Santo Domingo, the capital of the Dominican Republic. In 1975, he moved with his family to Perth Amboy, New Jersey, and later became a naturalized citizen of the United States. Díaz has held a variety of jobs, including copy shop assistant, dishwasher, steelworker, pool table delivery man, editorial assistant, and freelance writer. Díaz completed a bachelor of arts degree in literature and history at Rutgers University and a master of fine arts degree in creative writing at Cornell.

Díaz burst onto the literary scene with the publication of his short story collection *Drown* (Riverhead Books, 1996). The young author earned himself a six-figure advance that was unprecedented for someone who had only published five stories and who had nothing more than a one-page synopsis of a novel to show publishers bidding at auction. Success has not come without its price, however, for Díaz has published little in the years since his debut. In an interview for the *Latino News Network* online, quoted in *Contemporary Authors Online*, Díaz describes his meteoric success as "completely overwhelming." "I was not really mentally prepared for it. So instead of making mistakes—which meant . . . going nuts with the money or just going bananas and like changing who I was . . . what I did was shut down. . . . And I found it hard to write."

Díaz's stories have appeared in such prestigious publications as *Story*, *The Paris Review*, and *The New Yorker*, with two stories, "Ysrael" and "Fiesta, 1980," selected for inclusion in the *Best American Short Stories* anthology series. Subsequently, "The Sun, the Moon, the Stars" was included in *Best American Short Stories 1999*. Díaz was named one of *Newsweek* magazine's ten "New Faces of 1996." In 1999, *The New Yorker* magazine named Díaz one of the "twenty best fiction writers in America." In addition to being honored with a Lila Acheson Wallace-Reader's Digest Fund award

and a Guggenheim fellowship, Díaz was the 2002 recipient of the PEN/Malamud award for short fiction.

In early 2004, Díaz was teaching creative writing at Syracuse University and was at work on a novel tentatively entitled *The Cheater's Guide to Love.*

Plot Summary

Part 1

"The Sun, the Moon, the Stars" begins with the narrator claiming to be a good person even though he admits to cheating on his girlfriend. "I'm not a bad guy," he says. He rejects the stereotype of the philandering Dominican male as it applies to him. The narrator continues to rationalize his poor judgment, saying that everyone makes mistakes. He maintains his good character even after he reveals the presence of a letter that confirms his former girlfriend's opinion of him.

Looking back on his relationship with Magda, the narrator believes that their relationship had begun to improve once he began to express greater interest in her activities. "A nice rhythm we had going," he says. By then the affair with Cassandra has been over for months, yet the narrator cannot ignore the devastating impact her letter has had on his relationship with Magda and her family. He is now treated as an outcast, whereas he was once regarded as a son. He compares the damage to a "five-train collision."

The narrator continues to debate whether he should have admitted to the affair with Cassandra. His friends advise him to deny everything, but at the time he is too filled with remorse and too overwhelmed by the sight of Magda's pain to ignore the truth. "You have to listen to me, Magda. Or you won't understand," he begs.

The narrator describes Magda's physical appearance and personality. "She's a forgiving soul," one who attends Mass and asks nuns to pray for distant relatives. He is not the only one who has a high opinion of her, for "[s]he's the nerd every librarian in town knows, a teacher whose students fall in love with her." She is thoughtful and generous. "You couldn't think of anybody worse to screw than Magda," the narrator concludes.

The narrator then summarizes his attempts to win Magda back. Without shame, he recalls "[t]he begging, the crawling over glass, the crying" he did to convince her not to abandon their relationship. They discuss Cassandra, and the narrator placates Magda's curiosity by saying that he would have told her about the affair eventually. In the end, the narrator's love for Magda wins out over his sense of pride, yet that pride is not eliminated completely.

Nevertheless, the narrator senses that a profound change has occurred within Magda. "My Magda was turning into another Magda," he says. The narrator discovers that his girlfriend is no longer as accommodating as she once was. Rather than view her change in attitude as a result of his infidelity, he blames this change on the influence of her girlfriends, whom he believes are "feeding her a bad line." Even though he tries to ignore the fallout from the affair, every attempt he makes at reconciliation seems to confirm "something negative" about him. Magda's changes in attitude become more visible as time passes, bringing about improvements in her physical appearance and wardrobe, improvements that, as the narrator says, "would have alarmed a paranoid nigger."

Part 2

The scene changes to summer, and the narrator describes plans for a vacation to Santo Domingo. The vacation is put into doubt because Magda feels pressured to make a commitment which she is unprepared to do. The narrator, on the other hand, believes that a vacation will end the ambiguity and uncertainty that has plagued their relationship since Magda learned of the affair the previous winter. "Me and her on the Island. What couldn't this cure?" Once again, the narrator blames Magda's reluctance on her friends' influence.

The narrator momentarily forgets his worries as he reflects upon his hometown of Santo Domingo and the many things he has missed since he left the Dominican Republic for New York. With tenderness and affection, he recalls the hospitality of his fellow countrymen and the sense of camaraderie that binds them together. He remembers the affection they openly display toward one another.

However, the narrator cannot dwell for long on such memories because he must confront the harsh realities that forced him to leave Santo Domingo for a better life in the United States. "If this was another kind of story, I'd tell you about the sea," he says. He

Junot Díaz

would like to wax poetic about the beautiful Dominican landscape, but he cannot because that landscape is populated by "[m]ore albinos, more cross-eyed niggers, more *tígueres* [street children who often resort to stealing and prostitution in order to survive] than you'll ever see." The narrator is quickly distracted by thoughts of lovely young Dominican women before he resumes telling the reader about Santo Domingo and the dilapidated vehicles that roam the city's streets. He describes the shanties where a majority of Santo Domingo's citizens live, including his grandfather who still does not have running water or a flush toilet. The narrator recalls the place of his birth—Calle XXI (21st Street)—and wonders whether it will remain forever backward or make the strides toward modernity that are long overdue. In the end, the narrator, as confounded as ever by the lack of development in his homeland, says, "Santo Domingo is Santo Domingo. Let's pretend we all know what goes on there."

The narrator, whose name is Yunior, continues to believe that his relationship with Magda will be restored to its former level of intimacy if they observe the practices, such as visiting his relatives, that once established them as a couple. This time, however, Magda is bored, and, in what Yunior perceives to be a complete change in character, she tells him so. Yunior makes every attempt to be a good host, pointing out improvements, such as restaurant franchises, that have occurred since his last trip and telling her about some of his nation's history. Reluctantly, he admits that things are not going well, for Magda, who is normally very talkative, remains quiet throughout their bus trip from Santo Domingo to the country's interior.

Magda and Yunior continue to express differing opinions about how they should spend their vacation. Magda wants to go to the beach, whereas Yunior would prefer to spend more time in the countryside. Once again, he blames Magda's girlfriends for his difficulties, yet he manages to control his temper. Finally, he acquiesces and arranges for a bus to take them to the resort town of La Romana ahead of schedule.

Part 3

Once they arrive in La Romana, the tables turn, as it is now Yunior who becomes bored. His thoughts turn to sex rather than watching HBO. Yunior complains about how infrequently he and Magda have sex and how much more trouble he has seducing her than he did before. Sexual relations between them have become perfunctory, with no spark of passion or romance.

Yunior complains about their accommodations. It is not that the hotel accommodations are inadequate; it is that they are ostentatious and secluded from everything that might detract from the illusion of beauty and splendor. Yunior feels "walled away from everybody else," particularly the average citizens he has missed. He compares the resort to being in another country where "the only Island Dominicans you're guaranteed to see are either caked up or changing your sheets." They are served breakfast "by cheerful women in Aunt Jemima costumes."

The couple continues to argue over how much time they should spend apart from each other while on vacation. Magda says that she needs some time for herself "maybe once a day," but Yunior insists that they remain together. They compromise by taking a golf cart to the beach.

Yunior once again remarks upon the disparities between the resort and the rest of the country. "Casa de Campo has got beaches the way the rest of the island has got problems," he says. Having cataloged the many joys of Dominican life that are absent from the resort, Yunior next focuses on the scores of

white Europeans, the "budget Foucaults," who have flocked to the beach to contemplate beauty, especially that of the local girls. Yunior describes each one of the tourists as looking "like some scary pale monster that the sea's vomited up."

When he sees Magda dressed in a new bikini that her girlfriends helped to pick out, Yunior immediately believes that they have planned to "torture" him. Magda's beauty arouses Yunior's insecurities rather than restores his confidence. He admits to feeling "vulnerable and uneasy." The swagger and bravado associated with his sexual prowess now desert him, and Yunior finds himself begging Magda for a declaration of love. She refuses to be cajoled by him, ending the matter by calling him a "pestilence."

Yunior's insecurities worsen when he and Magda arrive at the beach. He fears that they do not look like a couple, and he becomes painfully aware that Magda, wearing her new bikini, has become the center of attention. Yunior, on the other hand, feels as though everyone regards him suspiciously.

An Assistant D.A. who, like Yunior, is a Dominican living in Quisqueya Heights, takes an interest in Magda and strikes up a conversation with her. Yunior becomes jealous and possessive, threatening the Assistant D.A. with physical violence. The Assistant D.A. espouses a profound empathy with his accused countrymen who come before him in a court of law. However, Yunior regards the Assistant D.A. as a traitor: "I'm thinking he sounds like the sort of nigger who in the old days used to lead bwana to the rest of us." Yunior's combative attitude toward the Assistant D.A. forces Magda to walk away in disgust. Yunior does not bother putting up an argument, for he already knows what Magda will say: "Time for you to do your thing and me to do mine."

That night Yunior decides to hang out around the pool and the local bar, Club Cacique, where he meets Lucy, a "Dominicana from West New York" who resembles Magda physically except that she, Lucy, is *Trigueña*, a woman with wheat-colored skin. Yunior is tempted by Lucy's beauty, but he resists temptation when he sees a "spiderweb of scars" covering her stomach. He then meets "two rich older dudes drinking cognac at the bar."

These two men are the Vice-President and Bárbaro, his bodyguard. According to Yunior, the Vice-President is "a young brother, in his late thirties, and pretty cool for a *chupabarrio*," though there is some doubt as to whether this streetwise man acquired his wealth legally. "I must have the footprint of fresh disaster on my face," thinks Yunior, for the Vice-President quickly orders shots of rum all around. Before long, the Vice-President and Bárbaro are giving Yunior advice about women, advice that is no different from that offered by Yunior's friends in Quisqueya Heights.

Yunior wonders whether his inability to remain faithful is truly a part of his nature. Did he cheat on Magda because he is Dominican? According to Magda's friends, "all us Dominican men are dogs." Yunior refutes the notion that his infidelity can be attributed to something like genetics, citing other reasons, namely what he refers to as "[c]ausalities." He attempts to assuage his wounded ego by saying that all relationships at one point or another experience "turbulence."

Yunior then recalls the beginnings of his relationship with Magda. He recalls with the accuracy of an accountant conducting an audit the ways in which they truly resembled a couple after a year of dating. Even though Yunior is willing to make the compromises that establish a harmonious, if somewhat monotonous, relationship, his restless nature reveals itself when he puts that first year with Magda in perspective: "Our relationship wasn't the sun, the moon, and the stars, but it wasn't [b——sh——t], either."

Yunior's thoughts turn to sex, and he rationalizes his eventual betrayal of Magda by citing the many opportunities for an affair which he has ignored previously. In other words, he is a victim of circumstance. He then reflects upon the origins of the affair with Cassandra. "First week of knowing her, I made the mistake of telling her that sex with Magda had never been topnotch," he confides. Though he does not completely accept responsibility for his role in the affair, as if to imply, once again, that he is but a hapless bystander and that Cassandra's strong sex drive is yet another "causality" that has led to the demise of his relationship with Magda, Yunior recalls how, even while in the throes of passion, he felt guilty for betraying the woman he loved.

Another day of vacation begins, and Magda and Yunior hardly speak to each other. The resort is throwing a party that night, and all guests are invited. As the couple dresses in front of the mirror,

Yunior admires Magda's appearance as he fondly recalls the first time he kissed her curls "shiny and as dark as night." Yunior's hope for a reconciliation returns, but it is dashed just as quickly when Magda informs him that tonight, of all nights, she wishes to be alone. A bitter argument ensues, with names called in anger. Finally, Yunior leaves, feeling sorry for himself, thinking, "I'm not a bad guy."

Yunior returns to Club Cacique, looking for Lucy but finding the Vice-President and his bodyguard instead. They sit at the quiet end of the bar, drinking cognac and discussing how many Dominican ballplayers are in the major leagues. "This place is killing me," says Yunior, and the Vice-President suggests that they take a drive. He wishes to show Yunior "the birthplace of our nation." Having nothing better to do, Yunior decides to go along for the ride. Before leaving, however, he casts one last glance around the room, only to find Lucy slightly disheveled but still very much a temptation. Reluctantly, Yunior accompanies the men out of the club.

The three men drive in a black BMW sedan on dark roads, the air sweet with the smell of sugar cane as insects "swarm like a Biblical plague" in front of the car's headlights. The Vice-President and Bárbaro talk at the same time as a bottle of cognac is passed around. Yunior wonders where they are going, but he dismisses any fears because, after all, he is with the Vice-President—and the Vice-President knows what he is doing or else he would not have become the Vice-President. Yunior has doubts about Bárbaro, however. The bodyguard's hand shakes as he tells Yunior about his former dreams of becoming an engineer, and this makes Yunior think that Bárbaro is anything but a bodyguard. Yunior really does not pay too much attention to either man, for his thoughts have once again returned to Magda and how he'll probably never have sex with her again.

Mosquitoes devour the men as they get out of the car and stumble up a slope covered with vegetation. Bárbaro carries a huge flashlight as the Vice-President tries to remember the way. Yunior reconsiders his opinion of the bodyguard when he sees him carrying a machine gun with authority, his hand as steady as ever.

Finally, the Vice-President locates the site, a hole in the red earth that Yunior identifies as bauxite. The hole is deep and "blacker than any of us," says Yunior, staring down into the hole. The Vice-President announces that the hole is the Cave of the

Jagua, "the birthplace of the Tainos." He ignores Yunior's attempts to correct his geography, saying that he is "speaking mythically," for the Vice-President regards the site with reverence. Bárbaro's flashlight barely penetrates the darkness as the three men continue to examine the hole.

When the Vice-President asks Yunior if he wants to see inside, Yunior cannot recall for sure what his answer was, though he realizes that he must have said yes, for he remembers Bárbaro handing him the flashlight before the men grabbed him by the ankles and lowered him into the hole. As he is lowered down, coins fly out of his pockets, *"bendiciones,"* or offerings, made to the spirits of his ancestors. Yunior cannot see much, "just some odd colors on the eroded walls" of the "cave" as he hears the Vice-President ask, "Isn't it beautiful?"

"This is the perfect place for insight, for a person to become somebody better," Yunior thinks as he hangs upside down. He imagines that this is the place where the Vice-President first caught a glimpse of "his future self," the person who would overcome poverty to become a successful businessman. Yunior also imagines Bárbaro, his dream of becoming a benefactor of the people not quite extinguished, buying a concrete home for his mother and showing her how to operate the air conditioner. Instead of looking at his future self, as he imagines the others must have done, Yunior looks toward the past, to the time he first met Magda during their college days at Rutgers. "And that's when I know it's over," he realizes. "As soon as you start thinking about the beginning, it's the end." Yunior starts to cry, forcing the men to pull him up. The Vice-President, seeing that Yunior has failed to make the most of this opportunity, chides Yunior for being less than a man.

Part 4

Looking back on the events that took place on the night he visited the Cave of the Jagua, Yunior realizes that "some serious Island voodoo" must have been at work, for the ending he saw came true. He and Magda returned to the United States the very next day, cutting their vacation short.

Five months later, Yunior receives a letter from Magda saying that she is dating someone new, a "very nice guy." "Dominican, like me," observes Yunior. Even though Yunior has a new girlfriend, seeing Magda's handwriting has a devastating ef-

fect on him. He realizes now that their relationship is finally over.

Yunior berates himself for being such a fool. He then narrates the sad demise of his relationship with Magda on a night that once promised joyous celebration. In a flashback, he describes how he returned to the bungalow, where he found Magda with her bags packed, her eyes red and swollen from crying. "I'm going home tomorrow," she tells him. He sits down next to her and takes her hand, hopeful that she'll give him one more chance. "This can work," he says. "All we have to do is try."

Characters

The Assistant D.A.

Like Yunior, the Assistant D.A. is a native of Quisqueya Heights who has returned to his native country for a brief vacation. The Assistant D.A. strikes up a conversation with Magdalena after meeting her on the beach at Casa de Campo, arousing Yunior's jealousy. Ironically, Yunior observes that the Assistant D.A. "loves his people" even though he is responsible for putting many of them behind bars. "'Better I'm their prosecutor,'" says the attorney. "'At least I understand them.'" Yunior views the Assistant D.A. as a traitor, comparing him to "the sort of nigger who in the old days used to lead bwana to the rest of us."

Bárbaro

Bárbaro is the Vice-President's bodyguard. Even though the weather is hot and humid, he wears an ascot to conceal a knife wound he received from a soldier. His expensive suit is often rumpled, and his hand shakes while he smokes, which makes Yunior believe that he is not a very good bodyguard—that is, until he sees him carrying a huge machine gun. A self-described modest man, Bárbaro is also regarded as something of a philosopher since he takes a slightly romantic view toward his job and freely dispenses advice about women. He once had hopes of becoming an engineer and building schools and hospitals for his village, but these hopes, like so many held during the Trujillo and Balaguer regimes, were ruined by the government's poor economic policies. In Spanish, his name means "barbarous," which contrasts his actions with the more sophisticated ways of his employer.

Cassandra

Cassandra works with Yunior and has an affair with him. With an ample bust and "tons of eighties freestyle hair," she is a femme fatale who initiates an affair with Yunior, who is much too weak to resist. Cassandra is a woman who knows what she wants and knows how to get it. Her aggressive personality contrasts with that of Magdalena, who is much more studious and reserved sexually. Though their affair is over, Yunior thinks of Cassandra frequently while on vacation in Santo Domingo, especially when the Vice President advises him to find another woman, one who is "bella [beautiful] and negra [black]." Cassandra's name evokes that of the ancient Greek prophetess who was granted the ability to foretell the future by the god Apollo. However, everyone who heard her prophecies believed them to be lies instead of truths, and thus a blessing became a curse. Ironically, Cassandra's letter to Magdalena is taken as the truth.

Claribel

A loyal and true friend, Claribel provides Magdalena with support during her break-up with Yunior. Yunior describes Claribel, a native of Ecuador, as "chinita," a woman having almond-shaped eyes like an Asian. Like Magda and Yunior, she is college-educated, graduating with a biology degree. Because Magda still lives at home, Claribel provides an alibi for her whenever she stays over at Yunior's apartment. Claribel is the only one of Magda's friends who is mentioned by name.

Her Girls

These women provide Magdalena with moral support and counsel throughout her relationship with Yunior, especially once she learns of his infidelity. Magda phones her girls throughout her vacation in the Dominican Republic. Yunior describes them as "the sorest losers on the planet" and often projects his resentment toward Magda onto them, believing that they conspire against him. For example, he believes that they helped Magda pick out a bikini just so she could "torture" him.

His Boys

These unnamed characters give Yunior advice on his love life and appear off-stage, as it were.

Media Adaptations

- Audio Editions (http://www.audioeditions.com) offers *The Best American Short Stories 1999* on cassette, each story read by its author. The set contains four abridged cassettes and features, in addition to Junot Díaz, such noted authors as Pam Houston, Jhumpa Lahiri, Aleksandar Hemon, and Tim Gautreaux.

They act like a Greek chorus, commenting upon Yunior's actions. They espouse many of the behaviors that earn Dominican men a reputation as liars and womanizers.

Lucy

Lucy meets Yunior at the resort in La Romana while Magda enjoys a night alone. Lucy lives in West New York but has returned to her native Dominican Republic for a vacation. Physically, she resembles Magda with her dark curly hair and light complexion. Yunior describes her as a *Trigueña*, a woman with a wheat-colored complexion. Lucy bears a "spiderweb of scars across her stomach," which may account for why she prefers to spend time with her teenaged cousins on the town rather than remain at home. Lucy's socioeconomic status compares dramatically with other natives of Santo Domingo, such as Yunior and the Assistant D.A., who have immigrated to Quisqueya Heights. Lucy is beautiful, but her beauty is often flawed. In this respect, she represents the Dominican Republic symbolically. Yunior finds Lucy's beauty tempting, but he resists.

Magda

Magda is Yunior's nickname for Magdalena. A native of Cuba, Magda is Yunior's long-suffering girlfriend. She learns of Yunior's affair when she receives a letter from Cassandra. Yunior describes Magda as a "forgiving soul," a devout Catholic who regularly attends Mass and who implores a group of nuns in Pennsylvania to pray for her family. Magda is a popular teacher with her students, and she continues to pursue an education even though she has earned a degree. "She's the nerd every librarian in town knows," says Yunior. Magda is very striking physically, with "big eyes and big hips and dark curly hair you could lose a hand in." With her red lips and voluptuous figure, she is the physical embodiment of what it is to be Latina. Magda is normally a very talkative person, but she can be sullen when she feels she has been wronged. As the story progresses, Magda becomes more assertive, taking time for herself and her interests despite pressure from Yunior to have sex. She asserts her independence on the night the resort sponsors a party, leaving Yunior to entertain himself. Five months after the end of their relationship, Yunior receives a letter from Magda that testifies, one would assume, to her forgiving nature.

Magdalena

See Magda

The Vice-President

A "young brother, in his late thirties," the Vice-President has all the hallmarks of a successful businessman, particularly one who comes from the slums of Santo Domingo. Not only is he well educated but he drives a BMW automobile, drinks cognac, and dresses fashionably—the essence of worldly accomplishment and sophistication. His business dealings may not all be legitimate, however. Yunior turns to the Vice-President for advice on women, and he dispenses it freely, with an air of worldly charm. The Vice-President respects his island ancestors, for he takes Yunior to the Cave of the Jagua, the mythical birthplace of the Tainos, with the hope that Yunior will be able to complete this rite of passage with manly pride and dignity.

Yunior

Yunior is the story's narrator and protagonist. He is a native of Santo Domingo who now resides in Quisqueya Heights, a district of Washington Heights in upper Manhattan that is home to many Dominican expatriates. Although Yunior is a well-educated professional who refers to characters from literature like Bartleby the scrivener, the hero of Melville's eponymous tale, and to Michel Foucault, a renowned French philosopher, he espouses the attitudes of the street. He refuses to believe that he is a

"bad guy" even though he freely admits to having an affair with Cassandra. Throughout the story, he struggles against the stereotype of the Dominican male who is constantly on the prowl for sexual adventure. Yunior's *macho* attitudes are often at odds with his personality, which is rather sentimental.

Themes

Relationships

Díaz's main theme is personal responsibility and the ways in which it sustains an intimate relationship. From the very beginning of the story, Yunior tells the reader—and himself—that he is not such a bad guy even though he cheated on his girlfriend. He makes these comments retrospectively, once the relationship with Magda has ended and there is no longer any hope of reconciliation. Even so, Yunior still fails to accept responsibility for his actions, attributing his infidelity to "causalities" rather than to his selfish behavior. When he and Magda were together, he viewed their relations as an extension of "a nice rhythm [they] had going" or "the momentum of the past" rather than a deliberate effort to establish harmony. Furthermore, he fails to see Magda's change in behavior—she becomes more aloof—as a result of his thoughtlessness. On the contrary, Yunior blames Magda's girlfriends for influencing her change in attitude toward him.

In addition to the loyalty one partner should demonstrate toward the other, Díaz addresses the loyalty demonstrated among friends. Magda and Yunior know that they can rely on their friends to support them unwaveringly. His boys and her girls staunchly defend their respective friend's position without making judgments. Though this type of blind loyalty can occasionally yield disastrous results, the two main characters act knowing that they will not have to face their problems alone.

Relationships between family members remain important throughout the story. When Magda's family learns of Yunior's infidelity, they immediately cut him off, as though he has been ostracized from the family. He is no longer treated like a son but like the *"sucio"* Magda accuses him of being.

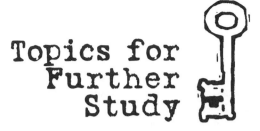

Topics for Further Study

- Research the U.S. occupation of the Dominican Republic. Who were some of the major players? Was the U.S. government welcome? How did the occupation affect the Dominican Republic's economy? How did the occupation affect the Dominican Republic's relations with other countries throughout Latin America?

- Who were the *parigüayos*? Where does their name come from?

- Explore the ways in which Díaz uses words that share a common origin in the English and Spanish languages. Cite examples. How does Díaz's use of language reflect his characters' environment?

- Who were the Tainos? What geographical region did they occupy? Did they really come from South America, as Yunior suggests? Are the Tainos an extinct race of people, or are their descendents alive today? Examine the cultural history they left behind.

- Research the Cave of the Jagua. Is it an actual place, or, as the Vice-President suggests, does it possess a more mythical importance? What symbolic connotations does it have in the story?

- How important a role does tourism play in the Dominican Republic? What other industries form the basis of this nation's economy? Research the rise and fall of the sugar cane industry in the countries of Central America and the Caribbean.

- In the story, the Vice-President and Bárbaro debate the actual number of Dominican ballplayers in the major leagues. Name some of the more famous Dominican ballplayers and compare their careers. Do Dominican ballplayers tend to play one position more than others? What accounts for the relatively high number of players from the Dominican Republic as opposed to, say, other countries in Latin America?

- When Columbus sailed to what is modern day Haiti and the Dominican Republic, he named the island Santa Esmeralda. Why? Research the expeditions of other European countries to the New World. Why did the French exert such a strong cultural influence on Haiti and not the Spanish?

- Haiti, the Dominican Republic's western neighbor, was known as a country where voodoo was practiced as of the early 2000s. Trace the origins of voodoo to West Africa. To what extent was the slave trade responsible for spreading voodoo's influence in the New World? How does voodoo compare with other religious practices in the region? For example, do the practices of Santeria and voodoo share any beliefs?

Indeed, Magda's father is so filled with rage upon hearing of Yunior's betrayal that he can hardly speak. "You no deserve I speak to you in Spanish," he tells Yunior. Magda's family makes every effort to protect her from further injury. Likewise, Yunior's family is important to him. Yunior honors tradition by visiting his *"abuelo"* immediately upon arriving in Santo Domingo, and he respects the hard work his grandfather did as a laborer in the cane fields.

National Pride

Yunior takes great pride in being from the Dominican Republic. "Let me confess: I love Santo Domingo," he says. He loves the people and their superstitious ways; he loves the "shredded silver" color of the sea after it has been "forced into the sky through a blowhole"; he loves the taste of Island rum. It is Yunior's love for his country and its beauty that causes him to feel outrage when he witnesses the abject poverty so many of his countrymen endure. Because he feels so much pride for his country, Yunior is willing to champion the underdog, as witnessed in his exchange with the Assistant D.A., whom he believes does more harm than good to the community of Dominicans living in Quisqueya Heights.

The Vice-President is another character who exhibits national pride. He takes Yunior to the Cave of the Jagua, "the birthplace of the Tainos," the first island residents. The Vice-President speaks solemnly and respectfully of this place even though its historical and anthropological value remains uncertain. He carries with him a sense of pride that bestows more importance on the cave than is perhaps justified, for its ability to transform Yunior lies in its mythical and symbolic power.

Economic and Social Divisions

When Yunior arrives in Santo Domingo, he faces the stark reality that is life in the Dominican Republic. He would like to tell the reader more about the beauty of this island nation, but the impoverished conditions of its people confront him at every turn. "More albinos, more cross-eyed niggers, more *tígueres* than you'll ever see." Children make their living in the street, selling candy or else resorting to stealing and prostitution. Yunior describes Santo Domingo as "a cosmology of battered cars, battered motorcycles, battered trucks, and battered buses, and an equal number of repair shops, run by any fool with a wrench." The entire city has fallen into disrepair. People live in shanty towns, their dilapidated houses lacking running water and toilets. Yunior recalls the street where he was born and cannot decide whether it qualifies as a slum. Despairing of his hometown's poverty, Yunior closes by saying, "Santo Domingo is Santo Domingo. Let's pretend we all know what goes on there."

Contrasted with the abject poverty of Santo Domingo is the opulence of La Romana's Casa de Campo, "The Resort That Shame Forgot." Casa de Campo is the wealthiest resort on the island, and it resembles in many ways an entire country unto itself. The resort has its own airport, beaches, and golf course. Security guards, or *"guachimanes,"* patrol the resort while peacocks strut among the "ambitious topiaries" that dot the landscape. Everywhere there is an air of sanitized purity, of separation from all that is unsightly. This is where the rich come to play and make deals that will increase their wealth. A majority of the hotel's clientele are white Europeans. Ironically, the only Island Dominicans seen at the resort are the ones who clean the rooms and serve food. Yunior sums up the disparities between the resort and the Dominican Republic as a whole when he says, "Casa de Campo has got beaches the way the rest of the island has got problems."

Race

Díaz is less concerned about addressing differences between whites and blacks than he is with exploring differences between people of African American descent. (Here the adjective *American* refers to people whose origins are in Central and South America as well as North America or the United States.) These latter differences mainly concern skin color and the ideal of feminine beauty. For example, Magda becomes the focus of men's attention the moment she arrives in the Dominican Republic, much to Yunior's chagrin. Men walk right up to her and compliment her on her appearance, hoping to win her favor. "You know how it is when you're on the Island and your girl's an octoroon," explains Yunior. "Brothers go apesh—t." (By "Brothers," he refers to men with dark skin.) Lucy, on the other hand, is referred to as a *Trigueña*, a woman with light, wheat-colored skin. She is regarded as beautiful, though perhaps not as beautiful as Magda, whose skin color is slightly darker.

Style

Point of View

The story is narrated in the first person by Yunior, the story's main protagonist. Yunior's energetic, colloquial tone invites the reader to listen attentively to his story. Yunior is also an unreliable narrator. He often contradicts himself, as when he tells the reader that Cassandra was not advertising falsely about her prowess in bed; previously, he tells Magda that sex with Cassandra was "lousy." The advantage Díaz gains in using this type of narrator is that the reader only hears one side of the story, thus underscoring the ironies that continue to confound Yunior long after his relationship with Magda has ended. Furthermore, the theme of responsibility is highlighted by the selective manner in which Yunior reveals his actions and by the way he interrupts his narrative to make passing remarks about women. Inadvertently, he proves that Magda's opinion of him is indeed correct.

Language

Borrowing the slang of New York's streets, Yunior refers to himself obliquely when he describes Magda's sudden physical transformation: "About a month later, she started making the sort of changes that would have alarmed a paranoid nigger." The word *nigger*, often used in the United

States as a derogatory term, is used by Yunior in the story to establish a more objective view of himself and to denote the affection and camaraderie he shares with his boys. They, in turn, address Yunior as "Nigger" when they desire his full attention and wish to impart advice about his relationship with Magda.

Díaz combines English with Spanish words and phrases that indicate Yunior's bi-cultural perspective of the world. He moves fluently between languages, using the language that best expresses his state of mind, even when he seems most confused. For example, when Yunior walks out of the hotel room in La Romana, effectively severing his relationship with Magda forever, he struggles to understand what has just happened while at the same time he maintains a facade of self-respect.

> This is the endgame, and instead of pulling out all the stops, instead of *pongándome más chivo que un chivo*, I'm feeling sorry for myself, *como un parigüayo sin suerte*. I'm thinking, I'm not a bad guy.

Moreover, Díaz challenges his reader's familiarity with other cultures and languages by using Spanish to express thoughts that would otherwise be considered vulgar if rendered in English. Thus, he maintains the story's narrative tone without compromising his artistic vision or the integrity of the characters he has created. Díaz is not in the least reluctant to use profanity, but he does use it for a purpose; namely, profanity illuminates the cultural perspective of the character at the moment the word is uttered. For example, when Yunior wishes to express a common sentiment, one that is often dismissive but not damaging, he will use English because that language, for him, lacks the power and authority he associates with his native tongue. On the other hand, when Yunior wishes to express a passionate state of mind, whether one aroused by erotic thoughts or extreme displeasure, he usually chooses Spanish. There is one occasion, however, when he uses English to make an emphatic point. He dismisses Magda's would-be suitors at the beach by saying, "Why don't you beat it, *pancho*?" Yunior expresses his disdain by using a word white North Americans use derogatorily to refer to someone of Latin heritage, a word that, in this case, compounds the slight because it does not even refer to the proper noun (i.e., *Pancho*).

Stereotypes

Díaz employs the stereotype of the femme fatale to underscore Yunior's sense of irresponsibility and to elucidate his *macho* tendencies. A femme fatale is a woman who is dangerously seductive and whose charms lead an unsuspecting man to ruin. Physically, Cassandra fits the stereotype, for Yunior describes her as "*bella* and *negra*," a beautiful black woman with "a big chest and a smart mouth," a "chick" with "tons of eighties freestyle hair" who wears denim skirts. She comes on to Yunior almost immediately after starting her new job, touching his pectoral muscles and complaining about her boyfriend, a "*moreno*," or brown-skinned man. Though Cassandra is quite feminine, she also knows how to hang out with the guys, organizing a football pool at work. She is competitive in a way that appeals to the male sensibility. Yunior quickly falls into the habit of having lunch with her, especially once he learns the intimate details of her sex life. Here Díaz employs yet another stereotype to initiate Yunior's undoing. When Cassandra, referring to her boyfriend, tells Yunior, "Black guys don't understand Spanish girls," he, a dark-skinned Dominican, cannot resist the challenge of proving her wrong. Although Yunior never reveals why Cassandra wrote the letter, his affair with her becomes one of the "causalities" which, he says, contribute to his breakup with Magda.

Díaz also uses stereotypes as a device to propel the action of his story. At the outset, Yunior tells the reader that he is not like other Dominican men; he is not a "*sucio*" who runs around chasing women. "I'm not a bad guy," he says. "I'm like everybody else: weak, full of mistakes, but basically good." He admits, however, to having cheated on Magda, and from this point forward Yunior attempts to persuade the reader that, regardless of what Magda or her friends might say, he does not conform to stereotype. The story is filled with anecdotes about what a thoughtful and considerate boyfriend he is, but then, as though enthralled by a self-fulfilling prophecy, Yunior will reveal his thoughts about another woman, thus proving Magda and her friends correct.

Historical Context

Pre-Columbian Culture and Peoples

When Christopher Columbus first arrived on Hispaniola, the former name for what is now Haiti and the Dominican Republic, there were an estimated 400,000 indigenous Taino Indians inhabiting the island. The word *Taino* means "men of the good," for the Taino were a gentle race of people whose lives where inextricably linked with their natural surroundings. The Tainos were a seafaring people who lived on the verge of dense jungle, but they also developed sophisticated agricultural practices that produced cassava, corn, squash, and peanuts. They wandered about naked, their bodies decorated with colorful dyes made from earth, and they bathed in the rivers near their homes, which were constructed of thatch and Royal Palm. They greeted Columbus and his men with the kindness and generosity that were honored Taino values. However, the Taino population decreased rapidly as a result of exposure to disease brought by the Europeans and by forced labor. The *encomienda* system, which allotted the Tainos to colonizers operating mines and farms and instructed the laborers in the tenets of the Catholic faith, forced many Tainos to commit suicide or abort pregnancies rather than endure a life of slavery. Eighteen years after Columbus' arrival on Hispaniola, the Taino population had dwindled to a mere 22,000.

Dictatorship in the Dominican Republic

For most of the twentieth century, the Dominican Republic, a Spanish-speaking country, experienced non-representative rule. The Dominican Republic has a history of changing ownership, with countries such as Spain, France, Haiti, and the United States governing the island nation. The United States, in particular, has intervened in the political affairs of the Dominican Republic, most notably in the years from 1916 to 1924, when United States military forces occupied the island, and between 1930 and 1961, when Rafael Leónidas Trujillo, backed by the U.S. government, ruled as dictator.

Trujillo won favor with the U.S. government in the wake of World War II largely because of his anti-communist stance. He encouraged foreign investment in the Dominican Republic by initiating a number of public works projects that were designed to create the illusion of prosperity. However, Trujillo's administration was rife with corruption, and, by the late 1950s, the social and economic gulf between the rich and poor in the Dominican Republic had widened. Trujillo's domestic problems were compounded by his intervention in the political affairs of other nations in Latin America and the Caribbean. Kidnappings and assassinations were linked to Trujillo and his government, forcing the Organization of American States to enforce harsh sanctions against the Dominican Republic before that organization severed all diplomatic ties. On May 30, 1961, Trujillo was assassinated by members of the military.

The government's brutality did not end there, however. The dictator's son, Ramfis Trujillo, assumed power briefly before being overthrown and exiled. Joaquín Balaguer, a former associate of Rafael Trujillo, attempted to stabilize the government, but opposition to his administration, an opposition that had been oppressed by more than thirty years of dictatorship, forced Balaguer, through demonstrations and strikes, to permit greater freedom of expression. Political parties formed, and national elections were promised. However, a military coup ensued, forcing Balaguer into exile. His efforts at democratization put him in good stead when he returned in 1966 after the United States military forces intervened in a Dominican civil war between constitutionalists, led by former Dominican president Juan Bosch, and a civilian *junta*, or council, led by businessman Donald Reid Cabral, whose antidemocratic stance was perceived by a majority of Dominicans as a front for the military.

Like his predecessor Trujillo, Balaguer instituted public works projects in an attempt to mollify the citizens of his country and to improve the reputation of the Dominican Republic internationally. Schools, clinics, dams, bridges, and many other projects designed to improve daily life were devised, but, unfortunately, distribution of income remained unequal in the country and Balaguer's projects, viewed by many as public relations stunts, were never realized.

Critical Overview

Unfortunately, there is no criticism available for "The Sun, the Moon, the Stars" because Díaz has yet to publish the story in a collection. Although the story is included in the anthology *Best American Short Stories 1999*, reviews of that book generally refer to the composition of the volume as a whole, offering plot summaries of a few selected stories rather than focusing on the individual achievements of their authors.

According to *Contemporary Authors Online*, the critic reviewing Díaz's short story collection *Drown* for *Publishers Weekly* noted that Díaz's intensity gives the collection "a lasting resonance," and the critic writing for *Kirkus Reviews* observes that "Díaz's spare style and narrative poise make for some disturbing fiction." In an interview with Marina Lewis, Díaz himself elaborates upon his strengths as a writer:

City slums of Santo Domingo as described in ''The Sun, the Moon, and the Stars''

What I write really well is silence, the things that the characters don't say, the gaps between people's sentences, the ellipses between what we feel, what we see, and what we recognize. I think that's where it all comes in."

Criticism

David Remy

Remy is a freelance writer in Warrington, Florida. In this essay, Remy considers Díaz's methods of characterization.

In "The Sun, the Moon, the Stars," Junot Díaz creates a narrator who is at once charming, naïve, and disingenuous. Nevertheless, Yunior is an engaging character, one who practically leaps off the page in an effort to convince readers—and himself—that, despite appearances to the contrary, he really is not such a "bad guy." Because Yunior seems genuinely perplexed by past events, the reader is at first sympathetic and eager to learn more about his romantic troubles. As the reader soon discovers, however, Yunior is his own worst enemy, and his word remains suspect. Thus, through Yunior's use of language and the disparity between his thought

and action, Díaz brings Yunior's character to light in a display of first-person narration fraught with unintended revelations.

One way in which Díaz portrays Yunior's character is through his use of language. A resident of Quisqueya Heights, a Dominican enclave in New York City, Yunior blends the rhythms of the street with a university education as he narrates his tale in both English and Spanish. For example, Yunior often refers to his "boys," his male friends, as though they comprised a gang. They affectionately address one another with epithets like "nigger," a term Yunior uses on occasion when referring to himself in the third person. He makes a show of using slang and strong language, as though trying to maintain a façade of impregnability against impending disaster. Using slang and profanity conceals Yunior's sensitive nature as it affords him a measure of identity, a sense of belonging he urgently needs once his relationship with Magda encounters difficulty.

Díaz makes language an inseparable aspect of character as he brings his narrator to life, for it is through Yunior's choice of language, both the manner in which he speaks as well as the language itself, that he reveals, however unintentionally, those aspects of his personality that permit the reader a more

What Do I Read Next?

- A native of the Dominican Republic, Julia Alvarez moved with her family to New York to escape Trujillo's regime when she was ten years old. Based in part on her early experiences as an immigrant, her novel *How the García Girls Lost Their Accents* follows the exploits of four sisters who move to the United States from the Dominican Republic. One of the sisters, Yolanda, is the protagonist of Alvarez's novel *¡Yo!* Alvarez addresses Trujillo's brutal dictatorship in her novel *In the Time of the Butterflies*, which is based on the true story of the Mirabal sisters who were murdered at the hands of Trujillo's secret police. The novel was later adapted into a film of the same name starring Salma Hayek, Edward James Olmos, and Marc Anthony.

- In 1984, Sandra Cisneros, a Mexican American writer, published *The House on Mango Street*, a book constructed of vignettes that may be read as short stories or prose poems. Narrated by Esperanza, a poor Latina girl who longs to have a room of her own and to become a writer, *The House on Mango Street* addresses the isolation from mainstream American culture many immigrants experience as it focuses on issues of poverty, identity, and cultural repression. Junot Díaz has cited Sandra Cisneros as one of his early influences.

- Edwidge Danticat evokes the rich cultural history of her native Haiti in novels and story collections such as *Breath, Eyes, Memory* (1994) and *Krik? Krak!* (1995), both of which have won her popularity with readers. However, it is Danticat's novel *The Farming of Bones* (1998) that is perhaps the more mature and enriching work of fiction. Narrated by Amabelle Desir, a young Haitian woman who was raised in the Dominican Republic after being orphaned, the novel's action occurs in 1937, with the massacre of Haitian workers by Dominican soldiers serving as a backdrop. Some 12,000 to 15,000 Haitians were slaughtered in what would be called an act of "ethnic cleansing." Amabelle survives the massacre, but she suffers deep psychological wounds in its aftermath as she contemplates the suffering of her fellow Haitians and the guilt of their Dominican oppressors. *The Farming of Bones* exposes one of the most horrific incidents in Latin American history as it honors the resilience of the human spirit.

- Junot Diaz's collection of stories *Drown* won the young author critical acclaim and a reputation as one of America's most talented writers. The stories, which feature characters that reappear throughout the book, are often set against the backdrop of drug culture and immigrant life, particularly that of young Dominicans who find their environment overwhelming. In these stories that create memorable portraits of characters from the *barrio*, Díaz explores familial relationships, sexual coming of age, and racial attitudes. His story "How to Date a Browngirl, Blackgirl, Whitegirl, or Halfie" addresses some of the themes in "The Sun, the Moon, the Stars," though it serves as a satirical how-to guide for poor Latino men on the make. *Negocios*, a Spanish-language edition of *Drown*, is available as a Vintage paperback.

- Mario Vargas Llosa, combines historical fact with fiction in his novel *The Feast of the Goat* (2002). Moving backward and forward in time, Vargas Llosa juxtaposes the stories of Urania Cabral, a successful New York lawyer who has returned to Santo Domingo to see her father, with that of the seven men who conspire to murder the Dominican leader Rafael Trujillo. In a third narrative strand, Vargas Llosa portrays Trujillo as a man frustrated by an elusive yet encroaching enemy: advancing age. Determined to preserve what little vitality he has left, Trujillo, nicknamed "The Goat" for his frequent sexual escapades, becomes obsessed with his grooming and personal hygiene, only to be confronted with incontinence and a recurring case of impotence that serves as a metaphor for his diminishing power as a ruler. Vargas Llosa describes the end of a brutal dictatorship as he offers an eloquent meditation on the moral and physical corruption of power.

comprehensive understanding of the story's events. Yunior's sense of identity is enforced by his use of Spanish, a language that conveys his sentiments directly. Yunior uses his native tongue to express feelings that demand immediate expression, such as those that convey his sexual desire for Magda or his intense displeasure when he is confounded by the alleged schemes of her girlfriends ("*cabronas*"). Yunior's use of both English and Spanish demonstrates his bicultural perspective on life, a perspective that occasionally creates conflict for him as he struggles to determine which cultural code applies in his relationship with Magda. He wants to be faithful to Magda, as a contemporary American male is expected to be, but at the same time he is eager to indulge his sexual appetite, something which Magda has never been able to satisfy. In other words, by demonstrating the way in which Yunior vacillates between roles as a compliant "boyfriend" and a macho male on the prowl, Díaz reveals the ambiguity that resides at the core of his protagonist, an ambiguity that molds Yunior's character as it propels the story forward.

Díaz also uses language to provide readers with a glimpse of Yunior's educational background and the social mobility that contributes to the composition of his complex character. Psychologically, Yunior's use of street language contrasts sharply with the cultural references he uses to underscore his opinions. He is obviously well versed in the humanities, for he refers to American literature and psychology on a couple of occasions to make what are, compared with the vulgar pronouncements of the *barrio*, subtle distinctions. When Yunior complains about Magda's reluctance to accept his invitations, he appropriates one of Herman Melville's most memorable characters and transforms the proper noun into a verb: "A lot of the time she Bartlebys me, says, 'No, I'd rather not.'" Furthermore, Yunior's description of white European tourists as looking like "philosophy professors, like budget Foucaults" on the beaches of Casa de Campo highlights the cultural, as well as the socioeconomic, disparities between tourists and Dominicans at the resort. These references to literature and psychology demonstrate a more calculated and less impulsive side of Yunior's character, one that is at odds with his tough, streetwise image.

As Yunior's language divulges his true character, so, too, does the disparity between his thought and action. By introducing a letter from Magda as a plot device (a letter which, true to his nature, Yunior does not reveal until the end of the story), Díaz

> "As Yunior's language divulges his true character, so, too, does the disparity between his thought and action."

provides a spark that ignites a welter of memories, filling Yunior with nostalgia and doubt. The letter serves as a catalyst for Yunior's recollections, which, in turn, lead him to reveal more about himself, albeit unconsciously. As Yunior reflects upon the letter (the contents of which are known only to him) as well as the one Cassandra sent Magda nearly a year earlier, Yunior divulges key aspects of his personality though he takes pains to disguise them by making oblique references to "causalities," the destructive chain of events his actions set in motion. Because the story is told in the first person, the reader hears only one side of the story, and Yunior, the narrator, takes full advantage of this, moving from Quisqueya Heights to Santo Domingo and back again as he tells his tale of failed romance. "I'm not a bad guy," he begins, and thus Yunior narrates his tale of romantic woe as a means of justifying his actions to Magda, himself, and the reader, yet, in the end, he proves to be an unreliable narrator. From this point forward, Yunior attempts to explain, rationalize, and excuse the reasons why he had an affair with Cassandra and subsequently failed to salvage his relationship with Magda once the affair was discovered. Even though Yunior refers to the affair as "that particular bit of stupidity," he never reforms his ways completely. He continues to look at other women while vacationing with Magda at a Santo Domingo resort, casting his eyes on the lovely Dominican girls he would not mind "kickin' it" with. In particular, he is attracted to Lucy, a Dominican girl from New York, whom he entertains thoughts of seducing; then, at the last minute, he reconsiders. Yunior may believe himself to be a dutiful boyfriend, but his actions clearly demonstrate otherwise.

Yunior wants to be a faithful and devoted lover, yet he cannot bear the thought of limiting himself to one partner, as Díaz makes clear through his protagonist's alternating bouts of resentment and self-recrimination. Díaz enhances characterization further by introducing the stereotype of the philandering Latin male as a negative ideal which Yunior, fully aware of the cultural influences at work upon him, must struggle against. If, according to Magda and her friends, all Dominican men are "dogs" (that is, "womanizers"), then Yunior must avoid completing a self-fulfilling prophecy. This struggle causes Yunior to commit actions that, although they may seem naïve and harmless, are disingenuous and harmful to his relationship with Magda. He tells "white lies" in the interest of preserving a delicate balance, one that could easily tip against him. For example, when Magda asks Yunior if he enjoyed sex with Cassandra, he responds matter-of-factly, "To be honest, baby, it was lousy." The reader later discovers Yunior's lie when he claims that Cassandra was not advertising falsely when she boasted of her sexual prowess. Thus the disparity between Yunior's statements and the actions he recounts reveal his true personality, that of a hopelessly ambivalent young man who wants nothing more than to have his way regardless of others' feelings.

For all of his attempts to pacify Magda, Yunior does not really change. Throughout his narrative, Yunior alternately plays the role of the heartsick lover and the wannabe player; he cannot bear the thought of losing Magda, yet at the same time he cannot help but wonder if a more exciting woman is not waiting for him around the next corner. As the final line of the story indicates, he is forever hopeful that his romantic life will change for the better. From the beginning of the story to the very end, however, Yunior's words and actions contradict him at every turn, revealing a character who remains as confused as ever by desire, never once humbled by experience.

Source: David Remy, Critical Essay on "The Sun, the Moon, the Stars," in *Short Stories for Students*, Gale, 2005.

Douglas Dupler

Dupler is a writer, teacher, and independent scholar. In the following essay, Dupler discusses the contradictions that appear in "The Sun, the Moon, the Stars."

In "The Sun, the Moon, the Stars," a short story by Junot Diaz, the title alludes to subtle contradictions that appear in the story, as well as to the pairings of opposites that show up in certain facets of the narrative. Upon first glance at the title, the reader is apt to think that the story has a romantic or idyllic

quality to it; for what is more charming than an image of the guiding lights of nature, the sun, moon, and stars? However, in the middle of the story, the narrator describes a failing relationship by declaring that the "relationship wasn't the sun, the moon, and the stars" after all. Furthermore, within the title is a pair of opposites, the sun and the moon, or, figuratively, the day and the night, the light and the shadow. This pairing of opposites of perception can further be observed in the way the narrator presents himself, his girlfriend, the relationship between them, and the country that gives the narrator his identity, Santo Domingo, known as the Dominican Republic. By presenting the story with elements of the light and dark, or the positive and negative sides of things, the narrator ultimately provides the reader with a more comprehensive view of a fictional world, despite the fact that the narrator at times seemingly contradicts himself.

The first glaring contradiction occurs with the opening line of the story, when the narrator suspiciously declares that he is not a "bad guy," but "basically good." However, he then presents a reflection of himself that he observes from his girlfriend Magdalena (or Magda), who describes him unfavorably, even in profane terms. The first paragraph continues as a confession to a dark deed, an act of betrayal lying under the surface of things, described as a "bone . . . buried in the backyard of your life." The narrator further incriminates himself by the admission that he would have kept this betrayal a secret, if not for a letter that was sent to his unsuspecting girlfriend. The narrator, however, does not seem to lose the reader's trust by admitting these negative aspects of himself. By providing a portrait of himself that shows both sides of his character, the bright and dark sides, the narrator builds empathy in the reader.

Another contradiction in the story is the narrator's description of his girlfriend. He describes her early on as a "forgiving soul," but then reverses this assessment when he notes that the relationship is getting "worse and worse," because of her inability to forgive his betrayal. The reader also sees two sides of this woman throughout the narrative. The narrator recounts the positive and warm qualities of Magdalena while reminiscing about their love affair, while at the same time she is becoming colder and more distant in the present time of the story.

The narrator also has a complex perception of his native country, Santo Domingo. He says, "Let me confess: I love Santo Domingo," and he describes the country as a mixture of beauty and ugliness, of noble people and impoverished surroundings. His hometown has been in a "state of indecision for years," perhaps echoing the narrator's own state. Admitting to his complex outlook of his country, the narrator says that he would "pretend" to "know what goes on there." Finally, despite his return to his beloved country, it is there that the relationship with Magda completely unravels and there that the narrator feels a painful alienation from the world.

The narrator also shows two sides of his identity as a Dominican man. He loves his country and has such faith in it that he believes a trip there with his girlfriend will restore their relationship. At the same time, he tends to believe that others view his ethnicity negatively. For instance, he writes that his girlfriend considers him a "typical Dominican man," which he thinks is a negative opinion. He also believes that Magda's friends attribute his betrayal to his nationality, because "Dominican men are dogs." The narrator's perception of his own nationality shows varied sides. He takes pride in the impoverished and hectic side of the country, but his girlfriend wants to go to an upscale resort that he jokes could get his "ghetto pass revoked." At this resort, the sight of Europeans offends him, and he stereotypes them as "philosophy professors." The narrator struggles with the fact that being from America enables him to afford time at the upscale resort, the same place that corrupt politicians go "to relax after a long month of oppressing the masses." Finally, the narrator's identity issues cause him to insult a Dominican man from America who is talking to Magda. This man is a successful attorney who "loves his people," but the narrator reveals anger and envy toward him.

The presence of Magda in Santo Domingo increases the narrator's confusions. When Magda becomes emotionally distant and requests space, the narrator says to her, "I feel like you rejected my whole country." His insecurity about being Dominican shows up when he compares himself to Magda. When she looks attractive on the beach, he feels "vulnerable and uneasy." He writes that when Magda smiles, men "ask for her hand in marriage," while when he smiles, "folks check their wallets." The narrator sees a reflection of himself in other people that is unfavorable or vulnerable and contains elements of prejudice and self-loathing over his own background.

> "Another contradiction in the story is the narrator's description of his girlfriend. He describes her early on as a 'forgiving soul,' but then reverses this assessment when he notes that the relationship is getting 'worse and worse,' because of her inability to forgive his betrayal."

In the field of psychology known as Jungian studies, the concept of the *shadow* is an important idea in understanding how people perceive the world. In Jungian theory, the shadow is part of the unconscious mind, the part of the personality that we cannot be completely aware of, because it exists under the surface of everyday activities. Jungian theorists believe that this part of the unconscious mind will eventually reveal itself by projecting outwards onto other people and things, which the conscious mind can then observe. If the conscious mind is the light, that which people are in touch with, then the unconscious mind contains the shadow that goes along with that light. This theory might provide insight into the narrator in "The Sun, the Moon, the Stars." When the narrator sees an unfavorable reflection of himself in other people, this might indicate turmoil in the unconscious part of himself that desires to be understood. Furthermore, the negative image of himself that the narrator constantly sees reflected back from Magda may indicate internal and unresolved feelings of guilt.

The narrator's perception of his home country, Santo Domingo, may also contain elements of the shadow, as evidenced by the way the narrator describes this place. After telling the reader how much he loves this country and giving a positive and detailed portrait of its energetic life, the narrator suddenly interjects negative elements. For instance, after pointing out American chain restaurants such as "Pizza Huts and Dunkin' Donuts," the narrator notes that "this is where Trujillo and his Marine pals slaughtered the *gavilleros*," and where another leader "sold his soul to the devil." Amidst this, "Magda seemed to be enjoying herself." This is very revealing. In these quick and subtle descriptions, we can almost feel the conflict the narrator has about living in America, as it is implied that American presence in the country is connected to injustice and violence. Furthermore, the narrator projects this guilt onto his girlfriend and thus reveals it in himself. In another description, that of the resort where the narrator and Magda go to relax, the narrator is offended by a Dominican American man who is an attorney in New York, connecting the idea of America with the idea of political power as well as with envy and anger.

Two other characters enter the story who are described in shady terms and have connections with political intrigue, the Vice President and his bodyguard, Barbaro, whom a soldier once "tried to saw open" at the neck. The narrator believes these men observe his face as a "footprint of fresh disaster," again revealing inner feelings of insecurity in the reflections of others. The Vice President, who studied in America, has the mysterious presence of an underworld character; only the narrator's mother back in America will know what his political connections really are. In the final scene of the story, the narrator goes in a black car with these two characters, and the bodyguard is lamenting his failure to become a civil engineer and to "build schools and hospitals," another failure of civil life in the country connected to men who once lived in "upstate New York." Then, in a strange move, the two men lower the narrator into a dark hole, where the coins drop from his pockets and he symbolically loses everything. Going into this shadow world may be "the perfect place for insight, for a person to become somebody better," claims the narrator; the only way to heal the shadow is to observe it. This dark hole is the place where the Vice President recognized the dark side of politics and corruption. This place is also where the narrator realizes his relationship with Magda is finally over. Ultimately, this dark mysterious cave, containing "serious Island voodoo," is a concluding symbol of the pain, guilt, and negativity that the narrator has been carrying deep within the shadow of his own mind.

Source: Douglas Dupler, Critical Essay on "The Sun, the Moon, the Stars," in *Short Stories for Students*, Gale, 2005.

Joyce Hart

Hart, a former writing teacher, is a freelance writer and author of several books. In this essay,

Hart examines how Diaz infuses his story with the concept of conflicting realities.

Right from the very first line of Junot Díaz's short story "The Sun, the Moon, the Stars," readers are warned that this is a tale of conflict. And from that point onward, whether it is a disagreement between the two main characters, the inconsistency of dire poverty superimposed onto commercial tourism, or one man's personal struggle of contradictory desires, Díaz floods his story with the sounds and sights of seemingly unavoidable collisions. These impacts occur when one reality clashes with another; when two separate visions, whether personal or environmental, conflict. This is a story in which people have trouble hearing what another person is saying, in which people do not understand what another person is feeling, and, worse yet, in which some of the characters appear to be living within a divided personal world in which they do not seem able to truly comprehend even themselves. Díaz's characters are just plain out of sync, and the consequences are that experiences becomes distorted. Even the title, which purposely suggests a fairy-tale romance, conflicts with the body of this story, which hopes to be a romance but ends up being quite the opposite.

Díaz wastes no time setting up the conflicts that permeate this short story. In the first paragraph of "The Sun, the Moon, the Stars," the narrator points out that Magdalena, his girlfriend, does not agree with him. And if the truth be known, even the narrator has trouble agreeing with himself. Although he will not admit that he is bad, he is hard pressed to convince the reader (or himself) that he is good. The narrator immediately qualifies his goodness: he is only basically good, he states. And it is upon this basic goodness that he sets the foundation of his argument—he does not deserve to lose his girlfriend, no matter what her friends advise and no matter what the narrator has done to destroy his relationship with her. The narrator admits that he has cheated on Magdalena, but he justifies his deception. It was just a fling, something he could not control. The woman, Cassandra, was all over him. How could he resist? And why, oh why is Magdalena making such a fuss over the affair? It is done with, having happened a long time ago, buried like an old bone in the backyard. It was performed at a time when his and Magdalena's relationship was not going as smoothly as it was right before Cassandra's letter arrived, unveiling the truth of the short-lived affair. So, in the narrator's mind, Magdalena should forgive him, although during most of the remaining story, he doubts she ever will.

That is the narrator's world. But Magdalena lives in another reality, one that is built on truths very different from the narrator's. Magdalena does not understand how her boyfriend could have done such a thing. How could he have had an affair? She takes his action as a personal attack against herself. She had trusted him to be monogamous. Her love for him was based on his fidelity. And like a parent who is scolding a child, Magdalena does her best, through her actions as well as her words, to let the narrator know that once trust is broken, there is no way of fixing it.

It takes the narrator a long time to comprehend Magdalena's message that something is seriously wrong with the relationship. And even when he catches hints of what Magdalena is trying to tell him, the narrator closes his eyes and wishes it away. He tries to convince Magdalena to forgive him, to persuade her to recreate their relationship, to show her there is another world that they can enter if she will just forget about Cassandra (even though the narrator has trouble doing this).

But Magdelena's world has been shattered, and the narrator is the cause of this disaster. Her dreams have changed. But even though she knows this, Magdalena does not fully comprehend how the change is affecting her. Therefore, she has to live somewhere in between the world she once shared with the narrator and a new world she has yet to completely shape. For instance, she feels she has to go along with plans they made earlier. The reason for this is that Magdalena cannot fully determine her new emotions because she is neither here nor there. And until she watches her feelings play out, until her new world is formed, she will not know what she thinks, not just about her boyfriend but about herself as well. Does she still love him? Can she forgive him? Can she continue to be who she was? And if not, who will she become?

The narrator and Magdalena travel to Santo Domingo where the narrator was born and raised. Although it is unclear in the narrator's mind whether he truly loves Magdalena (or does he just not want to take the time to find a new girlfriend), the narrator knows one thing for sure. He loves Santo Domingo. And he is hoping that in taking Magdalena to his tropical birthplace, she will learn to love him. Santo Domingo is one thing that is for real, he says. And it is here that the narrator believes he has his clearest

> "Their worlds are so different it is as if they speak different languages, use different expressions, and think in different terms. There are no more bridges linking their worlds. They have all been destroyed by conflict."

vision. He does not romanticize the island and its culture, its poverty, and its natural beauty. He sees it all for what it is, much more so than he sees anything else in his life, including himself and Magdalena. It might be this clarity that pulls him back to Santo Domingo. Something tells him that if in no other place on earth, here he will find the truth. Here, he hopes, he and Magdalena will discover a coming together of their hearts, their spirits, and their hitherto diverse worlds.

The narrator points out that although Santo Domingo provides a tropical setting of beautiful beaches and palm trees, his homeland is in no way a world of fantasy. It has a warm ocean, which offers gentle sea breezes, but it also has mosquitoes, extreme poverty, and filth. It is uncomfortably hot and humid, and, in Magdalena's mind, it is also boring. In other words, Santo Domingo itself represents a world of conflict. The heat of the tropical setting makes it the perfect place for an abundance of fruited plants and lush vegetation. The warmth of the ocean attracts visitors from all over the world. But not all of Santo Domingo's year-round inhabitants enjoy the benefits that their tropical homeland provides. Many women, for instance, are reduced to working as slave-costumed servants. Others work as prostitutes, serving the rich businessmen who come to Santo Domingo and staying in the walled-up sanctuaries of air-conditioned rooms. Most people who live in the shanties that abound throughout the country have never seen past these hotel walls, the narrator informs his readers. And those who stay inside these luxurious inns have little regard for what exists outside them. These two worlds are so far apart, one would think there was no chance of collision. But the narrator hints that there is trouble brewing. However, those circumstances need to be told in another story.

But it is inside these walls, in this artificially contrived paradise, that the narrator and his girlfriend finally end up. Magdalena insists they go there. Whereas the narrator had envisioned returning to Santo Domingo to share his history with Magdalena, her head is full of only the beautiful images taken from travel magazines. She is not interested in the narrator's relatives, their stories, and their way of life. She has not come to Santo Domingo to gain a more fully detailed account of her boyfriend's beginnings. To the contrary, she suggests that this trip is her reward for having endured the pain he has caused her. She goes with him to Santo Domingo to enjoy herself as much as she can, and then she suggests she will cut him loose upon their return to the States. She will tolerate the visit to his family, but her world, her dream, does not include them in any great proportion. After a couple of days during which she shares their company, she is ready for satin sheets on clean, cool beds and dress-up parties in a hotel ballroom. And even this is not enough for Magdalena, who finally admits that she also needs time alone, time to enjoy this luxury without having to share it with the one who is quickly becoming her ex-boyfriend.

The narrator in the meantime is having trouble accepting all of these changes in Magdalena. He cannot imagine how she is coming up with these ideas. Her concepts have nothing to do with his world, so he cannot relate to them. He thought that bringing her to Santo Domingo would make her fall in love with him all over again. He thought that in her agreeing to come, she was stating she was ready to commit to their relationship. The narrator never accepts what he sees or hears from Magdalena. He tells his readers that this is because he is such an optimist. The readers, on the other hand, are probably all saying it is rather because he is so blind and deaf. But Diaz might well be making the point that it is because these two people, the narrator and Magdalena, live in such disparate worlds. Their worlds are so different it is as if they speak different languages, use different expressions, and think in different terms. There are no more bridges linking their worlds. They have all been destroyed by conflict.

In the end, the only thing the narrator can conclude is that he must have been on drugs to

imagine a world in which he and Magdalena could co-exist. He finally starts listening to what she is saying, and, when he finally hears her, he realizes that he does not know her. It is at this point that Magdalena begins to grasp the definitions of her new world. She realizes that she has left the world in which she saw herself and the narrator as one. Like the proverbial caterpillar, she has cracked the cocoon and has emerged as a butterfly. No wonder the narrator does not recognize her. But even after the narrator's trip to the Cave of the Jagua, the deep black hole of creation, where he sees the future and that future does not include Magdalena, he still clings to a world that no longer exists. Unlike Magdalena, the narrator has not yet experienced a metamorphosis. He continues to hang in suspension. It is as if he is living in a vacuum and keeps asking Magdalena to join him. However, Magdalena, in essence, tells him that their worlds have separated forever. There will be no more collisions because they have at last drifted too far apart.

Source: Joyce Hart, Critical Essay on "The Sun, the Moon, the Stars," in *Short Stories for Students*, Gale, 2005.

Sources

Atkins, Christine, "Junot Díaz and Edwidge Danticat," in *New York State Writers Institute—Writers Online*, Vol. 1, No. 3, Spring 1997, at http://www.albany.edu/writers-inst/olv1n3.html#danticat (last accessed April 19, 2004).

Díaz, Junot, "Contributors' Notes," in *The Best American Short Stories 1999*, edited by Amy Tan and Katrina Kenison, Houghton Mifflin, 1999, p. 378.

———, "My First Year in New York; 1995," in the *New York Times Magazine*, September 17, 2000, Sec. 6, p. 111.

———, "The Sun, the Moon, the Stars," in the *New Yorker*, February 2, 1998, pp. 66–71.

"Junot Díaz," in *Contemporary Authors Online*, Gale, 2003 (last accessed April 4, 2004).

Lewis, Marina, "Interview with Junot Díaz," in *Other Voices*, Vol. 36, at http://www.webdelsol.com/Other_Voices/DiazInt.htm (last accessed April 26, 2004).

Rouse, Irving, *The Tainos: Rise and Decline of the People Who Greeted Columbus*, Yale University Press, 1992, pp. 5–25.

Stanton, David, "Junot Díaz: On Home Ground," in *Poets & Writers*, July/August 1998, pp. 26–37.

Stewart, Barbara, "Outsider with a Voice," in the *New York Times*, New Jersey section, December 8, 1996, p. 4.

Wiarda, Howard J., and Michael J. Kryzanek, *The Dominican Republic: A Caribbean Crucible*, Westview Press, 1992, pp. 41–48.

Further Reading

Bretón, Marcos, and José Luis Villegas, *Away Games: The Life and Times of a Latin Baseball Player*, University of New Mexico, 2000.

> Journalists Marcos and Villegas follow the career of Miguel Tejada as he rises from promising rookie to become one of the stars of the American League. (In 2002, Tejada was named league MVP [Most Valuable Player].) Tejada, who as of 2004 played shortstop for the Oakland Athletics, is just one of many Dominican players who left the *barrio* for the major leagues. The book addresses the impoverished backgrounds many ballplayers come from as well as the language and cultural barriers that await them in the United States.

Howard, David, *Coloring the Nation: Race and Ethnicity in the Dominican Republic*, Signal Books, 2001.

> Howard examines how ideas of skin color define Dominicans' idea of themselves as well as their Haitian neighbors. For decades, the Dominican Repub-lic has defined itself as white, thereby disassociating itself from its black, or African, roots and making it superior, in the eyes of many, to Haiti. According to the author, perceptions of race and the unwillingness to accept "blackness" in Dominican cultural and political life have created divisions of race, color, and ethnicity that mold relations within Dominican society.

Sagás, Ernesto, *Race and Politics in the Dominican Republic*, University Press of Florida, 2000.

> Sagás examines the use of *antihaitianismo* by Dominican leaders, particularly Trujillo, to portray Dominicans as a predominantly white, Catholic people, as compared to their neighbors in Haiti, who have been depicted as spirit-worshipping Africans. Although these racist and xenophobic attitudes first developed in the colonial era, they continue to be manipulated by conservative politicians in contemporary Dominican politics.

Yewell, John, Chris Dodge, and Jan DeSirey, eds., *Confronting Columbus: An Anthology*, McFarland, 1992.

> This anthology addresses a wide variety of subjects relating to the Spanish conquest of the New World, including the influence of the Catholic Church on indigenous peoples, the importance of sugar as a major export crop, and slavery. Most important, the book raises the specter of genocide, an issue that has gone largely ignored until the late twentieth century.

To Room Nineteen

Doris Lessing

1963

"To Room Nineteen," one of the collected stories in Doris Lessing's *A Man and Two Women* (1963), has been singled out as one of her best stories. It centers on a middle-aged English woman, whose world in a mid-twentieth century London suburb revolves around her husband, her four children, and her home. Everyone thinks Susan and her husband Matthew are the perfect couple, who have made all the right choices in life. When Susan packs her youngest children off to school, however, she begins to question the "intelligent" decisions she has made. When she discovers that her husband has been having extramarital affairs, she embarks on a journey of self-discovery that ultimately becomes a descent into madness.

This well-crafted story explores the warring impulses of intellect and instinct, mind and heart, against the backdrop of early 1960s London, when women were caught in the social conservatism of the past and unable to see the promise of a future that would encourage choice, fulfillment, and personal freedom. Lessing's tragic story illuminates the restrictions placed on women of this era and the devastating consequences of those restrictions. "To Room Nineteen" cemented Lessing's reputation as one of the century's finest short story writers.

Author Biography

Doris Lessing was born Doris May Tayler on October 22, 1919, in Kermanshah, Persia (now Iran) to two transplanted British expatriates, Alfred Cook Taylor (a farmer) and Emily Maude McVeagh. In 1924 the family moved to a farm in Southern Rhodesia, where they stayed for twenty years. Doris's education began at a convent school and later at a government school for girls. Her formal education ended when she was twelve. After two failed marriages, she kept her second husband's name and moved to London where she resided as of 2004.

Her first novel, *The Grass is Singing*, (1950) which focused on the horrors of apartheid and colonization, was well received. Fiona Barnes, in her article on Lessing for *Dictionary of Literary Biography*, notes, however, that Lessing worried about being labeled as too narrowly political, as she noted in her description of what it was like to be a writer from Africa. She admitted her situation had "many advantages," which included "being at the centre of a modern battlefield; part of a society in rapid, dramatic change." Yet ultimately, she saw her experience as "a handicap" for a writer, arguing that "to wake up every morning with one's eyes on fresh evidence of inhumanity; to be reminded twenty times a day of injustice, and always the same brand of it, can be limiting."

Although several of her works did center on the politics within her Middle-Eastern homeland, over her more than four decades of work, Lessing broadened her literary focus to include explorations of other important issues of the later half of the twentieth century. In her story "To Room Nineteen," for example, her focus is on the limited roles for women in 1960s London. Gail Caldwell, in her article for the *Boston Globe*, writes that Lessing has "written prolifically on everything from British colonialism . . . to the failure of ideology" and notes that she has "taken on the apocalyptic potential of a futuristic, Blade Runner London, the perils of the color bar in Africa, [and] the life of a young girl growing up on the veld." Lessing, who over the span of her literary career has written short stories, autobiographies, novels, and plays, has been celebrated as one of the most important writers of the age.

Her major awards include the Somerset Maugham Award, Society of Authors, 1954, for *Five: Short Novels*; Austrian State Prize for European Literature, 1981; German Federal Republic Shakespeare Prize, 1982; W. H. Smith Literary

Doris Lessing

Award, 1986, Palermo Prize, 1987, and Premio Internazionale Mondello, 1987, all for *The Good Terrorist*; Grinzane Cavour award (Italy), 1989, for *The Fifth Child*; honorary degree, Princeton University, 1989, and Harvard University, 1995; James Tait Black Memorial Book Prize, University of Edinburgh, and *Los Angeles Times* Book Prize, both 1995, both for *Under My Skin*; and finally the David Cohen British Literary Prize, 2001, for her life's work.

Plot Summary

Part 1

The story begins with a description of the history of Susan and Matthew Rawlings's marriage, which has been a very practical union. They married in their late twenties after having known each other for some time and after having experienced other relationships. They, and their friends, consider them to be "well matched."

Before their children came, Susan worked in an advertising firm while Matthew was a sub-editor for a London newspaper. They began their family in a house in Richmond, a suburb of London, and they eventually had four children. Their life together was happy but rather flat. They privately began to wonder about the central point of all of the work they did—Matthew outside the home and Susan inside. They did, however, love each other and were determined to have a successful marriage. As a result then, they convinced themselves that "things were under control."

One night Matthew comes home late and admits that he has been with another woman. Both he and Susan determine that the event was not important and would not damage their relationship. Yet, they both become irritable. Susan begins to wonder about her importance to Matthew and thinks about the ten years of her fidelity. Eventually, they determine that the sensible thing to do is to forget the entire incident. Matthew continues his infidelities, however, prompting Susan to consider the emptiness of her life and her lack of freedom.

Part 2

By the time they are in their early forties, Susan begins to think about what she would do when all of her children go to school. On the day that she drops the twins, her youngest, off for their first day of school, Susan returns home and spends a restless morning, not knowing quite what to do with herself. The restlessness evolves into a state of panic until she convinces herself that her feelings are quite normal and that it would take time to discover her own needs after caring so long for others' needs. Yet, she spends the day helping their maid take care of the house.

This pattern continues until the school holiday, when she feels resentment that she will no longer have any freedom, even though she has carefully avoided freeing herself from her domestic duties. She experiences a growing sense of restlessness and emptiness but hides her feelings from Matthew, because they are not "sensible."

On the fourth day of the holiday, her irritation grows to the point that she snaps at her children. Matthew's understanding and comfort help her regain control of herself, but the sense of restlessness returns when the children go back to school. In an effort to find a place where she can be alone and gain some measure of freedom, which has become increasingly important to her, Susan takes a spare room in the house for her own where she can enjoy some privacy. Matthew and the children respect her time there and determine not to take her for granted in the future.

Susan's restlessness, however, is not abated by the time in her room. Her increased impatience and anger frighten her, especially one afternoon when she thinks she sees a man in her garden, stirring a snake coiled at his feet. As she determines that this devilish man has brought on the emotional turmoil she is caught up in, he disappears.

Part 3

One afternoon, Susan decides to rent a room in London for a day so that she can be truly alone. Yet when the hotel's proprietress will not leave her in peace, Susan leaves, feeling defeated. At home, her maid complains that she did not like having the responsibilities of the house fall on her for the entire day while Susan was gone.

When Susan takes a holiday in Wales, she feels no relief since her husband and children call her each day with their questions and concerns. Returning home, she insists to Matthew that they need an au pair to help run the house. Recognizing that Susan has already spiritually removed herself from her family, Matthew reluctantly agrees.

Sophie, the au pair, becomes a great success in the household, embraced by all of its members. As a result, Susan feels that she will not be missed if she spends time away from home. Three days a week, she rents a shabby room in London where she sits alone, reveling in her freedom. Her time in the room allows her to endure her domestic roles at home. Soon the three days turn into five.

One night, assuming that she has taken a lover, Matthew asks her whether she wants a divorce. Susan dodges the question. The next day she discovers that Matthew has found out about her room, and as a result, she feels her freedom slipping away. When she returns home, she sees her daughter Molly being consoled by Sophie, and "blinks tears of farewell" in response.

Later, while trying to explain to Matthew what she was doing in the room, she decides that it would be easier to tell him that she does have a lover. This relieves Matthew, who admits that he is having an affair as well with a friend of theirs. The next morning, Matthew proposes that the four of them meet with each other and get everything out in the open. Susan panics, blurting out that her lover, "Michael Plant," is out of town. Determining that suicide will be the only way to quiet "the demons" in her head and achieve the freedom she so desperately needs, Susan returns to Room Nineteen, turns on the gas, and drifts "off into the dark river."

Characters

Mrs. Parkes

Mrs. Parkes, the Rawlings's housekeeper, is "one of the servers of this world, but she needed someone to serve." She does her job well, but cannot handle the responsibility of making any household decisions while Susan is away. She impedes Susan's freedom until Sophie is hired.

Matthew Rawlings

When the story opens, Matthew Rawlings is in his forties, as is his wife Susan. He is a "sensible" man who seems to have made all of the right choices in life. He married in his late twenties and only after he had experienced other relationships, unlike his friends who married young and "regretted lost opportunities." He chose Susan because he thought that they were "well matched" in temperament. Matthew is known for his moderation, his humor, and his "abstinence from painful experience," and so, he has become known as a reliable friend. Others depend on him for his levelheadedness. Matthew's job fits his personality and so satisfies him. He is a sub-editor for a large London newspaper where he is "one of the essential background people who in fact steady, inspire and make possible the people in the limelight."

Matthew's sensible nature does not let him blame his wife when he begins to feel a "certain flatness" to his life. He "never was really struck, as he wanted to be, by joy." Yet, his shallowness surfaces when he accepts the cultural "inevitability" that men will be tempted by other women at parties their wives cannot attend, since they are home with the children. When Matthew begins to have extramarital affairs, however, they initially leave him feeling guilty.

Readers begin to doubt Matthew's "intelligence" in his response to Susan's problems. His conventional nature refuses to allow him to see what is really wrong with her and so he cannot offer any help. As a result he withdraws from her when she stops acting sensibly and rationally according to the unwritten rules of their marriage. When he confronts her about the time she is spending in Room Nineteen, he is relieved when she insists that she is having an affair. His inability to face any really troubling reality causes him to fall back into his conventionality.

It is easier for him to believe that Susan has been unfaithful than to realize that there are serious problems in their marriage. He would rather find any way to avoid divorce, even though they have not been married in any real sense for some time. In an effort to ease the tensions of the admitted infidelities on both sides, Matthew proposes that they all be "civilized" about the situation and meet. Revealing his expertise at hiding his emotions, in this case jealousy, he suggests "reasonably" and "sensibly" that they could become "a foursome."

Molly Rawlings

Molly, one of Susan's twins, gives Susan the final impetus to commit suicide. As she watches Sophie comfort Molly through the window, Susan realizes that she is no longer needed by her family and that perhaps they would be better off without her.

Susan Rawlings

Susan is introduced as a mirror image of her husband. They share the same qualities: levelheadedness, intelligence, a good sense of humor, and dependability. Like Matthew, she also has trained herself to avoid any unpleasant experience. Both of them use "their intelligence to preserve what they had created from a painful and explosive world." She easily adapts to the change she undergoes when she and Matthew marry, giving up her job in a "concession to popular wisdom," and moving to the suburbs to care for her family. Both she and Matthew appear to have "an infallible sense for *choosing* right," and a determination that they would "not make the same mistakes" that they see their friends make.

Susan and Matthew have learned to control their emotions. "[T]he inner storms and quicksands were understood and charted." Susan selflessly gives up her independence for her family and even comes to accept Matthew's occasional infidelities, insisting that they are not his fault. Her "intelligence barred, too, quarrelling, sulking, anger, silences of withdrawal, accusations and tears." Gradually though, her emotions, so long suppressed, begin to emerge as Matthew's behavior, coupled with her closeted life in the suburbs, makes her feel more and more that her life "had become a desert, and that nothing mattered." She recognizes that the "essential Susan" was "in abeyance, as if she were in cold storage."

Unsure of what the essential Susan really is, she soon falls into an uncontrollable restlessness, which eventually forces her to abandon her traditional domestic duties. She begins to resent her lack of freedom and so tries to find places to be alone. Initially, her desire for freedom causes her to feel remorseful, especially when Matthew cannot understand her feelings. Soon she recognizes that the "conscious controlled decency" by which she lives makes her feel even more isolated and "nearly drove her crazy." Ironically, as she begins a search for her true self, which is continually impeded by her husband and family's requirements, her "sensible" nature reasserts itself, leading her to believe that she is being irrational.

Susan does begin to lose her sanity as she fails to find the freedom she so desperately needs. She begins to see "demons" in her garden and tries to escape them by fleeing to her room in London. When Matthew threatens to rob her of the freedom she finds there, she breaks and commits suicide, not having "the energy to stay" with her family.

Sophie Traub

Sophie, the Rawlings's au pair, is a young, healthy, German girl who cheerfully takes over all of Susan's duties in the household and becomes "a success with everyone." The entire family soon turns their attention to and their dependence on her, which enables Susan to spend her days in Room Nineteen. Feeling that Sophie could care for her family better than she, and concluding that Sophie "was already the mother of those children," Susan leaves her "big, beautiful white house . . . silently dedicating it to Sophie."

Themes

Conformity and Restriction

Susan experiences social as well as personal pressure to conform to specific cultural dictates. Her class, place, and gender all place social restrictions on her. Her class (middle) and place (suburbia) have been proscribed by specific cultural boundaries. Since she is in the middle class, she must own an expensive, large home in suburbia and maintain it well, which involves a great deal of time and money. As she attends to her home, her position in suburbia cuts her off from the more active life of the city. Her interaction in the community is limited to other middle-class homeowners and the servants who work for them.

The most pressing social restrictions, however, are placed on Susan as a result of her gender. She, not Matthew, must confine herself to the house in the suburbs because that is what was expected of women in England during the mid-twentieth century. Before she married Matthew, she worked in London in an advertising firm, where she could be an active part of the diverse city life, and where she could enjoy a measure of freedom. When she married, however, she made a "concession to popular wisdom" and along with Matthew, decided they would buy a house and start a family.

Susan acquiesces to and reinforces the restrictions placed on her. Without a second thought, she adopts the role of housewife and mother because her culture insists that this is the "intelligent" choice. She has learned to carefully order her life according to "sensible discrimination," which dictates an "abstinence from painful experience." Thus she avoids any challenge to the rules that might cause problems for her or her husband. She strives to achieve "everything right, appropriate, and what everyone would wish for, if they could choose." Of course, ironically, Susan really has no choice. To ensure that she maintains a "balanced and sensible family," she allows society to dictate her life.

Self-Discovery

While Susan has to admit that she and Matthew "had everything they had wanted and had planned for," she soon feels a sense of flatness and restriction. As the youngest two of her four children begin school, she realizes that she has given up her identity for her family and struggles to recapture a sense of self. In order to accomplish this, Susan must reject the traditional roles that she has previously accepted. This means that if she no longer accepts her role as wife and mother, she, by the standard definition, will no longer be acting sensibly and rationally. Lessing prompts us to wonder in this instance whose world is the more rational—Susan's, where attaining an authentic sense of self becomes a priority, or Matthew's, where any deviance from the norm is considered "madness." This conflict causes the reader to reexamine the word "intelligence" as it is applied to the Rawlings's marriage.

Madness

The tragedy of "To Room Nineteen" is that Susan's search for an authentic self leads to madness and ultimately suicide. Ironically, the insights she gains during her search reveal her inherent sanity. Susan cannot exist without a sense of freedom, which is a fundamental human desire. Denying that basic need, which Susan does for years, can be considered a form of madness. Thus, when she asserts her right to experience and satisfy this desire, she is acting sanely. This ironic interplay between insanity and madness becomes most evident in the final pages of the story.

In order to preserve the measure of freedom that she has achieved in Room Nineteen, Susan concocts a "rational" story for her time there. Her manufactured infidelity appears to be a reasonable explanation for her abandonment of her traditional duties as wife and mother. Susan recognizes Matthew's need to have a sensible explanation for her absences—a behavior that matches and thus condones his own infidelities.

Susan recognizes the irony of this situation in the room when she declares, "Oh, how ridiculous! How absurd! How humiliating!" The irony is extended by the description of her suicide, which becomes a "fructifying dream that seemed to caress her inwardly, like the movement of her blood." Susan's tragedy is that she believes suicide offers her the only pathway to true selfhood and freedom, so she drifts "off into the dark river" of death.

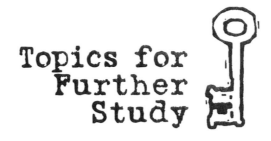

Topics for Further Study

- Think about how a dramatic version of "To Room Nineteen" could be produced. How would you deal with the background information on the Rawlings's developing relationship before the story begins? How would you depict Susan's descent into madness?

- Compare and contrast Michael Cunningham's novel *The Hours* with "To Room Nineteen," focusing on madness and its consequences in both works.

- Research the developments of political and literary feminism in Britain and relate them to the story.

- "Swinging London" became the center of 1960s culture. How would you rewrite "To Room Nineteen," placing it in this influential era?

Style

Narrative

Fiona Barnes, in her article for *Dictionary of Literary Biography*, argues that Lessing's "stories benefit from the creative tension caused by the unsettling contrast between the ethical, at times political, commitment of her vision and the cool, frequently humorous, detachment of her ironic tone." Lessing displays this ironic tone masterfully in "To Room Nineteen." From the opening line, the narrator sets up the tension between Lessing's political focus in the story and the detached narrative tone: "This is a story, I suppose, about a failure in intelligence: the Rawlings's marriage was grounded in intelligence."

The "I suppose" undercuts the suggestion that what drives Susan to suicide is the "failure" of her intelligence—her inability to control her emotions and her deep-seated desire for freedom. The narrator continues this subterfuge of the accepted judgment of Susan's condition throughout the story. For example, when the narrator notes that both Susan and Matthew feel a certain flatness in their marriage, she immediately insists "well, even this was expected. . . . [I]t was natural they sometimes felt like this." This statement though is immediately countered with the question "like what?" which suggests that the couple is actively avoiding any emotional introspection, which is the ultimate cause of the failure of their marriage and Susan's subsequent suicide.

By the end of the story, however, as Susan slips further into madness, the story's narrative voice shifts. The previously detached narrator now reflects Susan's point of view and presents a different irony. At this point, Susan is clear about the hypocrisy of her life as she slowly drifts "off into the dark river," for her the only route to true freedom.

Symbols

Glenna Bell, in her article for *The Explicator*, analyzes Lessing's use of color in the story, arguing that colors help symbolize Susan's descent into madness. The beginning "lacks color imagery altogether but, as Susan gradually becomes a more desperate personality, Lessing's references to color become more frequent, more noticeable, and more significant for the understanding of Susan's character." Bell suggests that the white house symbolizes the absence of color in Susan's life, reflecting the void she feels within her, while the greenness of her garden is representative of "the naturalness of a fertile and productive life."

The demonic figure in the garden is more complex. He suggests both the attraction and danger of her desire to reject "rationality" and to allow her emotions to surface. Later though, he represents all the voices of reason that have restricted her. When Susan allows her emotional self to take control in her final visit to Room Nineteen, "the demons" disappear, "gone forever, because she was buying her freedom from them."

Historical Context

A Woman's Place

During the first few decades of the twentieth century, feminist thinkers on both sides of the Atlantic engaged in a rigorous investigation of female identity as it related to all aspects of a woman's life. Some declared the institution of marriage to be a form of slavery and thus recommended its abolition. Others derided the ideal of the maternal instinct, rejecting the notion that motherhood should be the ultimate goal of all women. The more conservative feminists of this age considered marriage and motherhood acceptable roles only if guidelines were set in order to prevent a wife from assuming an inferior position to her husband in any area of their life together. A woman granted equality in marriage would serve as an exemplary role model for her children by encouraging the development of an independent spirit.

The early feminists in America and England, such as Eleanor Rathbone, who became a leading figure in England's National Union of Women's Suffrage Societies, were able to gain certain rights for women, including the right to vote. They were not able, however, to change society's view of a woman's place within the home. During World War II, American and British women were encouraged to enter the workplace, where they enjoyed a measure of independence and responsibility. After the war, however, they were forced to give up their jobs to the returning male troops. Hundreds of thousands of women were laid off and expected to resume their place in the home.

Training began at an early age to ensure that girls would conform to the feminine ideal—the perfect wife and mother. Women who tried to gain self-fulfillment through a career were criticized and deemed dangerous to the stability of the family. They were pressed to find fulfillment exclusively through their support of a successful husband. Television shows, popular magazines, and advertisements all encouraged the image of woman-as-housewife throughout the 1960s. The small number of women who did work outside the home often suffered discrimination and exploitation as they were relegated to low-paying clerical, service, or assembly-line positions. Women would have to wait until the 1970s to gain meaningful social and economic advancement.

Sexuality

Traditional attitudes about sex began to change during the 1960s. Dr. Alfred Kinsey's reports on the sexual behavior of men and women (1948, 1953) helped bring discussions of this subject out in the open. The public was intrigued by movie stars like Marilyn Monroe and Brigitte Bardot, who openly flaunted their sexuality. During this decade, relaxed moral standards resulted in an age of sexual freedom.

London was at the forefront of the cultural revolution of the 1960s, which promoted freer attitudes toward sexuality as well as other behaviors that had been restricted in the 1950s. "Swinging London" became the international center for what was most current in music, fashion, art, and film. The rise of youth culture, coupled with the energy generated by creative people in the arts, centered on Carnaby Street, made household names of Mary Quant, the Beatles, the Rolling Stones, Terrence Stamp, and Vidal Sassoon. Sexual expression and experimentation became one of the cultural hallmarks of this era.

Critical Overview

"To Room Nineteen" was first published in *A Man and Two Women*, a collection of Lessing's short stories that helped cement her reputation as an important short story writer. Most reviewers praised Lessing for her literary artistry. Paul Pickrel in *Harper* wrote that the "best of her work [in the

Compare
&
Contrast

- **Early 1960s:** In 1960, in a landmark obscenity trial *Regina v. Penguin Books Limited*, the court determines that D. H. Lawrence's long-banned novel *Lady Chatterley's Lover* is not obscene.

  Today: Reflecting the relaxed sexual mores of the twenty-first century, explicit sexual acts can be viewed on cable television as well as on the Internet. However, the Bush administration has increased funding in the annual federal budget for trying obscenity cases.

- **Early 1960s:** In 1963, Soviet cosmonaut Valentina Tershkova becomes the first woman in space.

  Today: Women continue to travel in space as well as run large corporations. Media mogul Oprah Winfrey is one of the wealthiest and most powerful people in the world.

- **Early 1960s:** In 1963, *The Feminine Mystique* by Betty Friedan is published. The book chronicles the growing sense of dissatisfaction women feel about the unequal treatment they are receiving in the home, the workplace, and in other institutions.

  Today: Women have made major gains in their fight for equality, although the Equal Rights Amendment, intended to codify the equality of men and women, has yet to be passed. It was introduced to every Congress between 1923 and 1972. In 1972 it was passed and then sent to the states to be ratified, but it failed to gain the approval of the required number of states. It has been introduced to every Congress since 1972.

collection] is equal to the best short stories now being written in English."

Dorothy Brewster, in her article on the author in *Twayne's English Authors Series Online*, applauds Lessing's focus on human relationships "with no particular significance in themselves, but successful in suggesting the flow of life around us" and her questioning "about what people mean to each other." A review in the *Times Literary Supplement* finds the stories in "this most notable collection" to be "intensely imagined." Peter Deane in *Book Week* concurs, arguing that the stories "all evidence a sound intelligence and often a very acute, intuitive insight. They are written with exacting care." Deane, however, finds the lack of "a personal tone" in the stories, "a sense of something necessitous or deeply felt."

A *Newsweek* reviewer determined that "To Room Nineteen" is the best in the collection. Critical response to the story has been consistently strong. Linda H. Halisky, in her article for *Studies in Short Fiction* praises Lessing's ability to bring her readers "to the brink of potentially healing new insights" about the relationships between men and women. Maria Elena Raymond, in *Feminist Writers* argues that the story is "on a par with the works of Poe, and reminiscent of Charlotte Perkins Gilman's 'The Yellow Wallpaper'."

Criticism

Wendy Perkins

Perkins is a professor of American and English literature and film. In this essay, Perkins examines the theme of self-knowledge in Lessing's short story.

D. H. Lawrence centered many of his novels and short stories on the difficulties inherent in what he called in his Foreword to *Women in Love* "the passionate struggle into conscious being." Lawrence's work traces the chronological development of his characters' growing awareness of themselves and their relation to their world. He also explores

What Do I Read Next?

- *The Awakening* (1899) is Kate Chopin's masterful novel of a young woman who struggles to find self-knowledge and inevitably suffers the consequences of trying to establish herself as an independent spirit.

- In the play *A Doll's House* (1879), Henrik Ibsen examines a woman's restricted role in the nineteenth century and the disastrous effects those limitations have on her marriage.

- Lessing's *The Fifth Child* (1989) is a harrowing portrait of a mother's struggle to raise a "disturbed" child, raising important issues about the nature of family and a woman's role within it.

- Michael Cunningham's novel *The Hours* (2002) focuses on similar themes of madness and traditional notions of a woman's place.

- Kate Millet's *Sexual Politics* (1969) studies the history and dynamics of feminism.

---

the antithetical forces that can impede an individual's quest for self-knowledge.

Lawrence believed that we gain knowledge of ourselves through two contradictory processes: our minds (what he called "mental consciousness") as well as our physical selves (our "blood-consciousness"). He explains in his December 8, 1915, letter to Bertrand Russell that the blood-consciousness "exists in us independently of the ordinary mental consciousness." Lawrence writes:

> And the tragedy of this our life, and of your life, is that the mental and nerve consciousness exerts a tyranny over the blood-consciousness, and is engaged in the destruction of your blood-being or blood-consciousness, the final liberating of the one, which is only death in result.

Doris Lessing joined the discussion generated by Lawrence's narratives of female and male self-discovery, which include his concentration on these antithetical impulses, but adapted them to her own historical moment. Lawrence's focus in the early decades of the twentieth century was a focus on the quest for an authentic self through the process of sexual awakening, reflecting the age's rejection of Victorian notions of propriety. Fiona R. Barnes, in her article on Lessing for the *Dictionary of Literary Biography*, notes that Lessing's works become "historical records that tackle the central political, spiritual, and psychological questions of the last half of the twentieth century."

One such work is her celebrated short story "To Room Nineteen." As Lawrence had done several decades earlier, Lessing centers on her character's internal quest for an authentic self grounded in the historical moment of the story, here in the early 1960s, when women were struggling to find an identity outside of the domestic sphere. In this story, Susan Rawlings experiences a battle of wills between her mental consciousness, which insists that she accept her traditional role as wife and mother, and her blood consciousness, which sparks her quest for absolute freedom.

During the first-wave feminist movement in America and Great Britain, which occurred from the late nineteenth century to early twentieth century, women made great strides in their push for equality in the areas of voting rights and birth control. During World War II, the American and British government encouraged women to join the workforce, where they added to the accomplishments of the early women's rights activists by succeeding in positions outside the home.

When the war ended, however, women were forced to give up their jobs, along with their newly developed sense of independence, and to retreat into the traditional roles of wife and mother. Post-war America and Britain returned to a renewed sense of domesticity and social conformity. The second-wave feminist movement did not begin to make significant gains in the fight for equality until the mid 1960s, when in America, the Civil Rights Act was passed, prohibiting sexual and racial employment discrimination.

Barnes writes, "despite her disavowal of feminism [Lessing] is perhaps most successful (and most renowned) for her portrayals of the changing female consciousness as it reacts to problems of the age." The problem for Susan Rawlings is that she marries before the second-wave activists begin their push for female autonomy. Susan is caught in the middle stage between the two waves of feminism—in the social conformity of the 1950s and early 1960s, a time when the "intelligent" thing to do is to adopt traditional male and female roles.

For the first ten years of her marriage, Susan has allowed, in Lawrence's terms, her mental consciousness to exert "a tyranny over the blood-consciousness" by dictating her life choices. Yet, as the last of her children start school, Susan's "blood consciousness" begins to emerge, threatening the fabric of her family, as well as her sanity.

Susan and Matthew have handled their relationship "sensibly," marrying late in their twenties, moving to the suburbs, and adopting conventional roles. Their "foresight and their sense" prompted them to decide that Susan would give up her job with an advertising firm and take care of the house and the children while Matthew would support them, both determining that "children needed their mother to a certain age." In the early days of their marriage, they, along with their friends, were certain that they had chosen "everything right, appropriate, and what everyone would wish for, if they could choose." Their "intelligence" kept them from wanting more and ensured that they would appreciate what they had.

Yet at the beginning of the story, this "balanced and sensible" couple begins to experience a sense of flatness, which becomes most pronounced for Susan. Initially, she responds by throwing all of her energy into the care of her children and the upkeep of the house. She struggles, though, to find a point for her hard work, a raison d'être, for she could not say "for the sake of *this* is all the rest." The closest she comes to finding a reason for her sacrifice is in their love for each other. Yet, she feels a growing sense that this is not enough, not "important enough, to support it all," especially when she discovers that Matthew is having sexual relationships with other women.

> " Yet, as the last of her children start school, Susan's 'blood consciousness' begins to emerge, threatening the fabric of her family, as well as her sanity."

Susan finds that she has little to say to Matthew when he comes home, other than the details of the day-to-day life of the household. She has become dependent on him to connect her to the outside world that she had once been an active part of. As she struggles to keep in check her hidden resentment, she does not, according to her "intelligent" sensibility, "make the mistake of taking a job for the sake of her independence." Her mental consciousness asserts its influence as "the inner storms and quicksands were understood and charted. So everything was all right. Everything was in order. Yes, things were under control."

As the narrator notes, however, in the first line, "this is a story . . . about a failure in intelligence," the intelligence on which the Rawlings' marriage is based. Susan reaches a point where she can no longer suppress her passionate desire for freedom. When her youngest children begin school, she embarks on an intense process of self-examination. As a result, she acknowledges that in order to survive, she must break the hold that her intelligence has had over her and follow the instincts of her blood consciousness, which impel her to establish self autonomy—physically and emotionally.

Yet Susan's struggle to break the tyranny of her mental consciousness, which compels her to resist the urge to abandon her family, pushes her to the verge of madness. As she recognizes that even the embrace of her beautiful twins becomes a "human cage of loving limbs," she begins to visualize a void, at first "something was waiting for her" at home, then "an enemy," then a "demon," then a "devil," that appears to her in her garden. She gains solace only in an empty hotel room, the Room Nineteen of the title. When Matthew spies on her daily sojourns there, he shatters the sense of freedom she gains and unwittingly forces her to attempt what she determines to be her only outlet—suicide. After turning on the gas in the hotel room, Susan drifts "off into the dark river" that "seemed to caress her inwardly, like the movement of her blood" echoing Lawrence's assertion that blood-consciousness "is one half of life, belonging to the darkness."

The story presents an ironic reversal, however, of Lawrence's insistence that death will result when mental consciousness takes over. Lessing suggests the reverse—that Susan's consuming desire to be free, to allow her blood consciousness to take control, leads her to suicide, the only option she sees. Susan's tragedy results from her inability to allow her "unreasonable" emotions and desires to surface earlier and more gradually. The battle that inevitably ensues between her intellect and her emotions drives her mad. Yet her madness becomes her path to freedom, as she slips "into the dark fructifying dream."

Linda H. Halisky, in her article for *Studies in Short Fiction*, notes the ironic use of madness in the story. As Susan's true self is emerging, those around her, including Susan, determine that she is not "herself." Halisky insists that when Susan expresses this thought, what she means is that "she is no longer the self she set herself willingly, sensibly, reasonably to become. Some deeper self has hold of her; some inexplicable, non-rational self is rearing its head and asserting its due." Susan has been "programmed, by the reason her culture has taught her to consider definitive, to label the expression of that self 'madness.'"

Janina Nordius writes in her article for *The Explicator* that in "To Room Nineteen," Lessing offers a "woman's perspective on the alienation fostered by modern society and its celebration of 'intelligence.'" As Lessing explores the mid-twentieth century restrictions placed on women's freedom and search for an authentic self, she also engages in a dialogue with D. H. Lawrence and his views on the interplay of contradictory human impulses. "To Room Nineteen" reflects this dialogue as it details the tragic result of the tyranny of the intellect.

Source: Wendy Perkins, Critical Essay on "To Room Nineteen," in *Short Stories for Students*, Gale, 2005.

Janina Nordius

In the following essay, Nordius explores Lessing's use of T. S. Eliot's "The Waste Land" as a subtext in "To Room Nineteen."

In her illuminating discussion of Doris Lessing's debt to T. S. Eliot, Claire Sprague traces allusions to *The Waste Land* and other poems in four of Lessing's novels. In addition to those instances, *The Waste Land* is also an important subtext in Lessing's short story "To Room Nineteen." Charting the failure of communication and subsequent decline of love in a mid-twentieth-century marriage, Lessing both pursues one of Eliot's most central themes in *The Waste Land* and writes back from the woman's point of view.

"To Room Nineteen" addresses Eliot's tableau in part 2 of *The Waste Land* that features a woman sitting before a mirror, brushing her hair:

Under the firelight, under the brush, her hair
Spread out in fiery points
Glowed into words, then would be savagely still.

The scene is reproduced twice in Lessing's story, as Susan Rawlings sits "running the brush over her hair again and again, lifting fine black clouds in a small hiss of electricity," while watching her husband in the mirror. In Lessing as well as Eliot, this scene stands out as an icon of the failure of genuine communication, even between would-be lovers, that both writers clearly blame on the general cultural and spiritual climate of the twentieth century; this might also, by some readers, be seen as a phenomenon of gender. The discourse of "intelligence," which so completely dominates the Rawlingses in Lessing's story, effectively excludes speaking of any other, not-so-rational experience. And whereas historically, on a broader scale, this discourse may be seen as resulting from the seventeenth-century "dissociation of sensibility," from which Eliot famously claims "we have never recovered," it is often viewed by feminist readers as working specifically to the disadvantage of female self-expression.

By shifting the focus from the man to the woman in the sterile scene in front of the mirror, Lessing radically transforms Eliot's "story." Thus, whereas the anonymous woman in *The Waste Land* comes across as plain neurotic and totally insensitive to her partner's more refined inner monologue, in "To Room Nineteen" the man is the one who fails to appreciate the register used by his wife. As Susan Rawlings gives up on intelligence, her experience of self "glows into" another kind of "words"—into the "his, his" of her hair under the brush, for example. The "hiss, hiss" in Lessing's story signifies much and draws as much on the imagery and the literary and mythical allusion used by Eliot as on *The Waste Land* itself. In this register of imagery and allusion, never voiced except as "hissing" but nonetheless manifest in Susan's thoughts, we are given an alternative story of Susan Rawlings.

In this alternative story, Lessing has her protagonist intuit the decline of her marriage in images of general cultural decay by drawing—like Eliot—on biblical as as well as classical mythology. The Edenic garden which is the prominent setting of the "happy" marriage soon turns into an arid "desert" as innocence is lost: Matthew embarks on his extramarital affairs and Susan finds herself a prisoner in her role as self-sacrificing angel-in-the-house. But perhaps the loss of the golden age might in fact be inherent in the construct of "intelligent" and responsible marriage itself. Thinking of her husband's affairs, Susan finds herself "secretly wishing [. . .] that the wildness and the beauty could be his"—the "wildness" and "beauty," we are to understand, of unrestricted joy and delight, unhampered by marital bonds or moral obligations. But, she realizes, "he was married to her. She was married to him. They were married inextricably. And therefore the gods could not strike him with the real magic, not really."

Just as Eliot did in *The Waste Land,* Lessing conspicuously uses the images of river and water as vehicles for her protagonist's critique of modern marriage. For Susan Rawlings, water comes to represent the vitalizing element in the dubious domestic bargain she enters into with her husband, a bargain that sentences "her soul" to stay put in the house, "so that the people in it could grow like plants in water." It is by turning to the river for comfort, "taking it into her being, into her veins," that Susan barely survives the draining of her powers implicit in this nurturing commitment. As it runs past the Rawlingses' garden-turned-wasteland at Richmond, the river Thames also serves to evoke, once more, the lost vitality of love. The contrast between "civilized" love gone stale and its lost "wildness" is poignantly captured in the image of the Rawlingses' "big civilised bedroom overlooking the wild sullied river." Yet, the river is also said to be "sullied," if not by the "empty bottles, sandwich papers, [. . . and] other testimony of summer nights" that litter Eliot's "Sweet Thames," then by the same cultural squalor and spiritual decay affecting love and marriage that made Eliot look back to Spenser's wedding song for a lost golden age.

Whereas in Eliot the use of myth and allusion seem ultimately to suggest some hope and consolation, no such relief awaits Lessing's protagonist. The "hissing" that we attribute to the snake in the garden and hear literally reproduced by the stream of gas sends her drifting "off into the dark river." It suggests, in the end, only insanity and death. This, then, is perhaps Lessing's most significant departure from Eliot: She uses his nostalgia to produce a woman's perspective on the alienation fostered by modern society and its celebration of "intelligence," then finally dismisses this nostalgia, too, as an impracticable approach to contemporary life.

Source: Janina Nordius, "Lessing's 'To Room Nineteen,'" in *Explicator*, Vol. 57, No. 3, Spring 1999, pp. 171–73.

Glenna Bell

In the following essay, Bell delineates the color imagery in "To Room Nineteen."

Doris Lessing's "To Room Nineteen" is a story of repression, alienation, and suicide. Lessing describes Susan Rawling's search for inner tranquility, during which she vacillates between "the big white house" in Richmond—an image that consistently suggests the emptiness, stagnation, and constraint of her lifestyle—and the green garden with its "slow-moving brown river"—green and brown being associated here with the freedom of nature and procreation. Susan is "driven" to seek peace of mind away from the estate—first, in the "ordinary and anonymous" room of Miss Townsend's hotel, then on the hillsides of Wales, "brilliant with ferns and bracken, jewelled with running water," and finally in the green-accoutred room 19 of Fred's Hotel, which constitutes an artificial surrogate for the natural green sanctuary of the garden.

Lessing imbues the main settings that Susan encounters in her progression from the white house to the green room 19 with colors appropriate to her character's changing mental state. Accordingly, the outset of the story lacks color imagery altogether but, as Susan gradually becomes a more desperate personality, Lessing's references to color become more frequent, more noticeable, and more significant for the understanding of Susan's character. Not until the Rawlings have moved to the white house does Lessing explicitly indicate that something is "wrong" with their marriage. She says that outwardly it appeared as if "they had everything they had wanted and had planned for. *And yet . . .* there must be a certain flatness . . ." Susan repeatedly attempts to rationalize and subjugate her discontent with her artificially controlled life. Gradually, Lessing reveals the extent to which Susan is hopelessly bound to her roles as wife and mother—eventually calling the house in Richmond "the big white house, on which the mortgage still cost four hundred a year"—using white to intensify the representation of the house as the embodiment of Susan's seemingly inescapable existence, with all its purposelessness and its absence of individuation. The white house, like Susan's life, is a prison, "for she knew that this structure . . . [and everything that was associated with it] depended on her, and yet she could not understand why, or even what it was she contributed to it." Even the holidays in the white house with her family were "like living out a prison sentence."

Susan goes to the garden to escape. In the story's imagery, the "emerald grass" and the "brown river" of the garden typify the naturalness of a fertile and productive life—the antithesis to Susan's "colorless," structured, and barren subsistence in the stark white house. Where white is present in the garden, it reinforces the meaning of the white house. Susan's "white stone seat" is a static, lifeless object like the house, like the inert routine of her daily life, which contrasts strikingly with the movement of the river, or the movement of crowds on the street, which Susan later longs to join. Likewise, the "snakelike creature," "whitish and unhealthy to look at," enhances the picture of Susan's entrapment; it is "twisting about, . . . in a kind of dance of protest." The snake's writhing protest is imagistically associated with Susan's disillusionment with her lifestyle. Lessing tells us that "something inside her [Susan] howled with impatience, with rage . . . And she was frightened."

Susan attempts to evade her impending self-awareness as she dreams of "having a room or a place, anywhere, where she could go and sit, by herself, no one knowing where she was." She finds this place in Fred's Hotel. Room 19 "had a single window, with thin green brocade curtains, a three-quarter bed that had a cheap green satin bedspread on it, . . . and a green wicker armchair." The green of the room, like that of the garden, suggests the verdant existence that Susan has been denied. Yet this color—an artificial green obviously associated with debased sexuality (evidently prostitutes commonly patronized the place)—accentuates Lessing's portrayal of the room as Susan's "last resort," a "hideous" substitute for the natural garden. This artificial green venue provides Susan temporary relief from her emotional turmoil until Matthew's detective discovers the hideaway, and all is ruined. Thereafter, "several times she returned to the room, to look for herself there, but instead she found the unnamed spirit of restlessness, a prickling fevered

hunger for movement, an irritable self-consciousness . . ." Again, Susan's emotions—anger and betrayal over her discovery—challenge her, stirring up this "irritable self-consciousness" that she has heretofore managed to suppress by creating a new identity as the anonymous Mrs. Jones, the inhabitant of room 19.

Susan returns to the room several times looking for "herself"—that is, Mrs. Jones—and encounters Susan Rawling and her "demons [emotions] that made her dash blindly about, muttering words of hate . . ." She knows now that she must once more move onward in her quest for emancipation from her inner discord. Ultimately, Susan returns to the artificial green surroundings of room 19 to find that this time "the demons were not here. They had gone forever, because she was buying her freedom from them." Susan's struggle ends as she listens to "the faint soft hiss of the gas that poured into the room, into her lungs, into her brain, as she drifted off into the dark river"—the eternally moving natural current of death. This is the final tie between the green room and the green garden, where she had previously gone "by herself, and looked at the slow-moving brown river; . . . and closed her eyes and breathed slow and deep, taking it into her being, into her veins." In fact, the "dark river" in the artificially green room 19 seems a more fitting destiny in view of Lessing's subtle and constant use of color as a motif embodying and intensifying the story's depiction of Susan's ever-growing need for release.

Source: Glenna Bell, "Lessing's 'To Room Nineteen,'" in *Explicator*, Vol. 50, No. 3, Spring 1992, pp. 180–83.

Irene G. Watson

In the following essay, Watson applies a Jungian interpretation to Lessing's "To Room Nineteen."

The Devil that appears to Susan Rawlings in Lessing's "To Room Nineteen" does not entice her to "partake of forbidden fruit" but to "open her eyes." Total insight into Susan's dilemma for both Susan and the reader rises or falls upon a correct view of the "son of the morning." Failure to apply a Jungian interpretation to the demon has caused critics to prematurely evaluate "To Room Nineteen" as a "horrifying study of insanity creeping on," or as "a meaningful story about a personal failure in marriage that represents a failure of the relationship between man and woman in our society."

Calling the demon, who appears in a garden with "a long crooked stick [that he uses] to stir around in the coils of a blindworm or a grass snake"—obvious phallic symbols—an image of Susan's latent evil nature and sensual cravings leads to the interpretation that Susan resents her husband's infidelities and wishes for equal sexual freedom. Her statement describing the devil as one who "wants to get into me and to take me over" might seem to support such a theory. However, a feminist evaluation, and Lessing has been called a feminist writer, or a Freudian interpretation in "Young Goodman Brown" style offers no clarification of the reasons for and consequences of Susan's inability to attain individuation. Ironically, Jung, who has been criticized for his "failure to understand feminine consciousness, with consequent errors in literary evaluations and interpretations," has the illuminating theory that adds great depth and understanding to Lessing's Susan. A Jungian interpretation of the devil and the accompanying phallic symbols gives insight to Susan's demon and Susan's female consciousness simultaneously. As Susan later says in regard to making love, "The idea made her want to cry with sheer exhaustion. She had finished with all that . . . [it] made her want to run away and hide from the sheer effort of the thing." Clearly, a Freudian analysis fails to understand the nature of Susan's trauma. There is much more at stake than latent physical desire.

The devil, as the personification of Susan's animus in Jungian theory, as the complement to her Ego, as the Self who reveals the deficiencies in Susan's life and character, is an ally rather than an enemy. His stick is still a phallic symbol, but one which represents potency, life, and strength rather than sexual desire. The second time Susan sees him, he carries a "leafy twig." Indeed the leaves are evidence of the life-producing capabilities of the twig. Susan's trauma has resulted from her subjugation of her talents and strengths—"her old firm, missing her qualities of humour, balance, and sense, invited her often to go back"—to her husband—she is "now dependent on a husband for outside interests and money"—and to her children—"Children needed their mother to a certain age, that both parents knew and agreed on." Susan is impotent. She needs to recognize the power, the wholeness, the strength her devil/animus represents and incorporate him, allow him "to get into [her]" and complete the process of individuation, "a conscious dialectic relationship between ego and Self."

Tragically, Susan fails to understand and accept her animus. She erroneously looks for health by rejecting both her Self and her current role as mother and wife and by seeking solitude in Room Nineteen in a dingy hotel. Jung says, "The connection between ego and Self is vitally important to psychic health. . . . When the connection is broken the result is emptiness, despair, meaninglessness and in extreme cases psychosis or suicide." Obviously, Susan's solitude is not healing. Her condition deteriorates until she is "impelling herself from point to point like a moth dashing itself against a windowpane" and finally enters Room Nineteen for the last time to "[listen] to the faint soft hiss of the gas that poured into the room, into her lungs, into her brain." The nature of Susan's demon is understood and her actions and subsequent suicide are predictable when a Jungian approach is applied.

Source: Irene G. Watson, "Lessing's 'To Room Nineteen,'" in *Explicator*, Vol. 47, No. 3, Spring 1989, pp. 54–55.

Sources

Barnes, Fiona R., "Doris Lessing," in *Dictionary of Literary Biography*, Vol. 139, *British Short-Fiction Writers, 1945–1980*, edited by Dean Baldwin, Gale Research, 1994, pp. 159–72.

Bell, Glenna, "'To Room Nineteen,'" in the *Explicator*, Vol. 50, No. 3, Spring 1992, pp. 180–83.

Brewster, Dorothy, "Doris Lessing," in *Twayne's English Authors Series Online*, G. K. Hall, 1999.

Caldwell, Gail, "Doris Lessing," in the *Boston Globe*, November 13, 1994, p. B1.

Deane, Peter, Review of *A Man and Two Women*, in *Book Week*, October 13, 1963, p. 16.

Halisky, Linda H., "Redeeming the Irrational: The Inexplicable Heroines of 'A Sorrowful Woman' and 'To Room Nineteen,'" in *Studies in Short Fiction*, Vol. 27, No. 1, Winter 1990, pp. 45–54.

Lawrence, D. H., "Foreword," in *Women in Love*, Modern Library, 1950, pp. ix–x.

———, *The Selected Letters of D. H. Lawrence*, edited by James T. Boulton, Cambridge University Press, 1977, pp. ix–x.

Lessing, Doris, "To Room Nineteen," in *A Man and Two Women*, Simon and Schuster, 1963.

Nordius, Janina, "'To Room Nineteen,'" in the *Explicator*, Vol. 57, No. 3, Spring 1999, p. 171.

Pickrel, Paul, Review of *A Man and Two Women*, in *Harper*, November 1963, p. 227.

Raymond, Maria Elena, "Lessing, Doris," in *Feminist Writers*, edited by Pamela Kester-Shelton, St. James Press, 1966.

Review of *A Man and Two Women*, in *Newsweek*, October 14, 1963, p. 62.

Review of *A Man and Two Women*, in *Times Literary Supplement*, October 18, 1963, p. 821.

Further Reading

Dean, Sharon, "Marriage, Motherhood, and Lessing's 'To Room Nineteen,'" in *Doris Lessing Newsletter*, Vol. 5, 1981, pp. 1, 14.

These subjects are explored in Lessing's story.

Pruitt, Virginia, "Crucial Balance: A Theme in Lessing's Short Fiction," in *Studies in Short Fiction*, Vol. 18, 1981, pp. 281–85.

Pruitt examines this dominant theme in Lessing's stories.

St. Andrews, Bonnie, *Forbidden Fruit: On the Relationship between Women and Knowledge in Doris Lessing, Selma Lagerlöf, Kate Chopin, Margaret Atwood*, Whitston, 1986.

St. Andrews explores the treatment of self-knowledge in Lessing's work and that of other authors.

Tiger, Virginia, "Taking Hands and Dancing in (Dis)Unity: Story to Storied in Doris Lessing's 'To Room Nineteen' and 'A Room,'" in *Modern Fiction Studies*, Vol. 36, 1990, pp. 421–33.

Tiger compares Lessing's two stories, focusing on their structure and voice.

The Veldt

Ray Bradbury
1951

"The Veldt" is the first story in Ray Bradbury's anthology, *The Illustrated Man*. Published in 1951 by Doubleday, the book was a great success with readers and critics alike. It was the perfect follow-up to Bradbury's successful publication of *The Martian Chronicles* the year before, and it cemented his reputation as a great writer. The anthology is a collection of short stories, most of which had been previously published individually in pulp and slick magazines. Bradbury tied these stories together with the framing device of the Illustrated Man himself. Each story is represented by a drawing upon the Illustrated Man's body and the stories come to life and tell themselves as he brings each new illustration into view. Bradbury's use of a sideshow character as a framing device reflects his own interest in the world of the carnival and sideshow. As a young boy, Bradbury was fascinated by the grotesque and sinister aspects he found lurking there, and these themes pervade many of his later works.

The rise in the popularity of television had a direct influence on Bradbury's story "The Veldt." At the time the story was written, many American families were acquiring their first television sets, and no one was sure exactly how this new technology would impact the relationships among family members. Some people were afraid that watching too much television would lead to the total breakdown of the family unit. This fear is directly reflected in "The Veldt," but in the story, Bradbury

heightens the odds by creating a machine that not only allows children to detach emotionally from their parents, but one that can also physically destroy the parents, as well.

Author Biography

Ray Bradbury was born on August 22, 1920 in Waukegan, Illinois to Esther Moberg and Leonard Spaulding Bradbury. The family moved often during Ray's childhood. From 1926 to 1933 they moved back and forth from Arizona twice. Finally, in 1934, they settled permanently in Los Angeles. Bradbury attended Los Angeles High School, where he developed a true love for writing. He joined the Los Angeles Science Fiction League and became active in the "fandom" subculture in which groups of science fiction fans would publish their own magazines known as "fanzines." In 1939, Bradbury produced four issues of his own fanzine, *Futuria Fantasia.*

Bradbury graduated from high school in 1938 but lived with his parents while continuing to write. He began trying to sell his short stories to science fiction pulp magazines and was successful in 1941 when his first paid publication, a short story titled "Pendulum," appeared in *Super Science Stories.* By the early 1940s, Bradbury's short stories appeared regularly in the popular pulp magazine *Weird Tales,* and by 1945 Bradbury was selling stories to the more prestigious "slick" magazines. Bradbury quickly gained recognition as a talented writer. In 1946 Bradbury met Marguerite Susan McClure. The two were married in Los Angeles on September 27, 1947. The couple eventually had four daughters: Susan (1949), Ramona (1951), Bettina (1955), and Alexandra (1958).

In 1947 Bradbury's first book, *Dark Carnival,* was published, and his reputation as a talented writer continued to grow. With the publication of his acclaimed book *The Martian Chronicles* in 1950, Bradbury moved to the forefront as one of the premier science fiction writers of the day. In 1951 he followed up this success with the publication of *The Illustrated Man,* an anthology containing the short story "The Veldt." This book was also extremely popular with readers and solidified Bradbury's reputation. Throughout the following years, Bradbury continued to build upon his success with the publication of *Fahrenheit 451* (1953),

Dandelion Wine (1957), and *Something Wicked This Way Comes* (1962).

Through the remainder of the century, Bradbury continued to write novels and short stories but also branched out to many other formats and media. He has written play scripts, screenplays, teleplays, and poetry. His works have been translated into numerous languages and have been adapted many times over. In 1964 three of his short stories, were presented on stage in *The World of Ray Bradbury* and in 1969 a film version of *The Illustrated Man* was released. Bradbury also produced his own cable television series, *Ray Bradbury Theater* from 1985 to 1992. Bradbury's work has won innumerable awards and honors including the O. Henry Memorial Award, the 1977 World Fantasy Award for Lifetime Achievement, the 1988 Nebula Grand Master Award from the Science Fiction Writers of America, and the National Book Foundation Medal for Distinguished Contribution to American Letters.

Plot Summary

Lydia and George Hadley live in a Happy-life Home, a technological marvel that automatically tends to their every need. It dresses them, cooks the food, brushes their teeth, and even rocks them to sleep. The house also contains a high-tech nursery. Lydia tells George that she thinks something might be wrong with the nursery, and she wants him to take a look at it. They go to the nursery, and as they stand in the center of the room, the nursery's previously blank walls and ceiling come to life. The room is transformed into a genuine African veldt, complete with a blazing hot sun and all the authentic sensory experiences that would accompany such a setting. The couple stands and watches the antelopes and vultures that roam the plains. There are also lions off in the distance that seem to be feeding upon a recent kill. Suddenly the lions turn and run toward George and Lydia. The two run out of the nursery and slam the door.

Lydia is still terrified that something has gone wrong and that the nursery settings are becoming too real. George assures her, however, that it is just the machinery of the room creating a realistic environment. The machine works through telepathy. It reads a person's thoughts and then projects them onto the walls to create the environment. George tells Lydia that the children have been reading a lot about Africa and that is why they have created the veldt. Lydia is still not convinced, and she insists that George lock the nursery for a few days. George is hesitant at first because he remembers the tantrums the children threw the last time he locked the nursery as a punishment. He relents, however, and locks the door. Lydia then suggests that they turn off the entire house for a few days. She is worried that she is becoming unnecessary because the house can perform the duties of wife, mother, and nursemaid. She notes that George seems to feel unnecessary too. As the two are talking in the hallway, the door of the nursery trembles as if something has jumped against it from the other side. Lydia is frightened, but George reassures her that the lions in the nursery are not real and therefore they cannot pose any real danger.

Later that day, George and Lydia are eating dinner at their automated table. George is still thinking about the events in the nursery. Because the nursery creates its environments by telepathically reading the children's thoughts, he is concerned about the images of death that seem to pervade the African veldt that they have created. George and Lydia both wonder why the children no longer want to create beautiful fantasy scenes like they used to. George decides to go and double-check the nursery once again. He walks in and finds himself in the middle of the veldt. Knowing that the room is programmed to react to thoughts, he attempts to change the room into a scene from Aladdin and his magic lamp. The room will not change, however. George returns to the table and tells Lydia about his inability to change the setting in the room.

Wendy and Peter return home and their father questions them about the African scene in the nursery. They deny that there is an African veldt. They take their parents to the nursery and show them that it contains a lovely green forest. George suspects that they are lying, however, and he sends them to bed. Before George and Lydia leave the room, they find a wallet lying on the floor. It is one of George's old wallets. It has been chewed and has blood smears on each side. George and Lydia leave the nursery and lock the door.

That night the couple are lying awake in bed discussing the nursery problem. They believe that it has caused Wendy and Peter to become spoiled and rather cold towards them. George decides that he will invite the children's psychologist, David McClean, over to take a look at the nursery to see

Ray Bradbury

what he thinks. A moment later, George and Lydia hear screams and the roar of lions coming from the nursery. The screams sound familiar, but the couple is not exactly sure why.

The next day Peter asks his father if he is going to lock up the nursery permanently. George says that he is considering turning off the entire house for a while. Peter threatens his father that he had better not do that. Soon, David McClean arrives. George takes him to the nursery where the children are playing. It has once again been turned into an African veldt. George and David can see the lions feeding off in the distance. They send the children out. After studying the African scene for a moment, David admits that he has a very bad feeling about what is taking place. He says that the children seem to care more about the room than they do about their parents and that the situation has become quite dangerous. He suggests tearing down the nursery. As David and George leave, George asks whether there is any way that the lions in the nursery environment could become real. David says he does not think so. The two then find a bloody scarf belonging to Lydia on the floor.

George begins switching off the house while the children cry and beg him to stop. George says that it is time they all went on a little vacation together and that he has asked David McClean to come over to take care of the house. The children plead for just one more moment in the nursery before George continues switching it off. Lydia urges her husband to let them have a few more minutes, and he relents. The children go to the nursery while Lydia and George go upstairs to change clothes. They suddenly hear the children calling them from the nursery. They rush in, but the children are not there. The nursery is once again the veldt, and the lions are approaching from the distance. Suddenly, the door of the nursery slams. George and Lydia run to escape but discover the children have locked the door from the outside. The lions approach as George and Lydia scream. Suddenly they realize why the screams coming from the nursery had always sounded so familiar. They had been their own screams.

The children calmly greet David McClean at the nursery doorway. He enters and sees the lions again off feeding in the distance. Then, Wendy politely offers David a cup of tea.

Characters

George Hadley

George Hadley is a father who wants to provide the best for his family. He loves his children, and is concerned about their welfare. He does not like acting as a disciplinarian, but will punish the children when necessary. Throughout the story, George slowly becomes frustrated with the effect the house is having on his family. He cares more for his family than he does for the convenience the automated house can provide; and therefore, he has no problem turning off the house. George does not jump to conclusions and tries to take a very logical approach to problems. George's logical nature is the reason that he does not realize the true danger of the nursery until it is too late.

Lydia Hadley

Lydia Hadley is a caring mother who loves her husband and her children. She is concerned that the high-tech home they are living in is having a negative effect upon the family relationships, and she longs for a return to a more traditional setting. Lydia has a strong intuition about the threat the nursery

poses. Lydia wants to do what is right, but she has a hard time following through with discipline and tends to give in to her children.

Peter Hadley

Peter Hadley is a spoiled ten-year-old boy who does not like to be told "no." He dominates his twin sister, Wendy, and often orders her around. Peter is very strong-willed and is not afraid to stand up to his father. He has a high I.Q. and is especially knowledgeable when it comes to technology. Peter is a cold and calculating little boy who will do whatever it takes to get what he wants. He is not above using threats and even murder to accomplish his objectives.

Wendy Hadley

Wendy Hadley is ten years old and is Peter's twin sister. She is a follower who obeys the wishes of her brother. She is extremely emotionally dependent upon the nursery and is devastated when her father threatens to turn it off permanently. Wendy has no emotional connection to her parents whatsoever and, therefore, has no remorse for setting them up to be killed.

David McClean

David McClean is a psychologist and a family friend. He is astute when it comes to recognizing the threat that some children's fantasies allude to. He immediately recognizes the dangerous state of mind that the children are in and wants to try and help George repair the emotional damage the nursery has caused.

Themes

Abandonment

Abandonment occurs on two levels in Bradbury's story. First, the children are figuratively abandoned by their parents when they are left in the care of a technological baby sitter. As the character of David McClean tells George, "You've let this room and this house replace you and your wife in your children's affections. This room is their mother and father, far more important in their lives than their real parents." This accidental abdication of parental responsibility sets the children up to become emotionally attached to the nursery. Then, when George threatens to turn off the nursery, the children are terrified because now they are going to be abandoned by their new, surrogate parent, the nursery.

Alienation

Alienation occurs when one feels cut off or estranged from what used to be comfortable and familiar. A sense of isolation and uneasiness takes over. In "The Veldt," this theme is embodied in the character of Lydia. She is the first to recognize that there is something unfamiliar happening in the house and urges George to take a look at the nursery because, it "is different now than it was." Lydia clearly recognizes her own feelings of alienation when she admits very early in the story, "I feel like I don't belong here."

Consumerism

George Hadley embodies the theme of consumerism because he believes in providing the best that money can buy for his family. George believes that he can show his family love by buying them things. Allowing material possessions to stand in for direct human interaction and expressions of love, however, is what ultimately sets George up as the enemy to his children. The theme is succinctly summed up near the end of the story when George asks Lydia, "What prompted us to buy a nightmare?" and she replies, "Pride, money, foolishness."

Dystopia

A dystopia is a place in which people lead fearful, dehumanized lives. It is the opposite of a utopia. Dystopias often serve as warnings of potential dangers that can be brought on through the misuse of technology or power. In "The Veldt," Bradbury turns the Hadley's Happy-life Home into a dystopia that gradually dehumanizes the children and destroys the parents. The dangers are revealed slowly through the story as George begins to realize that the wonderful home that he has provided for his family might not be so wonderful at all. His dream home actually turns into a nightmare.

Illusion versus Reality

The ability to distinguish illusion from reality and the co-mingling of the two is a key theme in "The Veldt." George ultimately agrees to turn on the nursery one more time, thus putting himself and his wife in jeopardy, because he believes that there

Media Adaptations

- *The Illustrated Man* was adapted as a film in 1969 by Jack Smight. The film stars Rod Steiger as the Illustrated Man and features only three stories from the book, including "The Veldt." This is widely regarded as a terrible adaptation of Bradbury's work, and Bradbury himself has commented that he "hates" this film version. It is available from Warner Studios Home Video.

- *The Fantastic Tales of Ray Bradbury* is a 2002 audiobook adaptation of several of Bradbury's notable stories, including "The Veldt." The stories are read by the author himself. It is available from Random House Audible audio downloads at http://www.audible.com.

- Another audio adaptation of "The Veldt" can be found in Books on Tape's 1988 edition of *The Illustrated Man*. This time the classic tales are read by Michael Prichard.

- "The Veldt" was also adapted as a stage play by Bradbury himself in a compilation called *The Wonderful Ice Cream Suit and Other Plays* (1972). This publication is available from Bantam Books.

is a definite distinction between illusion and reality. Something that is an illusion can never become truly "real." This is why George believes that the lions pose no real threat. They are only part of a machine that creates wonderful illusions, "Walls, Lydia, remember; crystal walls, that's all they are. Oh, they look real, I must admit—Africa in your parlor—but it's all dimensional superactionary, supersensitive color film and mental tape film behind glass screens." What George fails to understand is, in the world of this short story, illusion and reality are transposable. One can become the other at any moment.

Man versus Machine

One of the major conflicts in Bradbury's story is that of man versus machine. The story is built around the struggle to control and direct the

 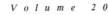

Topics for Further Study

- "The Veldt" deals with human beings who use technology to perpetrate evil. Can you think of any other stories or films that have a similar theme? Can you think of some stories or films where technology is used for good? If you were going to write a similar story, would you portray technology as good or evil? Why?

- The early 1950s was a time when the United States was gripped by a fear of Communism known as the Red Scare. Research the form of government known as Communism. What are the main ideas behind this system of government? Why do you think it seemed so threatening to the United States in the middle of the twentieth century?

- In psychoanalysis, people's thoughts and feelings are analyzed in order to help them sort out problems. What if George had sent Wendy and Peter to a psychoanalyst immediately upon realizing that the nursery was becoming a threat? Do you think the story would have turned out differently? Why or why not? What do you think

Wendy and Peter would have told the psychoanalyst? Write an imaginary conversation between these three characters.

- If you were going to design your own Happy-life Home, what automated conveniences would you put in it? Would you put in any safety mechanisms in case something went wrong? If so, what kind of mechanisms would you install?

- Research an African veldt. What kinds of plants and animals can be found there? Do you think Bradbury's description in the story is accurate?

- In his story, Bradbury uses careful descriptions and similes to create the sensory experience of the African veldt for the reader. Research another environmental setting, such as a tropical rain forest or the Arctic tundra. What descriptive words or phrases could help convey this environment to a reader? Can you think of some similes that would help the reader really "feel" the environment? Write a descriptive passage that evokes this sensory experience.

---

destructive power of the nursery's technology. Whoever controls the machine will have the ultimate power. In this story man is destroyed by the machines in two ways: not only are George and Lydia murdered by the nursery's technology, but the children's humanity is also destroyed. By identifying so closely with the nursery, the children have become less than human. They feel no guilt, remorse or regret when their parents die, and it is clear that they have become as cold and emotionless as the machinery that controls the nursery.

Revenge

"The Veldt" can be read as the ultimate children's revenge story. Children often feel powerless against adults and create elaborate fantasies in which they have the power to conquer any adult who refuses to give them what they want. George trig-

gers these fantasies in Peter and Wendy when he forbids them to take the rocket to New York. The children are used to getting their own way, and they become very angry when they cannot have what they want. Thus the cycle of revenge is set in motion.

Telepathy

Telepathy plays an important role in "The Veldt" as it provides the medium through which the weapons are deployed. The room manifests thought patterns on its walls, thus creating the possibility for evil thoughts to conjure up evil things. The children are able to use their telepathy to direct their destructive powers into the nursery images, thus creating a deadly setting for their parents. In the scientifically advanced world of this short story, thoughts have now become weapons, and children can kill their parents just by wishing them dead.

Style

Ambience

Ambience is the emotional tone that pervades a work of fiction. In "The Veldt" Bradbury sets up a tense, oppressive ambience in the story through his use of description and dialogue. He conveys the hot, oppressiveness of the African veldt through specific descriptive passages such as "The hot straw smell of lion grass, the cool green smell of the hidden water hole, the great rusty smell of animals, the smell of dust like a red paprika in the hot air." These descriptive passages create a sensory atmosphere and add to the sense of dread that pervades the story. The ambience lets the reader know that this is not a cheerful, happy comedy and that there is a good possibility that something terrible might happen.

Foreshadowing

Foreshadowing is a technique in which a writer drops hints about what is to happen later in a story. Bradbury uses this technique to hint at the fate of George and Lydia Hadley. While the two are lying in bed, they hear screams coming from the nursery, and Lydia comments, "Those screams—they sound familiar." Later, the reader realizes that the screams sound familiar to Lydia because they are actually her screams and those of her husband.

Science Fiction

Science fiction deals with the impact of imagined science upon society or individuals. Science fiction stories are often set in the future, but they do not have to be. One of the generally accepted rules of science fiction is that the events which occur in a science fiction story must be plausible based upon current scientific understanding. Bradbury follows these principles in "The Veldt." At the time the story was written, television was becoming a major force in American family life. Bradbury postulated what might happen if the items on these screens could eventually cross over from the world of simulated reality to the world of reality.

Simile

A simile is a comparison of two objects using the term "like" or "as." Bradbury uses similes throughout "The Veldt" to heighten his descriptive passages. When Wendy and Peter return home Bradbury describes them as having "cheeks like peppermint candy, eyes like bright blue agate marbles." The similes here serve to emphasize the fact that these are two cute, energetic children who might be found in any typical middle-American family. Bradbury also uses similes to heighten the tension of the short story. For example, after George Hadley turns off the house, he writes, "It felt like a mechanical cemetery." This description provides a clear mental image for the reader and also underscores the themes of technology and death.

Personification

The technique of personification involves attributing human characteristics to things that are not human. Bradbury uses this technique to great effect throughout "The Veldt." He personifies the nursery and the house itself by attributing emotions to these inanimate objects, "'I don't imagine the room will like being turned off,' said the father. 'Nothing likes to die—even a room. I wonder if it hates me for wanting to switch it off?'" By turning the house into a living, breathing entity through personification, Bradbury heightens the tension and the threat. Now the parents are not only fighting their children, they are also pitted against a technological monster that is working to destroy them.

Point of View

The story is told from a third-person point of view which means the narrator does not directly take part in the story but reports the events to the reader. The narrator is closely aligned with the character of George Hadley, however. He follows George's movements throughout the house and does not usually break away to report on scenes in which George is not involved. The story only breaks this pattern at the end, when George and Lydia are already dead and the narrator continues to report on the scene between Wendy, Peter and David McClean.

Historical Context

Nuclear Proliferation and the Cold War

World War II ended in 1945 when Germany and Japan surrendered to the Allied forces but, unfortunately, the war's end set the stage for a major struggle between the United States and the Soviet Union. These countries had very different goals for the post–World War II world. The United States supported free market capitalism while the Soviet Union believed in a communist society in which property and resources are owned by the nation as a whole, and production is controlled by the national

Compare & Contrast

- **Early 1950s:** The minimum wage is $0.75 per hour.

  Today: The minimum wage is $5.15 per hour.

- **Early 1950s:** Pulp fiction magazines are widely read, but their popularity is on the decline due to competition from television, comic books, and the paperback novel.

  Today: Very few pulp fiction magazines exist. Most books are now printed on more expensive paper and some only exist in electronic form.

- **Early 1950s:** Approximately 23.5 percent of American households own a television set. All sets are black and white.

  Today: Ninety-eight percent of American households have a television and of these, 76 percent have more than one. Ninety-nine percent of all televisions owned are color televisions. High definition and plasma televisions are now available.

- **Early 1950s:** Businessman Frank MacNamara and his friend Ralph Schneider introduce the Diners Club card. This is the first credit card in history, allowing members to charge food and drinks at twenty-eight participating New York City restaurants.

  Today: Travelers can carry one credit card that is accepted in countries all over the world. There are hundreds of different types of credit cards.

- **Early 1950s:** Treating children through psycho-analytic techniques is a new practice. The main interest in using these techniques on youngsters is sparked by the publication of Anna Freud's *The Psychoanalytic Treatment of Children* in 1946. It is several years before the practice is widely adopted.

  Today: Child psychology is a well-established field that can be studied in major universities across the country. Some psychoanalytic techniques are still in use in the field.

- **Early 1950s:** American children play with the Slinky toy and the Candyland board game.

  Today: Children spend a great deal of time playing video games.

---

government. Each country's people thought that their own political and economic system was the best, and they were very suspicious of outsiders. The Soviet Union was particularly worried because the United States had used nuclear bombs during the war. The Soviets were also concerned about the United States being the only superpower to have nuclear capabilities, so they quickly began to develop their own nuclear weapons. The Soviet Union successfully tested its first atomic bomb in 1949, long before the United States expected the Soviets to have the capability of creating such a device. The United States also learned that the Soviets had stolen state secrets in order to accelerate their nuclear weapons program. A state of deep paranoia developed in both countries and this feeling of competition and threat began what came to be known as the cold war. The war gained this name because even though there was a struggle between the two superpowers, their armies never fired a shot at each other. The Cold War lasted for more than forty years.

The Red Scare

During the cold war, many Americans were afraid that the Communists were infiltrating the country, and they began to try and seek out and punish Communist sympathizers. This fear of Communism became known as the "Red Scare" and it pervaded all areas of American life. In 1947 the United States government formed the House Un-American Activities Committee (HUAC) to investigate whether Communists had infiltrated Hollywood. A series of hearings were led by Senator

Joseph McCarthy in which he questioned artists who were suspected of being Communist sympathizers. Many careers were ruined during these hearings. The United States also became concerned that the government itself had been infiltrated. In 1950, Alger Hiss, a State Department employee, was accused of selling state secrets to the Soviets. He was tried and convicted of lying to Congress.

The Korean War

One country in which the Cold War played out very specifically was Korea. After World War II ended, the Soviets controlled the northern part of the country, while the United States controlled the south. On June 24, 1950, North Korea invaded South Korea. President Harry Truman immediately ordered American troops to aid South Korea. Soon after that, the Chinese sent troops to help North Korea. The two pushed each other back and forth until they finally ended with a face-off at the 38th parallel of latitude, where the war had originally begun. An uneasy truce was in place for the next eighteen months. In July, 1953, the two sides came to an agreement that they would consider the whole thing a draw.

The Move to the Suburbs

After World War II, suburban housing developments began to spread across the United States. Many families now could afford an automobile, which allowed them to live further from the city. People could now own a home in a quiet suburban community and commute to work downtown.

Pulp Magazines

Pulps were popular magazines that were printed on cheap gray wood pulp paper. They were inexpensive and were extremely popular among young readers. Each pulp fiction magazine grouped stories by genre. There were western pulps, sports pulps, romance pulps, horror pulps and science fiction pulps, among others. They were usually very sensationalistic and had titles such as *Weird Tales* and *Amazing Stories*. The proliferation of the pulp fiction magazines throughout the 1940s gave many writers their first chance to publish their work. Numerous writers began their careers by selling stories to these publications.

Television

Television became an important force in American life during the late 1940s and early 1950s. Through the medium of television, viewers could see sights from around the world that they were never able to see before. In 1951 the program *See It Now* broadcast simultaneous live images of the Golden Gate and Brooklyn Bridges. At this time, approximately one-fourth of American households owned a television set. Television quickly became a major force in popular culture across the country. In 1951 *I Love Lucy* debuted and established Lucille Ball as a national television star.

Critical Overview

Ray Bradbury gained critical acclaim early in his career, with the publication of *The Martian Chronicles*. This was an unusual situation because Bradbury was writing in the science fiction genre, a genre not usually very well-respected among the literary elite. Despite this, he was able to break through the prejudice and win many admirers. As Willis E. McNelly states in *Voices for the Future*,

> Ray Bradbury, hailed as a stylist and a visionary by critics such as Gilbert Highet and authors such as Aldous Huxley and Christopher Isherwood, remained for years the darling, almost the house pet, of a literary establishment other wise (*sic*) unwilling to admit any quality in the technological and scientific projections known as science fiction.

In fact, it was Isherwood's praise of *The Martian Chronicles* that first propelled Bradbury into the limelight and helped him find a wider audience of dedicated fans.

Bradbury followed this success with the publication of *The Illustrated Man*, another book that showcased his talent for writing in the short story format. *The Illustrated Man* was popular with critics and casual readers alike and has continued to be one of Bradbury's most influential works. As Robin Anne Reid notes in her book *Ray Bradbury: A Critical Companion*, *The Illustrated Man* "is widely considered one of Bradbury's strongest works." "The Veldt" has been a particularly popular story from the collection as evidenced by the fact that it was chosen for inclusion in the 1969 feature film and the stage play that Bradbury himself adapted from the book.

Though Bradbury is usually known as a science fiction writer, this label has been in dispute throughout his entire career. For purists, the definition of a science fiction story is one that uses present scientific knowledge to create events that are plausible. *Plausibility* is the key here, and it is this element that has caused disagreement about how to classify Bradbury's work. Because Bradbury sometimes creates implausible situations, some critics argue that he is a fantasy writer. As Damon Knight notes in his essay, "The purists are right in saying he does not write science fiction, and never has." Donald A. Wollheim also comments in *The Universe Makers* that "Ray Bradbury is not really a science-fiction writer at all."

Labels notwithstanding, over the years Bradbury's reputation has continued to grow, and he has been recognized as one of the most important American writers of the past fifty years. In his introduction to a collection of critical essays on Bradbury, Harold Bloom calls him, "one of the masters of science fiction and fantasy," and Wollheim praises him as "a mainstream fantasist of great brilliance." The fact that *The Illustrated Man* remained in print for over fifty years since it was first published in 1951 is evidence that the themes contained in these stories continued to hold a fascination for readers through the decades. It is also a testament to Bradbury's talent. The stories contained in *The Illustrated Man* have found an audience for over five decades, and they continue to delight a new generation of readers in the early 2000s.

Criticism

Beth Kattelman

Kattelman holds a Ph.D. in theater. In this essay, Kattelman examines Bradbury's use of literary devices to create his taut, well-crafted short story.

Writing a well-crafted short story is not easy. To be a good short story writer, the writer must know how to use many literary devices. Because the finished piece will not be very long, each word must be carefully chosen to deliver the maximum impact. Edgar Allen Poe, master of the short story, believed that a good short story must provide a "single effect." In other words, the action of a short story should be concentrated to deliver one strong emotional jolt, especially if that story is dealing with horror, suspense, or terror. Ray Bradbury openly acknowledges that he as a young writer was influenced by Poe, and he always strives to create the single, concentrated effect suggested by Poe. Bradbury masterfully uses similes, metaphors, dialogue, point of view, tone, and many other literary devices to draw the reader in and to heighten the

emotional experience. In his story "The Veldt," for instance, there are many fine examples of how Bradbury uses these literary devices to create a story that is engaging, clever, and shocking.

Bradbury always has a very strong start to his stories, and this is true of "The Veldt" as well. The story opens with the following bit of dialogue:

> George, I wish you'd look at the nursery.
> What's wrong with it?
> I don't know.
> Well, then.
> I just want you to look at it, is all, or call a psychologist in to look at it.

From these five brief lines the reader learns several things. First, he/she learns that there is a problem with the nursery and that one of the characters is concerned enough about it to ask for a second opinion. Also, through the somewhat unusual request for a psychologist, the reader gets the idea that the problem with the nursery is somehow connected with the human mind, thus raising the possibility that the story is taking place on another planet or during another time far in the future. The opening definitely lets the reader know that something strange is going on here. By dropping bits of provocative information right at the beginning, Bradbury piques the reader's interest and propels the reader into the story. This opening exchange also clues the reader in to what will become the central problem in the story—the nursery. From these few lines of dialogue, one immediately knows that the nursery is going to somehow be important, and now that Bradbury has accomplished this set-up, he can slowly reveal the strange world of the story bit by bit.

Bradbury often builds his themes around things that should be familiar but that are slightly altered in some way. He uses this idea in "The Veldt." Many people have an idea of what a nursery is, and they usually picture it as a safe, happy place in which children can play and interact with their caregivers. In this story, however, Bradbury has injected a twist. He has kept the idea of the nursery being a place for play and interaction, but he has replaced the typical caregivers—parents or a nanny—with an inanimate, unfeeling machine. This change becomes the catalyst for all of the disastrous events that take place in "The Veldt." Because the children have shifted their emotional attachments from their parents to the mechanistic nursery, it becomes both caregiver and an instrument of destruction. The nursery remains a safe, happy place for the children, but it becomes something entirely different for the parents. It becomes a mechanized beast. This tech-

What Do I Read Next?

- *I Sing the Body Electric! and Other Stories* is an excellent collection of classic Ray Bradbury short stories. The book is filled with great science fiction and fantasy pieces that are similar to those in *The Illustrated Man*. Although first published in 1976, the book contains work that spans Bradbury's early career from the 1940s through the 1970s.

- *Selected Stories of Philip K. Dick* (2002) collects some of the very best short stories from this master of mind-bending science fiction. Dick often writes about realities that have been manufactured by media, governments, and big corporations, and his stories have been the basis for numerous science fiction films including *Bladerunner, Total Recall,* and *Minority Report.* This volume is an excellent introduction to the work of this provocative author.

- Published in 2003 by Pocket Books *Great Tales and Poems of Edgar Allen Poe* collects some of the best works of this famous author. The edition also contains a selection of critical excerpts and suggestions for further reading.

- *The Science Fiction Hall of Fame, Volume I* contains twenty-six of the greatest science fiction stories ever written. The book was originally published in 1970 in order to honor the best science fiction writers of the day. Isaac Asimov, Arthur C. Clarke, Robert A. Heinlein, and Daniel Keyes are just a few of the great writers whose works are represented.

- *Forest J. Ackerman's World of Science Fiction* is a book by one of the premier experts on science fiction. Ackerman has also been a lifelong friend of Ray Bradbury's. Published in 1997, this lavishly illustrated volume presents Ackerman's take on the history and major authors of the science fiction genre. He also discusses the pulp magazines and science fiction on television and in film.

---

nique of taking something very familiar and altering it in some way is one that is used by Bradbury consistently. In the volume *Voices for the Future,* Willis E. McNelly comments upon how Bradbury's use of this technique provides not only an interesting story, but adds an element of social commentary as well,

> He pivots upon an individual, a specific object, or particular act, and then shows it from a different perspective or a new viewpoint. The result can become a striking insight into the ordinary, sometimes an ironic comment on our limited vision.

The atmosphere or ambience in a short story helps to build a reader's expectations and to set him or her up for the "single effect" that Poe lists as a short story's desired result. Two literary devices that Bradbury employs to help create a strong atmosphere in his stories, and thus to achieve his desired effect, are similes and metaphors. In his essay "When I was in Kneepants: Ray Bradbury,"

Damon Knight calls these similes and metaphors Bradbury's "trademarks," and he remarks that the use of these devices is one of the primary features that sets Bradbury apart from other, more traditional science fiction writers. Throughout "The Veldt" there are excellent examples of how Bradbury uses similes and metaphors to help create the ambience in the story. For example, when George is eating dinner and thinking about his recent experience in the nursery, Bradbury uses the phrases, "That *sun.* He could feel it on his neck, still, like a hot paw." This simile serves two purposes. Not only does it heighten the description of George's sensation by making the sun's heat seem much more tangible, it also foreshadows the ending of the story when George and Lydia are attacked by lions. Bradbury also uses a metaphor effectively near the end of the piece when he has George ask, "Lord, how did we ever get in this house? What prompted us to buy a nightmare?" By using the metaphor of house as

---

> This ability to manipulate and combine words for maximum effect is what has set Bradbury apart from many other short story writers. It is what has cemented Bradbury's reputation as an important and influential American writer."

nightmare, Bradbury not only conveys the fact that George has become very concerned but also that he still believes everything will turn out all right. After all, a nightmare is only an illusion. Or, at least that's what George believes.

While reading "The Veldt," one may notice that there are no very long passages describing what the characters are thinking. Bradbury sometimes provides brief phrases to let the reader know what is going on in a character's mind, but never more than a few carefully chosen words. This is typical of a well-written short story. Since there is no time for extended descriptions or long discussions, the author's choice of words must convey as much information as possible quickly and succinctly. As Robin Anne Reid comments in her *Ray Bradbury: A Critical Companion*, in short stories "more character development occurs through dialogue and description of actions than through in-depth descriptions of characters' thoughts and emotions." Bradbury is a master at this technique. He is always economizing and making his descriptive passages and dialogue serve a dual purpose. One fine example of this occurs in the following exchange between George and his son, Peter:

> Will you shut off the house sometime soon?
>
> We're considering it.
>
> I don't think you'd better consider it any more, Father.
>
> I won't have any threats from my son!
>
> "Very well." And Peter strolled off to the nursery.

Here, the reader should notice that, rather than whining or crying when his father says the house

might be shut off, Peter very calmly says, "I don't think you'd better consider it any more, Father." This well-spoken sentence, coming from a little boy who is upset, clues the reader into the fact that Peter is not your average ten-year-old. The measured, almost overly-subdued tone also conveys a coldness about the child. The reader gets the idea that Peter is a very calculating boy who is well in control of his own emotions. Even the fact that Peter replies with the phrase, "Very well," rather than saying "okay" provides a clue that this young boy is different than other boys of his age. The word choices convey a subtle creepiness about the boy. Another instance of effective dialogue occurs in the following exchange between George and Lydia:

> Those screams—they sound familiar.
>
> Do they?
>
> Yes, awfully.

This is a wonderful instance of foreshadowing, as well as a subtle pun. The phrase, "awfully familiar" usually means extremely familiar. By breaking it up and inserting it into the dialogue in the manner above, however, Bradbury subtly evokes another meaning. Now the screams are not only awfully familiar, but they are also familiar as well as awful.

Bradbury is indeed a skilled writer, who brings together many important literary elements in "The Veldt." This ability to manipulate and combine words for maximum effect is what has set Bradbury apart from many other short story writers. It is what has cemented Bradbury's reputation as an important and influential American writer. It is this skill that has also sustained Bradbury's popularity throughout his long and varied career. In her essay, "Ray Bradbury and the Gothic Tradition," Hazel Pierce explains the ultimate appeal that Bradbury has had for fans throughout the years. She notes that, while readers admire his imagination and creativity, they also appreciate his artistry. "Devoted readers of Bradbury have long recognized him as a poet in the fullest sense of the word—a maker and doer with words." Critics and fans alike recognize that Bradbury is a gifted artist who is constantly striving to write the very best story he can. His short stories continue to provide that "single effect" for readers, and they also stand as a fine example for other writers of what can be accomplished if you know how to use the tools correctly. As Damon Knight notes in the essay collection titled *Ray Bradbury*, "He is a superb craftsman, a man who has a great gift and has spent fifteen years laboriously and with love teaching himself to use it."

Source: Beth Kattelman, Critical Essay on "The Veldt," in *Short Stories for Students*, Gale, 2005.

Joyce Hart

Hart, a former writing teacher, is a freelance writer and author of several books. In this essay, Hart examines the reversal relationships that make up the heart of this story.

Ray Bradbury has a point to make in his short story "The Veldt." It is a rather simple and obvious point—Bradbury does not like machines. But the more interesting part of this story is not his dislike of a mechanical world but rather it is Bradbury's explanation of why he does not look upon a world run by machines as some kind of utopia in which human beings are free to pursue things other than the mundane chores of every day living. Quite contrary to the notion of a utopia, in Bradbury's view, machines turn the world upside down, ruining human relationships and destroying the minds of children. Instead of leaving time for people to ponder the higher thoughts of spirituality and philosophy, a world run by machines leaves people open to boredom and thoughts riddled with fear, anger, and vengeance. And it is these results that make Bradbury very unhappy.

Bradbury's husband and wife protagonists, George and Lydia Hadley, live in what Bradbury calls a Happylife Home, a place any person in their right mind would drool over, or at least that is what the Hadleys thought when they plunked down the cash to convert their normal habitat into one they thought would solve all their problems. The house was energy efficient, turning lights off and on when people entered or left a room. The house was soothing, rocking them and their children to sleep at night. The house was nurturing, fixing their meals, dressing them, and keeping their environment as clean as if they had a twenty-four-hour maid. Who could ask for more from a house?

Well, as some people believe, there is no such thing as utopia. And this concept partially forms the foundation of Bradbury's story. In the least, Bradbury contends that an existence heavily dependent on machines will cause as much strife as it eases. It might be fun to imagine fantastic realities but attempting to put them into play in a material world causes unforeseen hardships or maybe even fatal catastrophes. Something always seems to go wrong. In the case of Bradbury's creation, a lot of things go wrong, and the Hadleys' world is turned on its head. Something is wrong, they suspect, but they do not

> " Instead of leaving time for people to ponder the higher thoughts of spirituality and philosophy, a world run by machines leaves people open to boredom and thoughts riddled with fear, anger, and vengeance."

quite know what it is. What they do know is the heart of this unnamed flaw is located somewhere in the nursery.

The Hadleys are well intended parents who do not let money stand in the way of their children's happiness. They have installed something that Bradbury has imagined well before its time, a personal virtual reality room, which in turn would provide them with well-balanced, happy little minds. But the Hadley children's minds, as it turns out, are only happy at their parents' expense, and the debt involves a lot more than their parents' money.

It takes a while for the Hadleys to realize that something is amiss in the nursery. When George steps into the room one day he suddenly is overwhelmed by the heat. And the lions! They seem so real. Is it possible that the virtual reality machine has converted itself, has moved up a notch closer to being less virtual and more real? And what has happened to George, once ruler and lord of his household? He seems incapable of doing anything to change the course of the foreshadowed disaster that looms in the nursery. Even though he tries to avert a catastrophe and recapture the power that once was his, his attempts come up short. He locks the room and threatens to shut the machine off, but the children overthrow his rule. George is a king dethroned in his own castle.

The children, the narrator informs the reader, have taken over the parental role, whether or not George and Lydia want to face this. They throw tantrums when George locks them out of the nursery. And George, the misguided parent that he is, wants his children to be happy. After all, this is the reason he bought the Happylife Home in the first place. So the tantrums work. George does not want to see his children cry. Tantrums make no one happy. George backs down yet another degree as the children mastermind a plot to ensure total authority over their parents.

Next, in steps fear. Lydia is afraid of the nursery. Those virtual reality lions look like they are ready to pounce on George and Lydia. But then Lydia thinks this thought out again. Maybe she is just growing paranoid. After all, she has so much time to think now that she has less to do around the house. As a matter of fact, it is not that she has less to do, rather she has nothing to do at all. And that is another problem. The Happylife Home has left her with too much leisure. The mechanisms of her Happylife Home were supposed to give Lydia time to relax and have fun. So why does George examine his wife and tell her she looks tired? And why does Lydia say that maybe they need a vacation from this perfect little home? What has happened to their initial concept that this house will alleviate all their burdens?

This house that does everything for them is obviously making their life worse. Surely the Happylife Home keeps their house clean, feeds and cares for them in every way a full range of maids and butlers would, but the Happylife Home has also robbed George and Lydia of something very precious to them—their roles. It has taken away Lydia's need to be a wife, mother, and nursemaid. This is what her dream was. With the Happylife Home having rid Lydia of these chores, in Lydia's mind, she has no other reason to exist. The house has also corrupted George's role as head of household and makes George feel superfluous. This makes George very nervous. He smokes and drinks more than he should and is confused about how to handle his children. Whereas he thought the house would make his son and daughter happy and therefore grateful, they have instead turned into vile and spoiled children. This so-called utopian invention is giving them the opposite of what they want.

On top of this, everyone in the Hadley household appears to be stuck in a rut. Lydia wants the family to run away from the home, but the children will not hear of it. George wants to change the course of their lives, but as soon as the children complain, he reverses his intent. The children, too, seem to be stuck. Or at least, their parents think so. George and Lydia have never known their children to become so involved in one nursery theme for such a long time. Why are they so interested in Africa? And worse yet, why are they so fascinated with death?

In an act of desperation, the parents consult David McClean, the psychologist who understands the virtual reality machine and uses it to evaluate the health of children's minds. The mechanisms are suppose to clean (as in David's last name) all the bad parts of a child's psyche by allowing them to play out their neuroses. But when David walks into the nursery, he immediately senses that something is not right. The room has evolved into something unintended by the psychologists. Instead of alleviating negativity, it has drawn the Hadley children toward destructive thoughts. It has encouraged them to run amuck in childhood alienation. As the Hadleys will soon find out, the children's anger has actually developed more fully with the help of the virtual reality room, and the Hadley kids have become preoccupied with getting rid of their parents. The good doctor, although he suggests that George and Lydia immediately get rid of the mechanisms in the children's nursery, points his finger of blame not at the virtual reality diagnostic tool but rather at the parents. They have spoiled their children, he tells them, more than most parents would do. And in many ways, as the Hadleys attempt to rein their children in, they are now disappointing them. The children, David tells them, have replaced their parents with their room. The children believe that their parents are disposable. They have everything they need. As a matter of fact, they could quite easily function much better without mom and dad, or so they think.

Turn it all off, the doctor suggests. And George follows his orders. It is not too late, David says, to save the children. But everyone must go through retraining. It appears that George is finally learning a very important lesson. But Lydia is lagging behind him. The children throw tantrums again, and Lydia suggests that they give the children one more trip to the nursery. George gives in. Anything to keep the children happy. Of course, this is just what the children want. They set the trap, and the parents walk right into it and disappear.

But the story does not end here. The doctor returns to make a visit. He engages the children in their room. They seem content, but not everything looks well. That sun, which represents the children's anger, is still visible and very hot. And now it is the psychologist's turn to sweat. In addition,

George and Lydia are nowhere to be found. But there is even more going on, things that Bradbury just leaves to the reader's imagination. Although the children believe that things have once more gone topsy-turvy in their favor as they relish what they imagine to be a new-found freedom, readers might question just how free they are in allowing the nursery to replace their parents. The children sit there in their room in apparent calm, acting as adults as they entertain the doctor and offer him some tea. But what is really to become of them? How long can they pull off this charade? Just how much of a benefactor is this Happylife Home? Will it provide the children with food forever? What is the source of its energy? And more importantly, who will pay the bills? The children may be smart, but it is easy to conclude that they have not thought out all the consequences of their actions. They are, after all, just children. So by the end of Bradbury's story, the factual reality sets in. Despite all the promises of the mechanical world, Bradbury seems to be saying, machines will never fully replace humans. And in the process of humans making machines to improve the world, people should, unlike the Hadleys, think through their choices and the consequences of those choices.

Source: Joyce Hart, Critical Essay on "The Veldt," in *Short Stories for Students*, Gale, 2005.

John J. McLaughlin

In the following review, McLaughlin discusses the problems of adapting science fiction such as "The Veldt" to the stage.

To Ray Bradbury a toaster is an idea encrusted in chrome. A small idea, perhaps—one involving the relationship of heat to bread—but nevertheless an idea. More complex machines such as automobiles, TV sets, computers and missiles conceal ideas of a more complex sort. We are surrounded by these machine-ideas, says Bradbury, and we scarcely give them a thought. Yet they influence our lives more directly than Plato's forms or Aristotle's universals ever did.

Bradbury is a man who is seriously concerned with the ideas that machines have woven around us. One of the most prolific and widely read science fiction writers, he has written more than 300 short stories and several novels. Much of the bulk of his fiction has been concerned with a single theme—the loss of human values to the machine. Now Bradbury

> As a genre, science fiction combines the plot and moral tone of melodrama with the fantasy of romance, a combination which is a genuine literary novelty."

has brought his message to a new medium, the theatre, and, typically, he has mustered all the resources of imagination, talent and ingenuity available to make the stage speak for him with the effectiveness of the printed page.

"The World of Ray Bradbury," an evening of three one-act plays, opened in Los Angeles to generally favorable reviews. The appearance of a theatrical company dedicated to producing his own work represents more than dabbling in a new literary form for Bradbury. It is a full commitment to put time, energy and money into the theatre. He has spent $20,000 out of his own pocket, gathered a professional group of actors and stage technicians, and set out to establish a permanent theatre where his plays can be staged for as long as he cares to write them.

Two of the three plays now runing, *The Pedestrian* and *The Veldt,* examine the future effects of two of our most proliferating machines: the automobile and the television set. One of the favorite techniques of science fiction writers is to take a contemporary problem and push it to its logical extreme. What happens, for example, when cars and TV sets insinuate themselves increasingly into our lives? Quite simple: no one walks any longer. So *The Pedestrian* is set in 1990—as are all three of the plays—when it is illegal to be out on the street at night on foot. A nonconformist drags his friend away from his TV set to sample the forbidden fruit: the smell of night air, the sound of crickets, the sight of a jeweled sky, the feel of grass. They are detected by a patrol car, robot driven, speaking in a voice taped by someone long since dead, and the dangerous pedestrian is carted away to a psychiatric center.

In *The Veldt*, television is pushed to the point where it becomes a "complete environment"—a room where one is surrounded by three-dimensional pictures that reproduce any spot on earth with perfect realism. A man and his wife install such a TV playroom for their children and bustle them off to the room to keep them from under foot. But instead of duplicating the wonders of Egypt, the spectacle of Niagara, or any of the other enticements in the machine's repertory, the children keep the dial locked on a single ominous scene: an African veldt inhabited by lions that tear flesh from unidentified carcasses. The denouement is not too surprising: the children, psychotic from lack of love, lock their parents in the room, and during a blackout the audience hears them being torn to pieces by lions that have somehow become all too real.

The final play, and in many ways the best of the three, deals with a theme that has concerned Bradbury for some time—mediocrity, and whether or not it has any value. In *To the Chicago Abyss* Bradbury sings a Whitmanesque song in praise of junk. The action takes place after an atomic holocaust when famine and dearth are so complete that remembering the affluent times of the past is forbidden. But an old man appears who cannot forget and cannot keep from talking. He remembers "the junk of a race-track civilization"—the cigarette packages, candy bars, the look of the dashboard on a Cadillac, and the sound of the Duncan sisters. He becomes a fugitive who is doomed because "somehow my tongue moves" and he is compelled to recite his catalogues. Roses are nourished by manure, he says, therefore the "mediocre must be, so that most excellent fine can bloom."

Bradbury buffs will recognize the plots of these plays because all three appeared originally as short stories. There is, of course, nothing new about adapting narrative material to the stage, but in the case of science fiction it presents several difficult problems. As a genre, science fiction combines the plot and moral tone of melodrama with the fantasy of romance, a combination which is a genuine literary novelty. The methods of melodrama are easily accommodated on the stage, but successful fantasy occurs more naturally in narrative fiction where the imagination can create worlds that never were. When fantasy is dramatized, it is usually combined with music, dance and comedy—the worlds of *Camelot* or *Brigadoon* are best evoked by the arts of song and dance. Film is much more congenial to science fiction than the stage because special-effects technicians are able to take the most fantastic imaginings of the writer and actually con-

struct them from plastic or plaster-board. In a movie we don't have to use our imagination—the Martian landscape is there before our eyes.

How is a playwright to place science fiction on the stage? Will a bare stage and an appeal to the audience's imaginative powers be adequate for a play like *The Veldt*? Can we believe in such a machine without some hint of what it looks or sounds like? Bradbury's solution to these problems has been the same as the film maker's: turn it over to the technician. We are presented with a stunning array of futuristic projections and costumes, control panels with blinking lights, and a persistent sound track that bleeps and hums like a satellite orbiting around the balcony.

All this is done with a professionalism that commands admiration, for Bradbury has assembled a technical staff that includes such top Hollywood special-effects men as John Whitney who did many of the futuristic effects for the New York World's Fair. The sound is, on at least one occasion, terrifyingly effective: in the final scene of *The Veldt* where, sitting in the darkness amid horrifying screams, you hear lions about to spring into your lap. But for the most part the technical éclat intrudes upon the play—it becomes gimmicky rather than theatrical, crushing the drama rather than supporting it. The sounds, projections and costumes are attempts to *tell* us rather than to *suggest* what the future may be like. They are particularly obtrusive in the final play, *To the Chicago Abyss,* where Bradbury insists on actually showing the trivia his old man is describing—producing it magically by sleight of hand. The effect is a little like Lady Macbeth doing the sleepwalking scene carrying a bottle of cleaning fluid. This is especially sad, for the play doesn't need the technical hokum; it is sensitively written and well acted and is quite able to get by on its own dramatic values.

Many of the defects of the three plays can be attributed to the difficulties a playwright is bound to encounter when he creates a theatre for his own work. In Bradbury's case the complications were compounded by the fact that this was his initial experience in theatrical production and he had to defer to the judgment of the professionals who surrounded him. Yet he was compelled to make the final decisions—it was his money, after all, and he was the producer. Taking into account inexperience, it is not too surprising that the theatrical balance, which one would expect to be weighted toward action and dialogue in a play-wright's theatre, was instead shifted noisily in the direction of stagecraft.

One of the problems that might have emerged in a theatre company so completely dominated by the playwright never occurred; there was no clash of ego between the author and his professional cast of Equity actors. Bradbury is a man of benign manner but intense loyalty, and he easily won the respect and admiration of his company. His actors, most of whom work in television and films, turned in consistently fine performances. Harold Gould was particularly notable as the memory-plagued survivor in *To the Chicago Abyss*.

When asked recently whether he would do it the same way again, Bradbury refused to make excuses. "The final decisions were mine and I take full responsibility for what appears on the stage," he said. He did admit, however, that if he had learned anything from his first attempt to stage his own work it was "to trust the word." "You've got to believe in your own language," he said. But he is not defensive about his new theatre. "I don't think much of most of the theatre I see today," he said. "I'm not interested in writing an Albee play or a Baldwin play because it's the fashionable thing to do. I'm interested in experimenting with something different and in having fun doing it."

He intends to run the current program until he recovers his investment and then to produce three more. After that he has three comedies ready. He is also making plans to film the three one-acters now running and there is a possibility that they will be produced off-Broadway.

Bradbury is in an enviable position as a playwright, having made enough money from his writing to subsidize his own company, and prolific enough as a writer to keep it going indefinitely if he chooses. In effect, he has found his own cure for one of the endemic sicknesses of the American theatre: the playwright's subservience to the profit motive. This independence is made possible, of course, by the fact that he has a large pool of professional actors and technicians to draw from in Los Angeles, but also because he apparently has a ready-made audience of pre-conditioned Ray Bradbury fans anxiously awaiting his latest work for the stage.

He professes not to understand why other established writers with yearnings toward the theatre don't produce their own plays with their own company. "Why shouldn't a writer take risks on his own

work?" he asks. "I'm not the only writer who saves his money; besides, it doesn't cost that much. The fun I'm having is well worth it."

Source: John J. McLaughlin, "Science Fiction Theatre," in *Nation*, Vol. 200, No. 4, January 25, 1965, pp. 92–94.

Sources

Bloom, Harold, "Introduction," in *Ray Bradbury*, Modern Critical Views series, Chelsea House, 2001, p. 1.

Bradbury, Ray, "The Veldt," in *The Illustrated Man*, 1951, reprint, William Morrow, 2001, pp. 7–25.

Knight, Damon, "When I Was in Kneepants: Ray Bradbury," in *Ray Bradbury*, edited by Harold Bloom, Modern Critical Views series, Chelsea House, 2001, pp. 4–6.

McNelly, Willis E., "Ray Bradbury—Past, Present, and Future," in *Voices for the Future: Essays on Major Science Fiction Writers*, edited by Thomas D. Clareson, Bowling Green University Popular Press, 1976, pp. 167, 171.

Pierce, Hazel, "Ray Bradbury and the Gothic Tradition," in *Ray Bradbury*, edited by Harold Bloom, Modern Critical Views series, Chelsea House, 2001, p. 61.

Reid, Robin Anne, "The Illustrated Man," in *Ray Bradbury: A Critical Companion*, Greenwood Press, 2000, pp. 37, 39.

Wollheim, Donald A., "We'll Make a Star or Die Trying!" in *The Universe Makers: Science Fiction Today*, Harper & Row, 1971, p. 99.

Further Reading

Disch, Thomas M., *The Dreams Our Stuff Is Made Of: How Science Fiction Conquered the World*, Free Press, 1998.
   This book explores the impact that science fiction has had upon American culture. It shows how science fiction has been a catalyst for new realities and also how it has helped us to adjust to those realities.

Eller, Jonathan R., and William F. Touponce, *Ray Bradbury: The Life of Fiction*, Kent State University Press, 2004.
   This is the most comprehensive textual and cultural study of sixty years of Bradbury's work. It looks at his entire career, from the earliest writings to his most recently published novel, *Let's All Kill Constance*.

Haining, Peter, *The Classic Era of American Pulp Magazines*, Chicago Review Press, 2001.
   This book provides a comprehensive review of the various types of pulp magazines that were popular in America during the first half of the twentieth century. Each chapter explores one particular genre.

McCaffery, Larry, *Across the Wounded Galaxies: Interviews with Contemporary American Science Fiction Writers*, University of Illinois Press, 1991.

In this book, famous writers such as Ursula LeGuin, William Burroughs, Gene Wolf, and Octavia Butler discuss their work.

Stein, R. Conrad, *The Great Red Scare*, Silver Burdett, 1998. Stein's book is an overview of America's fear of Communist subversion during the late 1940s and early 1950s and is directed toward a young adult reader. The book also examines how Senator Joseph McCarthy was able to exploit America's fear of Communism to further his own agendas.

Glossary of Literary Terms

A

Aestheticism: A literary and artistic movement of the nineteenth century. Followers of the movement believed that art should not be mixed with social, political, or moral teaching. The statement ''art for art's sake'' is a good summary of aestheticism. The movement had its roots in France, but it gained widespread importance in England in the last half of the nineteenth century, where it helped change the Victorian practice of including moral lessons in literature. Edgar Allan Poe is one of the best-known American ''aesthetes.''

Allegory: A narrative technique in which characters representing things or abstract ideas are used to convey a message or teach a lesson. Allegory is typically used to teach moral, ethical, or religious lessons but is sometimes used for satiric or political purposes. Many fairy tales are allegories.

Allusion: A reference to a familiar literary or historical person or event, used to make an idea more easily understood. Joyce Carol Oates's story ''Where Are You Going, Where Have You Been?'' exhibits several allusions to popular music.

Analogy: A comparison of two things made to explain something unfamiliar through its similarities to something familiar, or to prove one point based on the acceptance of another. Similes and metaphors are types of analogies.

Antagonist: The major character in a narrative or drama who works against the hero or protagonist. The Misfit in Flannery O'Connor's story ''A Good Man Is Hard to Find'' serves as the antagonist for the Grandmother.

Anthology: A collection of similar works of literature, art, or music. Zora Neale Hurston's ''The Eatonville Anthology'' is a collection of stories that take place in the same town.

Anthropomorphism: The presentation of animals or objects in human shape or with human characteristics. The term is derived from the Greek word for ''human form.'' The fur necklet in Katherine Mansfield's story ''Miss Brill'' has anthropomorphic characteristics.

Anti-hero: A central character in a work of literature who lacks traditional heroic qualities such as courage, physical prowess, and fortitude. Anti-heroes typically distrust conventional values and are unable to commit themselves to any ideals. They generally feel helpless in a world over which they have no control. Anti-heroes usually accept, and often celebrate, their positions as social outcasts. A well-known anti-hero is Walter Mitty in James Thurber's story ''The Secret Life of Walter Mitty.''

Archetype: The word archetype is commonly used to describe an original pattern or model from which all other things of the same kind are made. Archetypes are the literary images that grow out of the ''collective unconscious,'' a theory proposed by psychologist Carl Jung. They appear in literature as incidents and plots that repeat basic patterns of life. They may also appear as stereotyped characters. The ''schlemiel'' of Yiddish literature is an archetype.

Autobiography: A narrative in which an individual tells his or her life story. Examples include Benjamin Franklin's *Autobiography* and Amy Hempel's story ''In the Cemetery Where Al Jolson Is Buried,'' which has autobiographical characteristics even though it is a work of fiction.

Avant-garde: A literary term that describes new writing that rejects traditional approaches to literature in favor of innovations in style or content. Twentieth-century examples of the literary *avant-garde* include the modernists and the minimalists.

B

Belles-lettres: A French term meaning ''fine letters'' or ''beautiful writing.'' It is often used as a synonym for literature, typically referring to imaginative and artistic rather than scientific or expository writing. Current usage sometimes restricts the meaning to light or humorous writing and appreciative essays about literature. Lewis Carroll's *Alice in Wonderland* epitomizes the realm of belles-lettres.

Bildungsroman: A German word meaning ''novel of development.'' The *bildungsroman* is a study of the maturation of a youthful character, typically brought about through a series of social or sexual encounters that lead to self-awareness. J. D. Salinger's *Catcher in the Rye* is a *bildungsroman*, and Doris Lessing's story ''Through the Tunnel'' exhibits characteristics of a *bildungsroman* as well.

Black Aesthetic Movement: A period of artistic and literary development among African Americans in the 1960s and early 1970s. This was the first major African-American artistic movement since the Harlem Renaissance and was closely paralleled by the civil rights and black power movements. The black aesthetic writers attempted to produce works of art that would be meaningful to the black masses. Key figures in black aesthetics included one of its founders, poet and playwright Amiri Baraka, formerly known as LeRoi Jones; poet and essayist Haki R. Madhubuti, formerly Don L. Lee; poet and playwright Sonia Sanchez; and dramatist Ed Bullins. Works representative of the Black Aesthetic Movement include Amiri Baraka's play *Dutchman,* a 1964 Obie award-winner.

Black Humor: Writing that places grotesque elements side by side with humorous ones in an attempt to shock the reader, forcing him or her to laugh at the horrifying reality of a disordered world. ''Lamb to the Slaughter,'' by Roald Dahl, in which a placid housewife murders her husband and serves the murder weapon to the investigating policemen, is an example of black humor.

C

Catharsis: The release or purging of unwanted emotions—specifically fear and pity—brought about by exposure to art. The term was first used by the Greek philosopher Aristotle in his *Poetics* to refer to the desired effect of tragedy on spectators.

Character: Broadly speaking, a person in a literary work. The actions of characters are what constitute the plot of a story, novel, or poem. There are numerous types of characters, ranging from simple, stereotypical figures to intricate, multifaceted ones. ''Characterization'' is the process by which an author creates vivid, believable characters in a work of art. This may be done in a variety of ways, including (1) direct description of the character by the narrator; (2) the direct presentation of the speech, thoughts, or actions of the character; and (3) the responses of other characters to the character. The term ''character'' also refers to a form originated by the ancient Greek writer Theophrastus that later became popular in the seventeenth and eighteenth centuries. It is a short essay or sketch of a person who prominently displays a specific attribute or quality, such as miserliness or ambition. ''Miss Brill,'' a story by Katherine Mansfield, is an example of a character sketch.

Classical: In its strictest definition in literary criticism, classicism refers to works of ancient Greek or Roman literature. The term may also be used to describe a literary work of recognized importance (a ''classic'') from any time period or literature that exhibits the traits of classicism. Examples of later works and authors now described as classical include French literature of the seventeenth century, Western novels of the nineteenth century, and American fiction of the mid-nineteenth century such as that written by James Fenimore Cooper and Mark Twain.

Climax: The turning point in a narrative, the moment when the conflict is at its most intense. Typically, the structure of stories, novels, and plays is one of rising action, in which tension builds to the climax, followed by falling action, in which tension lessens as the story moves to its conclusion.

Comedy: One of two major types of drama, the other being tragedy. Its aim is to amuse, and it typically ends happily. Comedy assumes many forms, such as farce and burlesque, and uses a variety of techniques, from parody to satire. In a restricted sense the term comedy refers only to dramatic presentations, but in general usage it is commonly applied to nondramatic works as well.

Comic Relief: The use of humor to lighten the mood of a serious or tragic story, especially in plays. The technique is very common in Elizabethan works, and can be an integral part of the plot or simply a brief event designed to break the tension of the scene.

Conflict: The conflict in a work of fiction is the issue to be resolved in the story. It usually occurs between two characters, the protagonist and the antagonist, or between the protagonist and society or the protagonist and himself or herself. The conflict in Washington Irving's story "The Devil and Tom Walker" is that the Devil wants Tom Walker's soul but Tom does not want to go to hell.

Criticism: The systematic study and evaluation of literary works, usually based on a specific method or set of principles. An important part of literary studies since ancient times, the practice of criticism has given rise to numerous theories, methods, and "schools," sometimes producing conflicting, even contradictory, interpretations of literature in general as well as of individual works. Even such basic issues as what constitutes a poem or a novel have been the subject of much criticism over the centuries. Seminal texts of literary criticism include Plato's *Republic,* Aristotle's *Poetics,* Sir Philip Sidney's *The Defence of Poesie,* and John Dryden's *Of Dramatic Poesie.* Contemporary schools of criticism include deconstruction, feminist, psychoanalytic, poststructuralist, new historicist, postcolonialist, and reader-response.

D

Deconstruction: A method of literary criticism characterized by multiple conflicting interpretations of a given work. Deconstructionists consider the impact of the language of a work and suggest that the true meaning of the work is not necessarily the meaning that the author intended.

Deduction: The process of reaching a conclusion through reasoning from general premises to a specific premise. Arthur Conan Doyle's character Sherlock Holmes often used deductive reasoning to solve mysteries.

Denotation: The definition of a word, apart from the impressions or feelings it creates in the reader. The word "apartheid" denotes a political and economic policy of segregation by race, but its connotations—oppression, slavery, inequality—are numerous.

Denouement: A French word meaning "the unknotting." In literature, it denotes the resolution of conflict in fiction or drama. The *denouement* follows the climax and provides an outcome to the primary plot situation as well as an explanation of secondary plot complications. A well-known example of *denouement* is the last scene of the play *As You Like It* by William Shakespeare, in which couples are married, an evildoer repents, the identities of two disguised characters are revealed, and a ruler is restored to power. Also known as "falling action."

Detective Story: A narrative about the solution of a mystery or the identification of a criminal. The conventions of the detective story include the detective's scrupulous use of logic in solving the mystery; incompetent or ineffectual police; a suspect who appears guilty at first but is later proved innocent; and the detective's friend or confidant—often the narrator—whose slowness in interpreting clues emphasizes by contrast the detective's brilliance. Edgar Allan Poe's "Murders in the Rue Morgue" is commonly regarded as the earliest example of this type of story. Other practitioners are Arthur Conan Doyle, Dashiell Hammett, and Agatha Christie.

Dialogue: Dialogue is conversation between people in a literary work. In its most restricted sense, it refers specifically to the speech of characters in a drama. As a specific literary genre, a "dialogue" is a composition in which characters debate an issue or idea.

Didactic: A term used to describe works of literature that aim to teach a moral, religious, political, or practical lesson. Although didactic elements are often found in artistically pleasing works, the term "didactic" usually refers to literature in which the message is more important than the form. The term may also be used to criticize a work that the critic finds "overly didactic," that is, heavy-handed in its delivery of a lesson. An example of didactic literature is John Bunyan's *Pilgrim's Progress.*

Dramatic Irony: Occurs when the reader of a work of literature knows something that a character in the work itself does not know. The irony is in the contrast between the intended meaning of the statements or actions of a character and the additional information understood by the audience.

Dystopia: An imaginary place in a work of fiction where the characters lead dehumanized, fearful lives. George Orwell's *Nineteen Eighty-four,* and Margaret Atwood's *Handmaid's Tale* portray versions of dystopia.

E

Edwardian: Describes cultural conventions identified with the period of the reign of Edward VII of England (1901–1910). Writers of the Edwardian Age typically displayed a strong reaction against the propriety and conservatism of the Victorian Age. Their work often exhibits distrust of authority in religion, politics, and art and expresses strong doubts about the soundness of conventional values. Writers of this era include E. M. Forster, H. G. Wells, and Joseph Conrad.

Empathy: A sense of shared experience, including emotional and physical feelings, with someone or something other than oneself. Empathy is often used to describe the response of a reader to a literary character.

Epilogue: A concluding statement or section of a literary work. In dramas, particularly those of the seventeenth and eighteenth centuries, the epilogue is a closing speech, often in verse, delivered by an actor at the end of a play and spoken directly to the audience.

Epiphany: A sudden revelation of truth inspired by a seemingly trivial incident. The term was widely used by James Joyce in his critical writings, and the stories in Joyce's *Dubliners* are commonly called ''epiphanies.''

Epistolary Novel: A novel in the form of letters. The form was particularly popular in the eighteenth century. The form can also be applied to short stories, as in Edwidge Danticat's ''Children of the Sea.''

Epithet: A word or phrase, often disparaging or abusive, that expresses a character trait of someone or something. ''The Napoleon of crime'' is an epithet applied to Professor Moriarty, arch-rival of Sherlock Holmes in Arthur Conan Doyle's series of detective stories.

Existentialism: A predominantly twentieth-century philosophy concerned with the nature and perception of human existence. There are two major strains of existentialist thought: atheistic and Christian. Followers of atheistic existentialism believe that the individual is alone in a godless universe and that the basic human condition is one of suffering and loneliness. Nevertheless, because there are no fixed values, individuals can create their own characters—indeed, they can shape themselves—through the exercise of free will. The atheistic strain culminates in and is popularly associated with the works of Jean-Paul Sartre. The Christian existentialists, on the other hand, believe that only in God may people find freedom from life's anguish. The two strains hold certain beliefs in common: that existence cannot be fully understood or described through empirical effort; that anguish is a universal element of life; that individuals must bear responsibility for their actions; and that there is no common standard of behavior or perception for religious and ethical matters. Existentialist thought figures prominently in the works of such authors as Franz Kafka, Fyodor Dostoyevsky, and Albert Camus.

Expatriatism: The practice of leaving one's country to live for an extended period in another country. Literary expatriates include Irish author James Joyce who moved to Italy and France, American writers James Baldwin, Ernest Hemingway, Gertrude Stein, and F. Scott Fitzgerald who lived and wrote in Paris, and Polish novelist Joseph Conrad in England.

Exposition: Writing intended to explain the nature of an idea, thing, or theme. Expository writing is often combined with description, narration, or argument.

Expressionism: An indistinct literary term, originally used to describe an early twentieth-century school of German painting. The term applies to almost any mode of unconventional, highly subjective writing that distorts reality in some way. Advocates of Expressionism include Federico Garcia Lorca, Eugene O'Neill, Franz Kafka, and James Joyce.

F

Fable: A prose or verse narrative intended to convey a moral. Animals or inanimate objects with human characteristics often serve as characters in fables. A famous fable is Aesop's "The Tortoise and the Hare."

Fantasy: A literary form related to mythology and folklore. Fantasy literature is typically set in non-existent realms and features supernatural beings. Notable examples of literature with elements of fantasy are Gabriel Garcia Marquez's story "The Handsomest Drowned Man in the World" and Ursula K. LeGuin's "The Ones Who Walk Away from Omelas."

Farce: A type of comedy characterized by broad humor, outlandish incidents, and often vulgar subject matter. Much of the comedy in film and television could more accurately be described as farce.

Fiction: Any story that is the product of imagination rather than a documentation of fact. Characters and events in such narratives may be based in real life but their ultimate form and configuration is a creation of the author.

Figurative Language: A technique in which an author uses figures of speech such as hyperbole, irony, metaphor, or simile for a particular effect. Figurative language is the opposite of literal language, in which every word is truthful, accurate, and free of exaggeration or embellishment.

Flashback: A device used in literature to present action that occurred before the beginning of the story. Flashbacks are often introduced as the dreams or recollections of one or more characters.

Foil: A character in a work of literature whose physical or psychological qualities contrast strongly with, and therefore highlight, the corresponding qualities of another character. In his Sherlock Holmes stories, Arthur Conan Doyle portrayed Dr. Watson as a man of normal habits and intelligence, making him a foil for the eccentric and unusually perceptive Sherlock Holmes.

Folklore: Traditions and myths preserved in a culture or group of people. Typically, these are passed on by word of mouth in various forms—such as legends, songs, and proverbs—or preserved in customs and ceremonies. Washington Irving, in "The Devil and Tom Walker" and many of his other stories, incorporates many elements of the folklore of New England and Germany.

Folktale: A story originating in oral tradition. Folktales fall into a variety of categories, including legends, ghost stories, fairy tales, fables, and anecdotes based on historical figures and events.

Foreshadowing: A device used in literature to create expectation or to set up an explanation of later developments. Edgar Allan Poe uses foreshadowing to create suspense in "The Fall of the House of Usher" when the narrator comments on the crumbling state of disrepair in which he finds the house.

G

Genre: A category of literary work. Genre may refer to both the content of a given work—tragedy, comedy, horror, science fiction—and to its form, such as poetry, novel, or drama.

Gilded Age: A period in American history during the 1870s and after characterized by political corruption and materialism. A number of important novels of social and political criticism were written during this time. Henry James and Kate Chopin are two writers who were prominent during the Gilded Age.

Gothicism: In literature, works characterized by a taste for medieval or morbid characters and situations. A gothic novel prominently features elements of horror, the supernatural, gloom, and violence: clanking chains, terror, ghosts, medieval castles, and unexplained phenomena. The term "gothic novel" is also applied to novels that lack elements of the traditional Gothic setting but that create a similar atmosphere of terror or dread. The term can also be applied to stories, plays, and poems. Mary Shelley's *Frankenstein* and Joyce Carol Oates's *Bellefleur* are both gothic novels.

Grotesque: In literature, a work that is characterized by exaggeration, deformity, freakishness, and disorder. The grotesque often includes an element of comic absurdity. Examples of the grotesque can be found in the works of Edgar Allan Poe, Flannery O'Connor, Joseph Heller, and Shirley Jackson.

H

Harlem Renaissance: The Harlem Renaissance of the 1920s is generally considered the first significant movement of black writers and artists in the United States. During this period, new and established black writers, many of whom lived in the region of New York City known as Harlem, published more fiction and poetry than ever before, the first influential black literary journals were established, and black authors and artists received their first widespread recognition and serious critical appraisal. Among the major writers associated with this period are Countee Cullen, Langston Hughes, Arna Bontemps, and Zora Neale Hurston.

Hero/Heroine: The principal sympathetic character in a literary work. Heroes and heroines typically exhibit admirable traits: idealism, courage, and integrity, for example. Famous heroes and heroines of literature include Charles Dickens's Oliver Twist, Margaret Mitchell's Scarlett O'Hara, and the anonymous narrator in Ralph Ellison's *Invisible Man*.

Hyperbole: Deliberate exaggeration used to achieve an effect. In William Shakespeare's *Macbeth*, Lady Macbeth hyperbolizes when she says, "All the perfumes of Arabia could not sweeten this little hand."

I

Image: A concrete representation of an object or sensory experience. Typically, such a representation helps evoke the feelings associated with the object or experience itself. Images are either "literal" or "figurative." Literal images are especially concrete and involve little or no extension of the obvious meaning of the words used to express them. Figurative images do not follow the literal meaning of the words exactly. Images in literature are usually visual, but the term "image" can also refer to the representation of any sensory experience.

Imagery: The array of images in a literary work. Also used to convey the author's overall use of figurative language in a work.

In medias res: A Latin term meaning "in the middle of things." It refers to the technique of beginning a story at its midpoint and then using various flashback devices to reveal previous action. This technique originated in such epics as Virgil's *Aeneid*.

Interior Monologue: A narrative technique in which characters' thoughts are revealed in a way that appears to be uncontrolled by the author. The interior monologue typically aims to reveal the inner self of a character. It portrays emotional experiences as they occur at both a conscious and unconscious level. One of the best-known interior monologues in English is the Molly Bloom section at the close of James Joyce's *Ulysses*. Katherine Anne Porter's "The Jilting of Granny Weatherall" is also told in the form of an interior monologue.

Irony: In literary criticism, the effect of language in which the intended meaning is the opposite of what is stated. The title of Jonathan Swift's "A Modest Proposal" is ironic because what Swift proposes in this essay is cannibalism—hardly "modest."

J

Jargon: Language that is used or understood only by a select group of people. Jargon may refer to terminology used in a certain profession, such as computer jargon, or it may refer to any nonsensical language that is not understood by most people. Anthony Burgess's *A Clockwork Orange* and James Thurber's "The Secret Life of Walter Mitty" both use jargon.

K

Knickerbocker Group: An indistinct group of New York writers of the first half of the nineteenth century. Members of the group were linked only by location and a common theme: New York life. Two famous members of the Knickerbocker Group were Washington Irving and William Cullen Bryant. The group's name derives from Irving's *Knickerbocker's History of New York*.

L

Literal Language: An author uses literal language when he or she writes without exaggerating or embellishing the subject matter and without any tools of figurative language. To say "He ran very quickly down the street" is to use literal language, whereas to say "He ran like a hare down the street" would be using figurative language.

Literature: Literature is broadly defined as any written or spoken material, but the term most often refers to creative works. Literature includes poetry, drama, fiction, and many kinds of nonfiction writing, as well as oral, dramatic, and broadcast compositions not necessarily preserved in a written format, such as films and television programs.

Lost Generation: A term first used by Gertrude Stein to describe the post-World War I generation of American writers: men and women haunted by a sense of betrayal and emptiness brought about by the destructiveness of the war. The term is commonly applied to Hart Crane, Ernest Hemingway, F. Scott Fitzgerald, and others.

M

Magic Realism: A form of literature that incorporates fantasy elements or supernatural occurrences into the narrative and accepts them as truth. Gabriel Garcia Marquez and Laura Esquivel are two writers known for their works of magic realism.

Metaphor: A figure of speech that expresses an idea through the image of another object. Metaphors suggest the essence of the first object by identifying it with certain qualities of the second object. An example is ''But soft, what light through yonder window breaks?/ It is the east, and Juliet is the sun'' in William Shakespeare's *Romeo and Juliet.* Here, Juliet, the first object, is identified with qualities of the second object, the sun.

Minimalism: A literary style characterized by spare, simple prose with few elaborations. In minimalism, the main theme of the work is often never discussed directly. Amy Hempel and Ernest Hemingway are two writers known for their works of minimalism.

Modernism: Modern literary practices. Also, the principles of a literary school that lasted from roughly the beginning of the twentieth century until the end of World War II. Modernism is defined by its rejection of the literary conventions of the nineteenth century and by its opposition to conventional morality, taste, traditions, and economic values. Many writers are associated with the concepts of modernism, including Albert Camus, D. H. Lawrence, Ernest Hemingway, William Faulkner, Eugene O'Neill, and James Joyce.

Monologue: A composition, written or oral, by a single individual. More specifically, a speech given by a single individual in a drama or other public entertainment. It has no set length, although it is usually several or more lines long. ''I Stand Here Ironing'' by Tillie Olsen is an example of a story written in the form of a monologue.

Mood: The prevailing emotions of a work or of the author in his or her creation of the work. The mood of a work is not always what might be expected based on its subject matter.

Motif: A theme, character type, image, metaphor, or other verbal element that recurs throughout a single work of literature or occurs in a number of different works over a period of time. For example, the color white in Herman Melville's *Moby Dick* is a ''specific'' *motif,* while the trials of star-crossed lovers is a ''conventional'' *motif* from the literature of all periods.

N

Narration: The telling of a series of events, real or invented. A narration may be either a simple narrative, in which the events are recounted chronologically, or a narrative with a plot, in which the account is given in a style reflecting the author's artistic concept of the story. Narration is sometimes used as a synonym for ''storyline.''

Narrative: A verse or prose accounting of an event or sequence of events, real or invented. The term is also used as an adjective in the sense ''method of narration.'' For example, in literary criticism, the expression ''narrative technique'' usually refers to the way the author structures and presents his or her story. Different narrative forms include diaries, travelogues, novels, ballads, epics, short stories, and other fictional forms.

Narrator: The teller of a story. The narrator may be the author or a character in the story through whom the author speaks. Huckleberry Finn is the narrator of Mark Twain's *The Adventures of Huckleberry Finn.*

Novella: An Italian term meaning ''story.'' This term has been especially used to describe fourteenth-century Italian tales, but it also refers to modern short novels. Modern novellas include Leo Tolstoy's *The Death of Ivan Ilich,* Fyodor Dostoyevsky's *Notes from the Underground,* and Joseph Conrad's *Heart of Darkness.*

O

Oedipus Complex: A son's romantic obsession with his mother. The phrase is derived from the story of the ancient Theban hero Oedipus, who unknowingly killed his father and married his mother, and was popularized by Sigmund Freud's theory of psychoanalysis. Literary occurrences of the Oedipus complex include Sophocles' *Oedipus Rex* and D. H. Lawrence's ''The Rocking-Horse Winner.''

Onomatopoeia: The use of words whose sounds express or suggest their meaning. In its simplest sense, onomatopoeia may be represented by words that mimic the sounds they denote such as ''hiss'' or ''meow.'' At a more subtle level, the pattern and rhythm of sounds and rhymes of a line or poem may be onomatopoeic.

Oral Tradition: A process by which songs, ballads, folklore, and other material are transmitted by word of mouth. The tradition of oral transmission predates the written record systems of literate society.

Oral transmission preserves material sometimes over generations, although often with variations. Memory plays a large part in the recitation and preservation of orally transmitted material. Native American myths and legends, and African folktales told by plantation slaves are examples of orally transmitted literature.

P

Parable: A story intended to teach a moral lesson or answer an ethical question. Examples of parables are the stories told by Jesus Christ in the New Testament, notably ''The Prodigal Son,'' but parables also are used in Sufism, rabbinic literature, Hasidism, and Zen Buddhism. Isaac Bashevis Singer's story ''Gimpel the Fool'' exhibits characteristics of a parable.

Paradox: A statement that appears illogical or contradictory at first, but may actually point to an underlying truth. A literary example of a paradox is George Orwell's statement ''All animals are equal, but some animals are more equal than others'' in *Animal Farm*.

Parody: In literature, this term refers to an imitation of a serious literary work or the signature style of a particular author in a ridiculous manner. A typical parody adopts the style of the original and applies it to an inappropriate subject for humorous effect. Parody is a form of satire and could be considered the literary equivalent of a caricature or cartoon. Henry Fielding's *Shamela* is a parody of Samuel Richardson's *Pamela*.

Persona: A Latin term meaning ''mask.'' Personae are the characters in a fictional work of literature. The persona generally functions as a mask through which the author tells a story in a voice other than his or her own. A persona is usually either a character in a story who acts as a narrator or an ''implied author,'' a voice created by the author to act as the narrator for himself or herself. The persona in Charlotte Perkins Gilman's story ''The Yellow Wallpaper'' is the unnamed young mother experiencing a mental breakdown.

Personification: A figure of speech that gives human qualities to abstract ideas, animals, and inanimate objects. To say that ''the sun is smiling'' is to personify the sun.

Plot: The pattern of events in a narrative or drama. In its simplest sense, the plot guides the author in composing the work and helps the reader follow the work. Typically, plots exhibit causality and unity and have a beginning, a middle, and an end. Sometimes, however, a plot may consist of a series of disconnected events, in which case it is known as an ''episodic plot.''

Poetic Justice: An outcome in a literary work, not necessarily a poem, in which the good are rewarded and the evil are punished, especially in ways that particularly fit their virtues or crimes. For example, a murderer may himself be murdered, or a thief will find himself penniless.

Poetic License: Distortions of fact and literary convention made by a writer—not always a poet—for the sake of the effect gained. Poetic license is closely related to the concept of ''artistic freedom.'' An author exercises poetic license by saying that a pile of money ''reaches as high as a mountain'' when the pile is actually only a foot or two high.

Point of View: The narrative perspective from which a literary work is presented to the reader. There are four traditional points of view. The ''third person omniscient'' gives the reader a ''godlike'' perspective, unrestricted by time or place, from which to see actions and look into the minds of characters. This allows the author to comment openly on characters and events in the work. The ''third person'' point of view presents the events of the story from outside of any single character's perception, much like the omniscient point of view, but the reader must understand the action as it takes place and without any special insight into characters' minds or motivations. The ''first person'' or ''personal'' point of view relates events as they are perceived by a single character. The main character ''tells'' the story and may offer opinions about the action and characters which differ from those of the author. Much less common than omniscient, third person, and first person is the ''second person'' point of view, wherein the author tells the story as if it is happening to the reader. James Thurber employs the omniscient point of view in his short story ''The Secret Life of Walter Mitty.'' Ernest Hemingway's ''A Clean, Well-Lighted Place'' is a short story told from the third person point of view. Mark Twain's novel *Huckleberry Finn* is presented from the first person viewpoint. Jay McInerney's *Bright Lights, Big City* is an example of a novel which uses the second person point of view.

Pornography: Writing intended to provoke feelings of lust in the reader. Such works are often condemned by critics and teachers, but those which can be shown to have literary value are viewed less harshly. Literary works that have been described as pornographic include D. H. Lawrence's *Lady Chatterley's Lover* and James Joyce's *Ulysses.*

Post-Aesthetic Movement: An artistic response made by African Americans to the black aesthetic movement of the 1960s and early 1970s. Writers since that time have adopted a somewhat different tone in their work, with less emphasis placed on the disparity between black and white in the United States. In the words of post-aesthetic authors such as Toni Morrison, John Edgar Wideman, and Kristin Hunter, African Americans are portrayed as looking inward for answers to their own questions, rather than always looking to the outside world. Two well-known examples of works produced as part of the post-aesthetic movement are the Pulitzer Prize-winning novels *The Color Purple* by Alice Walker and *Beloved* by Toni Morrison.

Postmodernism: Writing from the 1960s forward characterized by experimentation and application of modernist elements, which include existentialism and alienation. Postmodernists have gone a step further in the rejection of tradition begun with the modernists by also rejecting traditional forms, preferring the anti-novel over the novel and the anti-hero over the hero. Postmodern writers include Thomas Pynchon, Margaret Drabble, and Gabriel Garcia Marquez.

Prologue: An introductory section of a literary work. It often contains information establishing the situation of the characters or presents information about the setting, time period, or action. In drama, the prologue is spoken by a chorus or by one of the principal characters.

Prose: A literary medium that attempts to mirror the language of everyday speech. It is distinguished from poetry by its use of unmetered, unrhymed language consisting of logically related sentences. Prose is usually grouped into paragraphs that form a cohesive whole such as an essay or a novel. The term is sometimes used to mean an author's general writing.

Protagonist: The central character of a story who serves as a focus for its themes and incidents and as the principal rationale for its development. The protagonist is sometimes referred to in discussions of modern literature as the hero or anti-hero. Well-known protagonists are Hamlet in William Shakespeare's *Hamlet* and Jay Gatsby in F. Scott Fitzgerald's *The Great Gatsby.*

R

Realism: A nineteenth-century European literary movement that sought to portray familiar characters, situations, and settings in a realistic manner. This was done primarily by using an objective narrative point of view and through the buildup of accurate detail. The standard for success of any realistic work depends on how faithfully it transfers common experience into fictional forms. The realistic method may be altered or extended, as in stream of consciousness writing, to record highly subjective experience. Contemporary authors who often write in a realistic way include Nadine Gordimer and Grace Paley.

Resolution: The portion of a story following the climax, in which the conflict is resolved. The resolution of Jane Austen's *Northanger Abbey* is neatly summed up in the following sentence: "Henry and Catherine were married, the bells rang and everybody smiled."

Rising Action: The part of a drama where the plot becomes increasingly complicated. Rising action leads up to the climax, or turning point, of a drama. The final "chase scene" of an action film is generally the rising action which culminates in the film's climax.

Roman a clef: A French phrase meaning "novel with a key." It refers to a narrative in which real persons are portrayed under fictitious names. Jack Kerouac, for example, portrayed various friends under fictitious names in the novel *On the Road.* D. H. Lawrence based "The Rocking-Horse Winner" on a family he knew.

Romanticism: This term has two widely accepted meanings. In historical criticism, it refers to a European intellectual and artistic movement of the late eighteenth and early nineteenth centuries that sought greater freedom of personal expression than that allowed by the strict rules of literary form and logic of the eighteenth-century neoclassicists. The Romantics preferred emotional and imaginative expression to rational analysis. They considered the individual to be at the center of all experience and so placed him or her at the center of their art. The Romantics believed that the creative imagination reveals nobler truths—unique feelings and attitudes—than those that could be discovered by logic or by scientific examination. "Romanticism" is also used as a general term to refer to a type of sensibility found in all periods of literary history and usually considered to be in opposition to the principles of classicism. In this sense, Romanticism signifies any work or philosophy in which the exotic or dreamlike figure strongly, or that is devoted to individualistic expression, self-analysis, or a pursuit of a higher realm of knowledge than can be discovered by human reason. Prominent Romantics include Jean-Jacques Rousseau, William Wordsworth, John Keats, Lord Byron, and Johann Wolfgang von Goethe.

S

Satire: A work that uses ridicule, humor, and wit to criticize and provoke change in human nature and institutions. Voltaire's novella *Candide* and Jonathan Swift's essay ''A Modest Proposal'' are both satires. Flannery O'Connor's portrayal of the family in ''A Good Man Is Hard to Find'' is a satire of a modern, Southern, American family.

Science Fiction: A type of narrative based upon real or imagined scientific theories and technology. Science fiction is often peopled with alien creatures and set on other planets or in different dimensions. Popular writers of science fiction are Isaac Asimov, Karel Capek, Ray Bradbury, and Ursula K. Le Guin.

Setting: The time, place, and culture in which the action of a narrative takes place. The elements of setting may include geographic location, characters's physical and mental environments, prevailing cultural attitudes, or the historical time in which the action takes place.

Short Story: A fictional prose narrative shorter and more focused than a novella. The short story usually deals with a single episode and often a single character. The ''tone,'' the author's attitude toward his or her subject and audience, is uniform throughout. The short story frequently also lacks *denouement*, ending instead at its climax.

Signifying Monkey: A popular trickster figure in black folklore, with hundreds of tales about this character documented since the 19th century. Henry Louis Gates Jr. examines the history of the signifying monkey in *The Signifying Monkey: Towards a Theory of Afro-American Literary Criticism,* published in 1988.

Simile: A comparison, usually using ''like'' or ''as,''of two essentially dissimilar things, as in ''coffee as cold as ice'' or ''He sounded like a broken record.'' The title of Ernest Hemingway's ''Hills Like White Elephants'' contains a simile.

Social Realism: The Socialist Realism school of literary theory was proposed by Maxim Gorky and established as a dogma by the first Soviet Congress of Writers. It demanded adherence to a communist worldview in works of literature. Its doctrines required an objective viewpoint comprehensible to the working classes and themes of social struggle featuring strong proletarian heroes. Gabriel Garcia Marquez's stories exhibit some characteristics of Socialist Realism.

Stereotype: A stereotype was originally the name for a duplication made during the printing process; this led to its modern definition as a person or thing that is (or is assumed to be) the same as all others of its type. Common stereotypical characters include the absent-minded professor, the nagging wife, the troublemaking teenager, and the kind-hearted grandmother.

Stream of Consciousness: A narrative technique for rendering the inward experience of a character. This technique is designed to give the impression of an ever-changing series of thoughts, emotions, images, and memories in the spontaneous and seemingly illogical order that they occur in life. The textbook example of stream of consciousness is the last section of James Joyce's *Ulysses*.

Structure: The form taken by a piece of literature. The structure may be made obvious for ease of understanding, as in nonfiction works, or may obscured for artistic purposes, as in some poetry or seemingly ''unstructured'' prose.

Style: A writer's distinctive manner of arranging words to suit his or her ideas and purpose in writing. The unique imprint of the author's personality upon his or her writing, style is the product of an author's way of arranging ideas and his or her use of diction, different sentence structures, rhythm, figures of speech, rhetorical principles, and other elements of composition.

Suspense: A literary device in which the author maintains the audience's attention through the buildup of events, the outcome of which will soon be revealed. Suspense in William Shakespeare's *Hamlet* is sustained throughout by the question of whether or not the Prince will achieve what he has been instructed to do and of what he intends to do.

Symbol: Something that suggests or stands for something else without losing its original identity. In literature, symbols combine their literal meaning with the suggestion of an abstract concept. Literary symbols are of two types: those that carry complex associations of meaning no matter what their contexts, and those that derive their suggestive meaning from their functions in specific literary works. Examples of symbols are sunshine suggesting happiness, rain suggesting sorrow, and storm clouds suggesting despair.

T

Tale: A story told by a narrator with a simple plot and little character development. Tales are usually relatively short and often carry a simple message. Examples of tales can be found in the works of Saki, Anton Chekhov, Guy de Maupassant, and O. Henry.

Tall Tale: A humorous tale told in a straightforward, credible tone but relating absolutely impossible events or feats of the characters. Such tales were commonly told of frontier adventures during the settlement of the west in the United States. Literary use of tall tales can be found in Washington Irving's *History of New York,* Mark Twain's *Life on the Mississippi,* and in the German R. F. Raspe's *Baron Munchausen's Narratives of His Marvellous Travels and Campaigns in Russia.*

Theme: The main point of a work of literature. The term is used interchangeably with thesis. Many works have multiple themes. One of the themes of Nathaniel Hawthorne's ''Young Goodman Brown'' is loss of faith.

Tone: The author's attitude toward his or her audience may be deduced from the tone of the work. A formal tone may create distance or convey politeness, while an informal tone may encourage a friendly, intimate, or intrusive feeling in the reader. The author's attitude toward his or her subject matter may also be deduced from the tone of the words he or she uses in discussing it. The tone of John F. Kennedy's speech which included the appeal to ''ask not what your country can do for you'' was intended to instill feelings of camaraderie and national pride in listeners.

Tragedy: A drama in prose or poetry about a noble, courageous hero of excellent character who, because of some tragic character flaw, brings ruin upon him- or herself. Tragedy treats its subjects in a dignified and serious manner, using poetic language to help evoke pity and fear and bring about catharsis, a purging of these emotions. The tragic form was practiced extensively by the ancient Greeks. The classical form of tragedy was revived in the sixteenth century; it flourished especially on the Elizabethan stage. In modern times, dramatists have attempted to adapt the form to the needs of modern society by drawing their heroes from the ranks of ordinary men and women and defining the nobility of these heroes in terms of spirit rather than exalted social standing. Some contemporary works that are thought of as tragedies include *The Great Gatsby* by F. Scott Fitzgerald, and *The Sound and the Fury* by William Faulkner.

Tragic Flaw: In a tragedy, the quality within the hero or heroine which leads to his or her downfall. Examples of the tragic flaw include Othello's jealousy and Hamlet's indecisiveness, although most great tragedies defy such simple interpretation.

U

Utopia: A fictional perfect place, such as ''paradise'' or ''heaven.'' An early literary utopia was described in Plato's *Republic,* and in modern literature, Ursula K. Le Guin depicts a utopia in ''The Ones Who Walk Away from Omelas.''

V

Victorian: Refers broadly to the reign of Queen Victoria of England (1837–1901) and to anything with qualities typical of that era. For example, the qualities of smug narrow-mindedness, bourgeois materialism, faith in social progress, and priggish morality are often considered Victorian. In literature, the Victorian Period was the great age of the English novel, and the latter part of the era saw the rise of movements such as decadence and symbolism.

Cumulative Author/Title Index

Nationality/Ethnicity Index

African American

Baldwin, James
  The Rockpile: V18
  Sonny's Blues: V2
Bambara, Toni Cade
  Blues Ain't No Mockin Bird: V4
  The Lesson: V12
  Raymond's Run: V7
Butler, Octavia
  Bloodchild: V6
Chesnutt, Charles Waddell
  The Sheriff's Children: V11
Ellison, Ralph
  King of the Bingo Game: V1
Hughes, Langston
  The Blues I'm Playing: V7
  Slave on the Block: V4
Hurston, Zora Neale
  The Eatonville Anthology: V1
  The Gilded Six-Bits: V11
  Spunk: V6
  Sweat: V19
Marshall, Paule
  To Da-duh, in Memoriam: V15
Toomer, Jean
  Blood-Burning Moon: V5
Walker, Alice
  Everyday Use: V2
  Roselily: V11
Wideman, John Edgar
  *The Beginning of
    Homewood:* V12
  Fever: V6
Wright, Richard
  Big Black Good Man: V20
  Bright and Morning Star: V15

  *The Man Who Lived Under-
    ground:* V3
  *The Man Who Was
    Almost a Man:* V9

American

Adams, Alice
  The Last Lovely City: V14
Agüeros, Jack
  Dominoes: V13
Aiken, Conrad
  Silent Snow, Secret Snow: V8
Alexie, Sherman
  *Because My Father Always Said
    He Was the Only Indian Who
    Saw Jimi Hendrix Play "The
    Star-Spangled Banner" at
    Woodstock:* V18
Anderson, Sherwood
  Death in the Woods: V10
  Hands: V11
  Sophistication: V4
Asimov, Isaac
  Nightfall: V17
Baldwin, James
  The Rockpile: V18
  Sonny's Blues: V2
Bambara, Toni Cade
  Blues Ain't No Mockin Bird: V4
  The Lesson: V12
  Raymond's Run: V7
Barth, John
  Lost in the Funhouse: V6
Barthelme, Donald
  The Indian Uprising: V17

  *Robert Kennedy Saved from
    Drowning:* V3
Beattie, Ann
  Imagined Scenes: V20
  Janus: V9
Bellow, Saul
  Leaving the Yellow House: V12
Berriault, Gina
  The Stone Boy: V7
  Women in Their Beds: V11
Bierce, Ambrose
  The Boarded Window: V9
  *An Occurrence at Owl Creek
    Bridge:* V2
Bisson, Terry
  The Toxic Donut: V18
Bloom, Amy
  Silver Water: V11
Bowles, Paul
  The Eye: V17
Boyle, Kay
  Astronomer's Wife: V13
  Black Boy: V14
  The White Horses of Vienna: V10
Boyle, T. Coraghessan
  *Stones in My Passway, Hellhound
    on My Trail:* V13
  The Underground Gardens: V19
Bradbury, Ray
  There Will Come Soft Rains: V1
  The Veldt: V20
Brown, Jason
  Animal Stories: V14
Butler, Octavia
  Bloodchild: V6

Subject/Theme Index